# Lecture Notes in Computer Science　8463

Commenced Publication in 1973
Founding and Former Series Editors:
Gerhard Goos, Juris Hartmanis, and Jan van Leeuwen

Monica Chiarini Tremblay
Debra VanderMeer   Marcus Rothenberger
Ashish Gupta   Victoria Yoon (Eds.)

# Advancing the Impact of Design Science: Moving from Theory to Practice

9th International Conference, DESRIST 2014
Miami, FL, USA, May 22-23, 2014
Proceedings

 Springer

Volume Editors

Monica Chiarini Tremblay
Florida International University, Miami, FL, USA
E-mail: tremblay@fiu.edu

Debra VanderMeer
Florida International University, Miami, FL, USA
E-mail: vanderd@fiu.edu

Marcus Rothenberger
University of Nevada Las Vegas, Las Vegas, NV, USA
E-mail: marcus.rothenberger@unlv.edu

Ashish Gupta
University of Tennessee Chattanooga, Chattanooga, TN, USA
E-mail: gupta@utc.edu

Victoria Yoon
Virginia Commonwealth University, Richmond, VA, USA
E-mail: vyyoon@vcu.edu

ISSN 0302-9743                                    e-ISSN 1611-3349
ISBN 978-3-319-06700-1                            e-ISBN 978-3-319-06701-8
DOI 10.1007/978-3-319-06701-8
Springer Cham Heidelberg New York Dordrecht London

Library of Congress Control Number: 2014937552

LNCS Sublibrary: SL 3 – Information Systems and Application,
incl. Internet/Web and HCI

*Typesetting:* Camera-ready by author, data conversion by Scientific Publishing Services, Chennai, India

Printed on acid-free paper

Springer is part of Springer Science+Business Media (www.springer.com)

# Preface

This volume contains the papers presented at DESRIST: 9th International Conference on Design Science Research in Information Systems and Technology held during May 22–23, 2014 in Miami, Florida. The DESRIST Conference continued the tradition of advancing design research within the information systems discipline. As in previous years, scholars and design practitioners from many areas, such as information systems, computer science, industrial design, medical informatics, and software engineering came together to solve human problems through the innovative use of information technology and applications. The outputs of DESRIST, new and innovative constructs, models, methods, processes, and systems provide the basis for novel solutions to design problems in many fields.

DESRIST 2014 further built on the foundation of eight prior highly successful international conferences held in Claremont, Pasadena, Atlanta, Philadelphia, St. Gallen, Milwaukee, Las Vegas, and Helsinki. The title of this volume, "Advancing the Impact of Design Science: Moving from Theory to Practice", reflects the idea that as design science research matures to an established research paradigm, the focus is shifting from searching for legitimacy to informing practice and education.

Forty-nine research manuscripts and 22 short papers describing prototype demonstrations were submitted to the conference for review. Each paper was reviewed by at least two referees. In all, 19 full papers, seven research-in-progress papers, and 18 prototype demonstrations were accepted. The program also included an industry panel, one industrial keynote, as well as poster presentations. The accepted papers were evenly distributed between exemplars of design and theory development. As in previous years, a substantial majority of the papers described the application of design science research to real-world design problems in both industry and government.

We thank the authors who submitted their papers to DESRIST 2014 and we trust that the readers will find them as interesting and informative as we did. We would like to thank the members of the Program Committee as well as the additional referees who took the time to provide detailed and constructive reviews for the authors. We would also like to thank the other members of the Organizing Committee, as well as the volunteers whose dedication and effort helped bring about another successful conference. We believe the papers in these proceedings provide several interesting and valuable insights into the theory and practice of design science, and they open up new and exciting possibilities for research in the discipline.

May 2014                                   Monica Chiarini Tremblay
                                                      Debra VanderMeer
                                               Marcus Rothenberger
                                                            Ashish Gupta
                                                           Victoria Yoon

# Organization

## Program Committee

| | |
|---|---|
| Richard Baskerville | Georgia State University, USA |
| Sven Carlsson | Lund University, Sweden |
| Samir Chatterjee | Claremont Graduate University, USA |
| Roger Chiang | University of Cincinnatti, USA |
| David Darcy | Florida International University, USA |
| Brian Donnellan | National University of Ireland at Maynooth, Ireland |
| Kaushik Dutta | National University of Singapore, Singapore |
| Riitta Hekkala | Aalto University, Finland |
| Keumseok Kang | Florida International University, USA |
| Helmut Krcmar | Technische Universität München, Germany |
| Bill Kuechler | University of Nevada at Reno, USA |
| Subodha Kumar | Texas A&M University, USA |
| Mikael Lind | University of Borås / Viktoria Institute, Sweden |
| Peter Loos | Saarland University, Germany |
| Jan Mendling | Wirtschaftsuniversität Wien, Austria |
| Andreas Oberweis | Universitaet Karlsruhe, Germany |
| Balaji Padmanabhan | University of South Florida, USA |
| Tero Päivärinta | Luleå University of Technology, Sweden |
| Jinsoo Park | Seoul National University, South Korea |
| Jeffrey Parsons | Memorial University of Newfoundland, Canada |
| Henderik Proper | Public Research Centre Henri Tudor, Luxembourg |
| Sandeep Purao | Penn State University, USA |
| Hajo A. Reijers | Eindhoven University of Technology, The Netherlands |
| Matti Rossi | Aalto University, Finland |
| Gerhard Schwabe | Universität Zürich, Switzerland |
| Alexander Simons | University of Liechtenstein, Liechtenstein |
| Henk Sol | University of Groningen, The Netherlands |
| Thant Syn | University of Miami, USA |
| Oliver Thomas | University of Osnabrueck, Germany |
| Tuure Tuunanen | University of Jyväskylä, Finland |
| Karthikeyan Umapathy | University of North Florida, USA |

John Venable              Curtin University, Australia
Jan Verelst               University of Antwerp, Belgium
Joseph Walls              University of Michigan, USA
Axel Winkelmann           University of Wuerzburg, Germany
George Wyner              Boston University, USA

## Additional Reviewers

Akkaya, Cigdem            Petkov, Plamen
Castellanos, Arturo       Proper, Henderik
Castillo Alfred           Päivärinta, Tero
Cater-Steel Aileen        Quick, Reiner
Dadgar Majid              Rosenberg, Zuzana
De Reuver Mark            Schumann, Matthias
Dinter, Barbara           Shrestha, Anup
Drechsler, Andreas        Sjöström, Jonas
Gleasure, Rob             Stahlbrost, Anna
Heckmann, Carl            Sunyaev, Ali
Helfert, Markus           Thapa, Devinder
Krawatzeck, Robert        Toleman, Mark
Maedche, Alex             Vom Brocke, Jan
Meyer, Martin             Walls, Joseph
Miske, Carel              Zadeh, Pouyan
Morana, Stefan            Zhang, Guang
Nyström, Tobias           Ågerfalk, Pär
Peffers, Ken              Özcan, Deniz

# Table of Contents

## Design Science

## Emerging Themes

## Meta Issues

## Methods

## Supporting Business Processes

## Team Support

# Work In Progress Papers

# Prototypes

# Designing Information Systems for Sustainability – The Role of Universal Design and Open Innovation

Moyen Mohammad Mustaquim and Tobias Nyström

Department of Informatics and Media, Uppsala University
Box 513, 751 20 Uppsala, Sweden
{moyen.mustaquim,tobias.nystrom}@im.uu.se

**Abstract.** Although sustainability is a key concern in today's world, more efforts towards achieving sustainability are needed. User inclusion in the information system design process could enhance the outcome of a system's action towards sustainability. It is, however, important to understand the design procedure of a system to achieve such goals. A framework denominating as the inclusive innovation framework presented in this paper incorporated analyses from open innovation, universal design, and sustainability to motivate the initiation of internal and external driving factors towards sustainability goals. The derived framework could promote the information system's enabled sustainable goals by combining the use of universal design principles and the concept of open innovation. A requirement engineering model was also proposed that was interoperable within the three subjects of interest discussed in the paper and was necessary for understanding the application of an inclusive innovation framework. Two use cases were then presented as an illustration for arguing the validation of the proposed inclusive innovation framework. The findings from the use cases indicated that the use of universal design principles along with an open innovation concept could increase information systems' enabled sustainability goals. This could be done by enhancing a system's successfulness along with the increased user satisfaction.

**Keywords:** Sustainability, Open Innovation, Universal Design, Inclusive Innovation Framework.

## 1  Introduction

During the recent decades the impact of human activities on the Earth's eco-systems has become a growing concern. Research connected to sustainability issues in the information system field has increased due to larger awareness of environmental issues, climate change, and the risk of global warming [32], [45]. Information systems are ubiquitous in our society and they play an important role in confronting some of the adverse effects on the environment [46]. It is important to acknowledge that the increased use of the information system has constituted a growing environmental concern in itself, e.g. increased power consumption for running an IT system and the need of scarce resources to build IT artifacts [11]. The information system artifact is a tool that mediates activities and is different from a simple IT artifact. This is because

M.C. Tremblay et al. (Eds.): DESRIST 2014, LNCS 8463, pp. 1–16, 2014.

the information system artifact is considered to be an intricate socio-technical system defined as an "integrated and cooperating set of people, processes, software, and information technologies to support individual, organizational, or societal goals" [45]. Also there seems to be a strong public belief in the information system as an enabler of sustainability [46]. All larger systems are influenced by a variety of stakeholders that determines its future [17] and this is also implied for the information system. While no definite definition of the open innovation concept exists and the newness of open innovation itself was argued [42], the concept has usually proclaimed that a single organization could not innovate in solitude (closed innovation) any longer [9]. Therefore open innovation is dependent on reaching and involving more stakeholders [6] which could be described as a paradigm shift for setting innovation strategy and managing the innovation process. The information system could make it easier for stakeholders to organize and share ideas to reach a common set of goals [12]. Although initiated as a focused design concept for accessibility issues, universal design has broadened its scopes and has become popular in interdisciplinary design research. One way of looking into universal design out of the accessibility domain is its ability to increase user involvements through design. Since the 1960s it has been generally acknowledged that user participation in the information system development process could increase the likelihood of project success [2], [16], [41]. User involvement is therefore likely to result in increased user satisfaction [18], [41] and the perceived usefulness of the application [16], [41].

It was argued in this paper that a universal design concept incorporated into information system development would increase user participation in the design process and thus could contribute in achieving a target goal. If a link could be created between system development and the external social world, we would see that the same concerned social world that could be affected by sustainability issues would be a cause of the system's development decisions. Taking this into account, information system design incorporating the concept of universal design presented in this paper has an increased chance to influence sustainability goals. The underlying research question considered in this research paper is: "How universal design concepts may be used for improving sustainability achievement goals through the information system design?" A theoretical framework titled as "Inclusive Innovation Framework" was proposed, which explained how to design an information system inclusively by additional interactive stakeholder involvement and also as an iterative development process in order to achieve user satisfaction, successfulness of the system, and eventually the desired sustainability goals.

This paper is divided into eight sections. After this introduction section, necessary understandings of sustainability, open innovation, and universal design were introduced in the background section. The inclusive innovation framework (Fig. 1) showed how to support and improve the information system development that enables sustainability achievements, presented in Section 3. A requirement engineering model (Fig. 2) was presented in Section 4, based on the activities from a cognitive decision-making model to clarify how the proposed inclusive innovation framework could practically be used. The method section was presented in Section 5 followed by the results in Section 6, where two use cases were presented to validate the proposed framework. Section 7 presented a thorough discussion and future research possibilities that were initiated from this research work followed by a conclusion given in Section 8.

# 2    Background

## 2.1    Sustainability

One key definition of sustainable development, i.e. sustainability, was given by the world commission on environment and development, "that it meets the needs of the present without compromising the ability of future generations to meet their own needs" [47], also known as the Brundtland definition. Subsequently, to work for sustainability is to enhance a process to minimize or reverse the negative impact of that process on sustainability, both currently and in the future. The majority of research in green IT has focused on how to improve sustainability through more power-efficient computers [10] and thereby reduce greenhouse gas emission. Sustainability should perhaps not only focus on a particular perspective like the environment. An improved and more holistic way could be to use Elkington's triple bottom line (TBL) which consists of three components, namely: economic performance, society, and the natural environment [40]. For instance, promoting sustainable design could be found from the previous work of the authors, in which the TBL perspective was used in designing sustainable IT systems [33]. To remedy sustainability, problems that are based solely on technological solutions are futile since information systems are embedded in a societal development, and the information system could have a crucial role as part of a comprehensive approach [21] by influencing organizational and individual behaviors towards sustainability in all three components of TBL.

Research in the information system could contribute by taking a holistic view of an entire system, its design, and its aim to reach sustainability [11]. From an organizational perspective, all organizations have a set of goals to create values and the organization implements strategies to achieve these goals [7]. Shareholder wealth is often the main goal but could be viewed as a form of narrow self-interest. This individual rationality does not, however, always lead to collective rationality [46], e.g. sustainability could be viewed as a collective rationality goal shared by all stakeholders. Reaching sustainability and minimizing environmental impact therefore could largely be derived from the capability to find new solutions to innovation and the probability to do so could be increased by acquiring more resources, e.g. getting more stakeholders involved.

## 2.2    Open Innovation

The number of approaches to innovation is numerous and some are similar or become similar depending on researchers and the lack of an agreed clear definition [15], [30], [42]. Open innovation increases the probability to capture innovation opportunities by including external stakeholders, e.g. customers, suppliers, and competitors etc. in the innovation process. Gassman and Enkel [19] found three archetypical processes in open innovation: "outside-in process", "inside-out process" and "coupled process." A distinction between open innovation and von Hippel's "User Innovation" is that the latter is solely centered on the user [3] and not as the prior that also includes suppliers, competitors, and others, e.g. inter-organizational innovation is very important [43].

For example, previous research has showed that external stakeholder involvement and expansion to academic research is important for the design of open innovation

[34]. Research has also shown that the collective intelligence of groups-many minds are often better than one—seemed to be good at idea generation [4] that is shared with crowdsourcing [29] whereas crowdsourcing seems to be mostly focused on solving a predefined task and could be seen as outsourcing to the crowd [15]. More users and active user participation should therefore leverage the "wisdom of crowds" [29] to harvest the collective intelligence.

In the context of this paper an interesting question related to open innovation that still remained was: What could be the different driving forces that would motivate an organization towards the use of the information system in having a higher impact towards sustainability goals? More stakeholders given by utilizing the power of open innovation should give a better chance to move towards sustainable goals [33]. Also an amended way could be to design a sustainable system with the help of different stakeholders, e.g. user involvement [18] that could promote a positive motivation to reach sustainable goals in the system design. To design a sustainable system could perhaps remedy the recognized needs of sustainable practices [12] that could fit multiple levels of practices and also consider multidimensionality, i.e. TBL.

## 2.3     Universal Design and its Principles

Although universal design, inclusive design, and design for all are alternative words for the similar basic concept [35]. The customary understanding of universal design is that it improves the user experience through design across a broad range of users. Thus by meeting different requirements of the excluded user group, universal design promises to improve product experience through a comprehensive range of users without any special need for adaption or specialized design by the users [5]. One of the present vulnerabilities in universal design is that sometimes it becomes more of a design concept than a design strategy by promising too much to the users. However, the universal design concept could offer more than just design for people with disabilities and it is thus important to explore those possibilities to be utilized in a broader perspective. Foster and Franz highlighted user involvement need in the early stages of system development [16] and universal design should thus be embedded within the design and development process for improved user involvement resulting in enhanced designed products, systems, and services.

One approach to seek user's involvement is framed in the concept of open innovation design space presented in this paper. In the context of this research interest we believe that universal design could help in introducing different driving factors for achieving sustainability. Use of the open innovation concept could therefore support practicing universal design, leading towards a successful system design for achieving the sustainability goals. The original set of universal design principles are copyrighted to the Center of Universal Design and developed by a group of U.S. designers and design educators from five organizations in 1997 [39]. These principles are Equitable Use, Flexibility in Use, Simple and Intuitive Use, Perceptible Information, Tolerance for Error, Low Physical Effort, and Size and Space for Approach and Use. In this research, three design principles (Equitable Use, Size and Space for Approach and Use, and Tolerance for Error) were ignored. Our interpretation was that they address the accessibility issue of a designed system where accessibility is solely meant for reflecting physical limitations or disabilities that were not the present scope of interest.

# 3     The Inclusive Innovation Framework

The core argument behind the idea of this proposed framework was that by improving a system development process by an open innovation concept and the universal design principles would enable the maximum possible users to be active in the requirement capturing process. The relationships between different chosen factors in the framework were explained in this section. Since our assumption was that increased user participation in information system development by using the concept of universal design could increase the possibility of achieving sustainability goals, the four universal design principles were considered. These could increase external driving factors such as standards, user demand, pressure from a dedicated group, disclosure requirement etc., as well as internal driving factors of the information system such as social equity, simplicity in use, and strong learning ability. These internal and external motivation factors could help to achieve sustainability goals.

Tait and Vessey [40] addressed the need to reduce the number of factors being studied. Investigating all factors affecting user involvement and its impact on system success could be tedious and the main constructs that are central to influencing user involvement for the system's success should be narrowed down and analyzed [40, 41]. Reducing the number of factors and finding relevancies between them is therefore an important issue while designing a framework. Keeping this in mind, two contingent variables have been selected from the universal design principles: Flexibility in Use and Perceptible Information, which are in a relation with the next two variables also selected from the universal design principles: Low Physical Effort, and Simple, Intuitive Use.

The framework presented in Figure 1 acquired four universal design principles for consideration that could work in a circular process in the inclusive innovation design space. When an information system design is simple and used intuitively it would be perceived as a "flexible to use system" by its users. Furthermore, when the information presented in the system would easily be perceptible it would lead towards the "simple use" of a system through its design. An information system that takes less physical effort during its use could thus be perceived as a "flexible system" to its users. Since poor design could initiate limited stakeholder involvement, the proposed framework could contribute towards benefiting the user participation (inclusive innovation design space in Figure 1). It was understood from our previous discussion that by enabling the information system's supported actions the possibility to realize sustainability goals could become higher. Therefore it is important to consider the user satisfaction parameter, which would be promoted through the design strategies of the system. Furthermore, a combinatorial approach of two dependent variables, flexibility in use and perceptible information along with two other variables (low physical effort and simple, intuitive use) could realize user satisfaction that could lead towards sustainability goals (Figure 1). Since a system that is simple and spontaneous to use, easy to understand, remember, and learn should be able to promote any sustainability actions or goals as desired by the system designers, it would lead to the system success phase. Nevertheless, there could be other different factors that could influence a system to be defined as successful from the point of achieving sustainability goals, which were beyond the scope of this research.

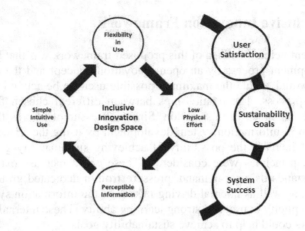

Fig. 1. Inclusive innovation framework for sustainability

## 4    Requirement Engineering Model

Designing a future information system requires a thorough understanding of organizations, user behavior, technology, and how all these are interrelated. The management of knowledge and intellectual assets is crucial for companies that desire to survive in the turbulent, ever more global and competitive environment [1]. Nuseibeh and Easterbrooks [36] defined requirement engineering as a series of decisions that lead from recognition of a customer problem to be solved (or a need to be satisfied) to a detailed specification of that problem. Typically requirement engineering is modeled as a process including a variety of sequential or iterative activities [26], [31]. Decision-making appears typically as embedded into one of the activities in the requirement engineering process. In the previous example [26], such an activity is "requirements analysis and negotiation." In another requirement, the engineering process described by Macaulay [31] is an activity of "feasibility and choice of options." This means that a requirement engineering model is important in several contexts. These different contexts could be considered as individual parameters for a requirement engineering model.

With the proposed inclusive innovation framework in hand it is thus important to realize how the activities in this framework could be practiced. A requirement engineering model could consequently help us understand what was proposed and described in this section. In order to raise the understanding of sustainability goals we call for an interactive approach in which distinguishing between the organizational and individual level of decision-making would be needed. Individual experts' work is full of choices, which may not be visible for upper organizational level actors, e.g. boards, management groups etc. In their cognitive process model Corner et al. [8] stressed these decision-making levels as four activities: attention, encoding, storage/retrieval, and choice, which were taking place iteratively at the organizational and individual levels. These four activities were considered and mapped in our requirement engineering model as four parameters that have relational connectivity within themselves. These parameters and the proposed model based on them were shown in Figure 2 and described below.

- Attention could determine the usefulness of a system, which means that the stakeholders would be aware of the usefulness of the system.
- Encoding could give information that would be determined as usability of the system in this research.
- Storage/Retrieval in our model would be mapped as sustainability awareness. Whether or not the stakeholders would be aware of sustainability, it could be used as an information bank that could be used to put impact on the other three parameters of our choice.
- Choice is an iterative process. It was mapped with the user participation and it would be the choice of the designers, whether or not they would be designing by considering any certain design principles for universal design.

Houdek and Pohl [22] noticed that requirement engineering activities were heavily intertwined and not seen as separate tasks by the participants of the process. We supported their argument and argued that decision-making could appear in intertwined requirement engineering activities for both individual levels, e.g. requirement engineering engineers' focus of attention and choices made, and collective levels, e.g. stakeholder communication, expert boards' work, and project management. The principle question behind this requirement engineering model's activities was: How could the information system's users successfully be driven to a decision towards sustainable awareness by the system's usefulness, usability, and inclusiveness of user participation? This model considered sustainability awareness to be its centralized objective since we previously discussed that an inclusive innovation framework could make stakeholders more involved and committed to a common sustainable goal. Active user participation would be helpful for discovering the usability of the system. Thus the user satisfaction parameter could be used to measure and derive usefulness of the system, which in turn would motivate increased user participation. On the other hand, positive feedback from the users of a useful system could motivate the designers to enhance the "design for all" concept for triggering user inclusion. Besides, an information system which could be perceived to be useful by its users should increase user satisfaction level. Furthermore, a higher user satisfaction acts as an external motivation factor to improve the system design. Therefore an improved usability outcome from a system would possibly result in useful system development by involving more user participations and this could make the whole process an iterative one. The combination of the usefulness of a system, a system's usability, and increased user participation could be an interoperable process to enhance sustainability awareness amongst the users of the system.

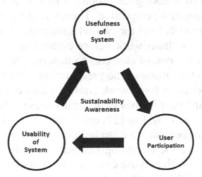

**Fig. 2.** A requirement engineering model for inclusive innovation framework

## 5    Method

The framework presented in Figure 1 was validated using use case methodology, which was important to clarify and organize system requirements. The use case is a popular and powerful method that gives a decent foundation for the verification of higher-level models. This usually is done by role-playing for the validation of different functional requirements. The sequences of interactions between a system and its users related to a specific goal are represented typically through the use cases.

For the validation of proposed inclusive innovation framework, two previous research articles were selected as our cases that could reflect similar research interests of sustainability and information system design. Two use cases were then derived on the basis of models presented in those two articles. These use cases showed how those models would behave within the context of our proposed inclusive innovation framework. In the first article by Kasarda, Termenny et al. [25], Design For Adaption (DFAD) methodology was discussed for achieving sustainable design goals. The first use case showed how inclusive innovation framework could contribute to DFAD methods to achieve sustainability goals. In the second article by Jabareen [24], the author presented a conceptual framework for sustainable development. The second use case thus showed how inclusive innovation framework could be applied in this conceptual framework for achieving sustainability.

The rationales behind choosing these two articles were that they were highly related to the similar aims of inclusive innovation framework in terms of goal, size, and complexity. The phenomenon presented in two selected articles was considered as two case studies. The proposed framework introduced a new way of achieving sustainability in information system design in which the organization level focuses were prioritized by using the concept of universal design and open innovation. Case studies should investigate contemporary phenomena in real life and the focus should be on organizational or managerial level [48] cited in [23] which was the instance here too. Thus the two selected models from the articles were considered to be our theoretical sampling as two cases. They were critical and extreme cases concerning the sustainability achievement. Through the help of use cases it was then shown how our proposed framework could act on these samples. Since it is often appropriate to choose multiple cases for theory testing and descriptions [23], two cases were chosen.

Since use case also focuses on the interaction of users in a particular situation of system by showing all possible system activities, it could thus make it easy to understand the difficulty of a large system by breaking the problems in to major functions and by stipulating applications from the user's perspective. Therefore different artifacts were identified from the two selected models from the two selected articles and were analyzed in the context of inclusive innovation framework before coming up with the use-case design. This was done by means of a group of elements to describe the behavioral views of two different cases presented in two articles. The presentation of two use cases to show how the proposed inclusive innovation framework could fit into the two selected cases conforms to the purpose of using case studies in qualitative research by Walsham [44] cited in [23], Eisenhardt [13] cited in [23], Lee [27] cited in [23], and Lee and Baskerville [28] cited in [23] where it was argued that case studies could be used to test theory within the positivist paradigm. Therefore the reasoning behind the choice of these two particular cases and thereby coming up with two use cases for the initial validation of the proposed theoretical framework was evidently unbiased.

# 6     Results

## 6.1     Use Case 1

Kasarda, Termenny et al. [25] presented two simple models for demonstrating the DFAD concept that explained how a control system analysis and design could be applied for adaptable product design. Our first use case therefore dealt with how an inclusive innovation framework could be used in the closed-loop feedback system.

The use-case diagram was shown in Figure 3. The suggested process of building this use case was then described. A closed-loop dynamic feedback system was redesigned by Kasarda, Termenny et al. [25] to a multivariable control system in which authors showed mathematically how multiple inputs and outputs could work as a nested loop. The components of the basic control system were mapped with the elements of inclusive innovation framework to show how the control system process could be sustainable by adding additional parameters from our proposed framework.

**Use Case:** Designing a control system for sustainability
**Level:** System
**Scope:** Changing the performances in different phases of control system to make the overall procedure more sustainable
**Primary Actors:** Designer of the control system (giving input or desired output response)
**Supporting Actors:** Users, System engineers (not shown on use-case diagram)
**Preconditions:** None
**Success Guarantees:** The team has good communication ability with its stakeholders and they are aware of the meaning of the sustainability goal in the context of their project.

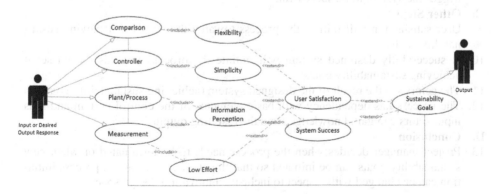

**Fig. 3.** Use cases for closed-loop control feedback system from [25] with inclusive innovation framework

**Stakeholders and concerns:**
- **Designers:** want to understand how to use inclusive innovation framework for increasing user satisfaction and achieving the system's success leading towards sustainability goals.
- **Users:** want to feel the system is simple, flexible, easy to perceive, and takes low effort to learn.
- **System Engineers:** want to understand the requirements of users and pass the information to designers accordingly.

**Trigger:** The designer decides to design the control system to be sustainable for enhancement of the user satisfaction.

**Success scenario:**

**A. Initialization of the Control Process**
1. The designers initiate the process by an input signal or desired output response signal. The input and out signals are compared.
2. Different components use algorithms to modulate actuator. The actuator is used to measure the changes.
3. The performance of the process or the system is to be controlled.
4. How the signals are detected and measured should be considered.

**B. Inclusive Innovation Design Space Process**
5. The comparison should be flexible with the context of the process or system. This increases user satisfaction.
6. The controller that is going to measure the changes should be simple enough so that the successfulness of a system can be increased based on this.
7. Users should be able to perceive the process information system easily so that it can lead towards system's success.
8. Low effort (physical or cognitive) should be given for the measurement and designers need to keep this in mind. This will improve user satisfaction. Measurement should also be given to consideration to be easily perceivable, which will trigger the system to be successful.

**C. Other Steps**
9. User satisfaction will initiate the process towards the phase of achieving sustainability goals.
10. A successfully designed system will initiate the process towards the phase of achieving sustainability goals.
11. The actors see the result of the designed system (achieving sustainability goals).
12. The process has dependency with basic elements of the control system and thus input actors can gain knowledge from the resulting output.

**D. Conclusion**
13. Project manager decides when the process needs to be terminated or when new sustainability goals can be initiated so that the elements of control process initiation can be changed with respect to inclusive innovation design space.

**Variations:**
1. The process is iterative so several iterations might be required before determining the true meaning of system success and user satisfaction based on the context of process or system of the designed system (achieving sustainability goals).

2.  Steps 5 and 6 should be performed parallel to steps 7 and 8.
3.  It may be needed to refine the understanding of sustainability goal with the context of selected system or plant after the first iteration for achieving system success and user satisfaction accordingly.

## 6.2   Use Case 2

Jabareen [24] developed a conceptual framework for sustainable development that was built on seven concepts. The central concept was the ethical paradox where sustainability (related to environment) and development (related to monetary variables) could have different practices based on the differences in ideological points of view. Natural capital stock represented all natural resources for the idea of maintaining it constant through time. Integrative management was the holistic view to integrate economic, environmental, and social matters in the management process. Utopia represented a vision for humans in which concepts of solidarity and justice are incorporated. Eco-Form was the design with ecological desired goals; in reality sustainable design. Global Agenda was a new political discourse based on sustainability. Equity was the social aspects of sustainable development and included economic, environmental, and social considerations and social values such as democracy, empowerment, freedom etc. The use-case diagram of inclusive innovation framework mapped into the framework of Jabareen [24] was shown in Figure 4. The purpose of Jabareen [24] was to understand the definition of sustainable development and the framework initiated this understanding from a multidisciplinary perspective. This framework was therefore considered important in order to understand what sustainable development could be in the context of the information system, its present and future development. The actors in the use case were the information system users who strive to reach any predefined sustainable goals. Eco format deals with design in a sustainable context and could be seen as sustainable design. Sustainable design should strive towards simple intuitive use since the information systems would then be characterized and seen as understandable and intuitive by the user.

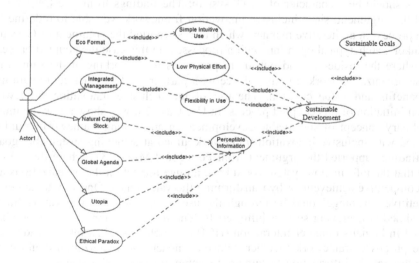

**Fig. 4.** Use cases of sustainable design with inclusive innovation framework

Also eco format could be seen as a parameter impacting the information system in a way in which the user should be given the possibility to use the information system without compromising any extra efforts (cognitive or physical). Ethical paradox could trigger perceptible information since it would have impact on the perceived legibility on information given by the system to the user. Natural capital stock belonged to the improved perceptible information parameter because the rule of keeping resources at a constant level is straightforward and also contributes to the legibility of the information system. Integrative management triggers flexibility in use, since the integration of economic, environmental, and social aspects could be done in many ways by the system. Utopia could activate perceptible information because the vision given by an information system could be said to identify universal goals (democracy, justice, empowerment etc.) that probably all users could agree with, were worth striving for, and could be internalized by users to give legibility to the information system. Global agenda also could trigger perceptible information because the new political discourse that was based on sustainability must provide legibility. As mentioned in Section 2.3, "Equitable Use" universal design principle was not considered in this research; the effect of equity into inclusive innovation framework was not discussed here.

## 7     Discussions and Future Work

The assumption stated in Section 3 was that increased user participation in information system development by using the concept of universal design could increase the possibility of achieving sustainability goals. The two use cases presented in the result section gave support to this. From the first case it was shown how a closed-loop feedback system can act more sustainably with the help of inclusive innovation framework. The DFAD concept for achieving sustainable system design was heightened by the help of inclusive innovation framework. Harmon et al. [20] found that an information system aiming for achieving sustainability should be able to redefine the process and this should be a character of an IT system. The findings from Use Case 1 supported this argument, since inclusive innovation framework was able to redefine the whole process in an iterative manner, which also supported the argument of Gassman and Enkel's archetypical open innovation processes (in this case the coupled process) [19], where the inside-out and outside-in processes were working at the same time and the organization worked in an alliance with partners and together could gain mutual benefits and value creation. The use of the inclusive innovation framework showed initiation of this coupled process. In Use Case 2 it was shown how the multidisciplinary concept of sustainable development in an existing framework could be practiced with inclusive innovation framework aimed at achieving sustainable goals. This finding supported the argument from Porter and Millar [37] where the authors wrote that the information system could have a huge impact on the organizations and their competitive achievement by transforming the value chain. One way to achieve a competitive advantage could be through the use of the inclusive innovation framework aimed at achieving sustainability goals. The transformation of the value chain initiated in human-computer interaction (HCI) research was taken into consideration by the proposed framework together with the impacts an organization could experience through the information system use by achieving sustainable goals.

Two important transfers were initiated from the findings of this research. Looking into universal design concept beyond physical disability was one major shift. The way universal design principles were used in the framework had nothing to do with design for people with disabilities. This supported the argument raised in the work of Mustaquim and Nyström [33] in which the authors used universal design principles to derive design principles for sustainability and argued that it was important to consider the universal design idea while aiming for sustainable design. Secondly, the concept of sustainable HCI was represented out of its traditional thoughts. Usually sustainable HCI referred design for changing human behavior towards ecological actions. This is often done by using cognitive dissonance to persuade and change users' behavior towards a predefined more sustainable behavior. The framework in this paper showed that this must not always be the case, to use HCI in a sustainable context. Instead HCI could represent its experience of sustainability in many different manners (universal design perspective, for example) and this could help building knowledge in the research of information system design and design science.

Smith and Reinertsen [38] argued that sharpening the front-end of the design and making the decisions earlier may have a better chance of attaining a direct effect on the goal of creating the product, such as by a successful marketing launch, higher user satisfaction, and increased usability of the product. Based on their argument and considering sustainability achievement as a goal to be affected, the proposed requirement engineering model could help identify the needs that could be essential to address in the earlier stages of system development. Because each decision might embody a commitment or abandonment to stakeholders' concerns, we stressed an active and reflective collaboration in the early phases using this requirement engineering model. Improved visibility into the requirement engineering process through the adoption of the open innovation concept should therefore enable better communication between different stakeholders.

A number of motivating research possibilities were initiated from the result of this research work. For instance, how to measure and perhaps benchmark an organization's information system in terms of achieving sustainability goals or sustainability measurement could be a highly interesting topic. What the appropriate methods to introduce would be when doing research on the requirement engineering model with organization could be another interesting research question for further study. Also it would be interesting to study how we could utilize collaborations in a stakeholder network to reach sustainability, together with a system's success and user satisfaction. Another research topic could be to investigate how different incentive systems could work in the inclusive innovation framework with the stakeholders involved in the process. Initiating information collection process for finding requirements from different user groups to measure sustainability goals through the inclusive information framework could be another issue that might commence from this paper. Empirical data collection from organizations using different information systems aiming for sustainable goals would be needed for this purpose. A combination of the inclusive innovation framework and the requirement engineering model in one unified model form could then be suggested, based on the findings from the empirical data analysis. Finally, it would also be interesting to see the possibilities to improve the usability of a system through measuring sustainability goals using the inclusive innovation framework.

## 8     Conclusions

In this paper the inclusive innovation framework was proposed, which showed how to achieve sustainability goals through the design of the information system. The framework included universal design principles and used the concept of open innovation in terms of creating a design space which was supported by a requirement engineering model. The findings from this research suggested that it would be worthwhile to practice inclusive innovation framework for achieving sustainability goals through the design of an information system. While research driven innovation is pulled by organizations and technology based innovation is pushed towards the organizations, design could play an important role for adding additional values towards improved usability of a system that could contribute in promoting design driven innovation for organizations. It was shown in this paper that it could be possible to use concepts from HCI to build new knowledge in information system study that would permit the collection of empirical data for further research.

## References

1. Amidon, D.M.: The Innovation Superhighway: Harnessing Intellectual Capital for Sustainable Collaborative Advantage. Butterworth-Heinemann, Amsterdam (2003)
2. Barki, H., Hartwick, J.: Measuring User Participation, User Involvement, and User Attitude. MIS Quarterly 18(1), 59–82 (1994)
3. Bilgram, V., Brem, A., Voigt, K.-I.: User-Centric Innovations in New Product Development – Systematic Identification of Lead Users Harnessing Interactive and Collaborative Online-Tools. International Journal of Innovation Management 12(3), 419–458 (2008)
4. Bonabeau, E.: Decisions 2.0: The Power of Collective Intelligence. MIT Sloan Management Review 50(2), 45–52 (2009)
5. British Standards Institute: BS 7000-6:2005 Design management systems, Managing inclusive design – Guide, BSI, London (2005)
6. Chesbrough, H.: The era of open innovation. Sloan Management Review 44(3), 35–41 (2003)
7. Chesbrough, H., Rosenblom, R.S.: The role of the business model in capturing value from innovation: evidence from Xerox Corporation's technology spin-off companies. Industrial and Corporate Change 11(3), 529–555 (2002)
8. Corner, P.D., Kinicki, A.J., Keats, B.W.: Integrating Organizational and Individual Information processing Perspectives on Choice. Organization Science 5(3), 294–308 (1994)
9. Dahlander, L., Gann, D.M.: How open is innovation? Research Policy 39(6), 699–709 (2010)
10. Dao, V., Langella, I., Carbo, J.: From green to sustainability: Information Technology and an integrated sustainability framework. Journal of Strategic Information Systems 20(1), 63–79 (2011)
11. Dedrick, J.: Green IS: Concepts and Issues for Information Systems Research. Communications of the Association for Information Systems 27, 173–184 (2010)
12. Di Gango, P.M., Wasko, M.: Steal my idea! Organizational adoption of user innovations from a user innovation community: A case study of Dell IdeaStorm. Decision Support Systems 48(1), 303–312 (2009)

13. Eisenhardt, K.: Building Theories from Case Study Research. Academy of Management Review 14(4), 532–550 (1989)
14. Elkington, J.: Towards the Sustainable Corporation: Win-Win-Win Business Strategies for Sustainable Development. California Management Review 36(2), 90–101 (1994)
15. Estellés-Arolas, E., González-Ladrón-de-Guevara, F.: Towards an Integrated Crowdsourcing Definition. Journal of Information Science 38(2), 189–200 (2012)
16. Foster Jr., S.T., Franz, C.R.: User involvement during information systems development: A comparison of analyst and user perceptions of system acceptance. Journal of Engineering and Technology Management 16(3-4), 329–348 (1999)
17. Freeman, R.E.: Strategic Management: A Stakeholder Approach. Pitman, Boston (1984)
18. Garceau, L., Jancura, E., Kneiss, J.: Object oriented analysis and design: A new approach to systems development. Journal of Systems Management 44(1), 25–33 (1993)
19. Gassman, O., Enkel, E.: Towards a theory of open innovation: three core process archetypes. In: Proceedings of the R&D Management Conference, Lisbon, Portugal, July 6-9, pp. 1–18 (2004)
20. Harmon, R.R., Demirkan, H., Raffo, D.: Roadmapping the next wave of sustainable IT. Foresight 14(2), 121–138 (2012)
21. Hilty, L.M., Hercheui, M.D.: ICT and Sustainable Development. In: Berleur, J., Hercheui, M.D., Hilty, L.M. (eds.) HCC9/CIP2010. IFIP AICT, vol. 328, pp. 227–235. Springer, Heidelberg (2010)
22. Houdek, F., Pohl, K.: Analyzing Requirements Engineering Processes: A case study. In: Proceedings of the 11th International Workshop on Database and Expert Systems Applications (DEXA), pp. 983–987. IEEE Press (2000)
23. Iacono, J.C., Brown, A., Holtham, C.: The use of the Case Study Method in Theory Testing: The Example of Steel eMarketplaces. The Electronic Journal of Business Research Methods 9(1), 57–65 (2011)
24. Jabareen, Y.: A New Conceptual Framework for Sustainable Development. Environment, Development and Sustainability 10(2), 179–192 (2008)
25. Kasarda, M.E., Terpenny, J.P., Inman, D., Precoda, K.R., Jelesko, J., Sahin, A., Park, J.: Design for adaptability (DFAD) - a new concept for achieving sustainable design. Robotics and Computer-Integrated Manufacturing 23(6), 727–734 (2007)
26. Kotonya, G., Sommerville, I.: Requirements Engineering, Processes and Techniques. John Wiley & Sons (1998)
27. Lee, A.: A Scientific Methodology for MIS Case Studies. MIS Quarterly 13(1), 33–50 (1989)
28. Lee, A., Baskerville, R.: Generalizing Generalizability in Information Systems Research. Information Systems Research 14(3), 221–243 (2003)
29. Leimeister, J.M., Huber, M., Bretschneider, U., Krcmar, H.: Leveraging Crowdsourcing: Activation-Supporting Components for IT-Based Ideas Competition. Journal of Management Information Systems 26(1), 197–224 (2009)
30. Lichtenthaler, U.: Open Innovation: Past Research, Current Debates, and Future Directions. Academy of Management Perspectives 25(1), 75–93 (2011)
31. Macaulay, L.A.: Requirements Engineering. Springer, London (1996)
32. Melville, N.P.: Information systems innovation for environmental sustainability. MIS Quarterly 34(1), 1–21 (2010)
33. Mustaquim, M.M., Nyström, T.: Designing Sustainable IT System – From the Perspective of Universal Design Principles. In: Stephanidis, C., Antona, M. (eds.) UAHCI/HCII 2013, Part I. LNCS, vol. 8009, pp. 77–86. Springer, Heidelberg (2013)

34. Mustaquim, M.M., Nyström, T.: Design principles of open innovation concept – universal design viewpoint. In: Stephanidis, C., Antona, M. (eds.) UAHCI/HCII 2013, Part I. LNCS, vol. 8009, pp. 214–223. Springer, Heidelberg (2013)
35. Mustaquim, M.: Gaze Interaction – A Challenge for Inclusive Design. In: Pichappan, P., Ahmadi, H., Ariwa, E. (eds.) INCT 2011. CCIS, vol. 241, pp. 244–250. Springer, Heidelberg (2011)
36. Nuseibeh, B., Easterbrook, S.: Requirements engineering: a roadmap. In: Proceedings of the Conference on The Future of Software Engineering (ICSE 2000), pp. 35–46. ACM (2000)
37. Porter, M.E., Millar, V.E.: How Information Gives You Competitive Advantage: The Information Revolution Is Transforming the Nature of Competition. Harvard Business Review 63(4), 149–160 (1985)
38. Smith, P.G., Reinertsen, D.G.: Developing Products Half the Time: New Rules, New Tools, 2nd edn. John Wiley & Sons, New York (1998)
39. Story, M.F.: Maximizing Usability: The Principles of Universal Design. Assistive Technology 10(1), 4–12 (1998)
40. Tait, P., Vessey, I.: The Effect of User Involvement on System Success: A Contingency Approach. MIS Quarterly 12(1), 91–108 (1988)
41. Terry, J., Standing, C.: The value of user participation in the E-commerce systems development. Informing Science Journal 7, 31–45 (2004)
42. Trott, P., Hartmann, D.: Why 'open innovation' is old wine in new bottles. International Journal of Innovation Management 13(4), 715–736 (2009)
43. Vanhaverbeke, W., Van de Vrande, V., Chesbrough, H.: Understanding the advantages of open innovation practices in corporate venturing in terms of real options. Creativity and Innovation Management 17(4), 251–258 (2008)
44. Walsham, G.: Interpreting Information Systems in Organizations. Wiley (1993)
45. Watson, R.T., Boudreau, M.-C., Chen, A.J.: Information systems and environmentally sustainable development: energy informatics and new directions for the IS community. MIS Quarterly 34(1), 23–38 (2010)
46. Watson, R.T., Corbett, J., Boudreau, M.C., Webster, J.: An Information Strategy for Environmental Sustainability. Communications of the ACM 55(7), 28–29 (2012)
47. WCED (World Commission on Environment and Development): Our Common Future. Oxford University Press, London (1987)
48. Yin, R.K.: Case Study Research: Design and Methods, 2nd, 3rd edn. Sage Publications (1994, 2003)

# Designing Business Models in the Era of Internet of Things*

## Towards a Reference Framework

Stefanie Turber[1], Jan vom Brocke[2], Oliver Gassmann[3], and Elgar Fleisch[4]

[1] Chair of Innovation Management, University of St Gallen, Switzerland
`stefanie.turber@unisg.ch`
[2] Hilti Chair of Business Process Mgt., University of Liechtenstein, Liechtenstein
`jan.vom.brocke@uni.li`
[3] Chair of Innovation Management, University of St Gallen, Switzerland
`oliver.gassmann@unisg.ch`
[4] Chair of Information Management, ETH Zurich, Switzerland
`efleisch@ethz.ch`

**Abstract.** The increasing pervasiveness of digital technologies, also refered to as "Internet of Things" (IoT), offers a wealth of business model opportunities, which often involve an ecosystem of partners. In this context, companies are required to look at business models beyond a firm-centric lens and respond to changed dynamics. However, extant literature has not yet provided actionable approaches for business models for IoT-driven environments. Our research therefore addresses the need for a business model framework that captures the specifics of IoT-driven ecosystems. Applying an iterative design science research approach, the present paper describes (a) the methodology, (b) the requirements, (c) the design and (d) the evaluation of a business model framework that enables researchers and practitioners to visualize, analyze and design business models in the IoT context in a structured and actionable way. The identified dimensions in the framework include the value network of collaborating partners (who); sources of value creation (where); benefits from collaboration (why). Evidence from action research and multiple case studies indicates that the framework is able to depict business models in IoT.

**Keywords:** Internet of Things, business model, value networks, digitization, service-dominant logic, collaboration, digital ecosystem, architecture.

## 1    Introduction

Today companies are exposed to highly dynamic business environments, driven by rapid developments and ever-increasing pervasiveness of digital technologies.

---

* An earlier version of this manuscript appeared in the Proceedings of the 22nd European Conference on Information Systems as "A Business Model Type for the Internet of Things", Research in progress, S. Turber and C. Smiela.

M.C. Tremblay et al. (Eds.): DESRIST 2014, LNCS 8463, pp. 17–31, 2014.
© Springer International Publishing Switzerland 2014

A driving force is that digital technology gets increasingly weaved in previously non-digital products, such as bikes, clothes and everyday household appliances. This phenomenon, referred to as "Internet of Things" (IoT) [1], is expected to have a major influence on the nature of products and services, and in consequence on overarching business models (BM) [2, 3], i.e. the overarching logic of how businesses work [4].

The "Nest", a digitized thermostat for private homes, is a popular, recent example to demonstrate how IoT is changing market dynamics: Equipped with sensors and connected to the internet, the "Nest" can be controlled remotely via a mobile app and can track the energy use of a household over time. These features open up numerous opportunities for novel services and business models within an emerging ecosystem of new collaborators. A current campaign for example includes energy providers as partners to reward users, when they let their "Nest" switch off the HVAC[1] during peak times[2]. From this lens "Nest" itself serves as platform, which brings multiple partners together to (co-) create and exchange valuable services (conf. [5]).

IoT in general inspires a wealth of new business models, which frequently involve diverse partners of thereby arising cross-industry ecosystems [6, 2]. This fact requires companies to rethink their firm-centered lenses in order to stay ahead in IoT driven market environments [5]. However, many companies have difficulties to capture and tap into the unprecedented ecosystem complexity around products and services in a structured way. Burkhardt [6] generally identifies the "absence of formalized means of representations (..) to allow a structured visualization of business model" as a major research gap. We applied existing methods for business modeling in workshops with companies, and found that the important characteristics of IoT ecosystems cannot sufficiently be addressed by these methods. Such characteristics, for instance, include multi-partner collaborations on digital platforms or the customers' enhanced role as value co-creator by providing user data [7, 8].

Our research addresses the need for a business model framework in IoT-driven market environments, which recognizes the specific impact of above-mentioned digitization. We chose a design science research (DSR) approach for our study to design a "framework for IoT business models" as the intended artifact. The artifact's design requirements build upon sources of justificatory knowledge across different domains: Marketing, strategic management and information systems.

The overarching research process is guided by the method described by Peffers et al [9]. All in all, the business model framework shall provide researchers with a framework to readily analyze business models in complex, IoT driven ecosystems. Practitioners are provided with an understandable and consistent framework to depict their organization's current and envisioned business models within complex IoT ecosystems.

In the following section we begin by outlining the method and procedure of our study in more details. We then set out related work and the requirements for the intended artifact. In section 4 we explicate the design of our business model framework by describing each dimension, including a brief rationale and an illustrative real-

---

[1] HVAC: Heating, ventilating, air conditioning.
[2] https://nest.com/thermostat/life-with-nest-thermostat/

world instantiation. The next section describes aspects of the evaluation to test and improve the design, as well as insights on the performance of the proposed artifact. We conclude by outlining key features and limitations of the artifact, as well as implications and an outlook on future research.

## 2    Research Design

As our primary goal is to create a new artifact, we chose a design science research approach. In this paper, the artifact, which we describe as business model framework for the Internet of Things, is an approach for visualizing, envisioning and analyzing complex business models in digital market environments. Our study mostly applies the method suggested by Peffers [9] and includes six iterative activities. Table 1 provides an overview of how we applied the method in our research. The first column outlines each activity $A_1$ to $A_6$. The second column provides details about applied methods and evaluation per activity. The last column includes outcome and status.

Important is that each activity is linked with an appropriate evaluation method to reach at the intended outcome, and less visible, that activity $A_{1-6}$ rather iterative than strictly subsequent. So we iterated in particular the prototyping and evaluation activities $(A_3)$ - the core activities of DSR - several times to continuously determine and improve the performance of the progressing artifact [10]. After several completed iterations we are approaching at the end of $A_3$ to continue with a cross-industry business model workshop as final proof-of-concept demonstration in $A_4$. At this point we see the artifact advanced to a level to share it with the wider scientific community. The present paper describes the artifact prototype prior to the proof-of-concept activity $(A_4)$ of the research process.

## 3    Background

Applying a DSR approach, we build our artifact upon relevant, extant work [11], which we find in three domains:

- Information Systems (IS) research provides us with essential insights regarding the nature of digital technology and digitized objects (3.1).
- Service-dominant (S-D) logic as part of recent marketing research provides a valuable extract about new market dynamics in the light of increasing digitization (3.2).
- Business Model (BM) research provides insights into useful building blocks by a large number of previous modeling approaches for different purposes [6] (3.3).

We proceed with a compact outline of each knowledge source and extract the relevant "bites" to inform the design of our business model artifact.

**Table 1.** Application of DSR for developing the IoT business model artifact [9]

| Activity | Method & Evaluation | Outcome |
|---|---|---|
| **A 1** Outlining the problem situation | Method/Stimulus: Real-world BM workshops with companies revealed the difficulty to visualize, develop and analyze business models in IoT driven business environments with extant BM approaches. Evaluation: • BM workshops in various industries, e. g. heating (5/13), home security (6/13), smart lighting (6/13), mobility (8/13), industry 4.0 (8/13), smart city (11/13) etc. • Literature review, review with researchers (IS, Management sciences), interview with practitioners (strategy, C-level) | • Clear design objective: A "BM for IoT context" • Justified research gap of high relevance • Preliminary assumptions on artifact requirements  Status: done (see: 1 Intro) |
| **A 2** Analyzing extant research for ideas and definition of solution requirements | Method: • Review of extant research at the intersection of management sciences, marketing and information systems research • Review of extant business model approaches • Derivation of requirements from theory  Evaluation: Cross-check w. experts and practitioners, test w. simple real-world IoT-business model instances (Nest) | • Relevant research streams identified, i.e. (1) IS: Digitized objects research; (2) BM research; (3) S-D logic • Justified artifact requirements  Status: done (see: 3 Background) |
| **A 3** Prototyping solutions & testing in practice | Method: • Prototyping by employing design principles [12] as interdisciplinary research team (IS, Strategy Management et al) • Several times: Testing and revisiting prototypes of the new artifact through 1. multiple case studies (cases: BM of startups and incumbents in the IoT context, in the smart home and smart city context specifically. 2. Action research: Business model workshops in IoT context (smart city)  Evaluation: As part of each testing. Evaluation criteria equals the criteria in A5 | • Validated artifact instances, in particular in smart home and smart city context  Status: done (see: 4 Artifact) |
| **A 4** Proof-of-concept demonstration of the applicability of the proposed framework | Method: • Action research: Cross-industry BM workshop with several companies, which are ecosystem partners, i.e. startups and incumbents in the overarching IoT context. Ideal: Wide range of industries represented  Evaluation: • Equals evaluation in A5 • By expert and practictioners | • Validated artifact instance in the overall IoT context  Status: ☐ planned in 2014 |
| **A 5** Summary evaluation | Method: • Semi-structured interviews with BM workshop participants after cross-industry workshop (A 4). • Review with experts from research and practice • Analysing  Evaluation: Structured evaluation according to following sets of criteria • Set 1: to evaluate DSR process by Hevner's Guidelines • Set 2: to evaluate DSR output (artifact) | • Field tested, actionable and justified artifact, ready to use for and researchers and practictioners.  Status: ☐ planned in 2014 |
| **A 6** Communication | Method: Four levels of communication • Academic conference / journal contributions (IS, Strat. Mgt) • Articles in practictioners outlet • Workshop concept to operationalize & apply the BM artifact in firms  Evaluation: • Feedback of wider IS research and BM community • Feedback by practice partners | • Peer reviewed publications  Status: ongoing |

## 3.1    IS: The Nature of Digitized Objects as Nucleus of Business Models in IoT

The Internet of Things, as stated, includes the universe of products and services, which are enabled by digital technology. They are internet-connected and able to directly communicate with each other [12]. According to Yoo et al [2] the incorporation of digital material causes physical objects to adopt all characteristics of digital technology, i.e. e. they become programmable, addressable, sensible, communicable, memorable, traceable, and associable. Yoo et al [3] further theorize that all digitized objects feature a layered architecture, which includes four layers (Fig. 1): The device layer comprises hardware, which can be any kind of devices, and an operating system to control the hardware; the network layer involves both the logical transmission plus network standards, and the physical transport; the service layer features direct interaction with the users through application programs, e.g. as the user create or consume content; the content layer hosts the data, such as texts, images or meta-data like geo-time stamps.

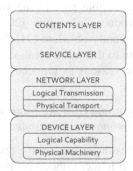

**Fig. 1.** The modular layered architecture of digital technology [5]

A key feature in the context of IoT business models is, that these four modular layers of digitized objects can be de-coupled. This way the digitized object represents a combination of elements across these layers, which are solely loosely interconnected through specified interfaces. "De-couplebility" of content, devices and information infrastructures allows multiple stakeholders to contribute across the four layers in an unforeseen way - interoperability provided [13, 14]. In the final analysis, the layers can be regarded as sources of value creation by multiple ecosystem partners [15, 16] and lay the foundation of business models, which distributively exist in multiple sites. For our artifact we adopt the four layers to naturally structure and organize value creation across multiple partners in digital ecosystems. We regard this as the nucleus of our business model framework in IoT.

## 3.2    Service-Dominant Logic Translates into Key Artifact Requirements

The increasing pervasiveness of digital technology is closely linked with the increasing ability to separate service and information from physical goods [3]. This special affordance of digital technology is a major reason for the emergence of new market dynamics and complex webs of activities between market partners. In this line, the S-D logic has evolved, as a new marketing paradigm seeking to describe the principles of these transformations [8]. As the S-D logic describes a type of market environments, which we envision our business model framework to operate, the S-D logic provides us with valuable input to define our artifact's requirements[3].

A first important cornerstone of S-D logic is the network-centric view. The focus is put on relationships between market partners and customers, which together build "value creation networks". The single firm appears, in the first place, as "organizer of value creation" [18]. In this light a firm's collaborative competence becomes a core premise for competitive advantage [19]. For our artifact we state the first requirement:

*R1: Provide a network-centric view to reflect multi-partner collaborations*

Another distinctive aspect is the assumed **role of the customer**. While traditional value creation models regard firms as the only value creators due to their production and distribution activities, S-D logic ties in with the opposing literature stream, which conceives the customer as an indispensible part in the value creation process: The customer as co-creator and co-producer of value [20]. The traditional producer/consumer divide becomes consequently obsolete [21]. The reason for customers – and entities in general - to contribute to the value creation process differ [22]. For the purpose of this study we classify the reasons as monetary and non-monetary benefits and derive further requirements:

*R2: Reflect customer's role as co-producer in the value network*
*R3: Reflect monetary as well as non-monetary reasons to collaborate*

The concept of customer as co-creator leads also to a revised notion of offerings in S-D logic, by which offerings are no longer conceived as output of a manufacturing process. Instead, offerings are seen as input feeding into the value co-creation process, or what Normann calls "artifacts designed to more effectively enable and organize value co-production" [20]. Offerings can be composed of a variety of artifacts, such as services or goods. In abstract terms, these artifacts represent "carriers" of certain competences [20], and ideally serve all as "a service platform that enables service exchange and value co-creation" [21]. In this light, physical products are conceived as medium to provide service. The traditional distinction between goods and services is finally transcended [21].

This view on artifacts features an important parallel with Yoo et al's layer model of digital innovation (2.1): In S-D logic the "artifacts" serve as platform to create value upon, which perfectly corresponds to the layer model, by which each single layer serves as platform on which other actors can build modules in other layers [23] and with each layer can be seen as source of value creation [conf. 15].

*R4: Reflect layer architecture to structure sources of value creation*

---

[3] Normann's approach is here framed as part of the S-D logic stream for proven similarities [20]

The S-D logic offers a fresh view on resources: The fact that firms always co-create value with the external environment implies that not only internal resources shall be regarded as relevant – as the prevalent resource-based view suggests [24] - yet also external resources that the firm can draw upon. Instead of an internal/external categorization, S-D logic therefore classifies resources as "operant" or "operand". The primacy is put on operant resources. They are dynamic and able to cause effects, such as knowledge, skills and technologies, and usually intangible. Operant resources are employed to act on other resources, while operand resources are acted on [21]. The latter are static and tangible, and include raw materials and goods. [7, 21]. Finally, in S-D logic a firm's external environment, its "ecosystem" of co-creating actors, is therefore seen as operant resource and important source of competitive advantage. It delivers the last requirement:

$R_5$: *Reflect ecosystem and value network partner as operant resource*

To summarize: There is a need for a business model framework featuring five solution requirements $R_{1-5}$, which can be derived from S-D logic (Table 2). These requirements guide the building process of the artifact in $A_3$. For the evaluation activities, the requirement serve as criteria the artifact has to meet.

**Table 2.** S-D logic translated into requirements for the business model artifact

| S-D Logic (extract) | Requirements (R) for the artifact: |
|---|---|
| • Collaboration is essential | $R_1$: Network-centric, rather than firm-centric |
| • Customer and partners are operant resource and co-producer of value | $R_2$: Reflects customer as co-producer, rather than solely receiver |
| • Incentives to participate in the ecosystem can be monetary and non-monetary | $R_3$: Take monetary and non-monetary benefit from collaborating into account |
| • Artifacts (=Yoo's "layers") are source of value creation | $R_4$: Reflect four layers of digital innovation as source of value creation |
| • Ecosystem is operant resource | $R_5$: Explicates all (potential) IoT ecosystem participants of the external environment |

### 3.3    Business Model Research Delivers the Main Building Blocks

So far literature does not provide a commonly acknowledged definition of "business model" and what elements it consists of [2, 28]. In general terms, as stated, the concept refers to the overarching logic of how a business works [4], or put differently, represents "a holistic picture of the business by combining factors located inside and outside the firm" [26].   A review of the extant literature by Mason [27] moreover has yet revealed a shift over time: Initially, the business models were intended to describe the roles of various network actors, especially in the narrow context of early internet and e-commerce businesses. Among them, Timmers' approach might be the most popular example [28]. As the business model concept became more widely applied beyond the context of digital businesses, the network-centric perspective has largely given way to a firm-centric view conceiving business models as undivided "property of the firm" [27]. Today, as digitization reaches all kinds of business and industries - vividly illustrated by the "Nest" example (section 1), we intend to revitalize the network centric view and tie in with early business model research [27, 28]. Not least this parallels with the first solution requirement $R_1$.

Moreover, we analyzed the extant business model approaches as of 1996 against the identified set of solution requirements $R_{1-5}$ as outlined in section 3.2. Our conclusion is that none of the prior studies found met all criteria for mainly two reasons: The approaches conceive business models as concept at firm level rather than network level, or are meant to explicate business models on a generic level and so are not supportive in capturing specifics of IoT ecosystems. As an exception can be seen the approach by El Sawy et al [2], emphasizing the evolutionary dimension of digital business models.

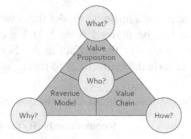

**Fig. 2.** Archetypal Business Model [32]

Despite the variety of business model approaches, it is noticeable that some continually recurring components exist although named differently [4, 26]: These essential elements can be summarized by the following dimensions (Fig. 2): *"Who"* defines the target customer to be addressed, *"What"* refers to the value proposition towards the customer, *"How"* addresses the value chain needed to deliver the value proposition. *"Why"* finally describes the underlying economic model to capture value. This basic approach traces back to Peter Drucker [4] and builds the foundation of business model research to this day [20]. For its archetypal character we elected this conceptualization as starting point to build a specialized business model artifact upon.

## 4        Artifact

In this section, we describe our artifact, a business model framework for IoT contexts, which we reached at after several iterations along the path of six activities as outlined in section 2. In general our research has led to a network-centric, 3-D framework consisting of three dimensions:

- Who: Collaborating partners who build the value network
- Where: Sources of value co-creation rooted in the layer model of digitized objects
- Why: Benefits for partners from collaborating within the value network

We explicate each dimension of the artifact including a short rationale and by referring to the requirements. We illustrate the dimension by the "Nest" case, as introduced in section 1, which also serves as instantiation in the evaluation section.

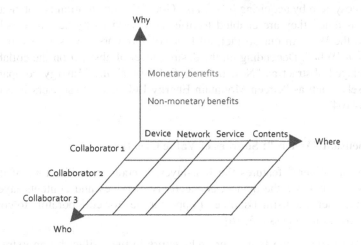

**Fig. 3.** Artifact: Framework design for a business model framework in the IoT context

## 4.1    Dimension "Who": Value Network of Collaborators

The first dimension "Who" encompasses all participants of an IoT ecosystem circling around digitized products. This includes partners, customers and all remaining stakeholders, which we refer to as "collaborators" in a wider sense and which are listed one by one. They can be specified at the intended level of abstraction.

*Rationale:* The explicit itemizing of all participants reflects the service-dominant logic's view that a company's external environment represents an "operant resource" offering the inherent opportunity for each participant to co-create value with other external participants as collaborators [19]. Moreover, customers are listed together with other collaborators on a single dimension, which conveys the philosophy, that value is always co-created with the customer, often even co-produced, especially in the digital context [7]. A distinction between partners and customers reflected by different dimensions was therefore redundant. *Requirements considered:* $R_1$, $R_2$, $R_5$.

*Instantiation "Nest":* In the "Nest" case the collaborating partners, i.e. value creators, are the following: (1) Nest Labs, a company which provides home owners with the "Nest", i.e. a learning thermostat plus an app, to remotely control the device (2) The "Nest" user, who contributes first in a monetary way by purchasing the "Nest" and later by using it as "Nest" feedbacks real-time data about the user's heating habits to Nest Labs (data layer). Nest Labs processes the data to customize the "Nest", i.e. adjusts it to the user's habits, to increase the overall user experience. So far (1) and (2) build a bilateral relationship. As Nest "owns" valuable data due to this relationship, also other partners are interested to collaborate and enhance the value-creation network: (3) Energy providers, who reward Nest users based on individual consumption data (data layer). E.g. if users run their "Nest" in the "rush hour reward" mode, so that the HVAC gets switched off during peak times. (4) Finally Google, who has recently joined the ecosystem by acquiring Nest Labs. Google's contribution is not clear at this point. It is assumed they are enabled to offer new services by access to behavioral data beyond the Web. In our artifact, all four collaborators are listed one by one on the dimension "Who". Depending on the desired level of abstraction the collaborators can be displayed abstract as "Nest users in California" and "Energy companies" or more precisely, such as "Green Mountain Energy Ltd" and "Nest users in San Francisco, CA 94104"[4]

### 4.2    Dimension "Where": Sources of Value Creation

The dimension "Where" features the four-layered modular architecture of digitized products, which includes the device, connectivity, services and contents layer (3.1). Each layer represents a distinct source of opportunities for collaborators to contribute to the value creation process [15, 16].

*Rationale*: We exposed the four-layer architecture in the artifact by an extra dimension, as the nucleus of business models in the IoT context (3.1). The layers naturally structure the collaborators according to their kind of contribution in the value creating process. Another benefit is, that the four layers are able to depict "co-opetition" aspects within the ecosystem landscape: Two players can be partners at one layer and compete on another layer in the same ecosystem [5]. *Requirements considered:* R4

*Instantiation "Nest"*: Along the four-layered structure, Nest Labs contributes on the device layer with the "Nest" thermostat, on the service layer by providing the app as interface to the "Nest" thermostat, and finally on the data layer by providing valuable user data. The user contributes on the device layer by purchasing the "Nest", the content layer by feedbacking real time data. Concerning co-opetition: Playing on different layers, Nest Labs and the energy provider are complimentary in the described scenario. Would the energy provider come up with an own internet-connected thermostat, they may still partner on the service layer, yet compete on the device layer.

### 4.3    Dimension "Why": Benefit for Collaborators

The dimension "Why" outlines each collaborator's "reason" to participate in the ecosystem. It is meant to depict all monetary as well as non-monetary benefits, which attracts collaborators to participate in the ecosystem [19].

*Rationale:* We find it essential to not only depict one company's revenue model, which "Why" is usually meant for (3.2), yet to consider all collaborators' benefits in a wider sense from their participation in the ecosystem. The reason is, that the collaborators

---

[4] In compliance with the prevailing privacy code of conduct.

in sum build the external ecosystem, i.e. e. an essential "operant resource" [7]. In consequence a healthy ecosystem features a competitive advantage, whose overall stability depends on each collaborator's satisfaction. Moreover, as the customer is likewise regarded as collaborator, it is no longer necessary to feature a customer-specific value proposition (in the traditional BM: "What", see 3.2), yet can be covered by the same dimension, "Why", which outlines all benefits occurring in the ecosystem. These can be monetary as well as non-monetary (fun, ethic reasons etc.) [19]. *Requirements considered: $R_1, R_3$*

*Instantiation "Nest":* Nest Labs derives first of all monetary benefits from being part of the ecosystem, i.e. e. revenues by selling the "Nest" device and by selling meaningful data. The "Nest" user's benefits from using "Nest" in the ecosystem context are varied, and may include haptic benefits (pleasant temperature), ethical benefits (saving energy), economic benefits (saving money, getting rewarded) or psychic benefits (benefits). The energy providers are attracted by the possibility to reduce the risk of energy shortage by influencing customers' behavior by monetary incentives. Google may benefit from new insights into consumers' behavior beyond the Web to leverage its data analytics competences into the internet of things[5].

## 5    Evaluation

In the first place, the new artifact should be useful and an effective solution to the problem of depicting IoT-driven business models (cf. "goal" in table 3). To assess whether we have reached at an artifact, which is equally rigor and relevant, we conducted evaluations at two levels: We evaluated (a) the artifact as research output and (b) the underlying research process. For the latter, we compared our overall DSR study with Hevner et al's suggested guidelines for building and evaluating design science research [29]. The following section outlines (a) the output evaluation, with regard to the overall evaluation scheme applied as well as major findings.

As performance is closely related to the intended use, we specifically compared the progressing artifact prototype with the initial goal, i.e. the effective depiction of IoT business models. We operationalized our goal by two sets of criteria: Criteria set 1 analysis whether and to what extent the artifact features good model properties, inspired by March et al [10]. Criteria set 2 examines whether and how well the solution requirements, we derived from S-D logic (section 3) are incorporated in the artifact.

To use appropriate methods for the evaluation of our framework artifact, we consulted prior DSR work specifying the evaluation of models and frameworks [10, 29–31]. We finally gathered a wealth of insights and evidence especially by using case studies and action research, enriched by expert and practitioner evaluations operationalized by questionnaires. Table 3 summarizes the applied evaluation scheme. In the following, we use first and foremost the "Nest" example (detailed in section 4) as instantiation to representatively indicate evidence in a concise way.

---

[5] http://www.wired.com/business/2014/01/googles-3-billion-nest-buy-finally-make-internet-things-real-us/

**Table 3.** Criteria and methods to evaluate the artifact's performance

| Goal of our DSR study | Criteria sets based on goal | Methods for gathering evidence |
|---|---|---|
| An effective solution... | **Set 1 Good model properties**<br>$M_1$: Fidelity with the real world<br>$M_2$: Completeness (=$R_1$-$R_6$)<br>$M_3$: Level of detail<br>$M_4$: Robustness | Interviews / expert evaluation multiple case studies, action research, instantiation |
| ...which is able to depict business models in IoT environments | **Set 2 Justified solution requirements**<br>$R_1$: Network-centric view<br>$R_2$: Customer as co-producer<br>$R_3$: (Non-) monetary reasons to participate<br>$R_4$: Value creation across four layers<br>$R_5$: Ecosystem as operant resource | |

Concerning criteria set 2 we may refer to the elaboration on the dimensions including the "Nest" case, which demonstrated that all solution requirements $R_{1-5}$ are incorporated in the artifact. Concerning set 1: The criteria *"Fidelity with the real world"* is seen reflected as the framework is able to describe the partner constellations and the value creation logic of "Nest" and other analyzed ecosystems, despite its strong simplification. The criteria *"completeness"* is inherent to the artifact by transitive relation: The requirements $R_{1-5}$, which are built in the artifact, reflect the central concepts of the S-D logic. The S-D logic itself is recognized to comprehensively depict digital market dynamics. Hence, we may argue $R_{1-5}$ justifies completeness. Regarding the criteria *"level of detail"* evaluation reveals that overall the artifact's dimension help to depict the core of an IoT ecosystem without getting lost in details. Except for dimension "Why", which carries the benefits for each partner from participating: Here the classification of "monetary" and "non-monetary" benefits helps to clarify on a generic level why partner collaborate. A more fine-grained dimension involving metrics could reveal further useful insights, such as the degree of partner's satisfaction and insights on the ecosystem' overall stability. The artifact's *"robustness"* we see reflected by the flexibility to work smoothly from several angles, e. g. in the Nest case, it is irrespective whether one looks at it from the energy provider's or Nest Labs' perspective. Moreover, the framework is evaluated applicable across different IoT themes and industries, e.g. to smart home, smart city and to any other IoT-driven context. In addition, what we learned as side effect from business model workshops with practitioners is that a method or instruction is desirable to complement the artifact and facilitate using it. A final proof of the value of the artifact is provided by a cross-industry business model workshop and summary evaluation, which are both still to come.

## 6      Conclusion

Although many business model approaches exist, there is no actionable business model framework to effectively depict business models in IoT ecosystems. We see this gap in sharp contrast to the overall importance and omnipresence of the topic[6]

---

[6] http://www.weforum.org/sessions/summary/new-digital-context

and in essence, our research approach attempts to address this need. This section is meant to summarize core features of the artifact and how it contributes to research and practice. We outline limitations and give an outlook on future research.

The specific features of our business model framework can be seen in three differentiating elements incorporated in the artifact: (a) IoT-driven market principles are recognized by applying solution requirements rooted in S-D logic, (b) the sources of value creation in IoT environments are recognized by applying the four layer model. (c) the relevance of the external environment is recognized by strictly applying a network-centric view. Another benefit can be seen in the applied design science research method [9] ensuring that the artifact is closely linked with theory and practice.

Our project is currently approaching at the proof of concept demonstration in $A_4$. Several "prototype and test" iterations in $A_3$ along defined criteria enabled us to determine whether both good model properties and solution requirements are represented in the artifact, and to refine accordingly. In a nutshell, we find the artifact as is well performing in both regards for IoT business models across industries. However, we see some limitations concerning the criteria "level of detail": In the present state the dimension "Why" allows only for a rough picture on each collaborators benefit, which restricts the artifact to solely manual use. To serve as basis for a business model software solution, as requested [6], the dimension needs to be further enhanced e.g. by an underlying metric. Moreover, the artifact works well as tool to depict business models in IoT, yet would benefit from a complementary method to facilitate its application. Furthermore, we tested the artifact so far in ecosystems involving IoT. We yet assume the artifact likewise applicable to digital ecosystems in general, which is another area of future research.

Our DSR study at its completion represents a business model framework, which contributes to both theory and practice: For theory, our work adds to the current business model research in the emerging context of Internet of Things by providing a both theoretically founded and field-tested business model framework. In this way researchers can readily use the framework to for example analyze IoT business model patterns in an efficient and structured way. Our paper also demonstrates, how DSR can be applied for developing a framework at the interface of three different domains: Strategic management, marketing and information systems. So far DSR has been commonly employed in IS research [11], yet is rarely used in management sciences.

For practitioners the artifact serves as tool for depicting, analyzing and envisioning business models in IoT. By making recent IoT-driven market dynamics and specifics of digitized goods explicit, the artifact is able to decidedly support business model development in complex IoT ecosystems. This is relevant, as without a clear view on market dynamics and collaborative value creation logic, it is hard to create sustainable IoT ecosystems and be a competitive part of it, which is the situation today for many companies, with roots in manufacturing in particular. Not least, resulting instance business models, specific to a certain IoT ecosystem, can be seen as mean of communication between current and future ecosystem partners.

**Acknowledgements.** The present work is supported by the Bosch IoT Lab at St Gallen University, Switzerland. An earlier version of this manuscript appeared in the Proceedings of the 22nd European Conference on Information Systems. The authors are grateful to the anonymous reviewers for thoughtful comments and helpful suggestions.

# References

1. Atzori, L., Iera, A., Morabito, G.: The Internet of Things: A survey. Comput. Networks 54, 2787–2805 (2010)
2. El Sawy, O.A., Pereira, F.: Business Modelling in the Dynamic Digital Space. Springer, Heidelberg (2013)
3. Yoo, Y., Lyytinen, K., Boland, R., Berente, N., Gaskin, J., Schutz, D.: The Next Wave of Digital Innovation: Opportunities and Challenges. In: Research Workshop: Digital Challenges in Innovation Research, pp. 1–37 (2010)
4. Magretta, J.: Why business models matter. Harv. Bus. Rev. 80, 86–92 (2002)
5. Yoo, Y., Henfridsson, O., Lyytinen, K.: Research Commentary —The New Organizing Logic of Digital Innovation: An Agenda for Information Systems Research. Inf. Syst. Res. 21, 724–735 (2010)
6. Burkhart, T., Krumeich, J., Werth, D., Loos, P.: Analysing the business model concept - A comprehensive classification of literature. In: International Conference on Information Science, pp. 1–19 (2011)
7. Vargo, S.L., Lusch, R.F.: Evolving to a New Dominant Logic for Marketing. J. Mark. 68, 1–17 (2004)
8. Yoo, Y., Boland, R.J., Lyytinen, K., Majchrzak, A.: Organizing for Innovation in the Digitized World. Organ. Sci. 23, 1398–1408 (2012)
9. Peffers, K., Tuunanen, T., Rothenberger, M.A., Chatterjee, S.: A Design Science Research Methodology for Information Systems Research. J. Manag. Inf. Syst. 24, 45–77 (2007)
10. March, S.T., Smith, G.F.: Design and natural science research on information technology. Decis. Support Syst. 15, 251–266 (1995)
11. Gregor, S., Hevner, A.R.A.: Positioning Design Science Research for Maximum Impact. Manag. Inf. Syst. Q. 37, 337–355 (2013)
12. Kominers, P.: Interoperability Case Study Internet of Things (IoT). Berkman Cent. Res. Publ. 7641 (2012)
13. Palfrey, J., Gasser, U.: Mashups Interoperability and eInnovation. Berkman Publ. Ser (2007)
14. Eaton, B., Elaluf-Calderwood, S., Sørensen, C., Yoo, Y.: Dynamic structures of control and generativity in digital ecosystem service innovation: the cases of the Apple and Google mobile app stores, LSE Working paper series 183. London (2011)
15. Mejtoft, T.: Internet of Things and Co-creation of Value. In: 2011 Int. Conf. Internet Things 4th Int. Conf. Cyber, Phys. Soc. Comput., pp. 672–677 (2011)
16. Yoo, Y., Henfridsson, O., Lyytinen, K.: Research Commentary—The New Organizing Logic of Digital Innovation: An Agenda for Information System. Inf. Syst. Res. (2010)
17. Vargo, S.L., Lusch, R.F.: Service-dominant logic: continuing the evolution. J. Acad. Mark. Sci. 36, 1–10 (2007)
18. Michel, S., Vargo, S.L., Lusch, R.F.: Reconfiguration of the conceptual landscape: A tribute to the service logic of Richard Normann. J. Acad. Mark. Sci. 36, 152–155 (2007)

19. Lusch, R.F., Vargo, S.L., O'Brien, M.: Competing through service: Insights from service-dominant logic. J. Retail. 83, 5–18 (2007)
20. Normann, R.: Reframing Business: When the Map Changes the Landscape. Wiley (2001)
21. Lusch, R.F., Nambisan, S.: Service Innovation, A Service-Dominant (S-D) Logic Perspective, MIS Q (forthcoming).
22. Lusch, R.F., Brown, S.W., Brunswick, G.J.: A general framework for explaining internal vs. external exchange. J. Acad. Mark. Sci. 20, 119–134 (1992)
23. Tiwana, A., Konsynski, B., Bush, A.A.: Research Commentary —Platform Evolution: Coevolution of Platform Architecture, Governance, and Environmental Dynamics. Inf. Syst. Res. 21, 675–687 (2010)
24. Penrose, E.T.: The Theory of the Growth of the Firm, vol. 1, pp. 1–23. John Wiley & Sons Inc., New York (1959)
25. Zott, C., Amit, R., Massa, L.: The Business Model: Recent Developments and Future Research. J. Manage. 37, 1019–1042 (2011)
26. Gassmann, O., Frankenberger, K., Csik, M., Weiblen, T.: The 4I - framework of business model innovation: a structured view on process phases and challenges. Int. J. Prod. Dev. 18 (2013)
27. Mason, K., Spring, M.: The sites and practices of business models. Ind. Mark. Manag. 40, 1032–1041 (2011)
28. Timmers, P.: Business Models for Electronic Markets. Electronic Markets 8, 3–8 (1998)
29. Hevner, A.R., March, S.T., Park, J., Ram, S.: Design Research in Information Systems. MIS Q. 28, 75–105 (2004)
30. Osterwalder, A.: The Business Model Ontology: a proposition in a design science approach. Inst. d'Informatique Organ. Lausanne, Switzerland, Univ. Lausanne, Ec. des Hautes Etudes Commer. HEC. 173 (2004)
31. Peffers, K., Rothenberger, M., Tuunanen, T., Vaezi, R.: Design Science Research Evaluation. In: Peffers, K., Rothenberger, M., Kuechler, B. (eds.) DESRIST 2012. LNCS, vol. 7286, pp. 398–410. Springer, Heidelberg (2012)
32. Gassmann, O., Frankenberger, K., Csik, M.: Revolutionizing the Business Model. In: Management of the Fuzzy Front End of Innovation, pp. 89–98. Springer International Publishing, Cham (2014)

# Co-creation Patterns between Designers and Users in the Design Process: A View of Reflexivity

Jaehyun Park[1,*] and Hyun-A. Park[2]

[1] Institute of Technology, Tokyo, Japan
park.j.ai@m.titech.ac.jp
[2] Konkuk University, Seoul, South Korea
kokokzi@naver.com

**Abstract.** In this paper, we empirically explore designer-user co-creation patterns in the design innovation process with a view of design reflexivity. This paper entails two propositions. First, co-creation between designers and users function as the core action in discovering and validating complex design information environments. Second, co-creation between designers and users can be identified by two reflexivity concepts: design reflexivity and role reflexivity. With these two propositions on designer-user co-creation, we ask the following research questions: (1) what do co-creation between designers and users characterize distinctive patterns in the design process? (2) How do designer-user co-creation patterns change a design routine in a design process? As an empirical approach, this study analyzed forty IT & design innovation project narratives and synthesized five designer-user co-creation patterns (two design reflexivity and three role reflexivity). The significance of this study is to open the importance of co-creation on the designer-user interaction, and it seeks to empirically explore the patterns of co-creation and suggests a theoretical / practical guideline for researchers and practitioners in the community of design process.

**Keywords:** Design & IT innovation Processes, Designer-User Co-creation, Reflexivity, Design Patterns.

## 1 Introduction

During the last forty years, the communities of design science, organization behaviors, and implementation have considered the importance of designer-user interactions in synthesizing better design outcomes in information systems (IS). In prior research, a few IS researchers have theoretically argued how IS designers could effectively understand IS users in user involvement (Ives & Olson, 1984; Kasper, 1996), information systems development (ISD) (Griffith, 1999; Levina & Vaast, 2005), and organizational learning for understanding the boundaries of users in ISD (Boland Jr, 1978; Carlile, 2002; Salaway, 1987). Based on their endeavors, IS systems design theories and methodologies have improved the theoretical knowledge and practices of

---

* Corresponding author.

M.C. Tremblay et al. (Eds.): DESRIST 2014, LNCS 8463, pp. 32–53, 2014.
© Springer International Publishing Switzerland 2014

designer-user interaction in IS. however, the established systems design methodologies do not consider how IS designers could co-create users more effectively. Also, the co-creation of designer-user has become a critical function for identifying the information boundaries of IS designers and IS users in the early stage of ISD. Moreover, these identified information boundaries between IS designers and users could lead successful IT artifacts and innovations in ISD. Therefore, this research deals with *how designers co-create with real users* in the design process. Based on the lack of co-creation between IS designers and uses in ISD, this research empirically explores the designer-user co-creation patterns and asks two research questions as follows:

*(1)  What do patterns of co-creation between designers and users encounter, occur in, and evolve in ISD?*
*(2)  What do roles between designers and users identify their co-creation patterns?*

To address these two research questions, this research posits a 'reflexivity' of designer-user interaction to demonstrate how designers co-create with real users in critical moments (Park, 2012; Park & Boland, 2012). Especially, this study takes a view of Bateson's reflexivity (Bateson, 1979, 2000) and Star and Griesmer's boundary objects (Star, 1989; Star & Griesemer, 1989) as theoretical foundations to support the issue of how IS designers could identify the information environments (boundaries) between designers and users in ISD. In this study, we explore ways in which reflexivity could identify effective interactions in the design process. Here, I highlight two reflexivity interactions: (1) one is *'design reflexivity'* by the designer-user interaction as a macro view addressing the first research question; and (2) the other is *'role reflexivity'* by designer-user interaction as a micro view addressing the second research question. As macro view of co-creation, the design reflexivity adopts Bateson's reflexivity in order to represent the *invisible loops* by designer-user co-creation. As a micro view of co-creation, on the other hand, the role reflexivity uses boundary objects in order to present *designer-user intangible purposes, actions and outcomes on the loops of designer-user co-creation.*

To empirically validate these two questions, this paper collected forty reflexivity project stories (twenty design reflexivity and twenty designer-user role reflexivity) associated with designer-user co-creation and conducted a grounded theory approach to synthesize the designer-user co-creation patterns. As a result, it elucidates five co-creation patterns of designer-user interaction, and it includes two-design reflexivity and three-role reflexivity patterns in the design process. The two design reflexivity patterns demonstrate how designer-user co-creation can identify different levels of problem solving and how designer-user problem solving interaction could identify different types of prototypes in the design process. The three-role reflexivity patterns portray how different types of designer-user co-creation by role reflexivity can develop the forms of designer-user interactions and the steps of design methods in the design process.

The contributions of this paper can be summarized: (1) it theoretically identifies five patterns of co-creation between designers and users in the design process; (2) it addresses the concept of reflexivity for arguing managerial dilemma between designers and users and their co-creation in the design process; and (3) it practically represents the contexts of how current IS designers could interplay with IS users with a view of reflexivity in the design process.

This paper is separated into five sub-sections to present the five reflexivity patterns as follows: (1) literature review; (2) theoretical foundation; (3) methodology; (4) findings; and (5) conclusions and implications.

## 2      Literature Review

This study explores co-creation patterns between designers and users with a view of reflexivity in the design process. To understand previous works of designer-user co-creation, it reviews the studies of designer-user interaction in participatory design research, which deals with co-creation in ISD focusing on user-driven innovation, and user-centered design, and the other related topics of in the design process.

### 2.1      Co-creation in Information Systems Development

Based on Churchman and Schainblatt (1965), IS researchers have considered the importance of mutual understanding between designers and users in creating successful managerial application. On his conceptual idea, some IS researchers have discovered multiple stakeholders' collaborations and their interaction in ISD (Barki & Hartwick, 2001; Kaiser & Bostrom, 1982; Levina, 2005; Robey, 1994). In addition, the community of user involvement research has considered the roles of users and focused on how users could be a more active stakeholder group in ISD (Ives & Olson, 1984; Kasper, 1996; Schonberger, 1980; Tait & Vessey, 1988). Moreover, only a few IS scholars have empirically tested designer-user interaction in order to validate the effectiveness of their interactions in ISD (Baskerville & Stage, 1996; Boland Jr, 1978; Marakas & Elam, 1998; McLean, 1979; Salaway, 1987). Yet, these multiple stakeholders' collaboration, user involvement, and designer-user interaction studies have challenges for identifying the co-creation between designers and users in the process of ISD.

In IS research, Hirschheim (1985) firstly maintains the idea of participative system design based on Scandinavia research tradition, in which he highlights the degree of users' involvement between social and technical contents in ISD. Although a few studies have considered designer-user interactions in terms of multiple stakeholders' collaboration, user involvement, and designer-user interaction in ISD; these research do not provide any research theories, methodologies, and practical directions of co-creation of designer-user interaction in ISD. Therefore, this research considers co-creation in participatory design in Scandinavia.

### 2.2      Co-creation in Participatory Design

Since 1970's, some scholars has historically developed participatory design in Scandinavia (Ehn, 1993; Kyng, 1991). Ehn (1988, 2008) contrasts participatory design and meta-design. To address these design approaches, he focused on the *things* modifying the space of interactions within a community of practice. He also focused on boundary objects in participatory design and infrastructures in meta-design. In his later paper, he defined design methods towards user participation as 'design-by-doing' and 'design-by-playing.' Thus, PD has two characteristics: (1) PD as empowerment and (2) PD as entangled design-games. PD as empowerment identifies users as co-designers based on the roots in movements towards democratization at work in the Scandinavian countries. On the other hand, the PD as entangled design-games conceptualizes participatory design as a pragmatic design theory referring to Wittgenstein and the language-game philosophy, 'communities-of-practice'(Lave & Wenger, 1998). PD as empowerment among multiple stakeholders' interactions entails the most important factors in a design process. Nygaard (1986) and Kyng (1996b) regard PD research as collaborative partnership or co-construction. The collaborative partnership encourages deep commitment of diverse stakeholders in order to cope with their design conflicts and contradictions in a design project. Cherkasky (2003) argues multidisciplinary design collaborations between designers and users. Kyng (1991) defines PD as an experimental inquiry or as a learning process that emphasizes mutual learning between designers and users in a design process. Gregory (2003) defines workplace democracy as a characteristic of PD, and suggests that workplace democracy combines multi-stakeholders' design actions such as work-oriented design, situated activity, and contextual inquiry in a system development. PD as entangled design-games conceptualizes language-based communication as a necessary part of the designer-user interaction (Ehn, 1988; Wittgenstein & Anscombe, 1997).

## 2.3    Users as Designers in PD

The tradition of meta-design considers that PD research offers a context-centered design approach that outlines conflicting interests and suggests a solution from the design process (Kyng, 1996a; Suchman, 1998). The context-centered design approach investigates the effectiveness of cooperating tools and techniques among participants in PD.

Fischer & Scharff (2000) propose 'meta-design' characterizing activities, processes, and objectives to create new media and environments that allow users to act as designers and be creative in the context of a particular system and participatory design processes. Fischer (2003) argues a fundamental objective of meta-design to create socio-technical environments that empower users to engage in informed participation. The suggested model explains how designers could incorporate users with the three conceptual stages: seeding, evolutionary growth, reseeding. This model demonstrates how designer-user interactions could support meta-design in the design process. Fischer & Giaccard (2006) outline the diversity of designers and users stemming from passive customer to meta-designer in the designer development. With this categorization, they demonstrate how designers could provide the opportunities of users as designers addressing and overcoming the problems of closed systems. This meta-design approach involves seeing the designer-user interaction as a collaborative construction of mutual knowledge with which design problems are defined and solutions are created. It shifts the focus from how users' current knowledge is revealed to designers to *how the interaction expands designers' and users' knowledge*. This approach works better for the actual design process where not only solutions but also problems evolve over time (Dorst & Cross, 2001; Suwa, Gero, & Purcell, 2000). Based on this approach, designers and users are encouraged to think beyond the knowledge within a person, department, or problem domain by reframing the current design problem and finding solutions from various domains.

## 2.4    User-Driven Innovation in PD

PD research has emphasized user-driven innovation in design methods and the concepts of collaboration. Buur et al. (2000) argue a critical issue of utilizing video in the ethnographic data or fieldwork materials, because visual data and material are the core objects to reflect real interactions with users and participants in the design process. Especially, non-participated stakeholders (e.g. designers, managers, and IT developers) could reflect the real moments of interactions in the fields based on the raw data. Buur & Bødker (2000) argue 'design collaboratorium' as a design approach that creates an open physical and organizational space where designers, engineers, users and usability professionals meet and work alongside each other. It illustrates how it is possible to reframe usability work and it discusses the new usability competence such as event-driven ways of working known from participatory design. Burr et al. (2004) posit the limitation of tangible user interaction of how projects and service design processes could highlight a particular user's tasks and contexts. To address this, they suggested two tangible user interactions techniques: (1) Hands-Only Scenario and (2) Video Action Wall. The Hands-Only Scenario is a ≈close-up version… of the dramatised use scenario, while the *Video Action Wall* is a technique of ≈live post-its… on a (projected) computer screen. Little snippets of action videos running simultaneously help designers understand user actions by the qualities they represent. Buur & Matthews (2008) overview three of the dominant approaches for engaging with users in co-innovation of products and services, in which they compared the three perspectives in terms of goals, methods and basic philosophy and discussed research directions of what they see as fundamental to the development of user-driven innovation.

## 2.5    Lessons from Literature Review

Co-creation of designer-user interaction has been theoretically and methodologically considered in ISD by most Scandinavian ISD researchers; however, it has become one of the most central issues in ISD, design science research, and information & organization research areas. Based on previous IS and PD researchers' endeavors, the issues and topics on co-creation by designer-user interaction can be summarized as the following concentrations. First, it has highlighted the importance of multi-stakeholders' collaborations with two characteristics in PD research development: (1) PD as empowerment and (2) PD as entangled design-games. Second, it considers meta-design as a context-centered design approach to outline conflicting interests and suggests a solution between designers and users. Third, PD research has supported to user-driven innovation in design methods and the ideas of design collaboration. Considering this research concentration into designer-user interactions focusing on co-creation with these three research orientations, IS researchers could consider the PD research as theoretical and practical propositions for identifing problems and solutions in-between IT and human-centered innovation. Yet, current problems of designer-user interactions in ISD and PD research do not provice any clear cut of theories, patterns, methods, protocols, and frameworks for the communities of researchers and practitioners of how they could understand the theoretical, methdological, or practical actions between IS designers and IS users in ISD. Thus, this research will highlight the patterns of co-creation that encouter, occur in, and evolve between designers and users in ISD.

## 3  Theoretical Consideration

To address the research questions, I adopt Bateson's reflexivity (Bateson, 1979, 2000) and Star and Griesmer's boundary objects (Star, 1989; Star & Griesemer, 1989) to elucidate the patterns of co-creation between designers and users in the design process. Using Bateson's reflexivity, this study supports the first research question focusing on design reflexivity--*What do patterns of co-creation between designers and users encounter, occur in, and evolve in ISD?* On the other hand, this argues the second research question on Star and Griesmer's boundary objects focusing on the roles of designer-user interaction --*What do roles between designers and users identify their co-creation patterns?*

Considering the characteristics of co-creation of designer-user interaction, it consists of intangible interactions between designers and users. To represent these invisible actions, previous theorists have developed a few theoretical knowledge and practice for understanding multiple stakeholders' behaviors and their information environments (Argyris & Schön, 1999; Bourdieu & Wacquant, 2004; Giddens, 1984; Goffman, 1967). In macro view on multiple stakeholders' interaction, Giddens (1984, 1991) argues the modularity between social structure and individuals for incorporating social meanings by constructing the given social structures. Bourdieu (1986; 2004) more emphasizes subjective interpretation in order to theorize the generative actions among multiple stakeholders in our societies. In micro dynamics of multiple stakeholders' behaviors, Argyris & Schön (1999) argue how the involved participants could share their ideas and take actions by negotiating them in the cycle of organizational learning. Goffman (1967, 1970) argues the different self-images between front state and back stage using a dramaturgical perspective. Yet, these theoretical concepts do not give a clear guideline for understanding co-creation between designers and users in terms of the changing *cycle* and the information environments (boundaries) by their interaction and co-creation in the design process. Thus, in this research, I interpret Bateson's reflexivity as macro reflexivity for demonstrating design reflexivity, which identifies co-creations between designers and users. Also, as micro reflexivity, I use boundary objects for understanding role reflexivity on the co-creation of designer-user interaction that identifies the latent loops and knowledge boundaries as information environments between designers and users in the design process.

## 3.1   A Proposed Model

To analyze the co-creation patterns between designers and users, this paper proposes a research model.

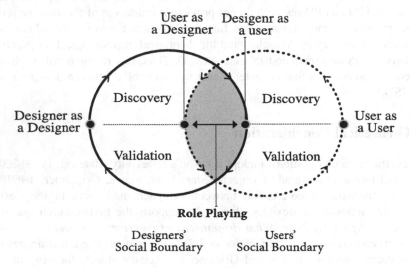

**Fig. 1.** Model of Co-creation of Designer-User Interaction

As Figure 1 presents, this model is made up of two different information boundaries. One is designer's boundary and the other is user's one. Looking at the boundaries (designer's and user's ones), there are two characteristics: (1) design action reflecting on design reflexivity, and (2) design roles by role reflexivity. Thus, each boundary consists of two design actions: discovery and validation. Also, the boundaries have two different roles (original and reversed roles). Based on these characteristics, each of the cycles of designers and users encounter, occur in, and evolve their information boundaries in the design process. Based on this proposed model, this study highlights the co-creation of designer-user interaction based on their design reflexivity and role reflexivity in the design process.

## 4     Methodology

During the interviews with designers, this study considers two questions associated with the co-creation of designer-user interaction by a view of reflexivity. The first question was about design reflexivity project experiences reflecting on the first research question. The other question was the project episodes about the designer-user role reversals in their design projects based on the second research question. Based on these two questions, only twenty designers answered and shared their project experiences among thirty five designers, because the other fifteen designers did not have any experience about design reflexivity and role reversed designer-user interactions in their design projects.

## 4.1 Data Collection

As Table 1 shows, the forty collected data deal with only twenty designers' experiences and their project stories. The collected *forty* design project stories are twenty project stories related to design reflexivity and twenty project stories are associated with designer-user role reversals in the design projects. This data include well-balanced types of design artifacts among projects, software / systems, and service design projects.

**Table 1.** Descriptive Summary of Interview Data

| Questions | Number of Data | Design Artifacts | | |
|---|---|---|---|---|
| | | Products | Software/Systems | Services |
| Reflexivity Projects | 20 | 11 | 7 | 2 |
| Role reversal Projects | 20 | 7 | 8 | 5 |
| Total | 40 | 18 | 15 | 7 |

**Table 2.** Summary of Interview Data Characteristics

| Collected Data | | Designer-User Interactions in the Design Process | | |
|---|---|---|---|---|
| Project Narratives (N) | Design Artifacts (N) | Research | Research & Synthesis | Research & Development |
| Reflexivity (20) | Products (11) | - | 2 | 9 |
| | Software/Systems (7) | - | 1 | 6 |
| | Services (2) | - | 1 | 1 |
| Role reversal (20) | Products (7) | - | 3 | 4 |
| | Software/Systems (8) | - | 5 | 3 |
| | Services (5) | - | 3 | 2 |
| Total: 40 Project Narratives | | 0 | 15 | 27 |

Table 2 shows the characteristics of the forty collected data in terms of design artifacts and processes. The data deal with well-balanced types of design artifacts; however, they only highlight Research & Synthesis (RS) and Research & Development (RD) in the design process, because 'reflexivity' requires the actual forms of cocreation between designers and users in the design process. Thus, the data show higher number of data in RS and RD.

## 4.2    Data Analysis

To analyze the design reflexivity and designer-user role reflexivity on the collected *forty* reflexivity project stories with the co-creation of designer-user interaction, I performed a grounded theory approach (Strauss & Corbin, 1990) to identify relevant frameworks, directions, and guidelines on collected project stories (episodes) as analytic methods. During this analysis, I highlighted the forms of reflexivity by co-creation of designer user interaction, in which reflexivity could determine the forms of co-creation of designer-user interaction and applied design methods in the moments of design process. With this view, I identified *five* designer-user co-creation patterns by a view of reflexivity.

To understand the co-creation patterns of designer-user interaction, I applied the micro dynamic pattern analysis to reveal designer-user interaction forms and methods for the collected forty project stories. In this data analysis process, I investigated forty project stories with a micro dynamic pattern analysis. In this data analysis process, I transformed all transcribed design project stories as visual process sequences to understand the micro dynamic patterns of how designer-user interaction went through a procedural path in creating design outcomes over time. In this analysis process, I used the sequence diagrams as an analytic tool for exploring the co-creation patterns between the designer-user interactions.

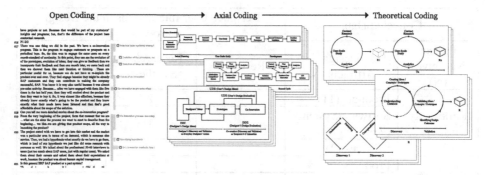

**Fig. 2.** Overview of Data Analysis Process

As Figure 2 presents, this data analysis followed the three steps of the grounded theory approach: from open, to axial, and to theoretical coding processes. In the open coding step, I reviewed every single line of the forty design project narratives to clarify codes, themes, and memos in the transcribed project stories using Atlas.ti, qualitative research software. Also, I analyzed the co-creation of designer-user interactions and the applied methods in the design processes. As a result from the open coding, I outlined each project story with characteristics of co-creation of designer-user interactions and applied design methods over time. Based on the open coding process, forty process diagrams were synthesized, which represent the co-creation of designer-user interactions and the applied design methods in the process of design projects in the axial coding step. In this step, I compared the similarities and differences and sought to categorize the forty project diagrams. After the axial coding process, I performed a theoretical coding process to incorporate the given process diagrams to synthesize co-creation patterns between designer-user interaction and their resulting outcomes in the sequence of design innovation and refinement.

During this grounded theory approach, I clarified eight designer-user interaction criteria to identify co-creation patterns on interaction between designers and users in the design process: (1) time (temporal versus longitudinal), (2) space (micro versus macro), (3) purpose (discovery versus validation), (4) history (with prior history versus without), (5) method (indirect versus indirect), (6) designer-user interaction leadership (designer-centered vs. user-centered vs. co-creation), (7) number of cycles (single versus multiple), and (8) problem-solving (problem-centered versus solution-centered). These eight criteria demonstrate the issues of scale / measurement how each pattern is identified through the data analysis process.

As an outcome, I elucidated five patterns (two design reflexivity and three designer-user role reflexivity) and created pattern diagrams and descriptions to theorize the relationships between the co-creation of designer-user interaction and design innovation in the design process. The next five co-creation patterns of designer-user interaction present how the co-creation of designer-user interactions can identify certain design outcomes (e.g. product, service, or IT system design) in the design process.

# 5    Finding: Five Co-creation Patterns of Designer-User Interaction

## 5.1    Two Co-creation Patterns in Design Reflexivity

Table 3 presents, I clarify two inter-related co-creation patterns in the design reflexivity based on twenty project stories: (1) problem solving reflexivity pattern (pattern 1) and (2) prototypes reflexivity pattern (pattern 2). The problem-solving reflexivity pattern focuses on designer-user problem solving actions, while the reflexivity in prototypes emphasizes the outcomes of how designer-user interaction could identify different levels of design outcomes in the design process. These two design co-creation patterns in the design reflexivity are inter-related each other for encouraging mutual understanding and involvement between designers and users in the design process.

**Table 3.** Two Co-creation Patterns in Design Reflexivity

| Patterns | | Co-creation Patterns by Design Reflexivity | Data (N) |
|---|---|---|---|
| Design Reflexivity | Pattern 1 | Design Reflexivity in Problem Solving | 11 |
| | Pattern 2 | Design Reflexivity in Prototypes | 9 |
| Total | | Two Design Reflexivity Patterns | 20 |

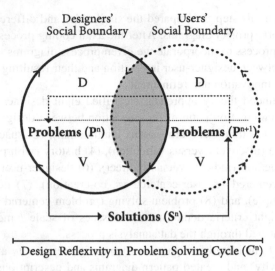

Fig. 3. Design Reflexivity in Problem Solving

## Co-creation Pattern 1: Design Reflexivity in Problem Solving

As Figure 3 presents, the first design reflexivity pattern demonstrates reflexivity of problem solving. In this pattern, designer-user interaction identifies problems of a design project and discovers solutions. After the problem-solving cycles, designers suggest / release the design solutions to users. Yet, users feel design problems on the suggested / released products or services, and they request the other design reflexivity. At this moment, designers' solutions encounter design problems and create other designer-user interaction cycle to identify the latent design problems and their solutions in a design process.

Designer-user interactions identify the problem solving reflexive pattern, and the cycles of designer-user interaction reveal the iterative problem solving. For example, some samples of the collected data (e.g. Taiwan package design, gymnastic equipment, and Korean Gas Safety Corp projects demonstrate how designer's problem solving interaction could identify new and refined design ideas, prototypes, and design solutions as the communication boundaries between designers and users. However, their efforts failed when they met user's boundary. Therefore, designer's outcomes stemmed from problem-solving actions understood as problems to users and it caused designers to discover the products or processes for new design solutions. In addition, Alpha's Arab TV (see Figure 4) and Beta's China automobile Service design (see Figure 5) illustrate how designers' problem solving met design dilemmas because of users' cultural differences. Users recognized designers' solutions as problems in their cultural boundary. Consequently, designers sought to understand different domains of knowledge and practice of identifying new problem statement in order to fit users' boundary in the design sequence.

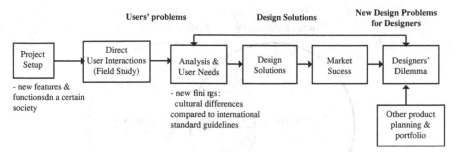

**Fig. 4.** A Case of Co-creation Pattern 1
(Design Reflexivity in Problem Solving)

## Story of Arab TV Project

As Figure 4 shows, this project was completed by Alpha's TV Company, the largest worldwide digital TV Company. The Alpha designers recognized the importance of users and their cultural environment in the early stage of design planning. Thus, the designers conducted a field study and observed cultural differences in the order of writing and reading compared to international standards and guidelines. The Arab culture followed left to right rather than right to left. Based on that, they used their ethnographic research results, and then they successfully released a new product into the market. However, designers encountered a new design dilemma, because they noticed an interesting phenomenon that Arab people used the other consumer electronic projects such as mobile phones and office hardware with the international standard—from left to right order. It made a new design dilemma for designers—should we follow the international guideline or cultural practices for their future design planning?

## Co-creation Pattern 2: Design Reflexivity in Prototypes

The second reflexivity pattern involves design reflexivity in prototypes as the outcomes by designer-user interaction in the design process.

As Figure 6 represents, this pattern shows how designer-user interaction reflexivity can generate different types of prototypes by enhancing the designer-centered discovery cycle and how they can expand their knowledge boundary by connecting with users. Different types of design prototypes can be explained about how this cycle can be reinforced by user validation. In this prototype reflexivity pattern, I summarize three prototypes issues: 1) prototypes for project setting and goal definition, 2) prototypes for the new product and service development, and 3) prototypes for communication with clients and users.

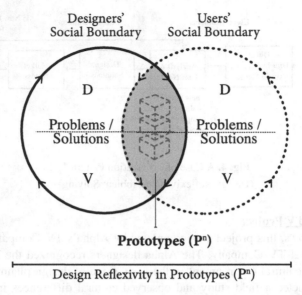

Prototypes (Pⁿ)

Design Reflexivity in Prototypes (Pⁿ)

**Fig. 5.** Co-Creation Pattern 2: Design Reflexivity in Prototypes

### 1) Prototypes for Project Setting and Goal Definition

With respect to prototypes for the *project settings and goal definitions*, the Han River, Gamma's game, and mobile product-business planning projects are examples. The Han River and mobile product-business planning projects offered a broad view about how designer-user interaction sought to define a new design innovation direction and project setting. These projects discovered and validated design ideas, concepts, and solutions based on direct interactions (e.g. field observations and interviews), because designers also should identify the project motivations, statements, and problems with a user-centered approach.

### Story of Gamma's Game Solution Project

The Gamma's game solution project showed the process identifying two different design-business prototypes using designer-user interaction. These two prototypes demonstrate how designer-user interaction can set up a project statement and orientation in the design-business project.

Gamma is one the biggest software, office, and game solution companies. To release new version of game solutions, they conducted preplanning, planning, and execution processes to identify and validate business and design impact. In this design planning and development process, designers conducted two steps of interactions: 1) business opportunities as "pretypes" and 2) design opportunities as prototypes. In these design processes, designer-user interaction sought to understand and create values for users in every stage of business-design development. The business prototypes deal with how the company can build a business direction, while the design prototypes consider design development based on the business goals. In this way, designer-user interaction encourages how the designers could understand effective ways of communications with real users in a certain design movement, and they synthesize different types of prototypes to communicate with users in the design project.

**2) Prototypes for the New Product and Service Development**
With respect to prototypes *for new product and service development techniques*, the insurance tool development and user testing projects demonstrate the processes about how designers sought to understand users' interactions and information environments, and then developed design prototypes as the outcomes of multiple design actions in the development process.

**3) Prototypes for Communication with Clients and Users**
With respect to prototypes for *social interactive tools to communicate with clients and users*, the S Company's design process and paper prototype stories represent how designers developed a series of prototypes to communicate with their users and clients to move their design process forward in negotiation and by persuasion with them. The S Company's design process story focused on why they should invite clients and users and how their participation workshops were effective for identifying clients' or users' hidden needs and requirements based on the multiple and different levels of prototypes. In addition, these design actions with prototypes provided a rationale about a design process to clients and users; therefore, they easily comprehended the designers' actions and challenges in the design process.

In this way, the design reflexivity in problem solving and prototypes should be mutually interplayed to develop the effective designer-user interactions in the design process. Most design projects consist of the recursive reflectivity between *problem solving* and *prototypes*. In the next section, I will explain the co-creation patterns of reflexivity by designer-user role reversal in the design process.

## 5.2   Three Co-creation Patterns in Designer-User Role Reflexivity

Table 4 presents, based on twenty project stories about role reflexivity of designer-user interaction, this section represents three co-creation patterns focusing on role reversals by designer-user interaction in the design process: (1) one way reflexivity; (2) two way reflexivity; and (3) one way double looped reflexivity pattern.

**Table 4.** Three Co-creation Patterns in D-U Role Reflexivity

| Patterns | | Co-creation by Designer-User Role Reversals | Data (N) |
|---|---|---|---|
| Role Reflexivity | Pattern 3 | One way reflexivity | 8 |
| | Pattern 4 | Two way reflexivity | 10 |
| | Pattern 5 | One way double looped reflexivity pattern | 2 |
| Total | | Three Role Reflexivity Patterns | 20 |

To address reflexivity, I define four roles of designer-user interaction in the design process: a designer as a designer, a designer as a user, a user as a user, and a user as a designer. Also, I define three interactions between the roles of a designer and a user: (1) communication; (2) role-playing; and (3) reflexivity. The communication deals with a designer and a user interact with their original roles. The role-playing entails how a designer and a user interact with the reversed roles. The reflexivity demonstrates how a designer and a user reflect on original or reversed roles. With this justification, I illustrate the following three role reflexivity patterns by designer-user interaction in the design process.

### Co-creation Pattern 3: One Way Reflexivity

As Figure 7 presents, the first role reversal co-creation pattern (pattern 3) is *one-way reflexivity*, which includes two paths. The one path demonstrates a designer as a user sees a user as a user, while the other describes a user as a designer sees a designer as a designer in the design process.

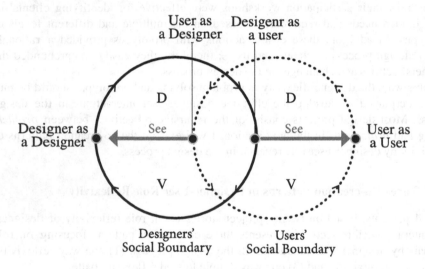

**Fig. 6.** One Way Reflexivity

The one-way path of designers observing users is commonly encountered in an ethnographic research or a field observation, in which a designer seeks to understand real users' interactions and activities within a users' boundary. On the other hand, the one-directional path of users seeing designers occurred during usability testing in the design validation process. Here, a user as a designer tried to provide feedback and suggestions to designers.

### Project Story of One Way Reflexivity Pattern

Gamma's China hotel project shows an example of this reflexivity pattern—the case of a designer as a user sees a user as a user. The objective of this project was to create a new hotel service design for international businessmen in China. In this project, designers conducted ethnographic research to understand businessmen's behaviors and to clarify requirements. In the ethnographic research process, the designers performed a mission --'Being the customer' (a designer as a user), and the designers separated different two different tasks: 1) a businessman with ample budget and 2) a businessman with a limited budget. Each designer conducted a series of tasks during their experience traveling as a rich or a moderately budgeted businessman from the Chinese international airport to the hotel. With this action, the designers identified design opportunities for synthesizing new hotel information service concepts as their future business-design models.

## Project Story of One Way Reflexivity Pattern

Delta's usability testing projects present this path of designer-user reflexivity, which describes a user as a designer sees a designer as a designer. User-centric usability S mobile device usability project demonstrated an example of this path. The S-mobile designers considered alternative alarm features and functions and they developed prototypes using multiple functional LED and vibrating. Therefore, the user-centric usability specialists validated the design prototypes what functions and features between the LED and vibrating combinations are effective as alternative signals. To do this, the usability specialists invited users and tested the prototypes. At the time, users evaluate them with the mode of a user as a user and they suggest some feedback and design ideas about on the prototypes. The result of usability test was users prefer the LED functions and features, but they were concerned about the vibrations. Also, they suggested light vibration with special alarm functions.

Based on the first one way reflexivity pattern (pattern 3), I interpret this pattern about the co-creation of designer-interaction as follows: current effective designer-user interaction methods imply theoretical understanding about the first role reflexivity with two major paths: 1) ethnographic research by designers and 2) usability testing by users. These two designer-user interaction methods assume that "designers believe that users cannot be designers, and users only can contribute their design ideas and suggestions under the control of designers in the user-centered design process."

## Co-creation Pattern 4: Two Way Reflexivity

As Figure 8 shows, the second co-creation pattern (pattern 4) by designer-user role reversal is *two-way reflexivity*, demonstrating a designer or a user with their original roles sees role-playing (role reversals) in the design process. This co-creation pattern has two paths: 1) a designer as a designer sees their role-playing process and 2) a user as a user sees the process of reversed role-playing. This pattern is mainly raised in participatory workshop and co-creation (co-innovation) in the design process. Especially, the participatory workshop and co-creation (co-innovation) have been considered effective approaches to understand user interactions and their environments and they have been applied with diverse versions of design methods or methodologies in the design process.

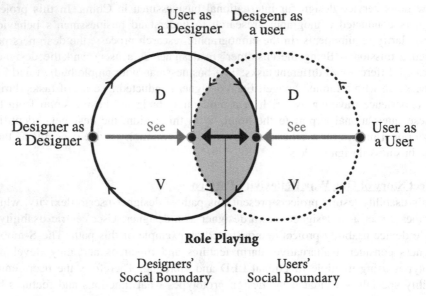

**Fig. 7.** Two Way Reflexivity

## Project Case of Two-Way Reflexivity

Epsilon's longitudinal participatory workshops for identifying new mobile interactions present an example of this pattern. The objective of this PD workshop was to
discover new interactions and validate them with users in the process of early design
stage. The PD workshop was separated with three steps. In the first workshop, designers and users understand the issues of projects and generated a shared knowledge
boundary as a project setting. From the first PD workshop, designers suggested for
users to write a diary about their device interactions reflecting their everyday interactions with other users, products, and services. In the second PD workshop, users presented their diaries in front of other designers and users. Here, designers and users
indirectly understood users' interactions. In the second PD workshop, users shared
their knowledge and practices to generate multiple versions of experiences. At the
same time, designers and users transformed a general user experiences and unique
experiences. In the third stage of PD workshop, designers and users pick several interesting, unique stores that they can develop as design opportunities. Here, designers
and users role reversals were conducted to generate more valuable design opportunities and concepts, which reveal real user stories. Therefore, in the third PD workshop,
users acted as designers and designers changed their role as users. Also, the designers
and users see their interaction with their original roles. Based on this series of PD
workshops, they conducted multiple design patent and developed specific design
ideas to release real design-business solutions.

For the second reflexivity pattern on designer-user interaction role, this pattern
partly admits users can be designers in a certain time in the design process. Also, the
user-centered designers have tried to build alternative methodological approaches to
listen to users' voices and observe their real interactions in the design development.

**Co-creation Pattern 5: One Way Double Looped Reflexivity**
As Figure 8 represents, the third co-creation pattern (pattern 5) by designer-user role reversal reflexivity deals with *one-way double looped reflexivity*, and it explains a designer as a designer sees how a designer as a designer sees a user as a user. This pattern usually meets in the time for design analysis. Especially, we call this design analysis process as 'design debriefing' with other designers. At this design analysis process, designers see the participated designer how the designer as a user sees a user as a user to identify design problems and opportunities by user interactions. In reality, this pattern is usually met in the sequence of design process because of time, financial, and resource limitations.

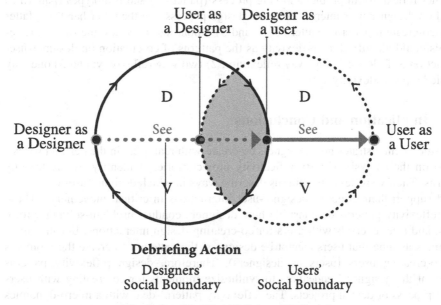

**Fig. 8.** One Way Double Looped Reflexivity

<u>**Project Case of One-Way Double Looped Reflexivity**</u>
Zeta's design debriefing process shows an example of this pattern. It refers to two-way interactions between designers and users. A designer conducted field or ethnographic studies to understand users (a user as a user) with the role of a designer as a user. After the field or ethnographic research, the designer come to his or her office and should share the direct experience and collected data to other designers that they did not have direct interactions with users. To share the observed and collected data, the designer should represent his or her experience (a designer as a user sees a user as a user) with the most objective way as possible. At this time, the designer tries to illustrate the real situations of fields without any subjective understanding, because the other designers should understand user's objective interactions and activities like the designer. In this design debriefing, the other designers see the designer's experience how the designer as a user understood a user as a user for identifying the facts

of users and their environments. Throughout the design debriefing process, the designers doubly see the user's information environment by the interaction of a participated designer's experience in the design process.

For the fifth co-creation pattern on designer-user interaction role, this pattern accounts for the process of how designers could create and share their design knowledge. Also, the debriefing process shows how designers could discover the effective process to understand users, concerning the given resources (e.g. members of designers, project budgets, and so on) in the design process.

In sum, this research synthesizes five co-creation patterns, which consider a view of reflexivity—design reflexivity and designer-user role reflexivity. The first two co-creation patterns (pattern 1 and 2) highlight how designer-user co-creation could lead designer reflexivity in problem-solving process (pattern 1) and prototypes (pattern 2) based on designer-user interaction in the design process. On the other hand, the latter three co-creation patterns (pattern 3, 4, and 5) emphasize how designer-user role reversals could identify three reflexivity as the patterns of co-creation on designer-user interaction as follows: 1) one way reflexivity; 2) two way reflexivity; and 3) one way double looped reflexivity.

# 6      Implication and Conclusions

This study demonstrates how designers co-create with real users in the design process. Based on the analysis of forty reflectivity project stories, I identify five reflexivity patterns. The five reflexivity patterns describe ways in which designer-user reflexivity could support their effective designer-user interactions in critical movements. These five reflexivity patterns demonstrate how designers conduct problem-solving, prototypes, and role reversals with users for co-creating design interactions. Because most designers assume that users cannot be designers, they attempt to create the moments for co-creating users (users as designers). Therefore, design reflexivity patterns represent the designers' endeavors to synthesize moments for co-creating with users in the process of design projects. The reflexivity patterns deal with a micro-dynamics of designer-user interaction and these patterns demonstrate co-creation between designers and users. Also, the two design reflexivity (pattern 1 and 2) and three role reflexivity patterns (pattern 3, 4, and 5) present the time temporality when the forms of the co-creation on designer-user interaction and the applied design methods are utilized in the design innovation.

Through this research, intangible five co-creation patterns between designers and users are elucidated. This conclusion makes the following contributions for the community of participatory design, information systems development, and information and organization studies in IS. First, it theorizes the patterns of co-creation on designer-user interaction in the design process. Second, it provides a methodology of how IS designers could understand effectively IS users in the design process. Especially, it highlights intangible micro dynamics between designers and users and their co-creation moments in the design process. Third, it suggests a practical guideline of co-creation about how IS designers could apply co-creation methods in order to interact with actual and virtual IS users in the design process.

# References

Argyris, C., Schön, D.A.: On organizational learning (1999)

Barki, H., Hartwick, J.: Interpersonal conflict and its management in information system development. Mis Quarterly 25(2), 195–228 (2001)

Baskerville, R.L., Stage, J.: Controlling prototype development through risk analysis. Mis Quarterly, 481–504 (1996)

Bateson, G.: Mind and nature: A necessary unity. Dutton, New York (1979)

Bateson, G.: Steps to an ecology of mind: Collected essays in anthropology, psychiatry, evolution, and epistemology. University of Chicago Press (2000)

Boland Jr., R.J.: The process and product of system design. Management Science 24(9), 887 (1978)

Bourdieu, P.: The forms of capital. [S.l.] (1986)

Bourdieu, P., Wacquant, L.J.D.: An invitation to reflexive sociology. Univ. of Chicago Press, Chicago (2004)

Buur, J., Bødker, S.: From usability lab to "design collaboratorium": reframing usability practice. Paper Presented at the Proceedings of the 3rd Conference on Designing Interactive Systems: Processes, Practices, Methods, and Techniques (2000)

Buur, J., Binder, T., Brandt, E.: Taking video beyond 'hard data' in user centred design. Paper Presented at the Participatory Design Conference (2000)

Buur, J., Jensen, M.V., Djajadiningrat, T.: Hands-only scenarios and video action walls: novel methods for tangible user interaction design. Paper Presented at the Proceedings of the 5th Conference on Designing Interactive Systems: Processes, Practices, Methods, and Techniques (2004)

Buur, J., Matthews, B.: Participatory innovation. International Journal of Innovation Management 12(03), 255–273 (2008)

Carlile, P.R.: A pragmatic view of knowledge and boundaries: Boundary objects in new product development. Organization Science 13(4), 442–455 (2002)

Cherkasky, T.: Designing Experience. International Journal of Engineering Education 19(1), 9 (2003)

Churchman, C.W., Schainblatt, A.H.: Commentary on "The Researcher and the Manager: A Dialectic of Implementation". Management Science 12(2), 2 (1965)

Dorst, K., Cross, N.: Creativity in the design process: co-evolution of problem–solution. Design Studies 22(5), 425–437 (2001)

Ehn, P.: Work-oriented design of computer artifacts. Umeå University (1988)

Ehn, P.: Scandinavian design: On participation and skill. In: Participatory Design: Principles and Practices, pp. 41–77 (1993)

Ehn, P.: Participation in design things. Paper Presented at the Proceedings of the Tenth Anniversary Conference on Participatory Design (2008)

Fischer, G.: Meta-design: Beyond user-centered and participatory design. Paper Presented at the Proceedings of HCI International (2003)

Fischer, G., Giaccardi, E.: Meta-design: A framework for the future of end-user development. In: End User Development, pp. 427–457. Springer (2006)

Fischer, G., Scharff, E.: Meta-design: design for designers. Paper Presented at the Proceedings of the 3rd Conference on Designing Interactive Systems: Processes, Practices, Methods, and Techniques (2000)

Giddens, A.: The constitution of society: introduction of the theory of structuration. Univ. of California Press (1984)

Giddens, A.: Modernity and self-identity: self and society in the late modern age. Polity press, Cambridge (1991)

Goffman, E.: Interaction ritual; essays in face-to-face behavior. Aldine Pub. Co., Chicago (1967)

Goffman, E.: Strategic interaction. Blackwell, Oxford (1970)

Gregory, J.: Scandinavian approaches to participatory design. International Journal of Engineering Education 19(1), 62 (2003)

Griffith, T.L.: Technology features as triggers for sensemaking. Academy of Management Review 24(3), 472–488 (1999)

Hirschheim, R.A.: User experience with and assessment of participative systems design. Mis Quarterly, 295–304 (1985)

Ives, B., Olson, M.H.: User involvement and MIS success: a review of research. Management Science 30(5), 586–603 (1984)

Kaiser, K.M., Bostrom, R.P.: Personality Characteristics of MIS Project Teams: An Empirical Study and Action-Research Design. MIS Quarterly 6(4), 43–60 (1982)

Kasper, G.M.: A theory of decision support system design for user calibration. Information Systems Research 7(2), 215–232 (1996)

Kyng, M.: Designing for cooperation: cooperating in design. Communications of the ACM 34(12), 73 (1991)

Kyng, M.: Designing for cooperation: cooperating in design. Communications of the ACM 34(12), 65 (1991)

Kyng, M.: Users and Computers-A Contextual Approach to Design of Computer Artifacts. DAIMI Report Series 25(507) (1996a)

Kyng, M.: Users and Computers: A Contextual Approach to Design of Computer Artifacts = Brugere og datamater: En kontekstuel tilgang til design af edb-systemer. Aarhus Universitet, Datalogisk Afdeling, Aarhus (1996b)

Lave, J., Wenger, E.: Communities of practice (1998) (retrieved June 9, 2008)

Levina, N.: Collaborating on multiparty information systems development projects: A collective reflection-in-action view. Information Systems Research 16(2), 109–130 (2005)

Levina, N., Vaast, E.: The emergence of boundary spanning competence in practice. Implications for implementation and use of information systems. MIS Quarterly 29(2), 335–363 (2005)

Marakas, G.M., Elam, J.J.: Semantic structuring in analyst acquisition and representation of facts in requirements analysis. Information Systems Research 9(1), 37–63 (1998)

McLean, E.R.: End Users as Application Developers. M&O Quarterly 3(4), 4 (1979)

Nygaard, K.: Program Development as a Social Activity. Paper Presented at the Information Processing 1986 (1986)

Park, J.: Designer-User Interaction as the Core of the Design & IT Innovation Process: A Socio-Cultural Perspective. In: ICIS 2012 Proceedings (2012)

Park, J., Boland, R.: Boundary Objects as Action in Information Systems Development (ISD): a Dramaturgical Perspective Using Sociodrama. AMCIS 2012 Proceedings. Paper 6 (2012)

Robey, D.: Modeling Interpersonal Processes During System Development: Further Thoughts and Suggestions. Information Systems Research 5(4), 439–445 (1994)

Salaway, G.: An organizational learning approach to information systems development. M&O Quarterly 11(2), 245 (1987)

Schonberger, R.J.: MIS design: a contingency approach. Mis Quarterly 4(1), 13–20 (1980)

Star, S.L.: The structure of ill-structured solutions: boundary objects and heterogeneous distributed problem solving. Distributed Artificial Intelligence, vol. 2, pp. 37–54. Morgan Kaufmann Publishers Inc. (1989)

Star, S.L., Griesemer, J.R.: Institutional Ecology, 'Translations' and Boundary Objects: Amateurs and Professionals in Berkeley's Museum of Vertebrate Zoology, 1907-39. Social Studies of Science 19(3), 387–420 (1989)

Strauss, A.L., Corbin, J.M.: Basics of qualitative research: grounded theory procedures and techniques. Sage Publ., Newbury Park (1990)

Suchman, L.: Human/machine reconsidered. Cognitive Studies 5(1), 1 (1998)

Suwa, M., Gero, J., Purcell, T.: Unexpected discoveries and S-invention of design requirements: important vehicles for a design process. Design Studies 21(6), 539–567 (2000)

Tait, P., Vessey, I.: The effect of user involvement on system success: a contingency approach. Mis Quarterly, 91–108 (1988)

Wittgenstein, L., Anscombe, G.E.M.: Philosophical investigations. Blackwell publ., Oxford, GB (1997)

# Design Principles for a Social Question and Answers Site: Enabling User-to-User Support in Organizations

Kevin Ortbach[1], Oliver Gaß[2], Sebastian Köffer[1], Silvia Schacht[2], Nicolai Walter[1], Alexander Maedche[2,3] and Bjoern Niehaves[4]

[1] European Research Center for Information Systems, University of Münster, Germany
{kevin.ortbach,sebatian.koeffer,
nicolai.walter}@ercis.uni-muenster.de
[2] University of Mannheim, Chair of Information Systems IV, Mannheim, Germany
{gass,schacht,maedche}@es.uni-mannheim.de
[3] University of Mannheim, Institute for Enterprise Systems, Mannheim, Germany
[4] Hertie School of Governance, Berlin, Germany
niehaves@hertie-school.org

**Abstract.** The adoption of consumer technology in organizations, termed as IT consumerization, alters the IT infrastructure of many organizations. Letting employees decide which IT tools to use for their work increases the complexity of the organizational IT landscape and immediately raises the question how to provide adequate support given the multitude of technologies. Bring-Your-Own-Device advocates argue that employees can provide IT support on their own. An established concept to provide user-to-user support are social questions & answers sites (SQA). While such community sites are perfectly suited for exploratory problem solving, they lack however suitability to help solving specific problems subject to a specific organization. Moreover, receiving fast ad-hoc help in SQA is rather unlikely, as communication is always indirect and experts to solve the problem are unknown beforehand. The work presented in this paper explores key design characteristics of SQA sites in organizations that overcome the shortcoming of public SQA sites. Based on existing IS literature, we identify four kernel theories that are relevant for SQA sites in organizations and derive meta-requirements from them. In a next step, we analyze five public SQA sites to identify common design principles of SQA sites that are already applied. The main part of our analysis matches the identified design principles with the formulated meta-requirements to address potential gaps with respect to an enterprise environment. We conclude our research with the suggestion of additional design principles for SQA sites that account for their application in an organizational context.

**Keywords:** IT consumerization, BYOD, user-to-user support, social questions and answer sites.

## 1 Motivation

The adoption of consumer technology in organizations, termed as IT consumerization [1], alters the IT infrastructure of many organizations. Inspired by experiences from

M.C. Tremblay et al. (Eds.): DESRIST 2014, LNCS 8463, pp. 54–68, 2014.

the private realm, people demand the use of sophisticated IT tools for work purposes that ideally can be chosen by themselves [2]. IT, once found solely in large organizational units, is now in the possession of single individuals. People have started to operate "complex and relatively large-scale individually owned IS" [3, p. 252]. In positive terms, IT selection by employees gives organizations the opportunity to apply technology more precisely to the individual needs of a particular knowledge [4]. In order to provide their employees with this choice, many organizations have launched "bring/choose-your-own-device" (BYOD/CYOD) initiatives [5]. However, letting employees decide which IT tools they want to use for work increases the heterogeneity of a company's IT landscape leading to various negative consequences. One particular problem is the question of enterprise wide IT support. By now, organizations have attempted to maintain control over devices, access points, interfaces and security controls in order to protect critical IT resources. However, "more devices, times more apps, equals exponentially more complexity for IT to support" [6, p. 4]. A recent survey found out that IT leaders termed "providing IT support for multiple mobile platforms" as a top challenge of BYOD [7]. Similarly, Niehaves et al. identified an increased support complexity as a major disadvantage of IT consumerization for organizations [8]. In this sense, every BYOD or CYOD strategy automatically creates a target conflict between higher freedoms for employees and comprehensive tech-support. The "growing variety of devices, computing styles, user contexts and interaction paradigms will make everything everywhere strategies unachievable" [9]. This complexity will challenge traditional support approaches that are often standardized to save costs or to be outsourced to an external provider.

BYOD advocates argue that employees that use privately owned devices for work can provide IT support on their own. Digital literacy has increased sufficiently to put the keys for IT support in the hand of the users. Younger generations are increasingly tech-savvy because they have grown-up with technology [10]. Wang et al. refuse this disparity between generations and replace it by a continuum of digital literacy that is influenced by demographical, psychological, organizational and social factors [11]. In any case, it is indisputable that people give more importance to IT, in both private and professional life. Consequently, people have built a familiarity with technology that they can transfer to the workplace to solve work problems [1]. Even complex problems can be solved if users receive expert assistance. The internet has brought up multiple social questions and answers sites (SQA), where users can give support to each other [12]. While such sites are perfectly suited for explorative problem solving, they lack suitability to help solving specific problems, for example, related to a particular business process, subject to a single organization. Moreover, receiving fast ad-hoc help in SQA is rather unlikely, as communication is always indirect and experts to solve the problem are unknown beforehand. When implementing SQA's in an organization, the aforementioned aspects can be healed. As employee skills are partially knowledge inside the organization, experts for specific problems can be identified enabling direct interaction. Furthermore, management practices can be used to encourage knowledgeable employees to share their know-how. In consequence, SQA implemented in an organization may address support challenges raised by BYOD or CYOD strategies. With this aim in view, our paper searches for principles that guide the design of SQA in organizations. Hence, we address the following research question:

RQ:    What are design principles of SQA in organizations to enable user-
to-support between employees?

The remainder of this paper is structured as follows. The next chapter lists related work about social software in organizations and SQA. After explaining our research method in Chapter 3, Chapter 4 presents a set of kernel theories, which we use to derive design principles for SQA in organizations. Following, in Chapter 5 we ana-lyze five online SQA regarding our identified principles. We discuss the findings in Chapter 6 and draw conclusions regarding the formulation of our design principles.

## 2     Related Work

### 2.1     Social Software in Organizations

Kaplan and Haenlein define social media as a „group of internet-based applications that build on the ideological and technological foundations of Web 2.0, and that allow the creation and exchange of User Generated Content" [13, p. 61]. Similarly, Kim et al. state that social web sites "make it possible for people to form online communities, and share user-created contents" [14, p.216]. Hence, the term social network sites focuses more on the networking aspects than the user generated content (UGC). Commonly the term is associated with web-based services that allow individuals to construct a public or semi-public profile, provide a list of other users they are con-nected to, and allow viewing this list of connections as well as those made by others within the system [15]. Typically, enterprise social software (ESS) is seen as a com-bination of social networking and social media for use in an enterprise [16].

Connected to the fact that most social software, whether in a private or a business context, is based on UGC, acceptance of these tools is crucial for their success. This is why several studies have targeted use behavior on these platforms. One important antecedent of use is the perceived network size [17], i.e., the total number of mem-bers, or, even more so, the number of peers [18]. Especially the latter was found to influence both the perceived usefulness as well as the perceived enjoyment of the particular platform [18]. While many studies have focused on explaining individual intention to use by means of established constructs from technology acceptance litera-ture [19, 20], use behavior has also been analyzed on a group level with respect to the we-intention to use the social system [21, 22]. In addition, different use types have been identified. For instance, in an enterprise context, Muller has differentiated be-tween passive („lurking") and active usage („contribution") of enterprise social media [23]. Similarly, in a private context, Pöyry et al. differentiate between participation and browsing [24]. With respect to UGC, the contribution of knowledge is an impor-tant behavior. In this context, Pi et al. found that especially subjective norm and a sense of self-worth positively influence the attitude towards knowledge sharing [25].

### 2.2     Social Question and Answer Sites

Previous research distinguishes between three types of question and answers sites (QA) currently found on the internet [26]: (1) Digital reference services are an online analogue of library reference services: information seekers direct questions to expert researchers who refer them to sources of useful information. (2) Expert services are topic centric and employ experts who provide information seekers with the required information. (3) Social question and answer sites (SQA) leverage the time and effort of everyday users to answer questions. Shah et al. define SQA as "a Web-based service for information seeking by asking natural language questions to other users in a network" [27]. SQA sites allow anyone to ask and answer questions and make use of various algorithmic strategies to allow a collaborative assessment of the quality of the content submitted [28]. Usually SQA focus on the information needs of an individual and do not specifically support the collaborative information accumulation of a group ([29]). Respectively, most SQA sites have little structural or role-based organization. However, many sites share characteristics of online communities as they have a base of regular users who engage in off-topic discussion, reply to one another instead of just asking or answering questions or take the role of a moderator [26].

One prominent research stream on SQA studies the behavior of users on SQA sites. For instance, Gazan identified two roles of question answerers – specialists and synthesists [29]. Specialists are knowledge experts who provide answers without referencing other sources, while synthesists are the ones who do not claim any expertise and provide answers with references to existing solutions. Furthermore, Gazan showed that answers from synthesists tended to be rated more highly than answers from specialists [29]. With regards to information seekers, Gazan found two types of questioners – seekers and sloths. Seekers demonstrate active engagement with the community and pursue communication regarding their questions. Sloths do not pursue further interaction with community members after receiving answers to their questions [29]. A second research stream focuses on design characteristics of SQA sites and tries to link them to user behavior or answer quality. A study of Tiwana and Bush found that most systems which do not allow social interaction with other users suffered from underuse or were abandoned outright [30]. Shah et al. examined Yahoo Answers and showed that its popularity is connected to its sophisticated reward features that intensify participation of users [27]. Adamic et al. argue that the approach of Yahoo Answers to allow exactly one answer as best, poses a potential weakness as several answers may be equally good and the standards by which answers are evaluated differ among individuals [31]. In turn, the possibility to annotate previous answers contributes to a higher user engagement as it creates a sense of collaborative information seeking [32].

## 3   Methodology

In order to investigate our research questions, we followed a two-step approach. First, we analyzed scientific literature to determine the relevant body of justificatory knowledge. Our literature search focused on such work which addresses three reoccurring themes of related work on SQA: (1) overall volunteer participation, (2) organization as a social network and (3) focus on knowledge storage and retrieval.

After consolidating all sources in joint discussions, we identified four research streams that provide guidance for core design questions of SQA artifacts in organizations [33] and furthermore establish theoretical links to system outcomes that can be empirically tested [34]. The results of this step, were summarized in form of eight meta-requirements (MR) that outline the scope and purpose of the anticipated class of SQA artifacts [35].

The second step included the development of design principles (DP) for SQA in organizations that satisfy the MR. The review of related work in Chapter 2 indicated that previous research as well as practice have already developed various DP for public SQA. To identify such design principles and determine gaps with regards to the anticipated private SQA applications inside organizations, we conducted an analysis of five popular public SQA on the internet. The analyzed SQA included stackoverflow.com, quora.com, discussions.apple.com, yahooanswers.com and success.salesforce.com. While some of these SQA are business oriented (e.g., stackoverflow.com), others are not limited to a context of question and answers (e.g., yahooanswers.com). We followed three consecutive steps in this SQA analysis. First, we identified all features of the selected SQA sites that related to our MR. Second, we clustered similar features across sites and derived commonly applied DP. Third, we matched the list of design principles with the MR derived from literature to determine whether the DP already addressed the MR completely or if additional DP were necessary to account for the particular requirements of an organizational context. If we identified a gap, we propose additional DP for SQA sites that are deployed in organizations.

# 4      Meta-Requirements Discovery

## 4.1      Knowledge Management

To prevent the loss of valuable knowledge, companies rely on strategies to manage knowledge effectively. Knowledge Management (KM) is "…the systematic and explicit management of knowledge-related activities, practices, programs and policies within the enterprise. Consequently, the enterprise's viability depend directly on: (1) the competitive quality of its knowledge assets and (2) the successful application of these asses in all its business activities […]" [36]. The KM process consists of knowledge (1) collection, (2) storage/retrieval, (3) transfer and (4) application [37]. Previous research provides a vast body of knowledge on collection, storage/retrieval and transfer. However, as Choi et al. state "… no matter how much knowledge is shared among team members, it cannot enhance team performance unless it is effectively applied" [38, p. 866]. Research on KM systems suggests that knowledge application increases, if the provision of knowledge is tailored to actual user needs – in particular to users' actual business process [39]. Consequently, we suggest that the (1) collection, (2) storage and especially retrieval, and (3) transfer of knowledge in a user-to-user support platform must be aligned to current user needs in order to enable knowledge application. This requires that the system be aware of the business context the knowledge is applied.

> MR1: A user-to-user support platform should monitor the user context in order to provide access to knowledge based on current needs.

Before the emergence of Web 2.0 applications, many companies relied on technologies such as databases or repositories in order to collect, store and transfer knowledge. However, many researchers like [40–42] realize that such central storage locations are used only seldom. Instead, they discover that individuals prefer to exchange their knowledge in direct communications [40]. Since organizational learning relies on externalization of knowledge, companies need to implement both, documentation of knowledge for indirect knowledge exchange, and multiple communication channels to enable direct knowledge sharing [43].

> MR2: A user-to-user support platform should provide integrated access to knowledge both, externalized in documents and provided by experts.

## 4.2 Social Presence

Social presence (SP), i.e., the feeling of human warmth and sociability based on the presence and perception of social cues [44], plays a major role in SQA. In contrast to face-to-face interactions, few social cues are available in online environments. Moreover, high anonymity leads to various negative effects for interpersonal relationship and community formation [45, 46]. As a consequence, many people desire online environments to be social as "social cues, such as pictures, can increase positive impressions of group communication (such as online discussions) and elicit warm feelings, causing users to have a more satisfying experience" [47, p. 9]. While SP can be designed [48], e.g., by providing options for using higher media richness such as profile pictures, in user-to-user platforms the users themselves have to act (e.g., use emoticons) in order to re-embed social cues [49]. Besides a feeling of a social environment, trust [50] and enjoyment [51] are further positive outcomes of SP.

While user-to-user support platforms are mainly designed to ask and answer questions, users also care about the impressions they make. Thus, beside the task-oriented character of SQA, presenting oneself and forming impressions is done by users intentionally and unintentionally [52]. One of the basic design elements of SQA is the user profile which gives room for self-expression [15, 53]. However, SQA may allow users to also ask questions anonymously. While pseudonyms or real anonymity may help to lower the barrier to ask questions [54], anonymous postings lack social cues and subsequently desirable outcomes of SP. Many studies show that social cues let others make judgments about others' personality and perceived SP subsequently [55, 56]. Therefore, we derive the following design principle:

> MR3: A user-to-user support platform should stimulate users to include many social cues in their user profiles by providing users enough room for self-expression.

While insights from the field of KM show that direct user-to-user communication is demanded, in terms of SP, the question is how this communication is specified. Studies have shown that direct communication which includes more social cues can positively benefit from SP [44]. However, high levels of SP might not always be necessary to accomplish a solution for easy to solve problems. For example, a simple information transfer through text-messaging can be sufficient [53]. As a result, SQA should intend to provide the best technical mediation for the interacting partners.

> MR4: A user-to-user support platform should provide options for direct user-to-user communication that reflect the continuum from basic text message functions up to the technological state-of-the-art.

## 4.3    Gamification

Deterding et al. [57, p. 10] define gamification as "the use of design elements characteristic for games in non-game contexts". In terms of SQA, gameful design elements are often used as interface design patterns like badges, leaderboards or level rankings [57, 58]. Since user participation in online communities is often carried out by only a small percentage of the overall users [23, 59], the gameful design is used in order to foster user participation and promote quality contributors. In SQA high participation and high willingness to share knowledge is essential. Wasko and Faraj show that people share their knowledge, if they perceive that sharing increases their professional reputation [60]. To this end, gameful design elements, that increase the reputation of users, are likely appropriate to support knowledge sharing in SQA. However, a careful design is necessary to harness the benefits of gameful design elements [58].

> MR5: A user-to-user platform should include gameful design elements that activate user behavior to support the use objectives of the platform.

In SQA it is particularly important that experienced users share their knowledge with the questioners. Welser et al. notice that users with many contributions do not necessarily provide value for the community in terms of knowledge sharing [61]. Consequently, gameful design elements for SQA must consider the quality of contributions as a crucial factor thereby an obvious target conflict between the individual and the platform operator exists. While knowledge seekers are motivated intrinsically to use the platform (motivated by receiving an answer to their question), special attention must be paid to motivate experts to contribute [62]. In the consumer sector, this is done by providing special services to please the best customers. In doing so, organizations use gameful design elements to enrich their services in order to influence user behavior [62]. For example, clothing stores offer special shop hours for premium customers or aviation companies provide special service like lounge entry or food selection for frequent travelers. In this sense, the application of gamified services could also be used in SQA for attracting experts to share their knowledge.

MR6:  A user-to-user platform should provide gamified services that lead to a new cognitive, emotional, social use of the core offer.

## 4.4    Social Network Theory

User-to-user support is based on knowledge exchange among users and, thus, can be considered a social network. Similar to SQA, one important aspect of social networks is participation, which goes along with the overall long- and short-term success of the platform [63]. Social network operators actively try to foster participation by establishing a close connection to the users over various communication channels, e.g., notification by email. These notifications have been found useful to increase participation in social networks [64]. In order to guarantee a rapid progress in the question-answer cycle, i.e., from the initial question until the approval of the best answer, a SQA may overtake this principle to provide real-time mechanisms to send user notifications.. There are multiple ways how such a feature may be implemented. For instance, notification icons that flash when a new answer or a comment is given to an asked subscribed question are quite common. Other possibilities to establish near real-time communication are notifications via RSS feed or email [65].

MR7:  A user-to-user support platform should inform the users about changes in order to speed up the support process by pointing out recent changes.

Another striving feature of social network is self-regulation. For example, this can be achieved by dedicated moderators who can delete or re-categorize questions [29]. In addition, the task may also be accomplished by active and encouraged users who flag redundant questions or merge them together. Beyond that, normal users, in the role of an evaluator, may be provided with the opportunity to report abusive behavior [66]. It has been shown, that measures of self-regulation are beneficial in the context of SQA sites [67]. Thus, it may be considered as MR for user-to-user support.

MR8:  A user-to-user support platform should implement measures for self-regulation in order to increase the overall quality of both structure and content of the support requests and answers.

## 5    Analysis of SQA Tools

In our analysis of popular SQA, we identified 27 DP. Table 1 summarizes the DP and relates them to the formulated MR. An "x" indicates that the DP is used to influence user behavior in the corresponding SQA.

The analysis shows that SQA already apply many DP related to the MR that were derived from the kernel theories. However, we argue that not all DP can be transferred simply to an organizational context without modifications. An analysis of possible modifications and extensions is presented in the following chapter.

**Table 1.** Overview of design principles used in popular SQA

| MR | Design principles | SO | YA | SF | QR | AP |
|---|---|---|---|---|---|---|
| MR1 | Follow watchlist to enable reuse | | x | x | x | |
| | Reputation bounties to motivate use | x | | | | |
| | Integration into work context | | | x | | |
| MR2 | Answers can be weighted | x | x | x | | x |
| | Questions can be weighted | | | | | x |
| | Experts are exposed (e.g., through badges) | x | x | | x | |
| | Direct communication | | | x | x | |
| MR3 | Pseudonyms as user names allowed | x | x | | | x |
| | Free choice of profile picture | x | x | x | x | x |
| | Text fields to provide personal information | x | | x | x | x |
| | History of user activities | x | x | x | x | x |
| | Links to users other profiles (e.g., twitter) | | | x | x | |
| MR4 | Direct text messaging | | | x | x | |
| MR5 | Badges | x | | x | | |
| | User level system | | x | | | x |
| | Point system | x | x | x | | x |
| | Number of contributions in user profile | x | x | x | | x |
| | Leaderboard | x | x | x | | |
| MR6 | Privileges for users with more points | x | | | | |
| MR7 | Notification icon | x | x | | x | x |
| | Sharing of posts | | x | x | x | |
| | RSS feeds | x | x | | x | |
| | E-Mail notifications | x | x | | x | x |
| MR8 | Question improvement (by another user) | x | | | x | |
| | Answer improvement (by another user) | x | | | x | |
| | Community tagging | x | | | x | x |
| | Report abusive behavior | | x | | | |

SO = stackoverflow.com; YA = yahooanswers.com; SF = success.salesforce.com

QR = quora.com; AP = discussions.apple.com

**Table 2.** Additional design principles for user-to-user support in an organizational context

| MR | Additional design principles |
|----|------------------------------|
| MR1 | Business process integration |
| MR2 | Integration with internal knowledge bases |
| MR3 | Post questions anonymously |
| MR4 | Direct audio- or video-chat |
|  | Collaboration support (e.g., screen-sharing) |
| MR5 | Quality emphasis of game-based elements |
| MR6 | Gamified services combined with real life |
| MR7 | Integrate with enterprise social media, rather than with public social media. |
| MR8 | Establish user hierarchy |

## 6    Discussion and Conclusion

This paper investigated design principles for user-to-user support platforms in an organizational context. From four kernel theories, we derived eight MR. By researching public web-based SQA, we found a set of DP that address the MR. Based on our analysis, we suggest additional DP for user-to-user support platforms that take into account the specific requirements of an organizational context. A summary of suggested design principles can be found in Table 2.

MR1. The detection of the overall context is necessary to provide knowledge that is adapted to user needs [39]. For example, Salesforce puts questions and answers in a particular context of development. An indirect form of context-awareness is the inclusion of follower or watch lists. By putting questions and answers in an entire stream of previous issues, users can understand current questions easily and adapt their answers accordingly. However, none of the SQA under investigation is embedded in actual working process of its users. Each platform is realized as a standalone application forcing users to interrupt their actual activities in order to ask questions or provide answers. In consequence, users are exposed to media disruptions. While it is difficult to define a comprehensive process embedment for public SQA, processes are defined within the context of an organization. In order to enable efficiency and decrease the amount of media disruption, we argue that such a DP will increase the value of the SQA.

MR2. All investigated SQA provide access to expert knowledge in the form of previous discussion streams. By asking questions open to an entire community, indirect communication between knowledge seekers and experts is enabled. In addition, weighing questions and answers enable users to get a quick overview on those comments that are most important or helpful. In organizations, however, many answers to questions are already captured in company-wide knowledge repertoires. While none of the SQA platforms include such externalized knowledge, the implementation of an organizational user-to-user support platform needs to consider existing internal knowledge bases enabling users to connect their questions and answers to externalized knowledge [43].

MR3. Creating answers and questions under a pseudonym is allowed for most of the analyzed SQA. However, none of the platforms allowed anonymous questions, since users had to register with their name and email address. In an organizational setting, anonymity, as a way to lower the barrier for asking questions [54], might be even more important, for example, people do not want to appear as incompetent, are afraid of mobbing or consequences of critical questions. While there were restrictions on user names, for profile pictures no obvious restrictions seem to be in place. Also, providing text-fields for self-expression ("about me") seems to be a standard feature. Less frequent was the option to make connections to users other profiles such as Facebook. Finally, histories of user activities (e.g., recently answered questions) were implemented in every platform. For an organizational context, room for self-expression and showing user activities is also important as this may increase SP and subsequently a climate of trust [47].

MR4. As SQA are mainly designed for public discussions, little direct communication measures were implemented. Other than Salesforce and Quora, no platform included direct user-to-user text messaging. In both existing cases, there were no features for self-expression such as emoticons, choice of fonts or text colors. More advanced direct communication functions such as video-chat, screen-sharing or remote desktop control could not be identified at all. In an organization, such features might be more important and used: Colleagues might be more willing to take the effort to work through a problem together (e.g., by having a shared-screen session). Credits taken and reputation gain is less virtual than in public SQA and might even help in being promoted. Colleagues also likely have no motives to harm (e.g., via a remote desktop session) [45, 46]. Also, the necessary IT infrastructure (e.g., webcams) might be implemented more easily under the lead of an IT department.

MR5. Besides Quora, all investigated SQA include gameful design elements to influence user behavior. It can be assumed that most of the badges, point and level systems are applied to motivate user participation. As public SQA strive for maximum participation, an organization should put emphasis on knowledge retrieval, transfer and application [37]. Thus, in an organizational setting the adjustment of such game-based approaches differs from public SQA. In particular, we argue that it must be ensured that people do not waste their working time to make contributions without value [61], just for gaining reputation in the gameful logic of the SQA. In this sense, in an organizational setting, game-based elements should focus more on quality than quantity adapted to the needs and goals of organizations and their members.

MR6. Gamified services in the SQA could be rarely identified in our analysis. This is likely due to the fact that public SQA have only a virtual binding to its users, so that a provision of real services can also only apply virtually. In an organizational context, the importance of the SQA can be enhanced by offering services that tackle the real world of contributors. For instance, an organization can award real badges instead of virtual ones. Moreover, organizations that want to foster knowledge transfer may even grant extra work hours for expert users so that they are relieved from other work duties. Here, the core service of more flexible work hours is enhanced with gameful experiences in the SQA that support the user's value creation [62].

MR7. All analyzed platforms have implemented some DP to point out recent changes to the users. Apart from Salesforce, all sites featured notification icons as well as the possibility to be notified by email or RSS if new posts or comments are added. In addition, several platforms allow users to share content on social media sites like Facebook or Twitter. This can be seen as an additional mechanism to keep users informed and, thus, to speed up response times and foster participation. However, in an organizational context, it has to be argued that this type of social media integration is likely to be unwanted by the enterprise as it would encourage employees to check their private accounts at work. Here, integrating the newsfeed with internal company portals or, if used, enterprise social media, may be more promising.

MR8. With respect to self-regulation, the platforms under investigation differ significantly. While Salesforce and Quora have implemented DP that allow other users to improve questions and answers as well as to tag existing posts, Yahoo Answers only allows users to report abusive behavior. Salesforce on the other hand did not allow for any self-regulation. In an organizational context, this aspect of self-regulation needs to be carefully considered as users are likely to know each other and may also be located on different hierarchy levels within the company. Thus, if usernames are tracked, this may lead to interpersonal issues affecting the working environment. This is highly dependent on the organizational culture. Here, allowing for anonymous change requests or assigning dedicated moderators (e.g., from the IT department) could help to overcome the issues.

Limitations and Outlook. Our study is beset with several limitations. First, our selection of relevant theories for the derivation of meta-requirements is not conclusive. While we believe that focusing on theories in the context of social interaction is a valid approach for identifying important aspects for a user-to-user support platform, other theories may have been used which would have led to a different set of MR and, thus, DP. Second, we only analyzed a small set of the SQA platforms currently available online. Therefore, it may be the case that some of the discussed improvements and current gaps are already addressed to some degree by other platforms. Future studies could target these limitations by incorporating other theoretical perspectives and expanding the number of analyzed platforms. In addition, research could focus on evaluating the potential of the discussed additional DP (e.g., process embedment or collaboration support) to improve the support process.

# References

1. Harris, J.G., Ives, B., Junglas, I.: IT Consumerization: When Gadgets Turn Into Enterprise IT Tools. MIS Q. Exec. 2012, 99–112 (2012)
2. Ortbach, K., Köffer, S., Bode, M., Niehaves, B.: Individualization of Information Systems - Analyzing Antecedents of IT Consumerization Behavior. In: International Conference on Information Systems (ICIS), Milano, ITA (2013)
3. Baskerville, R.: Individual information systems as a research arena. Eur. J. Inf. Syst. 20, 251–254 (2011)
4. Davenport, T.H.: Rethinking knowledge work: A strategic approach. McKinsey Q., 89–99 (2011)

5. Forrester: Key Strategies to Capture and Measure the Value of Consumerization of IT. A Forrester Consulting Thought Leadership Paper Commissioned by Trend Micro, Cambridge, MA, USA (2012)
6. Gens, F., Levitas, D., Segal, R.: Consumerization of IT Study: Closing the Consumerization Gap. IDC, Framingham, Massachusetts, USA (2011)
7. Barbler, J., Bradley, J., Macaulay, J., Medcalf, R., Reberger, C.: BYOD and Virtualization. Top 10 Insights from Cisco IBSG Horizons Study, San José, CA, USA (2012)
8. Niehaves, B., Köffer, S., Ortbach, K.: IT Consumerization – A Theory and Practice Review. In: Proceedings of the 18th Americas Conference on Information Systems, Seattle, Washington, USA (2012)
9. Gartner: Gartner Identifies the Top 10 Strategic Technology Trends for 2014, http://www.gartner.com/newsroom/id/2603623
10. Vodanovich, S., Sundaram, D., Myers, M.D.: Digital Natives and Ubiquitous Information Systems. Inf. Syst. Res. 21, 711–723 (2010)
11. Wang, E., Myers, M.D., Sundaram, D.: Digital Natives and Digital Immigrants - Towards a Model of Digital Fluency. In: Proceedings of the European Conference on Information Systems (ECIS), Barcelona, Spain (2012)
12. Von Hippel, E., Lakhani, K.R.: How Open Source Software Works: 'Free' User-to-User Assistance? Res. Policy 32, 923–943 (2003)
13. Kaplan, A.M., Haenlein, M.: Users of the world, unite! The challenges and opportunities of Social Media. Bus. Horiz. 53, 59–68 (2010)
14. Kim, W., Jeong, O.-R., Lee, S.-W.: On social Web sites. Inf. Syst. 35, 215–236 (2010)
15. Boyd, D.M., Ellison, N.B.: Social Network Sites: Definition, History, and Scholarship. J. Comput. Commun. 13, 210–230 (2007)
16. Kügler, M., Smolnik, S., Raeth, P.: Why Don't You Use It? Assessing the Determinants of Enterprise Social Software Usage: A Conceptual Model Integrating Innovation Diffusion and Social Capital Theories. In: Proc. 33rd Int. Conf. Inf. Syst., ICIS 2012 (2012)
17. Zhao, L., Lu, Y.: Enhancing Perceived Interactivity through Network Externalities: An Empirical Study on Micro-Blogging Service Satisfaction and Continuance Intention. Decis. Support Syst. 53, 825–834 (2012)
18. Lin, K.-Y., Lu, H.-P.: Why People Use Social Networking Sites: An Empirical Study Integrating Network Externalities and Motivation Theory. Comput. Human Behav. 27, 1152–1161 (2011)
19. Shipps, B., Phillips, B.: Social Networks, Interactivity and Satisfaction: Assessing Socio-Technical Behavioral Factors as an Extension to Technology Acceptance. J. Theor. Appl. Electron. Commer. Res. 8, 7–8 (2013)
20. Meyer, P., Dibbern, J.: An Exploratory Study about Microblogging Acceptance at Work. In: Proceedings of the Americas Conference on Information Systems (AMCIS), Lima, Peru (2010)
21. Cheung, C.M.K., Chiu, P.-Y., Lee, M.K.O.: Online Social Networks: Why Do Students Use Facebook? Comput. Human Behav. 27, 1337–1343 (2011)
22. Cheung, C.M.K., Lee, M.K.O.: A Theoretical Model of Intentional Social Action in Online Social Networks. Decis. Support Syst. 49, 24–30 (2010)
23. Muller, M.: Lurking as Personal Trait or Situational Disposition? Lurking and Contributing in Enterprise Social Media. In: Proceedings of the ACM 2012 Conference on Computer Supported Cooperative Work, New York, NJ, USA, pp. 253–256 (2012)
24. Pöyry, E., Parvinen, P., Malmivaara, T.: Can We Get from liking to buying? Behavioral differences in hedonic and utilitarian Facebook usage. Electron. Commer. Res. Appl. 12, 224–235 (2013)

25. Pi, S.-M., Chou, C.-H., Liao, H.-L.: A Study of Facebook Groups Members' Knowledge Sharing. Comput. Human Behav. 29, 1971–1979 (2013)
26. Harper, F., Raban, D.: Predictors of answer quality in online Q&A sites. In: Proc. SIGCHI Conf. Hum. Factors Comput. Syst. (2008)
27. Shah, C., Oh, J.S., Oh, S.: Exploring characteristics and effects of user participation in online social Q&A sites. First Monday 13, 18 (2008)
28. Gazan, R.: Social Q&A. J. Am. Soc. Inf. Sci. Technol. 62, 2301–2312 (2011)
29. Gazan, R.: Specialists and synthesists in a question answering community. Proc. Am. Soc. Inf. Sci. Technol. 43, 1–10 (2007)
30. Tiwana, A., Bush, A.A.: Continuance in Expertise-Sharing Networks: A Social Perspective. IEEE Trans. Eng. Manag. 52, 85–101 (2005)
31. Adamic, L., Zhang, J., Bakshy, E., Ackerman, M.S.: Knowledge sharing and yahoo answers: everyone knows something. In: Proceedings of the International Conference on World Wide Web, pp. 665–674 (2008)
32. Gazan, R.: Social Annotations in Digital Library Collections. D-Lib Mag. 14 (2008)
33. Hevner, A.R., March, S.T., Park, J., Ram, S.: Design Science in Information Systems Research. MIS Q. 28, 75–105 (2004)
34. Markus, M.L., Majchrzak, A., Gasser, L.: A Design Theory for Systems That Support Emergent Knowledge Processes. MIS Q. 26, 179–212 (2002)
35. Gregor, S., Jones, D.: The Anatomy of a Design Theory. J. Assoc. Inf. Syst. 8, 312–336 (2007)
36. Wiig, K.M.: Knowledge Management: An Emerging Discipline with a Long History. In: Despres, C., Chauvel, D. (eds.) Knowledge Horizons, pp. 3–26. Butterworth Heinemann (2000)
37. Alavi, M., Leidner, D.E.: Review: Knowledge management and knowledge management systems: Conceptual foundations and research issues. MIS Q. 25, 107–136 (2001)
38. Choi, S.Y., Lee, H., Yoo, Y.: The Impact of Information Technology and Transactive Memory Systems on Knowledge Sharing, Application, and Team Performance: A Field Study. MIS Q. 34, 855–870 (2010)
39. Gregor, S., Benbasat, I.: Explanations from intelligent systems: Theoretical foundations and implications for practice. MIS Q. 23, 497–530 (1999)
40. Julian, J.: How project management office leaders facilitate cross project learning and continuous improvement. Proj. Manag. J. (2008)
41. Petter, S., Randolph, A.B.: Developing soft skills to manage user expectations in IT projects: Knowledge reuse among IT project managers. Proj. Manag. J. 40, 45–59 (2009)
42. Koskinen, K.U., Pihlanto, P., Vanharanta, H.: Tacit knowledge acquisition and sharing in a project work context. Int. J. Proj. Manag. 21, 281–290 (2003)
43. Petter, S., Vaishnavi, V.: Facilitating experience reuse among software project managers. Inf. Sci. (Ny) 178, 1783–1802 (2008)
44. Short, J., Williams, E., Christie, B.: The Social Psychology of Telecommunications. John Wiley & Sons, Ltd. (1976)
45. Rockmann, K.W., Northcraft, G.B.: To be or not to be trusted: The influence of media richness on defection and deception. Organ. Behav. Hum. Decis. Process. 107, 106–122 (2008)
46. Zimbardo, P.G.: The human choice: Individuation, reason, and order versus deindividuation, impulse, and chaos. In: Nebraska Symp. Motiv., vol. 17, pp. 237–307 (1969)
47. Djamasbi, S., Siegel, M., Tullis, T., Dai, R.: Efficiency, Trust, and Visual Appeal: Usability Testing through Eye Tracking. In: 2010 43rd Hawaii International Conference on System Sciences (HICSS), pp. 1–10 (2010)

48. Walter, N., Ortbach, K., Niehaves, B.: Great to have you here! Understanding and designing social presence in information systems. In: ECIS 2013 Proc., pp. 1–12 (2013)
49. Walther, J.B., D'Addario, K.P.: The Impacts of Emoticons on Message Interpretation in Computer-Mediated Communication. Soc. Sci. Comput. Rev. 19, 324–347 (2001)
50. Cyr, D., Head, M., Larios, H., Pan, B.: Exploring Human Images in Website Design: A Multi-Method Approach. MIS Q. 33, 539–566 (2009)
51. Lombard, M., Ditton, T.: At the Heart of It All: The Concept of Presence. J. Comput. Commun. 3, 1–30 (1997)
52. Goffman, E.: The Presentation of Self in Everyday Life. Anchor Books (1959)
53. Walter, N.: Does Human Warmth Matter? – An Experiment on User Profiles in Initial Business Interaction. SIGHCI 2013 Proc. Paper 18 (2013)
54. Hertel, G., Schroer, J., Batinic, B., Naumann, S.: Do Shy People Prefer to Send E-Mail? Personality Effects on Communication Media Preferences in Threatening and Nonthreatening Situations. Soc. Psychol. (Gott) 39, 231–243 (2008)
55. Hess, T., Fuller, M., Campbell, D.: Designing Interfaces with Social Presence: Using Vividness and Extraversion to Create Social Recommendation Agents. J. Assoc. Inf. Syst. 10, 889–919 (2009)
56. Marcus, B., Machilek, F., Schütz, A.: Personality in cyberspace: Personal web sites as media for personality expressions and impressions. J. Pers. Soc. Psychol. 90, 1014–1031 (2006)
57. Deterding, S., Dixon, D., Khaled, R., Nacke, L.: From game design elements to gamefulness: defining gamification. In: Proceedings of the International Academic MindTrek Conference: Envisioning Future Media Environments, pp. 9–15. ACM (2011)
58. Kumar, S., Nepal, S., Colineau, N., Paris, C.: Using Gamification in an Online Community. In: 8th International Conference Conference on Collaborative Computing: Networking, Applications and Worksharing, pp. 611–618 (2012)
59. Nielsen, J.: Participation inequality: Encouraging more users to contribute, http://www.nngroup.com/articles/participation-inequality/
60. McLure Wasko, M., Faraj, S.: Why Should I Share? Examing Social Capital and Knowledge Contribution in Electronic Network of Practice. MIS Q. 29, 35–57 (2005)
61. Welser, H.T., Gleave, E., Barash, V., Smith, M., Meckes, J.: Whither the Experts? Social Affordances and the Cultivation of Experts in Community Q&A Systems. In: 2009 International Conference on Computational Science and Engineering, pp. 450–455. IEEE (2009)
62. Huotari, K., Hamari, J.: Defining gamification: A service marketing perspective. In: Proceeding Int. Acad. MindTrek Conf., pp. 17–22. ACM (2012)
63. Gyarmati, L., Trinh, T.: Measuring user behavior in online social networks. IEEE Netw. 24, 26–31 (2010)
64. Hsieh, G., Counts, S.: mimir: A market-based real-time question and answer service. In: CHI 2009 Proc. SIGCHI Conf. Hum. Factors Comput. Syst., pp. 769–778 (2009)
65. Gazan, R.: Microcollaborations in a social Q&A community. Inf. Process. Manag. 46, 693–702 (2010)
66. Agichtein, E., Castillo, C., Donato, D., Gionis, A., Mishne, G.: Finding high-quality content in social media. In: Proc. Int. Conf. Web Search Web Data Min., WSDM 2008, p. 183 (2008)
67. Anderson, A., Huttenlocher, D.: Discovering value from community activity on focused question answering sites: a case study of stack overflow. In: Proc. 18th ACM SIGKDD Int. Conf. Knowl. Discov. Data Min. (2012)

# Data Analytics and Human Trafficking

Kena Fedorschak, Srivatsav Kandala, Kevin C. Desouza, and Rashmi Krishnamurthy

Decision Theater
Arizona State University
Kena.Fedorschak@asu.edu

**Abstract.** Human trafficking is recognized internationally as an extreme form of violence against women, children, and men. Despite the fact that human trafficking is universally understood to be a burgeoning social problem, a paucity of data and insight into this issue exists. Data analytics has immense potential to elucidate trends in complex social data and inform future policy. We undertook a design science-inspired research approach to build datasets on human trafficking. Three prototypes are presented that describe the methodologies of human traffickers, display correlations between calls reporting suspected trafficking activity and various demographic data, and explicate the effectiveness of US anti-trafficking funding projects.

**Keywords:** human trafficking, sex trafficking, data analytics.

## 1 Introduction

In recent decades, discussions about big data have flooded the popular press and practitioner literature [1]. Big data refers large data sets that cannot be stored and analyzed by conventional database technologies. Harnessing big data has immense potential to elucidate complex social challenges and allow for effective policy interventions. For example, the New York City Department of Environmental Protection effectively used big data analytics to address illegal dumping of waste into sewers by restaurants. Data on restaurants that did not obtain a carting service certificate was combined with geo-spatial location tools to statistically estimate the likelihood of illicit activity – allowing city officials to eliminate 95% of illegal dumping [2].

Unfortunately, few useable human trafficking datasets are currently available. This is concerning given the adverse impact that trafficking in persons (TIP) has on society; it is believed that 21 million individuals are currently being trafficked worldwide – 50,000 of which are in the United States [3][4]. Despite policy efforts to eradicate TIP, human trafficking is one of the most lucrative and fastest growing forms of organized crime; its profits, estimated at $31.6 billion per year, are surpassed only by those of drug syndicates [5]. Conviction rates show that the risks of human trafficking are lower than the risks associated with trafficking illegal drugs or arms. Human trafficking is expected to surpass drug and arms trafficking in its incidence, cost to human wellbeing, and profitability to criminals within the next decade [6]. While many strategies have been tried to combat the issue of human trafficking, serious headway has not been made in terms of lowering the prevalence of TIP.

M.C. Tremblay et al. (Eds.): DESRIST 2014, LNCS 8463, pp. 69–84, 2014.

The current research overviews policy and data impediments to analytics and explains how data fusion can provide insight into human trafficking activity. The research represents initial efforts to develop a regional repository of data on human trafficking through a design science-inspired research approach. This data repository is the artifact that will eventually be constructed. However, prototype efforts were first necessary to understand proper procedures for collection, construction, and analysis of human trafficking related datasets. Three prototypes are presented that describe the methodologies of human traffickers, display correlations between calls reporting suspected trafficking activity and various demographic data, and explicate the effectiveness of US anti-trafficking funding projects. These studies demonstrate the ability to mine, fuse, and analyze data from various sources to generate intelligence on TIP on a smaller scale.

## 2     Data Analytics and Anti-Trafficking Policy

Despite the success of big data projects, large scale efforts to collect, store, and analyze human trafficking data have not occurred. Significant policy related advancements have been made since the turn of the century. However, since policy has rarely been informed by facts and evidence, it has been ineffective thus far. For example, the Trafficking Victims Protection Act (TVPA) was passed by Congress in 2000 and has had its funding subsequently renewed in 2003, 2005, 2008, and 2013; in the decade following the enactment of the TVPA, only 600 federal convictions for trafficking related crimes were secured – an extremely small number compared to the estimated prevalence of such behavior [7][8].

Policy can only be effective when information exists to inform policymakers' decisions. Data is lacking for almost every variable relating to trafficking; data collection and research is needed to explore what common methods and techniques are used by traffickers to evade detection, why a high demand for exploitative sexual behavior with non-consenting victims exists, which industries and locations commonly use forced labor, what specific variables or factors place individuals at risk for becoming victims of trafficking, and et cetera. While complete eradication of human trafficking is unlikely, policy can be designed to mitigate the issue significantly. This goal is achievable through context specific research and systematic data collection.

## 3     Lack of Data

The dearth of data, insight, and understanding of human trafficking networks can be attributed to four reasons: (1) traffickers operate clandestine networks, (2) victims of trafficking do not self-identify, (3) inadequate law enforcement efforts, and (4) lack of collaboration and data sharing initiatives. Extant explanations for each reason are explored below.

### 3.1    Traffickers Operate Clandestine Networks

Traffickers' livelihood depends on successful evasion of authorities, and they work tirelessly to avoid detection. There is no single modus operandi or code of conduct that human traffickers follow, which makes tracking and prosecuting offenders a challenge [9]. One federal agent noted:

> "Last week we had a case where a juvenile was lured into prostitution by a Facebook account... these girls use [cell] phones, the Internet ... Now everything, all the ads are being posted through the Internet. Child prostitution and prostitution is occurring from a computer to a hotel room [10]."

Many traffickers use front businesses to conceal their illicit activities. For example, 40-year-old Milagros Katz, and 17 of his colleagues, were arrested on November 20, 2012 for allegedly using an advertising firm as a money laundering front for a prostitution ring. The New York based firm, Somad Enterprises, Inc., had ties to human trafficking networks in China and South Korea – most of its prostitutes were imported from these countries. The organization advertised prostitution services on cable access TV, Craigslist, Backpage.com, and in other locations. In addition, the firm offered 'sophisticated' services such as airbrushing and search engine optimization (SEO), i.e., a 'propriety auto-posting system' was developed to allow for rapid posting and alteration of targeted ads for prostitutes and employed techniques to ensure that they remained at the top of internet search results. The organization laundered payments through a bevy of shell companies offering physical therapy services, business consultancy services, antiques, acupuncture, party planning, and more. Additionally, Johns were offered the option to purchase drugs, usually cocaine, along with a prostitute. According to New York Attorney General Eric Schneiderman, "It was quite a remarkable enterprise...like the mob goes to business school [11]."

The same technologies used by traffickers can be harnessed to fight TIP. Data collected from digital technologies constitutes an information trail that can be extremely useful for identifying, tracking, and prosecuting traffickers. Tools which gather this data from disparate sources and inform law enforcement have enormous potential. For example, researchers at the University of Southern California Annenberg Center on Communication Leadership and Policy (CCLP), recently developed a prototype software designed to detect possible cases of sex trafficking of minors online [12]. The software scans popular classified ad sites (e.g., Backpage, Adult Search, MyRedBook, and Cityvibe) looking for phone numbers associated with postings across different sites. In addition, the software scans for certain words and phrases that are likely to be associated with trafficking activity, e.g., terms like "visiting," "18," and "new." It is impossible to determine with 100% certainty that illicit activity is occurring, but likely instances of trafficking are displayed. This tool, and similar, should be adopted by law enforcement anti-trafficking task forces.

### 3.2    Victims of Trafficking Do Not Self-Identify

Violence inflicted by traffickers on victims is often severe. Rape, beatings, torture, assault, humiliations, abuse, degradation, threats, isolation, and physical confinement are common techniques employed by traffickers to break the will of human trafficking victims. Individuals rescued by law enforcement typically have acute physical and sexual trauma, mental illness, substance abuse, sexually transmitted diseases, and et cetera [8].

The Silence Compliance Model catalogues the reasons that victims tend to comply with traffickers [14]. Victims remain silent for three primary reasons: (1) coercion, victims are scared due to exposure to cruelty, brutality, torture, threats of harm to self and/or loved ones, and withholding food or other necessities; (2) collusion, victims are in survival mode due to dependence (for emotional, drug, or financial reasons), isolation, and brainwashing; (3) contrition, victims feel shame, guilt, culpability, remorse, regret, worthless, and abandoned. Furthermore, victims often become subject Stockholm Syndrome – a psychological phenomenon in which captives experience feelings of empathy and sympathy towards their captors [15]. Lastly, victims often will not self-identify out of fear that the criminal justice system will prosecute them, particularly if they do not fit the image of a young innocent trafficking victim, e.g., a victim who was coerced into prostitution to pay off smuggling debts may be too afraid of prosecution to cooperate with law enforcement [16].

Underreporting results in extreme difficulties tracking the prevalence of human trafficking activity. It limits the ability to gather real-time data on TIP, prevents accurate measurement of the problem, and impedes efforts to combat trafficking. Organizations have begun to collect data on TIP. For example, SumAll.org, a non-profit organization which focuses on data analytics services, has begun efforts to compile data in the fight against human trafficking. SumAll CEO Korey Lee notes, "[t]here's not a lot of data published out there, given that slavery and trafficking are illegal across the world. A lot of this information is locked up in PDF reports, hundreds of pages of U.N. documentation, and what not, so it's not easily accessible and available. So we wanted to transform that and make it a little easier to understand [17]." The Minnesota Department of Public Safety completes annual studies of human trafficking, including information on numbers of arrests, prosecutions, successful convictions, number of victims (including method of recruitment and discovery). In addition, trafficking routes and patterns are recorded, including states and countries of origin and destinations [18].

## 3.3    Inadequate Law Enforcement Efforts

Most law enforcement entities do not collect human trafficking related data. Farrell, McDevitt, & Fahy surveyed the chief or highest ranking officer in 3,189 municipal, county, and state law-enforcement agencies in a methodical attempt to uncover experiences and challenges that these agencies face when fighting human trafficking [16]. Their results show that less than 10% of police agencies investigated cases of human trafficking between 2000 and 2006 – the period directly following implementation of a Department of Justice (DOJ) program to fund anti-trafficking task forces. Agencies which did report investigating instances of human trafficking made minimal efforts; only 30% reported investigating both primary types of trafficking (labor and sex).

Lack of law enforcement initiative results in a failure to identify and combat instances of human trafficking. Training programs, anti-trafficking protocols and policies, and assignment of specialized personnel in task forces are common actions that law enforcement entities can take to combat trafficking. Training programs, which provide officers with vital information needed to identify and respond to instances of TIP, have been implemented by 19.7% of law enforcement agencies. Human trafficking protocols and policies, which provide a set of instructions on how officers should proceed if they believe that they have encountered human trafficking, have been implemented by 9.4% of law enforcement entities. Assignment of specialized personnel to combat trafficking is perhaps the most aggressive approach, and only 5.9% of law enforcement organizations have implemented such measures. However, Farrell, McDevitt, & Fahy's research found that the odds of identifying TIP cases increased 132% when training programs were made available to officers, by 288% when protocols and policies were enacted to guide officer identification and response, and by 98% when specialized personnel were assigned to combat trafficking [16].

In short, valuable data is never collected because law enforcement rarely makes human trafficking related arrests. Criminal records, location of crimes, conspirators, and other insights into the operations of trafficking syndicates gained through police activity can be enormously useful in the fight against TIP. However, even when relevant data is collected, it is rarely coded properly to ensure easy access and sharing. Furthermore, centralized databases to store trafficking information are virtually nonexistent. Proper data collection can only occur when law enforcement takes a proactive approach to human trafficking eradication.

## 3.4     Lack of Collaboration and Data Sharing

Federal policy efforts to promote interagency collaboration and TIP data sharing include (1) the 2005 reauthorization of the TVPA, which called for "an effective mechanism for quantifying the number of victims of trafficking on a national, regional, and international basis," and (2) the 2008 TVPA reauthorization required the FBI to include TIP data as a Part 1 crime in its annual report [19][20]. However, neither of these initiatives has resulted in the development of a comprehensive repository of information on human trafficking. Additionally, private sector work to collect human trafficking data is lacking.

Various impediments to collaboration and data sharing efforts exist. Restrictive laws and regulations can impede data sharing efforts. However, partnerships are emerging around data sharing and analysis. For example, the Polaris Project, a nonprofit organization committed to the eradication of human trafficking, has partnered with the United States government to manage the main human trafficking hotline in America. Since 2007, the Polaris Project has taken 72,000 calls, connected 8,300 survivors to support and services, and reported 3,000 cases of human trafficking to law enforcement. In early 2013, the Polaris Project announced a partnership with Google that will result in the launch of the Global Human Trafficking Hotline Network – an initiative committed to providing support to victims globally and leveraging data [21]. This effort highlights how effective collaboration can result in positive outcomes. However, interoperability challenges are often encountered when strategic partnerships are established – data is often coded differently and large IT investments are required to allow effective data sharing. Additionally, even agencies that have the ability to collect the necessary data (e.g., the intelligence community) have not made countering human trafficking a strategic priority.

# 4     Research Methodology

Given the current state of data on human trafficking, we chose to conduct a design science-inspired research project. Design science is a problem solving technique that seeks to create innovations in information systems (IS) through the development of new ideas, practices, technical capabilities, products, et cetera [22][23]. Collectively referred to as artifacts, new innovations are developed in an iterative manner – artifacts are developed, evaluated, and redeveloped continuously. In this paper we highlight three prototypes from our ongoing investigation that seek to use data analytics to uncover nuances of human trafficking. These prototypes can be considered mini-artifacts that help to uncover effective approaches to large-scale human trafficking database construction – the eventual aim of the research team.

We began our work by asking the following question: *what open data is available on human trafficking?* Mining the web, we found data on human trafficking news stories and cases. In addition, we found datasets that contained details of projects funded by the US government to combat human trafficking. Using these datasets, we began creating our first two prototypes. The prototypes focused on analytics and visualization of data. Next, we shared our outputs, the visualizations, with a series of stakeholder groups. These groups represented policy makers, researchers, students, and bloggers. Through feedback received, we iterated our models and visualizations. Following this, we engaged with one stakeholder, Truckers Against Trafficking (TAT), to analyze their proprietary data. True to the tenants of design science, we were able to engage this stakeholder by allowing them to add their design considerations to our existing prototypes. TAT data was integrated with our open datasets and novel visualizations and analytics were constructed. Based on the outcomes of these projects, we have now begun a more intensive engagement with one of the largest regional coalitions against human trafficking. All prior prototypes were shared with this stakeholder. In addition, it was the transmission of feedback directly between stakeholders (in this case between TAT and the Coalition Group) that enabled us to secure their engagement and data. A survey has been sent out to the coalition to begin to understand the kinds of data each agency has on trafficking and how data might be fused together. To the best of our knowledge, this project will be one of the first attempts to build a regional repository of data on human trafficking. Our work draws heavily on design science, albeit in an untraditional manner, to build mini-artifacts on human trafficking. While still in progress, our approach provides interesting insights on how to tackle data-poor problems through design science approaches.

# 5    Three Prototypes on Data Analytics and Trafficking

## 5.1    Human Trafficking News Article Analysis

This research was a prototype effort designed to explicate the viability of open data analytics to explore complex social issues. The project took place over the course of two months – August and September 2013. The research analyzed the abundant qualitative data which exists on human trafficking to uncover behavior patterns indicative of TIP activity. Five hundred articles, sourced from local news stations and online newspapers, were identified; an algorithm was designed to select articles published after the year 2000 that matched the following keywords: 'human trafficking,' 'sex trafficking,' and 'labor trafficking.' Stories were collected from major US publications from all areas of the country, e.g., the New York Times, The Boston Herald, Fox News Chicago, CBS Los Angeles, and et cetera. A coding system was developed and each article was assessed to determine if it contained all relevant information, i.e., perpetrator and victim demographic information (name, age, and location), venue(s) where crime occurred, and background data (prior convictions and occupation). Articles which did not contain complete information were discarded. Of the 500 analyzed articles, 39 cases were identified with complete information. These 39 articles were coded into an excel sheet for further analysis.

The results show that perpetrators generally tend to be in their mid-30's and 75% male. Traffickers often target individuals who are young, of low socioeconomic status, and lacking parental support (e.g., in the foster care system, homeless, et cetera). Many individuals fall victim to trafficking through the process of migration, e.g., in an attempt to secure a better future for themselves or their children, individuals are tricked by traffickers promising education, employment, and prosperity in a foreign country. Victims fit the profile of economically disadvantaged individuals lured away by the promise of money, shelter, and a better life. The results show that human traffickers generally recruit victims through one or more of the following methods: romance, offering material benefits, intimidation, imprisonment, offering legal employment, and international smuggling. Traffickers who recruit through using romance or offering material benefits methods typically spend time wining, dining, and seducing victims. For example, Roshaun Nakia Porter was indicted in federal court on April 30, 2012 after five different women told officers that they met Porter on Craigslist or seekingarrangements.com thinking they were entering into a monogamous relationship. Porter allegedly spent weeks showering the women with gifts and special treatment, before forcing them to turn tricks at a Motel 6 [24]. Intimidation and imprisonment methods involve threatening victims and detaining them against their will by force. For example, Donald L. Perinks was arraigned on charges of human trafficking and unlawful imprisonment on July 19, 2013. Perkins allegedly invited women to parties at his house, took them captive, forced them to perform sexual acts, and threatened to kill them if they resisted [25]. Offering legal employment and international smuggling models are typically used on economically disadvantaged individuals in developing countries. Traffickers offer financial incentives to victims willing to relocate. However, when victims arrive at their destination, they are forced into slavery. For example, Maximino Morales and Melinda Morales pled guilty on May 6, 2011 to federal charges of harboring Filipino nationals who they had illegally smuggled into the United States. Victims promised decent jobs in the United States, but were instead forced to work under abusive conditions in elder care facilities [26].

An analysis of crime location uncovered five primary venues where trafficking activity occurs: internet, home, hotel/motel, private businesses, and public locations (mostly used in combination). Public location was defined as spaces such as parks, rest stops, and streets. Private business described locations that were used as decoys for human trafficking operations, e.g., such as spas, massage parlors, restaurants, elder homes, farms, strip clubs, et cetera. The Internet was the most commonly cited venue; as discussed earlier, traffickers have begun rapidly using mobile technologies, social media sites, online classified sites, and other online platforms. However, this widespread use of the internet may indicate a bias in reporting designed to incite social commentary about the rapid growth of the internet. Articles which analyzed internet use tended to cite their intermediary role; traffickers generally initiate contact with victims over the internet, and then invite them to meet at a different location.

The capability to harness and leverage data from non-traditional sources is crucial. Open data efforts, which do not make use of sensitive or protected data, often do not require much political clout or resources to begin, i.e., projects can be initiated without first obtaining access to restricted data. Further studies should analyze movement patterns of human trafficking between geographic regions. Attention should be focused on large events, specific highways, airports, and et cetera. It is also imperative that the sample size be increased to ensure that conclusions drawn can be generalized.

## 5.2    Truckers against Trafficking

A second prototype study on human trafficking was conducted. This research was designed to demonstrate the benefits obtained from combining open data with proprietary data provided by Truckers Against Trafficking (TAT). TAT is a nonprofit organization that educates truckers in the United States about how to spot and properly report trafficking activity. The organization's mission, taken from its website, is to "educate, equip, empower, and mobilize members of the trucking and travel plaza industry to combat domestic sex trafficking [27]. This project took place during August and September 2013.

The TAT data, which spans a five year period from December 7, 2007 to September 31, 2013, describes call trends to the National Human Trafficking Resource Center (NHTRC). Location data was recorded for each call the NHTRC received. This location data was compared with various open data collected from Bureau of Labor Statistics (BLS) and the United States Census Bureau on unemployment, education spending, and crime for the year of 2009. The year 2009 was chosen as a midpoint for the 5 year data, as the most data was available for that year. Tableau (http://www.tableausoftware.com/) was used for analysis and visual representations.

The results showed a significant positive correlation between number of calls made to NHTRC violent crimes (fig. 1), education spending per pupil (fig. 2), and unemployment rate (fig. 3). Additionally, calls were compared against grades that Shared Hope – a nonprofit dedicated to eradication of TIP – assigned to each state denoting the strength of their legislative efforts to combat trafficking (fig. 4).

Fig. 1. Violent crimes per 100,000 population by state is displayed using a gun icon – larger icons indicate more crime and smaller icons indicate less crime. A red gradient displays the number of calls made to the NHTRC (darker red indicates more calls). While one might expect high levels of violent crime to be correlated with more human trafficking related calls, the data show just the opposite in Indiana and Ohio – these states have lower levels of violent crime but receive more calls.

Fig. 2. Education spending per pupil in each state is juxtaposed with the number of calls made to the NHTRC between December 7, 2007 and September 31, 2013. Number of calls to the NHTRC is shown as text relative to the value, with greater spending shown in bigger text. Education spending per pupil is displayed as a red gradient on the map with a green shade representing greater spending per pupil, above the national average, and red shade representing a lower amount allocated to education spending. Another positive correlation, though slight, is seen between these two variables.

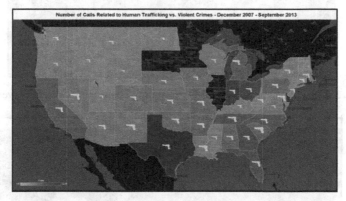

**Fig. 1.** Violent crime (icon) and human trafficking calls (gradient)

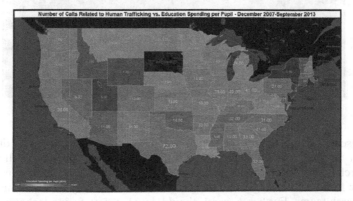

**Fig. 2.** Education spending per pupil (gradient) and human trafficking calls (text overlay)

Fig. 3. Unemployment rate and number of calls to NHTRC is mapped between December 7, 2007 and September 31, 2013. Unemployment rate is shown as a green to red gradient, with states that have an unemployment rate below the U.S. national unemployment rate shown in green and states with an unemployment rate above the U.S. national rate shown in red. The text displays number of calls to the NHTRC and are relative to size – greater number of calls are in larger text, lesser number of calls are in smaller text.

Fig. 4. Shared Hope's letter grades denote the relative strength of legislative efforts within the state. Trafficking-related calls are displayed on a gradient scale – darker blue states received more phone calls. The results are often contradictory; for example, Texas received a letter grade "B" while simultaneously receiving the highest number of calls.

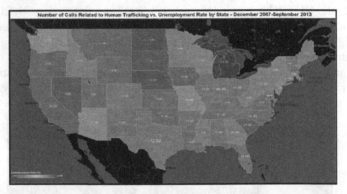

**Fig. 3.** Unemployment rate (gradient) and human trafficking calls (text overlay)

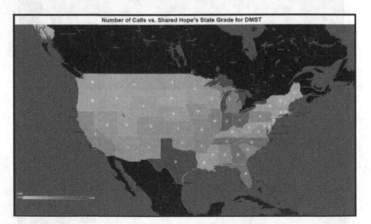

**Fig. 4.** Shared Hope's state grades (text) and calls (gradient)

This research demonstrates the potential for interesting insights to be drawn when open data is used in combination with proprietary data. The major limitation of this research is that only a small amount of call data was analyzed. Moreover, the data was never fused into a single dataset – there is no easy way to share this data with other research teams. Further research should develop data fusion techniques and best practices so that comprehensive databases consisting of fused data can be constructed and shared. Additionally, compiling call data from multiple sources would allow conclusions to be drawn with increased confidence levels.

### 5.3 Do Investments in Anti-Trafficking Programs Pay Off?

The third project conducted a preliminary analysis of the impact of federal government anti-trafficking investments made from 2003-2011. Since the enactment of the TVPA, government spending on anti-TIP efforts has increased from \$31.8 million in 2001 to \$185.5 million in 2010. Monetary aid is used to support law enforcement agencies that employ innovative technologies to apprehend traffickers, groups providing rehabilitation services to trafficking victims, and public awareness campaigns in affected communities to enhance detection and eradication of trafficking networks. However, it is unclear whether these efforts have resulted in decreased human trafficking activity. This research attempts to shed light on the effectiveness of anti-trafficking spending.

A comprehensive dataset was constructed to capture funding provided by US federal agencies to combat human trafficking from 2003-2011. We extracted information from the annual reports of the US Office to Monitor and Combat Trafficking in Persons (G/TIP) on the types of projects funded to combat human trafficking [28]. Additionally, data was collected to quantify trafficking activity on a global scale; data from the International Organization for Migration (IOM) was collected and statistically analyzed with tableau (fig. 5). Fig. 5. This graph displays the number of recorded human trafficking cases by region for 2010, 2011, and 2012. It is interesting to note the shifts in trafficking activity between each year; Europe saw an overall decline in recorded incidents of trafficking over the time period, while trafficking in South/Central Asia increased.

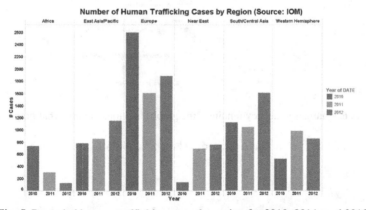

**Fig. 5.** Recorded human trafficking cases by region for 2010, 2011, and 2012

Data relating to project investments, funding agencies, recipient countries, project descriptions, regions, and governance characteristics was then aggregated. This data was not readily accessible, which is surprising given efforts in recent decades to increase transparency and data sharing. Consider the case of foreignassistance.gov, which is supposed to make data on foreign aid available for anyone to analyze and measure program efficacy. However, no data from the Office to Monitor and Combat Trafficking in Persons was available for analysis. Using a grounded theory approach [29], US anti-trafficking project descriptions were segmented into granular categories based on their investment objectives: rule of law, control for corruption, prosecution, prevention, protection, advocacy, intervention, resource, research, victim support services, and victimization. These categories could be applied as primary, secondary, or tertiary to account for multiple objectives per project. The World Bank's Rule of Law Governance Indicator was used as a control variable and served as a proxy to capture countries' levels of political stability. Transparency International's Corruption Perception Index was used as a proxy to control for level of corruption in the country. Visualization software was used to detect high-level spatial and temporal patterns between key variables.

Fig. 6. A combination of a bar and a line graphs are used. The line graph shows changes in funding by individual agencies from 2003-2011. The bar graph shows total funding by agency over that period. From Figure 7, it is clear that US agencies have awarded fluctuating amounts of funding to combat trafficking over the years. For example, the total amount awarded by the US Department of State rose from 2008-2010 and then fell from 2010-2011. In contrast, the total amount awarded by the US Department of Labor drastically dropped from 2010-2011.

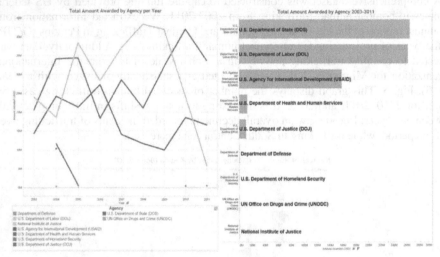

**Fig. 6.** Changes in agency funding (line graph) and total funding (bar graph)

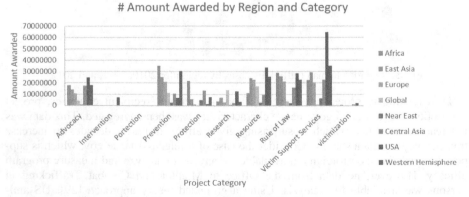

**Fig. 7.** Aid awarded by region and funding category

Fig. 7. The amount awarded by region and funding category is shown. USAID has made significant investments in victim support services, rule of law, advocacy and resource categories in USA when compared with other regions. Significant investments have been made in prevention and protection categories in Africa. In general, significant investments have been made by USAID in resources, rule of law and victim support services when compared to other categories. Victimization has the least amount awarded followed by research and protection categories.

Based on our research approach, we developed hypotheses to estimate the effect of US anti-trafficking investment on countries' compliance scores in three policy areas: prosecution, protection, and prevention. The prosecution principle ensures that the member countries punish the traffickers and their allies who have violated the rights of victims by enslavement. Protection involves assisting and providing adequate services to the victims to regain their freedom and reintegrate with their family to start a new life. Prevention capabilities ensure that countries adopt and implement comprehensive domestic policies and programs to combat human trafficking. Additionally, we also tested the effect of countries' governance characteristics (rule of law and control for corruption) on its capacity to combat corruption. Due to the nature of our dependent variables, we estimated a panel ordered logistic regression models [30].The hypothesis that US anti-trafficking investments would be positively associated with improvements in prosecution, protection, and prevention scores was not supported. However, the results did show that rule of law and control for corruption has a significant effect on Prosecution index. Rule of law has a significant impact on Protection index. Rule of law had a significant impact on Prevention index.

We also conducted analysis at the project level. We found that rule of law and control for corruption has a significant impact on investments made in Africa, East Asia Pacific and South and Central Asia. Both rule of law and control for corruption were not found to be significant in Europe and Eurasia region. However, rule of law (and not control for corruption) has been found to be significant in the near east region. A separate model has been to know the impact of unemployment on overall3P index as unemployment data was found to be missing in most of the project related information. Considering the unemployment variable in the model would have reduced the power of the statistical analysis (less data, less power). The Unemployment rate was found to be significant (negatively related) in impacting the overall3P index. It was found that rule of law and control for corruption have a significant impact on overall3P in investments made on advocacy, protection, prevention, research and rule of law categories.

The study's results have several implications at a policy level. Firstly, dividing investments into smaller categories gave us more information as to where resources were lacking and needed bolstering in an effort to help the anti-trafficking movement. Second, the results suggest that to fight trafficking, a country's governance factors must be taken into account. Allocating resources to improve these factors could help in combating the issue. Third, the study's results can help guide economic policy with respect to human trafficking issues that have multiple variables (such as rule of law, corruption, etc.) and time heterogeneity. The analysis highlights the difficulties in assessing the impact of effects of anti-trafficking investments and potential biases that may produce spurious estimates. Fourth, the study also created a consolidated dataset of US anti-trafficking investment information, removing the issues in analyzing multiple, heterogeneous datasets to assess the economic impact of these investments on policy outcomes.

This study exemplifies efforts to coordinate open data from disparate sources. It consolidates various investments made to anti-trafficking efforts, and can inform policymaker in their efforts to make evidence driven decisions. The research is primarily limited by measurement error, which could arise during any course of a funded project. Further research should explore investment data across greater time periods and across countries.

# 6    Future Analysis

Efforts to collect data from new sources must be undertaken. Mining data on human trafficking from social media sources could prove enormously beneficial. The research team is currently poised to undertake efforts to mine data from Twitter and other social media sources to elucidate the conversational dynamics that exist between anti-trafficking groups. Initially, we aim to gain an understanding of the structure and content of human trafficking tweets, i.e., what hashtags are used, where tweets originate from geographically, which users post human trafficking content, and other relevant information. Example hashtags: #Human Trafficking, #Child Trafficking, #Combat Trafficking, #Counter Trafficking, etc. Once a general understanding of the mechanisms behind human trafficking communications on twitter is obtained, data could be collected using key search terms consisting of messages/tweets (social media), relevant information (e.g., economics, number of cases registered, and other attributes), and location and temporal information. Location information obtained from the data could be linked to the census database to display data spatially. In addition, information pertaining to socio-economic characteristics such as unemployment rate, poverty, income status, et cetera could be obtained and used for analysis. This could lead to valuable information regarding the temporal and geographical distribution of human trafficking, socio-economic profiles, general sentiments held toward government sponsored anti-trafficking programs, and etc.

Several free software packages are being examined that could be used to extract data based on our search criteria, e.g., NodeXI and oAuth. Additionally, efforts are underway to catalogue collected data into a database. This database, which will eventually consist of data from myriad social media sources (e.g., Twitter, Facebook, Google Plus, Linkedin, Reddit, etc.), would allow researchers to conduct more in depth analyses. For example, search term-specific network analyses would allow for more in-depth exploration of certain topics and how they differ from others.

# 7    Conclusion

Design science approaches provide us with an ability to create artifacts in an iterative manner through mindful engagement of stakeholders. For social problems, such as countering human trafficking, this approach can help us make headway through building large datasets from the bottom-up. While not perfect, the research process described here helped us advance the cause of evidence-driven approaches to combatting human trafficking. As previously stated, the eventual aim of this work is to construct a large scale database on human trafficking; prototype efforts were necessary for the research team to uncover the best approaches to database construction. The prototypes demonstrate the ability to mine data from disparate sources and generate intelligence on human trafficking operations. As a first step, news articles were compiled and analyzed for trends and patterns. Second, call data from Truckers Against Trafficking compared with various social indicators and mapped visually in Tableau. Lastly, data on US government anti-TIP spending was collected and analyzed. Further research is necessary before database construction can begin, e.g., research which fuses twitter data with open data could provide insight into TIP.

# References

1. Manyika, J., Chui, M., Brown, B., Bughin, J., Dobbs, R., Roxburgh, C., Byers, A.H.: Big data: The Next Frontier for Innovation, Competition, and Productivity. McKinsey Institute (2011)
2. Feuer, A.: New York Times: "The Mayor's Geek Squad" (March 23, 2013), http://www.bridgetgainer.com/news/2013/03/new-york-times-the-mayors-geek-squad.html (accessed December 15, 2013)
3. International Labour Organization, ILO global estimate of forced labour: Results and methodology. International Labour Office, Geneva (2012)
4. Victims of Trafficking and Violence Prevention Act of 2000, P.L. 106-386 Stat. 114, 1464 (2000)
5. Belser, P.: Forced labour and human trafficking: Estimating the profits. Unpublished working paper, UN International Labour Organization, Geneva, Switzerland (2005)
6. Wheaton, E.M., Schauer, E.J., Galli, T.V.: Economics of human trafficking. International Migration 48(4), 114–141 (2010), http://dx.doi.org/10.1111/j.1468-2435.2009.00592.x
7. U.S. Laws on Trafficking in Persons (2013), U.S. Department of State website: http://www.state.gov/j/tip/laws/ (retrieved October 31, 2013)
8. Farrell, A., Fahy, S.: The problem of human trafficking in the U.S.: Public frames and policy responses. Journal of Criminal Justice 37(6), 617–626 (2009), http://dx.doi.org/10.1016/j.jcrimjus.2009.09.010
9. Fong, R., Cardoso, J.B.: Child human trafficking victims: Challenges for the child Welfare system. Evaluation and Program Planning 33(3), 311–316 (2010), http://dx.doi.org/10.1016/j.evalprogplan.2009.06.018
10. Tata, S.: Hundreds rally against human trafficking in Pomona (January 29, 2012), NBC website: http://www.nbclosangeles.com/news/local/Human-Trafficking-Not-Foreign-Problem-Pomona-138293964.html (retrieved November 2013)
11. "Remarkable" prostitution ring had its wwn ad firm to maximize SEO (November 20, 2012), Gothamist website: http://gothamist.com/2012/11/20/busted_prostitution_ring_had_it_adv.php (retrieved November 2013)
12. Latonero, M., Musto, J., Boyd, Z., Boyle, E., Bissel, A., Gibson, K., et al.: The rise of mobile and the diffusion of technology-facilitated trafficking. University of Southern California (2012)
13. Mechanic, M.: MetaFilter saved my pals from sex traffickers—exclusive interview (May 21, 2010), MotherJones website: http://www.motherjones.com/mojo/2010/05/metafilter-russian-sex-ring (retrieved November 2013)
14. Johnson, B.C.: Aftercare for survivors of human trafficking. Social Work & Christianity 39(4), 370–389 (2012)
15. Stolz, B.A.: Human trafficking policy. Criminology & Public Policy 9(2), 267–274 (2010), http://dx.doi.org/10.1111/j.1745-9133.2010.00625.x

16. Farrell, A., McDevitt, J., Fahy, S.: Where are all the victims? Understanding the determinants of official identification of human trafficking incidents. American Society of Criminology 9(2), 201–233 (2010), http://dx.doi.org/10.1111/j.1745-9133.2010.00621.x

17. Tennant, D.: Using big data to fight human trafficking (February 9, 2013), ITBusinessEdge website: http://www.itbusinessedge.com/blogs/from-under-the-rug/using-big-data-to-fight-humantrafficking.html (retrieved November 2013)

18. Human trafficking reports (2013), Minnesota Department of Public Safety website: https://dps.mn.gov/divisions/ojp/statisticalanalysiscenter/Pages/human-trafficking-reports.aspx (retrieved November 2013)

19. Trafficking Victims Protection Reauthorization Act of 2005, P.L. 108-193, Stat. 117, 2875 (2005)

20. William Wilberforce Trafficking Victims Protection Reauthorization Act of 2008, P.L. 110 457 Stat. (2008)

21. Kerr, D.: Google battles human trafficking with global hotline (April 9, 2013), CNET website: http://news.cnet.com/8301-1023_3-5757878893/google-battles-human-trafficking-with-global-hotline/ (retrieved November 2013)

22. Hevner, A., March, S., Park, K., Ram, S.: Design science in information systems research. MIS Quarterly 28(1), 75–105 (2004)

23. Denning, P.J.: A New Social Contract for Research. Communications of the ACM 40(2), 132–134 (1997)

24. Vargas, V.: Long beach man accused of forcing women into prostitution (May 1, 2012), National Broadcasting Company website: http://www.nbclosangeles.com/news/local/Long-Beach-Roshaun-Kevin-Nakia-PorterAccused-Human-Trafficking-Orange-County-Pimp-149777675.html (retrieved November 2013)

25. Harris, D.: 26-year-old Flint man charged with human trafficking, unlawful imprisonment (July 25, 2013), MLive website: http://www.mlive.com/news/flint/index.ssf/2013/07/26-year-old_flint_man_charged.html (retrieved November 2013)

26. Couple Pleads Guilty To Smuggling Filipino Nationals Into The US (May 6, 2011), CBS website: http://losangeles.cbslocal.com/2011/05/06/couple-pleads-guilty-to-smuggling-filipino-nationals-into-the-us/ (retrieved November 2013)

27. Truckers against trafficking (2012), Truckers Against Trafficking website: http://truckersagainsttrafficking.org (retrieved November 2013)

28. United States Office to Monitor and Combat Trafficking in Persons. U.S. Government Funded Anti-Trafficking Programs, http://www.state.gov/j/tip/response/grants/ (retrieved July 15, 2013)

29. Yin, R.: Case study research: Design and methods, 3rd edn. Sage Publications, Thousand Oaks (2003)

30. Greene, W.: Econometric Analysis. Prentice Hall, New Jersey (1993)

# The Design of a Multi-layer Scrutiny Protocol
# to Support Online Privacy and Accountability

Jonas Sjöström[1], Pär J. Ågerfalk[1], and Alan R. Hevner[2]

[1] Uppsala University, Sweden
{jonas.sjostrom,par.agerfalk}@im.uu.se
[2] University of South Florida, USA
ahevner@usf.edu

**Abstract.** Information systems design must balance requirements of privacy
and accountability for the good of individuals and society. Drawing from an
evolving theory of scrutiny, we propose a multi-layer protocol to support the
rigorous application of privacy rules and accountability rules in sensitive online
applications. We ground our study in the context of the design and development
of an eHealth system for psychosocial care. Privacy protections are balanced
with the need to provide for accountable interventions in well-defined critical
care situations.

**Keywords:** Privacy, Accountability, Privacy, Multi-layer protocols, Scrutiny,
Online psychosocial care, Anonymity, Design theory.

*"No one shall be subjected to arbitrary interference with his privacy, family, home or
correspondence, nor to attacks upon his honour and reputation."* United Nations: The
Universal Declaration of Human Rights [18, article 12].

*"Information accountability means the use of information should be transparent so it is possible to
determine whether a particular use is appropriate under a given set of rules and that the system
enables individuals and institutions to be held accountable for misuse."* Weitzner et al. [20].

## 1 Introduction

The rise of online communities and social media as a vehicle for large-scale social
interaction has accelerated the penetration of information technology (IT) into both
private and professional life [1] Arguably, a significant part of contemporary social
interaction is mediated by, or planned, using IT. While this evolution of human collaboration and social life may be beneficial in many ways, it also suggests a significant
threat to individual privacy. Two forces fuel the threat to privacy. The first force is the
growth of IT, which in itself enables increased functional capabilities, storage capaci-
ties, networking connections, and surveillance reach. The second force is that commercial actors find value in information about individuals, causing them to seek ways
to exploit technological opportunities to collect and capitalize on such information.

M.C. Tremblay et al. (Eds.): DESRIST 2014, LNCS 8463, pp. 85–98, 2014.

One's right to privacy, i.e. to "freedom from unauthorized intrusion" [12], is a human right as declared by the United Nations as seen in the above quote. The recent turmoil caused by former NSA employee Edward Snowden's leaked details of top-secret government mass surveillance programs shows the timeliness and importance of the online privacy discourse. One way to facilitate privacy is by means of providing anonymity. The topic of *anonymous* interaction between peers in an online community is at the heart of community design. People tend to behave differently in cyberspace than in real life, e.g. say and do things that they would not say or do face-to-face. This shift in behavior is known as the online disinhibition effect [16]. On the one hand, behavior may change in a way that is desired by the community provider, e.g. encouraging people to read and contribute to discussion fora. On the other hand, anonymity creates a risk of undesired behavior that negatively impacts the community provider's intentions, such as bullying or provision of links to buy illegal drugs. There are well-known examples of the consequences of unethical online behavior from discussion fora and online newspapers, such as the closedown of user comments on the Engadget forum [21]. Consequentially, the community provider may need to proactively monitor peer activity, identify undesired behavior, and take action when such behavior occurs. From the community provider perspective, such actions concern accountability, i.e. the means by which to hold people accountable when peer behavior deviates from the norms of the community.

Information accountability relies on transparency in IS design and use [20]. The tension between these two ideals – privacy and accountability – causes a challenge for designers to preserving privacy, while at the same time ensuring accountability. To address the challenge, we have developed a nascent *theory of scrutiny* – that is, a theory concerned with online interactive environments where privacy is guaranteed while accountability must be maintained and easily inspected. In Sjöström et al. [14] we conceptualized a supportive environment to maintain anonymity, yet one that preserves a meta-level of accountability and control. This paper extends our thinking on a theory of scrutiny via the design of a multi-layer protocol for supporting privacy and accountability in online applications.

The paper proceeds as follows. In section two we outline the theoretical background for the design. In section three, we present the multi-layer scrutiny protocol. Section four shows an application of the protocol to systematically scrutinize privacy and accountability in an organizational context and thus provides an informed argument [10] regarding the usefulness of the protocol. Section five concludes the paper.

## 2     Background

### 2.1     Privacy

Even though privacy is a well-known concept, it has never been as much in focus as it is currently. In addition to the technological development, developments in both the commercial and the public sector have given rise to increasing privacy concerns. Commercial organizations have identified new means to analyze consumers, and government intelligence exploits techniques to identify threats to society by analyzing online activity. Albeit deceptively straightforward, the term 'privacy' is not easily defined. A value-based definition views "general privacy as a human right integral to society's moral value system" [15, pp. 992–993]. While such a definition is highly normative, researchers in Information Systems and other social sciences frequently adopt other views, such as privacy as "the ability of individuals to control the terms under which their personal information is acquired and used" [4, p. 326]. In this work, we subscribe to the normative definition, while still acknowledging that the ability of individuals to maintain control of their information is an important consideration in IS design. A comprehensive survey and meta-analysis of IS research on privacy can be found in Belanger and Crossler [3].

## 2.2 Accountability

According to ethno-methodologist Harold Garfinkel [5, p. vii], actions that are accountable are "visibly-rational-and-reportable-for-all-practical-purposes", a notion that is at the heart also of information accountability in the context of online psychosocial care. In keeping with Weber's [19] classical definition of social action, i.e. that human behaviour to which the actor attaches meaning and which takes into account the behaviour of others and thus is directed in its course, Garfinkel's view suggests that an accountable IS must keep a record of the social actions performed through and by means of the system (both their social grounds and their social purposes) as a socio-pragmatic instrument for communication [6].

Weitzner et al. [20] approach accountability from a web infrastructure perspective. They propose three architectural features to be incorporated in the future web to facilitate transparency and information accountability.

- *First*, policy-aware transaction logs that record "information-use events" are required. Such logs should be kept by each endpoint in a de-centralized system. The point of the logs is that they facilitate follow-up on information use and misuse.
- *Second*, they point out the need for a common framework to represent policy rules. Semantic web technology would be the foundation for such frameworks, which would emerge through the collaboration of large overlapping communities on the web.
- *Third*, policy-reasoning tools would support users in understanding how the data they knowingly or unknowingly share may be used. Such information would be made possible through the policy rule frameworks.

## 2.3 Levels of Scrutiny

Drawing from the literature and our experiences in the design of privacy and accountability for a psychosocial online system, in [14] we describe four modes of scrutiny as shown in Table 1. Scrutiny is an activity that involves various stakeholders who engage in different types of action in relation to privacy and accountability.

**Table 1.** Four modes of scrutiny

| Mode | Scrutinizer | Accountable | Activity |
|---|---|---|---|
| Level 0 Scrutiny | Community member(s) | Community member(s) | At the peer-to-peer user level, mitigate community behavior that does not conform to the organizational norms |
| Level 1 Scrutiny | Staff member(s) | Community member(s) | At the staff-to-user level, mitigate community behavior that does not conform to the organizational norms |
| Level 2 Scrutiny | Provider Management | Staff member(s) | Log and monitor actions to protect privacy concerns and uphold accountability |
| Level 3 Scrutiny | External stakeholders | Provider Management | Audit organizations to validate compliance with legislation and ethics. |

The conceptual differentiation between these modes provides a structure to analyze an online system with respect to its capabilities to maintain organizational responsibilities and accountability, while protecting individual privacy. A fundamental preposition is that violation of privacy should be either (i) well-motivated based on organizational responsibility, or (ii) accounted for by someone.

Level 3 scrutiny explains the processes in society that shape and force stakeholders to comply with ethics and legislation regarding privacy and accountability. This level includes traditional external auditing practices but extends beyond what is legally required to encompass also tacit expectations that external stakeholders may impose on an organization.

In order for the organization to respond to such external scrutiny, there is a need for Level 2 scrutiny. Such scrutiny requires the organization to stay updated about the external requirements, and to setup internal processes to log and monitor use (and misuse) of sensitive information about individuals. This level is thus comparable to the traditional IT controller function in an organization but goes beyond budgetary control to include employee behavior in a wide sense. In order to adequately manage such control, the organization needs to monitor legislation changes and externally-imposed requirements for privacy and accountability.

Potential misuse may stem from Level 1 scrutiny where staff members monitor community activity in a responsible manner in accordance with organizational policies and external requirements. Less responsible staff behavior is a case of information misuse that should be 'detected' in level 2 scrutiny.

Privacy concerns are also subject to Level 0 scrutiny, which refers to the community members' peer control of, for example, personalization of visibility, their ability to block others, and report unauthorized content. Level 0 scrutiny also entails activities where community members take some responsibility for the societal discourse, the community providers' privacy policies, and staff behavior.

# 3    A Multi-layered Scrutiny Protocol

We begin the research process of generalizing our findings to a design theory of scrutiny that can be applied to a broader range of IS applications. Here we propose our initial understanding of how best to balance privacy and accountability via a multi-layered protocol based on the levels of scrutiny in Table 1. Scrutiny is an activity that involves various stakeholders who engage in different types of action in relation to privacy and accountability. Our design experiences allow us to inductively identify stakeholders in relation to scrutiny: *Societal institutions* (e.g. government agencies and the media), *principals* (e.g. community providers), *agents* (staff operating on behalf of principals) and *peers* (community members).

## 3.1    The Scrutiny Protocol Matrix

Given the above-identified stakeholders, we propose the Scrutiny Protocol Matrix (see Table 2) showing possible combinations of scrutinizers and scrutinized stakeholders. The columns in the matrix show four different types of accountability: Societal Accountability, Principal Accountability, Agent Accountability, and Peer Accountability. The rows in the matrix correspond to the different modes of scrutiny outlined in Table 1, denoted as Level 0 – Level 3. The conceptual differentiation between mode of scrutiny and type of accountability provides a sophisticated structure to analyze an organization with respect to its capabilities to maintain organizational responsibilities and accountability in relation to relevant stakeholders.

Societal Accountability means scrutinization of societal institutions and refers to society's self-sanitizing processes in terms of public discourse and policy development related to privacy (Level 3), and community provider managements' (Level 2), staff members' (Level 1) and community members' (Level 0) monitoring of laws and ethics that concern privacy. What is at stake here is the societal responsibility in relation to individuals and organizations.

Principal Accountability means scrutinization of community providers and refers to societal institutions' scrutiny of community providers' compliance with applicable privacy laws and ethics (Level 3), community provider managements' self-scrutiny, such as assessing that internal processes and policies fulfill stated and unstated privacy requirements (Level 2), staff members' (Level 1) and community members' (Level 0) scrutiny of corporate routines related to privacy and accountability. What is at stake here is community providers', as principals, responsibilities towards societal and individual interests.

Agent Accountability means scrutinization of individuals in their professional role and refers to scrutiny of staff behavior by societal institutions, such as law enforcement (Level 3), community provider managements' monitoring of staff members' privacy behavior in relation to internal policies (Level 2), staff scrutinization of their own behavior, such as following checklists (Level 1), and community members' scrutiny of staff interventions in the community (Level 0). What is at stake here is staff members' responsibility in relation to individuals, their employer and society at large.

**Table 2.** The Scrutiny Protocol Matrix

| Scrutinizer \ Scrutinized | Societal Accountability — Societal Institutions | Principal Accountability — Community Provider | Agent Accountability — Staff | Peer Accountability — Community Members |
|---|---|---|---|---|
| Level 3 Scrutiny — Societal Institutions | Public discourse on privacy and accountability | External scrutiny of community providers' compliance with privacy laws and ethics | External scrutiny of staff behavior | External audit / scrutiny based on direct access to community interaction data |
| Level 2 Scrutiny — Community Provider | Management monitors laws and ethics concerning privacy concerns | Management performs self-scrutiny, i.e. assessing if their processes and policies sufficiently fulfills privacy ideals | Management monitors that staff fulfills internal policies on how staff should behave according to privacy policies | Management scrutinizes community interaction data to identify privacy violations |
| Level 1 Scrutiny — Staff | Staff monitors laws and ethics concerning privacy concerns | Staff scrutinizes management routines related to privacy, e.g. labor unions protecting staff rights | Staff scrutinizes themselves | Staff scrutinizes community interactions to identify policy violations |
| Level 0 Scrutiny — Community Members | Clients monitor laws and ethics concerning privacy concerns | Clients scrutinize the community providers' policies and actions related to privacy protection and accountability. | Clients scrutinize how staff intervenes in the community | Clients scrutinize their peers and take action to control their own privacy. |

Finally, Peer Accountability means scrutinization of individuals in their role as community members and refers to scrutinization of individuals by societal institutions based on direct access to community interaction data (Level 3), scrutiny of community interaction data by community provider management to identify privacy violations

(Level 2) and by staff members to identify policy violations (Level 1), and community members (a) scrutinization of their peers and (b) actions to manage their own privacy (Level 0).

The four modes of scrutiny and their interdependencies outline a systematic protocol for accountability management in an organization. From the community provider point of view, any situation where privacy is breached in Level 1 scrutiny should be justified in keeping with the policies defined in the organization and conform to measures required to maintain Level 2 scrutiny, and should be logged for accountability purposes. If a Level 3 scrutiny is externally initiated, documentation from Level 2 scrutiny serves as an important source to account for the organization's actions, etc. What is at stake here is community members' responsibility in relation to peers, staff members, community providers and society at large.

## 3.2     Scrutiny Flows

On an abstract level, the interdependencies between the levels of scrutiny include (i) the privacy expectations that flow from higher levels to lower levels of scrutiny, and (ii) the information flow from lower to higher levels that enables accountability through transparent information use and misuse. We refer to these two flows as the **privacy expectation flow** and the **accountability flow**. The privacy expectation flow signals that stakeholders need to identify and interpret legislation, ethics, and policies at higher levels. Stakeholders – through their actions – render information traces that may be part of the accountability flow.

Our design work in the online psychosocial care setting continually highlighted trade-offs between accountability and privacy – an example of conflicting desires between the individual and the community provider. For the organization, there is a need to make balanced and well-informed decisions when to breech privacy [3]. If such decisions are done without appropriate reflection, there is a risk that it will decrease the community's trust in the organization. Unsolicited breech of privacy may also be against ethical standards or legislation. Therefore, in addition to scrutinizing what community peers are doing, there is also a need to scrutinize staff behavior. A systematic approach within the organization to manage both Level 1 and Level 2 scrutiny maintains the provider's capability to respond to level 3 scrutiny, i.e. external parties auditing the provider's compliance with legislation and ethics.

In addition to the flows as such, we propose two concepts to support the analysis of scrutiny flows. First, **flow awareness**, which we define as the knowledge within one stakeholder category about the meaning attached to the flow by individuals in the other stakeholder groups. Second, **flow disruptions** or 'flow flaws', which refer to disturbances in a flow preventing relevant information from propagating to subsequent levels of scrutiny.

## 3.3     A Model of Level 1 Scrutiny

The scrutiny matrix renders several questions about how to understand each level of scrutiny and well as their interdependencies. Here we elaborate further on Level 1 scrutiny performed by staff (Figure 1). Scrutinizing the activities in an online community is based on **content scanning**, which requires **content access**. Through scanning, staff may detect an **anomaly** that needs to be mitigated by **corrective action**. Such actions are performed to maintain **stakeholder responsibility**. Examples of corrective actions include blocking a forum post, banning a user from a community, or banning contributions to the discussion. Corrective action may require **actor access**. In some cases, the actor pseudonym is sufficient, e.g. when informing a community member about a rule. In other cases, the true identity of the actor may be required, e.g. when a community member violates legislation. In such cases, it may threaten individual **privacy**. From a provider's point of view, the model suggests that responsibilities should be clarified, and that 'anomalies' in the content that may threaten the organization, need to be mitigated. In the analyzed case study setting expanded in the next section, the moderator manual is an example of a design implication of this view.

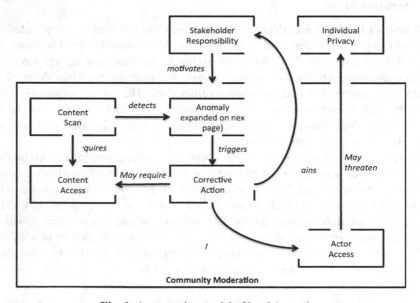

**Fig. 1.** An emerging model of level 1 scrutiny

# 4    Scrutiny in the U-CARE System

In this section, we briefly describe the U-CARE system as embedded in practice, and make some initial observations on how the scrutiny protocols are applied at various levels of stakeholder responsibility.

## 4.1    The Research Program

The system under study was designed and developed as part of a large multidisciplinary research program titled U-CARE. A major component of the project was the implementation of a complex software system for online psychosocial care. The program involves researchers and practitioners from psychology, medicine, information systems, caring sciences, and economics.

The research program aims at supporting people with potentially lethal somatic diseases to cope with posttraumatic stress caused by their diagnosis, which may lead to depression and anxiety. Such stress may also have a negative impact on the treatment of the somatic disease. For example, a depressive state may cause a patient to engage in less physical activity, develop sleeping problems, or forget to adhere to their medications. Internet-based self-help has proven effective for psychiatric disorders as well as for promotion of healthy behavior [2, 13]. It is promising both with regard to treatment efficacy and cost, by using less therapist time per effectively treated patient compared to face-to-face therapy [17].

The intended online support is based on a stepped-care strategy, which means that patients with mild depression or anxiety are directed to a self-help program, while patients with more severe depression or anxiety are offered a treatment program based on cognitive behavioral therapy (CBT) [13]. On top of this, patients become part of an online community, allowing them to interact with peers in discussion forums, online chats, and through internal messages.

## 4.2    Stakeholders and Privacy Concerns in U-CARE

The design of the U-CARE software system focused on issues related to information accountability, privacy, and anonymity. There are four different types of user-created content in the system: Forum threads and forum posts, public and private chat messages, internal messages (between peers), and public diary entries. Each type of content is subject to scrutiny, since others may view it. All users – staff as well as patients – are informed about the extensive logging of actions that takes place in the system, as well as the 'netiquette', i.e. the rules of conduct in the community. The stakeholder-oriented discussion below outlines at a high level privacy concerns in the U-CARE context.

**Peers.** From the perspective of individuals, privacy needs to be protected. Sensitive data must not fall into the wrong hands. Data should only be used for treatment, and (if informed consent is given) for other well-specified purposes. Implications for design include a need to adopt state-of-the-art technology and practices to ensure that data are well protected. Authentication and authorization schemes are necessary to appropriately allow access to data. De-identified data and personal identities should kept separate in order to increase security.

**Agents.** Health staff (e.g. therapists) needs to be able to provide care, insofar as possible without accessing the personal identity of the patients. However, when there is a risk for suicide or self-destructive behavior, there may be a need to 'breech' anonymity to take appropriate action to get in touch with the patient. For design, this means that most caregiving activities are performed with preserved anonymity for the patients. However, there is a need to be able to breech anonymity under certain circumstances.

**Principals.** As healthcare managers and decision makers, there is a need to explore the benefits of new technology, while at the same time maintaining the interests of individuals and professionals. An implication for design is that we need to facilitate follow-ups of privacy breeches to promote accountability. This motivates a logging of patient as well as staff action – and potential misuse of information in particular.

**Societal Stakeholders.** Several external stakeholders influenced the design process. First, each randomized controlled trial within U-CARE is granted approval from an ethical approval board with members appointed by the Swedish government. The objective of the board is to assess whether the societal value of a research initiative outweighs the potential negative impact (including privacy concerns) on individuals. Second, design deliverables (technology as well as practices) need to comply with legislation and ethics. An implication for design was that regulations from government agencies (e.g. the Swedish National Board of Health and Welfare and the Swedish Data Inspection Board) and legislation were scrutinized to promote a design compliant with those regulations.

### 4.3    Scrutiny Flows in U-CARE

In this section, we illustrate the privacy expectation flow and the accountability compliance flow in the U-CARE practice. We adopt the concepts and relations from our model of level 1 scrutiny to structure the presentation.

**Privacy Expectation Flow.** There is a vivid public discourse on issues related to privacy. Several cases of misuse and inadequate software design in the health context were exposed in Swedish media over the last few years. U-CARE as a community provider aims at high compliance with laws and regulations regarding information use and privacy. The Swedish Data Inspection Board – or other societal institutions – may initiate scrutiny of the organization. Given privacy expectations from societal institutions, legal and ethical aspects of management of participant data are continuous concerns, radically affecting the software design as well as managerial routines. Examples include the way participant data is logged and accessed, the adoption of two-step authentication for participants, role-based privileges to access information, and organizational and technical solutions to strengthen information security.

The privacy expectation flow also includes communication from U-CARE as a principal to staff and patients. Internal access policies are provided to staff to guide their work (i.e. content scanning and corrective actions), as well as information use policies and 'netiquette' communicated to patients. Psychologists, researchers, and health staff developed a 'moderator manual' (Table 3) describing problems (anomalies) that may occur that require staff scrutiny of peer activity. For each problem, there is a suggestion how to address the situation. In total, it consists of 15 anomalies, including pornographic content, insults, hate speech, advertising, propaganda *et cetera*. These anomalies represent four categories: Rule violations, medical/therapeutic claims without or contradictory to evidence, negative spirals, and

**Table 3.** Excerpt from the moderator manual

| Anomaly | Example | Corrective action(s) |
|---|---|---|
| Self-destructive or violent tendencies | A discussion revolves around self-destructive or suicidal thoughts. | Immediately contact the responsible therapist(s), who will in turn breech privacy to get in touch with the patient(s). Remove the content. |
| Respect for others | The real name of another participant is exposed in a public discussion. | Remove the content with a comment why it was removed. Write an internal message to the subject stating that it is not allowed to reveal the identity of other patients. |
| Promotion of illegal activity | A patient recommends illegal drugs and how to purchase them on the Internet. | Remove the content. Send internal message to the subject informing stating that illegal activities may not be promoted in the community. Contact the police in case there is reason to believe that someone is in danger. |

destructive tendencies. Explicit rules for privacy breeches serve as instruments to balancing privacy and accountability requirements. In this case the organization's goal is to offer an anonymous environment that should promote people's health and healthy behavior. Each anomaly should be understood as a deviation from what is desirable based on a stakeholder responsibility. The anomaly may lead to undesired consequence(s) for stakeholder(s). The negative spirals, for example, may lead to less healthy behavior, which contradicts the organization's goals as a caregiver.

**Accountability Compliance Flow.** While peer activity in a community may peak during non-office hours, there is a need for a filtered content access that supports staff in interpreting recent activity. Figure 2 shows the 'community monitor', i.e. the user interface for content scanning.

The bar chart at the top indicates the total amount of interactions per day. Below is a form to filter activity based on various parameters: Sender, recipient, keyword, message type, *et cetera*. An abuse detection function based on keyword scanning provides additional support to staff. Any message that contains abuse keywords is highlighted. Severe keywords – such as "suicide" – are more emphasized than the message in the example, based on a classification of keyword severity. In addition to the monitoring performed by staff, community peers are in control of their own communication. They may report forum posts, block other users, and personalize how they wish to display their profiles. They may also set their visibility to 'visible' or 'hidden'. In the latter case, no other users can see that they are online.

As shown in Table 3, corrective action does not always require the organization to reveal the personal identity of the patient. When identity is revealed, there is a clear rationale for it based on the organization's responsibilities. It is, however, feasible for staff to breech privacy at any given time. Any privacy breech will be logged, and the organization has setup routines to scrutinize breeches. The IT coordinator has the

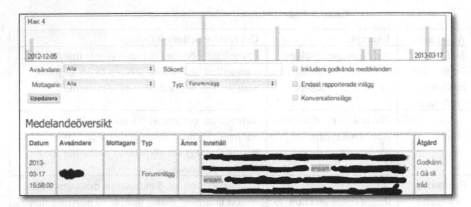

**Fig. 2.** Screenshot from community monitor view

responsibility to extract log data that is discussed in management meetings each month. Any breech of privacy that is not motivated by anomalies will be followed-up in order to hold staff accountable for potential information misuse. Staff members are informed about the privacy rules, both through documents in the organization and in the user interface of the software. The logging of privacy breeches and the routines to scrutinize the logs are part of the accountability compliance flow.

**Flow Awareness.** As shown above, the design work in U-CARE has taken into account many aspects of scrutiny, leading to software solutions as well as routines for staff operations and management. By systematically inquiring into the situation using the scrutiny protocol matrix, we can identify areas that require more attention. For instance, it is unclear to what extent patients *read* and *interpret* consent forms and netiquette rules in the user interface. That is; management knows what they communicate, but there is little knowledge of the actual impact on privacy expectations among their clients.

**Flow Disruptions.** In the case at hand, most attention to accountability compliance concerns the flows from level 0 to level 1 (staff monitoring patient communication) and from level 1 to level 2 (management monitoring privacy breeches by staff).

A risk in the context at hand is the potential misuse of information from technical staff, e.g. developers and technical supervisors with database access and/or access to other parts of the servers hosting the software. Such data access is not recorded in the current log files. In the U-CARE case, disturbances of this kind exist at present. Confidentiality agreements are signed by technical staff to mitigate the risks associated with these disturbances in the accountability compliance flow.

At present, there is an additional potential disruption in the accountability compliance flow related to the archiving routines among management. There is no formalized archiving function of the information related to management follow-ups on privacy breeches. The information is inferable from (i) the logs of previous breeches and (ii) notes and correspondence between U-CARE managers. However, a more systematic archiving of breeches and consequential follow-ups would prepare the organization better for external audits.

# 5    Conclusion

In this paper, we have drawn on our experiences in performing software systems design in the domain of online psychosocial care to develop and propose a theory of scrutiny. The theory addresses the relationships between accountability and privacy, explaining how these concepts relate to the interdependency between four modes of scrutiny. We have proposed an initial representation of the theory in the form of a multi-layered protocol that assigns clear responsibilities among peers, agents, management, and external stakeholders in an on-line community. The protocol supports a fuller understanding of the two key flows of privacy expectations and accountability and their points of communication and potential disruption.

The current version of the theory is a generalization from a single case study [11]. The current empirical setting – online psychosocial care – has served well to explore the problem (due to the sensitive character of personal information). It is, however, easy to find other settings where a community provider needs to relate to both accountability and privacy. Without elaboration, we argue that the theory of scrutiny would make an interesting foundation to inquire into communities of e-learning (e.g. MOOCs), online news, criminology, and scholarly peer review. Community providers in these example settings face similar situations where they provide an environment exposed to and threatened by social and technical vulnerabilities, which resonates with the purpose and scope of the theory.

Future work will include a more detailed analysis of implications for design through a systematic appropriation of meta-theorizing literature in design science research [7–9].

# References

1. Aakhus, M., Ågerfalk, P., Lyytinen, K., Te'eni, D.: Call for Paper: Information Systems for Symbolic Action: Social Media and Beyond. MIS Quarterly (2011)
2. Barak, A., Hen, L., Boniel-Nissim, M., Shapira, N.: A Comprehensive Review and a Meta-Analysis of the Effectiveness of Internet-Based Psychotherapeutic Interventions. Journal of Technology in Human Services 26(2/4), 109–160 (2008)
3. Bélanger, F., Crossler, R.E.: Privacy in the Digital Age: A review of information privacy research in information systems. MIS Quarterly 35(4), 1017–1041 (2011)
4. Culnan, M.J.: Consumer Privacy, Technology and Policy. In: George, J.F. (ed.) Computers in Society: Privacy, Ethics and the Internet, pp. 171–183. Pearson/Prentice Hall, Upper Saddle River (2003)
5. Garfinkel, H.: Studies in Ethnomethodology. Polity Press, Cambridge (1967)
6. Goldkuhl, G., Agerfalk, P.J.: IT Artefacts as Socio-Pragmatic Instruments: Reconciling the Pragmatic, Semiotic, and Technical. International Journal of Technology and Human Interaction 1(3), 29–43 (2005)
7. Gregor, S.: The Nature of Theory in Information Systems. MIS Quarterly 30(3), 611–642 (2006)
8. Gregor, S., Hevner, A.R.: Positioning and Presenting Design Science Research for Maximum Impact. MIS Quarterly 37(2), 337–355 (2013)

9. Gregor, S., Jones, D.: The anatomy of a design theory. Journal of the Association for Information Systems 8(5), 312–335 (2007)
10. Hevner, A.R., March, S.T., Park, J., Ram, S.: Design science in Information Systems research. MIS Quarterly 28(1), 75–105 (2004)
11. Lee, A.S., Baskerville, R.: Generalizing Generalizability in Information Systems Research. Information Systems Research 14(3), 221–243 (2003)
12. Merriam-Webster: Privacy, http://www.merriam-webster.com/dictionary/privacy
13. Riley, S., Veale, D.: The Internet & its Relevance to Cognitive Behavioural Psychotherapists. Behavioural and Cognitive Psychotherapy 27(1), 37–46 (1999)
14. Sjöström, J., Ågerfalk, P.J., Hevner, A.R.: Privacy and Accountability in Online Communities: Towards a Theory of Scrutiny. In: Helfert, M., Donnellan, B. (eds.) Proceedings of European Design Science Symposium 2013. To appear in CCIS. Springer (2013)
15. Smith, H.J., Dinev, T.: Information Privacy Research: An interdisciplinary review. MIS Quarterly 35(4), 989–1015 (2011)
16. Suler, J.: The Online Disinhibition Effect. Cyberpsychology and Behavior 7(3), 321–327 (2004)
17. Tate, D., Finkelstein, E.: Cost effectiveness of internet interventions: review and recommendations. Annals of Behavioral Medicine 38(1), 40–45 (2009)
18. United Nations: The Universal Declaration of Human Rights, http://www.webcitation.org/6LIK5GgYI
19. Weber, M.: Economy and Society. University of California Press, Berkeley (1978)
20. Weitzner, D.J., Abelson, H., Berners-Lee, T., Feigenbaum, J., Hendler, J., Sussman, G.J.: Information accountability. Communications of the ACM 51(6), 82–87 (2008)
21. Zhuo, J.: Where Anonymity Breeds Contempt. The New York Times (2010)

# Conceptual Design Science Research? How and Why Untested Meta-Artifacts Have a Place in IS

Rob Gleasure

Department of Accounting, Finance and Information Systems, University College Cork, Ireland
r.gleasure@ucc.ie

**Abstract.** This study presents both a rationale and a method for conducting conceptual design science research (DSR) that creates abstract and untested meta-artifacts. The DSR paradigm is centered upon a design-evaluate dynamic, in which designs are not only created but also put to the test in working environments. Yet there are occasions where the initial design theorizing is so challenging and complex as to warrant a contribution in its own right. Thus, a method is proposed for the design of meta-artifacts, based upon the systematic analysis and synthesis of existing artifacts. This method is demonstrated in the design of a meta-artifact for a novel crowdfunding platform that accommodates the pre-purchase of information and communication technology hardware products and services from businesses of all sizes, including medium-to-large enterprises.

**Keywords:** Design Science, Evaluation, Meta-Artifact, Theory-in-Use, Crowdfunding.

## 1 Introduction

Several decades have passed since scholars began calling for design-oriented approaches to Information Systems (IS) research [e.g. 37, 41, 55]. Since then the concept has matured significantly and numerous perspectives have been put forward as to how such research should be performed, including approaches that emphasize the IT artifact [30], approaches with a theoretical emphasis [26], approaches that seek to align design with existing action research techniques [49], and approaches that emphasize the pragmatism of a design-orientation [24]. Yet despite variations in focus, there has also been significant convergence between different frameworks into one cohesive design science research (DSR) paradigm [31, 58]. This convergence helps to create a unified paradigm that allows more reliable positioning and evaluation of the various types of contributions made by DSR studies [27]. Central to this unified paradigm are two recurring concepts, namely the role of embedded theory in design [c.f. 32, 47] and the importance of the evaluation of an IT artifact [c.f. 29, 46]. This study focuses on the latter of these concepts, specifically on the occasions where DSR theorizing can be undertaken without evaluation of an instantiated artifact.

With regard to the role of embedded theory in design, several levels of assumptions have been identified that lay the foundation for domain-specific instantiated designs. This includes generic 'kernel theory' from academia and practice that acts as a broad

M.C. Tremblay et al. (Eds.): DESRIST 2014, LNCS 8463, pp. 99–114, 2014.

conceptual lens for design [38, 55], the underlying explanatory models of target systems that describe causal relationships between technological and behavioral components of a target system [5, 33], and the abstract repeatable prescriptive design theory that the IT artifact uses to manipulate these technological and behavioral components [23, 26]. These layers are not always individually discussed in DSR studies, yet each may contribute to the design in some implicit or explicit way [21].

The second concept is the importance of the evaluation of instantiated artifacts in DSR, which is typically contrasted with theory-testing dynamic of traditional paradigms [e.g. 19, 30]. This evaluation component is especially important in the context of DSR because of the aforementioned layers of theoretical assumptions that comprise a design. These layers of assumptions present numerous opportunities for errors in theorizing, which a rigorous and contextually-meaningful evaluation may bring to light [46, 53]. Indeed, such is the nature of design that we often expect our at least some of our initial design features to fail, meaning we need to iteratively and repeatedly test designs within an actual environment to theorize reliably when adopting a DSR approach [29, 51].

Some scholars argue that the rigor with which an IT artifact is evaluated is what differentiates DSR from non-academic activities such as consultancy [44, 58]. Yet an absolute and unbending requirement for the rigorous evaluation of IT artifacts may be problematic, as Iivari [31, p.50-51] describes:

"there are two options to demarcate Information Systems as design science from inventions by practitioners. The first is to accept that there is no constructive research method that distinguishes the two, but that the difference lies in the evaluation… This is one option, but it easily leads to reactive research in which Information Systems as a design science focuses on the evaluation of existing IT artifacts rather than on the building of new ones… The second option is to try to specify a reasonably rigorous constructive research method for building IT artifacts… I would expect that this would make Information Systems as a design science more proactive, attempting to lead the evolution of IT and not merely react to it."

This study builds on this proposition, namely that there are situations where untested meta-artifacts, if designed appropriately, can present relevant and innovative contributions that pre-empt significant industrial developments. The next section looks at when such an approach may be appropriate, namely those situations where design theory and meta-artifacts are useful, yet their instantiation and evaluation is not feasible. Following this, a method is proposed for creating meta-artifacts in a systematic and rigorous manner. Finally, this method is demonstrated in the development of a meta-artifact for a novel crowdfunding platform to support the pre-purchase of Information and Communication Technology (ICT) products from producers of all sizes, including medium-to-large enterprises.

## 2    The Role of Conceptual Research in the Theorizing Process

Just as in DSR, the importance of testing theory in traditional paradigms is well-established [c.f. 45]. Yet within traditional paradigms it is accepted that theorizing is a gradual process, and that much of what is reported in a single study represents a snap-shot of some theory's ongoing development, rather than a finished product [c.f. 57]. Hence, purely conceptual (i.e. non-empirical) research has been common among pub-lished IS research in recent decades [11, 16, 28]. Despite the lack of empirical testing, many of these purely conceptual studies offer significant contributions by synthesiz-ing vast bodies of existing literature and/or offering radically new insights about some phenomena [e.g. 2, 14, 39]. Due to the scale and scope of the conceptual work per-formed in these studies, it is accepted that a sufficiently large step in the theorizing process has been performed, for which the lack of an empirical component is accepted as a reasonable limitation. The theorizing process in design-oriented studies is argua-bly more complex than that of traditional approaches, due to the need to not only understand the world as-is but also any number of possible new states [c.f. 51]. Thus, there are also likely to be many DSR studies where the initial theorizing process is so conceptually demanding and rich as to represent a significant contribution in its own right.

There is another more fundamental reason why DSR studies may seek to conduct purely conceptual theorizing work. Unlike traditional approaches which seek to test theory by observing an artifact or class of artifacts in use, DSR studies also seek to build such artifacts. This allows DSR studies a number of capabilities, such as the ability to introduce genuinely novel artifacts into industry as well as to test causal relationships in real world situations [32, 58]. It also presents new demands on the resources of DSR scholars, who must commit time and effort into build activities that are not required for those operating in traditional paradigms [6]. More importantly, the development of some artifacts is simply not feasible with the resources available to most researchers. On one hand, this may be due to a lack of the financial, technolo-gical, or personnel resources that are available to businesses operating in the target domain. On the other, it may be because the artifact is future-looking in a way that means the technological or infrastructural resources required to build it are still emerging, thus not yet mature enough to implement. This is illustrated in Figure 1.

The first issue can be addressed in some instances by partnering with industrial ac-tors. This assumes that such an opportunity presents itself, that the expectations and goals of partners are manageable, and that the industrial partner maintains sufficient flexibility to allow sufficient rigor to be maintained in design and evaluation. Such opportunities do periodically arise for researchers who maintain high levels of indus-trial contact. Unfortunately, the second issue is more difficult to address. This represents a significant limitation of the DSR paradigm, which as a consequence is left incapable of design theorizing that pre-empts radical future technological or infra-structural developments. Such design theorizing may be highly relevant to practition-ers operating in affected markets, as findings could be considered at the earliest stages in the development of their future products and services.

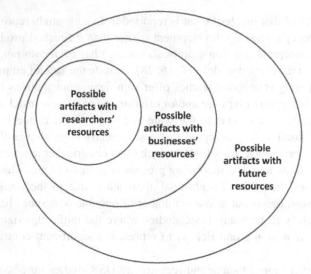

**Fig. 1.** The set of possible IT artifacts according to available resources

Thus, there are two instances where purely conceptual design may offer valuable and relevant contributions to IS, both of which reflect occasions where the novelty of the meta-artifact is particularly high. These are (1) when the scale and scope of design theorizing makes the initial stages of design theorizing unusually complex (2) when the resources required to build and evaluate an instantiated artifact are not yet available.

## 3    A Method for Conceptual Design Science Research

With the 'why' in place, attention can now be turned as to 'how' appropriate meta-artifacts could potentially be developed. Note that this is not intended as a single me-thodological solution but rather as the exploration of one possible approach to injecting rigor into initial design theorizing in the absence of the capacity to instantiate and eva-luate a situated artifact. Non-empirical studies in traditional paradigms do this using a range of techniques to compare and contrast existing research relating to the problem area [54, 56], as well as to analogize with better-understood phenomena in other fields or disciplines [52]. The techniques allow researchers to identify theoretical constructs and relationships in existing literature that describe phenomena relevant to the depen-dent variable being studied. Such constructs and relationships can then inform the crea-tion of some new theory on the basis of deductive reasoning processes.

This presents an interesting problem if conceptual DSR studies are to adopt a simi-lar approach. The novelty of the meta-artifact being developed means that existing artifacts studied by descriptive research will differ from it in fundamental and non-trivial ways. Hence, any attempts to theorize on the basis of such descriptive research cannot be presumed to be reliable. Similarly, comparable DSR studies will, assuming the adoption of this method is appropriate, be unlikely to cover the breadth of the behavioral outcomes of the meta-artifact. Put differently, an approach to theorizing in DSR studies based purely hypothetico-deductive logic may not appropriate in the absence of complementary abductive and inductive reasoning [19].

One possible solution to this problem is to leverage an assemblage of existing artifacts that manifest subsets of the desired behavioral outcomes for the meta-artifact being designed. Such behavioral outcomes can then act as 'meta-requirements' to guide the overall design [c.f. 55]. This parallels with traditional literature reviews, where searches are often bound within the context of some dependent variable(s), which dictates whether literature is relevant to the review being conducted [35].

Where the meta-artifact varies from existing artifacts in terms of scale and scope, this assemblage of artifacts may fall within similar classes, in the sense that they may address related problems in related domains. Where the meta-artifact pre-empts some technological or infrastructural developments, these artifacts may be assembled across more varied classes. For example, a meta-artifact for some large scale online community may be informed by analyzing a range of existing online communities demonstrating subsets of the desired behavioral outcomes. Conversely, a meta-artifact for an online community browsed by users using 3D virtual reality headsets may not be able to rely upon closely related artifacts, as they may not capture all of the desired behavioral outcomes. Instead, an analysis may need to be informed by existing online communities in combination with virtual world artifacts, motion sensor artifacts, gaming artifacts, etc.

The next step in the literature review process typically involves conceptualizing the topic by investigating the factors that contribute to the core phenomena being researched [e.g. 4, 13, 18, 54]. These can then be compiled into a concept matrix to determine relationships between constructs and help construct a theoretical model [56]. That approach can also be applied to the construction of a meta-artifact, where specific design features can be treated as independent variables and the instantiations of design principles. Where behavioral outcomes differ between existing artifacts, the design features of those artifacts can be contrasted to identify the elements of design contributing to different behaviors. This is illustrated in Figure 2.

The design features described may represent the technological and infrastructural characteristics of artifacts, i.e. the 'design product', or procedural characteristics of the development method, i.e. the 'design process' [c.f. 26, 55]. Analysis of the former may be more straightforward in the context of complete and situated artifacts developed by industrial practitioners. Yet the process by which design features are developed and introduced can have a significant impact on the outcomes of those features, meaning this development process may also need to be considered in some instances. Thus, in addition to looking at the static features of a design, in such cases researchers may also benefit from leveraging available historic data and observable trends concerning how these features were implemented.

This process is summarized as follows:

a) Identify the set of desired behavioral outcomes for the design
b) Identify a range of existing artifacts that, when taken together, capture the desired set of behavioral outcomes

c)  Identify the differentiating technological, infrastructural, and procedural characteristics of the selected existing artifacts
d)  Analyze the relationships between these key design features and associated behavioral outcomes and formalize this in the form of a meta-artifact

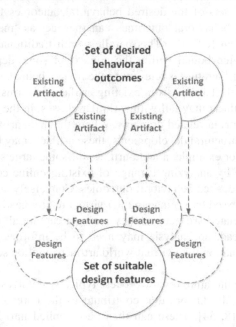

**Fig. 2.** The identification of suitable design features from existing artifacts

This method bases the design of the meta-artifact on design features used in existing artifacts, rather than relying solely upon theoretical descriptions of artifacts. The method shares some of the characteristics of a competitor analysis. However, instead of analyzing existing artifacts to determine the value of some behavioral outcomes, we are analyzing existing artifacts to determine the relationship between those behavioral outcomes and key design features. The method also shares some of the basic concepts of a literature review, however it differs in several important ways. Firstly, the unit of analysis in a literature review is typically a theoretical component describing some artifact(s), rather than the artifacts themselves. Secondly, these theoretical components are typically linked together by some descriptive, rather than prescriptive relationships. By targeting artifacts directly at a prescriptive level, we can afford design a greater abductive component and reduce the conceptual burden of translating descriptive findings to prescriptive theory (although complex theorizing may still be required to translate design practices across domains). This can then be triangulated with deductive reasoning that uses existing descriptive theory to hypothesize about the underlying causal mechanisms between identified design features and behavioral outcomes. Such triangulation allows opportunities for theoretical convergence to support the meta-artifact, as well as conflicting or tenuous assumptions to be identified.

The next section demonstrates how this method could be instantiated in the context of a novel crowdfunding platform.

# 4    An Example of Conceptual Design: A Crowdfunding Platform for Medium-to-Large Businesses

Crowdfunding is a phenomenon that has emerged in the last number of years, in which individuals use web platforms to collectively donate money to other individuals or organizations [c.f. 36, 42, 50]. This can take the form of peer-to-peer lending or equity investment, or charity, or it can take the form of project-based 'patronage' [17]. The last of these has received particular attention in IS literature recently [e.g. 7, 9, 59], due in part to the growth of platforms such as *Kickstarter*.

The platforms that enable project-based crowdfunding share the same basic dynamic, i.e. donors give to specific projects in return for some reward linked to the development of the project. Yet the nature of the different platforms and the types of projects they attract differ greatly. For example, while *Kickstarter, Indiegogo,* and *RocketHub* are all positioned as revenue-generating tools for start-ups and small business ventures, a comparison of the three platforms shows that the focus and character of each platform varies [c.f. 20]. *Kickstarter* and *RocketHub* promote their platforms as a means of supporting creativity, and consequently draw a user base that responds to novel technological and artistic artifacts. More recently, *RocketHub* has diverged from this focus by partnering with A&E Networks to emphasize the entrepreneurial aspect of the platform and allow greater exposure for the individuals and businesses behind specific projects [12]. *Indiegogo* on the other hand describes itself as a means of donor empowerment and as a vehicle for projects of passion. Hence, *Indiegogo* attracts more activism and ideologically-motivated projects than the other two platforms. This theme is also similar to that of the emerging platform *FundAnything*, which emphasizes not only business ideas, but also personal causes, medical expenses, tuition, celebration, etc.

## 4.1    Identify the Set of Desired Behavioral Outcomes for the Design

One feature of these leading crowdfunding platforms is that they each explicitly target the funding of projects put forward by individuals, start-ups, and small businesses, rather than those of established medium-to-large corporations. This is interesting, as many projects on these platforms seek to attract funding with economic incentives, most notably by rewarding donors with the product or service being funded once development is complete [15]. In such circumstances, donations acts as a pre-purchase of goods, which afford economic benefits to the creator, specifically the capacity for a pull-based inventory and inexpensive marketing, [8, 1] and could so also benefit donors by allowing them to purchase these products more cheaply than in standard marketplaces and keep up to date with new developments.

Thus, the crowdfunding of products and services from medium-to-large companies Information and Communication (ICT) hardware and software producers such as

Samsung, Apple, IBM, etc. has the potential to benefit both producers and consumers. Yet the absence of any established crowdfunding platform that actively seeks to enable this form of crowdfunding suggests that coming up with an appropriate design that generates real value is not trivial. As the implementation of such a platform is likely to require a scale of resources not readily available to full-time researchers, this represents a suitable opportunity to demonstrate the method for conceptual DSR.

In order to obtain the economic benefits described, the desired behavioral outcomes for the meta-artifact are three-fold (1) The platform must facilitate pre-purchase motivated users, rather than philanthropic or altruistic donations (2) The platform accommodate the crowdfunding of information and communication technology (ICT) products and services, and (3) The platform must facilitate high levels of interaction between funders and project coordinators.

### 4.2 Identify a Range of Existing Artifacts That, When Taken Together, Present the Desired Set of Behavioral Outcomes

In addition to the four platforms already discussed, several other project-based crowdfunding platforms have emerged with different approaches, typically specializing in some creative domains. For example, *PledgeMusic* is a 'direct to fan' platform in which artists seek the finances necessary to produce music or music-related products, such as books and tickets to live events. Core crowdfunding dynamics are also supported by traditional retail dynamics by which artists can sell released work to fans. *Pozible* is similar, dedicating itself to the crowdfunding of creative and artistic projects, including music, film, books, paintings, and theatre. Taken together, these six crowdfunding platforms manifest the desired behavioral outcomes. In terms of the prevalence of pre-purchase-based rewards, this is most common on the specialized music/art platforms, particular on *PledgeMusic*, where pre-purchase dynamics are ubiquitous. These dynamics can also be seen frequently on both *Kickstarter* and *RocketHub*, though many projects prefer other types of rewards, such as accompanying paraphernalia and accreditation. Pre-purchase is least common on *Indiegogo* and *FundAnything*, in which rewards are often purely philanthropic, humorous, or social in nature.

In terms of the prominence of crowdfunding campaigns for ICT products and services, each of the four generic platforms includes a large number of high-end technology products within dedicated technology sections of the websites. For *Kickstarter* and *RocketHub*, this subsection represents a standalone subsection of the website, whereas for both *Indiegogo* and *FundAnything* the technology section is embedded with 'entrepreneurial' and 'business ideas' sections, respectively. Unsurprisingly, for both *PledgeMusic* and *Pozible* the prominence of ICT products and services is low, although the technology section included on *Pozible* does include some related items, such as headphones and smartphone applications.

Lastly, the interactivity of all of the crowdfunding platforms is high. For each platform, creators are encouraged to maintain a profile, leave regular updates, and answer comments and questions presented by potential or actual donors. However, campaign organizers on *PledgeMusic* and *Pozible* are also encouraged to build a relationship with donors by offering additional bonus content, uploading videos that show how production is progressing. In the case of *PledgeMusic*, this also often involves uploading portions of completed music prior to full release.

### 4.3 Identifying the Differentiating Technological, Infrastructural, and Procedural Characteristics of the Selected Existing Artifacts

Four key differentiating technological, infrastructural, and developmental characteristics are evident in the sample of six crowdfunding platforms, namely (1) The funding scheme used (2) The manner in which the platform collects fees (3) The theme-specificity of projects seeking funding, and (4) The capacity for anonymous donations. A fifth characteristic arguably exists concerning whether the rewards offered to donors vary according to the level of donation. However, as all of the sample platforms rely upon a tiered system of rewards, this characteristic is not relevant.

As described already, the theme-specificity of *Kickstarter*, *RocketHub*, *Indiegogo*, and *FundAnything* is low, as projects are funded across a wide range of domains. *Pozible* is more specific than the previous four platforms and maintains a predominately artistic focus. However this distinction is less in recent times, during which *Pozible*'s scope has broadened to also include boutique food producers and even scientific research. *PledgeMusic* on the other hand remains highly specialized, with a focus entirely on music-related projects and a majority of campaigns dedicated to music production.

The funding structure falls into two categories. *Kickstarter*, *PledgeMusic*, and *Pozible* use a fixed funding scheme, in which a target sum is set by campaign coordinators. If this this sum is reached then the donations are processed and deposited to the coordinator. If it is not reached, then donations are returned to donors. *RocketHub*, *Indiegogo*, and *FundAnything* use an alternative flexible funding scheme. Here a target is again set, however while the campaign coordinator may receive additional benefits for reaching their target, donations are deposited to them immediately, regardless of whether or not this target is reached.

These funding structures also impact on the manner in which each platform collects fees. The three flexible funding platforms charge 8-9% of all funds collected, which is reduced to 4-5% if the target is reached. *Kickstarter*, *PledgeMusic*, and *Pozible* charge a fee only when a target is reached and a campaign coordinator collects funds. For *Kickstarter* and *Pozible* this fee is set at 5%, although on *Pozible* this drops to 4% on for project creators who have run previously successful projects. Payment processing fees of 2-5% are charged for each of these five platforms in addition to standard fees, which vary according to the types of payment options used and where payments originate. *PledgeMusic* differs from the rest, as a standard fee of 15% is deducted as soon as a target is reached, which absorbs all payment costs. In addition, *PledgeMusic* withholds 25% of the remaining sum until the project has been completed and the finished musical product is uploaded to the site.

Lastly, the capacity for anonymous donations also falls into two categories. *Kickstarter*, *RocketHub*, and *PledgeMusic* do not allow for anonymity and list both the identity of donors, as well as the amount contributed. This is contrasted by *Indiegogo*, *FundAnything*, and *Pozible* which allow donors not to disclose their identity, or alternatively, not to disclose the amount donated. These differences in design features and behavioral characteristics are illustrated in Table 1.

## 4.4    Analyze the Relationships between these Key Design Features and Associated Behavioral Outcomes and Formalize This in the Form of a Meta-Artifact

A fixed 'all or nothing' funding structure appears more suitable to the pre-purchase of products and services. This is likely because the target set in fixed funding campaigns is intended to represent the amount required to develop the proposed product or service. Hence, from a pre-purchase perspective it may be preferable to cancel the transaction if the product or service cannot be developed as initially described. On the other hand, where donations are ideologically-motivated donors may be more forgiving of late or incomplete products or services [40]. A fixed funding structure also appears more suitable to facilitate high levels of interaction between funders and project coordinators. This reflects the additional levels of hype and interest that are generated as a campaign reaches its conclusion under fixed funding conditions, whereby those involved look to discover whether or not production will go ahead [10].

In combination with a fixed funding structure, the set fee used by *PledgeMusic* appears most suitable to the pre-purchase of products and services. By not varying the amount, donors and campaign coordinators have more certainty regarding the value of and offering and can arguably plan their developments and rewards more accurately as a result. In addition, because of the up-front payments made in crowdfunding transactions, donors are arguably in need of protection from bad business practices [22]. Therefore, by withholding a proportion of payment until the product or service has been delivered to donors, the need for trust is lessened and donors are protected by a greater economic motivation for the campaign coordinator to fulfill their obligations. This may be important in the absence of the strong ideological component of other crowdfunding platforms.

Higher theme specificity within a platform also appears to further support the pre-purchase of products and services. This is presumably because donors that are interested in buying specific products or services are more inclined to frequent sites where those products or services are prominent. Conversely, donors who are interested in supporting projects for other reasons, such as a desire to enable artistic creativity, entrepreneurialism, or philanthropic goals, are less likely to be concerned with the specific nature of the product or service [3]. Theme-specific platforms also appear to demonstrate higher levels of interaction between funders and project coordinators. This may be because donors frequenting domain-specific platforms are likely to possess strong existing motivations to investigate and purchase items in that domain.

**Table 1.** Concept matrix of design features and behavioral outcomes from the sample of crowdfunding platforms

| | Behavioral Outcomes | | | Design Features | | | |
|---|---|---|---|---|---|---|---|
| | Pre-purchase dynamics used | ICT products/ services | Interactive user base | Main Funding Scheme | Fee structure | Theme specificity | Capacity for donor anonymity |
| *Kickstarter* | Medium | High | Medium-to-high | Fixed | 5% for successful projects | Low | No |
| *RocketHub* | Medium | High | Medium-to-high | Flexible | 8%, down to 4% if target is hit | Low | No |
| *Indiegogo* | Low-to-medium | Medium | Medium-to-high | Flexible | 9%, down to 4% if target is hit | Low | Yes |
| *FundAnything* | Low-to-medium | Medium | Medium-to-high | Flexible | 9%, down to 5% if target is hit | Low | Yes |
| *PledgeMusic* | High | Very low | High | Fixed | 15% plus staggered release of funds | High | No |
| *Pozible* | Medium | Low | High | Fixed | 4-5% for successful projects | Medium | Yes |

Lastly, the capacity for anonymous donations appears more suitable for pre-purchase motivated users. This is not intuitive, as one may assume that anonymity in purely economic transactions is more desirable than for ideological donations. Yet the desire for anonymity in crowdfunding donations is typically fuelled by social or reputational concerns, e.g. because donors are conscious of the size of their financial contribution, they are conscious of donating to their own projects, or they are out of sync with the donations preceding them [9]. Thus, it makes sense that there is less need for anonymous donations where donations are motivated by the pre-purchase of goods, rather than social or reputational concerns.

Thus, a meta-artifact for a crowdfunding platform that facilitates the pre-purchase of ICT products and services from manufacturers of all sizes, with high levels of interaction between funders and project coordinators, should include the following design features:

- o A fixed 'all or nothing' funding scheme should be applied, rather than a flexible scheme
- o A set fee  should be deducted that absorbs transactions and payment processing costs, and that withholds some proportion of payment until the finished product or service has been delivered to donors
- o The site should be limited in theme to ICT products and services, rather than encouraging funding campaigns across unrelated domains
- o There should not be the capacity for anonymous donations, but rather these donations should be attributed to specific people and institutions

## 5    Discussion and Conclusions

This study has presented a rationale and method for conducting conceptual DSR, i.e. DSR that creates untested meta-artifacts in a rigorous and repeatable manner. By demonstrating a role for conceptual DSR, the potential has been created for innovative and pro-active design studies in IS. Moreover, the method presented for such studies shows how a range of existing artifacts with subsets of the desired behavioral outcomes can be systematically analyzed to create a predictive meta-artifact. This idea of using existing artifacts and practices to inform design is not new, several researchers [e.g. 38, 48] have advocated the idea that legitimate kernel theory for design may be developed on the basis of practical 'theory in use'. However this study has demonstrated how such 'theory in use' can be systematically analyzed and synthesized in a manner comparable to established techniques for the analysis and synthesis of academic literature.

The usefulness of this method was demonstrated in the design of a meta-artifact for a novel crowdfunding platform to support the pre-purchase of ICT hardware products from manufacturers of all sizes, with high levels of interaction between funders and project coordinators. This example showed how such a platform could be mindfully designed, based upon the success of existing platforms with subsets of the desired behavioral outcomes. The meta-artifact offers a secondary contribution to the crowdfunding space by presenting an inter-platform perspective on crowdfunding. This not only theorizes as to how the proposed platform could be designed, but also examines the relationship between specific design features and the nature of crowdfunding on existing platforms.

A further contribution is offered to the DSR space by offering a critical reflection of one of the key pillars of DSR, namely the importance of evaluating a situated IT artifact. The intention in this paper is not to diminish the importance of such an evaluation for empirical DSR studies. Anyone who has performed IT-related design work has probably experienced that even the most well thought out of designs often fails to perform as expected 'when the wheels hit the road'. Thus, there is little doubt that a high proportion of empirical work is key to the quality of the broader DSR paradigm. Rather, the argument put forward in this study is that there are occasions where the initial stages of design theorizing offer both a significant practical contribution, as well as the theoretical richness to 'explain, predict, and delight' [57]. Hence, opening up this avenue of research may facilitate new forms of innovative and relevant DSR.

This leads onto the central limitation of the study, namely the lack of discussion concerning how situated artifacts are impacted by specific contexts. Recent developments in IS have highlighted the complexity of the process by which technologies become embedded within real-world socio-technical systems [e.g. 34, 43]. It is for this reason that DSR studies often speak of the theoretical component specific to such situated artifacts, e.g. as level 1 contributions [27], as demonstration [44], or as prototypes [25]. This challenges the ability to reliably abstract from existing artifacts in the proposed method, the reliability of the meta-artifact developed, as well as the ability to predict future technological developments. Such concerns are appropriate for all *a priori* design theorizing, yet such theorizing nonetheless represents an important stage in design, without which any planned utility-seeking interventions would be impossible. The proposed method offers a means to do this theorizing in a way that maximizes the theoretical rigor of this step of the design process. Furthermore, such a delineation of the early design process means that, should the meta-artifact be instantiated and tested in the future, the interpretation of emerging findings can more readily be related back to existing research and practice. Thus, this method for conceptual design theorizing, rather than offering a complete design process, offers a useful means of engaging with design challenges that may not otherwise be addressed at the height of their relevance.

# References

1. Agrawal, A.K., Catalini, C., Goldfarb, A.: Some Simple Economics of Crowdfunding. National Bureau of Economic Research, NBER working paper series No. w19133 (2013)
2. Alavi, M., Leidner, D.E.: Review: Knowledge management and knowledge management systems: Conceptual foundations and research issues. MIS Quarterly 25, 107–136 (2001)
3. Andreoni, J.: Impure altruism and donations to public goods: a theory of warm-glow giving. The Economic Journal 100, 464–477 (1990)
4. Bandara, W., Miskon, S., Fielt, E.: A systematic, tool-supported method for conducting literature reviews in information systems. In: Proceedings of the European Conference on Information Systems, Helsinki (2011)

5. Baskerville, R., Pries-Heje, J.: Explanatory design theory. Business & Information Systems Engineering 2, 271–282 (2010)
6. Baskerville, R., Pries-Heje, J.: Discovering the significance of scientific design practice: new science wrapped in old science? In: Proceedings of the IT Artefact Design & Workpractice Intervention Workshop, Tilberg, Netherlands (2013)
7. Beaulieu, T., Sarker, S.: Discursive Meaning Creation in Crowdfunding: A Socio-material Perspective. In: Proceeding of the International Conference for Information Systems, Milan, Italy (2013)
8. Belleflamme, P., Lambert, T., Schwienbacher, A.: Crowdfunding: Tapping the right crowd. In: International Conference of the French Finance Association, Antwerp, Belgium (2011)
9. Burtch, G., Ghose, A., Wattal, S.: An Empirical Examination of Users' Information Hiding in a Crowdfunding Context. In: Proceeding of the International Conference for Information Systems, Milan, Italy (2013a)
10. Burtch, G., Ghose, A., Wattal, S.: An Empirical Examination of the Antecedents and Consequences of Contribution Patterns in Crowd-Funded Markets. Information Systems Research (forthcoming)
11. Chen, W., Hirschheim, R.: A paradigmatic and methodological examination of information systems research from 1991 to 2001. Information Systems Journal 14, 197–235 (2004)
12. Connor, C.: Television Meets Crowdfunding: A&E Networks And RocketHub Launch 'Project Startup' For Entrepreneurs. Forbes, http://www.forbes.com/sites/cherylsnappconner/2013/04/18/television-meets-crowdfunding-ae-networks-and-RocketHub-launch-project-startup-for-entrepreneurs/ (retrieved June 01, 2014)
13. Cooper, H.M.: Organizing knowledge syntheses: A taxonomy of literature reviews. Knowledge in Society 1, 104–126 (1988)
14. DeLone, W.H., McLean, E.R.: Information systems success: the quest for the dependent variable. Information Systems Research 3, 60–95 (1992)
15. Dushnitsky, G., Marom, D.: Crowd Monogamy. Business Strategy Review 24, 24–26 (2013)
16. Dwivedi, Y.K., Kuljis, J.: Profile of IS research published in the European Journal of Information Systems. European Journal of Information Systems 17, 678–693 (2008)
17. Feller, J., Gleasure, R., Treacy, S.: From the Wisdom to the Wealth of Crowds: A Meta-triangulation of Crowdfunding Research. Working Paper v3, http://opennessandtransparency.net/sites/default/files/TOTO-Working-Paper-2013.01-v3.pdf (retrieved June 01, 2014)
18. Fink, A.: Conducting research literature reviews: from the Internet to paper. Sage, London (2010)
19. Fischer, C., Gregor, S.: Forms of reasoning in the design science research process. In: Jain, H., Sinha, A.P., Vitharana, P. (eds.) DESRIST 2011. LNCS, vol. 6629, pp. 17–31. Springer, Heidelberg (2011)
20. Gerber, E.M., Hui, J.S., Kuo, P.Y.: Crowdfunding: Why people are motivated to post and fund projects on crowdfunding platforms. In: Proceedings of the International Workshop on Design, Influence, and Social Technologies: Techniques, Impacts and Ethics. ACM, New York (2012)
21. Gleasure, R., Feller, J., O'Flaherty, B.: Procedurally Transparent Design Science Research: A Design Process Model. In: Proceedings of the International Conference for Information Systems, Orlando, USA (2012)

22. Griffin, Z.: Crowdfunding: Fleecing the American Masses. Case Western Reserve Journal of Law, Technology & the Internet (forthcoming), http://papers.ssrn.com/sol3/papers.cfm?abstract_id=2030001 (retrieved June 01, 2014)
23. Goldkuhl, G.: Design theories in information systems – a need for multi-grounding. Journal of Information Technology Theory and Application 6, 59–72 (2004)
24. Goldkuhl, G., Agerfalk, P.J.: IT Artifacts as Socio-Pragmatic Instruments: Reconciling the Pragmatic, Semiotic, and Technical. International Journal of Technology and Human Interaction 1, 29–43 (2005)
25. Goldkuhl, G.: The empirics of design research: Activities, outcomes and functions. In: Proceedings of the International Conference for information Systems, Milan, Italy (2013)
26. Gregor, S., Jones, D.: The anatomy of a design theory. Journal of the Association for Information Systems 8, 312–335 (2007)
27. Gregor, S., Hevner, A.R.: Positioning and presenting design science research for maximum impact. MIS Quarterly 37, 337–355 (2013)
28. Hamilton, S., Ives, B.: MIS research strategies. Information & Management 5(6), 339–347 (1982)
29. Hevner, A.R.: The three cycle view of design science research. Scandinavian Journal of Information Systems 19, 87–92 (2007)
30. Hevner, A.R., March, S.T., Park, J., Ram, S.: Design science in information systems research. MIS Quarterly 28, 75–105 (2004)
31. Iivari, J.: A paradigmatic analysis of information systems as a design science. Scandinavian Journal of Information Systems 19, 39–63 (2007)
32. Kuechler, B., Vaishnavi, V.: On theory development in design science research: anatomy of a research project. European Journal of Information Systems 17, 489–504 (2008)
33. Kuechler, W., Vaishnavi, V.: A framework for theory development in design science research: Multiple perspectives. Journal of the Association for Information Systems 13, 3 (2012)
34. Leonardi, P.M., Barley, S.R.: Materiality and change: Challenges to building better theory about technology and organizing. Information and Organization 18, 159–176 (2008)
35. Levy, Y., Ellis, T.J.: A systems approach to conduct an effective literature review in support of information systems research. Informing Science: International Journal of an Emerging Transdiscipline 9, 181–212 (2006)
36. Ley, A., Weaven, S.: Exploring agency dynamic of crowdfunding in start-up capital financing. Academy of Entrepreneurship Journal 17, 85–110 (2011)
37. March, S.T., Smith, G.F.: Design and natural science research on information technology. Decision Support Systems 15, 251–266 (1995)
38. Markus, M.L., Majchrzak, A., Gasser, L.: A design theory for systems that support emergent knowledge processes. MIS Quarterly 26, 179–212 (2002)
39. Melville, N., Kraemer, K., Gurbaxani, V.: Review: Information technology and organizational performance: An integrative model of IT business value. MIS Quarterly 28, 283–322 (2004)
40. Mollick, E.: The dynamics of crowdfunding: Determinants of success and failure. Journal of Business Venturing 29, 1–16 (2012)
41. Nunamaker Jr., J.F., Chen, M.: Systems development in information systems research. In: Proceedings of the Twenty-Third Annual Hawaii International Conference on System Sciences, Hawaii, USA

42. Ordanini, A., Miceli, L., Pizzetti, M., Parasuraman, A.: Crowd-funding: transforming customers into investors through innovative service platforms. Journal of Service Management 22, 443–470 (2011)
43. Orlikowski, W.J.: Sociomaterial practices: Exploring technology at work. Organization Studies 28, 1435–1448 (2007)
44. Peffers, K., Tuunanen, T., Rothenberger, M.A., Chatterjee, S.: A design science research methodology for information systems research. Journal of Management Information Systems 24, 45–77 (2007)
45. Popper, K.R.: Conjectures and refutations, vol. 28. Routledge & Kegan, London (1963)
46. Pries-Heje, J., Baskerville, R., Venable, J.R.: Strategies for Design Science Research Evaluation. In: Proceedings of the European Conference for Information Systems, Galway, Ireland (2008)
47. Purao, S.: Design research in the technology of information systems: Truth or dare. GSU Department of CIS Working Paper, Atlanta: Georgia State University, http://purao.ist.psu.edu/working-papers/dare-purao.Pdf (retrieved June 01, 2014)
48. Sarker, S., Lee, A.S.: Using a positivist case research methodology to test three competing theories-in-use of business process redesign. Journal of the Association for Information Systems 2 (2002)
49. Sein, M., Henfridsson, O., Purao, S., Rossi, M., Lindgren, R.: Action design research. MIS Quarterly 35, 37–56 (2011)
50. Stemler, A.R.: The Jobs Act and crowdfunding: Harnessing the power—and money—of the masses. Business Horizons 56, 271–275 (2013)
51. Simon, H.A.: The science of design: creating the artificial. In: The Sciences of the Artificial, pp. 111–138. MIT Press, Cambridge (1996)
52. Truex, D., Holmström, J., Keil, M.: Theorizing in information systems research: A reflexive analysis of the adaptation of theory in information systems research TF1FT. Journal of the Association for Information Systems 7, 797–821 (2006)
53. Venable, J., Pries-Heje, J., Baskerville, R.: A comprehensive framework for evaluation in design science research. In: Peffers, K., Rothenberger, M., Kuechler, B. (eds.) DESRIST 2012. LNCS, vol. 7286, pp. 423–438. Springer, Heidelberg (2012)
54. Vom Brocke, J., Simons, A., Niehaves, B., Riemer, K., Plattfaut, R., Cleven, A.: Reconstructing the giant: On the importance of rigour in documenting the literature search process. In: Proceedings of the European Conference for Information Systems, Verona, Italy (2009)
55. Walls, J.G., Widmeyer, G.R., El Sawy, O.A.: Building an information system design theory for vigilant EIS. Information Systems Research 3, 36–59 (1992)
56. Webster, J., Watson, R.T.: Analyzing the past to prepare for the future: Writing a literature review. MIS Quarterly 26, 13–23 (2002)
57. Weick, K.E.: What theory is not, theorizing is. Administrative Science Quarterly 40, 385–390 (1995)
58. Winter, R.: Design science research in Europe. European Journal of Information Systems 17, 470–475 (2008)
59. Zvilichovsky, D., Inbar, Y., Barzilay, O.: Playing Both Sides of the Market: Success and Reciprocity on Crowdfunding Platforms. In: Proceeding of the International Conference for Information Systems, Milan, Italy (2013)

# Knowledge Contributions in Design Science Research: A Meta-Analysis

Neelam Dwivedi[1], Sandeep Purao[1], and Detmar W. Straub[2]

[1] College of Info. Sci. and Tech., Pennsylvania State University, University Park, PA 16802
[2] College of Business, Georgia State University, Atlanta, GA
nxd22@psu.edu, spurao@ist.psu.edu, dstraub@gsu.edu

**Abstract.** This research analyzes patterns of artifact generation and knowledge contribution of design science researchers based on a meta-analysis of contemporary work. We derive these analyses based on prior classifications of design science artifacts and knowledge outcomes. Our analyses reveal a complex picture of what is produced and how by scholars in the design science community. The results allow us to characterize the evolution of design science research community, and point to possible gaps. We also show that empirical analyses of prior efforts are needed to complement the prescriptive work in the design science community. We hope that our findings will provide the research community a platform to reflect on their own work, improve the ability of individual researchers to position and communicate their work, and point to possibilities for building a cumulative knowledge base.

**Keywords:** design science research, knowledge outcomes, meta-analysis.

## 1 Introduction

Compared to other research paradigms such as natural and social sciences, design science research is in early stages of formulating its norms and practices ([38], [11]). Fundamentals such as what design science is or is not [3], methodologies ([34], [43]), evaluation methods ([6], [49]), and many other foundational elements that provide the means to legitimize design science research are being proposed and debated. Although mature scientific paradigms can have similar debates (see, e.g. [46] and [53]), they tend to refine rather than define the discipline, often building upon established norms for conducting scientific research. These norms include concepts and terms that have highly specific meanings, e.g., research questions, propositions, hypotheses, findings, etc. This enables scientists to communicate their research by following the (evolving) norms and accepted terminology within their communities. Recent work in design science research is aimed at establishing such norms and conventions.

We take a different perspective to contribute to this stream of work; – we offer a meta-analysis of contemporary research produced by the design science research community. Our intent is to understand the outcomes and knowledge contributions generated by the community via actual design science research (DSR) efforts. Our work is inspired by the intuition that while philosophy of science proffers how

M.C. Tremblay et al. (Eds.): DESRIST 2014, LNCS 8463, pp. 115–131, 2014.
© Springer International Publishing Switzerland 2014

research *should be done*, one needs to observe contemporary research to understand how it *actually gets done*. This is particularly true for design science research, where much work related to the building of innovative IT artifacts remains "hidden," i.e., only the researchers' perspectives about key artifacts and knowledge contributions are reported. Motivated by this intuition, we seek to answer following research question:

• What are the patterns of artifact generation and knowledge contributions by researchers via actual DSR efforts?

To address this question, we conduct a meta-analysis of published research in the design science conference. Our approach consists of four phases: selection of a corpus of papers, extraction of relevant data from papers in the sample, identification of artifacts and knowledge contributions, and discovery of patterns. The work iterated to interpret the outcomes described in DSR efforts; it also involves a mapping of these outcomes to prior statements about DSR artifacts and knowledge contributions.

Based on this meta-analysis, we make the following contributions. First, the analysis brings to the surface patterns of DSR artifact outcomes and knowledge contribution, including the influences acting on these. Second, the patterns allow an interpretation of how the DSR community is evolving. Third, we point to gaps and possibilities for future work to understand and prescribe norms for scholarly DSR work.

## 2    Background and Prior Work

We base our work on the idea that while philosophy of science [36, 20] and disciplinary work about DSR [11, 31, 39] have made definite advances in how research *should be done*, it is equally important to understand how contemporary research *actually gets done*. To understand the progression of thought about design science, we begin with a review of early work on DSR that recognized the fundamental differences between the sciences of design and the natural sciences, leading to the development of conceptual foundations of design science. This included the definition of the core building blocks underlying a design-based approach to science (see, e.g., [44, 45]). In the IS discipline, Walls et al. [51] identified design theory as a form of knowledge generated in DSR. March and Smith [25] classified DSR outputs into constructs, models, methods, and instantiations. Hevner et al. [14] extended this stream by proposing two categories – foundations and methodologies – that form the knowledge base in information system research framework. The first category, foundations, included artifacts proposed [22] along with theories, frameworks, and instruments. The second category, methodologies, focused on evaluation through data analysis techniques, formalisms, measures, and validation criteria. Kuechler and Vaishnavi [18] provided a perspective on how mid-level theories are generated when design researchers develop artifacts informed by kernel theories. More recently, Gregor and Hevner [11] extended the multi-level characterization of knowledge outcomes from Purao [37] with a longitudinal view to emphasize increasing levels of maturity across Level1 - a situated implementation, Level2 - nascent theory e.g. constructs and design principles, and Level3 - a mature design theory. Another form of knowledge outcomes – design principles – has also received much attention. Sein et al [43]) propose formalization of learning into design principles as part of an action design research approach (a sub-class of design science), and Gregor et al. [12] further classify and develop design principles into principles of form and function. These ideas build upon work that originated outside the design science community, such as technological rules to characterize products of management research [47], and Mode 2 knowledge[8]. Romme [40] extends this perspective by mapping it to design research as ideal-typical mode of research and further develops the idea of technological rules. Table 1 summarizes DSR *Outcomes* and *Knowledge Contributions* closely following the review above, along with examples. The table shows *Outcomes* that refer to the type of artifact designed by researchers; and the *Knowledge Contributions* that refer to the type of knowledge such as a theory, proposition, or a design principle, that is generated when researchers design and build the artifact. Although not comprehensive, the list is indicative of the recognition of various forms of outputs of DSR efforts. Our categorization is driven by prior statements related to such outcomes in design science research because of our focus on understanding how contemporary design science research *actually gets done* compared to how it *should be done*. More detailed analyses of different kinds of artifacts generated via DSR (following a larger sample of papers) are available elsewhere [30]; and a summary that conflates artifacts and knowledge outcomes for the early years from DESRIST is available in [41].

**Table 1.** A selective review of prior work about DSR *outcomes* and *knowledge contributions*

| Source | *Outcome;* Description | Example (by authors) |
|---|---|---|
| March and Smith [25] | *Construct*: A conceptualization to describe problems and their solutions within a domain | Roles in Group Decision Support Systems |
| | *Model*: A set of propositions or statements expressing relationships among constructs | Situation models in GDSS problem types |
| | *Method*: A set of steps used to perform a task. Methods are based on a set of underlying constructs (language) and a representation (model) | Generation and evaluation of ideas, automated facilitation in GDSS |
| | *Instantiation*: Realization of an artifact in its environment | An implemented GDSS |
| Gregor and Hevner [11] | *Level 1*: Situated implementation of artifact | Not provided |

| Source | *Knowledge Contribution;* Description | Example (by authors) |
|---|---|---|
| Walls et al. [51] | *Design theory:* A prescriptive theory that outlines design paths intended to produce effective information systems in a class | Design theory in the context of Executive Information System. |
| Gibbons et al. [8] | *Mode 2 Knowledge*: Application-based knowledge to solve a problem | Design of hypersonic aircraft |
| Romme [40] | *Design proposition:* "In situation S, to achieve consequence C, do A | Circular organizations, consensus driven decisions |
| van Aken [47] | *Technological rule*: a chunk of general knowledge, linking an intervention or artefact with a desired outcome or performance in a certain field of application. | In a factory, the use of constraining capacity group should be optimized. |
| | *Generative mechanism*: mechanism that produce an outcome in a particular context | The constraining capacity group determines the output of factory as a whole. |

**Table 1.** (*Continued.*)

| Kuechler and Vaishnavi [18] | *Mid-range theories:* Derived from kernel theory, can lead to testable hypotheses | Grammatical element salience in conceptual modeling (GESCM) |
|---|---|---|
| Sein et al. [43] | *Design principles:* Knowledge about creating artifacts that address a class of problems | Real-time capture for competence management systems |
| Gregor et al. [12] | *Principle of form:* structural aspects of the artifact that facilitate achievement of goals | For a jug: a shape that can hold liquid. |
| | *Principles of function:* series of actions that is necessary to achieve artifact's goals | For a jug: a handle to lift the jug |
| Gregor and Hevner [11] extending [37] | *Level 2:* Nascent theory as constructs, design principles, etc. | Not provided |
| | *Level 3:* Design theory | Not provided |

The selective review suggests some interesting interpretations. First, although the problem has vexed scholars for some time, there have been few comprehensive efforts to characterize DSR *outcomes* and *knowledge contributions.* Second, the work shows tension between theory-based and atheoretical outputs (although along a continuum instead of only extremes). Third, a cohesive structure of these different classes of outcomes/knowledge contributions is difficult to build across the proposals. However, overlaps across different proposals are clearly evident. For example, Level1, situated implementation [11], maps directly to instantiation, or realization of an artifact [25]. Finally, the table shows several dimensions scholars have used for classification, such as the dichotomy between substantive or operative knowledge (e.g., [47], drawing on [5]); type of artifact [25]; and maturity levels ([11] drawing on [37]). This review, thus, provided a sensitizing framework that informed our meta-analysis.

# 3     Research Method

The research problem calls for a review of contemporary DSR efforts following a systematic approach [52]. Quantitative meta-analysis can derive from the desire to summarize the findings of a research stream (usually via statistical analysis) or it can take the form of assessments that quantify the findings in variant ways ([10, 23, 54]). The research effort, however, goes beyond an analysis of textual content in published work, as in, for instance, a review of literature. The meta-analysis in this study required two additional elements. First, we allowed the textual analysis to be informed by statements about DSR outcomes and knowledge contributions (see summary in previous section). Second, we followed an iterative approach, repeatedly revisiting the papers because it allowed us to see modes of description as similar to or different from those encountered elsewhere. These two practices generated both a thematic description of each paper and a characterization of the outcomes and knowledge outcomes. Our effort was, thus, different from that reported in [31], where the authors examined only the title and abstract for a much larger set of papers to identify, what they termed design range and reach. In contrast, our process was more iterative, in-depth, and clearly subject to prior knowledge and biases on the part of the research team, which consisted of a first researcher who has been an active member of the design science community, a second who is a new entrant to the community, and a third whose interests span beyond the design science community. The process unfolded as follows. The second researcher analyzed a small set of papers. The outcomes were discussed with the first researcher. This process revealed new possibilities for interpretation that were added to the next round. Increasingly larger subsets of papers were analyzed in this manner punctuated by discussion. A final discussion with the third researcher provided a fresh perspective on the findings and interpretations.

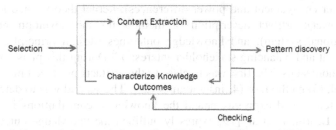

**Fig. 1.** Research Approach (extending Webster and Watson 2002)

The results, in the form of key attributes of research papers and characterization of outcomes and knowledge outcomes, were then used to discover patterns. The discovery of patterns itself was an iterative process. The overall research approach, thus, consisted of the following phases – selection, extraction, characterization, and analysis. Figure 1 outlines the research approach, which is elaborated next.

### 3.1    Selection of Corpus

The corpus for this meta-analysis was obtained from conference proceedings of DESRIST, the flagship design science conference in the IS discipline. The selection criterion was that the publication should report an actual DSR effort. The sample was further restricted to publications between 2011 and 2013 based on two key criteria. First, a limited scope of papers allowed an in-depth study (compared to [28]). Second, papers limited to DESRIST conferences provided a uniform context. Finally, it provided a window broad enough to study patterns but narrow enough to avoid interference from other factors such as time and different levels of research maturity. The papers excluded from the meta-analysis were, thus, papers such as literature review (e.g. [50]), prescriptions of methodologies or models for conducting DSR (e.g. [9]), and purely empirical evaluation (e.g., [4, 33]). The selection of 56 papers formed the corpus. Table 2 shows a summary of the population and the corpus selected.

**Table 2.** Selection of DSR Articles

| Source | Papers published | Papers analyzed |
|---|---|---|
| DESRIST 2011 | 34 | 14 (41%) |
| DESRIST 2012 | 30 | 16 (53%) |
| DESRIST 2013 | 45 | 26 (58%) |
| **Total** | **109** | **56 (51%)** |

## 3.2    Content Extraction

Following the approach described above, the content extraction phase proceeded in an iterative manner. During the first phase, we identified and extracted basic information such as a research-summary, artifact description, and the class of problems addressed by the authors. For example, examining the work by Lempinen et al. [21] yielded the following: "Summary (findings from an ADR project in a public organization where a new inter-organizational system was built, focusing on power relations between stakeholder organizations); class of problems (development problems related to stakeholder engagement and power differences); kernel theory (theories of organizational power); artifact description (a method for the development of an inter-organizational system); and knowledge outcomes (design principles such as early engagement and balancing stakeholder interests)." During this phase, we also carried out two more steps. The first was to classify the artifacts produced into : (1) construct, (2) model, (3) method, or (4) instantiation [25]. The second was to determine whether the researchers had expressly stated the knowledge contributions in the paper. For example, Lahrmann et al. [19] expressly outlined the knowledge outcomes as design principles; whereas Olsen et al. [32] chose not to expressly call out the knowledge outcome generated from their design effort. Extraction of content from each paper in this manner was important because it allowed the research team a shorthand to understand and characterize each paper.

## 3.3    Characterizing Knowledge Outcomes

Following the initial content extraction, we further examined the papers to characterize the knowledge generated by the authors, by comparing the knowledge contributions reported against the different knowledge forms (see Table 1). However, we allowed new knowledge forms to emerge if they could not be directly mapped to existing knowledge forms. During these iterations, we focused on characterizing two properties: (1) the *type* (see Table 1) and (2) the *source* of knowledge contributions.

The first property, *type* of knowledge contribution, was elaborated earlier along with a selective review of prior work (see Table 1). The second, *source* of knowledge was discovered during the analysis. For example, in some cases, authors of these works clearly reported prior (kernel) theories that informed and influenced their research (similar to the arguments in [51]). In other cases, the authors emphasized that it was the design process itself along with the accompanying research activities that generated the knowledge outcomes. We found this characterization similar to the notion of learning via building, i.e., knowledge generation from design and production [2] or the idea of substantive knowledge [5]. A third possibility was that knowledge was gained by putting the artifact to use, in simulated or real settings (similar to operative knowledge [5]). Here, one may argue that the source of knowledge was the interaction between the artifact as designed and the environment.

Although these statements appear to be fairly straightforward, we found that it was extremely difficult to tease apart the influence of these different sources. In many cases, multiple sources appeared to contribute to the knowledge generation effort.

Through a process of iteration and refinement, therefore, we, identified the following categories for *sources* of knowledge. The first category, *artifact design*, captured the source of knowledge as attributes of the artifact itself. This included internal attributes related to the structure or behavior of the artifact as well as external, use-oriented, functional properties of the artifact, whether influenced by kernel theories or not. We acknowledge that this category appears to conflate the internal and external properties. However, the intent was to distinguish this category from the other. The second category was identified as the *process of designing the artifact*. This included the activities and processes that gave rise to the design, re-design and implementation of the artifact; as well as the research-oriented activities that accompanied the design process. This phase – characterizing knowledge outcomes –proceeded in a deliberate manner, with identification of the *type* and *source* of knowledge contributions in each paper in the corpus with an ongoing check as the outer-loop (see Figure 1).

### 3.4    Discovering Patterns

The final phase included a re-examination of results to discover patterns. Following the tradition of quantitative meta-analysis research [54], this phase was carried out via exploratory analyses: generation of several tables and graphs. Each was subjected to cross-checks against others and interpreted to discover patterns. The relatively small number of papers describing actual DSR efforts and expressly stating knowledge contributions did not permit an extensive search for statistical patterns. Instead, we supplemented the analyses by returning to the papers to understand the details and further cement the interpretations. The outcomes are elaborated next.

## 4    Findings: Analysis and Interpretations

### 4.1    Conducting Design Science and Articulating Knowledge Contributions

The first observations from our analyses are aimed at articulating actual DSR conduct. From the 109 papers we examined, 56 actually described DSR efforts (see Table 2 earlier). Out of these 56, only 24 (less than half) articulated the knowledge contributions e.g., design theory, principles etc. Figure 2 shows these outcomes.

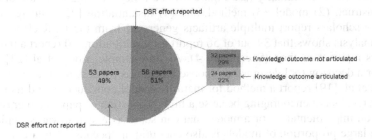

**Fig. 2.** DSR efforts reporting knowledge contributions

Papers that did not report actual DSR efforts were often aimed at investigating concerns such as the role of theory [48], prescriptions for evaluation [35], and methodological concerns [16]. These are appropriate as the DSR community tries to clarify underlying assumptions. Nevertheless, the relatively low number that report actual DSR efforts was alarming, in our view. It is also possible to interpret this data by arguing that the design science community is still nascent and, therefore, scholars in the community are still learning how to identify / articulate the findings. We analyzed the data further over the years. Figure 3 shows these results.

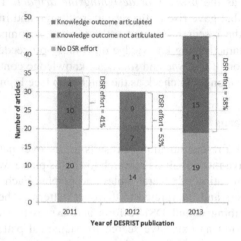

**Fig. 3.** DSR efforts reporting knowledge contributions (over time)

The results show that over time, papers that report DSR efforts have grown, proportionally. The number of papers that expressly articulate knowledge contributions shows a modest increase (4, 9 and 11 from 2011 to 2013), although its proportion shows an inconsistent pattern (44% in 2011, 56% in 2012, 42% in 2013). Together, these numbers suggest that DSR efforts are gaining momentum but scholars in the community are not consistently articulating the knowledge contributions yet.

## 4.2    Generating Different Types of Artifacts with Design Science Research

The second set of observations focus on the type of artifacts generated by scholars in the design science community (see Figure 4). We follow the classification of artifacts – (1) construct, (2) model, (3) method, and (4) instantiation [22]. Our results show that many scholars report multiple artifacts generated from the DSR effort. The aggregate analysis shows that 39 out of 56 report an instantiation, 30 report a model, and 21 papers report a method (See Figure 4). As an example, Looy et al [24] report a model for a decision tool designed to choose a business process maturity model while Lahrman et al. [19] report a method for maturity model construction and its instantiation. The results are encouraging because a high proportion of papers either report the result as an implementation or a model that can serve as a step towards implementation. The large proportion of models is also encouraging because they are a precursor to theory generation. Our findings echo those in [1] where research on decision support systems using the DSR paradigm was reviewed.

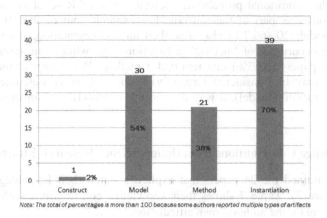

Note: The total of percentages is more than 100 because some authors reported multiple types of artifacts

**Fig. 4.** Generating artifacts via DSR efforts (number and proportion)

We investigated the data further to locate co-occurrence of different types of outcomes. For example, we found that out of the 39 papers that reported an instantiation, 20 (51.3%, reported as conditional probability) also described a model, 11 described a method, and 1 described a model as well as a method; only 7 reported an instantiation without an underlying model or method. Such lack of explication can hinder the knowledge articulation effort. Similar distributions were found in papers that reported other outcomes. We re-iterate that our intent was to compare how design science research is *actually done* compared to statements about how it *should be done*. As a result, more detailed analyses similar to those elsewhere (e.g. [30]) are not reported here. Table 3 shows the results of this analysis.

**Table 3.** Patterns of co-occurrence among different artifact types

| Artifact | Number (of 56) | Conditional Probability |
|---|---|---|
| *Instantiations* | 39 | |
| Instantiation only | 7 | 17.9% |
| Model + Instantiation | 20 | 51.3% |
| Method + Instantiation | 11 | 28.2% |
| Model + Method + Instantiation | 1 | 2.6% |
| *Models* | 30 | |
| Model only | 8 | 26.7% |
| Model + Method | 1 | 3.3% |
| Model + Instantiation | 20 | 66.7% |
| Model + Method + Instantiation | 1 | 3.3% |
| *Methods* | 21 | |
| Method only | 7 | 33.3% |
| Method + Instantiation | 11 | 52.4% |
| Construct + Method | 1 | 4.8% |
| Model + Method | 1 | 4.8% |
| Model + Method + Instantiation | 1 | 4.8% |
| *Constructs* | 1 | |
| Construct + Method | 1 | 100% |

Together, the conditional probabilities describe how DSR scholars combined the different outcomes as part of their efforts. For example, out of the 30 papers that described a model, 20 (66.7%) also described an implementation. Another notable outcome is the occurrence of 'method' in isolation (e.g., without an implementation) in 7 out of 21 papers (33.3%) that reported a method. We also note that only one reported what may be considered (arguably) a comprehensive outcome: a way of seeing a phenomenon (model), a way of working (method), and an implementation (instantiation).

## 4.3    Knowledge Contributions from Design Science Research Efforts

We further examined the 24 papers that explicitly stated their knowledge contributions (see Figure 2). Table 7 shows their knowledge contributions with illustrative examples, relying on the authors' own articulation.

**Table 4.** Self-reported knowledge contributions in contemporary DSR efforts

| Contribution | Number | An Example [Source] |
|---|---|---|
| Guideline | 2 (8.33%) | Differentiate functional requirements and incorporate more subjective information needs in Management Support Systems. [26] |
| Lesson | 2 (8.33%) | The design of environmental scanning systems is a top-down business project, and it should be communicated that way. [26] |
| Proposition | 3 (12.5%) | Adaptive parity proposition: the modularization in a volatile environment is the level where organizational adaptability is in parity with environmental volatility. [29] |
| Hypothesis | 2 (8.33%) | Impact of volatility hypothesis: As volatility increases for a choreography with a level of service abstraction set to mirror that of the "true" modular structure, the performance of the choreography will degrade. [29] |
| Design Principle | 9 (37.5%) | Balanced Inter-organizational system (IOS): Stakeholders' interest towards the IOS and power define their willingness to take part in the IOS [21] |
| Design Pattern | 2 (8.33%) | Preventive Control Pattern: Ensures that a check routine is automatically executed in conjunction with a certain process. Only if the check routine passes, the activity can complete. [42] |
| Design Requirement | 2 (8.33%) | Domain Specific Modeling Method for Multi-Perspective Hospital Modelling should provide a domain-specific modelling language for modelling clinical pathways. [13] |
| Design Recommendation | 1 (4.17%) | The bunch of management reports which typically exists in companies can easily be clustered through an electronic index and two types of information channels. [17] |
| Generative mechanism | 1 (4.17%) | Generative mechanisms for design of successful service engagements in KIBS domain: Development of high level interests, Perception of benefits, Creation of a value proposition, Organizing resources, Reconciling different values [22] |
| Total | 24  (See Figure 2) | |

The knowledge contributions show varying frequencies of occurrence, with 'design principle' being most frequent. The total number of papers is small with many cells less than 5, which can make any further statistical analyses, even nonparametric statistics, suspect. We did, however, examine how the authors conceptualized these knowledge contributions. One substantive finding from this analysis was that the knowledge contributions reported sometimes did *not* distinguish between descriptive and prescriptive knowledge. Consider, for example, the work by Lempinen et al. [21], who reported the building of an inter-organizational system (IOS). They described the design principle "Early Engagement" (in a prescriptive form) and a design principle "Balanced IOS" (in a descriptive form). This is an important distinction because much writing on DSR characterizes it as a science aimed at generating prescriptive knowledge (e.g., [44], [47]). The second key observation comes from a comparison of *reported* knowledge contributions (Table 4 above) against *expected* ones (see Table 1 earlier). A comparison across the two paints a striking picture (see Table 5 below).

**Table 5.** Knowledge contributions in DSR: Expected vs. Reported

| Knowledge Contributions Expected | Found in reported DSR efforts |
|---|---|
| Design Theory (Walls et al. 1992) | |
| • Mid-range theory (Kuechler and Vaishnavi 2008) | No |
| • Level 3: design theory (Gregor and Hevner 2013) | No |
| Mode 2 Knowledge (Gibbons et al. 1994) | |
| • Technological rule (van Aken 2004) | No |
| • Generative mechanism (van Aken 2004) | Yes |
| • Design proposition (Romme 2003) | Yes |
| • Design principle (Sein et al. 2011) | Yes |
| • Principle of form (Gregor et al. 2013) | Reported as Design Pattern, Requirement or Recommendation |
| • Principle of function (Gregor et al. 2013) | |
| Informally-specified knowledge contributions | |
| • Not a prescribed outcome in DSR | Guideline |
| • Not a prescribed outcome in DSR | Lesson |
| Knowledge contributions about interaction with context | |
| • Not a (directly) prescribed outcome in DSR | Hypotheses |

Table 5 shows two clear patterns. First, theory generation, although desirable, may be too demanding for DSR efforts (at least early work reported in conferences). We hope that this pattern will be less dominant with more work and a move to publications in archival journals. The second pattern suggests that some knowledge contributions (e.g. guidelines and lessons learned) may be of value, even if less well-specified. We see these as early versions of Mode 2 knowledge (e.g. via initial design-evaluate cycles), which may evolve into design principles or design propositions. Finally, we note that some knowledge contributions are also available as hypotheses that describe intended utilitarian outcomes, stated in a tentative form, i.e., subject to empirical tests indicating a need to test fitness of the designed artifact for a purpose (similar to [9]).

## 4.4     Variations in Source of Knowledge Contributions

The next set of analyses was aimed at understanding the source of knowledge contributions. This was a difficult proposition because it required inferring the mechanisms followed by the researchers to generate the knowledge contributions. As a first step in this process, we identified whether the researchers used any kernel theories as drivers for the research effort. Table 6 shows the results.

**Table 6.** Use of kernel theory in DSR efforts (see also Figure 2)

| Papers reporting DSR efforts | Kernel theor(ies) used | Kernel theor(ies) not used | Total |
|---|---|---|---|
| Articulated knowledge outcomes | 15 (62.5%) | 9 (37.5%) | 24 |
| Did not articulate knowledge outcomes | 10 (31.3%) | 22 (68.7%) | 32 |
|  | 25 | 31 | 56 |

The data showed that less than half (25 out of the 56) of the papers that reported DSR efforts identified kernel theories that influenced their work (few reported more than one). This number was spread differently across the papers that articulated / did not articulate the knowledge outcomes. Of the papers that articulated the knowledge outcomes, 62.5% specified kernel theories. This proportion dropped to 31.3% in papers that did not articulate knowledge outcomes. Over time, the number of papers that did not specify kernel theories actually increased, from 43% (6 out of 14 in 2011) to 69% (18 out of 26 in 2013). We note that our sample consists of conference publications where researchers may present early stage work. This may explain a greater focus on material artifacts rather than theoretical foundations.

To explore whether these are tenable explanations, we investigated the manner in which DSR scholars reported the knowledge contributions. The source of knowledge contributions from DSR efforts can be: (a) the design of the artifact itself, including any influence from kernel theories, or (b) the design / design research process adopted by researcher, including any influence from the research process. When the source is the design of an artifact, the knowledge contribution may be described in terms of a structural form or functional elements; when the source is an activity performed by researcher as part of the design / design research process, the knowledge contribution may be described in an action oriented form. Table 7 shows these results.

**Table 7.** Variations in source of knowledge contributions from DSR efforts

| Source | Count* | Example |
|---|---|---|
| Design of the Artifact, including influence from kernel theories | | |
| Form | 11 | Values of design parameters such as size, color, and tone of the warning messages in anti-phishing system [7] |
| Function | 18 | Elements of user interface to improve usability of an eWallet [32] |
| Design / Design Research Process, including a focus on specific design or research tasks | | |
| Design Process | 19 | Desirable activities in a design process for management support systems to improve user acceptance [28] |
| Research Process | 3 | Lessons from instantiating a recommendation system for coordinating immigrant child vaccination in Sweden [15] |

\* The total is higher than 24 because some papers describe multiple knowledge outcomes.

The results show that scholars in the DSR community reflect on both the designed artifacts as well as the processes that lead to the construction of these artifacts with a slight bias towards the former. The numbers also indicate that in most cases, scholars rely on multiple sources of knowledge.

# 5    Discussion and Future Research

These analyses suggest a number of possible interpretations. The most important concerns are the relative scarcity of actual DSR papers (see Table 2), the lack of explicit knowledge contributions in DSR (less than half of those papers, see Figure 2), and the different forms of knowledge contributions reported in actual DSR efforts compared to statements about DSR knowledge contributions (see Table 5). Together, we find that these results point to a lack of consistency among scholars in the DSR community, which can be an obstacle to building a cumulative knowledge base.

Not present in our analysis is a reporting of the scientific validation processes that would support the position that knowledge contributions had, indeed, been made (rather than simply asserted). DSR has a thin layer of such principles, mainly in the evaluation phase. We simply note that the lack of widely accepted validation principles may be hindering development of the DSR community. Over the last century the quantitative social sciences have evolved a set of terms for concerns that are important to this mode of inquiry, e.g. causation (internal validity), generalizability (external validity), measurement (content and construct validity; reliability), prediction (practical or predictive validity), and so forth. It would not be too far a stretch to say that the success of the social science paradigm is in some measure a tribute to the wide dissemination of these research standards in that community. The creation of analogous principles for DSR is not out of the realm of possibility. The articulation of such scientific principles would serve the DSR community well, in our view.

Returning to the data, they show that the dominant form of outcomes generated via DSR efforts is artifact instantiations although a number of researchers also generated models, often in conjunction with instantiations (see Table 3). These results indicate a focus on material artifacts more than abstract artifacts. We hope that as the design science community matures, we will see a more widespread occurrence of abstract forms including models and methods that must accompany instantiations. The incidence of an instantiation along with a model is also encouraging because it shows that researchers are not content with developing a model but take the additional step of implementation to subject the model to the rigors of translation into software.

A third significant finding was the use of kernel theories in only about half the papers reporting DSR efforts. This may indicate that design science research that is aimed at generating novel contributions begins as an atheoretical endeavor and only in retrospect and with much reflection can the researchers identify kernel theories that may provide a foundation for the work. We report these findings against the backdrop of an active debate: whether design science research should be informed by kernel theory (e.g., see [3], and how the absence of kernel theory can hinder explanation about why a design works [11]).

Next, the findings related to the source of knowledge contributions are interesting because they point out an important characteristic of DSR efforts. Both, the designed artifact as well as the process of design/design research can be sources of knowledge (see Table 7). In conjunction with the use of kernel theories, the emergence of knowledge contributions from DSR efforts can be complex because it can be influenced by the design / design research process, the kernel theories selected, as well as the designed artifact. These overlaps were evident in the results in Table 7.

Together, these patterns suggest one overwhelming concern. Although the design science research community has attempted to *prescribe* the knowledge contributions, these prescriptions may not have taken into account the peculiar nature of actual DSR efforts. As a result, the prescriptions may not match the realities of conducting DSR. We hope that the results reported in this paper will encourage further work that recognizes both, positions from philosophy of science as well as the nuances of actual DSR efforts. In particular, distinctions across different knowledge contributions and sources of knowledge may need more time and deeper thinking. Ensuring that we acknowledge the actual practice of DSR efforts will allow the emergence of norms for identifying and articulating knowledge contributions in a more consistent manner. The terms used to characterize knowledge contributions (e.g., design principle or guideline) are still in need of clear definitions. The informal knowledge contributions found in actual DSR efforts (see, for example, the bottom rows in Table 5) have no articulation in design science. As the DSR community clarifies these, including but not limited to maturity, sequence, and formalisms in each knowledge form, we hope that the attempts to establish such norms will be based on an inductive process that recognizes both the foundations from philosophy of science as well as actual DSR efforts in the community. Not recognizing the latter may lead to dysfunctional outcomes that unnecessarily straightjacket the design science researchers or force characterizations that run counter to the instinctive foundations of design science as aimed at intervention, problem-solving and creation of novel artifacts. This is a cautionary note we extend to the design science community.

We conclude by acknowledging that our analysis is restricted to DESRIST publications over a three-year period. It is possible to expand the set to include additional years as well as publications in other venues that publish DSR outcomes. In spite of this limitation, we hope that our work has provided a first step in a dialog to combine both prescriptive work and empirical analyses as the DSR community engages in an effort to develop and establish norms for conducting and reporting DSR efforts, and develop a cumulative knowledge-base.

# References

1. Arnott, D., Pervan, G.: Design Science in Decision Support Systems Research. Journal of the AIS 13(1), 923–949 (2012)
2. Baldwin, C.Y., Clark, K.B.: Design Rules, vol. 1: The Power of Modularity, 1st edn. The MIT Press (2000)
3. Baskerville, R.: What design science is not. European Journal of Information Systems 17(5), 441–443 (2008)

4. Becker, J., Beverungen, D., Matzner, M., Müller, O., Pöppelbuß, J.: Design Science in Service Research: A Framework-Based Review of IT Artifacts in Germany. In: Jain, H., Sinha, A.P., Vitharana, P. (eds.) DESRIST 2011. LNCS, vol. 6629, pp. 366–375. Springer, Heidelberg (2011)
5. Bunge, M.: Scientific Research II: The Search for Truth. Studies in the Foundations Methodology and Philosophy of Science, vol. 3/II. Springer-Verlag New York, Inc. (1967)
6. Cleven, A., et al.: Design alternatives for the evaluation of design science research artifacts. In: Proceedings of DESRIST (2009)
7. Chen, Y., Zahedi, F(M.), Abbasi, A.: Interface design elements for anti-phishing systems. In: Jain, H., Sinha, A.P., Vitharana, P. (eds.) DESRIST 2011. LNCS, vol. 6629, pp. 253–265. Springer, Heidelberg (2011)
8. Gibbons, M., et al.: The New Production of Knowledge: The Dynamics of Science and Research in Contemporary Societies. SAGE Publications (1994)
9. Gill, T.G., Hevner, A.R.: A Fitness-Utility Model for Design Science Research. In: Jain, H., Sinha, A.P., Vitharana, P. (eds.) DESRIST 2011. LNCS, vol. 6629, pp. 237–252. Springer, Heidelberg (2011)
10. Glass, G.V. (ed.): Integrating Findings: The Meta-Analysis of Research. Peacock, Ithasca (1978)
11. Gregor, S., Hevner, A.R.: Positioning and presenting design science research for maximum impact. MIS Quarterly 37(2), 337–355 (2013)
12. Gregor, S., et al.: Reflection, Abstraction, and Theorizing in Design and Development Research. In: Proceedings of the ECIS, pp. 1–12 (2013)
13. Heß, M.: Towards a Domain-Specific Method for Multi-Perspective Hospital Modelling – Motivation and Requirements. In: vom Brocke, J., Hekkala, R., Ram, S., Rossi, M. (eds.) DESRIST 2013. LNCS, vol. 7939, pp. 369–385. Springer, Heidelberg (2013)
14. Hevner, A.R., March, S.T., Park, J., Ram, S.: Design science in information systems research. MIS Quarterly 28(1), 75–105 (2004)
15. Holmberg, N., Steen, O., Carlsson, S.: Service Orienting the Swedish Vaccination Recommendation Activity with the Business Rules Centric Digital Service VacSam. In: Jain, H., Sinha, A.P., Vitharana, P. (eds.) DESRIST 2011. LNCS, vol. 6629, pp. 376–386. Springer, Heidelberg (2011)
16. Hovorka, D.S., Pries-Heje, J.: Don't Ignore the Iceberg: Timely Revelation of Justification in DSR. In: vom Brocke, J., Hekkala, R., Ram, S., Rossi, M. (eds.) DESRIST 2013. LNCS, vol. 7939, pp. 228–241. Springer, Heidelberg (2013)
17. Krönke, B., Reinecke, A., Mayer, J.H., Tischner, G., Feistenauer, H., Hauke, J.: Self-Service Management Support Systems— There's an App for That. In: vom Brocke, J., Hekkala, R., Ram, S., Rossi, M. (eds.) DESRIST 2013. LNCS, vol. 7939, pp. 420–424. Springer, Heidelberg (2013)
18. Kuechler, B.V.: Vaishnavi, On theory development in design science research: anatomy of a research project. European Journal of Information Systems 17(5), 489–504 (2008)
19. Lahrmann, G., Marx, F., Mettler, T., Winter, R., Wortmann, F.: Inductive Design of Maturity Models: Applying the Rasch Algorithm for Design Science Research. In: Jain, H., Sinha, A.P., Vitharana, P. (eds.) DESRIST 2011. LNCS, vol. 6629, pp. 176–191. Springer, Heidelberg (2011)
20. Lakatos, I.: Falsification and the methodology of scientific research programmes. In: Criticism and the Growth of Knowledge. Cambridge University Press (1970)
21. Lempinen, H., Rossi, M., Tuunainen, V.K.: Design Principles for Inter-Organizational Systems Development – Case Hansel. In: Peffers, K., Rothenberger, M., Kuechler, B. (eds.) DESRIST 2012. LNCS, vol. 7286, pp. 52–65. Springer, Heidelberg (2012)

22. Lessard, L., Yu, E.: Using Design Science Research to Develop a Modeling Technique for Service Design. In: Peffers, K., Rothenberger, M., Kuechler, B. (eds.) DESRIST 2012. LNCS, vol. 7286, pp. 66–77. Springer, Heidelberg (2012)
23. Lipsey, M.W., Wilson, D.B.: Practical Meta-Analysis. Sage Publications, Thousand Oaks (2001)
24. Van Looy, A., De Backer, M., Poels, G.: Towards a Decision Tool for Choosing a Business Process Maturity Model. In: Peffers, K., Rothenberger, M., Kuechler, B. (eds.) DESRIST 2012. LNCS, vol. 7286, pp. 78–87. Springer, Heidelberg (2012)
25. March, S.T., Smith, G.F.: Design and natural science research on information technology. Decision Support Systems 15, 251–266 (1995)
26. Mayer, J.H.: How Service Orientation Can Improve the Flexibility of Executive Information Systems—An Architecture Reworked from a Business Perspective. In: Jain, H., Sinha, A.P., Vitharana, P. (eds.) DESRIST 2011. LNCS, vol. 6629, pp. 306–320. Springer, Heidelberg (2011a)
27. Mayer, J.H.: Managing the Future—Six Guidelines for Designing Environmental Scanning Systems. In: Jain, H., Sinha, A.P., Vitharana, P. (eds.) DESRIST 2011. LNCS, vol. 6629, pp. 276–290. Springer, Heidelberg (2011b)
28. Mayer, J.H., Winter, R., Mohr, T.: Utilizing user-group characteristics to improve acceptance of management support systems— state of the art and six design guidelines. In: Jain, H., Sinha, A.P., Vitharana, P. (eds.) DESRIST 2011. LNCS, vol. 6629, pp. 291–305. Springer, Heidelberg (2011)
29. Nichols, J., Goul, M., Dooley, K., Demirkan, H.: Reconsidering modular design rules in a dynamic service context. In: Jain, H., Sinha, A.P., Vitharana, P. (eds.) DESRIST 2011. LNCS, vol. 6629, pp. 350–365. Springer, Heidelberg (2011)
30. Offermann, P., Blom, S., Schönherr, M., Bub, U.: Artifact Types in Information Systems Design Science – A Literature Review. In: Winter, R., Zhao, J.L., Aier, S. (eds.) DESRIST 2010. LNCS, vol. 6105, pp. 77–92. Springer, Heidelberg (2010)
31. Offermann, P., Blom, S., Schönherr, M., Bub, U.: Design Range and Research Strategies in Design Science Publications. In: Jain, H., Sinha, A.P., Vitharana, P. (eds.) DESRIST 2011. LNCS, vol. 6629, pp. 77–91. Springer, Heidelberg (2011)
32. Olsen, M., Hedman, J., Vatrapu, R.: e-wallet prototypes. In: Jain, H., Sinha, A.P., Vitharana, P. (eds.) DESRIST 2011. LNCS, vol. 6629, pp. 223–236. Springer, Heidelberg (2011)
33. Pedersen, R.U., Furtak, S.J., Häuser, I., Lauth, C., Van Kranenburg, R.: Mini Smart Grid @ Copenhagen Business School: Prototype Demonstration. In: vom Brocke, J., Hekkala, R., Ram, S., Rossi, M. (eds.) DESRIST 2013. LNCS, vol. 7939, pp. 446–447. Springer, Heidelberg (2013)
34. Peffers, K., et al.: A Design Science Research Methodology for Information Systems Research. Journal of Management Information Systems 24(3), 45–77 (2007)
35. Peffers, K., Rothenberger, M., Tuunanen, T., Vaezi, R.: Design Science Research Evaluation. In: Peffers, K., Rothenberger, M., Kuechler, B. (eds.) DESRIST 2012. LNCS, vol. 7286, pp. 398–410. Springer, Heidelberg (2012)
36. Popper, K.: The Logic of Scientific Discovery. Rouledge, London and New York (1992)
37. Purao, S.: Design Research in the Technology of Information Systems - Truth or Dare. Working paper (2002)
38. Purao, S., et al.: The Sciences of Design: Observations on an Emerging Field. Communications of the Association for Information Systems 23(29), 523–546 (2008)
39. Purao, S.: Truth or Dare: The Ontology Question in Design Science Research. Journal of Database Management 24(3), 51–66 (2013)

40. Romme, A.G.L.: Making a Difference: Organization as Design. Organization Science 14(5), 558–573 (2003)
41. Samuel-Ojo, O., Shimabukuro, D., Chatterjee, S., Muthui, M., Babineau, T., Prasertsilp, P., Ewais, S., Young, M.: Meta-analysis of Design Science Research within the IS Community: Trends, Patterns, and Outcomes. In: Winter, R., Zhao, J.L., Aier, S. (eds.) DESRIST 2010. LNCS, vol. 6105, pp. 124–138. Springer, Heidelberg (2010)
42. Schultz, M.: Enriching Process Models for Business Process Compliance Checking in ERP Environments. In: vom Brocke, J., Hekkala, R., Ram, S., Rossi, M. (eds.) DESRIST 2013. LNCS, vol. 7939, pp. 120–135. Springer, Heidelberg (2013)
43. Sein, M., et al.: Action Design Research. MIS Quarterly 35(1), 37–56 (2011)
44. Simon, H.A.: The sciences of the artificial. MIT Press, Cambridge (1996)
45. Suh, N.P.: Axiomatic design theory for systems. Research in Engineering Design 10(4), 189–209 (1998)
46. Sutton, R.I., Staw, B.M.: What theory is not. Administrative Science Quarterly, 371–384 (1995)
47. van Aken, J.E.: Management Research Based on the Paradigm of the Design Sciences. Journal of Management Studies 41(2), 219–246 (2004)
48. Venable, J.R.: Rethinking Design Theory in Information Systems. In: vom Brocke, J., Hekkala, R., Ram, S., Rossi, M. (eds.) DESRIST 2013. LNCS, vol. 7939, pp. 136–149. Springer, Heidelberg (2013)
49. Venable, J., Pries-Heje, J., Baskerville, R.: A comprehensive framework for evaluation in design science research. In: Peffers, K., Rothenberger, M., Kuechler, B. (eds.) DESRIST 2012. LNCS, vol. 7286, pp. 423–438. Springer, Heidelberg (2012)
50. Voigt, M., Niehaves, B., Becker, J.: Towards a Unified Design Theory for Creativity Support Systems. In: Peffers, K., Rothenberger, M., Kuechler, B. (eds.) DESRIST 2012. LNCS, vol. 7286, pp. 152–173. Springer, Heidelberg (2012)
51. Walls, J.G., et al.: Building an Information System Design Theory for Vigilant EIS. Information Systems Research 3(1), 36–59 (1992)
52. Webster, J., Watson, R.T.: Analyzing the past to prepare for the future: Writing a Literature Review. MIS Quarterly 26(2) (2002)
53. Weick, K., What, E.: theory is not, theorizing is. Administrative Science Quarterly 40(3), 385–390 (1995)
54. Wolf, F.M.: Meta-Analysis. Sage Publications, Beverly Hills (1986)

# Action Design Research in Practice: The Case of Smart Cities

Giovanni Maccani[1,*], Brian Donnellan[1], and Markus Helfert[2]

[1] National University of Ireland Maynooth, Co. Kildare, Ireland
{giovanni.maccani.2013,brian.donnellan}@nuim.ie
[2] Dublin City University, Dublin 9, Co. Dublin, Ireland
markus.helfert@computing.dcu.ie

**Abstract.** Smart Cities has emerged as an important research challenge among IS researchers in recent years. The grand claims that have been done about the potential of Smart Cities are grounded in a wide range of IT-related artifacts that were designed in theory and/or implemented in practice. Today, due to the growth of the level of knowledge maturity in this context, IS research in this field is more focused on the development of a nascent Smart City theory. The key concepts introduced in literature were collected through an eight-steps systematic literature review [19] and analyzed using [20]'s concept definition matrix. Based on this, this paper aims at reflecting upon research methodologies for conducting IS research in this field, and demonstrates the suitability of Action Design Research [43]. A Smart City research project that successfully used this methodology is also described to further support this statement.

**Keywords:** Smart Cities, Action Design Research, Systematic Literature Review.

## 1    Introduction: IS Research on Smart Cities

Smart Cities is more and more acknowledged as a relevant research challenge among IS researchers. The term Smart City was firstly introduced in [1]. In this seminal article the Smart City mission is defined as:

> *"The urban centre of the future, made safe, secure environmentally green, and efficient because all structures are designed, constructed, and maintained making use of advanced, integrated materials, sensors, electronics, and networks which are interfaced with computerized systems comprised of databases, tracking and decision making algorithms"*. [1, pp. 2]

However, greater attention by IS researchers started with the grand claims made by IBM [2][3] about the potential for such initiatives. Particularly the authors referred to the introduction of the concept of *"city as a system of systems"* [2, pp. 11]. In other words, their visionary articles aimed at demonstrating the potential value that is expected to be achieved through the application of different ICT solutions across a number of city's core systems, such as Transport, Communication, Water, and Energy

---

* Corresponding author.

M.C. Tremblay et al. (Eds.): DESRIST 2014, LNCS 8463, pp. 132–147, 2014.
© Springer International Publishing Switzerland 2014

to mention few. Then, their integration and interconnection would allow the creation of a holistic "system of systems" that is able to embed these city's core systems, and so to enable both a more efficient and effective management of the overall city [4], and a positive impact on its "triple bottom line" (economy, environment, society) [5]. Thus, the grand claims that have been done about the potential of Smart Cities are grounded in a wide range of IT-related artifacts that were designed in theory and/or implemented in practice. For example, their implementation across different city's domains can enable Intelligent Transportation Systems (e.g. [6]), or can increase water (e.g. [7]) and energy supply (e.g. [8]) efficiency, to mention some general instances. In the following years the IS research around Smart Cities significantly changed. In detail, the goals shifted from specific technological problem-solution analysis to more comprehensive studies regarding, for instance, innovative measurement frameworks [9] or overall strategies and business models [10][11]. In other words, from specific instantiation and implementation of software and process solutions, the IS research around Smart Cities is now concerned more with defining operational solutions, and so with structuring a new Smart City theory. In order to study how the research is moving in this way, we adopt Gregor and Hevner's framework [12] that outlines three levels of "contribution types" for Design Science Research (DSR) (see Figure 1). The DSR artifact has different natures [13] and the one that is assumed partially determines the type of contribution to knowledge. Other factors such as the state of the field of knowledge and the academic research conversation to which the research outcome is to be communicated are further variables that might be included when analyzing the nature of knowledge contribution [12].

| | Contribution Types | Example Artifacts |
|---|---|---|
| More abstract, complete, and mature knowledge | Level 3. Well-developed design theory about embedded phenomena | Design theories (mid-range and grand theories) |
| ↕ ↕ ↕ ↕ | Level 2. Nascent design theory—knowledge as operational principles/architecture | Constructs, methods, models, design principles, technological rules. |
| More specific, limited, and less mature knowledge | Level 1. Situated implementation of artifact | Instantiations (software products or implemented processes) |

**Fig. 1.** Design Science Research Contribution Types [12, pp.342]

In Figure 1, it is clear that the authors predict different levels of contribution types in relation to the level of maturity of the knowledge around the topic (i.e. *"problem maturity"*, [12, pp. 344]). As seen, the context of Smart Cities is then maturing and quickly evolved in academic literature since the publication of the seminal articles above mentioned. A plethora of suggestions regarding ICT solutions (artifacts) to make cities "smarter" is available in the literature to date [14]. Subsequently, a fundamental need to reflect on the Smart City concept, its construction and underlying assumptions to enable transparency and new readings was highlighted [15]. In other words, *"cities currently face a problem of standardization of the main building blocks of smart/intelligent cities in terms of applications, business model, and services. Standardization would dramatically reduce the development and maintenance costs of e-services due to cooperation, exchange, and sharing of resources"* [16]. Referring to the left cell in Figure 1, the maturity of the knowledge regarding Smart Cities is growing due the exponential growth of related academic publications. This shift is reflected in a change of the content and of the focuses upon which IS research on Smart Cities is conducted (from level 1 to level 2 in Figure 1). This paper aims at identifying a suitable research methodology for conducting IS research in the current context of Smart Cities. As a consequence, we conducted a systematic review of the literature (presented in section 2) to investigate the main concepts that IS authors introduced in this field to define what a Smart City is and which are the conceptual elements involved in such initiatives. It will allow us to identify a suitable research methodology (section 3) to systematically drive the research activities in the context of Smart Cities. Finally an example of a Smart City IS research project is provided in section 4, before the conclusions, where the main contributions of this paper are outlined.

## 2     Smart City Systematic Literature Review

Despite the plethora of suggestions regarding the design and instantiation of IT-related artifacts to improve the city's social, economical and environmental performances, the Smart City concept is still emerging, and the work of defining and categorizing it is in progress [17]. In fact, most of the definitions provided come from individual research needs or perspectives [18]. As a consequence we conducted a systematic literature review (SLR). This process adhered to Okoli et al's 8 steps [19] that are: (1) Purpose of the Literature Review, (2) Protocol and Training, (3) Searching for the Literature, (4) Practical Screen, (5) Quality Appraisal, (6) Data Extraction, (7) Synthesis of Studies, and (8) Writing the Review. Within the following sub sections, all of these steps will be described.

(1) *Purpose of the Literature Review:* in our case, this study was conducted to analyze the progresses of the stream of research connected to Smart Cities. Particularly, the main aim of this study is to extract all the relevant concepts that have been used in defining Smart Cities, and which are believed to be its enabler factors.

(2) *Protocol and Training:* within this second stage of the process, the specific steps and procedures to be followed have to be detailed. First, the key review questions must be defined. Consistently with the objectives outlined in step 1, two key review questions (RevQ) arose: what does the term Smart City mean? (RevQ1); which are the homogeneous dimensions that fully encompass all the enabler factors of Smart Cities? (RevQ2). The approaches that were followed were similar for both the RevQs. In detail to answer RevQ1 the first step was to collect all the definitions that have been published in literature. In order to systematically analyze these definitions, we defined a common syntactic structure made of different categories. The next step was about the development of a concept matrix, using as guidance the methodology proposed in [20]. Its development allowed us to have a complete overview of what have been said, how many times, and what a comprehensive definition of Smart Cities should include. The same approach was followed for RevQ2. The only difference was the subject under analysis. In fact, the analysis has taken into account all the contributions in which there was a clear attempt of defining and conceptualizing the Smart City concept with dimensions. These attempts can range from frameworks to simple lists of enabler factors. This process was externally validated by experts in the field of Smart Cities, and from experts in systematic literature review within the academic field.

(3) *Searching for the Literature:* The requirement for an article to be considered for this study was the presence of the word "Smart City/Smart Cities" either within the abstract, or the keywords, or the title of the paper. The sources of literature collection that we considered were three; in first place we looked at the most important journals' websites following journal rating charts such as the "AIS Basket of 8"; then, open access databases (Google Scholar) and specific subject databases (ACM Digital Library) were also included. In total we collected 908 articles. We then applied first exclusion criteria to titles (e.g. language), and there were 442 articles that were ordered and searched, and considered further.

(4) *Practical Screen:* The output of this step has to be a complete list of the literature that is considered for the review. In our case we went through it twice. First we reduced the total amount of articles by reading the abstracts of all the papers we had previously collected. Then, we carefully read all the papers. In particular, we verified their consistency with the two RevQs. In Figure 2 a summary of the process we implemented is provided.

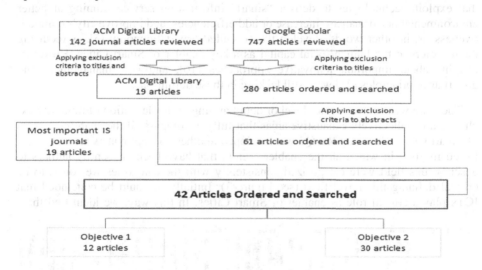

**Fig. 2.** Literature Selection Process

As a result we considered 12 contributions for answering RevQ1 and 30 for RevQ2.

(5) *Quality Appraisal:* this step involves a closer examination of the articles in order to assess their quality. However, given the novelty of the topic (almost 95% of the articles were published in the last two years), there were not problems relating to the amount of articles.

(6) *Data Extraction:* at this stage, a complete list of articles that comprised all of the materials needed to answer our RevQs was available. Therefore, we isolated the information relating to the two relevant objectives for this study. We listed all of the definitions in a table. We then extracted all the dimensions used to conceptualize Smart Cities. The output of this step was a complete list of relevant concepts from which we could synthesize our study and derive our conclusions.

(7) **Synthesis of Studies:** with respect to the definitions, we first looked at the syntax of the sentences. While doing so, we defined a common structure characterized by a number of main areas in which all the concepts that arise from these definitions can consistently fit. Examining the texts of the definitions we then classified at a high level of abstraction the components of such phrases, stating that: *"The Smart City is a [Context] that exploits / uses / leverages / develops an [Infrastructure] with-a-certain / implementing an [Approach] supported by [Factors] to enable [processes] to achieve/ improve / enhance / increase [Goals]"*. In other words, every single key concept that is stated in the definitions is related to one of these six main areas, i.e. context, infrastructure, processes, approach, factors, goals. So, after checking its validity, we've decomposed all the definitions into their key words or notions. Hence, with all the words/notions available, we followed the concept matrix method [20] in which each key word/notion is related to the author and grouped within the category to which it belongs (see Figure 3). After a preliminary investigation of the definition concept matrix, we could infer that a Smart City could be described as an initiative that exploits technologies to deliver "smart" information services aiming at better environmental performances, increase or add efficiencies, and improve city's competitiveness or, in other words, develop the so called Smart Economy [5]. A recurring theme refers to the human/social capital as a key enabler of Smart Cities. However, insights about important innovative approaches [16], and new management and governance principles [21] were still lacking in these definitions.

Then, we went into a greater level of detail aiming at the definition of mutually exclusive and collectively exhaustive areas that fully encompass all the enabling factors of Smart Cities. Based on RevQ2 we developed another concept matrix (already published in [14]) in which all the enabler factors that have been chosen by authors to describe this field were categorized consistently with the categories we found to be critical defining this novel field (see Figure 3). Initially, it could be concluded that ICTs play a crucial role as enabler of Smart Cities. In this way, we identified three

| Definitions | Context | | | | | | Infrastructure | | | | | | | Processes | | | | | Approach | | | | | | Factors | | | Goals | | | | | | | | |
|---|---|---|---|---|---|---|---|---|---|---|---|---|---|---|---|---|---|---|---|---|---|---|---|---|---|---|---|---|---|---|---|---|---|---|---|---|
| References: | Urban area | Mean | Way | Result | Initiative | Urban environment | Physical infrastructure | ICT | Intelligent City | Human capital | Social Capital | Relational Capital | Communication in infrastructure | Exploit information | Data collection | e-governance | Generate the knowledge-base | Delivering smart services | Triple-helix | Creative strategy | Knowledge intensive strategy | Government-driven | Participatory governance | Interactive information | Performance metrics | High-tech and creative industries | Stakeholders | Environmental sustainability | React quickly to problems | Make better decisions | Add efficiencies | Improve city's operations | Sustainable economic growth | Social performances | Urban growth | High quality of life |
| [Kanter] | | | | | | | | x | | | | | | x | x | | | | x | | | | | | | x | | x | x | x | x | | | | | |
| [Harrison] | x | | | | | | | | | | | | | | | | | | | | | | | | | | | | | | | x | | | | |
| [Castineira] | | x | | | | | | | | | x | | | | | | | | x | | | | | | | | | | | | | | | | | |
| [Helal] | | | x | | | | x | | | | | | | | | | | | x | | | | | | | | | x | | | | | | | x | |
| [Naphade] | | | | | | | | x | | | | | | | x | | | | | | | | | | | | | | | | | | x | | | |
| [Lombardi] | | | | | | | | x | | x | x | x | | | | | | | | | | | | | | | | x | | | | | | | | |
| [Tranos] | | | | | | | | x | x | | | | | | | | | | | | | | | | x | | | x | | | | x | x | x | | |
| [Kourtit] | | | | x | | | | | | | | | | | | | | | | | | x | x | | | | x | x | | | | x | x | x | | |
| [Leydedorff] | | | | | | | | x | x | | | | | | | x | x | x | | | | | | | | | | | | | | | | | | |
| [Kuk] | | | | | x | | | | | | | | | | | | | | | | x | | | | | | | | | | | | | | | |
| [Caragliu] | | | | | | | | x | | x | x | | x | | | | | | | x | | | | | | | | | | | | | | | | x |
| [Schuurman] | | | | | | x | | | | | | | | | | | | | | | | | x | x | | | | | | | | | | | | |
| Tot. | 1 | 1 | 1 | 1 | 1 | 1 | 1 | 6 | 2 | 2 | 3 | 1 | 1 | 1 | 2 | 1 | 1 | 1 | 3 | 1 | 1 | 1 | 2 | 1 | 1 | 1 | 1 | 5 | 1 | 1 | 1 | 3 | 3 | 2 | 1 | 1 |
| Tot. per Area | 6 | | | | | | 16 | | | | | | | 6 | | | | | 9 | | | | | | 3 | | | 18 | | | | | | | | |

Fig. 3. Smart City Definition Concept Matrix

fundamental milestones in building the technological background for Smart Cities, named the Spatial Intelligence of Cities [22]: Ambient Intelligence [23], Digital City [24], and the Intelligent City [25]. Respectively, they refer to the instrumentation, interconnection and intelligence steps presented in [2].

Furthermore, developing human resources and social capital are recognized, together with technology, as one of the enabler factors for Smart Cities by authors, e.g. [26]. According to literature, collaboration, participation, engagement, and partnerships are key words related to this field [5]. Hence, we need a collaboration model to actually establish technological and social components as enablers for Smart Cities. To support these approaches, researchers advocate the use of the "triple-helix" model which focuses in particular on relations between university, industry and government at an urban and regional scale [27]. Within this perspective, Living Labs methodologies [28] are stressed as being significant. Living Labs can be seen as a User-Centered Open Innovation Ecosystem [29] that aims at the integration of concurrent research and innovation processes within a "3P" (Public-Private-People) Partnership. Consistently, the balance between bottom-up and top-down strategies must be strengthened. To achieve these goals managerial interoperability across city's smart services, applications, and organizations is required [21]. At this point of development, we are in a good position to implement a Smart City strategy. Initially, we can state that the final goal of a Smart City is to provide services [5] in order to: improve city's inhabitants' quality of life [1], decrease city's carbon footprint [30], facilitate a sustainable economic growth [31], and increase or add efficiencies.

As a result of this process we identified all the key themes related to Smart Cities. At this stage we know what has been said, how many times and what a comprehensive definition should include. Thus, we define Smart City as *"an urban area that leverages its technological and social infrastructure implementing people-private-public partnerships supported by innovative governance in terms of policies, leadership and proper ongoing management principles, to enable smart information services, aiming at improving its critical capabilities"*. This definition encompasses all the critical aspects that arose from the literature currently available.

## 3    Choosing a Suitable Research Methodology

In the previous section we presented a SLR study on research to date within the topic of Smart Cities. Particularly, the concept definition matrix methodology allowed us to highlight what are considered the relevant concepts about conducting research in this emerging field. Furthermore, connecting to the introductory section of this paper, we highlighted with examples which is the current level of knowledge contribution of IS research projects in this field in relation to the level of knowledge maturity (see Figure 1). Hence, the aim of this paragraph is to find a suitable research methodology in order to enable the creation of prescriptive knowledge in terms of nascent Smart City design theory [32], considering all the relevant aspects arose from the SLR study. Particularly important for this scope is to consider the "Approach" category within both the concept definition matrixes previously introduced (see Figure 3 and [14]). Accordingly to literature, collaboration, participation, engagement, and partnerships are key words related to this field [33] [5]. Hence, Smart City projects need a collaboration model to actually establish technological and social components as actual enablers for Smart Cities. To promote these approaches the largest portion of literature refers to a model called "triple-helix" which focuses in particular on relations between universities, industries and government at an urban and regional scale [27]. This perspective is critical to bridge the gap between short-term city development priorities (demand pull) and long-term technological research and experimentation (technology push) [16]. This approach has been widely demonstrated by several case study researches as successful (among others [9][11]). As a consequence, one of the critical success factors for Smart Cities research projects is considered to be the establishment of a strong "Public Private Partnership" in which local government, IT industries and universities are involved in a highly participatory approach to design and deliver innovative artifacts in this domain. The main aim is placed at leveraging the awareness of the mechanisms that characterize cities (from the government side), and the technological infrastructure associated with cities (from the IT company side), with the knowledge arising from extant academic theory (from the university side). In this landscape, in the early stage interaction between these three main actors involved, the problem that is wanted to be solved arises. Particularly, the local government highlights a specific issue regarding the specific city context. Researchers from academia import a theoretical standpoint, by rigorously analyzing the progresses of literature connected to the specific problem. In the case in which a solution is not available in literature, a research gap is identified, and as a consequence a solution needs to be designed. The outcome, i.e. the artifact, is meant as a thing that has, or can be transformed into, a material existence as an artificially made object or process [34]. It is clear that, if considering the dearth in existing theory only, Design Science Research (DSR) is a suitable research methodology. DSR is defined as a construction-oriented view of IS research in which the main focus is around designing and building innovative artifacts [13]. Moreover, *"the artifact should be relevant to the solution of an unsolved and important problem"*. Thus, *"the development of the artifact should be achieved from existing and proved theories and knowledge and should be a solution of a defined problem"* [35]. On the other hand, if we consider the challenge articulated by the local government, a specific organizational solution is needed. As a consequence the rationale for the choice of DSR as the proper research methodology becomes weaker. According to [36], researches using design science are initiated by the researcher interested in developing technological rules for a certain type of issue. In fact, in DSR the organizational intervention is considered to be secondary [37]. Particularly the DSR methodology sees as a first priority to gain complete awareness about the problem, then design the artifact, followed by its evaluation, tracing the so called "build and then evaluate" path. As a consequence, the organization plays an active role within the evaluation of an artifact that had been already designed. Notwithstanding, some key authors in the topic of DSR (e.g. [13]) believe that the organization can play a key role also in shaping the problem that is wanted to be solved. However, none of them sees a participatory design of the solution itself as one of the main features of the methodology. Hence, if we did consider only the local government side of the research motivation, we would probably choose Action Research

[38], which can be seen as the combination of theory and researchers' intervention to solve immediate organizational problems [39]. It is clear here that the organization is at the core of this research approach. However, once the organization-related solution is designed and evaluated, various forms of the organizational context are inscribed into the artifact [40]. As a consequence the contribution to existing knowledge might suffer due to the lack of insights for the generalization of the problem and solution instances.

Thus, concerning this methodological challenge related to IS research in the context of Smart Cities, we have to incorporate an "action component" within a DSR approach, in order to meet the needs of the local government and ensure an original contribution to existing knowledge. In literature an interesting (and consistent to this study) attempt to combine these two approaches was done in [41, pp.9], and it is drawn from [42]. The scheme that is considered here involves a naturalistic evaluation, as opposed to the artificial one, as the class of artifacts that are taken into account are much more involving conceptual elements rather than technical ones (see Figure 1, Level 2 of DSR Contribution Types). We see here that the organizational involvement (the action research component) happens only during the evaluation of the already developed artifact. In the case of Smart Cities there are two main differences and inconsistencies. In first place, the local government (and so the organization), has to be involved since the very first stage of the research. Secondly, the artifact has to be designed and developed in a highly participatory approach with the organization and the practitioners (from the IT company side). We can conclude that both DSR (in its original formulation) and Action Research are not suitable for IS research projects in the field of Smart Cities. However, we can conclude that IS research in Smart Cities needs to be DSR that recognizes that the artifact emerges from the interaction with the organizational context (i.e. local government).

A method that addresses these issues is Action Design Research (ADR), which is defined as a *"research method for generating prescriptive design knowledge through building and evaluating ensemble IT artifacts in an organizational setting"* [43]. Its particular contribution is linked to the implementation of design science research to solve an organizational-related problem defined as an instance of a class of problems, in which the evaluation is conducted in a highly participatory process [44]. The ADR cycle is based on four main research stages: (1) Problem Formulation, (2) Building Intervention and Evaluation, (3) Reflection and Learning, and (4) Formalization of Learning. The first step involves the definition of the problem that is required to be solved. Here, the problem has to be identified, articulated, and scoped. Particularly important at this stage, is to relate the organizational problem to a broader class of problems. This first stage of the methodology is drawn upon two principles: (1) *Practice Inspired Research* and (2) *Theory-Ingrained Artefact* [43]. Generally, research on Smart Cities has been initially motivated by "practical" (as opposed to theoretical) issues. Some examples are the widely mentioned urbanization trend, the growing responsibility of cities for the world carbon footprint, and the dramatic change in the demographic composition of the population [45], that are stressing cities' balances and infrastructures. More specifically, earlier in this section we have underlined how the issue arising from the local government is translated and related to a research gap in theory by the academic side of the research team. Hence, a wide range of academic publications in IS literature in the context of Smart Cities demonstrates the effort that researchers are making to address these challenges with a theoretical perspectives, creating a range of original contributions to existing theories. The second stage of the ADR methodology is related to the process of building, intervention, and evaluation (BIE) of the artifact. Here again some principles are proposed in the ADR seminal article [43], that are (3) *Reciprocal Shaping*, (4) *Mutually Influential Roles*, and (5) *Authentic and Concurrent Evaluation*. After discovering initial theoretical contribution targets, the methodology also distinguishes between an IT-dominant-BIE (that is mainly focused on innovative technological design) and an organization-dominant-BIE (this format is related to the decision making processes within the organization). Both of these BIE types identify a highly participatory process, consistently with the calls for collaborative approaches made by several authors in the topic of Smart Cities (among others [46][47]). In detail, as concluded in [48], cities can be considered as densities in networks among at least these three relevant dynamics: that is, in the intellectual capital of universities, the industry of wealth creation, and their participation in the democratic government which forms the rule of law in civil society. The effects of these interactions can generate spaces within the dynamics of Smart Cities where knowledge production can be exploited. The evaluation phase is seen as a concurrent step, rather than a separate stage (principle 5). This particular approach allows identifying anticipated as well as unanticipated challenges related to the final solution. The importance of such an approach is ingrained in the concept of Living Lab [28], which it was demonstrated to be a successful way to design innovative artifacts in the context of Smart Cities by bringing together *"interdisciplinary experts to develop, deploy and test new technologies and strategies for design that respond to this changing world"* [49] (see also Special Issue on the Journal of Knowledge Economy [50]). The third step of ADR is crucial to ensure the contribution to knowledge of this research project, and it focuses on the reflection and learning process. This stage is drawn on the principle (6) *Guided Emergence*. In the context of IS research on Smart Cities, the final artifact is the result of the interplay that encompasses the relationship between the theories used and their application to the specific urban environment (including the local government, i.e. the organization) – related challenges [48]. Finally, the last stage proposed in [43] (i.e. Formalization of Learning) emphasizes once again the importance of having a (7) *Generalized Outcome* that can be further developed into general solution concepts for a class of field problems. The IS Smart City researcher is responsible of relating the specific city – solution to a significant contribution to theory by extracting the design pattern [51], understood as a generally reusable template solution to commonly re-occurring challenges (see [52]). The research outcome is then a theory-ingrained artifact, where theories allow the research team to both structure the organizational problem as an instance of a class of problems in literature, and guide the design [32]. The generalized outcome is achieved through the ongoing reflection and learning step, and the final formalization of learning one, by extracting the design principles [51] from the specific organizational-related solution. In this way, the organizational related problem can be solved without precluding the creation of an original contribution to existing knowledge.

Concluding, we found in ADR a relevant approach for providing systematic methodological guidance for current IS research conducted in the context of Smart Cities, and we demonstrated its suitability by relating its main principles to the key notions arose from a SLR study. This statement will be further demonstrated within the next section, in which it will be provided an example of successful application of ADR in a Smart City research project regarding the development of a Sustainable Connected City Capability Maturity Framework (SCC-CMF) [52].

# 4    ADR in Smart Cities: The SCC CMF

The aim of this section is to describe a successful usage of ADR in a Smart City research project. It was conducted by a research team that included representatives from the academic field (National University of Ireland Maynooth and Dublin City University), in collaboration with Dublin City Council (DCC) and Intel Corporation, and was focused on the development of a Smart City maturity model (SCC CMF) [52]. In this paper we focus on outlining how the research activities that were implemented are consistently related to the 7 principles of ADR [43]. In other words, we focus on the methodology that was used, rather than on the content of the final artifact itself that was already widely described in [52]. A "quadruple-helix" approach [53] was adopted, where the awareness and the influence of the city authority as well as the technological experience and insights of Intel Corp., could be combined with rigorous research from the academic field (ADR, *Principle 4*). Moreover, the involvement of representatives from the city council and citizens of Dublin ensured the presence of the "people component" in the people-private-public partnerships collaboration model that was established, which is considered critical in any Smart City project [16]. Hence, a strong partnership between the stakeholders involved was officially established [56], and it was followed by initial meetings in which objectives, roles of each member of the research team, priorities and deadlines were clearly defined. Thus a long-term commitment to the project was achieved (ADR, *Principle 3*). The first motivation for this research project came from an organizational-related problem. The DCC senior management team highlighted the need they had for a comprehensive model in order to assess the current position of the city's Digital Master Plan. According to Dublin Lord Mayor Naoise O'Muiri', the master plan will be modelled with the idea of promoting initiatives to create an *"everywhere digitally connected and sustainable city, from home to workplace, from streetscape to public park and from healthcare to education"* [55]. At this stage we can conclude that the research was *Practice Inspired* (ADR, *Principle 1*). In the city's managers opinion a solution should be also able to define an improvement strategy in relation to the city's characteristics, priorities, and constraints. On the other side, a SLR to identify the related research opportunities and gaps within the existing literature base was conducted. Here, it was found that, despite the definition of many static indexes to assess the "smartness of cities", e.g. [5][54], there was still a lack of dynamic assessment models [9]. Thus, after a highly participatory preliminary analysis of the project between the parties involved, two initial research questions were formulated: (1) How can Smart Cities be assessed in relation to their current and future ability of delivering services enabled by ICTs? (2) How can insights be given to city's managers to increase and optimize such capability?

It is clear here that the research addresses an organizational-related problem (DCC) defined as an instance of a class of problems identified through the SLR study. After discovering initial theoretical contribution targets, the research team had to select and customize the BIE cycle. Within the continuum between an IT-dominant-BIE and an organization-dominant-BIE, the project was much closer to the second option, as the artifact was designed with organization's participants input and ideas (ADR, *Principle 3*). Within the BIE cycle, the first version of the artifact was achieved as a part of a PhD program, by applying a theoretical lens to the dearth of existing theory, and by the usage of several research techniques (e.g. Grounded Theory [57], 8-steps SLR [19]), as described in [58] (ADR, *Principle 2*). The possibility of leveraging this first stage of the model by embedding the experience and competences from both DCC and Intel resulted in a significant change and improvement of the artifact, again consistently with *Principle 3* of ADR. Furthermore, as documented in [52], an ongoing evaluation of the artifact was achieved by involving Dublin City stakeholders since the first version of the solution was designed. Particularly, a city workshop was conducted involving city stakeholder representatives from those areas of the city in which Smart City ICT-related solutions are expected to be implemented. Among other activities that were implemented (e.g. individual and group-based assessment of the current level of maturity of Dublin City), the stakeholders had a further group discussion on potential improvements that can be done within the SCC CMF. Here they highlighted their ideas about future initiatives, potential benefits, as well as the challenges and obstacles that have to be overcome to allow their full implementation. As a consequence, the BIE cycle identifies a highly participatory process with the evaluation phase that can be seen as a concurrent step, rather than a separate stage (ADR, *Principle 5*). As a summary, the solution evolved since its first version through its usage by end users (i.e. responsible for the Dublin Digital Master Plan), and the inputs collected from stakeholders within the city (ADR, *Principle 6*). Concluding, by extracting the design pattern [52], the research team ensured that the outcome achieved with the design of the SCC CMF goes beyond the specific city solution (i.e. Dublin) (ADR, *Principle 7*). Despite filling the research gap previously identified, this research project gave constructive insights to the Smart City IS research community on how to systematically standardize this complex field. Furthermore, the SCC CMF is now being used to facilitate *"quantitative benchmarking across cities"* and as a *"standalone city assessment instrument"* [52]. In addition, the presence of researchers from academia facilitated this process, as their main interest was to keep the process rigorous and systematic.

Concluding, in this section an example of successful application of ADR in a Smart City project was described. Its consistency with [43]'s methodology was demonstrated by relating the research activities that were widely described in [52] to the 7 principles of ADR. These relationships will be summarized in the concluding section of this paper (see Table 1).

**Table 1.** ADR Principles in IS Smart City Research

| ADR Principles [43] | IS Smart City research | SCC CMF [52] |
| --- | --- | --- |
| Practice-Inspired Research | Smart City research activities are problem-inspired, from mega trends (e.g. urbanization) that are stressing cities' balances and infrastructures [2]. | The research project had as a starting point the issues articulated by the senior management team within DCC, i.e. need for an artifact to inform the strategy to become a Smart City. |
| Theory-Ingrained Artifact | The practical problem is related to a research gap in literature, and IS theories systematically drive the activities involved in the design of the artifact. | A mix of theories and research techniques was used for systematically drive the research activities (e.g. Grounded Theory [57], Maturity Models [59], 8-steps SLR [19]). |
| Reciprocal Shaping | The effects of the interactions-between local government, IT industry, and academia-generate spaces within the dynamics of cities where knowledge production can be exploited [48]. | The involvement since the beginning of the project of DCC (i.e. the organizational setting) ensured a participatory approach in designing the SCC CMF, which was then inevitably influenced by the specific context. |
| Mutually influential roles | The IT artifact is developed in a Triple-Helix environment [27], where IS theories (academic side) inform the practical knowledge related to the city (government side) and its technological landscape (IT industry side), and vice versa. | The final artifact is the result of the leverage of the awareness of the mechanisms that characterize cities (from Dublin City Council), and the technological infrastructure associated with cities (from Intel Corp.), with the knowledge arising from extant academic theory. |
| Authentic and Concurrent Evaluation | The importance of such an approach is ingrained in the concept of Living Lab [28], which was demonstrated to be a successful way to design innovative artifacts in the context of Smart Cities [50]. | An ongoing evaluation of the artifact was achieved by involving Dublin City stakeholders since the first version of the artifact was designed. Additionally, end users (i.e. responsible for the Dublin Digital Master Plan) actively participated in the design of the artifact. |
| Guided Emergence | The artifact is the result of the interplay that encompasses the relations between the theories used and their application to the specific urban– related challenges [48]. | The solution evolved since its first version through its usage by end users (i.e. responsible for the Dublin Digital Master Plan), and the inputs collected from stakeholders within the city. |
| Generalized Outcomes | The IS researcher is responsible of relating the specific city – solution to a significant contribution to theory by extracting the design pattern [51]. | The SCC CMF goes beyond the specific city solution. It is currently being used to facilitate *"quantitative benchmarking across cities"* and as a *"standalone city assessment instrument"* [52] |

# 5 Conclusions

This paper demonstrates the suitability of Action Design Research [43] to systematically focus on the complex research challenge associated with the topic of Smart Cities. As a summary we propose Table 1, in which the relations between the 7 principles of ADR with both general IS research on Smart Cities and the particular case described in the previous section (i.e. the SCC CMF), are outlined.

To support this statement, we firstly used [12]'s framework to describe the progresses to date of IS research in Smart Cities in terms of current research contribution targets in relation to the level of maturity of the knowledge in this field. Based on this, we conducted a SLR in order to investigate the key concepts upon which IS research on Smart Cities is currently grounded. The systematic identification of these concepts allowed us to both outline the methodological challenges that Smart City research projects are currently facing, and to demonstrate how ADR can be a suitable approach in this highly collaborative and practice inspired research landscape. Particularly, we showed how the main concepts arising from the SLR study are consistent with the 7 fundamental principles of ADR. In addition, we provided an example of successful application of ADR in this research domain, by focusing on the research activities implemented in the design of the SCC CMF [52].

**Acknowledgements.** This research is funded by Intel Corporation and the Irish Research Council (IRC). The authors would also like to thank Dublin City Council for their active contribution in shaping, designing, and refining this research.

# References

1. Hall, R.: The Vision of a Smart City. In: 2nd International Life Extension Technology Workshop, Paris (September 2000)
2. Dirks, S., Keeling, M.: A Vision of Smarter Cities. IBM Institute for Business Value (2009)
3. Harrison, C., Donnelly, I.A.: A Theory of Smart Cities. In: Proceedings of the 55th Annual Meeting of the ISSS, Hull, UK (2011)
4. Harrison, C., Eckman, B., Hamilton, R., Hartswick, P., Kalagnanam, J., Paraszczak, J., Williams, P.: Foundation for Smarter Cities. IBM Journal of Research and Development (August 2010)
5. Giffinger, R., Fertcher, C., Kramar, H., Kalasek, R., Meijers, E.: Smart Cities – Ranking of European Medium-size Cities. Vienna University of Technology (October 2007)
6. Chen-Ritzo, C.H., Harrison, C., Paraszczak, J., Parr, F.: Instrumenting the planet. IBM Journal of Research and Development (2009)
7. Venkatesen, M.: ICT as an Enabler for Smart Water Management. ITU (October 2010)
8. Stancic, Z.: Smart Electricity Distribution Network. European Commission Information Society and Media (July 2009)
9. Lombardi, P., Giordano, S., Farouh, H., Yousef, W.: Modelling Smart City Performance. Innovation – The European Journal of Social Science Research (June 2011)

10. Chourabi, H., Nam, T., Walker, S., Garcia, J.R., Mellouli, S., Nahon, K., Pardo, T.A., School, H.J.: Understanding Smart Cities: An Integrative Framework. In: 4th Hawaii International Conference on System Sciences (2012)
11. Caragliu, A., Del Bo, C., Nijkamp, P.: Smart Cities in Europe. In: 3rd Central European Conference in Regional Science – CERS (2009)
12. Gregor, S., Hevner, A.: Positioning and Presenting Design Science Research for Maximum Impact. MIS Quarterly 37(2), 337–355 (2013)
13. Hevner, A.R., March, S.T., Park, J.: Design Research in Information Systems Research. MIS Quarterly 28(1), 75–105 (2004)
14. Maccani, G., Donnellan, B., Helfert, M.: A Comprehensive Framework for Smart Cities. In: Proceedings of 2nd International Conference on Smart Grids and Green IT Systems (2013)
15. Wolfram, M.: Deconstructing Smart Cities: An Intertextual Reading of Concepts and Practices for Integrated Urban and ICT Development. REAL CORP 2012 Tagungsband, Schwechat (May 2012)
16. Schaffers, H., Komninos, N., Pallot, M., Trousse, B., Nilsson, M., Oliveira, A.: Smart Cities and Future Internet: Towards Cooperation Frameworks for Open Innovation. In: The Future Internet. Springer (2011)
17. Boulton, A., Brunn, S.D., Devriendt, L.: Cyber infrastructures and 'smart' world cities: physical, human, and soft infrastructure. In: International Handbook of Globalisation and World Cities, Cheltenham, UK (2011)
18. Abdulrahman, A., Meshal, A., Imad, F.T.A.: Smart Cities: Survey. Journal of Advanced Computer Science and Technology Research (June 2012)
19. Okoli, C., Schabram, K.: A Guide to Conducting a Systematic Literature Review of Information Systems Research. Sprouts (2010) ISSN 1535-6078
20. Webster, J., Watson, R.T.: Analyzing the Past to Prepare for the Future: Writing a Literature Review. MIS Quarterly 26(2), 13–23 (2002)
21. Nam, T., Prado, T.A.: Smart City as Urban Innovation: Focusing on Management, Policy, and Context. In: Proceedings of the 5th ICEGOV Conference, Tallin, Estonia, pp. 185–194 (September 2011)
22. Mitchell, W.: Intelligent Cities. e-Journal on the Knowledge Society (5) (2007) ISSN 1885-1541
23. Gasson, M., Warwick, K.: D12.2: Study on Emerging AmI Technologies. FIDIS Deliverables 12 (2) (2007)
24. van den Besselaar, P., Koizumi, S. (eds.): Digital Cities 2003. LNCS, vol. 3081. Springer, Heidelberg (2005)
25. Komninos, N.: Intelligent Cities: Innovation, knowledge systems and digital spaces. Routledge, London and New York (2002)
26. Toppeta, D.: The Smart City Vision: how Innovation and ICT can build smart, 'liveable', Sustainable Cities, Think! Report (2010)
27. Etzkowitz, H., Leydesdorff, L.: The Dynamics of Innovation: from National Systems and 'Mode 2' to a Triple Helix of Universities-Industry-Government Relations. Research Policy. Elsevier (2000)
28. Pallot, M., Trousse, B., Senach, B., Scapin, D.: Living Lab Research Landscape: From User Centered Design and User Experience towards User Cocreation. School'Living Labs - halshs.archives-ouvertes.fr (2010)
29. Chesbrough, H.W.: Open Innovation: The New Imperative for Creating and Profiting from Technology. Harvard Business School Press, Boston (2003)

30. Angoso, J.L.: Smart Cities: The ICT Infrastructure for Ecoefficient Cities. In: High Level OECD Conference (2009)
31. Doobs, R., Remes, J., Manyika, J., Roxburgh, C., Smit, S., Schaer, F.: Urban World: Cities and the Rise of Consuming Class. McKinsey Global Institute (June 2012)
32. Gregor, S.: The Nature of Theory in Information Systems. MIS Quarterly 30(3), 611–642 (2006)
33. Odendaal, N.: Information and Communication Technology and Local Governance: Understanding the difference between Cities in Developed and Emerging Economies. Environment and Urban Systems (2003)
34. Goldkuhl, G.: Anchoring Scientific Abstractions – Ontological and Linguistic Determination Following Socio-Instrumental Pragmatism. European Conference on Research Methods in Business and Management, Reading, UK (2002)
35. Peffers, K., Tuunanen, T., Rothenberger, M., Chatterjee, S.: A Design Science Research Methodology for Information Systems Research. Journal of MIS 24(3), 45–77 (2008)
36. Jarvinen, P.: Action Research is similar to Design Science. Quality and Quantity (41), 37–54 (2007)
37. Cole, R., Purao, S., Rossi, M., Sein, M.K.: Being Proactive: Where Action Research meets Design Research. In: Proceedings of 24th International Conference on Information Systems, pp. 325–336 (2005)
38. Davison, R.M., Martinsons, M.G.: Principles of Canonical Action Research. Information Systems Journal 14(1), 65–86 (2004)
39. Baburoglu, O.N., Ravn, I.: Normative Action Research. Organizational Studies (1992)
40. Nandhakumar, J., Rossi, M., Talvinen, J.: The Dynamics of Contextual Forces of ERP Implementation. Journal of Strategic Information Systems 14(2), 221–242 (2005)
41. Ivari, J., Venable, J.: Action Research and Design Science Research – Seemingly Similar but Decisively Dissimilar. In: 17th European Conference on Information Systems, Verona (2009)
42. Venable, J.R.: A Framework for Design Science Research Activities. In: Information Resource Management Association Conference, Washington DC (May 2006)
43. Sein, K.M., Henfridsson, O., Purao, S., Rossi, M., Lindgren, R.: Action Design Research. MIS Quarterly 35(1), 37–56 (2011)
44. Alsleben, M.: Creating Dynamic Capabilities: R&D Network Management for Globally Distributed Research and Development in the Software Industry. CreateSpace Independent Publishing Platform (2012)
45. Mulligan, L.: Smart Cities and Sustainable Technology. Siemens Ltd. (2010)
46. Steinert, K., Marom, R., Richard, P., Veiga, G., Witters, L.: Making Cities Smart and Sustainable. The Global Innovation Index (2011)
47. Schuurman, D., Baccarne, B., De Marez, L., Mechant, P.: Smart Ideas for Smart Cities: Investigating Crowd-sourcing for Generating and Selecting Ideas for ICT Innovation in a City Context. Journal of Theoretical and Applied Electronic Commerce Research (December 2012)
48. Leydesdorff, L., Deakin, M.: The Triple-Helix Model of Smart Cities: A Neo-Evolutionary Perspective. Journal of Urban Technology 18(2), 53–63 (2011)
49. MIT Living Labs, http://livinglabs.mit.edu
50. Komninos, M., Pallot, M., Schaffers, H.: Special Issue on Smart Cities and the Future Internet in Europe. Journal of Knowledge Economy (January 2012)
51. Martin, R.C.: Design Principles and Design Patterns. Object Mentor (2000)

52. Kenneally, J., Prendergast, D., Maccani, G., Donnellan, B., Helfert, M.: Sustainable Connected Cities: Vision and Blueprint towards Managing IT for City Prosperity and Sustainability. In: European Design Science Symposium. Communication in Computer and Information Science. Springer, Heidelberg (2013)
53. Carayannis, E.G., Campbell, D.F.J.: Mode 3 and Quadruple Helix: Toward a 21st Century Fractal Innovation Ecosystem. International Journal of Technology Management (2009)
54. Lee, J.H., Hancock, M.G.: Towards a Framework for Smart Cities: A Comparison of Seul, San Francisco & Amsterdam. Yonsei University (2012)
55. Digital Dublin, Digital Master Plan, http://digitaldublin.ie/masterplan/
56. Intel – DCC Partnership, http://newsroom.intel.com/community/en_ie/blog/2012/10/04/announcing-the-sustainable-connected-cities-dublin-collaboration
57. Glaser, B.G., Strauss, A.: Discovery of Grounded Theory. Strategy for Qualitative Research. Sociology Press, Mill Valley (1967)
58. Maccani, G., Donnellan, B., Helfert, M.: The Development of a Framework for Sustainable Connected Cities for Dublin, Ireland. In: 18th International Sustainable Innovation Conference, Surrey, UK (2013)
59. Mettler, T.: Maturity Assessment Models: a Design Science Approach. International Journal Society Systems Science 3(1), 81–98 (2011)

# Communicating Nascent Design Theories on Innovative Information Systems through Multi-grounded Design Principles

Peter Heinrich and Gerhard Schwabe

University of Zurich, Institute for Informatics, Binzmuehlestrasse 14, 8050 Zurich, Switzerland
{peterhe,schwabe}@ifi.uzh.ch

**Abstract.** One central goal of design science research (DSR) is to generate, extract and communicate knowledge about the design of an artifact. Design science researchers ultimately strive to contribute knowledge in the form of mature design theories; mere descriptions of the artifacts are not regarded as sufficient contributions to knowledge anymore in scholarly publications. There is an increasing body of guidelines on how to produce and publish mature design theories. However, not every research project is in that state. To publish intermediate results (i.e. nascent theories), only general, abstract publication schemes can be found in the recent literature making it difficult to publish design knowledge at that intermediate level. In this paper, we contribute an extension of an existing publication scheme, tailored towards the publication of such intermediate, work in progress design knowledge in the form of prescriptive design principles. This scheme was designed with respect to the complexity of today's information systems IT artifacts. To demonstrate the scheme's applicability, we will apply it to one of our recent scholarly publications in the CSCW area. We argue that this publication scheme extension will help to communicate design knowledge in earlier project stages, which allows a faster feedback to the knowledge base that will enable a broader community to participate in the "search process" for an optimal design solution.

**Keywords:** Design science research publications, design principles, design theory.

## 1 Introduction

Design oriented research is well established in IS research, particularly in Europe [1]. There is a vast body of literature that generally describes DSR in theory as well as in practice (i.e. [2–5]). There is general consensus that design science focuses on the acquisition of new knowledge through the design and evaluation of artifacts. "The fundamental principle of design science research is that knowledge and understanding of a design problem and its solution are acquired in the building and application of an artifact."[6]. But when it comes to practical research projects, the definition of what design science exactly is, starts to blur. The existing publication guidelines aim to be applicable for a wide variety of fields, methods and artifacts and therefore lack

M.C. Tremblay et al. (Eds.): DESRIST 2014, LNCS 8463, pp. 148–163, 2014.
© Springer International Publishing Switzerland 2014

specificity required to stringently describe practical projects in specific fields. Baskerville [7] highlighted the current ambiguities and misunderstandings by filling most of the space in an editorial describing what design science is not [7] and he is using one paragraph to advise the reader to make up their own minds by treating the DSR related articles in that journal issue as "best examples". Moreover, Gregor et al. [8] conclude that there is still a lack of clear understanding what defines a contribution to knowledge in the publications from DSR projects. To address the aforementioned problem, Gregor et al.'s article [8] provides a detailed framework for knowledge contributions and a schema for publishing DSR projects but in the end stays on an abstract level in order to be applicable to all kinds of practical DSR work.

For more mature knowledge however, i.e. design theories, there are several guidelines available [9, 10] on how to publish them, but not every research project is in that mature state. But as design science is regarded as an ongoing "search process" [2], it is from our point of view vital that design knowledge is contributed to the community especially in early stages. Otherwise the search process would be carried out by individuals rather than within a larger community.

Therefore, this paper aims to close that gap by extending Gregor et al. [8] in order to give specific guidance on the description of the artifacts and their design rationales with a focus on innovative information systems. Thus, the over all objective for that schema extension is to *foster the publication of nascent design knowledge in scholarly publications.* (In DSR terminology, this could also be called solution objective for the artifact, as discussed later in this article.)

This is a rather practical goal. However, by working on an artifact to reach this goal we can also contribute to the scientific knowledge base of DSR with its stream of literature on the publication of DSR results. The research question therefore addresses a gap in the current body of literature:

**Research Question:** *How can early design knowledge on information systems artifacts be rigorously communicated through nascent design theories at any time in the research process?*

To motivate the need for an extended DSR publication schema we report shortly on our experiences in communicating DSR. The past DSR activities in our research group often targeted the design of innovative IT artifacts in collaborative work environments like advisory service encounters. Although we (and our research group) published DSR related articles in the past years in the domain of travel agencies [11, 12] and the financial industry [13–15], we often faced a number of problems during the writing process, which sometimes even hindered the publication of valuable design knowledge. (1) During the course of such a projects, design knowledge exists at various levels of maturity at any given point in time (i.e. the time of writing). When publishing results from DSR activities we were often obliged to communicate knowledge with different levels of maturity simultaneously in order to describe our artifact and its design rationales stringently. However, we found it challenging to mix those levels of maturity while demonstrating overall rigor in a publication. (2) As the design space of possible artifacts is very large, it is in general impossible to address all design decisions in one single publication. Thus a selection of design aspects targeting the specified design goals have to be made and communicated transparently in order to avoid an impression of a random selection to readers. (3) As DSR activities are typically performed in a cyclic sequences [3] knowledge materializes at different stages in the process. This often does not seem to fit well into generic and linear structure of DSR publication schemas.

To address those problems, we will discuss the current literature on publishing DSR contributions to knowledge with a focus on designing and implementing IT-artifacts in real world contexts. We contextualize the current literature and existing publication schemes with our observed practical publication challenges and identify existing gaps. We then review the related literature and identify the necessary components and constructs to base the proposed framework upon. The main contribution of this article is the extended publication schema based on Gregor et al. [8] and a demonstration of its application to one of our previous research projects. The paper ends with a discussion of the proposed schema and its value to future research.

## 2    Related Work

The discussion of how to publish design knowledge already started decades ago. Walls et al. [16] provided a first structure for design theories. Walls et al.'s design theories were structured around 4 major components: "meta-requirements", "meta-design", "kernel theories", and "testable design hypothesis". The first component "meta-requirements" covers the description of the system objectives. The word "meta" was used to distinguish the project specific requirements from the more generic or abstract requirements covering the class of problems a design theory addresses [16]. The second component, the "meta-design", deals with describing the design abstractions, describing the essential rationales of the design solution. Again, the "meta"-prefix distinguishes the concrete artifact instantiation form its more generic or abstract counterpart in the design theory, that addresses a whole class of systems [16]. The third component, "kernel-theories" are meant to include justificatory knowledge for the developed theories. The fourth and last component, "testable design hypothesis", is used to provide evaluation criteria for the meta-design with respect to the meta-requirements [16].

Gregor et al. [8], also incorporating the work of Walls et al., developed a much more practical and recent framework for presenting design science research. This general framework provides a structure for complete DSR articles and includes the sections *introduction, background, method, artifact description, evaluation, discussion and conclusion*. For each section, the authors prescribe the nature of the expected content. However, as the article strives to addresses all possible kinds DSR projects, the descriptions are on an abstract and generic level. While most of the framework's sections may be directly applicable in many practical research projects, at least two of them are currently too general to be directly applicable. One of them is the "description of the artifact". In this section, the authors are required to give a "[...] concise description of the artifact at the appropriate level of abstraction [...]" [8]. But no guidance is given on how to describe the design of a complex information system. The other too generic section is the discussion section, where in the case of complex socio-technical systems an "[...] explicit extraction of design principles may be needed" [8]. There, too, no guidance is given on how to publish information in a rigorous way. Arguably, both sections might be the most important ones when it comes to demonstrating a contribution to knowledge using Gregor et al.'s publication scheme, especially as it is key to demonstrate an appropriate level of rigor [2] in such work. Gregor et al. [8] address that challenge by proposing two frameworks to categorize scholarly articles by (i.) the type of knowledge contribution, and (ii.) the level of knowledge maturity (and hence abstraction). The frameworks provide three categories for knowledge maturity (ranging from "situated artifact instantiation" to "mature design theories"), and four categories of knowledge contribution types ("routine design", "improvement", "exaptation" and "invention"). Kuechler et al. [17] published a framework to support the generation of intermediate design theories. They coined the term DREPT ("design relevant explanatory / predictive theory") to describe that type of theoretical knowledge. While providing a detailed framework to support theory generation from an epistemological and thus justificatory point of view, only sparse guidance is given on how to publish those results.

When designing innovative information systems in practice, many design decisions have to be made. Scholarly publications (should) ideally convey that design knowledge by extracting the essence of those innovative design factors. However, we found it hard to classify them into one distinct category of Gregor et al.'s frameworks [8]. On one hand, as for any innovative system of real world complexity, not all design decisions are justifiable by existing prior knowledge (or have been decided upon consciously or intentionally at all). If all design decisions were completely justifiable by prior knowledge, it would not be possible anymore to contribute to scientific knowledge bases as no new knowledge could be added. Such designs would be categorized as "routine design" and would be unpublishable by definition [8]. Thus, frameworks like [17] are not even applicable to portions of the design space, as the design knowledge is just to immature. On the other hand, based on our practical experience, it seems not even possible to fully describe the design for a class of systems within a single category of knowledge contribution or knowledge maturity. Knowledge contributions of real world systems are rather likely to fall into several (if not all) categories simultaneously. Some aspects of the system might be routine design (i.e. using existing platform libraries) while others might be transferred from foreign domains (exaptations) while still others might be improved versions of previously implemented constructs (improvements). A lack of clarity at this level could be a severe thread to the overall impression of the publication's rigor if not properly explicated.

A similar issue arises with communicating practical design knowledge on different levels of maturity. Gregor et al. [8] have developed a hierarchy of maturity levels, ranging from "artifact instantiation" up to "mature theories". However, as we often face the need to describe whole classes of information systems, it is again unlikely for a publication to only transport knowledge at one distinct level of maturity. But apart from that practical aspect, presenting abstract and generic knowledge (like design theories) also requires the description of the actual instantiation of an artifact [9]. Therefore, even publications that cover very mature knowledge are also likely to present knowledge at lower levels of maturity at the same time.

Thus we see the need to express the type of knowledge contribution as well as its maturity on a finer level of granularity in a publication.

## 2.1    Maturing of Knowledge within a DSR Project's Lifecycle

The design of innovative systems will always include a creative part of the designer (see Figure 1). Most likely, the creative part of the designer will be large when the project is novel and only little mature design knowledge is available. At any given time during a project's lifecycle, only parts of the design decisions can be justified through existing principles or (more mature) theories, while the rest is not (yet) formalized and thus can only be attributed to a designer's intuition (which equals intentionally taken design decisions) or is unconsciously made (which reflects the lowest level of maturity). One main concern of DSR is to formalize that "practical knowledge" [18] and thus transform the design knowledge into more mature forms. Gregor et al. [19] describe those transformations in maturity level as "passive causal analysis", where the effects of unconscious design decisions unfold during the evaluation and "abstraction and reflection" as a process of transforming intentional design decisions into more abstract representations such as design principles. As DSR projects typically encompass several build/evaluate cycles [3] design knowledge can mature with each iteration.

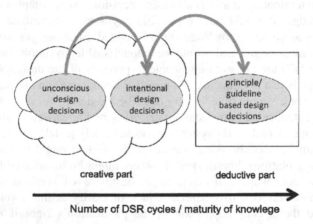

Number of DSR cycles / maturity of knowlege

**Fig. 1.** Flow of design decisions through maturity levels over time

However, to present a complete picture of the state of knowledge within a certain domain, we therefore see the need for a structure that allows the publication of a snapshot of the design-knowledge at any given time in a project in order to comprehensively describe the artifacts design rationales.

## 2.2    Design Principles as a way to Encapsulate Entities of Design Knowledge

To accomplish the task of encapsulating design knowledge of mixed levels of maturity and forms of contribution, we will use the concept of "design principles" as the primary format for formalizing design knowledge. At first glance, "design principles" seem to be a well-known and accepted form to convey design knowledge in design theories [10]. Gregor et al. acknowledge design principles as one way amongst others to communicate nascent design knowledge [8] as well as a corner piece of knowledge communication within mature design theories [9].

Van den Akker [20] offers the following generic structure of a design principle: "If you want to design intervention X (for the purpose/function Y in context Z), then you are best advised to give that intervention the characteristics A, B, and C (substantive emphasis), and to do that via procedures K, L, and M (procedural emphasis), because of arguments P, Q, and R." [20]. Depending on the nature of the design principle it may or may not be necessary to include both ABC as well as KLM. When the design principle focuses on process aspects KLM might be appropriated, where ABC may be more relevant when system features are to be described. PQR provide the grounding for the design principle.

However, this structure contains no explication of either the maturity level or the type of knowledge contribution per se. One candidate to operationalize the maturity level of a single design principle is its level of justification. For design principles used within design theories, Goldkuhl [18] suggests different forms of possible justification which he termed "grounding" that helps justify "theorized practical knowledge". The four grounding strategies are displayed in Figure 2 and a short summary of each strategy will be given in the following.

*Conceptual grounding:* Conceptual grounding is adequately expressed when all the concepts and phenomena related to a prescribed action and its goals are precisely defined through definitions and reasoning [18].

*Value grounding:* For every prescribed action a clear reference to an addressed goal should be presented, and, at the same time, the measure of goal achievement must be described [18].

*Explanatory grounding:* Justification for the prescriptive statements can be given through the incorporation of abstract theories, for example, like "kernel-theories" [18]. Kuechler et al. [17] provide a detailed description of how those external theories are epistemologically related with prescriptive or explanatory statements.

*Empirical grounding:* Through empirical grounding (in terms of instantiation and evaluation of the prescribed action) it can be investigated whether or not the prescribed action works in practice [18].

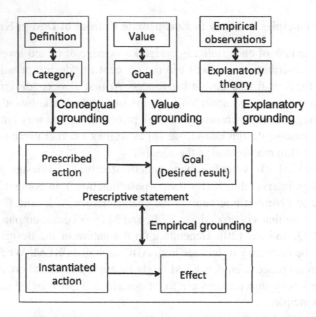

**Fig. 2.** Grounding of prescriptive statements (Goldkuhl [18])

As previously discussed, empirical grounding can be used to evaluate previously formalized design knowledge or give rise to completely new insights during the evaluation's execution [19]. From an epistemological point of view these are different evaluation strategies. Pries-Heje et al. [21] describe those different forms of evaluation for DSR projects in detail. An evaluation (in the sense of Goldkhul's empirical grounding) can only be of "ex-post" type, as the design principle has to be instantiated in the artifact to be testable. However, especially for multi-cycle DSR settings, the authors of [21] acknowledge the same evaluation also to be of the "ex-ante" type with respect to subsequent evaluations. To avoid any confusion within publication of DSR results, we see the need to clearly explicate the epistemological type of evaluation used, especially if one evaluation is used as "ex-post" type to provide empirical grounding as well as "ex-ante" type to derive new insights within the same publication.

## 3     Method

For this article, the method of design science research is applied, too. We follow the methodological step described by Peffers [4] involving the following activities: (1) *Problem identification and motivation*, (2) *Define the objectives for a solution*, (3) *Design and development*, (4) *Demonstration*, (5) *Evaluation*, (6) *Communication*. In this article, we apply this methodology as follows: In the introduction section we motivate (1) the problem from a practical perspective and define the central solution objective of the artifact. After reviewing the existing literature associated with the problem, we derive the requirements for the artifact (which is, in our case, the publication scheme) (2). Based on the background literature we develop the publication scheme (artifact) (3). We demonstrate (4) the artifact's applicability by following the publication scheme's structure with one of our previously published scholarly articles. The artifact is evaluated (5) by demonstrating one successful application with the aforementioned publication and by logic argumentation (discussion section) of why that artifact solves the described problems. This article fulfills the purpose of communicating the results (6).

# 4    Developing the Publication Schema

To guide the development of an appropriate publication scheme, we first synthesize a set of meta-requirements (MRQs), summing up our initial practical problem discussed within the context of the related work:

**MRQ1:** *The publication scheme shall allow the simultaneous presentation of design knowledge at different levels of maturity.*

**MRQ2:** *The scheme should clearly explicate the type of the contribution as well as the level of rigor that is available for each contribution to design knowledge.*

**MRQ3:** *The scheme should clearly explicate the selection process for the design knowledge.*

**MRQ4:** *The publication scheme shall allow the presentation of design knowledge from both, ex-ante and ex-post, abstractions simultaneously.*

To express the rationales for design decisions within a DSR project, we propose the structure in Figure 3. This structure emerged by combining the work of Walls et al. [16], Goldkuhl et al. [18], Gregor et al.[8, 19] and Kuechler et al. [17].  From top-down, and according to Walls et al.[16], *solution objectives* (SO) should be defined for the whole socio-technical system in question. A clear argumentation of why that objective is important in a certain context is mandatory. Walls et al. suggest to define the class of problems the design theory addresses through the definition of meta-requirements for the artifact. We argue, that Walls et al.'s meta-requirements are just refinements to the solution objectives as defined before. Thus they should be derivable from them. This is expressed in Figure 3 by the use of dashed arrows representing the semantics of "derived from" to link *meta-requirements* to solution objectives.

Continuing our description of Figure 3 from bottom-up, we now focus on *the instantiated design decisions*. Gregor et al. [8, 19] describe the different maturity levels for both, practical design decisions as well as for their abstract justification in the form of nascent theories containing principles or mature design theories. Kuechler et al.'s framework [17] promotes the different types of justificatory knowledge for a given artifact construction (meta-design). The interrelation of theory components and the other entities is represented by solid black arrows having the semantic of "justified by". "Unconscious design decisions" cannot be justified ex-ante by definition, as the designer was not even aware of them. However, they might still have an influence (represented by gray arrows) on the achievement of solution objectives.

Goldkuhl's grounding strategies (in particular value grounding) require a link between the principles (prescriptive statements) and the solution objectives (goals). However, as meta-requirements are already directly derived from the solution objective, they seem a good anchor point to which the value grounding should be attached to. The result is a directed graph (Figure 3) where ultimately for every design decision its contribution to a solution objective is traceable, thereby providing rigorous value grounding and also conceptual grounding by interrelating relevant concepts and phenomena within the shown hierarchy.

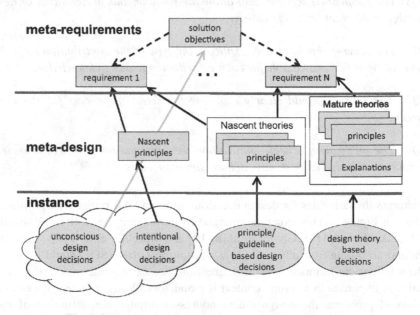

**Fig. 3.** Structure of entities within an immature DSR project

The central focus of this article is to cover as much of the design knowledge as possible through the formulation of design principles. Therefore, it should be an objective to provide as much grounding as possible, even for the nascent principles created through abstraction [19] from intentional design decisions. Besides the grounding provided by the described structure, further conceptual grounding can be performed by describing the domain's constructs and phenomena, the system is designed within [18], in detail. To ensure solid conceptual grounding, all those constructs and phenomena need to be defined properly. Empirical grounding can be achieved by applying the design principles in the course of the artifact's construction. Design principles are instantiated through design decision in the artifacts. Depending on the design of the evaluation, it might or might not be possible to provide direct empirical evidence to single design principles. Often, all design principles are applied altogether and the system is evaluated in terms of its solution objective achievement. This clearly is the weaker (implicit) form of empirical grounding but it is still valuable as a global indicator of success. But through observations, made during the course of evaluation, it might still be possible to draw inferences to particular design decisions, especially when they have led to problems or did not work as intended. Explanatory grounding provides one of the most rigorous forms of grounding. Strong logic argumentation and/or the use of external theories (kernel theories) [16, 18] can provide the required justification level here.

To sum up the discussion on grounding a single (nascent) design principle, we propose the structure presented in table 1 for the presentation of a multi-grounded design principle covering all described grounding strategies except of empirical grounding, because this requires the evaluation to have been executed.

**Table 1.** Proposed structure of a design principle

| Section | Contents |
|---|---|
| 1. Value grounding | Describe the requirement the principle should help to fulfill. |
| 2. Conceptual grounding | Make clear how the constructs used within the design principle interrelate with the domain objects. Clearly define any constructs not jet described. |
| 3. Explanatory grounding | If possible, provide explanations why the design principle should work in theory. Either justify the principle by logic argument or reference existing knowledge (maybe kernel theories) presented in the background section. |
| 4. Prescriptive statement | Precisely formulate an action that is applicable in the artifact's design. |

### 4.1 Proposed Adapted Publication Schema

To give practical advice on the publication of nascent design theories through design principles, we consolidate the previous aspects discussed into one publication schema. The aim was to merge the developed structures (figure 3 and table 1) into an existing, accepted and often cited publication scheme. The resulting scheme is an adapted version of Gregor et al.'s generic template for DSR publications [8] which has been extended (formatted in italics) to integrate the previously discussed constructs:

**Table 2.** Publication scheme adapted from Gregor et al. [8] (Extensions and refinements are formatted in italics)

| Section | Contents |
|---|---|
| 1. Introduction | Problem definition, problem significance/motivation, introduction to key concepts, research questions/objectives, scope of study, overview of methods and findings, theoretical and practical significance, structure of remainder of paper._Definition of the solution objectives (SOs) the intervention strives to achieve with a link to already described problems. The research gap should also be given here. An outlook to the scientific contribution that emerges should be given as an outlook for the paper's discussion._ |
| 2. Literature Review | Prior work that is relevant to the study, including theories, empirical research studies and findings/reports from practice._If existing design-principles or design theories are used, they have to be referenced here. As a conclusion of the literature review section, the gap in current literature should be stated._ |
| 3. Method | The research approach that was employed. |
| 4. Communication of design knowledge | _1. Meta-Requirements (MRQs) for the artifacts with clear reference to the SOs._  _2. A list of synthesized design principles (DPs) following the structure proposed in table 1. For each DP, its instantiation in the artifact should also be described here._  _4. Representation of the artifact as a whole as good as possible (screenshots of software, photographs of the environment it is supposed to be used within, etc.)_ |
| 5. Evaluation | _Presentation of the evaluation results. Presentation of data to support or reject the fulfillment of the SOs. If data is available to support or reject individual DPs it should be presented here._ |

**Table 2.** (*Continued.*)

| 6. Discussion | *1. Epistemologically close the loop between the sum of the design interventions and the achieved objectives.*<br><br>*2. If data (observations) are available that allow inferences on more detailed levels, link them back to MRQs or DPs whenever possible. If some of the design interventions did not work as intended, give possible explanations and point out further research opportunities.*<br><br>*3. If the evaluation motivates new design principle or refinements to previous ones (through the process of passive causal analysis [19]), derive new potential design principles (or refinements) here following the same structure as proposed in table 1. Of course in this case, empirical (ex-post) empirical grounding cannot be provided but may be subject for further research.* |
|---|---|
| 7. Conclusion | Concluding paragraphs that restate the important findings of the work.<br>Restates the main ideas in the contribution and why they are important. |

# 5    Application

To demonstrate how the publication schema could be applied in practices, we analyze one of our previous scholarly articles [15] that followed this structure. The article covers the topic of interpersonal relationship building when IT artifacts are collaboratively used in a dyadic setting. It communicates the results of a multi-cycle DSR project in the financial sector. In particular, that article contributes meta-requirements and design principles for IT-artifacts supporting interpersonal relationship building in financial advisory service encounter. As the research was carried out in a two-cycle DSR process, the scheme was slightly adapted to present the results in a cohesive manner. We will shortly discuss the structure of the article along the sections of the extended publication scheme (table 2):

***Introduction:*** In the introduction we briefly motivate the necessity to understand relationship-building in technology supported service encounters. A research question is formulated accordingly and a very rough outline of the paper is presented. Furthermore, the cyclic DSR setting is outlined and the specific structure of this DSR project is sketched as: build-evaluate (prototype 1) → abstraction & conceptualization → build/evaluate (prototype 2). As in this case the solution objective is justified by the empirical findings originating from the first evaluation, its presentation has been shifted to the "Communication of Design Knowledge" section.

*Literature Review:* The relevant literature covering the role of IT-artifacts in advisory encounters as well as literature covering relationship building in face-to-face collaboration is presented here. The design and primary evaluation of the first prototype was presented (in a seperate section) directly after the literature review part, as it was already published. However, for the purpose of that publication, the original evaluation of the first prototype was extended by the (previously unpublished) results regarding the failed relationship building aspect.

*Communication of Design Knowledge:* This section was split into two parts (meta-requirements / meta-design & instantiation) to ease the reading. In a first step, the solution objective of the artifact was presented: "Establish effortless relationship building in IT supported face2face advisory encounters". From there on, the (meta-) requirements are derived from three sources: existing literature, observations during the first evaluation, and a newly developed model of failed relationship building attempts. The derived requirements covered the design artifacts software, physical setting (environment), and process (organizational structure). Five meta-requirements were presented. One sample meta-requirement (originally called generic requirement in that article) governing the environmental aspects was: *"The physical effort to switch into the relationship building space has to be low. Avoid the need for body movement at all."* For each requirement, justification was given by means of referencing existing literature, the developed model or the evaluation observations (notably the first evaluation which was treated as an ex-ante evaluation).

In the meta-design & instantiation part, design-principles were presented and their instantiation within the artifact was described. Every design principle references at least one requirement and thereby provides value grounding. We strived for proper conceptual grounding by assuring that all constructs and entities were explained in the previous sections. Explanatory grounding was given in the form of logic argumentation. One sample design principle was: "Design-Principle 3 (to address generic requirement 3 and 5): Place the participants on adjacent sides around the table so that the RBS and AWS are reachable with minimal body and head movement. "[1]. Through the reference of the requirements value grounding is provided. To provide explanatory grounding, the relevant literature in the "literature-review" section is referenced directly with the design principle. To prepare the empirical grounding, explanations on the specific instantiation is given directly after the description of the principle: "[...] we raised the table by 15 cm to a comfortable height of approx. 70 cm. This allowed the participants to sit in a slightly tilted, diagonal position and use the table as an arm rest [...]. "

*Evaluation:* The evaluation contained a qualitative part of observations and interviews made with the participants as well as a quantitative measure of relationship building. Relationship building was operationalized indirectly by the time the participants mutually

---

[1] RBS and AWS are abbreviations of two (physical) states, participants could be within. Either a person works on the artifact (AWS) or he engages in relationship building (RBS) by seeking eye contact with the other person.

face gazed. From video recordings of the settings the gaze durations were sampled and compared between the two prototypes.

*Discussion:* In this section the results were discussed with respect to the overall solution objective as well as with respect to the previously defined requirements. We could demonstrate that the prototype, with our design principles implemented, could meet the solution objectives. However, a rigorous empirical grounding for individual design principles could not be achieved with the evaluation design used, as discussed in the limitations section.

# 6    Discussion and Conclusion

By applying the presented publication scheme, and its inner structure of the design principles to scholarly publications, we can address the practical problems discussed in the introduction. The problem of mixed knowledge maturity levels vanishes, as the scheme foresees design principles to communicate design knowledge, which can be formulated at all levels of maturity. The maturity of design principles can be explicated by their degree of justification, thereby not threatening the overall impression of rigor for the whole publication if only some design principles are immature. If all grounding strategies are successfully instantiated for all presented design principles, strongest rigor is demonstrated at this level. The selection of requirements for publications now follows a clear process: A requirement is included within a publication if design decisions (which are prescribed in the form of design principles) address it and at the same time the requirement is derivable from one or more of the presented solution objective. The structure explicitly foresees the communication of ex-ante and ex-post knowledge creation, while being always transparent on the rigor, and, thus, also on the maturity level of the communicated knowledge.

As we have shown in this article, it is likely for any practical DSR project to incorporate design knowledge on different levels of maturity on the meta-design level. However, also on the meta-requirements level, knowledge of different maturity levels can be incorporated. In the case of this article, the meta-requirements are derived form practical problems and gaps in the current literature. All meta-requirements address the central solution objective to "foster the publication of nascent design knowledge in scholarly publications".

From a DSR perspective, this article can also be seen as a nascent design theory by itself. This article provides central design principles on how to publish nascent design theories. The statement "Use the proposed structure in order to publish design knowledge" is prescriptive in a way that it suggests an action and formulates the desired goal. We provided proper grounding throughout the article by applying the described grounding methods: First, by a clear introduction of the relevant concepts based on existing literature. Second, conceptual grounding was provided for all relevant constructs used in the publication scheme. Third, value grounding was achieved by describing a desired goal, motivated by practical problems, and why that goal is important to the community. Fourth, only little explanatory grounding is provided, as it would involve theoretical models of how the publication process within the scientific community works and why. Most reasoning for the structure and constructs within the scheme are therefore of "conceptual grounding" or "value grounding" type. Empirical grounding is provided in the form of "proof by construction" [22] (also mentioned in Hevner [2]), as we presented one article that we could published with that structure applied.

Nevertheless, the empirical grounding in this article has to be treated as ex-ante evaluation because a large empirical base of published (or rejected) articles is still missing. Hence the design knowledge communicated within this article is at an intermediate maturity level and further research might be necessary to provide stronger (i.e. empirical) justification as well as refinements and adaptions to the described publication schema following the spirit of DSR as a "search process" carried out by the community.

In this paper we have discussed several practical writing problems of DSR related articles. By reviewing publication guidelines found in current literature, we identified a lack of specificity to describe design knowledge of practical DSR projects. Based on the literature on the concepts and methods of design research we derived a conceptual framework to arrange the knowledge entities within a publication (figure 3) in order to foster "conceptual grounding" [18] and "value grounding" [18] within those publications. The central entities of that schema are design principles as a way of formalizing design knowledge as prescriptive statements. We then applied the notion of multi-grounding from Goldkuhl et al. [18] to express the maturity level of a single design principle in terms of its "degree of grounding". To anchor those multi-grounded knowledge descriptions within a publication schema, we extended an existing scheme [8]. As a first instantiation, we could present one scholarly article that has been published following the prescribed structure. Hence, with this article we contribute a publication scheme that addresses our practical publication problems by providing a step-by-step guideline to publish design knowledge at any level of maturity and in any stage for practical DSR projects on innovative IT artifacts.

# References

1. Winter, R.: Design science research in Europe. Eur. J. Inf. Syst. 17, 470–475 (2008)
2. Hevner, A.R., March, S.T., Park, J., Ram, S.: Design Science in Information Sys-tems Research. MIS Q. 28, 75–105 (2004)
3. Hevner, A.R.: The three cycle view of design science research. Scand. J. Inf. Syst. 19, 87 (2007)
4. Peffers, K., Tuunanen, T., Rothenberger, M.A., Chatterjee, S.: A design science research methodology for information systems research. J. Manag. Inf. Syst. 24, 45–77 (2007)
5. Reinecke, K., Bernstein, A.: Knowing What a User Likes: A Design Science Ap-proach to Interfaces that Automatically Adapt to Culture. MIS Q. 37, 427–453 (2013)
6. Hevner, A., Chatterjee, S.: Introduction to Design Science Research. Design Research in Information Systems, pp. 1–8. Springer US (2010)
7. Baskerville, R.: What design science is not. Eur. J. Inf. Syst. 17, 441–443 (2008)
8. Gregor, S., Hevner, A.R.: Positioning and presenting design science research for maximum impact. Manag. Inf. Syst. Q. 37, 337–355 (2013)

9. Jones, D., Gregor, S.: The Anatomy of a Design Theory. J. Assoc. Inf. Syst. 8, 1 (2007)
10. Gregor, S.: The Nature of Theory in Information Systems. MIS Q. 30, 611–642 (2006)
11. Novak, J., Schwabe, G.: Designing for reintermediation in the brick-and-mortar world: Towards the travel agency of the future. Electron. Mark. 19, 15–29 (2009)
12. Schmidt-Rauch, S., Schwabe, G.: From telesales to tele-advisory in travel agen-cies: Business problems, generic design goals and requirements. ACM Trans. Manag. Inf. Syst. TMIS. 2, 17 (2011)
13. Nussbaumer, P., Matter, I., Schwabe, G.: "Enforced" vs. "Casual". Transparency – Findings from IT-Supported Financial Advisory Encounters. ACM Trans Manage Inf Syst. 3, 11:1–11:19 (2012)
14. Nussbaumer, M.P., Matter, D.I.I., à Porta, G.R., Schwabe, G.: Designing for Cost Transparency in Investment Advisory Service Encounters. Bus. Inf. Syst. Eng. 4, 347–361 (2012)
15. Heinrich, P., Kilic, M., Aschoff, F.-R., Schwabe, G.: Enabling Relationship Building in Tabletop-supported Advisory Settings. In: Proceedings of the 17th ACM Conference on Computer Supported Cooperative Work & Social Computing, pp. 171–183. ACM, New York (2014)
16. Walls, J., Widmeyer, G.: ElSawy: Building an Information System Design Theory for Vigilant EIS. Inf. Syst. Res. 3, 36–59 (1992)
17. Kuechler, W., Vaishnavi, V.: A Framework for Theory Development in Design Science Research: Multiple Perspectives. J. Assoc. Inf. Syst. 13 (2012)
18. Goldkuhl, G.: Design Theories in Information Systems - A Need for Multi-Grounding. J. Inf. Technol. Theory Appl. JITTA 6 (2004)
19. Gregor, S., Müller, O., Seidel, S.: Reflection, Abstraction And Theorizin. In: De-sign and Development Research. In: ECIS 2013 Complet. Res. (2013)
20. Van den Akker, J.: Principles and methods of development research. Design approaches and tools in education and training, pp. 1–14. Springer (1999)
21. Pries-Heje, J., Baskerville, R., Venable, J.: Strategies for Design Science Re-search Evaluation. In: ECIS 2008 Proc. (2008)
22. Nunamaker Jr., J.F., Chen, M.: Systems development in information systems research. In: Proceedings of the Twenty-Third Annual Hawaii International Conference on System Sciences, pp. 631–640. IEEE (1990)

# A Self-Service MSS Design from a New-Generation Manager Perspective

Jörg H. Mayer[1], André Röder[2], Jens Hartwig[2], and Reiner Quick[2]

[1] University of St.Gallen, Institute of Information Management,
Müller-Friedberg-Strasse 8, 9000 St.Gallen, Switzerland
joerg.mayer@unisg.ch
[2] Darmstadt University of Technology, Chair of Accounting and Auditing,
Hochschulstrasse 1, 64289 Darmstadt, Germany
{a.roeder,jens.hartwig}@stud.tu-darmstadt.de,
quick@bwl.tu-darmstadt.de

**Abstract.** More and more digital natives are populating the management levels of organizations. As such managers have higher expectations toward information systems (IS) accommodating their user self-service preferences, a more business-driven requirements analysis for management support systems (MSS) plays an increasingly dominant role. The objective of this paper is to develop both a set of MSS requirements that is more business-driven than the state of the art and—applying this approach—initial design guidelines for a new self-service MSS design. We demonstrate utility with a single-case study, evaluate our approach against the state of the art, and propose avenues for future research. The findings should lead to a better MSS design and be applicable to other IS domains as well.

**Keywords:** New-generation managers, management support systems (MSS), management reporting, information systems (IS) analysis and design, self-service IS, requirements analysis, principle of economic efficiency.

## 1    Design Problem

*Management support systems* (MSS) are information systems (IS) which are intended to support managerial work [1]. As an umbrella term, MSS covers management information systems (MIS), decision support systems (DSS), executive information systems (EIS), and—more recently—knowledge management systems (KMS) and business intelligence (BI) systems for managers [2]. Besides planning and preparing financial statements [3], the most important MSS function is (management) reporting [4].

Accommodating *user preferences* is particularly important for MSS design because the higher managers are positioned within an organization, the more likely they have multifaceted work experience that nurtures a highly individual attitude toward IS [5]. User preferences in IS research describe differences in the ways individuals want to use IS and have been a research topic since the 1970s. Mayer et al. [6] outline that, as

M.C. Tremblay et al. (Eds.): DESRIST 2014, LNCS 8463, pp. 164–179, 2014.

early as 1979, Zmud [7] asserts that "individual differences do exert a major force in determining IS success," for example, the technology acceptance model [8] and the IS success model [9] prove that user preferences play a predominant role in IS success.

Redesigning MSS is currently an interesting subject for two reasons: Firstly, digital natives increasingly populate organizations along with digital immigrants, who learned to engage with IS as adults and developed into mobile IS users over the years [10]. These new-generation managers make decisions faster than they have in the past [11] and want *self-service MSS* to support them to do so [11, 12]. Secondly, thanks to technical progress such as multi-touch, direct-manipulation user interfaces in recent years, even senior managers should be able to operate IS themselves [13]. Under these considerations, we state our research questions as follows:

- What is a *set of requirements* that is more business-driven than the state of the art?
- Applying this approach, what are *initial design guidelines* for a new self-service MSS design?

In our context, business-driven means that we derive requirements from new generation managers which are not only conceptually or technically possible but also economically feasible.

We follow design science research (DSR) in IS [14] and apply Peffers et al.'s [15] six-step process model. We motivate our research by identifying gaps in MSS design for new-generation managers and suggest a more business-driven set of requirements to address them (Sect. 1). After that, we reflect the state of the art and derive a future MSS research agenda (Sect. 2). Then, we propose a set of business-driven MSS evaluation criteria (Sect. 3), demonstrate utility of our proposal in a case study (Sect. 4), and—applying this approach—conclude with initial design guidelines for a new self-service MSS design. We evaluate our approach against the state of the art (Sect. 5) and suggest avenues for future research (Sect. 6).

## 2 Literature Review

### 2.1 Search Strategy

Following vom Brocke et al.'s four step process for literature research [16], we started with a *journal search*. As Webster and Watson [17] claim that major contributions are in the leading outlets, we chose IS outlets provided by the London School of Economics [18]. The search was based on the three *scholarly databases* AIS Electronic Library, EBSCOhost, ProQuest and we considered title and abstract. In addition, the standard Google search was used to cover recent practitioner contributions. With just six publications, our first *keyword search* focused on MSS and management reporting leads to an inadequate number and content to start our research (marked with "*" in the appendix "publications researched in the literature review").

Thus, we did both expanding our journal base with six ranked accounting journals[1] and complementing our search string. Based on prior research [19] our new keyword search (Table 1) within the new journal base yielded a total of 759 hits. After qualifying their titles, we end up with 60 hits. We scanned their abstracts and ended with 46 publications in total. A final *back and forward search* revealed 63 relevant publications (see appendix).

**Table 1.** Keyword search string

<table>
<tr><td colspan="2"></td><td colspan="6" align="center">OR</td></tr>
<tr>
<td rowspan="4">AND</td>
<td></td>
<td>Management support system</td>
<td>Executive information System</td>
<td>Management accounting system</td>
<td>(Group) Decision support system</td>
<td>Management information systems</td>
<td>Business intelligence</td>
</tr>
<tr>
<td rowspan="3">OR</td>
<td>Schedule</td>
<td>Stakeholder</td>
<td>Recipients</td>
<td></td>
<td>Management board</td>
<td>Board of directors</td>
</tr>
<tr>
<td>Management accounting</td>
<td>Requirements</td>
<td>Reporting</td>
<td></td>
<td>Report</td>
<td>Management</td>
</tr>
</table>

## 2.2　Framework for Classification

We structured the publications we examined in terms of the elements of IS design they employ and the meta categories of research in which they can be located.

**A. Elements of IS design** [20]: (1) *User requirements* are prerequisites, conditions or capabilities needed by managers using IS to solve a problem or achieve an objective [21]. They can be considered from both a functional and non-function perspective [22]. Functional requirements address "what" IS are supposed to or must do (purpose). Non-functional requirements, in contrast, reflect "how well" IS performs within its environment fulfilling its function [23]. (2) *Design guidelines* go beyond requirements to serve as predefined actions specifying how MSS are brought to life [24]. They cover the span from a generic type [14] to a more in-depth IS specification we propose in this paper. Models outline IS features or combinations of these [25]. Complementary methods describe the process of designing MSS [26]. (3) A more *business-driven IS design* should cover a user analysis segmenting user groups and different user group characteristics that influence managers' MSS use. The effects of use occurring to managers while using IS, complement our framework for literature research for a better MSS design proposal [27, 28].

**B. Meta categories of research:** Publications can be classified by their basic research approach and scientific domain. (4) The *research approach* covers twofold. Publications with a behavioral focus explain phenomena from practice and rely on observations as well as empirical methods. Design approaches involve ideas and frameworks for IS recommendations to create a better world [14, 20]. (5) Another relevant classification in our work is the *research domain* in which the researched publications are released. Since MSS levitate between the domains of management literature and IS we chose these domains as our categories. Figure 1 depicts our results.

---

[1] Accounting Review, Contemporary Accounting Research, Journal of Accounting Research, Management Accounting Research, Review of Accounting Studies, and Journal of Management Accounting Research.

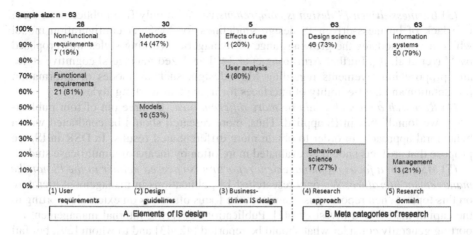

**Fig. 1.** Classification of the publications within our framework

## 2.3    Results: Current Shortcomings and Future Research Agenda

Our researched state of the art is shown in Figure 1 and we discuss the shortcomings as follows: (1) *Lack of MSS user requirements focusing on management reporting:* 21 of 63 publications focus on functional MSS requirements and seven of 63 on non-functional MSS requirements. However, there are various requirements for individual MSS aspects which do not focus on management reporting. For example, Tricker [29] describes manager information needs without stating specific reporting requirements. Both, Aders et al. [30] and Cheung and Babin [31] focus on individual aspects for decision-making, such as the right selection of data sources and KPIs, but they do not integrate these into the holistic concept of MSS.

The researched publications focus on the graphical design of MSS [32] and the ability to guide users within MSS. Furthermore, the researched list approaches lack a rigorous framework for requirements development and are most often incomplete. Existing studies [33] fail to provide an applicable set of MSS requirements with a rigorous basis. Finally, the researched requirements lists are most often outdated [34, 35] and do not cover the requirements of new-generation managers [36]. Thus, more current studies are needed.

*(2) Lack of MSS design guidelines for management reporting applying new IT-enabler:* 14 out of 63 publications cover methods which describe how to build MSS. 16 out of 63 publication focus on models. For example, Mayer [11] describes which areas should be reported and what they cover contentwise. Other publications emphasize the use of individual methods like environmental scanning [37], exception reporting [38] or real-time technologies [39] in the context of MSS. No publications provide comprehensive guidelines which serve as a suitable starting point for building a modern self-service MSS with a focus on management reporting. Marx et al. [36] is the only publication which build a rigorous criteria list and derived multiple principles for MSS design. However, they did not consider new-generation managers and new IT-enablers.

*(3) Business-driven IS design is comprehensive:* With only five publications, there is a lack of business-driven IS design guidelines for MSS. A configuration model which accommodates the growing range of managerial working styles was proposed by Mayer et al. [6]. Further Armstrong et al. [40] analyzed managers' cognitive styles and propose improvements regarding MSS design, such as modes of information presentation and the flexibility of interfaces for individual working styles.

*(4) Research approach could be more differentiated:* In three out of four publications, we found DSR in IS applied. Thus, more research should be conducted with a behavioral approach, in order to obtain more differentiated results. In DSR in IS, we propose that artifacts should be evaluated more often by means of a multi-case study.

*(5) MSS with a focus on management reporting is covered neither in the IS nor the management literature:* We only researched 13 publications in management literature on this topic. When reporting is examined, the focus often lies on external reporting to the capital market and investors [41]. Publications covering internal management reporting generally consider what should be reported [42, 43] and to whom [29], but fail to describe how this should be done. This outlines a lack of MSS literature focusing on management reporting regarding requirements and guidelines.

Summarizing our findings, there is a lack of a rigorous, ready-to-use set of business-driven user requirements from a new-generation manager business perspective with a distinct selection of criteria. Furthermore, initial guidelines for self-service MSS with focus on management reporting are also conspicuously absent.

# 3     Alternative Method

## 3.1     Principle of Economic Efficiency

The principle of economic efficiency is a well-known paradigm in business research which addresses the ratio between benefit and cost [44]. Thus, we propose business-driven evaluation criteria for MSS in contradiction to list approaches, structured equation models (SEM), TAM and IS success models. They should be oriented towards what is economically feasible (benefit-cost ratio) and not what is conceptually or technically possible. The following section is based on our prior research [19, 45].

Even if the IS costs can be identified by nature and amount, the ability to quantify IS value is limited [46]. Applying the "black-box method" [47] we differentiate between the basic criteria of IS output and input (Fig. 1). *System capabilities* (IS output) refer to the relevance of MSS to support managers' information needs.

*Resource requirements* (IS input), in turn, refer to the input needed to generate the IS output, such as primary information and manpower in terms of cost and time.

## 3.2     First Level of Specification: Design Criteria

We specify IS output by four design criteria following the St.Gallen Business Engineering approach [48] and Mayer et al.'s instantiation for MSS design [11, 19, 49].

The first layer of our design criteria, *strategic positioning* ("what" question) describes what purpose MSS fulfills accommodating different user requirements. In the *conceptual design* layer ("how" question) we describe MSS reports threefold regarding their content, visualization ("look & feel"), and process. The layer of *business/IT alignment* focuses on the flexibility of the underlying IT accommodating changing requirements within the layers above. In our context this layer covers the capability to handle changing information requirements and working styles in a timely manner [50]. *IT components* focus on the contribution of new IT-enablers for MSS design. By doing so, this fourth and final layer answers the "what with" question. IS standard components such as data warehouses are not examined, since they should not differ in detail and thus this aspect should be less interesting for research.

IS input specifies the required resources and therefore the effort to design MSS.

### 3.3    Second Level of Specification: Evaluation Criteria

While the design criteria remain at a more general level, we specify MSS evaluation criteria (EC) for all design criteria. They are derived from our literature review (Sect. 3), complemented by findings from both an expert focus group consisting of heads of management accounting or group business intelligence of large international companies from the competence center "corporate management systems" at the University of St.Gallen [51], and from our single-case study (Sect. 4).

The *MSS purpose* (EC 1) can be specified in terms of its recipient in the company. Besides management, we researched supervisory boards and parties responsible for external communication (e.g., investor relations) as complementary stakeholders of MSS design [29, 52, 53]. This criterion is rated by the scope of the report recipients, consistency, and synergetic efficiency.

The reporting content can be specified by four evaluation criteria. Firstly, the selection of *key performance indicators* (KPIs, EC 2) is evaluated in terms of its completeness in several information categories: profit and loss statement, balance sheet, cash flow statement, value-based management (including a value driver tree for traceability), as well as the current use of non-financial indicators [11, 30, 54]. Secondly, we take into account the extent to which the *information clusters* of financial accounting, management accounting, cash flow and liquidity management, compliance management and program management are covered [11, 55]. Furthermore, the KPIs are analyzed regarding their *dimensions of analysis* (e.g., divisional or regional) and temporal reference (i.e. actual or forecast, EC 3). The criterion is rated by the completeness of coverage of the mentioned information clusters, adequate information breakdowns, as well as a solid mixture of actual, planned and forecast values. The last criterion in this category, *advanced performance management* (EC 4), covers the use of ancillary reporting concepts like compliance/risk management, environmental scanning systems, and exception reporting [37, 38, 56]. The level of completeness of the aforementioned concepts is used for the rating.

To assess the visualization capabilities, we evaluate the *graphic design and data visualization* of MSS (EC 5) in terms of layout and the use of different types of information media like mobile devices and static documents [13], the existence of different types of dialog control [32], the use of different graphic types with or without interaction [32, 57], as well as self-service user guidance.

The MSS *reporting process* (EC 6) is evaluated by means of the reporting schedule which covers when recipients receive which report version, such as flashes (a shorter or preliminary report) or final reports [58]. The earlier the management receives the MSS information, the more time it has for decision-making.

Business/IT-alignment is appraised by the customization capabilities and we propose specifying IS flexibility. EC7 explores the question of how *flexible* MSS can accommodate individual information requirements [57] and working styles [6].

IT components evaluate the use of new IT-enablers in MSS design. This includes *mobile (MSS) use scenarios* (EC 8) focusing on the management reporting [59, 60]. Different *information media* (e.g., paper, PDF, website) are also evaluated (EC 9) [61]. Furthermore, *collaboration/commenting* (EC 10) features are rated by their capability to cover commenting and newer technologies such as RSS feeds or instant messaging [62, 63]. The final criteria in this layer evaluate the coverage of *real-time management* leveraging in-memory technologies (EC 11) [39, 64], as well as *predictive analytics on big data* (EC 12) [33, 65] in terms of their completeness and benefits.

Finally the *effort* (EC 13) consists of cost (i.e. budget spent on the MSS conceptual design, implementation, and maintenance of the IS) and time, i.e. time spent generating the most important MSS reports [66, 67].

**Table 2.** Evaluation criteria for MSS design

| Principle of economic efficiency | Design criteria | | Evaluation criteria | | | Description |
|---|---|---|---|---|---|---|
| Solution capabilities (IS output) | Strategic positioning (WHAT) | Purpose | EC | 1 | Stakeholder and complementary reports for additional recipients [29, 52, 53] | • Who are the recipients of the report? <br> • What is the coverage and volume of the reports? |
| | Conceptual design (HOW) | Content | EC | 2 | Key performance indicators (KPIs) [11, 30, 54] | • What KPIs are primarily used? <br> • Are they traceable by a value-driver-tree? |
| | | | EC | 3 | Dimensions of analysis [11] | • Which information clusters are covered? <br> • How are the performance indicators split up? <br> • What is their temporal reference? |
| | | | EC | 4 | Advanced performance management [37, 38, 56] | • Which ancillary concepts are applied in the management reports? Compliance/Risk management, environmental scanning? <br> • Exception reporting: Is it possible to define exceptions? |
| | | Visualization | EC | 5 | Graphical design and data visualization [32, 57, 68] | • How is the first "look&feel" and is the basic screen design consistent? <br> • Which types of (interactive) graphics are used? <br> • Are drill-functionalities, filter, and sorting mechanisms supported? |
| | | Process | EC | 6 | Reporting process [58] | • When are which reports provided to recipients? <br> • When do the recipients discuss the reports? |
| | Business/IT-alignment | Flexibility | EC | 7 | Flexibility [6, 57] | • How flexible is the MSS for accommodating individual information requirements and working styles? |

**Table 2.** (*Continued.*)

| | IT components (WHAT WITH) | New IT-enabler | EC | 8 | Mobile use scenarios [59, 60] | • How comfortable is it to adapt stationary desktop design to smart devices (e.g., report transformation for smart devices)? |
|---|---|---|---|---|---|---|
| | | | EC | 9 | Information media [61] | • Are there different information media (Paper, PDF, web, app) available to the recipients? |
| | | | EC | 10 | Collaboration/ commenting [62, 63] | • Is it possible to add comments to support collaboration across the company? |
| | | | EC | 11 | Real-time management [39, 64] | • Is in-memory technology used to foster new kind of insights or faster processes? |
| | | | EC | 12 | Predictive analytics on big data [33, 65] | • Are techniques from statistics, modeling, machine learning and data mining integrated into big data? |
| Resource requirements (IS input) | Effort | Adequacy | EC | 13 | Cost and time adequacy [66, 67] | • What is the budget and time allocation for MSS design and implementation?<br>• What is the budget and time allocation for on MSS operation and maintenance? |

## 4    Demonstrate

We demonstrate the utility of our findings by means of a *single-case study* and—applying our approach—conclude with some initial design guidelines for a new MSS design. We chose a case study approach, because it examines real-life situations and, thus tests the utility of artefacts for "creating a better world" [20]. A single-case study examines a subject in-depth and is therefore useful when a phenomenon is broad and complex. However, a case study approach is prone to bias as a result of subjectivity, which has been addressed by the authors accordingly, as described below.

We applied our set of requirements (Sect. 5) to a large raw materials and technology company (2012, revenue: USD 40 bn.; employees: 156,000). This company was selected, because its MSS capabilities have recently been reworked and should thus be a representative state of the art from practice.

The objective of the project was to evaluate the MSS status with a focus on management reporting and to investigate the benefit of new IT-enablers such as mobile or predictive analysis. We used a five-point Likert scale [69] to evaluate the company's MSS EC by EC (Table 1). The first point on the Likert scale indicates that the EC is not fulfilled at all, while a "five point" rating shows that it is achieved completely.

A team of three researchers (authors of this paper) and three company representatives—the heads of management accounting, planning, and risk, as well as the head of group reporting—were present at all times to reduce *misunderstandings*, *subjectivity*, and ensure a *comprehensive documentation* (i.e. transcript of audio recording) of all relevant information. We chose the following approach for our data collection: (1) Basic presentation of the MSS by the company's representatives and joint "Q&A" with the researchers to provide a general understanding, (2) analysis of the (monthly) top management report and the associated executive summary ("front page"), (3) a semi-structured detailed interview using our criteria list, explaining each EC, and letting the company representatives respond, followed by two feedback rounds to discuss certain topics in-depth, (4) presenting our findings to the representatives and giving them the opportunity to discuss the outcome, (5) final (minor) adjustments by the researchers. The findings lead to the following design guidelines for a new MSS design:

(1) *Value-driver trees are losing relevance (EC2)—an EBIT decomposition is gaining importance.* Detailed value-driver trees (with regard to value-based management) are no longer in the focus of new-generation managers, instead, EBIT (earnings before interest and taxes) decomposition is becoming more significant. A visual decomposition into the components could help managers to understand the individual impact factors on the final KPI.

(2) *Exception reporting currently uses separate information media (EC4)— therefore MSS should be able to send proactive "push" information when a certain threshold is crossed.* In order to use MSS as a single "point of truth," we propose an integration of exception reporting. The manager could set different thresholds for performance indicators and is notified if the threshold is exceeded. He or she is then able to perform an instant analysis and reply with edits or comments, without leaving the app.

(3) *"Modern" graphics are lacking (EC5)—a table-centric reporting can be enriched by (micro)charts.* Microcharts offer, within a small space (especially relevant for mobile MSS devices), a good overview of recent developments and contextual information. In addition, they can reveal even more details on demand, by showing tooltips.

(4) *There is a lack of leveraging for the new IT-enabler (EC8-12)—"mobile" is on the list for 2014 as most important.* The company neither uses mobile devices to support their managers, nor any kind of in-memory technology to accelerate its reporting process or enable new insight analyses. An implementation of mobile use with tablets is planned, so as to facilitate self-service use of the MSS.

(5) *Commenting/collaboration functions are lacking (EC10)—different media and commenting/collaboration features should be integrated into MSS.* A basic commenting function for every KPI would be a first step, especially with regard to the growing self-service use of MSS. The managers can use the functions to check back with the accountants, and for discussions with other managers or annotations for upcoming meetings (e.g., monthly regional meeting).

Evaluating *time & cost adequacy (EC13)*, the application of our method was limited. The company could no longer quantify their expenses for the MSS in retrospect and —looking forward to a multi-case study—such information is too sensitive to share. We propose that this is not a major issue with respect to the applicability of our method, because the costs of new MSS designs can be calculated and are usable for internal consideration.

As a result, the researched company is taking our findings for further MSS development. Especially in aspects where the current MSS performed subnormally, changes are required. Therefore, these findings can be used as a set of requirements for the evaluation of MSS frontend applications for mobile and stationary usage.

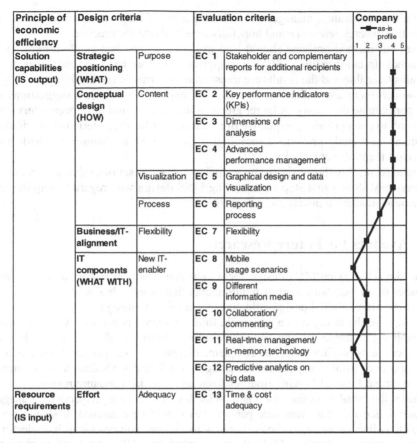

| Principle of economic efficiency | Design criteria | | Evaluation criteria | | Company as-is profile 1 2 3 4 5 |
|---|---|---|---|---|---|
| Solution capabilities (IS output) | Strategic positioning (WHAT) | Purpose | EC 1 | Stakeholder and complementary reports for additional recipients | |
| | Conceptual design (HOW) | Content | EC 2 | Key performance indicators (KPIs) | |
| | | | EC 3 | Dimensions of analysis | |
| | | | EC 4 | Advanced performance management | |
| | | Visualization | EC 5 | Graphical design and data visualization | |
| | | Process | EC 6 | Reporting process | |
| | Business/IT-alignment | Flexibility | EC 7 | Flexibility | |
| | IT components (WHAT WITH) | New IT-enabler | EC 8 | Mobile usage scenarios | |
| | | | EC 9 | Different information media | |
| | | | EC 10 | Collaboration/ commenting | |
| | | | EC 11 | Real-time management/ in-memory technology | |
| | | | EC 12 | Predictive analytics on big data | |
| Resource requirements (IS input) | Effort | Adequacy | EC 13 | Time & cost adequacy | |

**Fig. 2.** Evaluation of the company's MSS according to our criteria list (case study results)

## 5    Evaluate

To evaluate our approach on hand, we differentiate between rigor and relevance [70]. *Relevance* is given when the research addresses the problems faced and the opportunities afforded by the interaction of people, organizations, and IT [14]. *Rigor* is achieved through application of scientific theories, methods, experience, and expertise [71]. Comparing our findings and associated lessons learned from the case study with the state of the art (Sect. 2) we can discuss our approach as follows:

The *principle of economic efficiency* enjoys broad acceptance in business management research. Thus, it marks a rigorous (and generally accepted) starting point for requirements analysis structuring the examined requirements criteria [45]. This should be true for developing EC which are based on the findings from a *literature review* and complemented by findings from a manager expert group. This two-sided approach should lead to a relatively complete set of distinct requirements.

This paper confronts organizational changes in management (the upcoming digital natives) and MSS accommodating the rising self-service issues and increasing mobility of a new-generation managers. Developing a set of MSS requirements from their perspective ensures *relevance* and hopefully direct advice for practice.

Thus, our method on hand should lead to better results than single criteria or list approaches. In comparison to SEM, our approach is more hands-on, however, it still maintains traceable and the results are transparent in terms of intelligibility.

However, there are limitations as well. The expert focus group's suggestions can only approximate the reality. A larger group of managers could have been interviewed on-the-job to get a broader perspective of requirements for the criteria list. Additionally a single-case study prevents a meaningful quantitative evaluation and with just a single case it entails subjectivity.

Summarizing this short evaluation, we believe that our set of evaluation criteria for self-service MSS is a first step to improving MSS design with regard to requirements from a new-generation managers' perspective.

# 6    Avenues for Future Research

Taking the self-service MSS design for a new-generation managers as an example, this paper developed both a set of requirements that is more business-driven than the state-of-the-art and initial design guidelines for an new IS design.

To improve the utility of our approach, future research is needed. A first avenue is to complete the single-case profile with findings from a *multi-case study*. Furthermore, these as-is profiles should be complemented with a *to-be profile*. It should cover the perspectives from new-generation managers on future MSS design or summarize most important forward-looking findings from an expanded literature review.

Besides the initial guidelines for a new MSS design (software perspective), managers' *end-user device selection* (hardware perspective) should be examined. It should not be difficult to define a company's choice, but how to examine patterns for such a selection is likely to be more challenging [6]. Furthermore, managers' *MSS use situations* should be captured more in detail. Gender, age, temperament, self-efficacy in IS knowledge, expertise, and prior IS experience could be taken into account, as well as cultural factors.

The *functional perspective* on MSS design should be specified as well, especially whether there are changes due to the 2008/2009 economic crisis and the ongoing financial turbulences in Europe [11]. Last, but not least, the approach on hand has been applied to MSS design as an example. However, as another avenue of future research, the findings should be applicable to other IS domains as well.

# References

1. Carlsson, S.A., Henningsson, S., Hrastinski, S., Keller, C.: An Approach for Designing Management Support Systems: The Design Science Research Process and its Outcomes. In: Vaishanvi, V., Baskerville, R., Purao, S. (eds.) Fourth International Conference on Design Science Research in Information Systems and Technology (DESRIST), pp. 1–10. ACM Press, Malvern (2009)
2. Clark Jr., T.D., Jones, M.C., Armstrong Curtis, P.: The Dynamic Structure of Management Support Systems: Theory Development, Research Focus, and Direction. MIS Quarterly 31(3), 579–615 (2007)

3. Marx, F., Wortmann, F., Mayer, J.H.: A Maturity Model for Management Control Systems - Five Evolutionary Steps to Guide Development. Business & Information Systems Engineering 4(4), 193–207 (2012)
4. Arnott, D., Pervan, G.: A Critical Analysis of Decision Support Systems Research. Journal of Information Technology 20(2), 67–87 (2005)
5. Winter, R.: Design of Situational Artefacts—Conceptual Foundations and Their Application to IT/Business Alignment. In: Pokorny, J., Repa, V., Richta, K., Wojtkowski, W., Linger, H., Barry, C., Lang, M. (eds.) Information Systems Development, pp. 35–49. Springer, New York (2011)
6. Mayer, J.H., Winter, R., Mohr, T.: Situational Management Support Systems. Business & Information Systems Engineering 4(6), 331–345 (2012)
7. Zmud, R.W.: Individual Differences and MIS Success: A Review of the Empirical Literature. Management Science 25(10), 966–979 (1979)
8. Davis, F.D.: Perceived Usefulness, Perceived Ease of Use, and User Acceptance of Information Technology. MIS Quartely 13(3), 319–340 (1989)
9. DeLone, W.H., McLean, E.R.: The DeLone and McLean Model of Information Systems Success: A Ten-Year Update. Journal of Management Information Systems 19(4), 9–30 (2003)
10. Vodanovich, S., Sundaram, D., Myers, M.: Digital Natives and Ubiquitous Information Systems. Information Systems Research 21(4), 711–723 (2010)
11. Mayer, J.H.: Current Changes in Executive Work and How to Handle Them by Redesigning Executive Information Systems. In: Mancini, D., Vaassen, E., Dameri, R.P. (eds.) Accounting Information Systems for Decision Making, vol. 3, pp. 151–173. Springer, Heidelberg (2013)
12. Stodder, D.: Achieving Greater Agility with Business Intelligence: Improving Speed and Flexibility for BI, Analytics, and Data Warehousing. TDWI Report, Renton, USA (2013)
13. Wixom, B.H., Watson, H.J.: The BI-Based Organization. International Journal of Business Intelligence Research 1(1), 13–28 (2010)
14. Hevner, A.R., March, S.T., Park, J., Ram, S.: Design Science in Information Systems Research. MIS Quarterly 28(1), 75–105 (2004)
15. Peffers, K., Tuunanen, T., Gengler, C.E., Rossi, M., Hui, W., Virtanen, V., Bragge, J.: The Design Science Research Process: A Model for Producing and Presenting Information Systems Research. In: 1st International Conference on Design Science in Information Systems and Technology (DESRIST), pp. 83–106. Claremont Graduate University, Claremont (2006)
16. vom Brocke, J., Simons, A., Niehaves, B., Riemer, K., Plattfaut, R., Cleven, A.: Reconstructing the Giant: On the Importance of Rigour in Documenting the Literature Search Process. In: Newell, S., Whitley, E., Pouloudi, N., Wareham, J., Mathiassen, L. (eds.) 17th European Conference on Information Systems (ECIS), Verona, pp. 2206–2217 (2009)
17. Webster, J., Watson, R.T.: Analyzing the Past to Prepare for the Future: Writing a Literature Review. MIS Quarterly 26(2), 13–23 (2002)
18. Willcocks, L.P., Whitley, E.A., Avgerou, C.: The Ranking of Top IS Journals: A Perspective from the London School of Economics. European Journal of Information Systems 17(2), 163–168 (2008)
19. Hauke, J., Mayer, J.H., Quick, R., Feistenauer, H.: New-Generation Managers' Business/IT Alignment Perspective for a More Business-Driven IS Design. In: Abramowicz, W. (ed.) BIS Workshops 2013. LNBIP, vol. 160, pp. 73–88. Springer, Heidelberg (2013)
20. Walls, J.G., Widmeyer, G.R., El Sawy, O.A.: Building an Information System Design Theory for Vigilant EIS. Information Systems Research 3(1), 36–59 (1992)
21. IEEE: IEEE Recommended Practice for Software Requirements Specifications. Institute of Electrical & Electronics Engineers (1998)

22. Sommerville, I.: Software Engineering. Pearson, München (2010)
23. Paech, B., Kerkow, D.: Non-functional Requirements Engineering - Quality Is Essential. In: Regnell, B., Kamsties, E., Gervasi, V. (eds.) 10th Requirements Engineering: Foundation for Software Quality (REFSQ), pp. 237–250. Universität Duisburg-Essen, Riga (2004)
24. Dietz, J.L.G.: Architecture. Building Strategy into Design. Academic Service, The Hague (2007)
25. Gregor, S.: The Nature of Theory in Information Systems. MIS Quarterly 30(3), 611–642 (2006)
26. March, S.T., Smith, G.F.: Design and Natural Science Research on Information Technology. Decision Support Systems 15(4), 251–266 (1995)
27. Benbasat, I., Nault, B.R.: An Evaluation of Empirical Research in Managerial Support Systems. Decision Support Systems 6(3), 203–226 (1990)
28. Powell, P.L., Johnson, J.E.V.: Gender and DSS Design: The Research Implications. Decision Support Systems 14(1), 27–58 (1995)
29. Tricker, B.: Editorial: What Information do Directors Really Need? Corporate Governance: An International Review 5(3), 109–111 (1997)
30. Aders, C., Hebertinger, M., Schaffer, C., Wiedemann, F.: Shareholder Value-Konzepte–Umsetzung bei den DAX100-Unternehmen. Finanz Betrieb 5(11), 719–725 (2003)
31. Cheung, W., Babin, G.: A Metadatabase-Enabled Executive Information System (Part B): Methods for Dynamic Multidimensional Data Analysis. Decision Support Systems 42(3), 1599–1612 (2006)
32. Few, S.: Information Dashboard Design: The Effective Visual Communication of Data. O'Reilly Media, North Sebastopol (2006)
33. Ghazanfari, M., Jafari, M., Rouhani, S.: A Tool to Evaluate the Business Intelligence of Enterprise Systems. Scientia Iranica 18(6), 1579–1590 (2011)
34. Houdeshel, G., Watson, H.J.: The Management Information and Decision Support (MIDS) System at Lockheed-Georgia. MIS Quarterly 11(1), 127–140 (1987)
35. Rockart, J.F., Treacy, M.E.: The CEO goes on-line. Harvard Business Review, 82–88 (January-February 1982)
36. Marx, F., Mayer, J.H., Winter, R.: Six Principles for Redesigning Executive Information Systems - Findings of a Survey and Evaluation of a Prototype. ACM Transactions on Management Information Systems 2(4), article 26 (2012)
37. Işık, Ö., Jones, M.C., Sidorova, A.: Business Intelligence Success: The Roles of BI Capabilities and Decision Environments. Information & Management 50(1), 13–23 (2013)
38. Wu, J.: Harnessing the Power of Exception Reporting. DM Review 15(9), 16–68 (2005)
39. Watson, H.J., Wixom, B.H., Hoffer, J.A., Anderson-Lehman, R., Reynolds, A.M.: Real-time Business Intelligence: Best Practices at Continental Airlines. Information Systems Management 23(1), 7–18 (2006)
40. Armstrong, S.J., Cools, E., Sadler-Smith, E.: Role of Cognitive Styles in Business and Management: Reviewing 40 Years of Research. International Journal of Management Reviews 14(3), 238–262 (2012)
41. DeFond, M.L., Francis, J.R.: Audit Research after Sarbanes-Oxley. Auditing: A Journal of Practice & Theory 24(s-1), 5–30 (2005)
42. Axson, D.A.: Best Practices in Planning and Performance Management: From Data to Decisions. Wiley (2007)
43. Galloway, D.L.: Achieving Accurate Metrics Using Balanced Scorecards and Dashboards. Performance Improvement 49(7), 38–45 (2010)
44. Samuelson, P.A.: Foundations of Economic Analysis. Harvard University Press, Cambridge (1983)

45. Mayer, J.H., Marx, F.: Systematic Development of Business-Driven Requirements – Using Next-Generation EIS Design as an Example. In: Winter, R., Zhao, J.L., Aier, S. (eds.) DESRIST 2010. LNCS, vol. 6105, pp. 506–521. Springer, Heidelberg (2010)
46. Patas, J., Bartenschlager, J., Goeken, M.: Resource-Based View in Empirical IT Business Value Research–An Evidence-Based Literature Review. In: 45th Hawaii International Conference on System Science (HICSS), Maui, HI, pp. 5062–5071 (2012)
47. Todd, P., Benbasat, I.: Process Tracing Methods in Decision Support Systems Research: Exploring the Black Box. MIS Quarterly 11(4), 493–512 (1987)
48. Österle, H., Blessing, D.: Business Engineering Modell. Business Engineering, pp. 65–85. Springer, Heidelberg (2003)
49. Mayer, J.H., Winter, R.: New-Generation Managers and Their IS Support—Getting It Right with the Corporate Navigator. In: vom Brocke, J., Hekkala, R., Ram, S., Rossi, M. (eds.) DESRIST 2013. LNCS, vol. 7939, pp. 432–437. Springer, Heidelberg (2013)
50. Aier, S., Riege, C., Winter, R.: Unternehmensarchitektur – Literaturüberblick und Stand der Praxis. Wirtschaftsinformatik 50, 292–304 (2008)
51. Competence Center. Corporate Management Systems, http://uss.iwi.unisg.ch
52. Granlund, M., Mouritsen, J.: Special Section on Management Control and New Information Technologies. European Accounting Review 12(1), 77–83 (2003)
53. Dutta, S., Wierenga, B., Dalebout, A.: Designing Management Support Systems Using an Integrative Perspective. Commun. ACM 40(6), 70–79 (1997)
54. Sharma, A.K., Kumar, S.: Economic Value Added (EVA)-Literature Review and Relevant Issues. International Journal of Economics and Finance 2(2) (2010)
55. Singh, S.K., Watson, H.J., Watson, R.T.: EIS Support for the Strategic Management Process. Decision Support Systems 33(1), 71–85 (2002)
56. Houghton, R., El Sawy, O., Gray, P., Donegan, C., Joshi, A.: Vigilant Information Systems for Managing Enterprises in Dynamic Supply Chains: Real-Time Dashboards at Western Digital. MIS Quarterly Executive 3(1), 19–35 (2004)
57. Yigitbasioglu, O.M., Velcu, O.: A Review of Dashboards in Performance Management: Implications for Design and Research. International Journal of Accounting Information Systems 13(1), 41–59 (2012)
58. Leidner, D.E., Elam, J.J.: Executive Information Systems: Their Impact on Executive Decision Making. Journal of Management Information Systems 10(3), 139–155 (1993)
59. Andersson, B., Henningsson, S.: Developing Mobile Information Systems: Managing Additional Aspects. In: European Conference on Information Systems (ECIS), Pretoria (2010)
60. Mayer, J.H., Bischoff, S., Winter, R., Weitzel, T.: Extending Traditional EIS Use to Support Mobile Executives Online and Offline. MIS Quarterly Executive 11(2), 87–96 (2012)
61. Lawson, R., Desroches, D., Hatch, T.: Scorecard Best Practices: Design, Implementation, and Evaluation. Wiley (2008)
62. Parr Rud, O.: Business Intelligence Success Factors: Tools for Aligning Your Business in the Global Economy. John Wiley & Sons, Hoboken (2009)
63. Shim, J.P., Warkentin, M., Courtney, J.F., Power, D.J., Sharda, R., Carlsson, C.: Past, Present, and Future of Decision Support Technology. Decision Support Systems 33(2), 111–126 (2002)
64. Demirkan, H., Delen, D.: Leveraging the Capabilities of Service-oriented Decision Support Systems: Putting Analytics and Big Data in Cloud. Decision Support Systems 55(1), 412–421 (2013)
65. Nemati, H.R., Steiger, D.M., Iyer, L.S., Herschel, R.T.: Knowledge Warehouse: An Architectural Integration of Knowledge Management, Decision Support, Artificial Intelligence and Data Warehousing. Decision Support Systems 33(2), 143–161 (2002)
66. Schober, F., Gebauer, J.: How Much to Spend on Flexibility? Determining the Value of Information System Flexibility. Decision Support Systems 51(3), 638–647 (2011)

67. Charles, T.H.: Regular Article: Management Accounting: This Century and Beyond. Management Accounting Research 6(3), 281–286 (1995)
68. Pijpers, G.G.M., Bemelmans, T.M.A., Heemstra, F.J., van Montfort, K.A.G.M.: Senior Executives' Use of Information Technology. Information and Software Technology 43(15), 959–971 (2001)
69. Norman, G.: Likert Scales, Levels of Measurement and the "laws" of Statistics. Advances in Health Sciences Education 15(5), 625–632 (2010)
70. Venable, J., Baskerville, R.: Eating our own Cooking: Toward a More Rigorous Design Science of Research Methods. Electronic Journal of Business Research Methods 10(2), 141–153 (2012)
71. Hevner, A.R.: The Three Cycle View of Design Science Research. Scandinavian Journal of Information Systems 19(2), article 4 (2007)

# Appendix: Publications Researched in the Literature Review

| # | Author(s) | Year | Title | Publication | Elements of IS design | Research approach | Domain |
|---|-----------|------|-------|-------------|----------------------|-------------------|--------|
| 1 | Aders et al. | 2003 | Shareholder Value-Konzepte–Umsetzung bei den DAX100-Unternehmen | Finanz Betrieb | Functional requirements | Behavioral Science | Management* |
| 2 | Andersson, B., Henningsson, S. | 2010 | Mobile IS: Managing Additional Aspects | European Conference on Information Systems | Model | Design Science | IS |
| 3 | Armstrong et al. | 2011 | Role of Cognitive Styles in Business and Management: Reviewing 40 Years of Research | International Journal of Management Reviews | User analysis | Design Science | Management |
| 4 | Arnott, D., Pervan, G. | 2005 | A critical analysis of decision support systems research | Journal of information technology | Method | Behavioral Science | IS |
| 5 | Axson, D.A. | 2007 | Best practices in planning and performance management: from data to decisions | Book | Method | Design Science | Management |
| 6 | Barua, A., Whinston, A.B. | 1998 | Decision support for managing organizational design dynamics | Decision Support Systems | Model | Design Science | IS |
| 7 | Cavalcanti, E. P. | 2005 | The Relationship between Business Intelligence and Business Success | Journal of Competitive Intelligence and Management | Functional requirements | Behavioral Science | IS |
| 8 | Cheung, W., and Babin, G. | 2006 | A Metadatabase-Enabled EIS (Part A): A Flexible and Adaptable Architecture | Decision Support Systems | Functional requirements | Design Science | IS |
| 9 | Chi, R. T., and Turban E. | 1995 | Distributed Intelligent Executive Information Systems | Decision Support Systems | Model | Design Science | IS |
| 10 | Clark Jr et al. | 2007 | The Dynamic Structure of Management Support Systems: Theory Development | MIS Quarterly | Model | Design Science | IS |
| 11 | DeFond, M.L., Francis, J.R. | 2005 | Audit research after Sarbanes-Oxley | Auditing: A Journal of Practice & Theory | Functional requirements | Behavioral Science | Management |
| 12 | Dekkers et al. | 2007 | Organising for Business Intelligence: A Framework for Aligning the Use and Development of Information | BLED | Model | Design Science | IS |
| 13 | Demirkan, H., Delen, D. | 2013 | Leveraging the capabilities of service-oriented DSS: Putting analytics and big data in cloud | Decision Support Systems | Functional requirements | Design Science | IS |
| 14 | Deng, X., Chi, L. | 2013 | Understanding Postadoptive Behaviors in IS Use | Journal of Management Information Systems | Functional requirements | Design Science | IS |
| 15 | Donlon, B. | 2007 | Designing Next-Generation Dashboards | DM Review | Non-functional requirements | Design Science | IS |
| 16 | Dutta, S., Wierenga, B., Dalebout, A. | 1997 | Designing Management Support Systems Using an Integrative Perspective | Communications of the ACM | Method | Design Science | IS |
| 17 | Eckerson, W. | 2010 | Performance Dashboards: Measuring, Monitoring, and Managing Your Business | Book | Method | Design Science | IS |
| 18 | Fernández-Medina, E. et al. | 2006 | Access Control for the Multidimensional Modeling of DW | Decision Support Systems | Functional requirements | Design Science | IS |
| 19 | Few, S. | 2006 | Information Dashboard Design | Book | Non-functional requirements | Design Science | IS |
| 20 | Galloway, D. L. | 2010 | Achieving Accurate Metrics Using BSC and Dashboards | Performance Improvement | Functional requirements | Design Science | Management |
| 21 | Ghazanfari, M., Jafari, M., Rouhani, S. | 2011 | A tool to evaluate the business intelligence of enterprise systems | Scientia Iranica | Functional requirements | Design Science | IS |
| 22 | Horngren, C.T. | 1995 | Management accounting: this century and beyond | Management Accounting Research | Functional requirements | Design Science | Management |
| 23 | Houdeshel, G. and Watson, H. J | 1987 | The Management Information and Decision Support (MIDS) System at Lockheed-Georgia | MIS Quarterly | Non-functional requirements | Design Science | IS |
| 24 | Houghton, R. et al. | 2004 | Vigilant Information Systems for Managing Enterprises in Dynamic Supply Chains: Realtime Dashboards At Western Digital | MIS Quarterly Executive | Method | Design Science | IS |
| 25 | Hung, S.-Y. | 2003 | Expert versus novice use of the executive support systems: an empirical study | Information & Management | Model | Behavioral Science | IS |

| 26 | Işık, Ö., Jones, M.C., Sidorova, A. | 2013 | Business intelligence success: The roles of BI capabilities and decision environments | Information & Management | Non-functional requirements | Behavioral Science | IS |
|----|----|----|----|----|----|----|----|
| 27 | Lawson, R., Desroches, D., Hatch, T. | 2008 | Scorecard best practices: design, implementation, and evaluation | Book | Functional requirements | Design Science | Management |
| 28 | Leidner, D. E., Elam, J. J. | 1994 | Executive Information Systems: Their Impact on Executive Decision Making | Journal of Management Information Systems | Model | Behavioral Science | IS |
| 29 | Marx, Frederik, Jörg H. Mayer, and Robert Winter | 2011 | Six principles for redesigning executive information systems—findings of a survey and evaluation of a prototype | ACM Transactions on Management Information Systems | Method | Design Science | IS |
| 30 | Mayer, J. H. | 2012 | Using the Kano Model to Identify Attractive User Interface Software Components | International Conference on IS | Functional requirements | Behavioral Science | IS |
| 31 | Mayer, J. H., Quick, R., Hauke, J. | 2013 | Taking a New-Generation Manager Perspective to Develop Interface Designs | International Conference on IS | Method | Design Science | IS |
| 32 | Mayer, J., Steinecke, N., Quick, R. | 2011 | Improving the Applicability of Environmental Scanning Systems: State of the Art and Future Research | Governance and Sustainability in IS. | Method | Design Science | IS |
| 33 | Mayer, J.H. | 2013 | Current Changes in Executive Work and How to Handle Them by Redesigning EIS | Accounting IS for Decision Making | Model | Design Science | IS |
| 34 | Mayer, J.H. | 2010 | Organisatorische Veränderungen durch die aktuelle Wirtschaftskrise – Bestandsaufnahme und Implikationen für Unternehmenssteuerungssysteme | Deutscher Controlling Congress | Functional requirements | Design Science | Management |
| 35 | Mayer, J.H. | 2011 | Managing the Future—Six Guidelines for Designing Environmental Scanning Systems | Service-Oriented Perspectives in DSR | Method | Design Science | IS |
| 36 | Mayer, J.H., Bischoff, S., Winter, R., Weitzel, T. | 2012 | Extending Traditional EIS Use to Support Mobile Executives Online and Offline | MIS Quarterly Executive | Non-functional requirements | Design Science | IS |
| 37 | Mayer, J.H., Winter, R., Mohr, T. | 2012 | Situational Management Support Systems | Bus Inf Syst Eng | User analysis | Design Science | IS |
| 38 | Nemati, H.R., Steiger, D.M., Iyer, L.S., Herschel, R.T. | 2002 | Knowledge warehouse: an architectural integration of knowledge management, decision support, artificial intelligence and data warehousing | Decision Support Systems | Method | Design Science | IS |
| 39 | Nowduri, S. | 2011 | Management information systems and business decision making: review, analysis, and recommendations | Journal of Management and Marketing Research | Method | Design Science | IS |
| 40 | Parr Rud, O. | 2009 | BI Success Factors: Tools for Aligning Your Business in the Global Economy | Book | Model | Design Science | IS |
| 41 | Popoviča et al. | 2012 | Towards business intelligence systems success: Effects of maturity and culture on analytical decision making | Decision Support Systems | Functional requirements | Behavioral Science | IS |
| 42 | Powell P. L., and Johnson J. E. V. | 1995 | Gender and DSS Design: The Research Implications | Decision Support Systems | Effects of use | Behavioral Science | IS |
| 43 | Power, D. J., and Sharda, R. | 2007 | Model-Driven Decision Support Systems: Concepts and Research Directions | Decision Support Systems | Model | Design Science | IS |
| 44 | Rainer, R.K., Watson Hugh, J. | 1995 | What does it take for successful executive information systems | Decision Support Systems | Method | Design Science | IS |
| 45 | Reimann, B.C., Waren, A.D. | 1985 | User-oriented criteria for the selection of DSS software | Communications of the ACM | Functional requirements | Design Science | IS |
| 46 | Rockart, J. F. and Treacy, M. E. | 1989 | The CEO goes on-line | End-user computing: Concepts, issues, and applications | Non-functional requirements | Design Science | Management |
| 47 | Salmeron, J. L. | 2002 | EIS Data: Findings From An Evolutionary Study | The Journal of IS and Software | Functional requirements | Design Science | IS |
| 48 | Sankar, C. S., Ford, N., and Bauer, M. | 1995 | A DSS User Interface Model to Provide Consistency and Adaptability | Decision Support Systems | Model | Design Science | IS |
| 49 | Schober, F., Gebauer, J. | 2011 | How Much to Spend on Flexibility? Determining the Value of IS Flexibility | Decision Support Systems | Model | Behavioral Science | IS |
| 50 | Sharma, A.K., Kumar, S. | 2010 | Economic value added (EVA)-literature review and relevant issues | International Journal of Economics and Finance | Functional requirements | Behavioral Science | Management |
| 51 | Shim, J. P. et al. | 2002 | Past, Present, and Future of Decision Support Technology | Decision Support Systems | Method | Design Science | IS |
| 52 | Singh, S. K., Watson, H. J., Watson, R. T. | 2002 | EIS support for the strategic management process | Decision Support Systems | Model | Design Science | IS |
| 53 | Starovic, D. | 2002 | Performance Reporting to Boards: A Guide to Good Practice | Chartered Institute of Management Accountants | Functional requirements | Design Science | Management* |
| 54 | Taipaleenmäki, J., Ikäheimo, S. | 2011 | On the convergence of management accounting and financial accounting – the role of information technology in accounting change | Journal of Accounting Information Systems | Functional requirements | Design Science | Management |
| 55 | Tricker, B. | 1997 | Editorial: what information do directors really need? | Corporate Governance: An International Review | Functional requirements | Design Science | Management* |
| 56 | Vandenbosch, B., Huff, S.L. | 1997 | Searching and Scanning: How Executives Obtain Information from Executive Information Systems | MIS Quarterly | Model | Behavioral Science | IS |
| 57 | Walstrom, Kent A., and Rick L. Wilson | 1997 | An examination of executive information system (EIS) users | Information & Management | User analysis | Behavioral Science | IS |
| 58 | Watson et al. | 2006 | Real-time Business Intelligence: Best Practices at Continental Airlines | Information Systems Management | Method | Behavioral Science | IS |
| 59 | Winter, Robert | 2011 | Design of Situational Artefacts—Conceptual Foundations and Their Application to IT/Business Alignment | Information Systems Development | User analysis | Behavioral Science | IS |
| 60 | Wixom, B., and Watson, H. J. | 2010 | The BI-Based Organization | International Journal of BI Research | Model | Design Science | IS |
| 61 | Wu, J. | 2005 | Harnessing the Power of Exception Reporting | DM Review | Functional requirements | Design Science | IS |
| 62 | Yigitbasioglu, O. M., and Velcu, O. | 2012 | A Review of Dashboards In Performance Management: Implications for Design and Research | International Journal of Accounting IS | Non-functional requirements | Design Science | IS |
| 63 | Young, D., Watson, H.J. | 1995 | Determinates of EIS acceptance | Information & Management | Model | Behavioral Science | IS |

# Towards a Design Science-Driven Product-Service System Engineering Methodology

Christina Niemöller, Deniz Özcan, Dirk Metzger, and Oliver Thomas

Information Management and Information Systems,
Osnabrueck University, Osnabrueck, Germany
{christina.niemoeller, deniz.oezcan,
dirk.metzger, oliver.thomas}@uni-osnabrueck.de

**Abstract.** Customers are increasingly demanding integrated solutions so that Product-Service Systems (PSS) have been proliferated in the global economy. The resulting PSS effects of utilization are of versatile nature for both suppliers and demanders. Especially the field service is characterized by the integrated provision of product and service wherefore service technicians need support by mobile information systems (IS). Although different PSS Engineering methods exist, a fundamental base, including the triple of Product, Service and the support through IS, is needed for the conceptual development of PSS. Therefore, within the Design Science Research (DSR) field established concepts are inspected for their applicability in the PSS Engineering process. Goal of this contribution is to extend the scope of information systems in order to derive a methodology which enables a design science oriented development of IS as an essential part of PSS.

**Keywords:** Product-Service System, Service Science, Design Science Research.

## 1 Introduction

The number of Product-Service Systems (PSS) has increased proliferated in recent years, which is reducible to a growing share of the service sector [1]. According to current statistics, the German economy for example registered a growth of the performance of the service sector in 2012 in defiance of a simultaneous decrease of the manufacturing and building industry [2]. Especially in leading industrialized countries the service sector represents a considerable ratio of the gross domestic product (GDP) which makes it to an indispensable branch of industry in the global economy [3][4].

In order to persist in the economic competition, companies increasingly internalize to act as a solution provider on the market, which are highly characterized by their combined offer of both products and services [5]. This results from the fact that customers are increasingly demanding integrated solutions to meet their individual needs [6]. In this way, a value generation in form of hybrid value bundle takes place, which is also called hybrid value creation [7][5]. Also known under the name Product-Service System, the concept of the integrated provision of goods and services offers benefits and potentials for providing companies [8]. Monetary benefits [6], a clear

M.C. Tremblay et al. (Eds.): DESRIST 2014, LNCS 8463, pp. 180–193, 2014.
© Springer International Publishing Switzerland 2014

distinction from competitors and as well as increasing customer satisfaction [9] and the concomitant enhanced customer loyalty [10] may result as useful effects from PSS.

Since the machinery and plant engineering constitutes an important industry and is also characterized by the use of services as parts of their portfolio, PSS are discovered especially in this industry field [11]. In addition to the manufacture of machinery and equipment, the Technical Customer Service (TCS) is furthermore taking care of product-specific requirements and is, to this end, in interaction with the customer [12]. The tasks service technician has to cope with are characterized by diversity which makes an assistance system to a necessity to master the service complexity. Beside technical problems, the TCS also has to be equipped with commercial skills that are incurred as part of a service process, such as procurement of spare parts, guarantee measures and invoicing [13]. In addition, the TCS has an important function by its role as an interface to the customer [14], what makes him able to provide feedback about product-specific and customer-specific properties back to the company [15]. The quality of service is mainly influenced by the TCS, which is why a support of the service technician for service delivery and an efficient arrangement of the considered PSS is indispensable [16].

A research gap exists thereby through the fact that PSS-Engineering (PSSE) methodologies in the context of Design Science Research (DSR) have not been analyzed to date. The scope of our work is the investigation of existing PSSE methodologies and the development of a design science oriented PSS approach in order to create evaluation-driven, relevant and rigorous PSS.

The following section describes the concept of Design Science Research as an initial situation for the construction of a design science oriented PSS. In Section 3 the concept of Product-Service Systems is introduced by investigating relevant components of PSS. Further, an analysis of PSS-Engineering methodologies reveals former used approaches in the field of PSS research. On this basis, we established a DSR oriented Product-Service System Engineering Methodology, which is presented in Section 4. In Section 5 we will transfer our developed concept into a case study of the machinery and plant engineering to show the application. Section 5 concludes our approach and indicates further research.

## 2     Design Science Theory

### 2.1     Concepts of Design Science Research

The design science paradigm is a legitimate Information System Research paradigm to create an innovative Information Technology (IT) artifact to address a certain problem [17][18]. To specify this paradigm HEVNER ET AL. has established seven guidelines that describe characteristics of well carried out research [17]. These guidelines are also reflected in the Design Science Research (DSR) Cycle View presented in figure 1. The *Design Cycle* as the core cycle iterates between building artifacts and evaluating them against certain requirements [18] until the utility, quality and efficacy is rigorously proved [17]. These certain requirements are considered in the *Relevance Cycle* that not only provides the problem to be addressed but also defines the satisfying criteria for the final evaluation of the research result [18]. As DSR is motivated to improve the environment [19] by solving a relevant business problem with innovative and purposeful artifacts, HEVNER ET AL. argues that a combination of technology-based artifacts such as system conceptualization, organization-based artifacts like structures and people-based artifacts as for example training and the process for building these, have to be designed [17]. DSR artifacts can be in the form of constructs, models, methods and instantiations applied in the development and use of information systems [20].

For being rigorously proved, the *Rigor Cycle* is aimed at providing grounding scientific theories and methods along with domain experience and expertise [18]. Those evaluation methods, which are obtained in the current knowledge base, contain observational methods like case or field studies as well as analytical, experimental, testing and descriptive methods [17]. Furthermore, the Rigor Cycle not only provides foundations but also return new knowledge generated by the conducted DSR [18]. Finally, the results of DSR have to be presented to researchers who study the artifacts in context and extend them, to practitioners who implement them in a technical way and to a management-oriented audience that apply the artifacts within the organization.

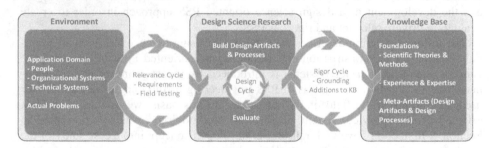

**Fig. 1.** Design Science Research Cycles [18]

PEFFERS ET AL. developed a Design Science Research Methodology (DSRM) Process Model [21], which i.a. obtains the DSR guidelines and the understanding of the DSR Cycles mentioned before (see figure 2). The first step (1) comprises the identification of the problem to show the relevance. After that, (2) the objectives of a solution are defined and (3) the actual designing and development (d&d) phase begins. After the first instance of the artifact has been build, the functionality will be demonstrated in a convenient context (4). In the more formal evaluation phase (5), it should be observed how well the designed artifact suits to solve the defined problem using relevant metrics and analysis techniques. Thereafter, the process either iterates back to the d&d phase to improve the artifact or, if the artifact is already satisfying, the communication of the results (6) takes place.

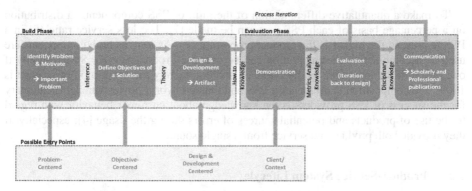

**Fig. 2.** DSRM Process Model (referring to [21][37])

In reality not every DSR process proceeds from step 1 until 6. Hence, PEFFERS ET AL. defined possible research entry points like a problem-centered (start-step: 1), an objective-centered (start-step: 2), a d&d-centered (start-step: 3) or a client/context initiation (start-step: 4). [21] As we can see DSR is conducted in an iterative research process with the aim to generate new knowledge. The presented DSR research contributions already propose frameworks for the successful usage of generic DSR and provide elementary concepts for a clear contribution into the application environment. As the DSR methodology is already established to create innovative IT artifacts and IS should be an essential part of PSS engineering, the insights of DSR are used to improve the PSS Engineering process, which is presented in the following.

# 3    Product-Service System

## 3.1    Constituent Parts of Product-Service Systems

PSS represent hybrid products that consist of an immaterial component, the service part, as well as a material good, the product [22][23]. While traditionally products and services are developed independently and organized in different departments, the concept of PSS targets to an integrated product and service offering [4]. Depending on the PSS configuration variable amounts of service and product can be present and the ratio can continuously change over time, for example due to technological developments or of changing customer needs [8]. Figure 3 illustrates the structure of PSS.

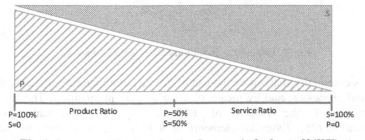

**Fig. 3.** Structure of Product-Service Systems (referring to [24][7])

To make a quantitative differentiation of the ratio of PSS components, a distribution on a percentage basis of each PSS part can be made [7]. The less service ratio (S) in a PSS is present, the higher is the product proportion (P). As long as both components are used as a combination the integration can be called a Product-Service System. Only if one of the PSS components is discontinued and e.g. merely the proportion of product is 100%, the composition is no longer a PSS and thus no hybrid power bundle. Elementary for the success of PSS providers is the knowledge about customer behavior with regard to the use of products and potential sources of errors during the usage [4]; especially, if they provide both product and service from a single source.

## 3.2     Product-Service System Lifecyle

Towards a PSS, requirements of different origin can exist. PSS developers, -providers and within the context of PSS involved stakeholders as well as customers that demand for PSS have claims on a Product-Service System, which need to be fulfilled and regarded in the development process. In addition to these actors, additional components of a PSS are also software and processes that are required for a value proposition [25]. A special requirement and at the same time also essential characteristic of PSS is the extension of the product life cycle, because within a product's life cycle it is possible to provide in all of its phases a physical good combined with services [7].

In order to include the needed requirements for a PSS systematically already in the development phase, the consideration of existing industrial structures is necessary. Hence, it is important to support the developer of a PSS with the integration into an overall concept. Figure 4 illustrates the considerable elements of a PSS within a lifecycle [25].

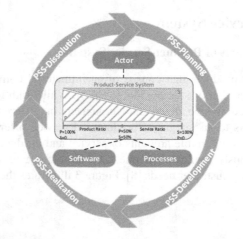

**Fig. 4.** Underlying Requirements of a PSS-lifecycle

A PSS is essentially marked by the use of product and material interests, the use of software and processes, and by means of actor's value proposition. The life cycle of PSS consists of the phases of PSS-planning, -development, -realization and -dissolution [25]. Essential elements of a PSS are, in addition to the service and the product, the interplay of actors, software and the identification of processes.

For the design of PSS it must be clearly defined, which actors are present, which are in interaction with the PSS, what processes exist and what software is needed to run the expenses incurred in connection of PSS activities efficiently. So, before a user-oriented design of PSS can take place, the requirements of the user need to be considered first.

### 3.3 Engineering Methodologies for Product-Service Systems

In the field of service research a plethora of conceptualizations of PSS already exists but only few consider specific methodologies for Product-Service System design from the view of development [26].

The wider approach of SPATH AND DEMUß examines services during product design and determines the development of PSS as a socio-technical system, which is characterized by the interaction on human and machine. The foundation for the design is appropriated through an integrated requirements engineering within the development process of the physical good [27].

MCALOONE treat the development of Product-Service Systems in two different ways. First of all, they take the product life cycle and afterwards attach a dedicated service lifecycle to the usage period of the product. So, they propose to design services when they are needed during the use of the product [28].

Another approach for the design of Product Service Systems was found by WEBER ET AL. and their application of the Property-Driven-Development (PDD) on Product-Service Systems. They basically decide between structure-based and behavior-based characteristics of Product-Service Systems and design them through different iterations in an integrated way also regarding customer integration by beginning with customer needs [29].

THOMAS ET AL. describe the design of PSS by employing an engineering cycle. The focus is given for material and service characteristics that are designed in an iterative process consisting of two cycles (customer cycle and developer cycle) on the base of customer requirements. The development, which ends with the finished PSS, begins with recording customer requirements and, consequently, with the problem identification. Furthermore, the integration of the customer and developer cycle allows also both the demonstration and the evaluation of the created artifact [26].

According to ISAKSSON ET AL., the development of PSS represents the engineering work to transform requirements to solutions which means that the engineering design of PSS has a wider range of what design parameters are available. The provided process of a functional product development (FDP) starts with the integration of customer needs and the objective of developing a solution [30].

BOUGHNIM AND YANNOU see the development of PSS similar to service development and provide a map of a PSS system using the Blueprinting Method according to SHOSTACK [32] and regarding all processes, actions and interactions inside as well as outside the company [31].

MAUSSANG ET AL. identified, in their research of current approaches for designing PSS, two different research priorities, the design of PSS from the system point of view and the design from the product point of view. From a system point of view the designer of the PSS focusses a new combination of technological artifacts on the basis of functional parameters while within the product point of view the designers consider that both services and products should be developed in an integrative manner. Based on that, they have designed a two stage approach for PSS development. First the elements of PSS are defined and second a detailed design phase is determined to define technical solutions [33].

Another PSSE methodology is presented by LEE AND KIM who investigate the functional modelling of PSS by including also information of service providers and receivers. They provide a functional modelling framework to facilitate the arrangement of product and service elements to produce various PSS concepts [34].

TAN ET AL. defined four dimensions and methodology steps which cover the essential design elements of a PSS. The analysis of value proposition, product life cycle, activity modelling cycle and the actor network enable the alignment as well as a good understanding of how products and systems work [35].

Overall, for all the approaches the focus is given for the design of services and products combined, iteratively and on the basis of customer demands. However, the basis for most of the modern services and products is the IT-Infrastructure that serves as enabler. This is why the product-service engineering methods have to be adapted to include the development of IT artifacts. From the analysis of the methodologies proposed in literature we ascertained that most of them focus implicit on the first three DSR process steps embracing the problem identification, definition of the objective of a solution as well as the design and development of PSS. Merely, the PSSE methodology from THOMAS ET AL. contains five steps of the DSRM Process Model according to PEFFERS ET AL. including the demonstration phase by the transition of the engineering process result, the construction of a PSS and back to the customer, where also the evaluation takes place [21]. Based on our literature findings we construct in the following adjusted design science oriented PSSE methodology drawing on THOMAS ET AL. The superior aim is to transfer DSR methodologies on PSS research in order to show the applicability and relevance of the design science paradigm to service science.

# 4    Construction of a Design Science Oriented Product-Service System

Although the DSR approach is primarily aimed at the field of Information Systems, it has implication for information technology associated areas such as engineering disciplines [18][35]. So far it has been used to construct a wide range of socio-technical artifact as for instance decision support systems, governance strategies, methods for the IS evaluation and chance interventions [36].

Due to the build-evaluate pattern of DSR, it is only about proving the usefulness of an artifact. According to SONNENBERG AND VOM BROCKE a rigorous DSR process also requires the validation of the artifact design decisions before evaluating the artifact in the field [37]. Hence, they proposed three principles that should be considered in the building phase. They claim to have multiple evaluation episodes during a single iteration of the DSR process to evaluate not only the usefulness of the artifact (exterior modes: ex post evaluation) but also the constituents and the design decisions (interior mode: ex ante evaluation). In addition to that, the prescriptive knowledge should be documented in a particular way, meaning that i.a. also justificatory knowledge (why an artifact may work in a given context) or information about the expository instantiations to reason about the feasibility and applicability at build time in the interior mode. Performing the documentation already during the build phase and not just after the evaluation has been conducted, immediately effects the way the upcoming evaluation can be accomplished. [37]

This is why the given PSSE Framework [26] should be extended by evaluation cycles in the build phase as it is shown in figure 5. Considering that, SONNENBERG AND VOM BROCKE propose exemplary evaluation criteria and evaluation methods, which are used in the following [37].

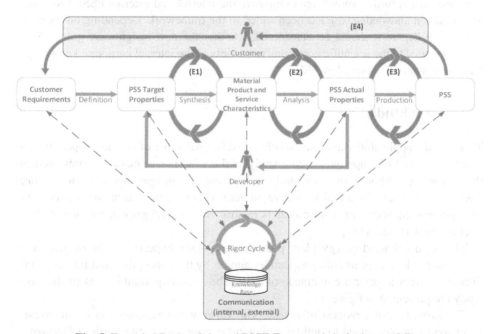

**Fig. 5.** Extended Design Oriented PSSE Framework (referring to [26])

After the customer requirements have been translated into target properties and the material products and service characteristics have been defined, they should be evaluated against criteria such as the applicability, the suitability, the importance, the novelty and the feasibility using methods like a literature review, reviews of practitioner initiatives, interviews of expert or focus groups or surveys with customer (E1). Having conducted the evaluation, the characteristics became justified design objectives. To evaluate the actual PSS properties for getting a validated design specification criteria like the feasibility, simplicity, completeness, consistency and operationally should be considered. Those can be evaluated by demonstration or simulation, benchmarking or again surveys and interviews (E2). After the actual PSS properties have been defined and a component has been build, the artifact should be proved of applicability in an artificial setting. By prototype experiments or demonstrations of the components to a focus or expert group the ease of use as well as the effectiveness and efficiency, the robustness and the suitability of the instance can be evaluated (E3). The fourth evaluation step (E4) already exists in the present PSSE Framework: By evaluation through the customer for instance in a case study, a field experiment or a survey the artifact instance can be validated in a naturalistic setting. As described in Section 2 HEVNER ET AL. considers a three cycle view to conduct DSR [18]. The relevance cycle view and the design cycle view have been implemented already through the four evaluation steps (E1-E4); however, the rigor cycle is still missing so far. Heretofore, there is not any knowledge management activity explicitly designated. To ground the PSSE steps and to add further knowledge to improve the internal and external PSSE processes and results, a knowledge base has been added to the framework. Depending on the confidentiality degree it should be considered, whether the new insights are going to be communicated to the scientific community or solely to the internal corporate knowledge base for instance in case of key PSS.

## 5     Case Study

To show the applicability and the associated additional value of our developed design science oriented PSS approach a case study of the wind power market is presented in the following. Although the case study is fictional, the insights and experiences are based on a project with a real PSS development. Due to actual discussion of renewable energies the sector of wind power is raising with annual growth rate about 28% over the past 15 years [38].

The regarded wind energy plant provider is already experienced in building the provided products; uncertainties especially appear by the conception and implementation of services to offer a combined solution. The most important results of the case study are presented in figure 6.

The provider got a request of investors in form of the management of an investment fond who demanded to build a new wind energy park in the north of Germany. Given by the fact that the investors are just a group of financiers without any capabilities to care of the wind power plants themselves, they were searching for a solution provider who offers a package of combined products and services to warrant a viable wind energy generation.

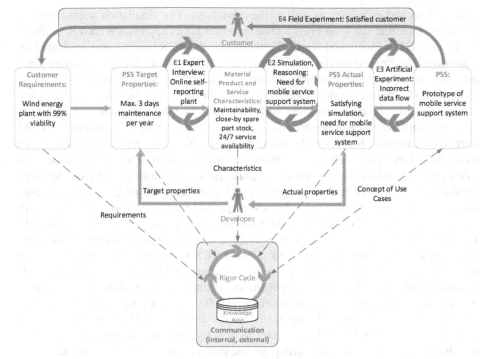

**Fig. 6.** Results of the Case Study

The recorded customer requirements consisted of four wind energy plants that should be viable 99% of the year. In a next step, the customer requirements were translated into the PSS target properties as a basis to communicate in the specialized terminology: 99% viability requires that the plant runs at least 362 days in a year implicating that there are only three days in a year to service and maintain the plants. The characteristic synthesis from the target properties for the PSS was mainly characterized by the experience of the developer. In the following, the central material products and service characteristics are presented without discussing the detailed construction process, because the paper focusses on concept of hybrid bundle and not on the construction of a product itself. Due to the properties of short service cycles, the developer determined the product to be constructed as an easily maintainable plant. Spare parts have to be stored in close-by stocks with a convenient infrastructure and the TCS consisting of the service center and the technicians themselves have to be available 24 hours a day. After the characteristics had been defined the first evaluation cycle started. Experts in form of PSS researchers were interviewed about the feasibility, simplicity, completeness, consistency and operationally of the concept. Meanwhile, it became apparent that the wind energy plants have to be online to immediately report back malfunction. The concept of an online plant was added to the characteristics and the actual PSS Properties were defined: the products and the IT-systems were designed and a training concept for the TCS technicians was created. Subsequently, the plant itself was evaluated by simulation to get an impression of the effectiveness and efficiency as well as the robustness. The simulation was successful due to the fact, that the wind energy plant provider is already experienced in building the plant itself as mentioned above. Furthermore, the TCS process was evaluated by reasoning. The process models were analyzed and potentials for improvement were detected: to support the complete process chain, the TCS technicians have to be connected via mobile service support system. To meet the short service time, the technician have to receive the order with all necessary plant information at the point of service, in case of repair services he needs to order the spare parts immediately and after having finished his service he has to document his work steps for further service requests. For the specification the outcomes of the second evaluation were added and a first prototype of the mobile service support system was built. Thereby the developers draw on the scientific knowledge base using the concept of Use Cases, to construct a support system, that considers every possible use case representative for all eventual activities of TCS processes (for further information see [39], [16] and [13]). The instance of the first prototype was evaluated in an artificial setting. An experiment conducted by the developer and selected TCS technicians took place. On that point, the whole process beginning by the wind energy plant reporting back a malfunction up to the TCS technician repairing the plant using the mobile service support systems was tested. As a result an incorrect data flow between the technician and the service center was detected. In the next step, the errors were fixed and the scenario could be evaluated in the field. Necessary to that, the PSS was shown to the customer and the earlier contacted expert group of researchers. Due to the fact, that the focus group was satisfied, there was no further iteration of the PSSE Cycle necessary. The PSSE Cycle was finished with the roll-out of the product and signing the service contracts.

During the PSSE process the developers not only referred to already existing research theories and practical methods but also stored the relevant information about the customer requirements, the specification of the PSS and the construction itself into the internal knowledge database to create the possibility to transfer them to further developments. In addition to that, the innovative mobile service support system was presented to researchers and practitioners on a leading trade fair for industrial technology in Germany.

## 6    Discussion of the Results

Lessons learned from the case study were in particular that the revised framework provided the user and developer of a Product-Service System with more input from different participants. With the inclusion of different groups such as experts, customers, users, etc. the development team had the chance to evaluate and judge the potential PSS from different views already during the development phase. Those additional evaluation activities lead to several insights that supported the developer, especially the inexperienced one, with the creation of a successful PSS. The chance of having a PSS that successfully cover the customer expectations and needs improves. However, one of the downsides of this approach is the extended development period and the higher costs. This might be in particular in a fast moving market an unwanted effect that has to be assessed thoroughly before taken into account. In the case study presented within this paper the market does not awaits the fast moving actions which is why the PSS Development approach is appropriate. In addition to that, oncosts for adaptations after the finished product has been presented drop for the reason that the customer and expert groups are already included in the build phase where adaptations are not that enormous as in the aftermath.

Another positive aspect of the approach was the inclusion of the Knowledge Base. Although most of the companies use the knowledge they gain implicitly in their next projects this explicit approach of adding all information to a dedicated database in order to reuse parts of them is beneficial. As the Knowledge Base might as well be further used in cooperation with scientists this leads to the positive aspect that new scientific findings might get included in new PSS and vice versa. Altogether the aspects of the revised framework assist the development of successful PSS and add vital parts to the conventional approach.

# 7    Conclusion and Outlook

The development of Product-Service Systems needs to be viewed from a process-oriented perspective in virtue of the complexity that exists in the provision of an appropriate integrated solution to meet customer needs. Especially in the service field, an optimal design of processes and supporting activities is important for the service delivery in order to create customer satisfaction and loyalty. For this purpose, the development of PSS has been considered from a methodological point of view with due regard to the Design Science Research paradigm. Thereto, elementary concepts of DSR which need to be considered during the design of an artifact and that are suitable for the process-oriented design of PSS were introduced. A PSSE approach was derived by investigating existing literature in PSS research and exemplified by a case study of the TCS within the wind power market. The combined consideration of these two research fields allowed us the construction of a design science oriented Product-Service System methodology as a basis for the support of the design of PSS processes in the context of hybrid value creation. This paper is a first step to extend the scope of information systems containing a design science oriented development of IS as an essential part of PSS.

Our derived PSSE methodology does not claim to be exhaustive but rather presents an integrated approach on how a PSS can be developed conceptually and considering DSR requirements. In order to improve the validity of our findings, in future we schedule to extend the scope of our investigation by different branches to achieve more results with the aim to provide a guidance and signpost for the design of PSS. Further we plan to examine applied approaches and engineering methodologies within research projects comprising the development of PSS in order to ascertain distinctions and to reveal potentials for the improvement of our presented PSSE methodology.

# References

1. Boehm, M., Thomas, O.: Looking beyond the rim of one's teacup: a multidisciplinary literature review of Product-Service Systems in Information Systems, Business Management, and Engineering & Design. Journal of Cleaner Production 51, 245–260 (2013)
2. Statistisches Bundesamt: Pressekonferenz Bruttoinlandsprodukt 2012 für Deutschland (2013), https://www.destatis.de/DE/ PresseService/Presse/Pressekonferenzen/2013/BIP2012/ Statement_Egeler_2012_PDF.pdf?__blob=publicationFile
3. Maglio, P.P., Vargo, S.L., Caswell, N., Spohrer, J.: The service system is the basic abstraction of service science. Information Systems and e-Business Management 7(4), 395–406 (2009)
4. Meier, H., Roy, R., Seliger, G.: Industrial Product-Service Systems—IPS2. CIRP Annals - Manufacturing Technology 59(2), 607–627 (2010)
5. Leimeister, J.M., Glauner, C.: Hybride Produkte – Einordnung und Herausforderungen für die Wirtschaftsinformatik. Wirtschaftsinformatik 50(3), 248–251 (2008)
6. Becker, J., Beverungen, D., Knackstedt, R.: The challenge of conceptual modeling for product–service systems: status-quo and perspectives for reference models and modeling languages. Information Systems and e-Business Management 8(1), 33–66 (2009)
7. Becker, J., Beverungen, D., Knackstedt, R.: Wertschöpfungsnetzwerke von Produzenten und Dienstleistern als Option zur Organisation der Erstellung hybrider Leistungsbündel Empirische Erkenntnisse zur Bedeutung. In: Becker, J., Knackstedt, R., Pfeiffer, D. (eds.) Wertschöpfungsnetzwerke - Konzepte für das Netzwerkmanagement und Potenziale aktueller Informationstechnologien, pp. 3–31. Springer Physica, Heidelberg (2008)
8. Goedkoop, M.J., van Halen, C.J.G., te Riele, H.R.M., Rommens, P.J.M.: Product Service systems, Ecological and Economic Basics. VROM/EZ, The Hague (1999)
9. Kuo, Y.F., Wu, C.M., Deng, W.J.: The relationship among service quality, perceived value, customer satisfaction, and post-purchase intention in mobile value-added services. Computers in Human Behaviour 25(4), 887–896 (2009)
10. Kumar, V., Batista, L., Maull, R.: The Impact of Operations Performance on Customer Loyalty. Service Science 3(2), 158–171 (2011)
11. Bamberger, R., König, A., Pflaum, A.: Mobile Servicewelten im Maschinenbau. VDMA-Verlag. Frankfurt am Main (2010)
12. VDMA: Entscheidungshilfe zur Einführung von Service management systemen. VDMA Verlag. Frankfurt am Main (2008)
13. Fellmann, M., Özcan, D., Matijacic, M., Däuble, G., Schlicker, M., Thomas, O., Nüttgens, M.: Towards a Mobile Technical Customer Service Support Platform. In: Daniel, F., Papadopoulos, G.A., Thiran, P. (eds.) MobiWIS 2013. LNCS, vol. 8093, pp. 296–299. Springer, Heidelberg (2013)
14. Deuse, J., Wischniewski, S., Birkmann, S.: Knowledgebase für die kontinuierliche Innovationsarbeit im Technischen Kundendienst. In: Herrmann, T.A., Kleinbeck, U., Ritterskamp, C. (eds.) Innovationen an der Schnittstelle zwischen technischer Dienstleistung und Kunde, pp. 155–176. Physica, Heidelberg (2009)
15. Zolkiewski, J., Lewis, B., Yuan, F., Yuan, J.: An assessment of customer service in business-to-business relationships. Journal of Services Marketing 21(5), 313–325 (2007)
16. Özcan, D., Niemöller, C., Fellmann, M., Matijacic, M., Däuble, G., Schlicker, M., Thomas, O., Nüttgens, M.: A Use Case-driven Approach to the Design of Service Support Systems: Making Use of Semantic Technologies. In: Proceedings of the International Symposium on Services Science (ISSS), Leipzig, pp. 105–116 (2013)
17. Hevner, A.R., Salvatore, T.M., Park, J., Ram, S.: Design Science in Information Systems Research. MIS Quarterly 28(1), 75–105 (2004)

18. Hevner, A.R.: A Three Cycle View of Design Science Research. Scandinavian Journal of Information Systems 19(2), 87–92 (2007)
19. Simon, H.A.: The sciences of the artificial. MIT Press (1996)
20. March, S.T., Smith, G.F.: Design and Natural Science Research on Information Technology. Decision Support Systems 15(4), 251–266 (1995)
21. Peffers, K., Tuunanen, T., Rothenberger, M.A., Chatterjee, S.: A Design Science Research Methodology for Information Systems Research. Journal of Management Information Systems 24(3), 45–77 (2007)
22. Baines, T.S., et al.: State-of-the-art in product-service systems. Proceedings of the Institution of Mechanical Engineers, Part B: Journal of Engineering Manufacture 221(10), 1543–1552 (2007)
23. Aurich, J.C., Fuchs, C., Wagenknecht, C.: Life cycle oriented design of technical Product-Service Systems. Journal of Cleaner Production 14, 1480–1494 (2006)
24. Tukker, A.: Eight Types of Product-Service System: Eight ways to Sustainability? Experiences from Suspronet. Business Strategy and the Environment 13, 246–260 (2004)
25. Laurischkat, K.: Wandel des traditionellen Dienstleistungsverständnisses im Kontext von Product-Service Systems. In: Thomas, O., Nüttgens, M. (eds.) Dienstleistungsmodellierung 2012 - Product-Service Systems und Produktivität, pp. 75–95. Springer Gabler, Wiesbaden (2012)
26. Thomas, O., Walter, P., Loos, P.: Design and usage of an engineering methodology for product-service systems. Journal of Design Research 7(2), 177–195 (2008)
27. Spath, D., Demuß, L.: Entwicklung hybrider Produkte—Gestaltung materieller und immaterieller Leistungsbündel. In: Service Engineering, pp. 463–502. Springer (2006)
28. McAloone, T.: Teaching and Implementation Models for Sustainable PSS Development. Sustainable Consumption and Production: Opportunities and Challenges 23, 125 (2006)
29. Weber, C., Steinbach, M., Botta, C., Deubel, T.: Modelling of Product-Service Systems (PSS) Based on the PDD Approach 2. In: International Design Conference - Design 2004, Dubrovnik, pp. 1–9 (2004)
30. Isaksson, O., Larsson, T.C., Rönnbäck, A.Ö.: Development of Product-Service Systems: Challenges and Opportunities for the Manufacturing Firm. Journal of Engineering Design 20(4), 329–348 (2009)
31. Boughnim, N., Yannou, B.: Using Blueprinting Method for Developing Product-Service Systems. In: International Conference on Engineering Design, pp. 1–16 (2005)
32. Shostack, G.L.: How to Design a Service. European Journal of Marketing 16(1), 49–63 (1982)
33. Maussang, N., Sakao, T., Zwolinski, P., Brissaud, D.: A Model for Designing Product-Service Systems using functional Analysis and Agent based Model. In: International Conference on Engineering Design, ICED 2007, Paris, France, pp. 1–11 (2007)
34. Lee, S.W., Kim, Y.: A Product-Service Systems Design Method Integrating Service Function and Service Activity and Case Studies. In: Proceedings of the 2nd CIRP International Conference on Industrial Product Service Systems, pp. 275–282 (2010)
35. Tan, A., MacAloone, T., Lauridsen, E.: Reflections on Product/Service System (PSS) conceptualisation in a course setting. International Journal of Design Engineering (2009)
36. Gregor, S., Hevner, A.R.: Positioning and Presenting Design Science Research for Maximum Impact. MIS 37(2), 337–355 (2013)
37. Sonnenberg, C., vom Brocke, J.: Evaluations in the Science of the Artificial – Reconsidering the Build-Evaluate Pattern in Design Science Research. In: Peffers, K., Rothenberger, M., Kuechler, B. (eds.) DESRIST 2012. LNCS, vol. 7286, pp. 381–397. Springer, Heidelberg (2012)
38. Global Wind Energy Council: Global Wind Energy Outlook 2012 (2012)
39. Cockburn, A.: Writing Effective Use Cases. Addison-Wesley, Boston (2000)

# A Reference Model for the Information-Based Support of Enterprise Transformations

Nils Labusch, Stephan Aier, and Robert Winter

Institute of Information Management, University of St. Gallen,
St. Gallen, Switzerland
{Nils.Labusch,Stephan.Aier,Robert.Winter}@unisg.ch

**Abstract.** Enterprises from time to time have to go through radical changes, oftentimes referred to as enterprise transformations (ETs). Depending on the type of ET that is conducted, different information requirements exist. In order to support ETs, a reference information model should therefore distinguish different ET types. Based on the empirical analysis of ETs that is used to determine four ET types with different information requirements, we construct such a reference model in the paper at hand. The application of the model is exemplified with the case of enterprise architecture management as an information provider.

**Keywords:** enterprise transformation, information model, enterprise architecture management.

## 1    Introduction

Enterprises from time to time have to go through changes that are not routine but fundamental and radical. These changes are designated as enterprise transformations (ETs) [1]. ETs substantially alter an organization's relationships with its key constituencies like customers or suppliers [1]. Examples of such fundamental changes are adaptions of the business model [2], mergers and acquisitions [3], or introductions and replacements of enterprise-wide information technology [4, 5, 6]. Conducting ETs is challenging and many efforts fail [5, 7]. ETs are also discussed under the terms "business transformation" [8, 9, 10, 11] or "organizational transformation" [6, 12, 13, 14].

Research concerning ETs is conducted since decades in different research disciplines; including information systems (IS) research. However, Besson & Rowe [15] conclude that past and current work mostly focusses on psychological and socio-cognitive inertia (e.g., employee resistance) – socio-technical and economic inertia are underestimated, or seem to be overlooked in ET research. We thus consider ETs a topic that offers huge research potentials for IS researchers due to the holistic perspective that IS can offer about people, tasks, and technology. Supporting ET managers with this perspective also provides significant potentials for practice.

During an ET, many stakeholders are involved which have extensive and diverse information requirements. These oftentimes need to be fulfilled by ET managers (e.g., program managers, C-level executives). Providing decision relevant information for

M.C. Tremblay et al. (Eds.): DESRIST 2014, LNCS 8463, pp. 194–208, 2014.

an ET is a mission critical task [16] and the availability of information at the right time to monitor and troubleshot the ET is described as a major success factor [17].

ET information requirements can be met by sourcing and integrating information from many different information systems. Since ETs affect the entire enterprise, the most important information is usually sourced from enterprise-wide information systems like transactional (ERP) systems, data warehouses, function-specific information systems (e.g., Human Relations), or project/program management IS. Important sources of information are systems that are already build to support enterprise-wide coordination – like, e.g., Enterprise Architecture Management (EAM) information systems. In order to utilize these systems in an ET, an information reference model would be helpful, that allows identifying the relevant information requirements.

However, depending on their drivers, their criticality, affected functions, and other contingencies, ETs are very different. As a consequence, the information requirements of ETs are different. Therefore we need to understand the different types of ET from an information perspective in order to provide appropriate and tailored information support. Our goal therefore is not to propose a 'one size fits all' information reference model for ET support, but instead to leverage the knowledge prevalent in design science research to construct a reference information model that allows distinguishing different ET types. Thus, we pose the following research question:

*RQ: How can information requirements in ETs be structured in a reference information model that allows distinguishing different ET types?*

We proceed as follows: We discuss related work in section two. We go on with introducing our research and design approach. We present results from the classification process of ETs from an information requirements perspective in section four. A demonstration based on EAM as an information provider is presented in section five. The paper is concluded with a summary and limitations in section six.

## 2    Related Work

In academic research, typically two understandings of change are prevalent [18]: On the one hand, evolutionary views assume that organizational change is incremental and continuous. Fundamental differences result from the accumulation of small changes over long periods. On the other hand, punctuated equilibrium models [19] assume that fundamental organizational change occurs in short periods of discontinuous, revolutionary change, which punctuate long eras of relative stability represented by incremental, convergent changes [14].

ET research is rooted in the latter research stream. Examples of such fundamental changes are ETs of the business model [2], mergers & acquisitions [3], or introductions and replacements of enterprise-wide IT systems [4, 5, 6]. Especially because of the latter example and the assumed potential of IT to impose ETs [20], the topic gains attention in the IS community [e.g., 21, 22].

When transforming an enterprise, a high number of decisions, some of them with major consequences, have to be taken. In order to take these decisions on a thorough foundation, manifold information has to be collected and consolidated in short time

[23, 24, 25, 26]. Thus, a fit between the information requirements and the information provision is crucial [16, 27, 28, 29].

However, what is missing in order to take appropriate design decisions for the information provision are details about the information needed most. Thus, a classification is valuable that allows distinguishing different types of ETs and explicates the occurring information demands. While very few classifications exist in order to distinguish ETs [e.g., 1], none of them classifies ETs from an information requirements perspective. We aim at closing these gaps by understanding, which types of ET exist from an information requirements perspective and providing an information reference model for ETs.

Reference models are well-known in IS research. Such a model is considered to be a conceptual framework that can be used as a draft for IS design and development [30]. Reference models exist for different areas, e.g., logistics [31] or quality management [32]. In order to be useful, reference models need to be adaptable to certain situations in an efficient manner and thus need to provide guidance on their adaption [33]. We aim at integrating the determined ET types in order to simplify the adaption and configuration of the proposed model.

## 3     Research Approach

Existing classifications of ETs focus on the respective goals, not on information requirements. However, to allow for a tailoring of information systems concerning the information requirements of an ET, we need a classification that is based on these requirements (and not, e.g., the ET goals). In order to derive such a classification and to identify ET types based on the information requirements, we base our research process on the guidance given by Winter [34] and Bucher & Klesse [35].

### 3.1     Identification of Contingency Factors and Information Requirements

In order to understand the diversity of ETs, we need to identify relevant contingency factors and information requirements. Basically, these are differentiated into three groups: the environment of the ET ("the organization"), the ET itself (goals, reasons, figures, etc.) and the information requirements of ET managers.

In order to identify contingency factors concerning the ET and the organization, we conducted a literature survey in databases (EBSCO and ISI) and top journals of information systems and management science. We followed the Basket of Eight [36] (eight journals) and the European JOURQUAL ranking [37] (journals ranked equal or higher than B in the partial rankings information systems (26 journals) and management (21 journals)). We applied the search term "(((organizational OR enterprise OR business OR radical) AND transformation) OR "radical change")" in the title in combination with the term "(type* OR archetype* OR class* OR categor* OR taxonom* OR segment* OR dimension*)" in the abstract. The search revealed 397 results in total, after reviewing the abstracts; we considered 23 papers relevant for further analysis. We further included sources from forward and backward analysis. We surveyed these sources (mostly empirical studies or cases) in detail, in order to extract concrete contingency factors for the analysis. Examples are goals of the ET [38], affected departments [39], reasons for the ET [14], and figures like the involved resources [e.g. 40].

In order to analyze the information requirements during ETs, we incorporate work that we conducted earlier. In two papers we identified information needs that ET managers potentially would have. One study is based on literature [41] the other on interviews with experts [42]. We consolidate the identified information items from the studies above in one list (see the provided information model in figure 2 for details) with different groups of information and the single information requirements. This list is provided to the ET experts as part of the study. The goal is to identify, whether all of these information requirements were existing during all ETs, or if differences could be identified.

## 3.2    Empirical Analysis

We provided the contingency factors and information objects to four practitioners in one organization in order to evaluate if they were comprehensible and if major aspects were missing. The participants had different job positions that deal with ETs (e.g., project managers, process manager). We wanted to make sure that the contingency factors and information objects are unambiguous and can be judged in reasonable time. During this pilot phase we noticed that filling in the questionnaire takes about 30 minutes. Due to the complexity of the problem domain we consider this amount of time reasonable.

During the pilot phase some information objects needed to be rephrased to increase their clearness and to preserve the meanings from the source papers. In addition, this pretest was meant to identify further contingency factors or information objects that we would need to add. Interestingly, no more factors were added by the experts, which might serve as a quality indicator for the ones we originally choose.

After the pre-test, we provided the questionnaire to a total of 30 highly knowledgeable informants that are able to describe ETs as the unit of analysis. These were for example ET managers, CEOs, or program managers. The informants were asked to rate the items based on a five point Likert scale [43]. We were able to collect data from a variety of industries (see table 1, multiple answers allowed). We consider including multiple industries an advantage due to avoiding industry-specific bias and thus increasing the general applicability of the artifact.

**Table 1.** Overview of participating industries

| Industry | Amount |
|---|---|
| Education | 1 |
| Power Supply | 7 |
| Financial Services | 6 |
| Healthcare | 3 |
| Information & Communication | 8 |
| Production | 4 |
| Transport & Logistics | 1 |
| Insurance | 2 |
| Other | 3 |

## 4     Design Process

### 4.1     Identification of Enterprise Transformation Types

We conducted a hierarchical cluster analysis (Ward's method, squared Euclidian distance) based on the information requirements illustrated above (see the concrete information items in Fig 2.). In order to use as many cases as possible for the analysis, we handled missing values by replacing the missing with column (variable) means. If more than 10% of values were missing, we omitted the case. This procedure left us with 21 ETs that were used for the cluster analysis.

An important challenge when designing a reference model is to determine the number of configurations it supports. Whenever too many configurations exist, the number of organizations decreases were a particular configuration can be applied. A 'one size fits all' model or a model that supports too few configurations, on the other hand, is not considered to be useful because specific requirements cannot be met to a sufficient extent [44, 45]. We determined the number of configurations for our model based on the goal to provide meaningful guidance for the ET support but at the same time adhere to statistical criteria.

A two cluster solution would have been most appropriate concerning the cluster distance (measured by the squared Euclidian distance). However, with this configuration, cluster one would contain two cases while the second cluster would contain the others. With a three cluster solution, clusters would not be a helpful foundation for design since differences of information requirements among the clusters were not concise. In the four cluster solution, clusters are more differentiated concerning their information requirements and hence provide more appropriate guidance for the design step. Five or six cluster solutions do not provide enough differences to warrant another differentiation in the following model design. In consequence, we choose a four cluster solution to guide the following design steps. Figure 1 provides an overview of the summarized mean values in the respective groups of information.

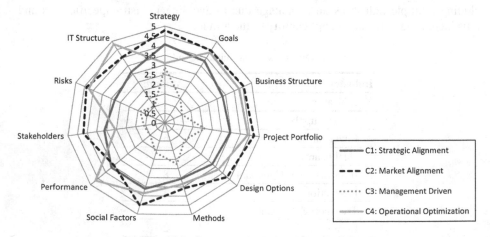

**Fig. 1.** Information demands in the different clusters

Cluster one, *strategic alignment,* represents ETs that are driven by strategic changes or the introduction of new products and necessary changes in the IT. Corporate management, but also IT departments guide these ETs. The strongest goal is optimization (thus, achieving more efficiency, e.g., in processes or IT systems). A second goal is increasing the flexibility of the company (thus, being able to react to future changes in the market environment). Information that was considered most important in this cluster is related to strategy (e.g., business strategy, ET drivers) or goals (e.g., goal descriptions). Information that was considered least important is about locations, information relevant to outsourcing, information about affected stakeholders. Furthermore, information about shareholders, suppliers, internal guidelines, and IT security were of least importance. The average level of information considered necessary, is rather in the middle (compared to the other clusters).

Cluster two, *market alignment* ETs, represents ETs that are driven by the introduction of new products and services or by changes of the addressed market segments. ETs are guided by corporate management and marketing departments. It seems to be consequent that goals of these ETs are mostly repositioning in the market and optimization of internal structures. Thus, in this cluster, the changes in the market environment already happened and triggered a respective reaction by the organization. On average, the information requirement in cluster two is higher than in the first one. Information that is considered to be important in this cluster is similar to the strategic alignment cluster concerning the top-most important ones – especially concerning strategy and goals. However, some information is important that is highly related to the cluster-specific goals, e.g., skills of employees, product portfolio, legislative rules, customers, etc. Less important information is about benefits, current costs as much as quantitative and qualitative monitoring of the success.

Cluster three, *management-driven* ETs, represents ETs that are driven by changes in corporate management and changes of the company structure. They are guided by corporate management. The strongest goal is repositioning. For this kind of ETs the market environment, an overview of projects, redundancies between those projects, etc. were considerably important. However, most values about the importance of the information are very small compared to the other clusters and the overall average of the dataset. ETs in this cluster do not need much information because they are conducted by managers that rely solely on their experience implementing their vision about the organization. Thus, from an information perspective, the support in this cluster can only occur on a very low level.

The ETs represented by cluster four, *operational optimizations* are driven by changes of the environment (e.g., legal-wise) and by necessary adaptations of supporting IT systems. Additional drivers are performance crises or structural changes in the company. It is not surprising that such ETs are guided by the technology/IT departments and the corporate management. The main goal is optimization, partially also repositioning. Most important information that is specific in this cluster is about applications, IT infrastructure, redundancies between projects, capabilities of employees, processes, etc. What are considered least important information are ET drivers, market environment, and most information about external stakeholders. Thus, the ETs that are described in this cluster are mostly internally visible and external impact is less considered.

Based on the findings from literature and the empirical analysis, we are able to design a reference model that consolidates these findings.

## 4.2     Design of an Enterprise Transformation Information Model

We used the clusters above, in order to provide guidance, which information are most considerable in which ET type. We found the median to be an appropriate decision criterion due to its stability concerning outliers. When the information item was rated with the median value itself, it was included in the ET type. Thus, the model below (figure 2) allows for configuration of information systems concerning the four differentiated ET types. This allows for a much more efficient application of the model depending on the ET type, the organization has to conduct.

The model is comprised of eleven information groups that contain more detailed information items. For each information item an indicator label is assigned that provides configuration guidance. Each ET is supposed to mostly belong to one of the clusters introduced above. Once the ET type is determined, the indicator color next to the information item provides guidance about the relevance of the information item for this specific ET type. When the indicator is colored white, the information item is not relevant for the corresponding cluster. Consider for example the information item "important steps" in the "strategy" information group. It is relevant for all types of ET, except the management-driven (Cluster 3) ones.

Due to the level of abstraction in the model, we do not provide detailed relations between the information groups, since information needs to be combined and exchanged in many ways that are depending on the concrete ET in the concrete organization. In very broad terms, the information groups relate together as follows: In order to prepare a sufficient strategy for the ET, the transformation's most important steps, its market environment, its drivers, and the business strategy are needed to be known. Based on the ET strategy, ET managers need to determine the goals of the ET. Strategy and goals of the ET define how the ET changes business and IT structures. Based on the goals, strategy, and existing structures, different design options can be proposed and evaluated. Operationally, the ET has to be broken down in projects and project portfolios that leverage the available skills and resources. During the ET, the performance needs to be monitored. Different stakeholders that are involved in the ET need to be known and addressed. They impose social factors that heavily influence the ET. In order to ensure the success of the ET, risks need to be assessed and handled. All of the above aspects can be improved by applying methods that are designed in order to support ETs.

In concrete ETs, however, organizations need to further discuss and evaluate the model concerning their particular ET. In addition, organizations need to determine, which departments, disciplines, or information systems can provide which information that is considered to be necessary. On the other hand, designers of, e.g., information systems can use the model to analyze, in which ETs their system could be applied and add value. We use the IS enterprise architecture management (EAM) in order to demonstrate its role for the information supply in different ETs in the next section.

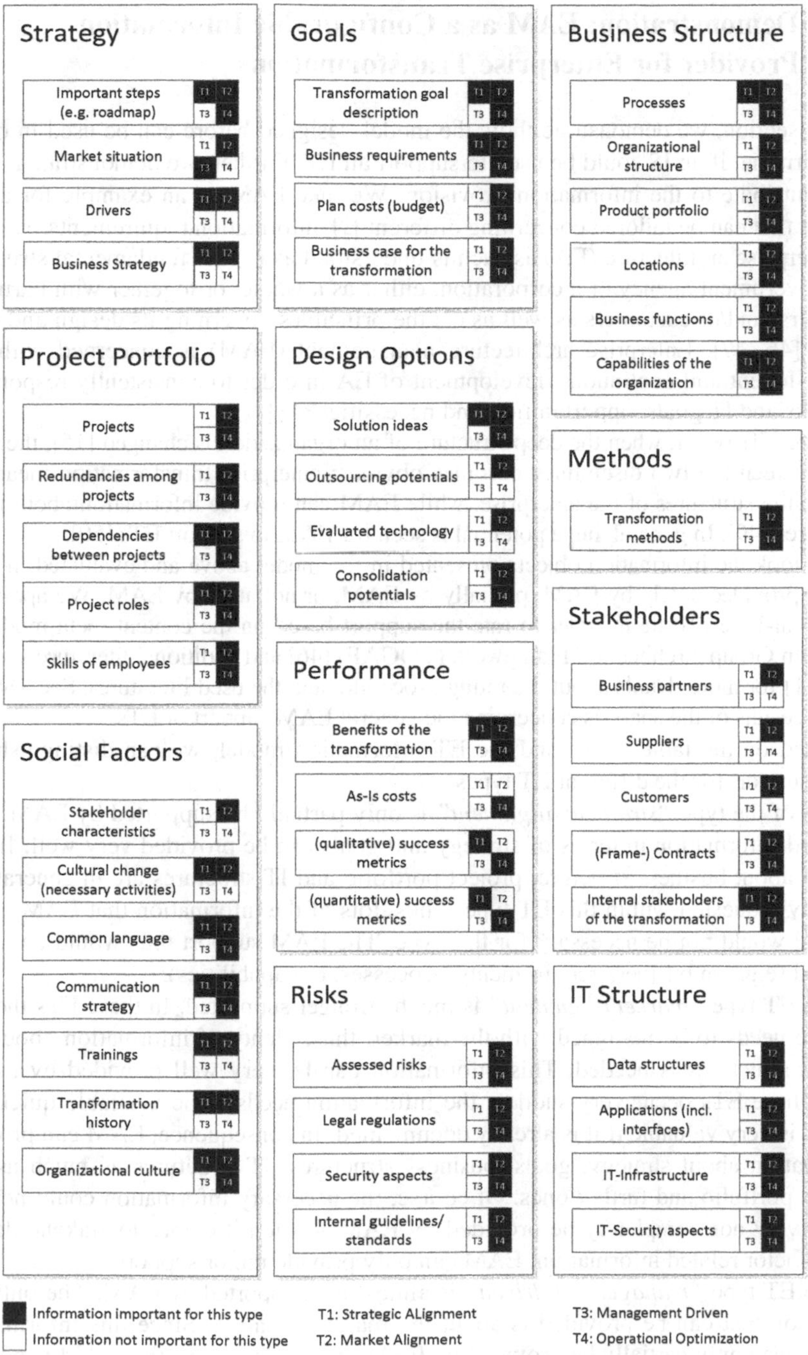

## Strategy

- Important steps (e.g. roadmap) — T1 T2 T3 T4
- Market situation — T1 T2 T3 T4
- Drivers — T1 T2 T3 T4
- Business Strategy — T1 T2 T3 T4

## Goals

- Transformation goal description — T1 T2 T3 T4
- Business requirements — T1 T2 T3 T4
- Plan costs (budget) — T1 T2 T3 T4
- Business case for the transformation — T1 T2 T3 T4

## Business Structure

- Processes — T1 T2 T3 T4
- Organizational structure — T1 T2 T3 T4
- Product portfolio — T1 T2 T3 T4
- Locations — T1 T2 T3 T4
- Business functions — T1 T2 T3 T4
- Capabilities of the organization — T1 T2 T3 T4

## Project Portfolio

- Projects — T1 T2 T3 T4
- Redundancies among projects — T1 T2 T3 T4
- Dependencies between projects — T1 T2 T3 T4
- Project roles — T1 T2 T3 T4
- Skills of employees — T1 T2 T3 T4

## Design Options

- Solution ideas — T1 T2 T3 T4
- Outsourcing potentials — T1 T2 T3 T4
- Evaluated technology — T1 T2 T3 T4
- Consolidation potentials — T1 T2 T3 T4

## Methods

- Transformation methods — T1 T2 T3 T4

## Social Factors

- Stakeholder characteristics — T1 T2 T3 T4
- Cultural change (necessary activities) — T1 T2 T3 T4
- Common language — T1 T2 T3 T4
- Communication strategy — T1 T2 T3 T4
- Trainings — T1 T2 T3 T4
- Transformation history — T1 T2 T3 T4
- Organizational culture — T1 T2 T3 T4

## Performance

- Benefits of the transformation — T1 T2 T3 T4
- As-Is costs — T1 T2 T3 T4
- (qualitative) success metrics — T1 T2 T3 T4
- (quantitative) success metrics — T1 T2 T3 T4

## Stakeholders

- Business partners — T1 T2 T3 T4
- Suppliers — T1 T2 T3 T4
- Customers — T1 T2 T3 T4
- (Frame-) Contracts — T1 T2 T3 T4
- Internal stakeholders of the transformation — T1 T2 T3 T4

## Risks

- Assessed risks — T1 T2 T3 T4
- Legal regulations — T1 T2 T3 T4
- Security aspects — T1 T2 T3 T4
- Internal guidelines/ standards — T1 T2 T3 T4

## IT Structure

- Data structures — T1 T2 T3 T4
- Applications (incl. interfaces) — T1 T2 T3 T4
- IT-Infrastructure — T1 T2 T3 T4
- IT-Security aspects — T1 T2 T3 T4

■ Information important for this type
□ Information not important for this type

T1: Strategic ALignment
T2: Market Alignment
T3: Management Driven
T4: Operational Optimization

**Fig. 2.** ET reference information model

## 5    Demonstration: EAM as a Configurable Information Provider for Enterprise Transformations

In this section, we demonstrate, how the model designed before can be used in order to determine, if an IS could be used to support an ET. Further, we demonstrate how it can contribute to the information provision. We take EAM as an example for an IS artifact that can be tailored concerning different ET information requirements.

Enterprise architecture (EA) as such is understood as (1) the fundamental structure of a government agency or a corporation, either as a whole, or together with partners, suppliers, and/or customers as well as (2) the principles governing its design and evolution [46, 47]. Enterprise architecture management (EAM) is concerned with the establishment and continuous development of EA in order to consistently respond to business and IT goals, opportunities, and necessities [48].

Since ETs occur, when the deep structure of an organization is changed [15], the relation between the two disciplines becomes obvious: enterprise transformation means to change the structures of the enterprise, while EAM can provide information about these structures [49]. In general, huge potential is seen for EAM to support ETs [50].

We took the information objects presented in the model above and evaluated, if they can be provided solely by EAM, partially by EAM, or not at all by EAM. We applied a five point-Likert-Scale in order to rate the support based on the content meta-model of the Open Group Architecture Framework (TOGAF) [46] and additional literature sources (see [41] for more details about the rating procedure and the used literature). See Table 1 for the results of the analysis concerning the general EAM support of ETs.

Based on the table above and the ET information model, we can distinguish the EAM support for the different ET types.

ETs of the type *"strategic alignment"* is only partially be supported by EAM. The required information in terms of strategy and goals can be provided very well. Information about business structure, project portfolio and IT structures are in general not strongly requested within this ET type. Thus, lots of the information that EAM could provide would not be necessary for this type. The EAM support thus would be much focused (e.g., on business requirements, processes, or capabilities).

The ET type *"market alignment"* is much stronger supported. In these ETs the enterprise needs to be realigned with the market, thus, plenty of information about the current structures is needed. This information can be very well provided by EAM. Since these ETs occur very sudden, the information needs to be available quickly – thus, it is very valuable if it is already documented. In consequence, EAM can provide information about strategy, goals, business structures, IT structures as much as the project portfolio and further ones. Of course, the necessary information could neither exclusively nor completely be provided by EAM – when it comes to stakeholder or social factor related information, EAM can only provide minor support.

The ET type *"management driven"* is almost not supported by EAM. The only information that can be provided is about the market situation. Since this information can anyway only partially be provided by EAM, the model shows that EAM is not the preferred discipline/information system to support the ET type.

**Table 2.** EAM support of ETs

| Information | EAM Support |
|---|---|
| Strategy | Support differs, business strategy and drivers could be provided very appropriately, market situation rather partially, important steps (e.g. in terms of a roadmap) could be provided very well. |
| Goals | Goals and requirements are direct meta-model elements of EAM, information to determine budgets and develop business cases could be partially provided. |
| Business Structure | Knowledge about structures is often considered the core of EAM, thus these are all direct part of the content meta-model and the support is very strong. |
| Project Portfolio | Information about projects and skills are also considered core of EAM. |
| Design Options | EAM can partially contribute in providing design options, however, many more stakeholders need to be involved. |
| Methods | The content meta-model does not consider ET methods, minor support could be possible since architects are often keen on methods. |
| Social Factors | Social factors are usually not contributed by EAM. Establishing and designing a common language is part of EAM. |
| Performance | EAM is able to collect benefits of ETs and additional qualitative measures. Financial side is out of EAM scope. |
| Stakeholders | Concerning Stakeholders, EAM is able to provide information about contracts, suppliers and internal stakeholders of the ET since these are content meta-model elements. |
| Risks | Guidelines/standards can be provided. |
| IT Structure | Providing Information about IT structures is core of EAM. |

For *"operational optimizations"* EAM again can provide valuable information. According to the model, strategic aspects are almost not important and ETs of this type rather require fundamental knowledge about the business and IT structure of the company in order to realize optimizations. Thus, these ETs directly address again the core of EAM.

Figure 3 illustrated the summary of the EAM system support differentiated by ET type.

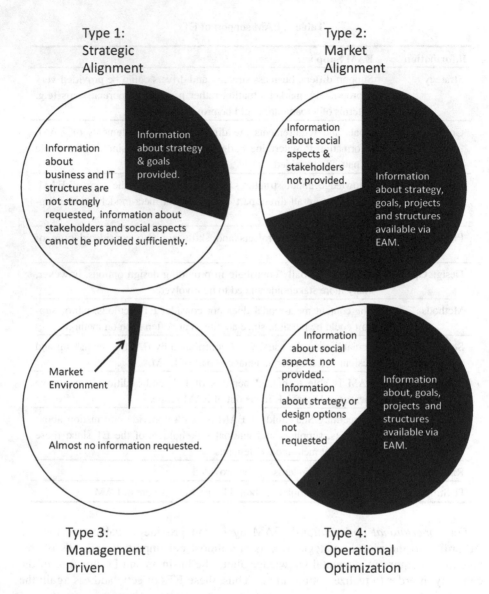

**Fig. 3.** EAM system support differentiated by ET type

## 6    Summary, Limitations and Outlook

In the paper at hand we provide a reference information model that allows distinguishing different types of ETs based on the information that ET managers require. The model distinguishes four different ET types that have been identified with an empirical analysis of ETs. Based on the model, we demonstrate how the information provision by EAM needs to be configured, in order to fulfill ET-type dependent information requirements. The demonstration shows that certain types of ET can be much better supported by IS than others. Our contribution to the body of ET literature therefore is a model that allows for providing information during ETs much more focused. Further, the model provides a dense overview of information that is necessary in ETs.

In order to identify, how the best information support for the identified ET types can be assured, the demonstration that we conducted should be repeated with other information systems beyond EAM. Candidates are ERP systems, business intelligence systems, or other enterprise-wide IS.

Some limitations occur in the presented research. It could be the case that further clusters exist that we did not identify due to a limited amount of transformation cases. This problem occurs whenever complex real-world phenomena are researched and abstracted in a model. Future work and an increased empirical foundation of the model will show, if the identified types need to be revised or if they will be confirmed. Due to the highly knowledgeable informants that we collected the responses from, we are reasonably confident to assume the latter. Further, each ET in the evaluated set of data is described by one respondent. Due to the manifold roles that conduct ET management (e.g., program managers, C-level executives), role-specific differences about required information could occur. Based on the current amount of data collected, we are not able to account for these differences. However, such different information requirements by different roles provide an interesting field for future research.

Additional future work planned in the project is to provide the model to practitioners that deal with EAM during ETs. Focus groups or interviews with these experts will provide valuable feedback and input to the model in order to further increase its applicability and utility, especially in the domain of EAM. We invite researches that primarily deal with other IS to extent and apply the model in their domains.

**Acknowledgement.** This work has been funded by the Swiss National Science Foundation (SNSF).

# References

1. Rouse, W.B.: A Theory of Enterprise Transformation. Systems Engineering 8(4), 279–295 (2005)
2. Aspara, J., Lamberg, J.-A., Laukia, A., Tikkanen, H.: Strategic management of business model transformation: lessons from Nokia. Management Decision 49(4), 622–647 (2011)
3. Johnston, J., Madura, J.: Valuing the Potential Transformation of Banks into Financial Service Conglomerates: Evidence from the Citigroup Merger. The Financial Review 35(2), 17–36 (2000)
4. Bhattacharya, P.J., Seddon, P.B., Scheepers, R.: Enabling Strategic Transformations with Enterprise Systems: Beyond Operational Efficiency. In: ICIS 2010 Proceedings, p. 55 (2010)
5. Sarker, S., Lee, A.S.: IT-enabled organizational transformation: a case study of BPR failure at TELECO. The Journal of Strategic Information Systems 8(1), 83–103 (1999)

6. Hock-Hai Teo, B., Tan, C.Y., Wei, K.-K.: Organizational Transformation Using Electronic Data Interchange: The Case of TradeNet in Singapore. Journal of Management Information Systems 13(4), 139–165 (1997)
7. Kotter, J.P.: Leading Change: Why Transformation Efforts Fail. Harvard Business Review 73(2), 59–67 (1995)
8. Ashurst, C., Hodges, J.: Exploring Business Transformation: The Challenges of Developing a Benefits Realization Capability. Journal of Change Management 10(2), 217–237 (2010)
9. Ash, C.G., Burn, J.M.: Assessing the benefits from e-business transformation through effective enterprise management. European Journal of Information Systems 12, 297–308 (2003)
10. Daniel, E.M., Wilson, H.N.: The role of dynamic capabilities in e-business transformation. European Journal of Information Systems 12, 282–296 (2003)
11. Davidson, W.H.: Beyond Re-Engineering: The Three Phases of Business Transformation. IBM Systems Journal 32(1), 65–79 (1993)
12. Dixon, S.E.A., Meyer, K.E., Day, M.: Stages of Organizational Transformation in Transition Economies: A Dynamic Capabilities Approach. Journal of Management Studies 47(3), 416–436 (2010)
13. Orlikowski, W.J.: Improvising Organizational Transformation Over Time: A Situated Change Perspective. Information Systems Research 7(1), 63–92 (1996)
14. Romanelli, E., Tushman, M.L.: Organizational Transformation as Punctuated Equilibrium: An Empirical Test. Academy of Management Journal 37(5), 1141–1166 (1994)
15. Besson, P., Rowe, F.: Strategizing information systems-enabled organizational transformation: A transdisciplinary review and new directions. Journal of Strategic Information Systems 21(2), 103–124 (2012)
16. Galbraith, J.R.: Organization Design: An Information Processing View. Interfaces 4(3), 28–36 (1974)
17. Keller, S., Meaney, M., Pung, C.: McKinsey Global Survey results: What successful transformations share (2010)
18. Wischnevsky, J.D., Damanpour, F.: Punctuated Equilibrium Model of Organizational Transformation: Sources and Consequences in the Banking Industry. Research In Organizational Change and Development 15, 207–239 (2005)
19. Gersick, C.J.G.: Revolutionary Change Theories: A Multilevel Exploration of the Punctuated Equilibrium Paradigm. Academy of Management Review 16(1), 10–36 (1991)
20. Cooper, R.B.: Information technology development creativity: a case study of attempted radical change. MIS Quarterly 24(2), 245–276 (2000)
21. Thorogood, A., Reynolds, P., Yetton, P.: Performing Under Pressure: IT Execution in a $1.4bn Business Transformation. In: ICIS 2010 Proceedings, p. 164 (2010)
22. Sammon, D., Adam, F.: Justifying an ERP Investment: Critical Success Factors for Transformation Investments. In: ICIS 2008 Proceedings, p. 60 (2008)
23. Tichy, N.M.: Managing Organizational Transformations. Human Resource Management 22(1-2), 45–60 (1983)
24. Fry, L.W., Vitucci, S., Cedillo, M.: Spiritual leadership and army transformation: Theory, measurement, and establishing a baseline. The Leadership Quarterly 16, 835–862 (2005)
25. Singh, R., Mathiassen, L., Stachura, M.E., Astapova, E.V.: Dynamic Capabilities in Home Health: IT-Enabled Transformation of Post-Acute Care. ournal of the Association for Information Systems 12(2), Article 2 (2011)
26. Klein, A., Krcmar, H.: DCXNET: E-Transformation at DaimlerChrysler. In: ICIS 2003 Proceedings, p. 103 (2003)

27. Galbraith, J.R.: Designing Organizations: An Excecutive Guide to Strategy, Structure, and Process. Jossey-Bass, San Francisco (2002)
28. Galbraith, J.R.: Designing Complex Organizations. Addison-Wesley, Boston (1973)
29. Galbraith, J.R.: Organization Design. Addison-Wesley, Reading (1977)
30. Fettke, P., Loos, P.: Perspectives on Reference Modeling. In: Fettke, P., Loos, P. (eds.) Reference Modeling for Business Systems Analysis, pp. 1–20. Idea Group Publishing, Hershey, PA and London (2007)
31. Holten, R., Melchert, F.: Das Supply Chain Operations Reference (SCOR)-Modell. In: Becker, J., Knackstedt, R. (eds.) Wissensmanagement Mit Referenzmodellen. Konzepte für die Anwendungssystem- und Organisationsgestaltung, pp. 207–226. Physica, Heidelberg (2002)
32. European Foundation for Quality, M.: The EFQM Excellence Modell. EFQM Representative Office, Brüssel (1999)
33. Becker, J., Delfmann, P., Knackstedt, R.: Adaptive Reference Modeling: Integrating Configurative and Generic Adaptation Techniques for Information Models. In: Becker, J., Delfmann, P. (eds.) Reference Modeling, pp. 27–58. Physica, Heidelberg (2007)
34. Winter, R.: Problem Analysis for Situational Artefact Construction in Information Systems. In: Carugati, A., Rossignoli, C. (eds.) Emerging Themes in Information Systems and Organization Studies, pp. 97–113. Physica, Heidelberg (2011)
35. Bucher, T., Klesse, M., Kurpjuweit, S., Winter, R.: Situational Method Engineering - On the Differentiation of "Context" and "Project Type". In: Situational Method Engineering - Fundamentals and Experiences, pp. 33–48. Springer, Geneva (2007)
36. Association for Information, S.: Senior Scholars' Basket of Journals. Springer, Heidelberg (2010)
37. Schrader, U., Hennig-Thurau, T.: VHB-JOURQUAL2: Method, Results, and Implications of the German Academic Association for Business Research's Journal Ranking. BuR - Business Research 2(2), 180–204 (2009)
38. Baumöl, U.: Strategic Agility through Situational Method Construction. In: Proceedings of the European Academy of Management Annual Conference 2005, München (2005)
39. Porter, M.E.: Competitive Advantage: Creating and Sustaining Superior Performance. Free Press, New York (1985)
40. eurostat (ed.): NACE Rev. 2 Statistical classification of economic activities in the European Community, Luxembourg (2008)
41. Labusch, N., Winter, R.: Towards a Conceptualization of Architectural Support for Enterprise Transformation. In: Proceedings of the European Conference on Information Systems (ECIS) 2013, Utrecht, NL (2013)
42. Labusch, N., Aier, S., Rothenberger, M., Winter, R.: Architectural Support of Enterprise Transformations: Insights from Corporate Practice. In: Tagungsband Multikonferenz Wirtschaftsinformatik 2014, pp. 1048–1060. Universität Paderborn, Paderborn (2014)
43. Likert, R.: A Technique for the Measurement of Attitudes. Archives of Psychology 22(140), 1–55 (1932)
44. vom Brocke, J., Thomas, O.: Designing Infrastructures for Reusing Conceptual Models - A General Framework and its Application for Collaborative Reference Modeling. In: Proceedings of the Ninth International Conference on Business Information Systems (BIS 2006), Klagenfurt, Austria (2006)
45. Becker, J., Delfmann, P., Knackstedt, R., Kuropka, D.: Konfigurative Referenzmodellierung. In: Becker, J., Knackstedt, R. (eds.) Wissensmanagement mit Referenzmodellen. Konzepte für die Anwendungssystem- und Organisationsgestaltung, pp. 25–144. Physica, Heidelberg (2002)

46. The Open Group: TOGAF Version 9.1 (2011)
47. Winter, R., Fischer, R.: Essential Layers, Artifacts, and Dependencies of Enterprise Architecture. Journal of Enterprise Architecture 3(2), 7–18 (2007)
48. Aier, S., Gleichauf, B., Winter, R.: Understanding Enterprise Architecture Management Design – An Empirical Analysis. In: Proceedings of the 10th International Conference on Wirtschaftsinformatik WI 2.011, Zurich, pp. 645–654 (2011)
49. Gardner, D., Fehskens, L., Naidu, M., Rouse, W.B., Ross, J.: Point-Counterpoint: Enterprise Architecture and Enterprise Transformation as Related but Distinct Concepts. Journal of Enterprise Transformation 2(4), 283–294 (2012)
50. Winter, R., Townson, S., Uhl, A., Labusch, N., Noack, J.: Enterprise Architecture and Business Transformation: The Difference and Synergy Potential. 360° – The Business Transformation Journal (2012)

# Mining Configurable Process Fragments
# for Business Process Design

Nour Assy, Walid Gaaloul, and Bruno Defude

Computer Science Department, Telecom SudParis
UMR 5157 CNRS Samovar, France

**Abstract.** As business requirements become increasingly challenging in today's fast changing environments, cross-organizational collaboration gains more and more attention for a successful business process design. Since many organizations may work on similar processes with some variations, *configurable reference models* have been proposed as a key aspect for a flexible process design. However, the complexity introduced by such models remains an open issue. The designer ends up with one model that integrates a family of process variants making the process design and update a complex task. In this work, we propose to assist the designer with *configurable process fragments*. However, instead of building the configurable process fragment from existing process models, we propose to use event logs as input. Such recorded executions capture the *real behavior* of processes which cannot be derived from their designed models. Then, using these logs we derive *guidelines* that direct the configuration of the resulted fragment. Our approach has been implemented as a plugin in the ProM framework and tested using a collection of event logs.

## 1 Introduction

The fast changing in today's business requirements forces organizations to adopt new paradigms for increasing their processes' adaptability. In such a highly dynamic environment, process design becomes a complex, time-consuming and less-effective task. Therefore, multiple organizations tend to share their processes experience in a common infrastructure to enable learning best practices from each other [1]. To this end, *configurable process models* [2,3] have been proposed to enable a flexible cross-organizational collaboration.

A configurable process model integrates a family of process variants into one consolidated model using configurable elements. At design-time, configurable elements are configured by selecting only the relevant parts according to process design requirements. In this way, business designers can derive individual process models that fit to their specific needs without an extra design effort. Recently, some approaches proposed to build configurable process models from a collection of existing process variants [4–6]; Others tried to mine one configurable process model out of collections of *event logs* [7–9]. However, these approaches have three main drawbacks. First, they may encounter the problem of managing the complexity of the resulted configurable model when input variants are large and

M.C. Tremblay et al. (Eds.): DESRIST 2014, LNCS 8463, pp. 209–224, 2014.
© Springer International Publishing Switzerland 2014

varied [10]. Second, they provide only the possibility of deriving and reusing **entire** existing process models. And last, they do not assist the configuration of the process by exploring the **usage** of existing processes.

In our previous work [11], we addressed the first issue by proposing an approach that assists business designers with *configurable process fragments* built from process models. Nevertheless, process models are not a source always available and do not provide the real behavior of their executions. To this end, process mining has gained a huge interest in business process management researches [12] as event logs record the real behavior of the processes and they are always available in all today's information systems. Therefore, in this work, we propose to use process mining techniques to discover the configurable process fragment from a collection of event logs. Moreover, to handle the second and third issue, we propose a frequency-based approach that guides the configuration of the resulted fragment. Concretely, we explore the (in)frequent executions in the event logs in order to derive *ranked guidelines* that help in deriving a suitable configuration.

The remainder of this paper is structured as follows: Our motivation is presented in Section 2. In Section 3, some notions on configurable process fragments and process mining are provided. Section 4 elaborates our approach to mine a configurable process fragment. In Section 5, we detail our proposition to extend the discovered fragment with guidelines. Section 6.2 illustrates our experimental results. Some related work is depicted in Section 7 and we conclude in Section 8.

## 2    Motivation

Let us consider a car rental agency that has two branches in different countries. These branches execute different variants of the same process that slightly differ in their structure and behavior according to the country and customers needs (see Fig. 1). The two variant models depicted in the right of Fig. 1 and modeled in BPMN (Business Process Modeling Notation) illustrate the corresponding event logs (on the left of Fig. 1). In the first variant, the customer submits a request through a web form (activity $x$) which is received by the agency (activity $a$). Then, it checks the customer's credit (activity $b$) and the car availability (activity $c$). Based on a processing step (activity $z$), if the request is accepted, its details are saved (activity $d$). Afterwards, the user profile is updated (activity $f$) and a confirmation email is sent to the customer (activity $e$); and last a customer feedback is received (activity $p$). In the other case, the request is aborted (activity $g$) and a cancellation email is sent to the customer (activity $h$). In the second variant, the customer sends his request by email (activity $y$). Compared to the previous variant, the customer personal information (activity $i$) is registered along with checking customer's credit (activity $b$) and car availability (activity $c$). After the request is saved (activity $d$), either a confirmation (activity $e$) or cancellation email (activity $h$) is sent. And before receiving the customer feedback (activity $p$), new services are offered (activity $o$). If the request is rejected, others' cars propositions are given (activity $l$). Next, they are sent to the customer (activity $m$) and the request is archived (activity $n$). Each process

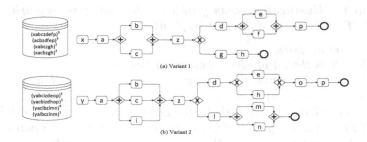

**Fig. 1.** Two event logs with their corresponding variant models of a car rental process

execution is logged as an instance in the event log; For example, in Fig. 1(a), five instances of the execution $xabczdefp$ are logged.

Suppose that (i) a new branch is opening and needs to define its own process or (ii) an existing branch needs to enhance or create a new variant of its existing process. In the first case, the business designer starts modeling the process with the activity "a" followed by the activity "z". At this point, she may need some assistance to complete the process. In the second case, the designer may need to enhance or create a new variant from her process model by modifying only some parts causing efficiency degradation of the process; for example by modifying the fragment that includes the activity "z".

To benefit from past experience, one solution would be to search in the existing process models the activities that occur frequently with the selected one. However, designed process models do not provide information on their *usage* and they may be inaccurate when their real executions deviate from their expected described behavior. In addition, process models are not always explicitly defined and the only information we have is the recorded logs. Therefore, we propose in this work to discover from a collection of event logs a **configurable process fragment** that includes the selected activity (i.e. in our example "z") and its interactions with its neighbors. Afterwards, using the observed behavior in the event logs, we derive *guidelines* that assist the designer in deriving a *frequently* executed individual fragment. For instance, the designer may be interested to know that the activity "check car availability" is **often** executed with "check customer's credit" but **rarely** with "register customer information". Such information cannot be derived by looking only to the designed fragment model.

## 3 Preliminaries

### 3.1 Configurable Process Model

A process model can be represented as directed graph with labeled nodes that we call *Business Process Graph*. This notation is derived from the common constructs of most graph-based process modeling languages such as EPC (Event-Driven Process Chain), BPMN, UML, etc.

**Definition 1.** *(Business process graph).* *A business process graph*
$G = (N, E, T, L)$ *is a labeled directed graph where:*

- *$N$ is the set of nodes,*
- *$E \subseteq N \times N$ is the set of edges connecting two nodes,*
- *$T : N \to t$ is a function that assigns for each node $n \in N$ a type $t$ where*
  *$t \in \{activity, gateway\}$*
- *$L : N \to label$ is a function that assigns for each node $n \in N$ a label such*
  *that if $T(n) = activity$, then $L(n)$ is its name, and if $T(n) = gateway$ then*
  *$L(n) \in \{\vee, \wedge, \times\}$ where $\vee = OR$, $\wedge = AND$ and $\times = XOR$.*

Let $G = (N, E, T, L)$ be a business process graph and $n \in N$. We define
the pre- and postset activity of a gateway $g \in N$ as the set of preceding and
succeeding activities in its incoming and outgoing branches respectively.

**Definition 2.** *(preset activity $\bullet g$, postset activity $g \bullet$).* *The preset activity*
*of a gateway $g \in N$ is denoted as $\bullet g = \{a \in N : ((a, g) \in E) \vee (\exists g_1, g_2, .., g_k \in$*
*$N : (a, g_1), (g_1, g_2), ..., (g_k, g) \in E)\}$. Similarly, the postset activity of $g$ is denoted*
*as $g \bullet = \{a \in N : ((g, a) \in E) \vee (\exists g_1, g_2, .., g_k \in N : (g, g_1), (g_1, g_2), ..., (g_k, a) \in$*
*$E)\}$.*

For example, in Fig. 2, $\wedge_1 \bullet = \{a, b, i\}$, $\vee_5 \bullet = \{h, f, e\}$, etc.

A configurable process model is a process model that integrates multiple model
variants through configurable elements. A configurable element is an element
whose **configuration decision is made at design-time** [3]. Configurable elements can be *gateways* and/or *activities*. A configurable gateway has a generic
behavior which is restricted by configuration. For example, a configurable "$\vee$"
can be configured to an "$\wedge$" or an "$\times$" with(out) restricted incoming or outgoing branches. A configurable activity can be included (i.e. $ON$), excluded (i.e.
$OFF$) or optionally included (i.e. $OPT$). Moreover, configuration decision can be
assisted with *guidelines* that specify a suitable configuration for a given configurable element. In our approach, configurable elements are *gateways* since their
configurations include those of the activities. For instance, a restricted outgoing
configurable gateway's branch excludes the corresponding postset activities (i.e
the corresponding activities are $OFF$). In addition, we propose an approach to
derive guidelines ranked with *high*, *medium* or *low* depending on whether such
configuration is highly, moderately or weakly recommended.

**Definition 3.** *(Configurable process model).* *A configurable process model*
*is denoted as $G^c = (N, E, T, L, B, C, G)$ where:*

- *$N, E, T, L$ are as specified in Definition 1;*
- *$B : N \to \{true, false\}$ is a boolean function returning true for configurable*
  *nodes;*
- *$C : N \to conf$ is a function that assigns for configurable gateways a valid*
  *configuration $conf$ (see Definition 4);*
- *$G : N \to (C, R)$ is a function that assigns for a configurable node a guideline*
  *$(c, r) \in (C, R)$ where $c$ is a configuration and $r \in \{high, medium, low\}$ is a*
  *corresponding rank.*

**Definition 4. (Configuration C).** *Let $G^c = (N, E, T, L, B, C, G)$ be a configurable process. For each $g^c \in N$ such that $T(g^c) = gateway \land B(g^c) = true$, we define its configuration $C(g^c) = < g, \bullet g >$ in case $g^c$ is a join gateway and $C(g^c) = < g, g \bullet >$ in case $g^c$ is a split gateway where $T(g) = gateway$ such that:*

1. *$g \preceq g^c$ where $\preceq$ is a partial order that specifies which concrete gateway may be used for a given configurable gateway, i.e. $g \preceq g^c$ iff $T(g^c) = $ "$\lor$" or $T(g) = T(g^c)$*
2. *$g \bullet \subseteq g^c \bullet$, i.e. $g$ has restricted outgoing branches in case $g^c$ is a split gateway;*
3. *$\bullet g \subseteq \bullet g^c$, i.e. $g$ has restricted incoming branches in case $g^c$ is a join gateway.*

An example of a configurable model is depicted in Fig. 2, where configurable nodes are denoted by thick circles and an excerpt of guidelines are attached as a text annotation. One possible configuration of the configurable "$\land_1$" is $C(\land) = < \land, \{b, c\} >$ as $\land \preceq \land$ and $\{b, c\} \subset \{b, c, i\}$.

## 3.2 Process Mining

Process mining is a field in the process management that includes the set of techniques for extracting process information from event logs. The process discovery is defined in the context of process mining and aims at discovering a process model from recorded event logs [13–15]. A record, called *trace*, is a valid execution of a process. A trace $t = a_1 a_2 ... a_n$ is a sequence of executed activities where $a_1$ is the start activity and $a_n$ is the end activity; $|t| = n$ is the length of $t$ and $t[i]$ is the $i^{th}$ activity. The set of traces relative to a process form the event log $L = \{t_i : 1 \leq i \leq |L|\}$. The alphabet $A = \{a_1, a_2, ..., a_m\}$ defined over $L$ is the set of distinct activities in $L$ where $|A| = m$ denotes its cardinality.

We denote by $(a \prec b)_t$ the precedence relation between $a$ and $b$ in the trace $t$ iff $\exists 1 \leq i < j \leq n$, $a_i = a \land a_j = b$. Based on the *precedence* relation, we define four ordering relations that can be derived from an event log $L$.

- **Causal relation a $\rightarrow$ b** iff $\forall t \in L : a, b \in t \implies (a \prec b)_t \land \neg(b \prec a)_t$, i.e. for all traces containing $a$ and $b$, $a$ always appears before $b$.
- **Parallel relation a $\otimes$ b** iff $\exists t_1, t_2 \in L : a, b \in t_1 \land a, b \in t_2 \implies (a \prec b)_{t_1} \land (b \prec a)_{t_2}$, i.e. there exists a trace $t_1$ in which $a$ appears before $b$ and another trace $t_2$ in which $b$ appears before $a$.
- **Conditional relation a $\otimes$ b** iff $\exists t \in L : a \in t \land b \notin t$, i.e. there exists a trace in which $a$ appears without $b$.

It is worth noting that an obvious mapping function $M$ exists between the relations in a business process graph $G$ and a corresponding event log $L$ where: $M(\land) = \otimes$, $M(\times) = \otimes$ and $M(\lor) = \otimes \land \otimes$.

## 4  Mining Configurable Process Fragments

This section elaborates our approach to mine a configurable process fragment out of collections of event logs. Assuming the existing of an event log repository, we define $\mathbb{L} = \{L_i : i \geq 1\}$ as the set of available event logs and $\mathbb{A} = \{A_i : i \geq 1\}$ as the set of the corresponding alphabets. First, we extract from each event log a sublog relative to the neighborhood context of a selected activity (Section 4.1). Then, we merge the extracted sublogs into one sublog in order to mine one process fragment in which we identify the configurable elements (Section 4.2).

## 4.1   Deriving the Neighborhood Context Log

The neighborhood context log of an activity $a \in A$ derived from an event log $L$ represents the portions of traces in $L$ that contain "$a$" and its neighbors' activities. A *neighbor activity* is an activity connected to "$a$" via a causal, parallel or conditional relation (see Section 3.2). Since a causal relation $a \rightarrow b$ is general and assumes the existence of a flow of activities from $a$ to $b$, we define its length $k$ denoted as $a \rightarrow_k b$ in order to limit the causal neighbors of $a$. This definition in inspired from an earlier work on Petri-nets semantics [16]. Two activities $a$ and $b$ are in a $k^{th}$-causal relation if there exist $k$ flows between them.

**Definition 5. ($k^{th}$-causal relation):** *two activities $a$ and $b$ are in a $k^{th}$-causal relation in the event log $L$ denoted by $a \rightarrow_k b$ iff: $(a \rightarrow b) \wedge (\exists t = a_1 a_2 ... a_n \in L : a_i = a \wedge a_{i+k} = b : 1 \leq i \leq n$ such that $\forall t_x = a_1 a_2 ... a_n : t_x \neq t, a_i = a \wedge a_{i+l} = b \implies k < l)$.*

For example, in the event log in Fig. 1(a), $b \rightarrow_2 d$ since $b \rightarrow d$ and in the second trace (i.e $acbzdfep$) there is one activity $z$ between $b$ and $d$.

Based on a selected length $k$, we extract the neighborhood context log $L_a^k$ relative to the activity $a$ by projecting the traces in the initial log $L$ on the activities that are in 1 to $k^{th}$-causal, parallel and conditional relations with $a$. Formally, a projection function is defined as:

**Definition 6. (Projection $Pr(L, A)$).** *A projection function $Pr$ defined over an event log $L$ restricted by an alphabet $A$ is defined as follows: $\forall 1 \leq i \leq |L|$ : $t_i \in L \wedge t_i[j] \notin A, 1 \leq j \leq |t_i| \implies t_i[j] = $ "$-$".*

**Definition 7. (Neighborhood context log).** *The neighborhood context log of an activity $a$ derived from the event log $L$ and its corresponding alphabet $A$ is denoted as $L_a^k = \{t_i\}$ where:*

- $t_i = t_i^{Pr} \setminus (-)^*$, *and*
- $t_i^{Pr} \in Pr(L, A_a)$ *where* $A_a = \{a\} \cup \{a_i : a_i \in A\}$ *such that* $(a \rightarrow_l a_i \vee a_i \rightarrow_l a, 1 \leq l \leq k) \vee (a \oslash a_i) \vee (a \otimes a_i)$.

For example, in Fig. 1(b), the activities $b$, $c$, $i$, $d$ and $l$ are in $1^{st}$ causal relation with $z$ and the activities $a$, $e$, $h$ $m$ and $n$ are in $2^{nd}$-causal relation. There are no parallel and conditional relations with $z$. The alphabet for $k = 2$ is $A_z = \{z, a, b, c, i, d, l, e, h, m, n\}$ and the neighborhood context log is $L_z^2 = \{(abcizde)^5, (acbizdh)^3, (acibzlmn)^4, (aibczlnm)^3\}$.

## 4.2   Mining the Configurable Process Fragment

In order to mine a configurable process fragment, we propose to extract from each event log $L_i \in \mathbb{L}$ the neighborhood context log $L_a^k$ of the activity $a$. Then, we merge the corresponding neighborhood context logs into one sublog $\mathbb{L}_a^k = \cup L_a^k$. This sublog is used as an input for an existing mining algorithm in order to discover the corresponding process fragment which describes the behavior recorded in the merged sublog, yet it is not configurable. This is because existing mining algorithms are not able to explicitly specify the configurable nodes. Therefore, we provide in the following a simple approach to identify configurable gateways.

Let $G = (N, E, T, L)$ be the discovered process fragment from the merged sublog $\mathbb{L}_a^k$. We say that an activity $a$ is a **shared** activity if it is mined from **multiple** neighborhood context logs $L_a^k \in \mathbb{L}_a^k$; In other word, $a$ is shared if it belongs to multiple alphabets, i.e. $a \in \cap_{i \geq 2} A_a$ such that $i$ is the number of the corresponding alphabets. Otherwise, it is an **unshared** activity. Therefore, a split (respectively join) gateway is configurable if:

- it has at least one shared activity in its postset (respectively preset), or
- it has at least two unshared activities in its postset (respectively preset) and those activities are mined from different neighborhood context logs (i.e. they belong to different alphabets).

Consequently, we define a configurable process fragment as:

**Definition 8. (Configurable process fragment).** *Let $G = (N, E, T, L)$ be the discovered process fragment from the merged sublog $\mathbb{L}_a^k$. We define the corresponding configurable process fragment $G^c = (N, E, T, L, B, C, G)$ as:*

- *$\forall g \in N$ such that $T(g) = $ "gateway" $\wedge$ $g$ is a split gateway, then $B(g) = $ true iff $(\exists a_i \in g \bullet : a_i$ is shared$) \vee (\exists a_1, a_2 \in g \bullet : a_1, a_2$ are unshared $\wedge a_1 \in A_i \wedge a_2 \in A_j \wedge i \neq j)$. The same holds for a join gateway, however we handle the gateway preset instead of its postset.*
- *$C$ follows Definition 4*
- *$G$ is defined in Section 5.*

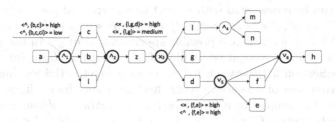

**Fig. 2.** The discovered configurable fragment of the activity $z$ within 2-neighbor areas

An example of the discovered configurable process fragment relative to the activity "$z$" in Fig. 1 for $k = 2$ is depicted in Fig. 2. For example, the split gateway "$\wedge_1$" is configurable since the activity $b \in \wedge_1 \bullet$ is shared (Note that

$c$ and $i$ are also shared activities); "$\wedge_4$" $m, n \in \wedge_4 \bullet$ are neither shared nor unshared and mined from different logs.

This example shows that even with a small number of configurable elements (i.e. 5 configurable gateways in our case), deriving a suitable configuration is far from trivial. The number of possible configurations may be too large. For instance, if the configurable fragment has $x$ configurable gateways, the number of possible configurations is $O(2^{\sum_{i=1}^{x} y_i})$ where $y_i$ is the cardinal of the preset or postset of the configurable gateway $x_i$. Therefore, the designer will be interested to know which activities are often executed together and how they interact in order to select a proper configuration. For example, to configure the gateway "$\wedge_1$", she would like to know that activities $b$ and $c$ are **often** executed together but **rarely** with $i$ so that she selects the configuration $C(\wedge_1) =< \wedge, \{b, c\} >$. In the next section, we present a frequency-based approach to derive guidelines that assist the designer in deriving a suitable configuration.

# 5   A Frequency-Based Approach to Mine Guidelines

This section elaborates our approach to derive *guidelines* that assist the configuration of the discovered process fragment. Basically, we propose to explore the recorded executions in the merged sublog in order to recommend the *frequently executed* paths as *ranked guidelines*. These guidelines are dynamic in the sense that they are updated after each configuration step in order to take the already chosen configurations into consideration. First, we model all traces recorded in the merged sublog in a frequency-based suffix tree (Section 5.1). Then, for each configurable gateway, we rank its possible configurations with *high*, *medium* or *low* depending on their frequencies recorded in the suffix tree and taking into account the previously chosen configurations (Section 5.2).

## 5.1   A frequency Suffix Tree for Configuration Executions

Let $G^c = (N, T, L, E, B, C, G)$ be a configurable process fragment discovered from the merged sublog $\mathbb{L}_a^k = \cup L_a^k$. A configurable split (respectively join) gateway $g^c \in N$ can be represented with respect to its type and postset (respectively preset) as $g^c =< g^c, g^c \bullet >$ (respectively $g^c =< g^c, \bullet g^c >$) where each configuration $C(g^c) =< g, g \bullet >$ is one possible specialization of $g^c$. In the sublog $\mathbb{L}_a^k$, a configuration can be recognized by identifying the *parallel* and/or *conditional* relation (see Section 3.2) between its preset or postset activities. Since the log traces are sequences of executed events, finding a specific configuration in an event log can be mapped to a *string pattern matching problem*. For example, finding a configuration $C =< \wedge, \{a, b\} >$ refers to searching for a parallel relation between $a$ and $b$; that is, searching for the traces including $a$ and $b$ in different orders. We say that $C$ has been executed $x$ times if, in $\mathbb{L}_a^k$, the postset activities $g \bullet$ appears $x$ times in the $g$ relation.

In light of the above presented insight, we propose to use *suffix trees* [17] to model all possible executed configurations and their frequencies. A suffix tree is an efficient data structure for storing all possible substrings of a given string in a linear time [18]. It provides linear-time solutions for string pattern matching problems and has been widely used in biological domain for DNA sequence analysis. A suffix tree for a string $S$ having $l$ distinct characters is a rooted directed tree where each edge is labeled with a nonempty substring of $S$ and each internal node has at least two children. Two edges issued from the same node cannot have the same labels. Furthermore, the concatenation of the edges' label of every path from a root to an internal node represents a suffix of $S$. Some variants of the suffix tree have been proposed such as the probabilistic suffix tree [19] and the weighted suffix tree [20]. In our work, we propose to use a frequency-based suffix tree where each node is labeled by the frequency of occurrence of the suffix starting from the root to that node in the corresponding event log. An example of a frequency suffix tree is illustrated in Fig. 3.

In order to build the frequency suffix tree, we propose to project the merged sublog $\mathbb{L}_a^k$ on the postset and preset activities of configurable split and join gateways respectively. The projected sublog is called *Configuration sublog*.

**Definition 9. (*Configuration sublog*).** *A configuration sublog $L^c$ built from a merged sublog $\mathbb{L}_a^k$ and a configurable process fragment $G^c$ is defined as $L^c = \{t_i : t_i = t_i^{Pr} \setminus (-)^*\}$ where $t_i^{Pr} \in Pr(\mathbb{L}_a^k, A^c)\}$ and $A^c = \{a_i \in N : i \geq 1\}$ such that $\forall a_j \in A^c : 1 \leq j \leq i, \exists g \in N : B(g) = true \wedge a_j \in g \bullet$ in case $g$ is a split gateway or $a_j \in \bullet g$ in case $g$ is a join gateway.*

For example, the configuration sublog $L^c$ built from the process fragment in Fig. 2 and the sublog $\mathbb{L}_z^2$ where $k = 2$ is $L^c = \{(bcdef)^5, (cbdfe)^4, (bcgh)^2, (cbgh)^3, (bcide)^5, (cbidh)^3, (cibl)^4, (ibcl)^1\}$. This configuration log is the projection of $\mathbb{L}_z^2$ on the alphabet $A^c = \{b, c, i, g, l, d, f, h, e\}$ as "$\wedge_1$", "$\wedge_2$", "$\times_3$", "$\vee_5$" and "$\vee_6$" are configurable and $b, c, i \in \wedge_1 \bullet; b, c, i \in \bullet \wedge_2; h, f, e \in \vee_5 \bullet$, etc.

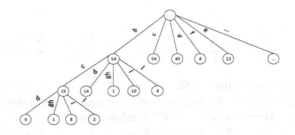

**Fig. 3.** An excerpt of a frequency suffix tree

Afterward, we build the generalized frequency suffix tree for the configuration sublog using Ukkonen's algorithm [18] which is a linear-time algorithm for building incrementally the suffix tree for a set of strings. An excerpt of the resulted frequency suffix tree for the configurable fragment in Fig. 2 is illustrated in Fig. 3. For example, in this tree, the suffix $bc$ is executed 19 times.

## 5.2   Deriving Ranked Guidelines

Using the frequency suffix tree, we compute for each configurable gateway the frequency of execution of all its possible configurations. Then, based on a specified execution frequency threshold, we attribute to each configuration a rank $r \in \{high, medium, low\}$. This process is repeated after each selected configuration in order to recompute the configurations' frequencies of the remaining configurable gateways with the previously chosen ones.

In the followings, we show that using the frequency suffix tree, we compute the frequency of an "$\wedge$" configuration, from which we derive the frequencies of the "$\times$" and "$\vee$" configurations using the set and statistical theories. We show the split gateway case; the same holds for a join gateway. To find the frequency of an "$\wedge$" configuration $C = < \wedge, \wedge \bullet >$, we search for all suffixes containing the postset activities in different positions. For example, searching in the suffix tree in Fig. 3 for the configuration $C = < \wedge, \{b, g, h\} >$ returns the suffixes $bcgh$, $bgh$, etc. For each matched suffix $m$, we denote by $f_m$ its frequency of occurrence. For example the frequency of the matches $bcgh$ and $bgh$ are $f_{bcgh} = 1$ and $f_{bgh} = 1$ respectively. In order, to find the frequency of the "$\wedge$" configuration $C$ denoted by $F_{\wedge \bullet}$, we sum the frequencies of all found matches:

$$F_{\wedge \bullet} = \sum_i f_{m_i} \tag{1}$$

The execution of an "$\times$" configuration represents the cases in which the corresponding postset activities are not executed together, and that of an "$\vee$" includes the "$\wedge$" and "$\times$" executions (see Section 3.2). Therefore, we propose to use the set theory to represent the executions of each activity in the postset as a set. Consequently, the "$\wedge$" configuration represents the intersection of the corresponding postset sets, the "$\times$" configuration represents their exclusive union and the "$\vee$" configuration represents their union (see Fig. 4). Then based on the statistical theory, we compute the frequency of an "$\times$" configuration denoted as $F_{\times \bullet}$ as:

$$F_{\times \bullet} = \sum_{i=1}^{n} f_{a_i} - \sum_{k\%2}^{n} k \times \sum_k F_{\wedge A_k} + \sum_{k\%2+1}^{n} l \times \sum_l F_{\wedge A_l} \tag{2}$$

where $n = |\times \bullet|$ is the cardinal of the postset of "$\times$" and $A_k$ (respectively $A_l$) is the set of $k$ (respectively $l$) permutations of first transitive postset. For example, the frequency of execution of the "$\times$" configuration $C = < \times, \{b, g, h\} >$ is $F_{\times(b,g,h)} = f_b + f_g + f_h - 2 \times (F_{\wedge(b,g)} + F_{\wedge(b,h)} + F_{\wedge(g,h)}) + 3 \times F_{\wedge(b,g,h)}$.

The frequency of execution of an "$\vee$" configuration denoted as $F_{\vee \bullet}$ is the sum of $F_{\wedge \bullet}$ and $F_{\times \bullet}$. Since $F_{\vee \bullet}$ would be the highest in all cases, **we omit ranking the "$\vee$" configuration** in our work, and we let its choice to the designer.

In order to rank a configuration $C = < g, g \bullet >$, we compute its frequency ratio $R_C$ as:

$$R_C = \frac{F_{C \bullet}}{max(\cup_i F_{C_i \bullet})} \tag{3}$$

**Fig. 4.** The representation of the three relations $\wedge$, $\times$ and $\vee$ using the set theory

where $F_C$ is the frequency of the corresponding configuration and $max(\cup_i F_{C_i \bullet})$ is the maximal frequency of all possible configurations of the corresponding gateway. A ratio equal to 1 denotes that the corresponding configuration appears in all possible executions, while a ratio equal to 0 denotes that it has been never executed. Based on $R_C$, we propose a set of *thresholds* to assign a rank $r \in \{high, medium, low\}$ where:

$$r = \begin{cases} high & if\ 0.7 \leq R_C \leq 1 \\ medium & if\ 0.3 \leq R_C < 0.7 \\ low & if\ 0 < R_C < 0.3 \end{cases} \tag{4}$$

Using Definition 4 and the above equations, we detail in Algorithm 1 the steps for deriving a list of ranked guidelines for configurable elements. The algorithm is applied after each configuration step. It takes as input the suffix tree, the set of configurable gateways and the set of previously selected configurations; it provides as output a list of ranked guidelines. Initially, there is no configured gateways, therefore for each configurable gateway we rank its possible configurations and we add them to the list of guidelines (Lines 3-8, 14-15). Afterwards, after each selected configuration (Lines 18-19), we update the configurations rankings of the remaining configurable gateways by taking into account their frequency of occurrence with the previously selected ones. To do so, we create the logical formula $LF$ by intersecting the previous configurations with the current one (Line 10). For example, in Fig. 2, suppose that $C(\wedge_1) = C(\wedge_2) = < \wedge, \{b, c\} >$, and $C(\times_3) = < \times, \{g, d\} >$; to compute the frequency of occurrence of $C(\vee_5) = < \wedge, \{f, e\} >$, one possible configuration of "$\vee_5$", along with $C(\wedge_1)$ and $C(\times_3)$, we derive the corresponding logical formula $LF = (b \wedge c) \wedge (g \vee d) \wedge (f \wedge e)$. Since, the frequency of an "$\wedge$" configuration is the basis for deriving the others frequencies, we transform the logical formula $LF$ into its disjunctive normal form $DF$ (i.e. the disjunction of conjunction) (Line 11). Having $DF$, we can now compute the final frequency $F_{\times DF}$ (Line 12). For example, the disjunctive normal form of $LF$ is $DF = (b \wedge c \wedge f \wedge e \wedge g) \vee (b \wedge c \wedge f \wedge e \wedge d) = A \vee B$ where $A = b \wedge c \wedge f \wedge e \wedge g$ and $B = b \wedge c \wedge f \wedge e \wedge d$; the corresponding frequency $F_{\times \{A,B\}} = F_A + F_B - 2 \times F_{\wedge \{A,B\}}$ which corresponds to the frequency of occurrence of the configuration $C(\vee_5)$ along with $C(\times_3)$ and $C(\wedge_1)$. The corresponding execution ratio is $R_C = \frac{F_{\times DF}}{max(\cup F_{C(\vee_5)})}$. In this way, we update the guidelines' rankings after each selected configuration by taking into consideration the previously selected ones until all configurable gateways are configured.

---

**Algorithm 1.** Algorithm for deriving ranked guidelines

---

1: **input**: suffix tree $S$, list configurable gateways $L^c = \{G_i^c =< g_i^c, g_i^c \xrightarrow{\bullet_a} >\}$, list of selected configurations $L = \{C_i =< g_i, g_i \bullet >\}$
2: **output**: list of ranked guidelines $L_{guid}$
3: **while** $L^c \neq \phi$ **do**
4:   **for** $G_i^c \in L^c$ **do**
5:     Get the set of all valid configurations based on Definition 4
6:     **for** each possible configuration $C$ **do**
7:       **if** $L = \phi$ {Initially no configured elements} **then**
8:         Compute the frequency $F_{\times C}$ and/or $F_{\wedge C}$ according to the gateways' type
9:       **else**
10:        get the logical formula $LF = \wedge_{i=1}^{|L|} C_i \wedge C$ where $C_i$ is a previously selected configuration and $C$ is the current one
11:        Get the disjunctive normal form $DN$ of $LF$
12:        Compute the frequency $F_{\times DN}$ of $DN$
13:      **end if**
14:      Compute the corresponding execution ratio $R_C$
15:      add the guideline $G =< C, r >$ to the list $L_{guid}$ where $r$ is the rank corresponding to $R_C$
16:     **end for**
17:   **end for**
18:   add the selected configuration to $L$
19:   remove the corresponding configurable gateway from $L^c$
20: **end while**

---

# 6   Validation

## 6.1   Proof of Concept

We have implemented our approach as a plugin in PRoM framework [1] which is a flexible framework for process mining environment. We extended the alpha algorithm [21], an existing mining algorithm, to mine a configurable process fragment. The output of the alpha algorithm is a Petri net. Therefore, we used the EPCConverion plugin available in PRoM to convert the petri net into the EPC notation. Since the computation of disjunctive normal forms (see Section 5) is NP-complete, we used a Shared Binary decision Diagram (SBDD) solver [2] that can derive disjunctive normal forms in a polynomial time. Due to the space limitation, further information about the plugin can be found at http://www-inf.it-sudparis.eu/SIMBAD/tools/mineFrag.

## 6.2   Experiments

Using our developed plugin, we conducted experiments on a set of generated event logs from a shared collection of business process models which has been

---

[1] http://www.promtools.org/prom6/
[2] We used the BDDC calculator available at: http://www-verimag.imag.fr/~raymond/tools/bddc-manual/bddc-manual-pages.html

used for the experiments reported in [22]. The set consists of 719 event logs for 560 different processes. The average number of traces in each log is between 50 and 299 traces. There exist in total 3003 distinct activities, from which 996 appear in multiple event logs (i.e. in average, an activity appears in 2 to 115 event log). In order to have focused results, we reduced the number of logs by taking those that contain the activities appeared in 10 to 20 logs. We were left with 223 event logs. To test the efficiency of our approach, we compute (i) the structural and behavioral *precision* and *recall* metrics proposed in [23] in order to quantify the amount of equivalence between our discovered configurable fragment and the previously existing ones, and (ii) the amount of reduction in the number of possible configurations using our guideline-driven approach.

**Precision and Recall Metrics:** The precision and recall metrics are well known metrics for evaluating the relevance of retrieved information. In our work, a high precision denotes the ability of the configurable fragment to generate only the existing fragment models, while a high recall denotes that the configurable fragment has a generic behavior and is able to derive new fragments that do not exist before. In [23], structural and behavioral precision and recall metrics were proposed in order to quantify the amount of equivalence between two process models. Structural precision and recall compare two models $M_1$ and $M_2$ based on their graphical structure and are defined:

$$Precision(M_1, M_2) = \frac{|E_1 \cap E_2|}{|E_2|}; \quad Recall(M_1, M_2) = \frac{|E_1 \cap E_2|}{|E_1|} \quad (5)$$

where $E_1$ and $E_2$ are the set of edges in $M_1$ and $M_2$ respectively. Behavioral precision and recall compare two models $M_1$ and $M_2$ on the basis of an existing event log $L$ that record a typical behavior and are defined as:

$$Precision(M_1, M_2, L) = \frac{\sum_{t \in L} \frac{\#t}{|t|} \sum_{i=0}^{|t|-1} \frac{|enabled(M_1,t[i],L) \cap enabled(M_2,t[i],L)|}{|enabled(M_2,t[i],L)|}}{|L|}$$

$$Recall(M_1, M_2, L) = \frac{\sum_{t \in L} \frac{\#t}{|t|} \sum_{i=0}^{|t|-1} \frac{|enabled(M_1,t[i],L) \cap enabled(M_2,t[i],L)|}{|enabled(M_1,t[i],L)|}}{|L|}$$

$$(6)$$

where $enabled(M_1, t[i], L)$ returns, if it exists, the activity in $M_1$ enabled by the event $t[i]$ in $L$. In our experiment, for each repeated activity, we discover its corresponding configurable fragment; then we discover the individual process fragments from existing event logs. We compute the precision and recall metrics of each of the individual fragments with the configurable one. The results for the minimal, maximal and average values are reported in Fig. 5(a) and the percentage of configurable fragments having a precision and recall values greater or equal to 0.5 are illustrated in Fig. 5(b). These results show that the precision and recall metrics record high values which is a desired result since our aim is to reproduce existing fragments (i.e. high precision) as well as new fragments that do not exist before but that are inspired from existing ones (i.e. high recall).

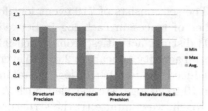
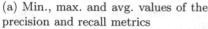

(a) Min., max. and avg. values of the precision and recall metrics

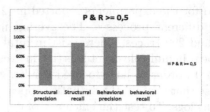

(b) Percentage of configurable fragments having a precision and recall values greater than 0.5

**Fig. 5.** Precision and recall metrics values

**Evaluating the Space of Valid Configurations:** In this experiment, we compute the average number of all possible configurations for each configurable process fragment. Then, we show that using our guideline driven approach, we restrict this number by assisting the designer in deriving a suitable fragment. We take the scenario for deriving the configurations having a rank $r = high$.

**Table 1.** The average number of possible configurations

|  | configurable elements | Total possible configurations | configurations $r = high$ |
|---|---|---|---|
| Avg. # | 25 | $68 \times 10^{19}$ | 1565 |

The results reported in Table 1 show that, using our approach, the space of possible configurations is strongly reduced while assisting the designer in deriving a frequently executed fragment.

## 7    Related Work

The work presented in this paper is inspired from [2,3] where configurable process models are introduced. To build a configurable process model, some approaches propose to merge a set of process models [4,5], others try to discover a configurable model out of collection of event logs [7–9]. However, the proposed approaches tend to merge or discover entire process models, thus they can encounter the problem of managing the complexity of the resulted model [10] making the design phase a complex task. In our previous work [11], we proposed to merge a set of fragment models into one configurable fragment. Whereas in this work, we propose to build a configurable process fragment from a collection of event logs that capture the real behavior of processes. Furthermore, we propose a frequency-based approach to assist the configuration of the discovered fragment through guidelines.

Buijs et al. [7] analyzed four approaches for mining configurable models. Their experimentation results show that the approach initially presented in [8] in which the event logs are merged into one log in order to mine one generale process model is beneficial for providing a model that considers the behavior and frequencies as recorded in the event logs. Different from them, instead of merging entire event logs, we extract from each event log a sublog relative to the neighborhood context of an activity and we merge the extracted sublogs into one subloglog in order to mine one fragment model. In order to identify the configurable elements, they "re-play" each single event log on the discovered model while in our approach, we propose a simple approach based on the shared and unshared activities in the mined fragment.

Jansen-Vullers et al. [9] propose an approach to derive a configuration (i.e an EPC model) given that a C-EPC exists and a log containing only data on the frequency of executed activities. They formulate the problem as an Integer Linear Programming in order to find the best configuration. In our work, we also derive configurations based on the frequency of execution. However, in our case the event logs record the sequence of executions, thus, we use a frequency-based suffix tree to solve the problem. Furthermore, we dynamically derive a configuration based on each selected configuration step.

La Rosa et al. [24] propose a questionnaire-driven approach for configuring reference models. They propose a framework built on a set of questions defined by domain experts and answered by designers experts. Compared to their work, we propose to use the knowledge resulted from process usage in order to derive configurations. We model the execution histories of processes in a frequency based suffix tree and use it to guide the configuration by recommending the frequently executed configurations together.

## 8   Conclusion

This paper provided an approach for assisting the business process design with configurable process fragments. We proposed an approach to mine a configurable process fragment out of collection of event logs. Since a configurable fragment captures a generalized behavior, we also proposed a dynamic guideline-driven approach to assist the configuration process using a frequency-based suffix tree.

In our future work, we intend to extend our configuration approach in two directions. First, we aim to take into account, besides the frequency information, other interesting information from the event log such as the performance information. For instance, an activity infrequently executed but with a high performance (e.g. short time, high quality) may be more valuable to be recommended in the configuration process. Second, we want to address the behavioral (deadlock-free, livelock-free) and syntactical correctness of the configured fragment by mining only those guidelines that preserve such correctness.

## References

1. van der Aalst, W.M.P.: Intra- and Inter-Organizational Process Mining: Discovering Processes within and between Organizations. In: Johannesson, P., Krogstie, J., Opdahl, A.L. (eds.) PoEM 2011. LNBIP, vol. 92, pp. 1–11. Springer, Heidelberg (2011)

2. Gottschalk, F., van der Aalst, W.M.P., Jansen-Vullers, M.H., Rosa, M.L.: Configurable workflow models. Int. J. Cooperative Inf. Syst. (2008)
3. Rosemann, M., van der Aalst, W.M.P.: A configurable reference modelling language. Inf. Syst. (2007)
4. Rosa, L., et al.: Business process model merging: An approach to business process consolidation. ACM Trans. Softw. Eng. Methodol. (2013)
5. Gottschalk, F., van der Aalst, W.M.P., Jansen-Vullers, M.H.: Merging event-driven process chains. In: Meersman, R., Tari, Z. (eds.) OTM 2008, Part I. LNCS, vol. 5331, pp. 418–426. Springer, Heidelberg (2008)
6. Derguech, W., Bhiri, S.: Merging business process variants. In: Abramowicz, W. (ed.) BIS 2011. LNBIP, vol. 87, pp. 86–97. Springer, Heidelberg (2011)
7. Buijs, J.C.A.M., van Dongen, B.F., van der Aalst, W.M.P.: Mining configurable process models from collections of event logs. In: Daniel, F., Wang, J., Weber, B. (eds.) BPM 2013. LNCS, vol. 8094, pp. 33–48. Springer, Heidelberg (2013)
8. Gottschalk, F., Aalst, W., Jansen-Vullers, M.: Mining Reference Process Models and their Configurations. In: EI2N 2008, OTM 2008 Workshops (2008)
9. Jansen-Vullers, M.H., van der Aalst, W.M.P., Rosemann, M.: Mining configurable enterprise information systems. In: Data Knowl. Eng. (2006)
10. Dijkman, R.M., Rosa, M.L., Reijers, H.A.: Managing large collections of business process models - current techniques and challenges. Computers in Industry (2012)
11. Assy, N., Chan, N.N., Gaaloul, W.: Assisting business process design with configurable process fragments. In: IEEE SCC 2013 (2013)
12. van der Aalst, W.M.P.: Process Mining: Discovery, Conformance and Enhancement of Business Processes. Springer Publishing Company, Incorporated (2011)
13. van der Aalst, W., Weijters, T., Maruster, L.: Workflow mining: Discovering process models from event logs. IEEE Trans. on Knowl. and Data Eng. (2004)
14. Weijters, A.J.M.M., van der Aalst, W.M.P.: Rediscovering workflow models from event-based data using little thumb. In: Integr. Comput.-Aided Eng. (2003)
15. Medeiros, A.K., Weijters, A.J., Aalst, W.M.: Genetic process mining: An experimental evaluation. Data Min. Knowl. Discov. (2007)
16. Weidlich, M., van der Werf, J.M.: On profiles and footprints – relational semantics for petri nets. In: Haddad, S., Pomello, L. (eds.) PETRI NETS 2012. LNCS, vol. 7347, pp. 148–167. Springer, Heidelberg (2012)
17. Aho, A.V., Hopcroft, J.E.: The Design and Analysis of Computer Algorithms. Addison-Wesley Longman Publishing Co., Inc. (1974)
18. Ukkonen, E.: On-Line Construction of Suffix Trees. Algorithmica (1995)
19. Bejerano, G., Yona, G.: Variations on probabilistic suffix trees: statistical modeling and prediction of protein families. Bioinformatics (2001)
20. Iliopoulos, et al.: The weighted suffix tree: An efficient data structure for handling molecular weighted sequences and its applications. In: Fundam. Inform. (2006)
21. van der Aalst, W.M.P., Weijter, A., Maruster, L.: Workflow mining: Discovering process models from event logs. IEEE TKDE (2003)
22. Fahland, D., et al.: Analysis on demand: Instantaneous soundness checking of industrial business process models. Data Knowl. Eng. (2011)
23. Alves de Medeiros, A.K., van der Aalst, W.M.P., Weijters, A.J.M.M.: Quantifying process equivalence based on observed behavior. Data Knowl. Eng. (2008)
24. Rosa, M.L., et al.: Questionnaire-based variability modeling for system configuration. Software and System Modeling 8(2), 251–274 (2009)

# Developing the Evaluation of a Pattern-Based Approach for Business Process Improvement

Philipp Griesberger

Chair of Business Engineering, University of Regensburg, Germany
philipp.griesberger@ur.de

**Abstract.** The evaluation of design science (DS) artifacts is a frequently discussed research issue, and many approaches have been developed for this DS activity. However, it is often stated that these approaches only provide rudimentary support for determining the appropriate evaluation methods for an individual DS project. In this paper, an evaluation method for a Business Process Improvement (BPI) pattern approach, which is currently under development, is elaborated. For that purpose, findings from reviewing relevant literature as well as general DS evaluation criteria are investigated to derive an evaluation method for the BPI pattern approach.

**Keywords:** Business Process Improvement, Patterns, Evaluation.

## 1 Introduction

Organizations nowadays are faced with permanent changes emerging from various sources (e.g. technological progress, increasing customer expectations, growing competitiveness, etc.) [1]. Thus, organizations have to be more and more flexible and responsive to quickly adapt e.g. to changing needs of customers [2]. All of these changes have to be considered in the daily work routines of organizations, which are represented by their business processes [3]. Thus, it is not surprising that BPI has gained major importance over the years [4]. Several approaches for BPI were developed all of them aiming at making business processes more effective and efficient, e.g. by increasing the output quality or by cutting development costs [5] (exemplary approaches: "Business Process Reengineering" [6], or "Process Innovation" [7]). However, taking into account that BPI projects are often encompassing and non-recurrent (see e.g. [2, 8]) makes the comparison of different approaches and the selection of the most appropriate one a challenging task. In spite of this large range of approaches in the field of BPI, it is remarkable that the implementation of improvement, i.e. the actual steps necessary to provoke improvement, is hardly addressed at all in BPI literature [9]. Thus, most approaches stop after the analysis of problems and identification of possible improvements (e.g. by means of generic activities like brainstorming) for a business process without covering the subsequent actual implementation of the necessary changes [10, 11]. To approach this problem, structured descriptions of former successful improvement measures for given problem statements are useful [12], so-called BPI patterns. By means of patterns, language-based

M.C. Tremblay et al. (Eds.): DESRIST 2014, LNCS 8463, pp. 225–240, 2014.
© Springer International Publishing Switzerland 2014

examples for successful problem solutions can be provided [13]. The attractiveness of a pattern approach lies in the simple dissemination of abstracted knowledge [14], the reduced development time of new solutions [15], or the predictable outcome of their application [16]. The embodiment of the BPI pattern approach is a structured list of successful improvement measures in the form of patterns which can be used depending on the underlying objective to be dealt with in a BPI project.

The overall research project, which this paper is part of, follows the Design Science research (DSR) paradigm, which, in a nutshell, seeks to create artifacts for specific tasks [17] to solve identified organizational problems [18]. The subsequently necessary evaluation of these created artifacts is a central activity and of utmost importance in DSR [19]. However, the question of how to actually perform the evaluation of created artifacts is controversially discussed (see e.g. [20-22]). Thus, despite there being numerous different evaluation methods, current literature provides little support for a researcher as to how to actually perform the evaluation [22, 23]. Besides, a proper DS evaluation may also be dependent on the constructed artifact type itself as well as on the artifact's underlying design assumptions. For example, applying new artifacts in case studies is a common evaluation method. However, a potential problem herein lies in the limited generalizability of single cases (see [21]) which e.g. hampers statements about assumptions made in a DS project. Against this background, and as there is no universal formula for DS evaluation, this paper treats this topic by reconsidering the applicability of different evaluation methods and concentrates on an individual DS project this evaluation has not been performed yet. It also discusses important issues associated with this goal, which are addressed in this paper, on the one hand by reviewing related work to analyze how the evaluation is performed therein, and, on the other hand, by considering general criteria that are important for evaluating DS artifacts. Together, inferences for evaluating the BPI pattern approach are drawn resulting in a method for the thorough evaluation of the BPI pattern approach.

The remainder of this paper is organized as follows. In section 2, relevant terms and topics that are essential for the paper at hand are introduced. The BPI pattern approach is presented in section 3, as far as it is needed for the research objective of the paper. In the section 4, insights from reviewing related work are discussed. After that, section 5 presents general criteria that have to be considered for the evaluation of DS artifacts. In section 6, the evaluation method for the BPI pattern approach is presented based on the findings generated from the preliminary work in the paper. Finally, section 7 concludes the paper and gives an outlook for further research.

## 2    Theoretical Background

### 2.1    Business Process Management and Improvement

The comprehensive concept of business process management (BPM) can be described as the "general managerial approaches of process orientation" [4]. Aligning an organization according to its business processes is meanwhile "regarded as a competitive advantage and fundamental to business success" [24]. BPM represents a life cycle comprising seven steps (identification, modeling (as-is), analysis, improvement (to-be), implementation, execution (to-do), monitoring/controlling) [25]. A major challenge still remains the fourth step of the life cycle ("improvement (to-be)") that is addressed in this paper, in which the basis for the positive effects of BPM is provided by configuring a business process in the best possible condition. The concept of BPI was originally coined by Harrington (1991) in his book "Business Process Improvement". According to him, BPI results in some kind of change and enhances the effectiveness and efficiency of a business process [26] which consequently improves its performance and increases the degree of accomplishing organizational goals [27]. These changes can occur at one (or more) of the elements of a business process, which are activity, control-flow, resources, organizational units, organizational assignment, input, output, and information flow [27].

## 2.2 Characteristics of the Design Science Research Paradigm

DS has gained high popularity in the field of IS and has become a legitimate IS research method [14, 28, 29]. Literature about DS offers a plenitude of general research activities which are problem identification, objectives of solutions, and evaluation of generated artifacts [30]. A process for carrying out DSR is the design science research methodology (DSRM) by Peffers et al. [31] which represents a synthesis of DS processes in IS and other disciplines and is used by various research projects in the field of DS [20]. The DSRM consists of six steps as depicted in Fig. 1.

**Fig. 1.** Design Science Research Methodology (DSRM) [31]

A DSR project has to be based on a solid theoretical foundation. It can be disadvantageous to over-emphasize the artifact which is not based on an adequate theory base, because the utility of the result stands or falls with a well-designed artifact and its inherent design criteria [18]. Thus, all assumptions underlying the construction of an artifact, which at the same time imply criteria for its evaluation, have to be transparent and made comprehensible in the best possible way, e.g. by embedment in the accepted knowledge base. There are various possibilities for the embodiment of artifacts, i.e. the output of a DS project. A widely accepted classification of artifacts [22, 32] distinguishes between *methods* (e.g. algorithms and practices), *models* (e.g. abstractions and representations), *instantiations* (e.g. software products or implemented processes), and *constructs* (e.g. vocabulary and symbols) [17, 18].

## 2.3 Guidelines for the Evaluation of Design Science Artifacts

Each artifact type which is built has to be evaluated scientifically to determine if the desired progress is achieved [17]. Without a rigorous evaluation of a created artifact, this DS outcome can be regarded as an unconfirmed declaration that the artifact meets its purpose [23], which makes it impossible to effectively judge the overall research efforts [17]. Thus, according to the results of the evaluation, it can be verified if the created artifact „works", i.e. if it is purposeful [18]. Additionally, as design is supposed to be an iterative activity, these results may provide valuable feedback about the initial design process and possible refinements that can be made to raise the quality of the resulting DS artifact [18]. Many approaches for carrying out an evaluation of a DS artifact have been proposed which are considered partly artifact-specific and partly artifact-neutral [20]. Thus, choosing the right evaluation approach has to be made against the background of the particular artifact [21, 31]. If the artifact is rather technical (e.g. an algorithm in programming code) and presents the artifact type *method*, dynamic aspects like the run-time performance would typically be of high interest which can be verifiable e.g. by means of an evaluation method which simulates artificial data to measure appropriate run-time metrics. If, on the contrary, the artifact is more of a theoretical nature (e.g. a conceptual model about a real-world phenomenon), which applies to the artifact type *model*, the validity and thus rigor of the artifact construction is of primary importance, i.e. an evaluation method has to address aspects of completeness and correctness of the artifact (verifiable e.g. by expert evaluation). Peffers et al. aimed at considering the artifact's influence for evaluation by considering the question if there are certain characteristics of artifacts that lead to certain kinds of evaluation methods [21]. As a result, they identified some patterns of evaluation types and DS artifacts which may provide researchers with examples as to how to carry out DS evaluation depending on an individual artifact [21]. The analyzed evaluation method types are approved in DS [21] and are listed in Tab. 1.

**Table 1.** Evaluation Method Types [21]

| Method Type | Description |
|---|---|
| *Logical Argument* | An argument with face validity. |
| *Expert Evaluation* | Assessment of an artifact by one or more experts (e.g. Delphi study). |
| *Technical Experiment* | A performance evaluation of an algorithm implementation using real-world data, synthetic data, or no data, designed to evaluate the technical performance. |
| *Subject-based Experiment* | A test involving subjects to evaluate whether an assertion is true. |
| *Action Research* | Use of an artifact in a real-world situation as part of a research intervention, evaluating its effect on the real-world situation. |
| *Prototype* | Implementation of an artifact aimed at demonstrating the utility or suitability of the artifact. |
| *Case Study* | Application of an artifact to a real-world situation, evaluating its effect on the real-world situation. |
| *Illustrative Scenario* | Application of an artifact to a synthetic or real-world situation aimed at illustrating suitability or utility of the artifact. |

In recent years, various frameworks for the selection of an evaluation method, which all synthesize former evaluation approaches and which do not only focus on the to be evaluated artifact, have been proposed. The framework by Pries-Heje et al., in essence, constitutes of the dimensions "what to evaluate" (design process or design product), "when to evaluate" (ex ante/ex post), and "how to evaluate" (artificial vs. naturalistic evaluation) [22]. Cleven et al. proposed a framework consisting of 12 variables, which are "approach", "artifact focus", "artifact type", "epistemology", "function", "method", "object", "ontology", "perspective", "position", "reference point", and "time" [20]. Each of these variables, which, according to the authors have been considered relevant in former research works, can assume different values and altogether form an evaluation method for a DS artifact. Sonnenberg/vom Brocke introduce evaluation patterns that "reflect the structure of DSR processes, DSR evaluation criteria, as well as existing DSR evaluation frameworks." [33] Thus, they also aim at identifying what has been done to evaluate DS artifacts, and record their findings in the form of reusable patterns, which are described according to their "intent", "context and applicability", "description", "implications", and "examples". These evaluation patterns can provide evaluation support for other DS projects with similar characteristics as the ones a pattern is recorded for. The above discussed approaches are surely helpful to reveal what possibilities exist to configure a certain evaluation method in general and support a researcher in doing so. However, by means of these approaches, it is not as simple as that to identify what evaluation approach should exclusively be applied in a particular DS project, without further analysis. The underlying situation or context, respectively, of a DS project obviously require for different needs of evaluation. If a DS project e.g. is rather practice-oriented and serves for the development of a new solution for a particular organizational need, the relevance of the created solution i.e. is the new solution really capable to solve the problem "in the real world", is the crucial question for evaluation (e.g. by means of subject-based experiments). If, in turn, a DS project strives to enhance the scientific knowledge base, evaluating the rigor and accuracy of the design process are the salient points (e.g. by means of an expert evaluation). Thus, characteristics like e.g. the problem domain, objectives of a solution, artifact design, artifact construction, and the artifact type represent situation-specific characteristics that have to be taken into account. Consequently, it seems necessary that for the ultimate configuration of an evaluation method these individual characteristics of a DS project are determinative and always have to be reflected against existing possibilities for evaluation. Thus, for the research at hand, an examination of existing evaluation approaches and their beneficial aspects can serve as a basis for further analysis and eventually for the configuration of the evaluation method for the BPI pattern approach.

## 3     The BPI Pattern Approach

The BPI pattern approach builds on previous BPI approaches adopting their effective aspects (procedure according to [11]) and adds as a new concept the special focus on the actual measures that are undertaken to transform a business process from its "as-is" to a desired "to-be"-state ("act of improvement"). The overall research project follows the DSRM by Peffers et al. (see sect. 2.2.), the included DSRM-steps 1 to 4 have already been dealt with in previous research papers and are subsequently only addressed in short. The problem description (DSRM-step 1: "Identify problem & motivate") of the overall research project, namely the missing support of the "act of improvement" of current BPI approaches, has been elaborated in section 1 (and in-depth in [27] and [12]). The development of reusable BPI patterns to address the identified deficit of DSRM-step 1 is the objective of the proposed solution (see [12]) (DSRM-step 2: "Define objectives of a solution"). A formalization of the BPI pattern approach was performed by developing a data model of a BPI pattern (DSRM-step 3:

"Design & Development"). This was reached by means of a literature review about pattern notations in the field of IS (see [12]). The next step in the DSRM is to show the general applicability of the developed solution (DSRM-step 4: "Demonstration") which, in case of the BPI pattern approach, was already successfully shown in a case study (see [34]), which also resulted in first findings about the general usefulness of the approach, which is the subject of DSRM-step 5 ("Evaluation"). The paper at hand, together with the papers mentioned further up in this section, all represent parts of the final DSRM-step 6, the "communication" of the results of the overall research project.

As the evaluation of artifacts (DSRM-step 5) is considered a main activity in DS [17] which asks for a rigorous examination of the utility, quality, and effectiveness of a DS artifact [18] and since this is the DSRM-step which is currently in progress, this issue is of special attention in the paper at hand. As the artifact type has an influence on the choice of a proper evaluation method (see sect. 2.3), it is important to define the artifact under consideration clearly. Thus, a careful look on the achieved results is necessary to determine what exactly is to be evaluated. As a first result, the relation between the derived attributes of a BPI pattern is shown by the corresponding data model (from [12]), which is depicted in Fig. 2.

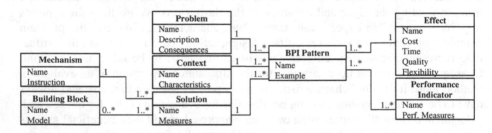

**Fig. 2.** Data Model of a BPI Pattern [12]

By means of this data model, the principal functioning of a BPI pattern can be explained. Every BPI pattern has a certain *name* and provides an *example* of its successful application. A BPI pattern provides a *solution* for a specific *problem* under consideration of the underlying *context*. The solution must be complemented by a *mechanism* occurring at an element of a process (e.g. delete activity) and can optionally be provided by a *building block*, i.e. a graphical representation of the proposed solution (i.e. pre-built models for implementation). Regarding the selection of suitable BPI patterns, they contain indications about their estimated *effects* (in terms of cost, time, quality, and flexibility). For measuring the success of applying a BPI pattern, it has to provide appropriate performance measures (e.g. waiting time etc.) to determine if the application has resulted in the desired change. Altogether, the identified attributes along with the data model contribute to a clear definition of BPI patterns and provide the basis for their derivation, i.e. the creation of single instances of BPI patterns. As a second result, a procedure for applying BPI patterns was proposed in the aforementioned case study [34], which is illustrated in Fig. 3 and explained afterwards.

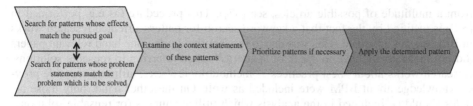

**Fig. 3.** Alternative procedures for the selection of a BPI pattern [34]

In a BPI project, the search for an appropriate pattern can either be started with a scan of the problem statements of all patterns and a filtering of relevant ones, or, if a specific goal is pursued, a search for those patterns which match the pursued goal (for both possibilities both steps have to be executed). Next, the context statements of the remaining patterns have to be investigated for aspects that hinder the application of a pattern. If several patterns remain after this step has been performed, the best solution has to be prioritized to be ultimately applied. In the case of the BPI pattern approach, according to the presented results, different artifact types can be identified making an evaluation even more challenging. The BPI pattern data model (see Fig. 2) represents the artifact type *model,* because it prescribes the general structure of a BPI pattern and the relationships among its inherent elements [17]. A derived BPI pattern, in turn, can surely be regarded as the artifact type *instantiation* of the superordinate BPI pattern type (and is therefore an operationalization of the BPI pattern data model) [17]. Lastly, considering the entire procedure of improving business processes (see Fig. 3) where BPI patterns (instances) are applied at the stage of anticipating the actual improvement, the procedure corresponds to the artifact type *method*, as it represents a "set of steps used to perform a task" [17]. Thus, for developing a proper evaluation method for the BPI pattern approach, these three different types of artifacts *model*, *instantiation*, and *method*, which were identified have to be taken into account.

## 4    Evaluation of Pattern-Based Approaches in the Field of BPM

As regards this paper which aims to show the way to thoroughly evaluating the BPI pattern approach it is interesting to see how related work has so far dealt with this topic. Thus, other pattern-oriented approaches in the field of BPM, i.e. research works that aim at providing reusable proven knowledge about BPM (see sect. 4.1) are investigated as to how the evaluation in these approaches is performed, or, if an evaluation is not performed, what indications are given as to what the evaluation must look like (see sect. 4.2). The focus is intentionally extended to the general field of BPM and to corresponding works that have a pattern-based approach of business processes in view, even if some of them cannot directly be attributed to supporting the act of improving business processes.

### 4.1    Procedure for the Selection of Related Work

Instead of conducting an exhaustive literature review (see [37]), it was considered more appropriate to perform an in-depth analysis of a limited number of carefully chosen papers that pursue a comparable approach as we are doing with the BPI pattern approach (so-called "representative literature review" by considering a sample from a multitude of possible articles, see [37]). This procedure (as e.g. performed in [38]) is justified by the fact that a keyword search for pattern-oriented research works in BPI was not adequate. This was due to the fact that on the one hand relevant papers did not mandatorily have to speak of "patterns" when referring to reusable solutions. Research works about "best practices", "methodologies" etc., utilizing reusable proven knowledge about BPM were included as well. On the other hand, only those articles should be included in the analysis which utilize patterns (or reusable solutions) that are applicable for improving business processes. In addition, an in-depth analysis of literature sources was necessary to identify those articles which share the same characteristics and requirements regarding the DS project (problem domain, artifact type etc.). This careful analysis is done to make reliable statements because the evaluation of a DS artifact depends to a large extent on the individual characteristics of a DS project (see sect. 2.3).

Thus, by means of a backward-/forward search [39] for pattern-oriented research works in the field of BPM, which started when beginning our DS project 3 years ago (see [27]), and evolved up to today, 34 articles were identified as being relevant to be analyzed. Next, only papers covering the artifact types that are contained in our own approach (*model*, *instantiation*, and *method*, see sect. 3) were considered as being useful. Thus, 3 papers that covered the artifact type *construct* were withdrawn.

Summarizing, the derived procedure for determining literature that deals with pattern-oriented approaches in BPM covering the artifact types *model*, *instantiation*, and *method* led to 31 papers that were analyzed. The criteria for examining these papers were the principal content of the paper (to assess the similarity to our own approach and enable an accurate analysis), the corresponding artifact type, i.e. what type of artifact the developed solutions in these works were assigned to. Finally, the type of the performed evaluation procedure (if available) was determined according to the different possible types of evaluation (based on Tab. 1 in sect. 2.2). On the basis of the results of this analysis, which are discussed in section 4.3, inferences could be drawn for deriving the evaluation method for the BPI pattern approach (see sect. 6).

## 4.2    Results of the Analysis

Following, the results of reviewing related work about the evaluation of pattern-based approaches in BPM are discussed. First, it should be noted that more than half of the investigated research works do not perform an evaluation of their pattern-related approach at all (17 out of 31 reviewed papers) ([5, 16, 36, 40-53]).

As to the remaining approaches which did conduct an evaluation, it was interesting to see what evaluation types (according to Tab. 1 in sect. 2.3) were applied to what kind of artifact types. To identify and allocate the evaluation types, it was necessary that a paper had a clearly evident section explicitly dealing with evaluating its underlying approach. For example, the simple mentioning of the utility of an approach in the concluding remarks of a paper was not regarded as sufficient to be allocated as a "logical argument". From the group of 17 papers which did not perform an evaluation, five at least made statements about what was planned in further research regarding an evaluation. Thus these papers will also be considered in our following analysis. As the results of our own DS project comprise the three different artifact types *model*, *instantiation*, and *method*, the key findings of the analysis are discussed in an artifact type-specific manner:

Artifact Type *Model*

- Barros proposes domain-specific reusable patterns that encapsulate high-level do-main-specific business knowledge and logic [35]. Evaluated by means of a case study, the author justifies the utility of the patterns predominantly with the fact that appropriate solutions are available and do not have to be found "ad-hoc".
- Stephenson/Bandara utilize an action research approach for pattern-based process modeling. Similarly to Barros, they report benefits like accelerated time frames and provisioning of quality (reusable) process models [54].
- In the papers of Andersson et al. and Jung/Sprenger, no evaluation is performed. Andersson et al. state that their created patterns are so far hypothetical and that an (subject-based) experiment is required to prove the validity for practical purposes [5]. Jung/Sprenger mention discussion rounds with experts as necessary for vali-dating their derived model of business process patterns [36].

Artifact Type *Instantiation*

- Gschwind et al. propose patterns for business process modeling which are based on workflow control-flow patterns to provide support for modeling business processes [15]. After demonstrating their approach in three different scenarios (focusing on applicability), they prove its utility by describing a prototype implementation.
- Nagayoshi et al. introduce conceptual level patterns for reducing exceptions in business processes of organizations [55]. Their assumed patterns in business processes are verified by means of a case study in a Japanese company. Due to the single case the authors admit a rather low generalizability of their patterns.
- Zimmermann develops a tool which utilizes patterns for process description sup-port based on a framework for describing a process description formalism [56]. The patterns are evaluated by two user tests (Subject-Based Experiment).
- Rogers/Salustri create a pattern language for quality function deployment [50]. They do not perform an evaluation in their work, but aim for testing and validating their patterns with industry partners (Subject-Based Experiments).

Artifact Type *Method*

- Hanafizadeh et al. develop a method for strategic business process redesign to evaluate the alignment of best practices from literature with an organizational strategy [57]. The method is tested in a case study aiming at showing the relevance of the identified best practices and the verification of their selection process.
- Reijers/Limam Mansar suggest a framework of best practices that can support the development of a radically improved process design [48]. A case study serves for va-lidating the framework especially focusing on the question if the framework covers the mandatory aspects practitioners look for when redesigning processes [58].
- Norta/Grefen propose a concept for electronic sourcing by means of patterns that improve the coordination of service provisions across several tiers of supply chains [59]. They show the utility of their framework by means of a case study.
- Paludo et al. develop a concept for business process patterns to be used in software developing [60]. A case study serves to show the relevance of the derived patterns, but has, however, a narrow focus and thus low generalizability.

- Pourshahid et al. introduce a framework for an automated suggestion of business process redesign patterns based on monitoring results [61]. By means of a case study, they demonstrate both their feasibility and utility for a real-world process.
- Turetken et al. introduce a set of patterns for capturing domain-specific representations of compliance requirements [62]. They apply their concepts in two case studies, whose objectives are testing the applicability and examining the expressiveness of patterns, i.e. if patterns are able to express requirements of diverse concerns.
- Niedermann et al. propose a platform for (semi-)automated optimization during the stages of process design, execution and analysis by means of patterns [16]. In an associated work they provide an example that shows the utility of employing their patterns (illustrative scenario) [63].
- Smirnov et al. present a concept for deriving so-called action patterns, which can be used during process modeling and are derived from a collection of process models by means of association rules mining [64]. In terms of validation, they conduct a technical experiment with the help of the SAP Reference Model.
- Zellner proposes a framework for deriving patterns for business process redesign [65]. The usefulness of these patterns is validated conducting a laboratory experiment (Subject-Based Experiment).

Tab. 2 summarizes the distribution of employed evaluation approaches (in columns) on the considered artifact types (in lines) in the investigated papers in which an evaluation was conducted (plus the intended evaluation approaches in brackets).

**Table 2.** Distribution of employed evaluation types

| Evaluation Type / Artifact Type | Logical Argument | Expert Evaluation | Technical Experiment | Subject-based Experiment | Action Research | Prototype | Case Study | Illustrative Scenario | TOTAL |
|---|---|---|---|---|---|---|---|---|---|
| Model | 0 | 0 (1) | 0 | 0 (1) | 1 | 0 | 1 | 0 | 2 (2) |
| Instantiation | 0 | 0 | 0 | 1 (1) | 0 | 1 | 1 | 0 | 3 (1) |
| Method | 0 | 0 | 1 | 1 | 0 | 0 | 6 (1) | 1 (1) | 9 (2) |
| TOTAL | 0 | 0 (1) | 1 | 2 (2) | 1 | 1 | 8 (1) | 1 (1) | 14 (5) |

### 4.3     Discussion of the Results of the Analysis

While performing the analysis described in the previous section, several general issues associated with the evaluation of DS artifacts arose. First, the majority of the approaches seem to interpret "evaluation" solely as demonstrating the utility of an artifact, i.e. the artifact's effectiveness. For example, an often stated positive effect of the use of patterns is that much effort is saved which would otherwise be wasted in developing new solutions from scratch (see e.g. [35]). In our opinion, evaluations should additionally make indications on how well a derived artifact supports the creation of a solution to a problem, in the sense of Peffers et al. who described evaluation as "Observe and measure how well the artifact supports a solution to the problem" [31], i.e. the artifact's efficiency. Second, it is important to consider if an evaluation rather pursues a practical or a theoretical purpose. Practitioners have completely different interests in and demands on a new solution (e.g. concerning applicability aspects) than researchers (focusing more on the development process of a new solution) [33]. A problem encountered with a rather practice-oriented evaluation occurs when DS projects are performed in too close cooperation with industry partners. In addition to the often prevailing need for early results, a too narrow view on the participating industry partner complicates general conclusions [14]. Moreover, business environments are subject to ongoing changes (see sect. 1), which might discount the value of generated artifacts in the future. Besides, the fact that 17 out of the 31 papers considered do not perform an evaluation confirms the statement that in DS more importance is attached to the creation and design of new artifacts ("build"-activity) than to the question if the developed artifact really meets its purpose ("evaluate"-activity) (see [66]). However, the investigated works which do perform an evaluation all miss an important aspect, namely to raise the question - before evaluating their approaches - what type(s) of evaluation exist and which one(s) of them actually is (are) suitable to give evidence about the quality of a created artifact. Thus, there is no comparison found in these works of (dis)advantages of different evaluation approaches for particular solutions. As it was already ascertained that the different evaluation approaches aim at different goals (see sect. 2.3), the question arises what really constitutes an adequate evaluation which does not just show the utility of an artifact, but also proves that it is better than anything that already exists. Thus, the results from the analysis conform to a fact mentioned earlier on, namely that there is no real consensus about what is desirable or acceptable in evaluating DS artifacts (see [21]). To solve this issue, the consideration of general evaluation criteria is helpful allowing for an assessment of the artifact performance against those criteria (see [17]).

# 5 General Evaluation Criteria

The evaluation of the BPI pattern approach has to take the three different artifact types *model*, *instantiation*, and *method* into account (see sect. 3). Appropriately, March/Smith propose a set of artifact-specific evaluation criteria (see Tab. 3), which are useful for deriving an eligible evaluation method. Some of these criteria are exclusively applicable to a single artifact type (e.g. "model" can be evaluated by the criteria "fidelity with real world phenomena"); on the other hand, there are artifact types; e.g. "method" and "instantiation"; which can both be evaluated by means of the criteria "efficiency" (see [33]). Besides these artifact-specific evaluation criteria, e.g. Hevner et al. enumerate artifact-neutral criteria which can be applied to evaluate the quality of DS artifacts. These criteria, which coincide with the ones by March/Smith, are "functionality", "completeness", "consistency", "accuracy", "performance", "reliability", "usability", and "fit with the organization" [18].

**Table 3.** Artifact-specific evaluation criteria ([17], cited from [33])

| Criteria | Model | Instantiation | Method |
|---|---|---|---|
| Completeness | X | | |
| Ease of use | | | X |
| Effectiveness | | X | |
| Efficiency | | X | X |
| Fidelity with real world phenomena | X | | |
| Generality | | | X |
| Impact on environment and the artifact's users | | X | |
| Internal consistency | X | | |
| Level of detail | X | | |
| Operationality | | | X |
| Robustness | X | | |

Summarizing, the decision of which evaluation criteria to use has to be made carefully considering the underlying context (resp. business environment) of a DS project (see also sect. 2.3), in the sense of justifying the utility of an artifact, if it satisfies the underlying requirements and if it really can be used to solve the problem it was created for (according to [18]). Besides, it is desirable to contrast the efficiency of problem solving by means of a new artifact with previously developed approaches by way of an evaluation in this case, too.

## 6    Evaluation Method for the BPI Pattern Approach

It has already been shown in [34] by means of a case study that our BPI pattern approach is feasible and useful. As we have been continuing our work, besides giving further proof of the utility of using BPI patterns, we demonstrate that actual progress has been achieved [17], i.e. considering the question as to what extent the usage of BPI patterns for supporting the act of improving business processes is better than relying on customary approaches for that purpose. Therefore, by considering the results from sections 4 (beneficial aspects from reviewing related work) and 5 (artifact-specific evaluation criteria, see Tab. 3), we pursue the following evaluation method.

Concerning the BPI pattern data model (artifact type *model*), we aim at interviewing experts (as in [36]) or conducting Subject-Based Experiments (as in [5]) (e.g. by questioning the effort for training) to assess the adequacy of the data model, which also includes the question if the included attributes are *complete* and conform to *real-world requirements*. Likewise, it is to be verified that the description of BPI patterns based on the data model is *detailed enough* to reach the underlying objective, namely to provide proper reusable means that provide abstracted knowledge to support the act of improving business processes (in accordance with [18]) and facilitates its dissemination (see [14]). In addition, we strive for a prototypical implementation of the data model in an adequate data modeling tool (similar to [15]). Thus, it is imaginable to enhance current business process modeling tools by implementing BPI patterns as situational measures, by which the efficiency of their application can be assessed (as in [36]), e.g. the time saved for the development of new solutions (see [15]).

Regarding the procedure of selecting an appropriate BPI pattern out of a repository (artifact type *method*), it has to be *generally* possible to apply a solution that helps to reach the objective of a BPI project by running the whole procedure (*operationality*) (e.g. by means of indicators such as the number or quality of suitable solutions, or the adaptability to differing needs). Thus, case studies or illustrative scenarios are suitable approaches to evaluate the BPI pattern procedure by comparing it with previous BPI approaches. However, a reported problem with case studies is that a too specific context hampers the generalizability of the results (as in [55, 60]), as real-world circumstances may influence the applicability [21]. Notwithstanding, assistance for generalizing research results obtained by case studies exists [67]. Besides, an illustrative scenario that enables the definition of an ideal context [21] allows for a comparison of different BPI approaches. The generated effort to apply the different BPI approaches enables feedback about the *efficiency* and the *ease of use*.

The evaluation of a single BPI pattern (artifact type *instantiation*) is a little more complex. Hevner et al. remark that instantiations show that models, methods, or constructs can be implemented in a working system and enable a concrete assessment of an artifact's suitability to its intended purpose [18], i.e. the expected outcome (see [16]) . The original intention of a single BPI pattern is that it provides proven practices from former BPI projects, which are described on the basis of the BPI pattern data model, to ensure their proper application by considering the underlying context *(environment)*. Thus, the contents of BPI patterns are validated by the fact that they already led to improvements *(effectiveness)*. For verifying their *efficiency*, it is possible to capture the above-mentioned illustrative scenario, which e.g. treats a typical problem of business processes and analyze how well this problem can be solved by means of single BPI patterns (e.g. by measuring cycle-times, process cost, or customer satisfaction) and what adjustments might lead to an improvement of their application.

# 7    Conclusion

There is an emerging trend regarding the reuse of proven knowledge of processes in the form of patterns [52]. However, most of the works share the lack of only marginally treating the topic of evaluating new solutions in respect of their underlying objectives (see sect. 4). An adequate evaluation of DS artifacts is a crucial task though [18], as, eventually, the results of the evaluation may provide evidence that the designed artifact is useful [19]. In general, there is plenty of literature on what possibilities exist to perform an evaluation of a DSR artifact (see sect. 2.3). However, at the same time, it is stated that researchers are not sufficiently provided with guidance on how an evaluation exactly should be conducted [23].

The contribution of this paper lies in addressing the issues that arise when evaluating DS artifacts by discussing a specific DS project, the BPI pattern approach, which is currently under development. Thus, the aim of this paper was to develop an individual evaluation method for a specific DS project and not to propose an evaluation method for DS projects in general. The results of this research are supposed to stimulate the widespread discussion about how to carry out DS evaluation.

This research is, however, not without limitations. The review of related work makes no claim for completeness, since only a representative sample of papers was analyzed. Nevertheless, as the evaluation of artifacts strongly depends on the given characteristics of a DS project, which makes a simple adaptation of former approaches impossible (see sect. 4), considering a total of 31 articles provides insight into how similar approaches treated the issue of evaluating new solutions.

In future research, we will concentrate on carrying out the derived evaluation method. An important issue will be the exact determination of performance indicators to prove the usefulness of the overall BPI pattern approach.

# References

1. Boerner, R., Moormann, J., Wang, M.: Staff training for business process improvement - The benefit of role-plays in the case of KreditSim. JoWL 24(3), 200–225 (2012)
2. Sidorova, A., Isik, O.: Business process research: a cross-disciplinary review. BPMJ 16(4), 566–597 (2010)
3. Fuglseth, A., Gronhaug, K.: IT-enabled Redesign of Complex and Dynamic Business Processes: the Case of Bank Credit Evaluation. Omega 25(1), 93–106 (1997)
4. Buavaraporn, N., Tannock, J.: Business process improvement in services: case studies of financial institutions in Thailand. IJQRM 30(3), 319–340 (2013)
5. Andersson, B., Bider, I., Johanesson, P., Perjons, E.: Towards a formal definition of goal-oriented business process patterns. BPMJ 11(6), 650–662 (2005)
6. Hammer, M., Champy, J.: Reengineering the corporation: a manifesto for business revolution. Harper Business, New York (1993)
7. Davenport, T.H.: Process Innovation - Reengineering work through Information Technology. Harvard Business School Press, Boston (1993)
8. Rosemann, M., de Bruin, T.: Application of a Holistic Model for Determining BPM Maturity. BPTrends, February 1-21 (2005)
9. Rjinders, S., Boer, H.: A Typology of Continuous Improvement Implementation Processes. Knowledge and Process Management 11(4), 283–296 (2004)
10. Nwabueze, U.: Process improvement: the case of a drugs manufacturing company. BPMJ 18(4), 576–584 (2012)
11. Snee, R.: Lean Six Sigma – getting better all the time. IJLSS 1(1), 9–29 (2010)
12. Falk, T., Griesberger, P., Leist, S., Johannsen, F.: Patterns for Business Process Improvement – A First Approach. In: ECIS 2013 Proceedings (2013)
13. Vaishnavi, V., Kuechler, W.: Design science research methods and patterns: innovating information and communication technology. Auerbach Publications, Boca Raton (2008)
14. Buckl, S., Matthes, F., Schneider, A.W., Schweda, C.M.: Pattern-Based Design Research–An Iterative Research Method Balancing Rigor and Relevance. In: vom Brocke, J., Hekkala, R., Ram, S., Rossi, M. (eds.) DESRIST 2013. LNCS, vol. 7939, pp. 73–87. Springer, Heidelberg (2013)
15. Gschwind, T., Koehler, J., Wong, J.: Applying Patterns during Business Process Modeling. In: Dumas, M., Reichert, M., Shan, M.-C. (eds.) BPM 2008. LNCS, vol. 5240, pp. 4–19. Springer, Heidelberg (2008)
16. Niedermann, F., Radeschütz, S., Mitschang, B.: Deep Business Optimization: A Platform for Automated Process Optimization. In: GI 2010: ISSS and BPSC Proceedings (2010)
17. March, S.T., Smith, G.F.: Design and natural science research on information technology. Decision Support Systems 15, 251–266 (1995)
18. Hevner, A.R., March, S.T., Park, J., Ram, S.: Design Science in Information Systems Research. MIS Quarterly 28(1), 75–105 (2004)
19. Venable, J., Pries-Heje, J., Baskerville, R.: A Comprehensive Framework for Evaluation in Design Science Research. In: Peffers, K., Rothenberger, M., Kuechler, B. (eds.) DESRIST 2012. LNCS, vol. 7286, pp. 423–438. Springer, Heidelberg (2012)
20. Cleven, A., Gubler, P., Huener, K.M.: Design Alternatives for the Evaluation of Design Science Research Artifacts. In: DESRIST 2009 Proceedings (2009)

21. Peffers, K., Rothenberger, M., Tuunanen, T., Vaezi, R.: Design science research evaluation. In: Peffers, K., Rothenberger, M., Kuechler, B. (eds.) DESRIST 2012. LNCS, vol. 7286, pp. 398–410. Springer, Heidelberg (2012)
22. Pries-Heje, J., Baskerville, R., Venable, J.: Strategies for Design Science Research Evaluation. In: ECIS 2008 Proceedings (2008)
23. Ostrowski, L., Helfert, M.: Design Science Evaluation – Example of Experimental Design. Journal of Emerging Trends in Computing and Information Sciences 3(9), 253–262 (2012)
24. Harmon, P.: Business Process Change: A Guide for Business Managers and BPM and Six Sigma Professionals. Morgan Kaufmann, Burlington (2007)
25. Rosemann, M.: Business Process Lifecycle Management. White Paper (4/2001) (2004)
26. Harrington, H.J.: Business Process Improvement - The breakthrough strategy for Total Quality, Productivity and Competitiveness. McGraw-Hill, New York (1991)
27. Griesberger, P., Leist, S., Zellner, G.: Analysis of Techniques for Business Process Improvement. In: ECIS 2011 Proceedings (2011)
28. Alturki, A., Gable, G.G., Bandara, W.: The Design Science Research Roadmap: In Progress Evaluation. In: PACIS 2013 Proceedings (2013)
29. Gregor, S., Hevner, A.R.: Positioning and presenting Design Science Research for Maximum Impact. MIS Quarterly 37(2), 337–355 (2013)
30. Gacenga, F., Cater-Steel, A., Toleman, M., Tan, W.-G.: A proposal and evaluation of a design method in design science research. EJBRM 10(2), 89–100 (2012)
31. Peffers, K., Tuunanen, T., Rothenberger, M.A., Chatterjee, S.: A Design Science Research Methodology for Information Systems Research. JMIS 24(3), 45–77 (2007)
32. Winter, R.: Design science research in Europe. EJIS 17, 470–475 (2008)
33. Sonnenberg, C., vom Brocke, J.: Evaluation Patterns for Design Science Research Artefacts. In: Helfert, M., Donnellan, B. (eds.) EDSS 2011. CCIS, vol. 286, pp. 71–83. Springer, Heidelberg (2012)
34. Falk, T., Griesberger, P., Leist, S.: Patterns as an artifact for business process improvement - insights from a case study. In: vom Brocke, J., Hekkala, R., Ram, S., Rossi, M. (eds.) DESRIST 2013. LNCS, vol. 7939, pp. 88–104. Springer, Heidelberg (2013)
35. Barros, O.: Business process patterns and frameworks. BPMJ 13(1), 47–69 (2007)
36. Jung, J., Sprenger, J.: Muster für die Geschäftsprozessmodellierung. GI 2006: DW (Integration, Informationslogistik und Architektur) Proceedings (2006)
37. Cooper, H.M.: Organizing knowledge syntheses: A taxonomy of literature reviews. Knowledge in Society 1, 104–126 (1988)
38. vom Brocke, J., Simons, A., Niehaves, B., Riemer, K., Plattfaut, R., Cleven, A.: Reconstructing the Giant: On the importance of rigor in documenting the literature search process. In: ECIS 2009 Proceedings (2009)
39. Levy, Y., Ellis, T.J.: A Systems Approach to Conduct an Effective Literature Review in Support of Information Systems Research. Informing Science Journal 9, 181–212 (2006)
40. Amescua, A., García, J., Sánchez-Segura, M.-I., Medina-Domínguez, F.: A Pattern-Based Solution to Bridge the Gap Between Theory and Practice in Using Process Models. In: Wang, Q., Pfahl, D., Raffo, D.M., Wernick, P. (eds.) SPW/ProSim 2006. LNCS, vol. 3966, pp. 97–104. Springer, Heidelberg (2006)
41. Appleton, B.: Patterns for Conducting Process Improvement. Pattern Languages of Program Design 3 (PLoP Conference) Proceedings (1997)
42. Atwood, D.: BPM Process Patterns: Repeatable Design for BPM Process Models. BPTrends (2006)
43. Dietz, J.L.G.: Generic recurrent patterns in business processes. In: van der Aalst, W.M.P., ter Hofstede, A.H.M., Weske, M. (eds.) BPM 2003. LNCS, vol. 2678, pp. 200–215. Springer, Heidelberg (2003)
44. Forster, F.: The Idea behind Business Process Improvement: Toward a Business Process Improvement Pattern Framework. BPTrends 1–13 (2006)

45. Harmon, P.: Process Change Patterns. BPTrends 3(6) (2005)
46. Kim, A., Jung, J.-Y.: Process Change Pattern Analysis in Collaborative Processes. In: ICIEOM 2011 Proceedings (2011)
47. Kim, D., Kim, M., Kim, H.: Dynamic Business Process Management based on Process Change Patterns. In: ICCIT 2007 Proceedings (2007)
48. Reijers, H.A., Limam Mansar, S.: Best practices in business process redesign: an overview and qualitative evaluation of successful redesign heuristics. Omega 33(4), 283–306 (2005)
49. Rinderle-Ma, S., Reichert, M., Weber, B.: On the formal semantics of change patterns in process-aware information systems. In: Li, Q., Spaccapietra, S., Yu, E., Olivé, A. (eds.) ER 2008. LNCS, vol. 5231, pp. 279–293. Springer, Heidelberg (2008)
50. Rogers, D., Salustri, F.A.: A quality function deployment method pattern language for efficient design. In: ICED 2009 Proceedings (2009)
51. Störrle, H.: Describing process patterns with UML. In: Ambriola, V. (ed.) EWSPT 2001. LNCS, vol. 2077, p. 173. Springer, Heidelberg (2001)
52. Tran, H.N., Coulette, B., Dong, B.T.: A UML-Based Process Meta-model Integrating a Rigorous Process Patterns Definition. In: Münch, J., Vierimaa, M. (eds.) PROFES 2006. LNCS, vol. 4034, pp. 429–434. Springer, Heidelberg (2006)
53. Weber, B., Rinderle, S., Reichert, M.: Change Patterns and Change Support Features in Process-Aware Information Systems. In: Krogstie, J., Opdahl, A.L., Sindre, G. (eds.) CAiSE 2007. LNCS, vol. 4495, pp. 574–588. Springer, Heidelberg (2007)
54. Stephenson, C., Bandara, W.: Enhancing Best Practices in public health: Using process patterns for Business Process Management. In: ECIS 2007 Proceedings (2007)
55. Nagayoshi, S., Liu, Y., Iijima, J.: A Study of the Patterns for Reducing Exceptions and Improving Business Process Flexibility. In: Albani, A., Aveiro, D., Barjis, J. (eds.) EEWC 2012. LNBIP, vol. 110, pp. 61–76. Springer, Heidelberg (2012)
56. Zimmermann, B.: Pattern-basierte Prozessbeschreibung und -unterstützung - Ein Werkzeug zur Unterstützung von Prozessen zur Anpassung von E-Learning-Materialien (Diss.). TU Darmstadt (2008)
57. Hanafizadeh, P., Moosakhani, M., Bakhshi, J.: Selecting the best strategic practices for business process redesign. BPMJ 15(4), 609–627 (2009)
58. Limam Mansar, S., Reijers, H.A.: Best practices in business process redesign: validation of a redesign framework. Computers in Industry 56(5), 457–471 (2005)
59. Norta, A., Grefen, P.: Discovering Patterns for inter-organizational business process collaboration. IJCIS 16(3&4), 507-544 (2007)
60. Paludo, M., Burnett, R., Jamhour, E.: Patterns Leveraging Analysis Reuse of Business Processes. In: Software Reuse: Advances in Software Reusabilty Proceedings (2000)
61. Pourshahid, A., Mussbacher, G., Amyot, D., Weiss, M.: An aspect-oriented framework for Business Process Improvement. In: Babin, G., Kropf, P., Weiss, M. (eds.) E-Technologies: Innovation in an Open World. LNBIP, vol. 26, pp. 290–305. Springer, Heidelberg (2009)
62. Turetken, O., Elgammal, A., van den Heuvel, W.-J., Papazoglou, M.: Enforcing Compliance on Business Processes through the Use of Patterns. In: ECIS 2011 Proceedings (2011)
63. Niedermann, F., Radeschütz, S., Mitschang, B.: Business Process Optimization Using Formalized Optimization Patterns. In: Abramowicz, W. (ed.) BIS 2011. LNBIP, vol. 87, pp. 123–135. Springer, Heidelberg (2011)
64. Smirnov, S., Weidlich, M., Mendling, J., Weske, M.: Action Patterns in Business Process Models. Universitätsverlag Potsdam, Potsdam (2012)
65. Zellner, G.: Towards a framework for identifying business process redesign patterns. BPMJ 19(4), 600–623 (2013)
66. Sein, M.K., Henfridsson, O., Purao, S., Rossi, M., Lindgren, R.: Action Design Research. MIS Quarterly 35(1), 37–56 (2011)
67. Lee, A.S., Baskerville, R.L.: Generalizing Generalizability in Information Systems Research. ISR 14(3), 221–243 (2003)

# Building a Software Tool for Transparent and Efficient Process Assessments in IT Service Management

Anup Shrestha, Aileen Cater-Steel, Mark Toleman, and Wui-Gee Tan

University of Southern Queensland, Toowoomba, Australia
{anup.shrestha,caterst,mark.toleman,wui-gee.tan}@usq.edu.au

**Abstract.** Process improvements provide a structured approach for organisations to improve the way they operate. A number of process improvement methodologies such as ISO9000, TQM, Six Sigma, Lean, and Agile have been proposed over the last few decades and subsequently software tools have been developed to apply these methodologies. However determination of process capability to measure improvement is predominantly conducted by expert process assessors and consultants with proprietary frameworks. We propose the use of the international standard for process assessment ISO/IEC 15504 for a transparent measurement of process capability. We also demonstrate development of a software tool based on the standard that can facilitate organisations to assess their processes efficiently. In this paper, we explain the development, implementation and preliminary evaluation of a software-mediated process assessment approach in the area of IT Service Management at a large public-sector IT organisation in Queensland, Australia. This paper's contribution is the integration of the design science research methodology with the task-technology fit theory for the development of the software tool as a research artefact. For practitioners the project demonstrates transparent and efficient assessment of IT service processes to facilitate continual improvement.

**Keywords:** Process Assessment, IT Service Management, Task-Technology Fit, Design Science Research, ISO/IEC 15504.

## 1 Introduction

Organisations have adopted methodologies such as ISO9000, TQM and Six Sigma for better business performance in terms of process effectiveness and efficiency [1]. Software developed to apply these methodologies such as Business Process Modelling tools have expedited process adoption and improvement [2]. However, measurement of process improvements, i.e., process assessments lack uniformity and transparency in the way they are conducted [3]. The lack of software tools for process assessments may be attributed to the lack of a standard structure in the way process assessments are conducted. Moreover it is reported that process assessments are costly and time-consuming [3, 4].

ISO/IEC 15504, the international standard for process assessment, was initially developed for the assessment of software development processes [5]. However this standard has now emerged as a general process assessment standard. COBIT has

M.C. Tremblay et al. (Eds.): DESRIST 2014, LNCS 8463, pp. 241–256, 2014.

recently adopted this standard for the assessment of IT governance processes [6]. In response to the paradigm shift of IT's focus from technology to service provision, the standard has published a process assessment model for IT services [7]. We intend to develop a software tool based on the model enabling organisations to self-assess IT service processes. Review of prior studies has found that software tools are primarily designed to support assessors in process assessment. In contrast, the software tool we developed is targeted for IT organisations to self-assess their IT service processes.

According to research conducted by Gartner, investment in IT services exceeded that in IT devices, IT systems and enterprise software in 2012 and is forecast to continue [8]. It is obvious that businesses will increasingly evaluate IT in terms of what value is offered by IT services rather than how the technologies are managed. The IT Service Management (ITSM) discipline has embraced a process approach along with service-oriented thinking in managing IT for business. The popular ITSM framework, Information Technology Infrastructure Library (ITIL®) and the international standard of ITSM (ISO/IEC 20000) stress the importance of process improvement for better IT services. In practice, ITSM is endorsed by an internationally active practitioners' forum called itSMF but there is limited scholarly work in this discipline [9].

The research problem that motivates this research is (a) the  lack of transparency in the way process assessments are conducted and (b) the lack of efficiency for organisations to repeatedly conduct process assessments.

We propose an approach called Software-mediated Process Assessment (SMPA): a standards-based process assessment approach by which organisations can self-assess their processes using a software tool. A research project in collaboration with academics, practitioners and standards committee members with combined expertise in ITSM and process assessment was initiated in 2011 to develop and evaluate the SMPA approach. The research team includes an industry partner, one of the world's leading assessment solution providers that provided its software platform to develop our tool. The research question of our research project is: *How can the software-mediated process assessment approach be developed and used in an IT organisation?* The objective of this paper is to report the development, implementation and evaluation of the software tool developed for the SMPA approach. We conduct this research as a Design Science Research (DSR) [10] project. The unique contribution to knowledge from this research is the application of fit profile from task and technology requirements to explicate rigorous design principles in building a software tool that addresses IT organisation problems of lack of transparency and efficiency in assessments.

The introduction section discussed the research problem and research question. The following section provides an overview of existing ITSM process assessment approaches. The research methodology is discussed next. The artefact development and demonstration are then explained in detail, followed by an account of the evaluation of the tool. The conclusion summarises the findings and suggests an agenda for future work.

## 2     Review of Prior Studies

In this section, we firstly review the existing approaches in ITSM process assessments in order to articulate the research problem of lack of transparency and efficiency in the prevalent approaches. We then provide an overview of the task-technology fit theory and the international standard of process assessment, ISO/IEC 15504 that are used in this design science research project.

## 2.1 Existing Approaches of ITSM Process Assessment

There are several commercial ITSM process assessment tools (e.g. [11]). These bespoke services can be considered as a black box since the rationale behind the assessment activities is not disclosed. We found three prominent ITSM Process Assessment approaches from the literature review: (a) Tudor's ITSM Process Assessment provides an overall approach to conducting process assessments based on ITIL and ISO/IEC 15504 [12]; (b) Standard CMMI Appraisal Method for Process Improvement (SCAMPI) using CMMI for Services (CMMI-SVC) as the measurement model [13]; and (c) ITIL Process Maturity Framework assesses ITIL processes based on five defined levels of maturity [14].

The existing ITSM process assessment approaches advocate their measurement framework for transparent process assessment. All process assessment approaches discussed in the literature and proprietary process assessment services offered by consultants in the IT industry appear to be based on one of the two related measurement models: Capability Maturity Model/ Integration (CMM/ CMMI) and the international standard of process assessment ISO/IEC 15504. Both measurement models for process capability determination originated from the software engineering discipline and are largely harmonized in their measures [5]. Moreover, the role of ISO/IEC 15504 as a consistent measurement framework for ITSM process assessment was confirmed by a systematic literature review [15].

Apparently none of the existing process assessment approaches encourage or demonstrate use of software tools for an efficient self-assessment of IT service processes for organisations. Several initiatives reported about the use of software tools in ITSM process assessments are either proprietary (hence not transparent and efficient) or developed only for the assessors to use (hence does not promote efficient self-assessments by IT organisations). We did not find any published research or industry initiatives towards developing a transparent approach to conduct self-assessments of processes by IT organisations. We base our research on this identified gap. Furthermore, there are industry reports of high costs and unstructured assessment approaches discouraging ITSM process assessments even though organisations see value in the idea of assessments [16]. Therefore this problem is also relevant in the IT industry.

## 2.2 Transparency and Efficiency Challenges

Addressing transparency and efficiency are two major challenges of process assessments [3]. These challenges are taken into account as important problems that must be solved with the proposed tool.

**Transparency.** For our task of process assessment, transparency is the concept of facilitating any course of action with accessible information regarding the assessment. Transparency can be improved by aligning the assessment activities with the ISO/IEC 15504 standard that provides guidance on conducting the assessment process. Moreover, there are process assessment tools that are 100% compliant with the normative and informative parts of the ISO/IEC 15504 standard (such as SPICE-Lite Assessment tool or SEAL software assessment tool). These assessment tools provide an interface to the assessors in assisting them to record evidence for standard indicators, rate process capabilities and produce assessment reports. These assessments are transparent in the sense that they align with the standard.

However there is still lack of objectivity in the assessment approach particularly in terms of data collection, analysis and presentation. The existing ITSM process assessment approaches have challenges in regards to transparency because they use interviews to map participant opinions to the standard indicators which are subject to interpretation by both the participant and the assessor. Moreover, assessment results are based on subjective evaluation of the assessors for process capability determination and process improvement recommendations. The issue of transparency is therefore a significant hurdle in conducting an objective and standardised process assessment. We therefore consider transparency is a critical task challenge that needs to be addressed by the tool.

**Efficiency.** Efficiency determines the degree of economy with which any assessment consumes resources, especially time and money [17]. We believe efficiency can be achieved in process assessments since a number of process assessment activities can be automated with the use of the tool. This translates to significant cost savings from not using expensive assessors and consultants while enabling repeated self-assessments for IT organisations. This opportunity can address the efficiency challenges for process assessment. We therefore consider efficiency as our second task challenge to consider while developing the tool.

## 2.3    Task-Technology Fit

In DSR projects, researchers are advised to use established kernel theories to inform and justify the research work [18]. We present the task-technology fit (TTF) theory [19] as the kernel theory in our research to advise how the task challenges of process assessment and technology requirements for a new software tool fit together to articulate artefact design and development. The choice of TTF theory is justified by the core focus of the research question to build a technology solution in response to task challenges.

TTF theory proposes that IT is more likely to have a positive impact on individual performance if the capabilities of the IT match the tasks that the user must perform [20]. TTF deviates from self-reported user evaluations and looks at the "fit" between the technology features and the task requirements to be supported by the technology. TTF theory was later applied for evaluation of group performance by verifying the fit with group support systems technology [19]. Since then the theory has been applied to a diverse range of information systems and is considered one of the prominent theories to explain the impact of IT on performance. We adopt Zigurs and Buckland's TTF theory for two primary reasons: (a) the software tool is a decision support tool that shares similar technology dimensions as proposed in the theory, viz. communication support, process structuring and information processing; and (b) our approach of designing an ideal fit profile to match task and technology is supported by this theory.

## 2.4    International Standard for Process Assessment

It is important to have a brief review of the international standard for process assessment, ISO/IEC 15504 which is the basis of the SMPA tool development and evaluation. The standard defines six process capability levels (CL0 to CL5) which in turn consist of a total of nine process attributes (PA1.1 to PA5.2) and further consist of generic practices [21]. Process assessment must be compliant with the ISO/IEC 15504 requirements where the assessors collect objective evidence against process indicators to determine capabilities of a process and to ultimately improve processes in an organisation. A process reference model provides all the indicators to determine process performance (CL1) which is specific to each process. Likewise the process assessment model provides generic indicators to determine higher levels of process capabilities in a standard manner. Fig. 1 illustrates the structure of the ISO/IEC 15504 process assessment model with five steps of process capability levels.

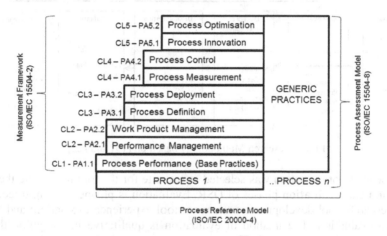

**Fig. 1.** Process Assessment Model based on ISO/IEC 15504 [21]

# 3    Research Methodology

We use Design Science Research (DSR) methodology [22] because this research is motivated to develop a novel artefact in order to solve an organisational problem [10]. We follow the six DSR methodology steps: problem identification and motivation, objectives of a solution, design and development, demonstration, evaluation, and communication [22]. We integrate the TTF theory process model with the DSR methodology and use it to explain the development and evaluation of the artefact.

The challenges of lack of transparency and efficiency in ITSM process assessments represent the first DSR phase of **problem identification and motivation**. The second DSR phase, **objectives of a solution** can be defined from the three technology dimensions derived from the TTF theory [19]: communication support; process structuring; and information processing. We use the technology dimensions as technology requirements for the tool development. Ultimately alignment between task challenges and technology requirements is represented with an ideal fit profile that proposes a set of design considerations for the tool development. The process of building the fit profile and ultimately the tool aligns with the **design and development** phase of DSR.

While most of the existing process assessments rely on process-specific indicators that demonstrate objective evidence of process capabilities, the software tool facilitates a top-down approach where assessment at each level is defined with a goal and then assessment is guided by explicit questions and metrics that are set to goal attainment. A top-down approach in process assessment ensures that the measurement follows a transparent workflow of assessment activities. This concept is guided by the Goal-Question-Metric (GQM) approach. The GQM approach defines a measurement model for software metrics on three levels: goal (conceptual level); question (operational level); and metric (quantitative level) [23].

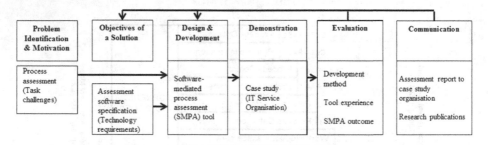

**Fig. 2.** Research Methodology based on [19] and [22]

A case study organisation was selected as test site for the tool to execute the **demonstration** and **evaluation** phases of DSR. Evaluation is planned during three stages of the research: tool development evaluation; tool experience evaluation; and SMPA approach evaluation. The method of evaluation is qualitative investigation through semi-structured interviews with IT service managers and process performers at the case study organisation. We present this paper as a publication of the **communication** phase of DSR to obtain feedback regarding the development and evaluation of the artefact.

## 4    SMPA Tool Design and Development

TTF theory has been associated with evaluative research where a fit of task requirements is sought from existing technologies [24]. We extend the application of TTF theory to understand the development of a new technology for particular task challenges. This approach is particularly suitable for DSR to exert rigour in explaining development of novel artefacts. This also makes sense in the practical world: we have learnt that requirements must be carefully considered before designing and developing a technology solution to overcome task challenges. Therefore, integration of TTF theory in the DSR process is a novel research approach illustrated in Fig. 2 and we propose this integration as a unique contribution of this paper.

In the context of the development of the tool, we now discuss three stages of tool design and development. In the first stage, requirements for assessment workflow and automation to be supported by the tool are discussed (technology requirements) based on task challenges. A fit profile is then established to provide a set of design principles to guide the development of the tool as the second stage. This is followed by the third stage of tool development based on the design principles of the fit profile.

## 4.1 Process Assessment Technology Requirements

We examine the existing challenges of lack of transparency and efficiency in the task of process assessment that need to be overcome by the software tool. We group our task challenges as a typical "decision task" since process assessments are conducted to make informed decisions on improving processes continually. According to the TTF theory, technology requirements for the challenges of a decision task must focus on "information processing" and "process structuring" dimensions of technology for enhanced performance [19]. We use the term "technology requirements" rather than "technology dimensions" as used originally in the theory. This is because we are not evaluating existing technology dimensions for a fit but trying to develop a technology solution that fits task challenges to technology requirements. The technology proposed for the software tool runs on a cloud-based platform for assessment facilitation and a web-based interface for online surveys.

- **Process Structuring.** The tool must define the assessment process workflow by which the entire procedure is conducted as explicitly documented in the standard [21]. Assessment workflow steps have been proposed to define a structure in the activities: Definition, Preparation, Assessment, Analysis, Results Presentation and Closure phases [12]. The technology requirements of process structuring should lead to the development of the tool that can facilitate the entire assessment process in a transparent manner. Transparency is achieved with the use of a software tool since the software can provide comprehensive coverage of all questions relating to the standard using online surveys. The approach of asking questions directly to the assessment participants and allowing the software tool to objectively calculate process capabilities based on the survey responses promote transparency. Moreover, the assessment report produces recommendations based on the ITIL® framework stored in the knowledge base of the software tool, thereby promoting transparency for process improvements since the recommendations are based on the questions that align with the assessment model of the standard.
- **Information Processing.** The ability to automate activities of process assessment is considered as the information processing requirement for the development of the tool. The steps of assessment data collection and validation, process capability ratings and reporting of the assessment results requires gathering, aggregating, evaluating and finally presenting information. Therefore, having an efficient information processing capability is an important requirement for the tool. Efficiency is achieved by the use of online surveys instead of assessment interviews for data collection; and the generation of process improvement recommendations based on the DSS tool. Process assessments using a software tool can enable cost-effective and repeatable assessments so that the organisations can spend their time and resources on process improvement activities rather than conducting assessments.

## 4.2     Design Principles

In this project, a fit profile provides design principles for the tool development based on the task challenges and technology requirements. The fit profile as shown in Table 1 answers the research question that we posed in section 1: *how can the software-mediated process assessment tool be developed and used in an IT organisation?*

Table 1. Fit profile as design principles

| Process Assessment (Task challenges) | SMPA tool (Technology Requirements) | Tool Design Principles | Resources Needed |
|---|---|---|---|
| Transparency | Process Structuring | Facilitate Assessment Workflow | International Standard for Process Assessment (ISO/IEC 15504) |
| Efficiency | Information Processing | Automate Assessment Activities | Decision support systems (DSS) tool |

In order to facilitate assessment workflow to address transparency issues, alignment with the international standard for process assessment is critical while developing the tool. Together with a thorough review of the standard [21], its process reference model [25] and the assessment model for IT services [7] were used. Similarly a DSS tool provides decision support by processing relevant information. We use a software tool to automate assessment activities during collection and analysis of process data directly from participants; and presentation of assessment results in the form of process capability and recommendations for decision support in process improvements.

We used the fit profile to present two design principles and the two key resources we needed before commencing the actual tool development. Based on the design principles and using the resources from the fit profile (see Table 1), our research artefact was developed to address the task challenges using technology requirements.

## 4.3     Development of the SMPA Tool

The GQM approach has been previously applied in the software industry. However use of this approach to develop a process assessment tool in ITSM is novel. The international standard defines a reference model where each process is defined in terms of purpose and outcomes [25]. Attainment of the process purpose by meeting the outcomes defines the "goal" component of the software tool.

Likewise, the standard provides a set of base practices to fulfil the process outcomes and a set of generic practices for Level 2 (process management), Level 3 (standardisation), Level 4 (quantitative measurement) and Level 5 (innovation) of process capability. These practices are used as assessment indicators by an assessor in a formal assessment. In our context, the emphasis is on providing information that can drive improvement of IT service processes. The practices specified in the standard were mapped into a set of 177 assessment questions. The tool allocates these questions to the respondents based on three process roles: process performers, process managers and process interfaces. This defines the "question" component of the tool.

Finally every question is rated using the scale: "Not" (N), "Partially" (P), "Large-ly" (L), "Fully" (F) and "Not Applicable" (NA) as defined in the standard. This rating is a knowledge metric of the process stakeholders. Rather than the assessment team making a subjective choice of the indicator rating, the software tool objectively meas-ures feedback from the process stakeholders directly from the questions and provides a transparent metric to determine process capability.

The application of an objective GQM approach for assessment workflow of the tool is the key facilitator for a transparent process assessment. The features of the SMPA tool automate many of the assessment activities as discussed next.

**Assessment Data Collection and Validation.** The tool accumulates responses from all the concerned process stakeholders using an online survey interface. Every ques-tion also features a free text comments box to capture qualitative contextual data that can be analysed to validate responses and provide specific recommendations. The approach of asking questions directly in a web-based survey environment represents a faster and more efficient data collection method compared to assessment interviews with the same level of rigour in service research [26].

**Process Capability Determination and Rating.** The software tool determines the final score for each process at each capability level. This is done by calculating the mean value of all the responses for a level by all the respondents. The coefficient of variation ($CoV$) of all the responses is also computed by the tool:

$CoV_x = \frac{\delta_x}{\bar{x}}$ where $CoV_x$ is the coefficient of variation, $\delta_x$ is the standard devi-ation and $\bar{x}$ is the mean value of $x$ responses for a particular process capability score.

$CoV$ is useful in determining reliability of the process score based on dispersion of the responses. The mean and the $CoV$ are simple statistical measures to understand what the critical mass of assessment respondents think about the processes being assessed. This is a new feature of the tool that is not explicitly stated in the standard.

**Assessment Reporting with Process Improvement Recommendations.** The SMPA tool is not only a stand-alone survey engine, it has embedded a knowledge base that stores contextual recommendations for process improvements tied to every assess-ment question. Using the knowledge base developed from best practice guidelines (ITIL®) for process improvements in ITSM, the tool performs gap analysis based on the collected response metrics and produces a report with improvement recommenda-tions. We developed the knowledge base with recommendation items at the question level for four IT service processes in our research project. For every question when the mean rating is either "partially" (P) or "not" (N), i.e. there is an element of risk in the process activity, a recommendation item associated with each question is ex-tracted from the knowledge base and the accumulated knowledge items are compiled to develop the final assessment report with process improvement recommendations.

# 5    SMPA Tool Demonstration

Agreement was reached with a large government organisation to trial the SMPA tool. The IT service department of the organisation has over 55 IT service staff and delivers IT services to residents across a large area in Australia servicing over 150,000 residents. The IT service department provides 34 identified services supporting IT functions in the organisation and typically manages 300 service requests per week.

Three ITSM processes were selected for assessment: Problem Management, Change Management and Configuration Management based on a process selection approach that provides decision support in selecting critical processes to improve [27]. Prior to implementing the SMPA tool, in April 2013 we conducted a conventional interview-based process assessment led by an experienced ISO/IEC 15504 certified expert assessor following the RAPID methodology [28], hereby referred as the manual assessment, at the organisation to enable the comparison of the SMPA outcomes with those of a manual assessment. The manual assessment scope was agreed to Capability Level 3 for the three processes. The manual assessment determined that while the capability of Problem Management and Configuration Management processes were both rated at Level 2 (Managed), the Change Management process was assessed at Level 0 (Incomplete) as shown in Table 2. The process capability ratings in

Table 2 were determined based on the objective evidence collected during interviews by three assessors. The final results were signed off following expert judgment by the lead assessor as fully complying with ISO/IEC 15504 standard.

**Table 2.** Process Capability results from the manual assessment

| Processes Assessed | Process Attributes | | | | |
|---|---|---|---|---|---|
| | 1.1 | 2.1 | 2.2 | 3.1 | 3.2 |
| Problem Management | F | L | L | L | L |
| Change Management | P | L | L | L | P |
| Configuration Management | F | F | L | L | L |

The trial of the online SMPA tool was conducted from October to November 2013. To facilitate the assessment, the organisation nominated a senior IT service manager who was trained to use the administrator's console of the tool. The assessment questionnaire was completed by three process managers, five process performers and five other process stakeholders for the three processes. The SMPA tool collected survey responses and generated an assessment report. The assessment report presented different process capability scores as shown in Table 3. The SMPA tool determined that the Problem Management process was at Capability Level 1 (Performed) while the Change and Configuration Management processes were assessed at Level 0 (Incomplete). The report also provided 319 process improvement recommendations and listed 46 user comments from the respondents.

Because of the information processing capability of the SMPA tool, there is no human judgment used in determining the process capability ratings. The scores were derived purely based on the analysis of the assessment data captured by the tool. Besides the ratings, Table 3 also presents the reliability score for each rating as shown in parenthesis. The reliability score is based on the number and variation of responses ($CoV$) and is determined based on the following simple rule: High (H) if $CoV < 30\%$; Moderate (M) if $30\% \leq CoV \leq 50\%$; and Low (L) if $CoV > 50\%$. The process capability results from the manual assessment are significantly different to the SMPA tool. These differences are discussed in section 6.2.

**Table 3.** Process Capability results from the SMPA tool

| Processes Assessed | Process Attributes | | | | | | | | |
|---|---|---|---|---|---|---|---|---|---|
| | 1.1 | 2.1 | 2.2 | 3.1 | 3.2 | 4.1 | 4.2 | 5.1 | 5.2 |
| Problem Management | L (H) | P (M) | P (L) | P (L) | P (M) | P (M) | N (M) | P (M) | P (M) |
| Change Management | P (M) | P (M) | P (M) | P (L) | L (H) | P (M) | P (M) | P (M) | P (M) |
| Configuration Management | P (L) | P (M) | P (L) | P (L) | P (H) | P (M) | P (M) | P (M) | P (M) |

# 6    SMPA Tool Evaluation

DSR projects require an evaluation phase in order to determine effectiveness of the artefact [10]. From the TTF theoretical perspective as well, we have discussed the design principles from the fit profile but evaluation of the fit needs to be reviewed by examining the utility of the tool at the case study organisation.

We organise our evaluation based on the design science evaluation framework [29]. The *ex-ante* evaluation took place in several iterations during the design and development of the artefact. The use of the TTF theory for a fit profile to obtain design principles for the tool, adherence to the international standard of process assessment, use of the GQM approach in facilitating assessment workflow, and software automation in several assessment activities – all of these contribute as evaluation checkpoints for effective tool design and development as detailed in section 4.

## 6.1    Tool Experience Evaluation

To perform the *ex-post* evaluation we conducted a focus group with the survey participants. Soon after the survey closed the focus group was conducted with seven people who participated in the SMPA assessments. The discussions sought feedback about the experience of the IT service process managers, process performers and other process stakeholders using the tool. Based on the Diffusion of Innovation theory [30], we constructed a focus group protocol to determine key discussion points that constituted the five innovation factors of the new technology use: compatibility, complexity, relative advantage, observability and trialability in order to evaluate experience with the use of the tool.

One of the researchers facilitated the focus group discussion. Participants reported that they found the tool easy to use and largely agreed that a self-assessment experience answering direct questions made the exercise more visible and less costly to implement than a manual assessment. For example:

*Assessment Facilitator.* *"The tool has the advantage of giving you a really broad dataset. So you can survey 50 people easily because you don't have to have them in a room at one time..."*

*Process Performer-2.* *"I can be honest as I am not being watched. I can answer truthfully because I'm not going to get in trouble. It gives you a voice. I mean, you can be anonymous with a survey and not worry that your boss is sitting next to you."*

*Process Manager-1.* *"...the survey can be very accurate, and is probably a better return on investment because you are not taking up everyone's time all at once. I would imagine it would be cheaper to do rather than have someone [expert assessor] across the table for that amount of time..."*

There were also constructive suggestions to improve the relevance and clarity of the assessment questions. For example,

*Process Manager-1.* *"I think the questions were relevant but the interpretation was the big barrier ... once you understand what was being asked and how it was being presented, it became a lot easier to answer the questions".*

### 6.2   SMPA Outcome Evaluation

After the SMPA report had been provided to the organisation in December 2013, interviews were conducted with three process managers to enable us to evaluate their perceptions on the validity and quality of the reports. Answers to these interview questions enabled a comparison of the outcomes of the manual assessment and SMPA approach.

There was consensus among the three process managers that the SMPA report produced accurate scores, in particular they commended the reliability score which they believed will help to determine the priority areas of improvement. For example:

*Process Manager-2:* *"What I like about the report from the tool is that it is backed up by solid evidence, and the reliability score is fantastic – it helps to determine if we are all thinking in the same direction or all over the place – I feel that the reliability score is more powerful than the process capability score in some instances."*

*Process Manager-1.* *"You can take an example of the configuration management process, we know that we don't do that well – in fact you can say the process is not even in place. Surprisingly the manual report said that configuration management is at Level 2 and I have to disagree. The report from the software rightly scored us a Level 0 for this process."*

All process managers also confirmed that the recommendations from the SMPA tool were valid and more actionable than the manual assessment report.

*Process Manager-3.* *"Since your recommendations are derived from the comprehensive guidelines of ITIL best practices, I think they are detailed enough for effective implementation ... recommendations provided in the manual assessment are very broad and holistic directions."*

*Process Manager-2.* *"Numbers speak for themselves. We have over 100 process improvement recommendations derived from the tool that can be traced back to the identified gap at every question. I think the manual assessment report had less than 20 recommendations that are not very specific."*

In an attempt to account for the dramatic differences between the scores of the two assessment reports (Table 2 and Table 3), the following suggestions were discussed:

- The influence of the lead assessor in the manual assessment may introduce bias resulting in judgment based on previous experience, a set of underlying assumptions, and perceptions and interpretations while determining the scores.
- Different staff participated in the two assessments: the manual assessment had 10 participants and the SMPA questionnaire was completed by 11 respondents. Only three process stakeholders participated in both assessments.
- The time lag between the two assessments was six months and a few significant changes during this time such as the implementation of a new ITSM tool and staff changes might contribute to changes in process capability ratings.
- The manual assessment was conducted in a group discussion environment including stakeholders from all roles for a particular process. Peer group discussions may be biased since senior managers and extroverts may dominate the discussion and assert their opinions leaving inactive participation from other process stakeholders. This limitation is removed in the SMPA tool as everyone had an anonymous and equal say about the processes in a more democratic manner through online surveys, therefore improving accuracy in understanding the true picture.
- Assessment questions were more granular in the SMPA tool. While the manual assessment focused on high level discussions and the assessors' judgment of specific assessment indicators based on those discussions, the SMPA approach focused on the standard asking very specific questions for every indicator to determine the process capability. A more granular approach improves the authenticity of the SMPA approach but this means a significant time imposition for survey respondents by examining specific aspects of a process in detail.

In summary, the evaluation in terms of tool experience and outcome confirmed the potential of the SMPA tool to address transparency and efficiency challenges in process assessments in the context of IT service processes. One of the significant achievements of the project is the intention to commercialize the SMPA tool by our industry partner, providing strong evidence of industry relevance of our research outcome and therefore maintaining an effective rigour-relevance balance in DSR [31].

# 7    Conclusion

The existing guidelines for process assessment lack transparency and assessments by external consultants are costly to conduct. We have developed an online process assessment tool aligned with the international standards to overcome this problem. The challenges to conduct a transparent and cost-effective process assessment and the technology requirements to address such challenges have been considered to develop the tool with the help of a theoretically grounded fit profile. In addition the growth of outsourcing of IT service functions and the use of virtual IT teams around the globe means that the tool with its online survey feature can be an efficient technology for repeated process assessments by IT organisations. The SMPA approach addresses transparency issues in process assessment by following a goal-oriented measurement of IT service processes using a standard process assessment model.

On reflection, it may have been better to select one process for design and evaluation rather than four since no significant benefits arose in terms of design knowledge and contribution with the addition of more processes. The evaluation revealed that it was the transformation of generic practices of the standard that requires more work. The base practices of the standards were well understood by the survey participants. In this regard, we could have focused on the generic practices (capability component) for design and evaluation of the tool rather than the process component.

Our contribution to knowledge is the application of the fit profile from task and technology requirements to develop design principles for the project. The integration of TTF theory with the DSR methodology is a novel approach. The implication of this research in practice is the presentation of a goal-oriented measurement based on the GQM approach for transparent and efficient assessments in IT service management.

We recognise limitations of this research: processes were assessed at only one organisation. Consequently, we do not claim generalisation of this research and call for future research to investigate and evaluate the SMPA approach in more organisations and in broader disciplines beyond IT service management. However, the design principles used in this study can be applied in other contexts beyond ITSM process assessments in the area of assessments of any general process-based management system, such as for COBIT in IT governance or in PMBOK or Prince2 methodologies for project management. Moreover, in practical terms, we do not claim that the SMPA approach can replace a formal and rigorous process assessment. The tool is developed with an intention to automate several activities of a standard process assessment and therefore enable organisations to repeatedly self-assess their processes for improvements rather than to assess via formal audit such as ISO/IEC 20000 certification.

In future, following repeated use of the tool, it will be possible to conduct a long-term outcome evaluation by observing the impact of the SMPA approach on service improvement. We believe the research has contributed towards achieving transparent and efficient process assessments with a well-structured design and development of the artefact. Future evaluation of the research will hopefully uncover more important implications for enhancement of the SMPA tool for process assessments.

# References

1. Harrington, H.J.: Business Process Improvement: The Breakthrough Strategy for Total Quality, Productivity, and Competitiveness, vol. 1. McGraw-Hill, New York (1991)
2. Aguilar-Saven, R.S.: Business Process Modelling: Review and Framework. International Journal of Production Economics 90(2), 129–149 (2004)
3. Lloyd, V.: ITIL Continual Service Improvement. The Stationery Office, London (2011)
4. Fayad, M.E., Laitinen, M.: Process Assessment Considered Wasteful. Communications of the ACM 40(11), 125–128 (1997)
5. Rout, T.P., Tuffley, A.: Harmonizing ISO/IEC 15504 and CMMI. Software Process: Improvement and Practice 12(4), 361–371 (2007)

6. De Haes, S., Van Grembergen, W., Debreceny, R.S.: COBIT 5 and Enterprise Governance of Information Technology: Building Blocks and Research Opportunities. Journal of Information Systems 27(1), 307–324 (2013)
7. ISO/IEC, ISO/IEC TS 15504-8:2012 - Information Technology - Process Assessment - Part 8: An Exemplar Process Assessment Model for IT Service Management. 2012, International Organization for Standardization: Geneva, Switzerland
8. Lovelock, J.-D.: Forecast Alert: IT Spending, Worldwide, 4Q12 Update. Gartner, Inc., Connecticut (2013)
9. Winniford, M., Conger, S., Erickson-Harris, L.: Confusion in the Ranks: IT Service Management Practice and Terminology. Info Sys. Management 26(2), 153–163 (2009)
10. Hevner, A.R., March, S.T., Park, J., Ram, S.: Design Science in Information SYstems Research. MIS Quarterly 28(1), 75–106 (2004)
11. PinkElephant. PinkSCAN$^{TM}$ - Online Process Maturity Assessment (2013) (cited May 12, 2013),
    http://www.pinkelephant.com/Products/PinkONLINE/PinkScan/
12. Barafort, B., Betry, V., Cortina, S., Picard, M., St-Jean, M., Renault, A., Valdès, O.: ITSM Process Assessment Supporting ITIL. In: Tudor, P.R.C.H. (ed.) Van Haren Publishing, Zaltbommel (2009)
13. CMMI, Standard CMMI® Appraisal Method for Process Improvement (SCAMPISM) A, Version 1.3: Method Definition Document, SEI: CMU University, MA, USA (2011)
14. MacDonald, I.: ITIL Process Assessment Framework. The Co-operative Financial Services, Manchester (2010)
15. Mesquida, A.L., Mas, A., Amengual, E., Calvo-Manzano, J.A.: IT Service Management Process Improvement based on ISO/IEC 15504: A Systematic Review. Information and Software Technology 54(3), 239–247 (2012)
16. Mainville, D.: 8th Annual ITSM Industry Survey. Consulting-Portal, Georgia (2013)
17. Roberts, L.: Process Reengineering: The Key to Achieving Breakthrough Success. American Society for Quality Press, WI (1994)
18. Venable, J.R.: The Role of Theory and Theorising in Design Science Research. In: 1st International Conference on Design Science Research in Information Systems and Technology, CGU, CA (2006)
19. Zigurs, I., Buckland, B.K.: A Theory of Task/Technology Fit and Group Support Systems Effectiveness. MIS Quarterly 22(3), 313–334 (1998)
20. Goodhue, D.L., Thompson, R.L.: Task-Technology Fit and Individual Performance. MIS Quarterly 19(2), 213–236 (1995)
21. ISO/IEC, ISO/IEC 15504-2:2004 – Information Technology – Process Assessment – Part 2: Performing an Assessment, International Organization for Standardization: Geneva (2004)
22. Peffers, K., Tuunanen, T., Rothenberger, M.A., Chatterjee, S.: A Design Science Research Methodology for Information Systems Research. Journal of Management Information Systems 24(3), 45–77 (2007)
23. Van Solingen, R., Basili, V., Caldiera, G., Rombach, D.H.: Goal Question Metric (GQM) Approach. In: Marciniak, J.E. (ed.) Encyclopedia of Software Engineering. John Wiley & Sons: Online Version (2002)
24. Fuller, R.M., Dennis, A.R.: Does Fit Matter? The Impact of Task-Technology Fit and Appropriation on Team Performance in Repeated Tasks. Information Systems Research 20(1), 2–17 (2009)

25. ISO/IEC, ISO/IEC TR 20000-4:2010 – Information Technology – Service Management – Part 4: Process Reference Model, International Organization for Standardization: Geneva, Switzerland (2010)
26. Deutskens, E., de Ruyter, K., Wetzels, M.: An Assessment of Equivalence Between Online and Mail Surveys in Service Research. Journal of Service Research 8(4), 346–355 (2006)
27. Shrestha, A., Cater-Steel, A., Toleman, M., Tan, W.-G.: A Decision Support Tool to Define Scope in IT Service Management Process Assessment and Improvement. In: vom Brocke, J., Hekkala, R., Ram, S., Rossi, M. (eds.) DESRIST 2013. LNCS, vol. 7939, pp. 308–323. Springer, Heidelberg (2013)
28. Cater-Steel, A., Toleman, M., Rout, T.: Process Improvement for Small Firms: An Evaluation of the RAPID Assessment-Based Method. Information and Software Technology 48(5), 323–334 (2006)
29. Pries-Heje, J., Baskerville, R., Venable, J.R.: Strategies for Design Science Research Evaluation. In: 16th European Conference on Information Systems, Galway, Ireland (2008)
30. Rogers, E.M.: Diffusion of Innovations, 4th edn. The Free Press, NY (1995)
31. Kuechler, B., Vaishnavi, V.: Promoting Relevance in IS Research: An Informing System for Design Science Research. Informing Science 14(1), 125–138 (2011)

# CM2: A Case-Based Conflict Management System

Guangxuan Zhang and Sandeep Purao

College of Information Sciences and Technology, The Pennsylvania State University, University Park, PA 16802
gxzhang@psu.edu, spurao@ist.psu.edu

**Abstract.** This paper presents the design of CM2: a case-based conflict management system. We envision the system as an aid to understand and manage conflict situations by referring to past conflict situations, which are stored as Vignettes - vivid yet analytical, theory-laden descriptions. A meta-model, developed on basis of prior kernel theories, is used to structure and represent the constructs and progression of each conflict vignette. The set of vignettes forms the foundation of a case-based reasoning system. CM2 implements the storage and case-based reasoning mechanisms. The paper illustrates CM2 with a use scenario, and concludes with an outline of planned evaluation, discussion about implications, and future work.

**Keywords:** Conflict management, Conflict management system, Case-based reasoning, Meta-model, Vignette.

## 1    Introduction and Motivation

Conflicts are pervasive in all projects [1]. A conflict refers to an interactive process that begins with incompatibility between interdependent parties [2, 3]. Prior research points out that conflicts may arise because of differences in goals, differences in ways of working, or interpersonal dissonance [4, 5]. Managing conflicts is becoming increasingly important as modern projects become large and complex [6]. Further, contemporary projects often involve several participants from different knowledge backgrounds [7], considered essential for unleashing creativity. These differences can also sow the seeds for conflicts.

Managing concurrent, prolonged or diverse conflict (in complex projects) is challenging for human beings because of inherent limits on our cognitive ability. Our actions are often subject to predictable bias and affect, which can lead to undesirable consequences in conflict situations [8]. The predictable bias indicates that people involved in a conflict will more be influenced by *recent* experiences. The influence of affect suggests that people tend to make irrational decisions with little deliberation when they are emotionally involved in a situation. These and other limitations can lead to inappropriate or even counterproductive decisions and behaviors.

A few tools (in the form of software support) have been proposed for conflict management [9, 10]. These tools either provide communication support (e.g. anonymous messages, procedural support, and voting) [11, 12] or offer rational solutions to conflicts (e.g. based on quantitative codification) [9, 13]. Although these types of systems

M.C. Tremblay et al. (Eds.): DESRIST 2014, LNCS 8463, pp. 257–272, 2014.

provide a suite of tools to manage the underlying data, they do not address the basic challenge: providing managers the ability to understand a wide variety of conflict situations, and make effective conflict management choices.

To address this challenge, we design and demonstrate a novel artifact – a conflict management system – that can help conflict parties make sense of conflict situations and become aware of conflict management behaviors in a systematic manner. To build the conflict management system, we follow a design science research approach [14–16]. In line with the direction proposed by Ross et al [10], the designed system utilizes case-based reasoning, enhanced by kernel theories that help structure past experiences about conflicts. These past experiences are captured as vignettes, i.e., vivid yet analytic descriptions of conflicts in practice [17]. Each vignette conveys key information about a conflict (e.g. claims, actions and strategies), that are structured on the basis of a meta-model we derive from kernel theories about conflict management. The design is instantiated in the form of a system, called CM2. We describe the architecture of CM2, briefly illustrate its implementation and demonstrate its use by outlining a use scenario. Specifications of testable hypotheses and proposed empirical evaluation, along with a discussion of implications complete the paper.

## 2    Background and Prior Research

### 2.1    Conflict and Conflict Management

Workplace conflict has been intensively studied in the fields of organization, psychology, and communication [1–3] to investigate a number of components of conflict. The selective review we present below emphasizes findings from prior research; and provides a structure that we can use to understand conflicts.

Understanding a conflict starts with examining its *cause*. Prior work suggests three broad types of conflicts: task, process and relationship [4]. *Task* conflicts arise because of incompatible viewpoints and opinions pertaining to essential ideas of the task, such as its goal, logic, and value. *Process* conflicts are triggered between people who have different viewpoints and opinions pertaining to duty, resource delegation, and schedule. *Relationship* conflicts can be traced to adverse emotions and feelings between people. Understanding the cause is important because it can both predict the outcome as well as suggest strategies for mitigation of consequences. For example, prior studies show that task conflicts have the potential to lead to beneficial outcomes while process and relationship conflicts can lead to dysfunctional consequences [18].

Understanding a conflict situation also means understanding it *as a process*. Conflicts may be conceptualized following a sequential model, or a more nuanced, punctuated model. The punctuated process model emphasizes events that occur as a conflict unfolds. In line with the punctuated equilibrium theory, the punctuated process model describes the conflict process as alternating between stasis and transition [19, 20]. Here, a transition refers to a short period of time when a conflict shifts substantially in terms of its intensity and its progress toward resolution. A transition is characterized by behaviors and emotions of parties to a conflict. The conflict escalation theory suggests that a conflict may undergo a combination of two types of transitions – conflict escalation and conflict de-escalation [21]. Conflict escalation occurs when a conflict is intensified with mechanisms such as more extreme strategies, emotional involvement, issue generalization, or increased number of participants. Conflict de-escalation occurs when conflict parties re-assess the conflict situation and change their language and behaviors to more moderate, collaborative ones.

Knowing the *roles* played by conflict parties is a precondition for understanding their behaviors. The parties involved in a conflict can be broadly classified into two categories: principal conflict parties and third parties. The term 'principal conflict parties' refers to individuals or groups who are interdependent with one another in the pursuit of their interests in spite of the incompatibilities between them [2]. The term 'third parties' refers to individuals or groups who intervene into the conflict either to fulfill their duties or because they have a stake in the conflict [22]. Understanding a conflict situation, thus, requires recognizing the perspectives and actions of both principal conflict parties as well as third parties who are affected by the conflict.

Prior work also outlines conflict management *strategies* to characterize the general intention of the principal conflict parties toward a conflict and the approaches they use for coping with the conflict [3]. Scholars have conceptualized conflict management strategies in a space defined by two dimensions – concern for self and concern for others. Combining these two dimensions results in five styles or strategies that the Principal conflict parties can use: collaborating (H-H), compromising (M-M), yielding (L-H), contending (H-L), and avoiding (L-L) [23]. A conflict management strategy, thus, represents a composite construct that characterizes the general orientation of a conflict party, not a specific action. This review of prior work (briefly described above) provides important constructs and kernel theories that guide this research.

## 2.2 Case-Based Reasoning for Managing Conflicts

Conflict management is a task full of uncertainty. Although conflict management strategies provide high-level explanations of conflict behaviors, knowledge about how to apply these strategies is still scarce. One important reason is that the behaviors of principal conflict parties' are influenced by a very large amount of external and internal factors. The relationship between these factors and the behaviors cannot be captured by structured and un-ambiguous rules. A case-based reasoning strategy provides a way to overcome this challenge.

Case-based reasoning (CBR) is different from rule-based reasoning. It is a problem-solving strategy based on previous experiences [10, 24]. A CBR system refers to a type of expert system or decision support system that applies reasoning based on matching of prior cases to the current situation. The intent is to assist users to understand and solve current problems by referring to similar problems that may have occurred in the past. A CBR system achieves this by storing and indexing a sufficient amount of previous experiences as cases. When a new problem arises, the user can identify past cases and adapt them to address the current problem.

CBR systems can be designed for two potentially overlapping concerns: problem solving and/or problem interpretation [24]. In the first instance, a CBR system is designed to propose almost-right solutions to new problems on basis of previous problem-solution pairs. In the second instance, a CBR system assists users to identify previous cases similar to current problem or situation for the purpose of generating deeper understanding and assessment of the current problem or situation. It is possible to analyze the potential usefulness of CBR for conflict management by comparing the problems related to conflict management elaborated in prior research, and the professed benefits of CBR [25, 26]. Table 1 summarizes these as the potential for application of CBR to assist users with conflict situations.

**Table 1.** Applicability of CBR for Conflict Management

| Factor | Elaboration |
|---|---|
| Lowering knowledge acquisition costs | Reduce cognitive efforts used for maintaining a collecting of conflict management experience/knowledge |
| Reasoning shortcut | Avoid repeating all reasoning steps in situations where a repetitive conflict occurs or a long chain of reasoning is required to understand and make decision for the conflict. |
| Reasoning focus | Indicate what are essential for understanding and solving conflict and reduce emotional impacts. |
| Error prevention | Avoid repeating mistakes made in previous conflict situations by indicating what cause failure in the past. |
| Learn over time | Accumulate knowledge about conflict and conflict management over time. |

To the best of our knowledge, only two CBR systems have been reported in the context of conflict management situations [10, 26]. Both have been designed to identify conflict resolutions within a limited problem domain (Nature Resource Dispute) and therefore, offer little direct help for understanding conflict situations and conflict management behaviors in other domains. Additionally, neither system has incorporated prior scholarly research about conflict and conflict management as kernel theories into the systems. The work we report breaks from these prior efforts because it represents a conscious application of the design science research paradigm and recognition of prior scholarly work as kernel theories that contribute to the design effort.

## 3     A Foundation for the Design

### 3.1     Conflict Vignettes

The foundation for our design science effort is a *Vignette*, analogous to but different in important ways from a *Case*. We make this choice because Cases form the basis of CBR systems. In CBR design, a case refers to a set of information that records previous experience or knowledge. The design of a CBR system involves three considerations: case representation, case retrieval and adaption, and case entry and maintenance [25]. Among these, case representation is crucial because it reflects the informational components and structure that provides the foundation of the CBR system.

Case representation is about structuring and formatting previous experience and knowledge in a well-packaged form [25]. Each case can be conceptualized in terms of a problem and a solution. In a CBR system, this problem description and circumstance is codified for the purpose of case indexing and retrieval. Such a design fits situations in which previous solutions can be readily applied to new problems [10]. However, this design has limited capacity to assist users to *understand* new, hitherto not encountered, problems and develop new solutions. To overcome this limitation, we draw upon and extend the notion of Case, to a new structure we call Vignette.

We define a Vignette as an analytical narrative of practice. It is constructed to convey information about a series of events taken to be representative, typical, or emblematic [27]. With regard to conflict management, vignettes have been shown to be a useful approach for conveying conflict management knowledge [28, 29]. In a more recent study, Zhang and Purao [17] adapt vignette as the key unit of data collection and analysis, pointing out possible benefits of creating and analyzing vignettes in the context of conflict management practice.

As shown in Table 2, vignettes are created to inspire thinking and reflection on how and why conflicts occur drawing on theoretical precursors, different from cases, which are constructed to explain what it is. Previous studies point out two features of vignette – richness and abstraction – that qualify it for analytical purpose [17].

**Table 2.** Comparison between Case and Vignette

|  | Case | Vignette |
|---|---|---|
| *Purpose* | Informative | Analytical |
| *Description Focus* | Solution | Process |
| *Format* | Experience-based | Theory-based |

Vignettes are rich because they contain the information necessary for readers to build a picture of a set of events by activating their imagination and interest [30, 31]. Although Vignettes are usually short, they provide adequate information about an experience that is limited in scope. By reading a Vignette, a reader is able to capture the essence of a past experience and develop a sense of "being there" [27]. A Vignette can achieve this by providing moment-to-moment description.

However, even a richly detailed Vignette is a reduced account and an abstraction of the original set of events [27]. It conveys information that reflects and sharpens only some details of the original events and leaves out others. The selection is conducted to heighten some analytical concepts [27] to stimulate reflection and thinking about these aspects [32]. The construction of vignette heavily, thus, relies on both the experience of creator or experts as well as prior theoretical constructs.

To ensure both richness and abstraction, we construct a meta-model of conflict vignettes on basis of constructs and relationships identified in prior research. Constructs represent the information sets that are important for understanding conflict and making conflict management decisions. Incorporating these in the meta-model of conflict vignettes, in essence, has the effect of treating these prior findings as kernel theories [14]. Table 3 shows the set of constructs used in the meta-model. Values of some constructs are specified in Table 4.

**Table 3.** Key Constructs in Conflict Vignettes

| Construct | Description | Source |
|---|---|---|
| *Conflict* | Conflict is a process in which incompatibility between *Claims* from *Conflict Parties* surfaces, and may be resolved. | (Thomas, 1992) |
| *Cause* | Cause refers to the underlying reasons for the incompatibility among *Claims*. | (Jehn and Mannix, 2001) |
| *Claim* | Claim represents an intrinsic interest, goal, or opinion of a *Conflict Party*. | (Thomas, 1992) |
| *Transition* | Transition refers to a moment when the nature of the *Conflict* shifts substantially. | (Gersick, 1988) (Putnam, 2004) |
| *Conflict Party* | Conflict party refers to individuals or groups who are engaged in a *Conflict*. | (Thomas, 1992) |
| *Role* | Role reflects the perspective of a *Conflict Party* involved in a *Conflict*. | (Putnam and Poole, 1987) |
| *Strategy* | Strategy represents the plan that *Conflict Parties* apply for coping with *Conflict*. | (Olekalns et al., 2008) |
| *Action* | Action is the behavior enacted by a *Conflict Party* following a *Strategy*. | (Rahim, 2010) |

**Table 4.** Values of Constructs

| Construct | Values |
|---|---|
| *Cause* | {Task, Process, Relationship} |
| *Transition* | Escalation: {Emotionalization, Extension} De-escalation : {Concession, Proposal} |
| *Role* | Principal parties: $\{P_{claim1}, ..., P_{claimN}\}$; Third party: {Mediator} |
| *Strategy* | {Collaborating, Compromising, Yielding, Contending, Avoiding } |
| *Action* | {Argue for, Argue against, Query, Inform, Emote, Propose} |

The constructs capture the lifecycle of a conflict, i.e., how the conflict may undergo transitions marked as key moments. The model recognizes that a conflict can arise if there are multiple conflict parties, each with a specific role. A conflict may arise, escalate and may be resolved based on the claims that each conflict party holds. To resolve a conflict, the conflict parties may employ various strategies based on their role and their interpretation of the conflict. These strategies are then enacted through actions, as the conflict unfolds. These actions may include directly arguing for or against specific claims, querying, informing and proposing solutions. As conflict parties interact with one another through a sequence of actions, the accumulated sequence of actions can sometimes lead to substantial shifts, i.e. transitions in the conflict. Figure 1 shows the meta-model we use to structure the vignettes, which includes constructs as well as relationships among the constructs.

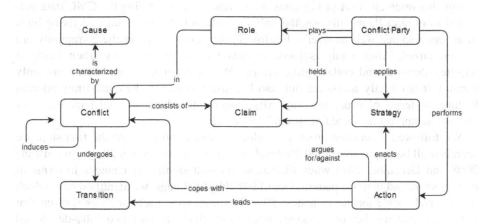

**Fig. 1.** A Meta-model for Conflict Vignettes

## 3.2    Capturing Vignettes from Computer-Mediated Communication Data

To achieve richness and abstraction, creating vignettes requires a large amount of raw data that cover the fine-details of facts.   One possible source of data (in some situations), therefore, is computer-mediated communications (CMC). CMC refers to communication conducted via IT tools, such as email, mailing lists, forums, and instant messages [33].

The increasing use of CMC provides an opportunity of overcoming the constraint in terms of data availability that has limited prior work on conflict management system development. First, CMC data can record a large portion of interaction between conflict parties. CMC tools have become the primary (sometimes, the only) communication channel in some projects. Reviewing messages exchanged between project participants, therefore, allows us to rebuild narratives. Second, CMC text includes interaction information. All CMC tools require reciprocation between users [34]. CMC text as the media between users conveys not only the content of communication but also information about how they interact. By examining the structure of comments (e.g. messages and replies) [35] and scrutinizing the content [36], the interaction between users can be conceptualized as narratives. Further, CMC text is able to provide a historical view that is more concise and reliable than the memory [37]. Third, CMC text has diverse informational content [38] because it tends to be rich in opinion and emotional information [39, 40]. For example, Nigam and Hurst [40] analyzed about 34,000 messages posted on a large collection of newsgroups and found that only 3 percent of the content contains topical information. Another study by Derks et al. [41] shows that emotional communication is more frequent and explicit in CMC than in face-to-face communication. The richness of CMC text makes it suitable to extract the vivid yet analytical descriptions necessary to generate vignettes.

For this research, a set of vignettes were created by examining the CMC data collected from bugzilla.mozilla.org, the online community for reporting and fixing bugs in an open source web browser – Firefox. Projects conducted in the community are self-organized. After a bug is filed, it turns into a 'project' only when fixing it requires decision and collaborative efforts. We selected this data source not only because it is directly accessible but also because projects in the community address features in terms of structure complexity, uncertainty, dynamics and pace, i.e. they provide an appropriate breeding ground for conflicts.

We followed a two-step process to select candidate projects. At the first step, we searched all bugs that were filed for Firefox version 3.0 to version 29.0 between June 2008 and December 2013 when Firefox underwent significant changes in terms of market share and upgrade pattern. Out of 948,746 filed bugs, we identified 657, which had the right scale for the vignettes: 50 to 120 messages. Early analysis showed that bugs with that number of messages were more likely to turn into fully-developed conflicts. The number of messages was still a reasonable number for manual processing. At the second step, we randomly selected projects from this population (657 instances), reviewed them, randomly selected 5% (approximately 30) to construct vignettes. These 30 formed the basis of our design science efforts.

We constructed the conflict vignettes by manually examining, analyzing and coding messages exchanged in each bug. To do this, first, we identified the conflict(s), including its cause and claims by reviewing all messages. Multiple conflict situations were identified in some bugs. Next, we coded the actions performed by the conflict parties, as expressed in each message. After that, we combined actions conducted by each participant to identify his/her role in the conflict and the strategy toward the conflict. Finally, we identified transitions in the conflict process by reviewing the actions in sequence. Table 5 presents an example vignette, and Table 6 presents a summary of the 30 conflict vignettes we created.

**Table 5.** An Example Vignette

| Construct | Description |
|---|---|
| *Conflict* | Keep or remove the properties context menu item in Firefox. |
| *Cause* | Task related |
| *Claim* | Claim 1: Remove the menu item<br>Claim 2: Keep the menu item |
| *Transition* | Escalation: {Emotionalization (12 times), Extension (12 times)}*<br>De-escalation: {Concession (1 time), Proposal (5 times)} |
| *Conflict Party* | 57 participants |
| *Role* | $P_{Claim1}$: 12 participants;    $P_{Claim2}$: 31 participants;<br>Mediators: 15 participants |
| *Strategy* | Participants of $P_{Claim1}$ mainly apply Contending strategy, supplemented with collaborating. Participants of $P_{Claim2}$ mainly apply Contending strategy, supplemented with yielding. |

Note: * Overlaps exist.

**Table 6.** A Summary of Created Conflict Vignettes

| Statistics | Results |
|---|---|
| Conflicts | Task-related (21), Process-related (9) |
| Number of Messages | Min (8), Max (119), Ave (74) |
| Duration | Min (1 Day), Max (9 Months) |
| Number of Participants | Min (7), Max (57), Ave (33) |
| Number of Transitions | Min (0), Max (28), Ave (15) |
| Share of Applied Strategies | Collaborating (9%), Contending (81%), Compromising (6%), Yielding (2%), Avoiding (2%) |

A sample of 30 conflict vignettes was considered sufficient because it allowed a representation of many constructs although a few were not fully reflected due to the domain features. For example, none of the vignettes showed an independent relationship conflict because all projects are conducted around bugs. We found that the dominant strategy was Contending, which could be explained as greater aggression correlated with a weak social relationship between conflict parties [42]. We expect that Compromising and Yielding are more frequently used in organizational settings.

## 4    CM2: A System for Reasoning with Conflict Vignettes

The set of conflict Vignettes provided the foundation for the case-based reasoning we designed. The system, called CM2 (Conflict Management System based on Computer-Mediated Communication), is presented (see Figure 2). CM2 is designed in accordance with the guidelines for CBR system design [25].

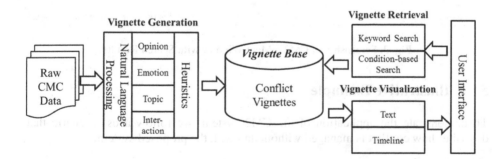

**Fig. 2.** System Architecture – CM2

At the front end, CM2 includes modules that interact with users to retrieve and display conflict vignettes. The direct manipulation user interface (see Figure 3) is linked to modules for vignette retrieval and vignette display. The vignette retrieval module provides two search options, keyword search and condition-based search. The retrieved conflict vignettes are presented in plain text format, along a visualization that depicts conflict process via timeline. The appearance of the timeline draws upon

Timeline and TimePlot, two widgets proposed by CSAIL [43]. The scale and interval used in our timeline is calculated based on the number of total messages exchanged for a conflict considering that computer-mediated communication is often asynchronous [34]. Following these decisions, data about the conflict vignettes was structured and stored in the form of a Vignette-base that was constructed on basis of the meta-model of conflict vignettes (see Figure 1 earlier). The base is now populated with the 30 manually generated vignettes. Vignette generation functions that simulate the manually process are under design.

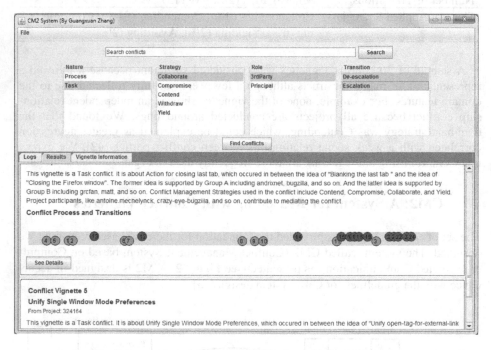

**Fig. 3.** Screenshot of CM2 – Main Window with Search Results

# 5     Illustrative Example

To demonstrate the application of the CM2 system, we follow a use scenario that describes how conflict is managed without and with the proposed system.

## 5.1     An Illustrative Scenario without CM2

Grant is the leader of an online community aimed at developing and maintaining open source software tools. Members of the community come from a number of backgrounds. These members, developers and users, use a mailing list to exchange ideas and make decisions about software design. Conflicts arise when, for instance, developers propose incompatible software designs or users express discontent with any software changes made by developers. After a new version of a software is released,

Grant observes multiple discussions in the mailing list that provide pointers to such conflicts. Grant realizes that he needs to better understand and manage these conflict situations. He senses that this is a daunting task not only because multiple conflicts are going on in parallel but also because of the lack of clues about how these conflicts would evolve, and how different participants would react.

Without any external assistance, Grant can only draw on his experiences to envision these conflicts, anticipate participants' reactions, and choose strategies for his actions. It is challenging to develop a reasonable vision of each conflict partly because of the sheer number of conflicts, and partly because he cannot always recall similar conflict situations and other participants. As a result, his understanding and decisions are largely influenced by his recent experiences, which may be misleading. For example, a recent conflict that resulted in favorable experience may cause Grant to develop an optimistic attitude to all conflicts he is now facing. This may then cause neglect or insufficient attention to the conflicts. Another potential mistake may be to misjudge the orientation of a conflict party. Unfavorable experience with an opponent in a recent conflict may lead Grant to be more aggressive when he interacts with the conflict party, even if the other conflict party tries to adopt a collaborative strategy.

## 5.2    Re-*visioning* the Scenario with CM2

Using CM2 can help Grant overcome challenges mentioned above. CM2 not only provides a repository of previous experience but also helps to organize the reasoning process. Without knowing what kind of conflicts he wants to review, Grant can start his reasoning by looking at what occurred in the past. As shown in Figure 3, the four list panels show the available selection criteria that can be used to search conflict vignettes. Each of the criteria has at least one conflict vignette that matches it.

With the assistance of these criteria, Grant can start his reasoning by categorizing the new conflicts and prioritizing them. Let's assume that Grant decides to start with handling task-related conflicts first, considering that they are more relevant to their development effort. He is interested in knowing how a typical task conflict evolves, how it can be solved in a collaborative way, and how third parties contribute to the resolution of a conflict. With these clues, Grant specifies the search conditions and searches for conflict vignettes. Figure 3 also shows the search results.

For each conflict, a Vignette is generated by using key information about the conflict narratives stored in the repository. After considering the retrieved vignettes, Grand may identify a few conflict Vignettes that are most appropriate to the ongoing conflicts. He can investigate those, most relevant, Vignettes by examining them more closely. The CM2 system will display all details about the conflict (see Figure 4) including parties, claims and transitions. Grant can drill down into each transition and examine how the conflict progressed to gain a better understanding and to assess whether the lessons may be applicable to the ongoing conflicts.

With the CM2 system, we envision that Grant would be able to manage conflicts in a more organized way. The vignettes would provide Grant a place to start the investigation when new conflicts arise. The kernel theories behind the system would provide a set of criteria that Grant can use to categorize and understandi new conflicts. Biases such as recency and others will be minimized because Grant would be able to access to a large base of vignettes along with pointers to those, which may be potentially useful. With the help of CM2, Grant would be able to develop a more realistic vision of new conflicts by referring to relevant conflict situations from the past. Grant would also have a better understanding of other conflict parties, especially those he may not be familiar with by looking at their pattern of actions. This insight would allow Grant an opportunity to adjust his strategy and tactics when he approaches them.

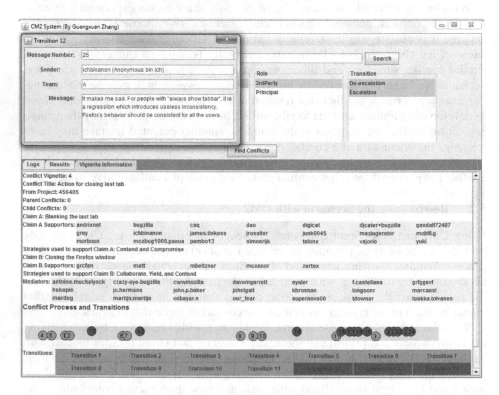

**Fig. 4.** Screenshot of CM2 – Conflict Vignette Details

## 6     Planned Evaluation

The design science artifact we have outlined – CM2 – is being refined and the base of vignettes is being further populated at this time. The evaluation for CM2 will follow. In this section, we outline hypotheses pertaining to the performance of CM2 – treating it as an instantiation that follows the model outlined in the paper. We specify these hypotheses and briefly operationalize how they can be tested [44]. A planned evaluation of this nature is not only essential for developing the knowledge contributions from our work [15], but also critical for ongoing design improvement and design knowledge accumulation [14]. This mode of specifying a planned evaluation along with testable hypotheses follows the work from Muller-Wienbergen et al. [44].

Because the design of CM2 is driven by the call for information systems that can support users to make better decisions for conflict management behaviors, the hypotheses we outline are aimed at this intended use. We expect that using CM2 will help users reflect on conflicts from the past, which will, in turn, result in better interpretation of the current problem situation and better conflict management decisions. We hypothesize that:

H1a: The use of systems instantiated following the CM2 model will result in better *interpretation* of conflict situation than *without* such use.

H1b: The use of systems instantiated following the CM2 model will result in better *interpretation* of conflict situation *compared* to the use of other systems.

H2a: The use of systems instantiated following the CM2 model will result in better *decisions* for conflict management than *without* such use.

H2b: The use of systems instantiated following the CM2 model will result in better *decisions* for conflict management *compared* to the use of other systems.

To test these hypotheses, we propose a laboratory experiment [44, 45]. H1a and H2a would require setting up a control group without access to a system. The experimental design can also be applied to test H1b and H2b with the help of a system that helps with basic data management tasks or a naïve version CM2 that does not store the vignettes nor provide any recommendations. The research design for the experiment would consist of a control group and a treatment group. Knowledgeable subjects would be randomly assigned into the groups. For the actual task (in the case of H1a and H2a), the subjects in the control group will be provided with copies of emails that have been used for creating the 30 conflict vignettes in their original format. Subjects in the experimental group will be provided with the CM2 system.

The experiment will consist of two tasks that both groups will complete in random order [44]. The first task will require them to interpret a new conflict situation; the second will require them to make a decision when faced with a new conflict situation. Another two new conflict vignettes will be created for the two tasks, respectively. To measure the 'goodness' of outcomes, we will rely on a pre-populated set of answers from a panel experts. The responses from the subjects will be compared against this set of answers and rated.

# 7    Implications and Future Work

Conflicts are a part of the modern, distributed workplace that relies on a geographically distributed and diverse set of knowledge workers. Conflicts, however, need not be the "dark side of the workplace." Instead, they can be beneficial when appropriately managed [18]. To assist managers to limit the negative aspects of conflict while promoting its positive aspects, we have proposed the design of a case-based conflict management system. The system, called CM2, can assist conflict parties to understand conflict situations and make better decisions by referring to experiences gathered from past conflict situations. The foundation for the design we have proposed is the notion of a conflict Vignette. We have defined a Vignette as similar to, yet distinct in important ways from a Case in that it is analytical and theory-laden. It represents key information pertaining to a conflict, such as cause, claims, transitions, actions, strategies, and other relevant information. These constructs are identified following kernel theories about conflict management in prior research.

The design we have outlined has the potential to make several contributions to theory and practice. First, the CM2 system, to our best knowledge, is the first system that tries to structure how assistance may be provided to managers for more effective conflict management behaviors. Second, the design we propose builds on a meta-model of conflict Vignettes, which can be applied for capturing and representing vivid yet analytical descriptions of conflict episodes. The notion of a Vignette is, in itself, an important contribution because it suggests a new structure that provides a new foundation for case-based conflict management system. Further, it also provides an approach that can be leveraged for capturing and representing theory-laden episodes in other domains beyond conflict management. Third, we claim that practitioners may benefit from CM2 in that it can improve their conflict management strategies, and may eventually develop more constructive attitudes toward conflict.

We acknowledge that there are some limitations to our design. First, the design effort and outcome reported in this paper can contribute only a "partial theory," that consists of constructs and a model along with an early instantiation. We describe this as the initial step in a journey toward a mature design theory [16]. More evaluation of the proposed system is also required to validate the design and understand the phenomenon in which the design is embedded. Second, we acknowledge that the usefulness of the system is determined by the scale of its repository. The more conflict vignettes it contains, the more likely it can provide relevant references to users. While computer-mediated communication produces a large amount of raw data, such data is not readily available for use and manual processing can be daunting. Automatic or semi-automatic approaches are required to help users to generate key information as specified in this paper through parsing and analyzing the raw communication data. The preliminary results from our work show that this can be realized through natural language processing techniques and heuristics. The former techniques, such as Recursive Neural Tensor Network [46], are able to parse CMC data into atomic information sets that can be used to generate conflict vignette constructs based on some heuristics. Third, as more conflict vignettes are populated into the system, users will also face the new challenge of locating the vignettes that are most appropriate and informative for current conflict situation. Some matching functions are necessary for enhancing performance of the system. Candidate approaches, such as nearest neighbor retrieval, inductive approaches, and knowledge guided approaches can be analyzed and added to enhance the system further. These are part of our future research agenda.

# References

1. De Dreu, C.K.W., Gelfand, M.J.: Conflict in the Workplace: Sources, Functions, and Dynamics across Multiple Levels of Analysis. In: De Dreu, C.K.W., Gelfand, M.J. (eds.) The Psychology of Conflict and Conflict Management in Organizations, pp. 3–54. Psychology Press (2008)
2. Putnam, L.L., Poole, M.S.: Conflict and Negotiation. In: Jablin, F.M., Putnam, L.L., Roberts, K.H., and Porter, L.W. (eds.) Handbook of Organizational Communication: An Interdisciplinary Perspective, pp. 549–599. Sage Publications (1987)
3. Thomas, K.: Conflict and Negotiation Process in Organizations. In: Dunnette, M.D., Hough, L.M. (eds.) Handbook of Industrial and Organizational Psychology, pp. 651–717. Consulting Psychologists Press (1992)

4. Jehn, K.A., Mannix, E.A.: The Dynamic Nature of Conflict: A Longitudinal Study of Intragroup Conflict and Group Performance. Acad. Manag. J. 44, 238–251 (2001)
5. Rahim, M.A.: Managing Conflict in Organizations. Transaction Publishers (2010)
6. Alderma, N., Ivory, C., McLoughlin, I., Thwaites, A., Vaughan, R.: Managing Complex Projects: Networks, Knowledge and Innovation. Routledge (2013)
7. Geraldi, J., Maylor, H., Williams, T.: Now, let's make it really complex (complicated): A systematic review of the complexities of projects. Int. J. Oper. Prod. Manag. 31, 966–990 (2011)
8. Kahneman, D.: Thinking, fast and slow. Macmillan (2011)
9. Madani, K., Rouhani, O.M., Mirchi, A., Gholizadeh, S.: A negotiation support system for resolving an international trans-boundary natural resource conflict. Environ. Model. Softw. 51, 240–249 (2014)
10. Ross, S., Fang, L., Hipel, K.W.: A case-based reasoning system for conflict resolution: design and implementation. Eng. Appl. Artif. Intell. 15, 369–383 (2002)
11. Chiravuri, A., Nazareth, D., Ramamurthy, K.: Cognitive Conflict and Consensus Generation in Virtual Teams During Knowledge Capture: Comparative Effectiveness of Techniques. J. Manag. Inf. Syst. 28, 311–350 (2011)
12. El-Shinnawy, M., Vinze, A.S.: Polarization and Persuasive Argumentation: A Study of Decision Making in Group Settings. MIS Q. 22, 165–198 (1998)
13. Fraser, N.M., Hipel, K.W.: Computer Assistance in Labor-Management Negotiations. Interfaces (Providence) 11, 22–30 (1981)
14. Gregor, S., Jones, D.: The anatomy of a design theory. J. Assoc. Inf. Syst. 8, 312–335 (2007)
15. Walls, J.G., Widmeyer, G.R., El Sawy, O.A.: Building an information system design theory for vigilant EIS. Inf. Syst. Res. 3, 36–59 (1992)
16. Gregor, S., Hevner, A.R.: Positioning and presenting design science research for maximum impact. MIS Q. 37, 337–355 (2013)
17. Zhang, G., Purao, S.: Using Vignettes to Study Conflict Management Practices in Enterprise Architecture Initiative. In: iConference 2013 Proceedings (2013)
18. Jehn, K.A.: A Multimethod Examination of the Benefits and Detriments of Intragroup Conflict. Adm. Sci. Q. 40, 256–282 (1995)
19. Gersick, C.J.G.: Time and Transition in Work Teams: Toward a New Model of Group Development. Acad. Manag. J. 31, 9–41 (1988)
20. Putnam, L.L.: Transformations and Critical Moments in Negotiations. Negot. J. 20, 275–295 (2004)
21. Pruitt, D.G.: Conflict Escalation in Organizations. In: De Dreu, C.K.W., Gelfand, M.J. (eds.) The Psychology of Conflict and Conflict Management in Organizations, pp. 245–266. Psychology Press (2008)
22. Pruitt, D.G., Kim, S.H.: Social Conflict: Escalation, Stalemate, and Settlement. McGraw-Hill Higher Education (2004)
23. Olekalns, M., Putnam, L.L., Weingart, L.R., Metcalf, L.: Communication Processes and Conflict Management. In: De Dreu, C.K.W., Gelfand, M.J. (eds.) The Psychology of Conflict and Conflict Management in Organizations, pp. 81–114. Psychology Press (2008)
24. Kolodner, J.L.: An introduction to case-based reasoning. Artif. Intell. Rev. 6, 3–34 (1992)
25. Main, J., Dillon, T., Shiu, S.K.: A Tutorial on Case Based Reasoning. In: Pal, S., Dillon, T., Yeung, D. (eds.) Soft Computing in Case Based Reasoning SE - 1, pp. 1–28. Springer, London (2001)
26. Kolodner, J.L., Simpson, R.L.: The MEDIATOR: Analysis of an early case-based problem solver. Cogn. Sci. 13, 507–549 (1989)

27. Erickson, F.: Qualitative methods in research on teaching. In: Wittrock, M.C. (ed.) Handbook of Research on Teaching, pp. 119–161. MacMillan Reference Books (1986)
28. McCabe, D., Knights, D., Wilkinson, A.: The politics of IT-enabled restructuring and the restructuring of politics through total quality management. Accounting, Manag. Inf. Technol. 8, 107–126 (1998)
29. Sabherwal, R.: The evolution of coordination in outsourced software development projects: a comparison of client and vendor perspectives. Inf. Organ. 13, 153–202 (2003)
30. Poulou, M.: The role of vignettes in the research of emotional and behavioural difficulties. Emot. Behav. Difficulties. 6, 50–62 (2001)
31. Huebner, E.S.: Bias in special education decisions: The contribution of analogue research (1991)
32. Angelides, P., Gibbs, P.: Supporting the Continued Professional Development of Teachers through the Use of Vignettes. Teach. Educ. Q. 33, 111–121 (2006)
33. Herring, S.C.: Computer-mediated communication: Linguistic, social, and cross-cultural perspectives. John Benjamins Publishing (1996)
34. Sack, W.: Conversation map: an interface for very-large-scale conversations. J. Manag. Inf. Syst. 17, 73–92 (2000)
35. Fu, T., Abbasi, A., Chen, H.: A hybrid approach to Web forum interactional coherence analysis. J. Am. Soc. Inf. Sci. Technol. 59, 1195–1209 (2008)
36. Herring, S.C.: Computer-mediated communication on the internet. Annu. Rev. Inf. Sci. Technol. 36, 109–168 (2002)
37. Viegas, F.B., Smith, M.: Newsgroup Crowds and AuthorLines: visualizing the activity of individuals in conversational cyberspaces. In: Proceedings of the 37th Annual Hawaii International Conference on System Sciences (2004)
38. Abbasi, A., Chen, H.: CyberGate: a design framework and system for text analysis of computer-mediated communication. Mis Q. 32, 811–837 (2008)
39. Subasic, P., Huettner, A.: Affect analysis of text using fuzzy semantic typing. IEEE Trans. Fuzzy Syst. 9, 483–496 (2001)
40. Nigam, K., Hurst, M.: Towards a robust metric of opinion. In: AAAI Spring Symposium on Exploring Attitude and Affect in Text, pp. 598–603 (2004)
41. Derks, D., Fischer, A.H., Bos, A.E.R.: The role of emotion in computer-mediated communication: A review. Comput. Human Behav. 24, 766–785 (2008)
42. Johnson, N.A., Cooper, R.B.: Power and Concession in Computer-mediated Negotiations: An Examination of First Offers. MIS Q. 33, 147–170 (2009)
43. Karger, D.: SIMILE Project, http://www.simile-widgets.org/
44. Müller-Wienbergen, F., Müller, O., Seidel, S., Becker, J.: Leaving the Beaten Tracks in Creative Work – A Design Theory for Systems that Support Convergent and Divergent Thinking. J. Assoc. Inf. Syst. 12, 714–740 (2011)
45. Poole, M.S., Holmes, M., Desanctis, G.: Conflict Management in a Computer-Supported Meeting Environment. Manage. Sci. 37, 926–953 (1991)
46. Socher, R., Perelygin, A., Wu, J.Y., Chuang, J., Manning, C.D., Ng, A.Y., Potts, C.: Recursive Deep Models for Semantic Compositionality Over a Sentiment Treebank. In: EMNLP (2013)

# Call for Action:
# Designing for Harmony in Creative Teams

Mateusz Dolata and Gerhard Schwabe

University of Zurich, Department of Informatics, Zurich, Switzerland
{dolata,schwabe}@ifi.uzh.ch

**Abstract.** Competitive markets force diverse organizations to intensively manage innovation. Many of them set up multifunctional teams responsible for generating novel and original ideas. Such teams often face higher risk of conflicts and tensions, being an inherent part of creative processes. Impact of this phenomena on creative performance of teams, even though extensively addressed in research, remains unclarified. We approach this issue while providing a novel interpretation framework inspired by the concept of *harmony* in *jazz improvisation*. We apply it to observations made with project teams in an organizational setting, and use it to inform design of a supporting collaborative solution. We postulate the need for further work on team *harmony* and creativity.

**Keywords:** creativity, harmony, jazz improvisation, task conflict, teamwork.

## 1    Introduction

The importance of innovative ideas in organizations has grown over the last decades. Creative performance of teams plays an important role in this change and requires a close consideration. Still, some aspects of group creativity remain unclarified, particularly in the longitudinal, organizational context. A prominent case is the phenomenon of intragroup disagreements or confrontations, hitherto interpreted and intensively researched in the context of team or group conflict. The output is a partially contradictory and inconsistent body of knowledge [16, 51, 75], failing to provide clear prescriptions regarding collaboration engineering and the design of appropriate support systems. The insufficiency may hails from the inadequate framing of relevant findings. Therefore, we introduce a framework relying on the concept of *harmony* in creative teams. It originates from the *jazz improvisation* (JI) metaphor already considered in a variety of contexts [27], including organizational change. In order to motivate the relation between JI and creative performance, a closer look at the organizational context of creativity, i.e., innovation is discussed.

Innovation used to be considered anything, but business as usual. Recently, the paradigm has changed, while turning innovation into an inevitable element of business and society. Due to the highly competitive markets and customer demands, role of innovation management has grown to become one of the organization core business processes [28, 68]. Simultaneously, the interest in creativity support has arisen. The dependency between creativity and innovation is widely discussed [3, 14, 74]. While

M.C. Tremblay et al. (Eds.): DESRIST 2014, LNCS 8463, pp. 273–288, 2014.
© Springer International Publishing Switzerland 2014

creativity is about conceptualization or development of *novel* and *useful* ideas for products (*value creation*), innovation is about implementing them in organizations (*value capture*) [2, 25, 74]. Other important factor is the *idea novelty*. Changes applied in the course of innovation processes possess the degree of *relative* novelty, while creativity results in *absolute* novelty [3, 14]. This distinction emphasizes the role of creativity for radical innovation. While incremental changes often emerge from work practices, radical ideas with large impact flourish under specific circumstances, such as dedicated environments or particular organizational climate [70]. One of the methods proposed within the concept of ambidextrous organizations [52] are separate divisions for exploratory and traditional units, possibly organized in teams.

Executive, administrative and other 'daily business' teams are expected to have different dynamics than creative teams, particularly due to the differences in goal setting [36, 37]. While using the analogy to music in general [1, 44], one could compare the traditional action teams to classical music ensemble, who interpret the masterpieces of art in a predefined, precisely described frame. At the same time, creative teams exhibits similarities with jazz musicians [6, 27], who improvise using underspecified 'minimal structures' [4, 35] to create *melody* through 'the suddenly arisen harmonic organization' [6]. Considering the managerial sciences, JI is primarily applied in the field of organizational change and innovation strategies [24, 35, 46, 72], as well as marketing [27]. In limited scope, it is also used to moderate creative collaboration in groups [6, 13]. Regardless of how popular is the analogy based on melody composition in jazz, *harmony*, also an important dimension of music, has not yet been attended extensively.

In the context of music, *harmony* "directs the attention to how patterns of *consonance* and *dissonance* unfold over time" [1]. It describes the relationship of tones as they sound simultaneously, as well as the organization of such relationships in time [60]. Whereas in classical music, *harmony* is the responsibility of the composer and the interpreter influences it only in a limited way, jazz musician take care of the *harmony* while they improvise [63]. They create high-tension moments through *dissonances* and resolve them on the go, through movement towards consonant intervals. In general terms, *dissonance* in music describes a situation when simultaneous combination of two or more frequencies is experienced as unpleasant. Recent studies show, that generalization of such experiences is somewhat possible [76]. Speaking figuratively, if somebody hits several 'incompatible' piano keys at the same time, the sound will be experienced as unpleasant by most of the listeners. *Dissonance* can vary in its intensity, and to a certain degree it is included in most music pieces generally considered harmonious, including even great masterpieces of classical music, not to mention spontaneously emerging jam sessions.

Terms like *harmony*, *consonance* or *dissonance* hardly ever appear in literature on innovation management, and if so, mostly without deeper grounding in the theory. Different authors refer to *harmony* when addressing topics such as cultural differences [29], team constellations [49], and team effectiveness [45], in the context of intragroup tensions or incompatibilities. However, they do not explain the analogy. Instead, they fall back to the well-established concepts from psychology, such as conflict and agreement. We, acknowledge that there exist a relation between the notions of conflict and *dissonance*. In particular, when considering task conflict as incompatibility of activities rather than dissent of goals [69], the analogy to the incompatibility of tones becomes obvious. In this situation, analyzing current literature on performance and conflicts in creative teams, as well as its shortcomings, seems to be the appropriate starting point.

Group creativity is approached by a vast amount of studies and is addressed by numerous literature syntheses [30, 47, 51, 56–58]. Due to the high capacity for cross-breeding of concepts, ideas and values, groups are considered potentially more creative than individuals or nominal group [55, 58, 67]. However, it is met with concern how little is known about turning this potential into real value [20, 40]. On the one hand, organizational scientist address creativity mostly on the level of individuals [20, 57]. On the other hand, psychology research discusses collective creativity, primarily, while considering brainstorming performance in lab experiments [21, 31]. Nevertheless, the emerging body of knowledge provides evidence for positive relation between creative performance and numerous other attributes, such as team size and diversity, as well as task and goal interdependence, shared vision, participative safety, task orientation and communication [30, 57].

Role of conflict and related factors for creative groups is frequently addressed in psychology and in organizational science [51]. Jehn [31] classifies team conflict into three categories: task conflict, relationship conflict, and process conflict. Studies prove the latter two to be detrimental to creative processes in groups. Interestingly, given this framing, no clear statement can be made in favor or against task conflict [51]. Still, any kind of disagreement and disharmony in groups may result in relationship conflict, thus negatively influencing creative performance [31, 75]. This is analogous to the *dissonance* produced by incompatible chords in a jazz performance, which, if not resolved or accented properly, may result in a poor aesthetic impression overall. We want to extend on this notion of group performance, while answering the first research question:

*RQ1. What is the constitution of team harmony in creative teams?*

As indicated before, conflicts may have negative influence on creative teams and lead to detrimental effects in a wider context. While there exist multiple IT systems to support creative teams at work through enhancing stimulation or providing means for parallelization of idea production, little has been done to support management of overall *harmony* in this specific situation [43, 71]. Given the importance of creativity for the value chain of modern organizations and potential influence of *dissonance* on creative performance, we seek to provide information on the following:

*RQ2. How to support teams at maintaining harmony by means of IT?*

This contribution is structured along these research questions. In the first line, it describes a literature study addressing the *harmony*-related issues in creative teams. It then provides a short summary of an exploratory study conducted prior to the literature review, which however confirms its results. Afterwards, implications for research and work practices are discussed.

## 2    Methodology

Overall structure of this study follows the paradigm of *Design Science Research* (DSR) [26]. In the introduction, we present the practical relevance of creative team research for organizational science and particularly emphasize on *harmony*, as a potentially influential factor for their performance. Second, we conduct a rigorous literature review of psychology and managerial science articles to analyze work done on conflict in the context of creativity. This leads to a synthesis of our working hypothesis on the potential of team harmony and related constructs, a kernel theory, complemented with prescriptive statements on creative group work. The proposed kernel theory is then evaluated based on observations made during an exploratory study done prior to the literature review. On the one hand, this procedure enables a better understanding of the observed events and tendencies. On the other hand, it deals as a first, limited and necessarily subjective [23, 48] sieve for the proposed set of assumptions and solutions. The above process forms the first cycle described in this paper, in which the concept of team harmony is treated as the artifact under consideration.

Subsequently, we discuss the possibilities of supporting harmony in creative teams. We attempt to match the developed requirements to existing group support systems addressing creativity. Due to the limited outcome of this inductive elaboration, we deduce an exemplary approach resulting from the concept of harmony. We finalize while proposing design principles that rely, primarily, on conceptual, value and explanatory grounding [21]. The remainder of this section addresses the particular methodologies applied to collect data.

The process of the literature search is aligned to the guidance proposed by vom Brocke [7]. We certainly acknowledge the need for documenting the literature search, as well as the literature selection process [53]. Our review is structured accordingly.

To collect a body of knowledge on relation between *harmony* and creativity, we started with querying several databases with use of the search service offered by *EBSCOhost* (www.ebscohost.com). We limited the choice of active databases to the following ones: *Academic Search Complete (ASC), Business Source Premier (BSR), eBook Collection, EconLit, ERIC, Information Science and Technology Abstracts, PsycARTICLES, PsycBOOKS, PsycEXTRA, PsycINFO, SocINDEX*. We used the following terms connected by Boolean 'AND' to query the databases: *'conflict management team creativity'*.[1] The overall number of hits including all listed terms was 122 (out of them 44 in *BSR*, 27 in *PsycINFO* and the remaining ones distributed over other databases) and after duplicate removal 82. All returned articles were published between 1980 and 2013. Review of all those contributions is out of scope of a conference paper, therefore we selected a subset according to the following criteria based on the coding of abstracts and titles.

---

[1] In our first tries, we queried the databases for concepts related to harmony in creativity, but quick investigation of results did not yield any or very few relevant hits (number in parenthesis represent overall hits in scholar journals and the relevant ones given the broad context of this article): *harmony innovation team (9/1), dissonance innovation team (2/0), consonance innovation team (0/0), harmony team creativity (3/1), consonance team creativity (0/0), dissonance team creativity (3/1)*. Given those results, we decided to focus on the well-established concept of *conflict management*, which we consider related to harmony, and extend the results by means of forward and backward search if possible (cf. Section 1).

- Focus primarily on creative teams or design teams or innovation teams;
- Focus on dynamics of teams (rather than team constant attributes like diversity);
- Reference to *harmony, conflict* or *conflict management* in the title or abstract;
- Journal listed in the *Association for Information Systems* (AIS) summary of MIS Journal Rankings [62] extended by the journals in the field of *innovation and technology change management* from the ABS Journal Quality Guide [22].

This procedure yielded a set of 19 journal articles meeting all the criteria. As none of the detected literature reviews referred to conference publications, we decided not to conduct extensive search in the conference proceedings. Instead, we manually assessed articles from the ACM Creativity & Cognition conference proceedings from last 5 years and extended the results set by two further articles. Additional review of ICIS 2013, ECIS 2013, and DESRIST 2013 proceedings did not provide any hits. However, backward and forward search [73] added another 26 journal articles, primarily from the flourishing field of psychological research on brainstorming performance. For the sake of precision and continence of the current publication, we give preference to studies conducted in organizations and/or with long term perspective, as well as pertinent meta-analysis, that were published between 2000 and 2013. Table 1 (p. 7) presents the final set of eleven studies along with additional comments and a summary of findings.

To collect knowledge on existing systems addressing needs of innovation and creative teams we applied a procedure similar to the above one. To start the search process, we query for *'creativity support information systems'*. This search returns 268 hits (345 before the removal of exact duplicates: 146 in *BSR*, 129 in *ASC*, and the remaining ones distributed over other databases) from years 1980 – 2013. We apply the following criteria to the articles based on their titles and abstracts:

- Focus on information systems and technology research.
- Reference to influence on creative or innovative performance.
- Focus primarily on creative teams or design teams or innovation teams.
- Journal listed in the AIS summary of MIS Journal Rankings [62].

This procedure returns 22 results compatible with all criteria. Review of conferences, analogue to the one mentioned earlier, yields further three contributions. Forward and backward search [73] extends this list by another nine positions. Regrettably, none of the systems or designs in the resulting set of studies directly approaches *harmony*, tensions or conflicts in creative teams in an organizational context. An extensive review goes, therefore, beyond the scope of this publication. Nevertheless, we address findings from this review in Section 5, while describing an exemplary system to support *harmony* in creative teams.

Another part of the current contribution, the exploratory study, relies upon observations made with ethnographically informed methods [23, 48] in a specific organizational context. It was conducted within a graduate course at a European University, in which students are encouraged to apply *Design Thinking* (DT) on a real-life innovation challenge, offered by industry partners. DT is a human-centered approach laid out along a structured process in order to produce breakthrough innovation with value to organizations and society [8, 17, 59]. It is an iterative procedure addressing need-finding, ideation, prototyping, testing, and (re)defining. This cycle is applied repeatedly along a process starting with a design space exploration, followed by long divergent and convergent phases, until finalization in a single prototype [11]. Characteristic for this approach is the demand for high ambiguity of ideas and prototypes to be achieved in the first stage of the project and number of choices to be made along the way towards the final prototype. Consequently, teams are exposed to major tensions at any point of time [65]. Even though, DT itself encourages *harmony maintenance*, teams encounter problems related to their diversity and distributed collaboration setting. Our study in the context of DT course focuses on three teams working from September 2012 to June 2013, with no breaks in between. The teams are coached by DT experts in two weekly sessions: once on the course level and once on the team level. Observations made in several of those sessions, as well as non-structured interviews with coaches and team members serve as basis for the study described in Section 4. Particularly, we focus on the occurrence of incompatible tendencies in teams, and on whether and how the team approaches them on its way throughout the course.

# 3    Theorizing on Harmony

The existing literature does not explicitly approach the holistic notion of *harmony*, as introduced in the current contribution. It does, however, extensively discuss the influence of tensions and conflicts on team performance, and in particular, creative performance [69]. However, as opposite to the role of *dissonance* in music, the impact of task conflict in creative teams has not been yet fully clarified [30, 51], though it is considered a relevant variable [56]. Resolving the conflict dilemma is out of scope of this publication. Instead, we propose a concise literature review and identify the most relevant constructs and relations to motivate our *harmony*-centered model of creative performance. Based on the extensive literature review described earlier, we selected a number of papers summarized in Table 1. We primarily included studies conducted in organizational context – we follow the assumption that this context, including team or work group history and goals, substantially moderates the important relationships. Also, we considered studies that generate or mimic such organizational context in university circumstances, if the observations made have a longitudinal character. Finally, we refer to two extensive literature meta-analysis to show the general tenor on relationship between conflict and creative performance of teams.

Even a short peek on the table unveils the main problem, confirmed by the meta-reviews [30, 51]: no clear, linear relation between task conflict and creative performance can be established. Whereas some studies suggest a linear or curvilinear relationship, others prove further dependence on project phase or team type, and additional factors like information exchange or participative safety. The picture does not get clear, even if laboratory studies in psychology, excluded from this review, are considered [56, 69]. Designing a system to address tensions in creative teams would be, in this situation, at least cumbersome. That is where the *harmony*-oriented approach comes into play.

**Table 1.** Selection of the reviewed articles on conflict and creativity sorted chronologically; along with the most relevant, statistically significant findings given the current topic. CP stands for *creative performance*, TC for *task conflict*, RC – *relationship conflict*, PC – *process conflict*. The notation used for results: A × B stands for *the correlation between construct A and construct B*, ↑ depicts a *positive* relation, and ↓ – a *negative* one.

| Reference | Character of study | Relevant variables | Relevant results |
|---|---|---|---|
| Jehn and Mannix, 2001 [33] | longitudinal, survey-based, university, project teams | TC, RC, PC, team CP, project phase | TC × project phase = inversely U-shaped for teams with high CP; TC × project phase = ↑ (sign. grow of TC in late phase) for teams with low CP |
| Lovelace et al., 2001 [42] | survey-based, organization, new product project teams | task disagreement (~TC), innovativeness (~CP) | TC × CP = ↓, moderated by *freedom to express doubts* and *collaborative or contentious* character of communication |
| Kurtzberg and Mueller, 2005 [41] | self-report-based, longitudinal, organization, teams | TC, RC, PC, individual CP, team creative synergy | TC × individual CP = ↑ one day after TC occurs; TC × team creative synergy = ↓ at the day TC occurs |
| Chen, 2006 [12] | survey-based, organization, project teams | TC, RC, team CP | TC × CP = ↑ in technology oriented teams; RC × CP = ↓ in service oriented teams |
| De Dreu, 2006 [15] | survey and interview-based, organization, various teams | TC, team CP, information exchange, collaborative problem solving | TC × CP = inversely U-shaped (slight shift towards low level of TC); TC × information exchange = inversely U-shaped; TC x collaborative problem solving = inversely U-shaped |
| Kratzer et al., 2006 [38] | survey-based, organization, project teams | team polarity (~ TC), team CP, project phase, degree of innovation | team polarity × CP in incremental innovation or late innovation phase = ↓; team polarity × CP in early innovation phase = inversely U-shaped (i.e., CP high at moderate level of CT, CP lower if CT high or low) |
| Hülsheger et al., 2009 [30] | meta-analysis, literature based | TC, RC, cohesion, internal communication, team CP | CP × cohesion = ↑; CP × internal communication = ↑; no significant results for TC or RC |
| Farh et al., 2010 [19] | survey-based, organization, project teams | TC, team CP, project phase | TC × CP = inversely U-shaped in the early project phase (slight shift towards high level of TC) |
| Jehn et al., 2010 [32] | in-class experiment, organization, work groups | conflict asymmetry, group CP | group task conflict asymmetry* × group CP = ↓ * the degree of dispersion in group regarding perceived conflict |
| Fairchild and Hunter, 2013 [18] | longitudinal, survey-based, university, design teams | TC, participative safety, team CP | TC × CP = ↑ only if high participative safety; low TC and low participative safety correlate with most original solutions |
| O'Neill et al., 2013 [51] | meta-analysis, literature based | TC, RC, PC, team type, performance, team CP | TC × team perf. = ↑ in decision-making; ↓ in production and project teams; no significant results for TC, PC or RC × team innovation performance (~ CP) |

On the one hand, team *harmony* stems from the previously mentioned JI metaphor. This results in the vocabulary choices and dependencies between constructs that describe the overall team *harmony*. On the other hand, it uses findings from the field of managerial sciences and psychology addressing the task conflict and intragroup tensions. This twofold motivation assures compatibility of the presented paradigm with the JI-motivated literature as well as the actual behavioral knowledge base.

An important issue in improvisation music is the ongoing *listening* to each other [13, 27]. This is a specific form of communication, as the message constructed by one musician (*melody*) is primarily not directed at the band, but the audience. Still, it is implicated that band members receive the message and interpret it appropriately. Also the creative teams mostly generate solutions addressed at external audience (users, customers, and partners), still the communication within the team remains substantial to the management of conflicts and tensions, as well as the creative performance [15, 42]. This dimension of *harmony* is referred to as *mutual listening* in our model.

As discussed before, jazz musicians, especially in jam sessions, generate *dissonances* to provide an emotionally involving performance. *Dissonances* are also natural to the creative processes, and as some research suggests, may be beneficial to the overall output. Still, as Jehn et al. [32] conclude, differences or lacking awareness of them may be detrimental to work performance. Therefore, we postulate that teams need to develop *dissonance awareness* and shall be supported at it.

Finally, if *dissonances* occur, *harmony* requires to manage them. Some *dissonances* are resolved straight away towards *consonance*, some others are deliberately accented and resolved afterwards. This process does not require dedicated reflection, but happens along the course of improvisation. Several studies provide evidence for a curvilinear dependency between conflict and creativity, others suggest moderating effects of, e.g., collaborative atmosphere [18, 19, 33, 42]. We follow up on their findings and postulate the importance of *dissonance resolution* in creative teams. Fig. 1 depicts the proposed *harmony* oriented view on creative performance along with the appropriate design requirements, to be considered when addressing this issue in collaboration engineering or design of creative support systems.

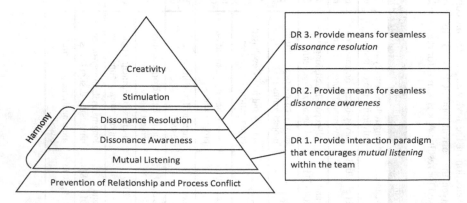

**Fig. 1.** Harmony-oriented view of creative performance and resulting design requirements

# 4    Exploratory Study

This exploratory study deals as an evaluation of the proposed *harmony*-oriented model of creative performance. At the same time, it motivates the design of a mechanism that shall support creative teams at maintaining their *harmony* while preserving most successful work practices. We focus on three teams chosen to represent the variety of collaborative settings encountered in the design thinking course. At the same time, those teams exhibit different patterns of *harmony*. All teams are working according to the same process and follow the same three milestones. They, also, use similar IT infrastructure mix, including a wiki page for documenting purpose, file sharing services and social platforms for asynchronous work, as well as IM-messaging and video conferencing for synchronous communication. Additionally, video and picture sharing platforms are used as a storage for the respective media.

Team A consists of seven members of two universities on different continents. Their challenge addresses innovative service design task for financial industry. Team members use the whole range of communication media, including biweekly video conferences. All of them also meet twice in real in the course of the project. Nevertheless, knowledge gaps arise regarding the state and objective of particular tasks. *Mutual listening* fails particularly at the boundary between the two participating universities. As the task conflict lasts for almost 90% of the project duration, it turns into process conflict. The team performance at the first and second milestone is below the average. The team is aware of the *dissonance* and seeks for its resolution during the final real meeting, short before the deadline. Team surprisingly performs above the average. The final prototype improves significantly over the last days during the final co-located session.

Team B consists originally of five students, however one lefts after the first milestone. It is a three universities – two continents team. Their challenge addresses the design of a social platform for sports industry. As opposite to Team A, in the early stage, Team B experiences only mild *dissonances* that are addressed and resolved in co-located settings. The team performs extremely well in the first milestone compared to others and it is above average in the second one. As everyone agrees on the course of action, team decides to distribute the tasks. Starting at this point, *mutual listening* is not as easy as before anymore, *dissonances* arise, of which the team members are only partially aware. The final co-located meeting unveils the *dissonances*, which the team is not prepared to deal with. Consequently, they remain partially unresolved and the team performs below expectations and below average.

Team C consists originally of three, and after first milestone four students, from two universities located in the same country. It aims at designing an innovative collaboration platform for financial industry. Due to the arrival of new team member, it has a period of active *harmony* maintenance, which is conducted seamlessly along the team tasks and activities. Intensive *mutual listening* produces awareness of *dissonances*, which are either immediately resolved or kept open for a short period of time. None of the strategies is detrimental to the team. On the contrary, it supports creative problem solution. Whereas the team was considered average in the first milestone, it outperforms other teams in the last one.

# 5    Artifact Design

While analyzing the previous cases, one recognizes the influence of team *harmony* on the overall creative process and the dynamics of particular groups. Creating novel products or business models requires constant supply of new ideas, which, in the described design thinking course, come primarily from the team as well as the potential users and their environment, coaches and project partners. Still, regardless of the idea origin, it is the team, who assembles the prototypes while converting the ideas and combining them with the domain-specific knowledge and observations. This creative process has particularly much in common with improvised jazz music, where music emerges harmonic and rhythmical combination of chords. Whereas a jam session is mostly a timely limited gathering, creative collaboration as described above is an ongoing improvisation performance lasting for several months.

As previously indicated, the presented teams perform pretty well if working synchronously at the same place. Mostly, they are able to deal with local, short-term *dissonances* and *consonances* in a way that supports their creative output. *Harmony* maintenance happens simultaneously to the main activities, without dedicated reflection and adjustment time. Even though, we cannot assume all co-located sessions to be absolutely optimal, the above analysis as well as received feedback suggest that they form the highlights of the development process. Traditionally, four modes of collaboration emerged which aligned to the dimensions of space (co-located/distributed) and time (synchronous/asynchronous) [61]. Unfortunately, some collaboration patterns, even if successful in co-located and synchronous setting, cannot be easily transferred and applied to the overall process of creative project work. In the innovation projects, there will necessarily be phases of distributed individual or subgroup work – this holds for the DT course as well as for creative innovation teams in organizations. The reasons range from the absence of a single team member up to the dissemination of team members across countries and time zones. Also, recent disputes show the fundamental role of individual work for creative introverts [10]. Given the importance of collaboration distributed across space or time, we ask how to support teams at maintaining *harmony* in settings others than synchronous work.

Hitherto, as the literature review on GSS (*Group Support Systems*) and CSS (*Creativity Support Systems*) unveils, little has been done to address team creativity in the context of *harmony* in asynchronous settings. Whereas CSS addresses such concepts as *playfulness, comprehension* and *specialization* of knowledge [71] as ways of stimulation, it does not explicitly address conflict that may occur in stimulated teams [34, 47, 64]. GSS addresses issues of consensus and effective decision making in creative problem solving, it does however primarily focus on co-located sessions [39, 50]. It provides process support through communication parallelization, anonymity, group memory, and media effects, as well as task and process structure, and task support [50]. Still, its usage for *harmony* maintenance is limited. While considering the JI metaphor, task *harmony* shall emerge from collaboration practices and not from intensive reflection, which lies in focus of *group decision support systems*, a branch of GSS. We intentionally stress the difference between explicit conflict management and tacit *harmony* maintenance, and model the latter while taking co-located, synchronous collaboration as our gold standard.

Given the dependencies depicted in Fig. 1, it seems natural to consider the level of *mutual listening* in the first line. Participators of off-line group ideation sessions find themselves in a situation, where listening to one another happens naturally and is mostly successful. However, as soon as teams are distributed, keeping awareness of who is sending something into the common communication channel and what is the content of the message is by far more difficult. There exist tools to support distributed synchronous teams working in a creative or problem-solving mode. They fall into the category of *conferencing systems, media spaces* [66] and *collaborative virtual environments* [5]. Teams working asynchronously, but at the same place, can manage this awareness by observing changes in the working environment (notes on the walls, prototypes left on side, etc.). Also, in file sharing services that are widely used for distributed, asynchronous work, some mechanisms for supporting awareness are implemented. However, they mostly focus on the issue of time- or dependency-based coordination of team activities [9] and fail to address some of the other user expectations [54]. This section explicitly addresses an extended view on asynchronous awareness aligned to the notion of *mutual listening* as derived from JI metaphor.

We describe a simple, exemplary interaction paradigm that supports team members at maintaining a constant mutual notion of what others do, thus allowing for early *dissonance awareness* and appropriate reaction to this. It also provides simple means to resolve *dissonances* or keep them to assure idea divergence, although it does by no means limit the teams in their choices. The mechanism, we propose, relics on the division of the common repository into two distinct spaces: (1) the individual spaces of team members, depicted in Fig. 2 by the peripheral bubbles with names, (2) the central team space, 'We', including elements currently relevant for the whole team and therefore describing the *general tenor* of development within the team. If, within a predefined period of time, an element is attended by more than the half of the team, it will automatically move to the middle, thus showing the team awareness of its content. If a specific element from 'We' remains unattended for a longer period of time, it returns to its owner, who is then able to discard it.

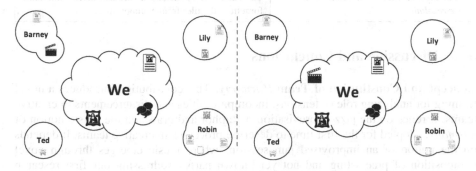

**Fig. 2.** Sketch representing basic notion of asynchronous *mutual listening* mechanism

We deliberately apply the word 'element' instead of 'file' or 'document'. It is natural, that in a process including co-located setting, some work artifacts are real things and may be represented in the repository in some underspecified form. Another important feature of the proposed mechanism is the versioning that allows to review team performance and attend forgotten elements. Team members can also 'un-attend' an element if they are not sure of its compatibility with the *general tenor*. Teams that stand in a phase of stronger *dissonance* realize it through the small size of the 'We'-space compared to the individual spaces.

Fig. 2 depicts the basic interaction mechanism introduced for this exemplary application of *harmony* perspective. In general, one can see the team members along with their individual spaces and the central space. Each team member can attend any element regardless of its location. One can see that *Robin* has four different elements she works on, while *Barney* has two, one depicted as a document and one as a video. It is indeed a video prototype of a new service he proposed to the team. He has been extensively working on it for the last days, which is signalized by the 'gemmating' bubble. If at least two other members open and watch the video within a week, it will automatically move to the 'We' space. We propose one week as the control period of time due to the character and rhythm of the design thinking course, but any other time frame is possible.

With this proposition we address all levels of *harmony* maintenance discussed in the previous chapters and propose the following design principles. Below we summarize them given the developed requirements.

**Table 2.** Requirements and design principles for support of team *harmony* in long-term setting

| Requirement | Design Principle |
|---|---|
| DR 1. Provide interaction paradigm that encourages *mutual listening* within the team | To reach DR 1, limit the number of elements considered common team output to the ones attended by the majority of team members. |
| DR 2. Provide means for seamless *dissonance awareness* | To reach DR 2, visualize the ratio of files within the common space and distributed among individual spaces. |
| DR 3. Provide means for seamless *dissonance resolution* | To reach DR 3, include a mechanism for automatic forgetting the files from common space. |

# 6     Discussion and Conclusions

**Concept and Constitution of Team *Harmony*.** This contribution introduces a novel framing for analyzing role of tensions, incompatibilities and disagreements in creative teams. It relies on the jazz improvisation metaphor and draws on the music notion of *harmony*, adopted for the first time to describe processes in creative teams. It depends on the notion of an improvised jam session, where music emerges through novel composition of preexisting and not yet known parts. Addressing our first research questions, we opened up with a rigorous literature review on task conflict and accompanying tension in creative teams. While focusing on studies from organizational and semi-organizational, long-term context, we elaborated on factors influencing or moderating creative performance and disagreements in teams. We ended up with a *harmony*-oriented view on team creative performance, which in its core includes a model of team *harmony* (cf. Fig. 1). It consists of the following layers: *mutual listening*, *dissonance awareness*, and *dissonance resolution*. We postulate that well performing creative teams will seamlessly maintain *harmony*, at least in synchronous, co-located sessions. We also assume, that it is possible to support teams at this particular activity by means of IT systems and process improvements. The concept of *harmony* and its constituents was evaluated through cognitive walkthrough, based on the observations made in a specific and creativity-oriented organizational context. The introduced model contributes to the knowledge base on conflict in creative teams and opens new possibilities to frame research questions and possible results.

**Designing Support for *Harmony*.** Given the capabilities coming with the introduced concept of *harmony*, we applied the collected insights in design of an exemplary system to support *harmony* in teams. It incorporates *harmony* maintenance in standard actions of users, thus supporting the idea of seamless interaction. It relies on a simple mechanism that limits the number of elements considered common team output and provides constant feedback on the ratio between individual, possibly incompatible or dissonant actions, and the concerted ones. Even though the proposed paradigm was designed to be implemented in an IT system, it is possible to adapt it as a process to creative teams working in different settings. Thus, it can be easily applied by practitioners and moderators of creative processes.

**Limitations and Outlook.** The current study discloses a practical gap in the field of CSS / GSS, and, at the same time, it contributes to a better understanding of processes in creative teams. Still, we do not postulate our research to be accomplished or terminating. On the contrary, we recognize that our literature review is not complete, even though rigorously conducted and documented. Nonetheless, it was sufficient to develop and motivate the proposed model of team *harmony*. Our primary focus on teams in organizational context excluded much valuable research done in classes or labs – attending this literature could provide further theoretical clues on *harmony* in creative contexts. Moreover, further practical evidence can be attained through implementation of the proposed paradigm in real teams. The latter could benefit from a holistic system that encompasses findings from the fields of CSS and GSS, thus a closer look in those fields is still pending. In that sense, we look forward to future research that uses the notion of team *harmony* and adds to it. Herewith, we call for further investigation of *harmony* issues in the context of creativity and innovation.

# References

1. Albert, S., Bell, G.G.: Timing and Music. Acad. Manage. Rev. 27(4), 574–593 (2002)
2. Amabile, T.M.: A Model of Creativity and Innovation in Organizations. Res. Organ. Behav. 10, 123–167 (1988)
3. Anderson, N., et al.: The routinization of innovation research: a constructively critical review of the state-of-the-science. J. Organ. Behav. 25(2), 147–173 (2004)
4. Barrett, F.J., Peplowski, K.: Minimal Structures Within a Song: An Analysis of "All of Me". Organ. Sci. 9(5), 558–560 (1998)
5. Benford, S., et al.: Collaborative Virtual Environments. Commun. ACM 44(7), 79–85 (2001)
6. Börjesson, S., Fredberg, T.: Jam sessions for collaborative management research. Collab. Res. Organ. Sage Lond. 135–148 (2004)

7. Vom Brocke, J., et al.: Reconstructing the giant: On the importance of rigour in documenting the literature search process. In: Proceedings of the European Conference on Information Systems, pp. 2206–2217. AIS, Verona (2009)
8. Brown, T.: Design Thinking. Harv. Bus. Rev. 86(6), 84–92 (2008)
9. Brush, A.J.B., et al.: Notification for Shared Annotation of Digital Documents. In: Proceedings of the SIGCHI Conference on Human Factors in Computing Systems, pp. 89–96. ACM, New York (2002)
10. Cain, S.: Quiet: The power of introverts in a world that can't stop talking. Random House Digital, Inc. (2013)
11. Carleton, T., Leifer, L.: Stanford's ME310 Course as an Evolution of Engineering Design. Presented at the 19th CIRP Design Conference, Cranfield, UK (March 31, 2009)
12. Chen, M.-H.: Understanding the Benefits and Detriments of Conflict on Team Creativity Process. Creat. Innov. Manag. 15(1), 105–116 (2006)
13. Crossan, M.M.: Improvisation in action. Organ. Sci. 9(5), 593–599 (1998)
14. De Dreu, C.K.W., et al.: Group creativity and innovation: A motivated information processing perspective. Psychol. Aesthet. Creat. Arts 5(1), 81–89 (2011)
15. De Dreu, C.K.W.: When Too Little or Too Much Hurts: Evidence for a Curvilinear Relationship Between Task Conflict and Innovation in Teams. J. Manag. 32(1), 83–107 (2006)
16. De Dreu, C.K.W., Weingart, L.R.: Task Versus Relationship Conflict, Team Performance, and Team Member Satisfaction: A Meta-Analysis. J. Appl. Psychol. 88(4), 741–749 (2003)
17. Dym, C.L., et al.: Engineering Design Thinking, Teaching, and Learning. J. Eng. Educ. 94(1), 103–120 (2005)
18. Fairchild, J., Hunter, S.T.: We've Got Creative Differences: The Effects of Task Conflict and Participative Safety on Team Creative Performance. J. Creat. Behav. 64–87 (2013)
19. Farh, J.-L., et al.: Task Conflict and Team Creativity: A Question of How Much and When. J. Appl. Psychol. 95(6), 1173–1180 (2010)
20. George, J.M.: Creativity in Organizations. Acad. Manag. Ann. 1(1), 439–477 (2007)
21. Goldkuhl, G.: Design theories in information systems-a need for multi-grounding. J. Inf. Technol. Theory Appl. JITTA 6(2), 59–72 (2004)
22. Harvey, C., et al.: Academic Journal Quality Guide: Version 4. The Association of Business Schools (ABS), London (2010)
23. Harvey, L.J., Myers, M.D.: Scholarship and practice: the contribution of ethnographic research methods to bridging the gap. Inf. Technol. People 8(3), 13–27 (1995)
24. Hatch, M.J.: Exploring the Empty Spaces of Organizing: How Improvisational Jazz Helps Redescribe Organizational Structure. Organ. Stud. Walter Gruyter GmbH Co KG 20(1), 75–100 (1999)
25. Hennessey, B.A., Amabile, T.M.: Creativity. Annu. Rev. Psychol. 61, 569–598 (2010)
26. Hevner, A.R., et al.: Design Science in Information Systems Research. MIS Q. 28(1), 75–105 (2004)
27. Holbrook, M.B.: Playing the Changes on the Jazz Metaphor: An Expanded Conceptualization of Music-, Management-, and Marketing-Related Themes. Found. Trends® Mark 2(3-4), 185–442 (2007)
28. Horn, C., Brem, A.: Strategic directions on innovation management – a conceptual framework. Manag. Res. Rev. 36(10), 939–954 (2013)
29. Hsieh, T.-J., et al.: The Impact of Top Management Team Conflict on New Product Development: A Cross-Cultural Perspective. Int. J. Innov. Technol. Manag. 7(2), 193–208 (2010)
30. Hülsheger, U.R., et al.: Team-level predictors of innovation at work: A comprehensive meta-analysis spanning three decades of research. J. Appl. Psychol. 94(5), 1128–1145 (2009)

31. Jehn, K.A.: A Qualitative Analysis of Conflict Types and Dimensions in Organizational Groups. Adm. Sci. Q. 42(3), 530–557 (1997)
32. Jehn, K.A., et al.: The Effects of Conflict Asymmetry on Work Group and Individual Outcomes. Acad. Manage. J. 53(3), 596–616 (2010)
33. Jehn, K.A., Mannix, E.A.: The Dynamic Nature of Conflict: A Longitudinal Study of Intragroup Conflict and Group Performance. Acad. Manage. J. 44(2), 238–251 (2001)
34. Johnson, H., Carruthers, L.: Supporting creative and reflective processes. Int. J. Hum. - Comput. Stud. 64(10), 998–1030 (2006)
35. Kamoche, K., Cunha, M.P.e.: Minimal Structures: From Jazz Improvisation to Product Innovation. Organ. Stud. 22(5), 733–764 (2001)
36. Kerr, N.L., Tindale, R.S.: Group Performance and Decision Making. Annu. Rev. Psychol. 55(1), 623–655 (2004)
37. Kozlowski, S.W.J., Ilgen, D.R.: Enhancing the Effectiveness of Work Groups and Teams. Psychol. Sci. Public Interest 7(3), 77–124 (2006)
38. Kratzer, J., et al.: Team Polarity and Creative Performance in Innovation Teams. Creat. Innov. Manag. 15(1), 96–104 (2006)
39. Kunifuji, S., Kato, N.: Consensus-Making Support Systems Dedicated to Creative Problem Solving. Int. J. Inf. Technol. Decis. Mak. 6(3), 459–474 (2007)
40. Kurtzberg, T.R., Amabile, T.M.: From Guilford to Creative Synergy: Opening the Black Box of Team-Level Creativity. Creat. Res. J. 13(3/4), 285–294 (2001)
41. Kurtzberg, T.R., Mueller, J.S.: The Influence of Daily Conflict on Perceptions of Creativity: A Longitudinal Study. Int. J. Confl. Manag. 16(4), 335–353 (2005)
42. Lovelace, K., et al.: Maximizing Cross-Functional New Product Teams' Innovativeness and Constraint Adherence: A Conflict Communications Perspective. Acad. Manage. J. 44(4), 779–793 (2001)
43. Lubart, T.: How can computers be partners in the creative process: Classification and commentary on the Special Issue. Int. J. Hum.- Comput. Stud. 63(4/5), 365–369 (2005)
44. Mantere, S., et al.: Music as a metaphor for organizational change. J. Organ. Change Manag. 20(3), 447–459 (2007)
45. McCrimmon, M.: Teams without roles: empowering teams for greater creativity. J. Manag. Dev. 14(6), 35–41 (1995)
46. Meyer, A., et al.: The Organization Science Jazz Festival: Improvisation as a Metaphor for Organizing. Organ. Sci. 9(5), 540–542 (1998)
47. Müller, S.D., Ulrich, F.: Creativity and Information Systems in a Hypercompetitive Environment: A Literature Review. Commun. Assoc. Inf. Syst. 32, 175–200 (2013)
48. Myers, M.: Investigating Information Systems with Ethnographic Research. Commun AIS. 2, 4es (1999)
49. Nemeth, C.J., Ormiston, M.: Creative idea generation: harmony versus stimulation. Eur. J. Soc. Psychol. 37(3), 524–535 (2007)
50. Nunamaker, J.F., et al.: Electronic Meeting Systems. Commun. ACM 34(7), 40–61 (1991)
51. O'Neill, T.A., et al.: Examining the "pros" and "cons" of team conflict: A team-level meta-analysis of task, relationship, and process conflict. Hum. Perform. 26(3), 236–260 (2013)
52. O'Reilly, C.A., Tushman, M.L.: The ambidextrous organization. Harv. Bus. Rev. 82(4), 74–83 (2004)
53. Okoli, C., Schabram, K.: A Guide to Conducting a Systematic Literature Review of Information Systems Research. Sprouts Work. Pap. Inf. Syst. 10, 26 (2010)

54. Pankoke-Babatz, U., et al.: Stories about asynchronous awareness. In: Cooperative System Design: Scenario-Based Design of Collaborative Systems, pp. 23–38. IOS Press (2004)
55. Paulus, P.: Groups, Teams, and Creativity: The Creative Potential of Idea-generating Groups. Appl. Psychol. 49(2), 237–262 (2000)
56. Paulus, P.B., et al.: Modeling ideational creativity in groups: Connecting cognitive, neural, and computational approaches. Small Group Res. 41(6), 688–724 (2010)
57. Paulus, P.B., Coskun, H.: Creativity. In: Levine, J.M. (ed.) Group Processes, pp. 215–239. Psychology Press, New York (2013)
58. Paulus, P.B.: Huei-Chuan Yang: Idea Generation in Groups: A Basis for Creativity in Organizations. Organ. Behav. Hum. Decis. Process. 82(1), 76–87 (2000)
59. Plattner, H., et al.: An unified innovation process model for engineering designers and managers. In: Design Thinking Understand, Improve, Apply. Springer, Heidelberg (2011)
60. Randel, D.M.: The Harvard Dictionary of Music. Harvard University Press (2003)
61. Rodden, T., Blair, G.: CSCW and Distributed Systems: The Problem of Control. In: Bannon, L., et al. (eds.) Proceedings of the Second European Conference on Computer-Supported Cooperative Work, pp. 49–64. Springer Netherlands (1991)
62. Saunders, C.: MIS Journal Rankings, http://ais.site-ym.com/?page=JournalRankings
63. Scheer, A.-W.: Jazz-Improvisation und Management (2002)
64. Shneiderman, B.: Creativity Support Tools. Commun. ACM 45(10), 116–120 (2002)
65. Sonalkar, N., et al.: Emotion in Engineering Design Teams. In: Fukuda, S. (ed.) Emotional Engineering, pp. 311–326. Springer, London (2011)
66. Steve, H. (ed.): Media Space 20+ Years of Mediated Life. Springer, Heidelberg (2009)
67. Thompson, L.: Improving the creativity of organizational work groups. Acad. Manag. Exec. 17(1), 96–109 (2003)
68. Tidd, J., Bessant, J.: Managing Innovation: Integrating Technological, Market and Organizational Change. John Wiley & Sons (2011)
69. Tjosvold, D.: Cooperative and Competitive Goal Approach to Conflict: Accomplishments and Challenges. Appl. Psychol. 47(3), 285–313 (1998)
70. Tschirky, H.: Managing innovation driven companies: approaches in practice. Palgrave Macmillan, Houndmills (2011)
71. Voigt, M., Niehaves, B., Becker, J.: Towards a Unified Design Theory for Creativity Support Systems. In: Peffers, K., Rothenberger, M., Kuechler, B., et al. (eds.) DESRIST 2012. LNCS, vol. 7286, pp. 152–173. Springer, Heidelberg (2012)
72. Walzer, N., Salcher, A.: Management by jazz – creating innovation from the principles of chaos and order. Ind. Commer. Train. 35(2), 67–69 (2003)
73. Webster, J., Watson, R.T.: Analyzing the Past to Prepare for the Future: Writing a Literature Review. MIS Q., xiii–xxiii (2002).
74. West, M.A., Farr, J.L.: Innovation at work. In: West, M.A., Farr, J.L. (eds.) Innovation and Creativity at Work: Psychological and Organizational Strategies, pp. 3–13. John Wiley & Sons, Oxford (1990)
75. De Wit, F.R.C., et al.: The paradox of intragroup conflict: A meta-analysis. J. Appl. Psychol. 97(2), 360–390 (2012)
76. Zentner, M.R., Kagan, J.: Infants' perception of consonance and dissonance in music. Infant Behav. Dev. 21(3), 483–492 (1998)

# An Empirical Account of Fitness-Utility: A Case of Radical Change towards Mobility in DSR Practice

Mudassir Imran Mustafa[1,2], Jonas Sjöström[1,2], and Jenny Eriksson Lundström[1]

[1] Department of Informatics and Media, Uppsala University, Sweden
{mudassir.imran,jonas.sjostrom,jenny.eriksson}@im.uu.se
[2] Department of Public Health and Caring Science, Uppsala University, Sweden

**Abstract.** Evaluation is an essential part of design science research - a means to demonstrate qualities of artefacts and knowledge abstractions. The utility-fitness model suggests that evaluation needs to move from 'usefulness' measures to utility functions that incorporate the long-term evolution and survival of an artefact in its design landscape. In this paper, we interpret a process of innovative change taking place within a design system, in order to provide an empirical account of utility-fitness. We propose that the utility-fitness model pays too little explicit attention to technological-ecological fit, accountability, and robustness: Three ideals that were prevalent in the scrutinized empirical setting.

**Keywords:** Design Science Research, Fitness, Utility, Evolution, Ecology, Diffusion of Innovation.

## 1 Introduction

Evaluation has been emphasized as a core activity in design science research (DSR). Through evaluation, the researcher demonstrates the usefulness and the efficacy of proposed design science artefacts [1]. Evaluation concerns both design outputs and theoretical contributions (i.e. artefacts and abstract contributions).

Gill & Hevner [2] provide a view on IT artefact quality that expands the prevailing focus on *utility as usefulness* in DSR. The fitness-utility model incorporates a set of characteristics of an IT artefact that are related to its long-term value in society, rather than its immediate usefulness. We conceive of the fitness-utility model as a conceptual elaboration of the notion of mutability as an aspect of design theory [3]. Gill and Hevner [2] propose that designers (in practice) base their designs on more or less explicit utility functions. These choices of the designers evolve over time, as they interact with various stakeholders in the design process. Usefulness, in this view, is one out of many choices in the utility function. The fitness-utility model proposes a tentative set of design candidate characteristics that are likely to impact the fitness of an artefact to its intended application environments. The characteristics include decomposability, malleability, and openness (all promoting modification of the artefact). Additional characteristics that affect fitness are novelty, elegance, and whether or not

M.C. Tremblay et al. (Eds.): DESRIST 2014, LNCS 8463, pp. 289–303, 2014.

the artefact is interesting. Finally, they argue that the *design system* that supports the emergence of the artefact is important for the long-term evolution and diffusion of the artefact in the evolving design landscape.

As a simple example, an artefact that does not continually evolve through design actions is like to become obsolete quicker than one that is frequently revised in accordance with new requirements from stakeholders in its application environment. Design systems may have different characteristics. Consider, for example, the difference between open source communities and closed communities of users and designers. Thus, Gill & Hevner [2] present utility as a construct to estimate fitness – which in itself is presented as an abstract concept. The true value of fitness "unfolds only over time" [2, p.5:2]. Further, they elaborate the meaning of utility, claiming that the IS DSR community tends to view it rather narrowly as a characteristic of the artefact, in relation to other qualities such as efficacy. They propose an exaptation from economics, where utility is posited as a function to rank choices in the context of decision-making. The utility function is thus formed as a function $f$ where each choice $x$ is expressed as a set of attributes, i.e.:

$$\text{Utility} = f(x_1, x_2, ..., x_N). \tag{1}$$

Two assumptions are important in economics with respect to the utility function. First, the choices are individual, and affected by social and cultural forces. Second, individuals seek to maximize their own utility. The utility-fitness model [2] thus makes a contribution to the idea of utility in IS DSR research through a definition of utility that goes beyond usefulness. Given that the fitness-utility model was recently introduced, there is a lack of empirical studies that show how designers relate to the design candidate characteristics in actual design practice.

The purpose of this paper is to explore empirically how the DSR utility function is enacted in software development practice.

We take an interpretive stance to analyse a process of innovation within a design system, investigating how a series of events unfolded as an implication of a proposal for innovative re-design of an IT artefact. As diffusion of innovation happens in a social context [4], in which the maturity and preconditions of the environment influences the innovation adoption rate, we also need an understanding of benefits and limitations of the new technology *given its context*. Consequently, we have complemented our analysis with innovation diffusion theory (ibid.) as an additional theoretical input for our analysis.

The paper is outlined as follows: We provide an introduction to research on utility characteristics of design artefacts, with a particular focus on the Utility-Fitness Model of Gill & Hevner [2]. We describe the method of our study and present the results. Then, we discuss the results of our investigation and its implications for the evaluation of artefact quality. In the final section we conclude and outline future work.

## 2     Research Setting and Research Approach

In this section, we introduce the approach for data collection and data analysis, followed by an overview of the empirical setting for the study.

## 2.1    Research Approach

The approach in this paper is to learn more about design practice by doing design, as explained by Baskerville et al. [5]. Their view resonates with the pragmatic idea that inquiry into a situation leads to an in-depth understanding of that situation [6], and that attempts to change a situation will disclose forces that prevent and support the attempted change. We investigate a process in which a team of developers was exposed to and acted upon ideas on how to adapt their web-based artefact to better support mobility; i.e. a re-design of the artefact to support use on a variety of devices such as smartphones and tablets. The developer team consists of four full-time developers, two PhD students working part-time as developers, and a senior researcher.

This study was conducted through a set of design activities, including design and development of software as well as formative workshops with the developer team. Data was collected during and between design and evaluation workshops. In total, 8 workshops were organized, engaging a great variety of stakeholders. Workshop discussions were documented and in some cases audio was recorded. In addition, field notes were taken. To provide additional corpus, data sources also include e-mail correspondence, presentations, meeting minutes, artefact source code revision history, and log messages. The first author of this paper was the originator and manager of the design process and participated in the development. The second author acted as a manager and developer in the design team. The last author was continually informed about the design process and participated in one of the workshops.

We appropriated an interpretive approach to data analysis following the principles of Klein and Myers [7]. As outlined by Orlikowski and Baroudi [8], interpretive research aims at understanding phenomena by attempting to understand the meaning that participants assign to them. In this case, the phenomenon at hand is to understand the meaning of 'fitness-utility' from the point of view of developers. Data was analysed iteratively by shifting between interpretation of data, theoretical studies, and development of theoretical interpretations. Analysis of actions, decisions, development efforts, and emergence of artefact attributes represent the parts while the evolving analysis results represent the *whole* [7]. The shift in focus between *parts* and the whole correspond to the fundamental *principle of the hermeneutic circle*. Following the *principle of contextualization*, we also factor in the historical background of the case environment to support interpretation. The data was also further analysis with keeping diffusion of innovation [4] theory in mind.

Given the interpretive approach, there is a need to mitigate the 'mediation of language and preconception' associated with understanding reality, to paraphrase Orlikowski and Baroudi [8]. A triangulation approach was employed to analyse data, motivated by the authors' different experiences from the design process and their varying 'distances' to the development team. The triangulation approach was beneficial to address the principle of interaction between the researchers and the subject [7]. Two researchers initially approached the process of interpretation independently. The final version of the interpretation was done in joint discussions where all three researchers discussed the consistency of the results and validated the resulting concepts against empirical data.

## 2.2     Research Setting

U-CARE (Uppsala University Psychosocial Care Programme) is a research programme aiming at designing and developing knowledge regarding Internet-reliant protocols for psychosocial care and cognitive behavioural therapy. Approximately 10 treatment protocols are part of ongoing studies, including for example paediatric oncological care, adult oncological care, cardiological care, and fear of birth among pregnant women. Typically, Randomized Controlled Trials (RCTs) are conducted to study the effect of a self-help programme via Internet on anxiety and depression. Research groups are interdisciplinary, including researchers from various disciplines such as caring sciences, psychology, economics, and information systems.

The U-CARE Portal is the web-based software to support treatment as well as research. The design of the portal was ingrained by viewpoints from a large number of stakeholders, including representatives from the different academic disciplines, practitioners such as nurses, medical doctors, and psychologists, and patients.

The software is still evolving in an ongoing design process. Bug fixes, refactoring and development of new features take place in an agile process. Development sprints last for two weeks, and the target of the organization is to release a new production version of the software every month. In total, 80+ design workshops were organized since the inception of the program in 2010, engaging a great variety of stakeholders. The stakeholder-centric [9] and iterative approach promotes a focus on value creation – a continuous assessment of the software as a means to contribute to the overarching goals of the U-CARE programme. The multi-disciplinary approach in U-CARE resonates well with the characteristics of rigorous evaluation in IS design research as put forth by Hevner et al. [1]. Contributions from psychology and economics, disciplines with a strong quantitative evaluation tradition, ingrain U-CARE research with evaluation methods. Relevance, design and rigor cycles [10] are part of the stakeholder-guided process through which the design emerges. The overarching ambition among the IS researchers in the U-CARE context is to employ design science research to develop novel design knowledge drawing from design experiences in the context of online psychosocial care.

We briefly present characteristics of the software to give an indication of its complexity. The software supports various activities in treatment and research, including Cognitive Behavioural Therapy (CBT), psychoeducation, chat, moderated forum discussions, decision support for therapists, design of new treatment protocols, manage reminders, survey design and data collection, data export, FAQs, patient diary keeping. As a backbone for these features, the software also supports role management and authorization, content management, logging, configurable reminders, and multi-linguality. The software consists of five subsystems, comprising in total ~50 000 lines of code and ~100 database tables. Since some of the RCTs are ongoing, new releases of the software are required to be stable to prevent damage to ongoing treatment and research.

## 3     Interpretation of Design Activities

In this section, we provide an account of the performed design activities, and the abstractions made from interpretation of those activities. We structure our description on a phase-model of design activities (Fig. 1) that correspond to the three first phases of the innovation-decision process [4].

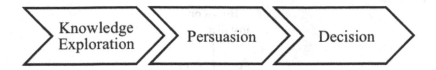

**Fig. 1.** Three stages of innovation-decision (after [4])

First, *knowledge exploration*, includes activities concerned with understanding the context of design, including requirements from the organization, the installed techno-logical base, and opportunities for innovation given the technological landscape. Second, *persuasion*, focuses on the set of activities through which design was guided to evolve in a direction to satisfy stakeholders. Third, *decision*, elaborates on the de-sign activities that were required to convince stakeholders to adopt the new design in their practice.

### 3.1   The Knowledge Exploration Stage

The process towards a mobile software started out explorative, with the purpose of better understanding (i) mobility needs and installed base, and (ii) the 'mobility land-scape', i.e. mobile technologies and development strategies that may be relevant in the current context.

**Mobility Needs and Installed Base.** Through a series of informal discussions with representatives of the organization, basic requirements for mobility were phrased. Mobility has been recognized as important since the inception of U-CARE, but it has never been at the fore in the design process. Early discussions, however, made it pos-sible to identify a set of requirements (R1-R4 below) for adaptations of the software for mobile use. Psychology researchers deemed mobility desirable but at the time the focus was to design rigorous studies on web-based treatment. Even though mobility was not required at the time it was emphasized that mobility, when provided, should be *accessible on patients' choice of devices* (R1) and *provide security and protect privacy of patients* (R2). IS researchers (who also acted as system analysts and soft-ware developers) expressed that trends towards mobility should be recognized in the design of U-CARE software. However, an adaptation to mobility should *require minimum development / maintenance effort* (R3) and be *designed on top of the exist-ing system infrastructure insofar possible* (R4). These requirements illustrate impor-tant preconceptions that governed the process of adapting the software for mobility.

**Mobility Landscape.** Literature and online resources (e.g., blogs and forums) were studied to learn more about the mobility landscape, including devices, operating sys-tems, frameworks, standards, regulatory organizations, and developer resources. A rudimentary model for comparison of development approaches (Fig. 2) was created. Given the requirements R1-R4, B is the ideal quadrant in the U-CARE setting, since it builds on the installed base *and* allows use of device capabilities (e.g. GPS and user interface components) to support design for a better user experience.

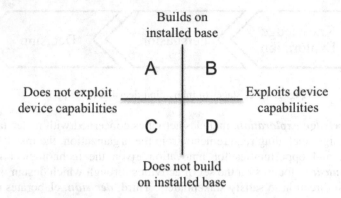

Fig. 2. A rudimentary model for comparison of development approaches

It is out of scope to present all identified approaches here, but a range of optional paths towards mobility were identified, ranging from completely native apps [D], to various hybrid app solutions mixing web and native code [B/D], responsive design frameworks to make a web site adapt to different screen sizes [A]. In addition, scripting frameworks such as jQuery mobile were identified that enables websites to get the look and feel of user interfaces of native mobile apps [B]. In addition to assessing the different approaches based on literature, experimental development was conducted to better understand each technological concept and its potential value in relation to the installed base and requirements from the organization.

## 3.2    The Persuasion Stage

The persuasion phase consisted of four design workshops and development efforts that took place as a consequence of decisions made during the workshops (Fig. 3).

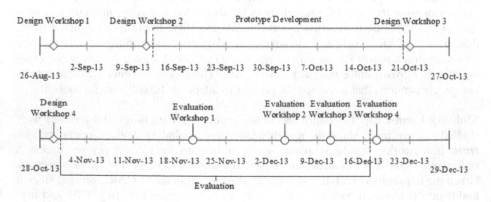

Fig. 3. Timeline of workshops

## Design Workshop 1

**Overview.** During the first workshop, mobility was presented as an innovation challenge of U-CARE. Open feedback on the issue was gathered from the scientific advisory board members of U-CARE, staff and associated researchers.

**Design Implications/Decisions.** There were two key results from the discussions: 'technology could be used more effectively in order to promote behaviour change' and 'enhance recruitment to intervention studies e.g. via the design of the portal's layout'. The workshop resulted in an increased awareness of mobility issues and triggered further discussion on the topic within U-CARE.

**Undertaken Design Actions.** The IS researchers planned a second design workshop to introduce and discuss mobility solution design choices.

## Design Workshop 2

**Overview.** Workshop 2 was the main design workshop. It included a presentation of mobility and motivations (see Fig. 2), a Q&A-session, and an open discussion that highlighted the following key characteristics:
    elegance and interessement for the user:

> *"the review of option we have is valuable ... I want to see if you run the (existing) system today on mobile devices, how can we find the minimum situations to adopt the system for better user experience...,*

elegance and interessement from a developer's perspective

> *"I am agreeing it is elegant to adopt the system using Bootstrap [CSS framework] ... one way forward is experimental refactoring and modernizing the development environment..."*

However, most evident was characteristics pertaining to the accountability and robustness of the existing design system and its ecology

> *"... there are architectural issues preventing mobile [native] app approach implementation ... if we redesign the entire software as platform .... then we can have apps to interact with platform ... right now app can't be considered as an option ...........while solving one problem we may creating more problem ... the change in the system is a risk too ..."*

> *"... we have to balance between long term goals/vision for the platform and the immediate requirements ... there are issues related to resource and our work is govern by organizational context we are working in ..."*

> *"...this was at the time most critical as the system was running in production environment and the (RCTs) studies were going on with real participants.*

*Any change in views without thoroughly testing could have resulted in dis-crepancies in the RCT-research data, disruption in information flow and scramble study material related to interventions. Ultimately this could have caused undesired (negative) effects on participants' health..."*

**Design Decisions/Implications.** The developers agreed to follow the *Mobile First philosophy* and to *implement responsive web design* on experimental basis *using a CSS framework*. At the time, the development team was working on a back-end refactoring of the existing software. The developers agreed that they should work on front-end refactoring as well as implement the mobility. The use of the Model-View Controller pattern (MVC) facilitated the simultaneous refactoring of both back-end and front-end design. The front-end refactoring required a revision of more than 400 view pages.

**Undertaken Design Actions.** The developers made the assessment that the software required substantive refactoring on the view side in order to be compatible with suit-able third-party technologies for mobility. A three-stage upgrade plan was devised. The first step was a conversion of existing views to 'razor', a view standard that was a prerequisite for the selected framework for responsive design. The second step was to implement the responsive design framework in the views (*designing for mobility*). The third step was to adapt the treatment content (images, audio, videos, text, etc.) to render better on multiple devices.

### Subsystem and System Prototype Development

**Overview.** Parallel development was employed on the existing and new systems by splitting development team into two teams E and M  (E for existing system, M for mobility). Using software versioning and revision control system (Subversion) a sepa-rate branch was created for prototype development in parallel to the existing system development. The goal of the subsystem prototype was to test the feasibility of the design and establish a proof of concept in the relevant environment by gradually im-proving and introducing additional functionality. Development started with a few web pages, files architecture (theme resource, JavaScript and CSS libraries, etc.). The development process was governed by two design principles, i.e. *design for One Web* and *rely on Web standards* out of ten proposed by W3C (mobile web guideline / best practices). The design principles correspond to the meta requirements elicited in the search process. During the development discussion, feedback and evaluation was continuously conducted between developers as well as between teams.

**Development Implications/Decisions.** As a result of these discussions it was decided that *application access using standard mobile browser with HTTPS only*, was to be provided, i.e. the same as provided for the existing web application. Furthermore the *data was not being stored on mobile devices* Once the system prototype was com-pleted the developers decided to have a design workshop to assess the prototype.

**Undertaken Design Actions.** Once the subsystem prototype was completed, devel-opers from both teams discussed the process, pros and cons of the prototype, and provided feedback. After thoroughly evaluating the prototype they decided to move forward and decided to convert all views. Iteratively the subsystem prototype was extended and expanded to a full system prototype, which exactly mirrored (visually) the existing system but created via the Razor view engine and upgraded syntax. Manual unit testing was performed on each view during development.

## Design Workshop 3

**Overview.** In the third workshop a demo of the prototype, description of changes in the code, and analysis of efforts required to synchronize both branches were presented.

**Design Implications/Decisions.** Overall developers were satisfied with the prototype and agreed to shift to the new code branch. The critical factor was the many changes in the views as it was risky to release them in the production environment without rigorous evaluation. On the one hand, here was a need for systematic testing to achieve a satisfactory confidence level in the system, on the other hand, to delay the process too much would have required extra efforts in code synchronization (due to parallel development) and further delaying step two (*designing for mobility*) development. The views were not covered by the unit test so automatic testing (which could be an ideal situation in this case) could not be carried out. A test plan and an approach to test the new system were deemed necessary.

**Undertaken Design Actions.** After discussions it was decided to schedule an evaluation planning workshop, and to allocate full development resources for parallel independent system testing once a week. All developers installed the latest development environment and the system prototype branch to work on it according to schedule.

## Design Workshop 4

**Overview.** During workshop 4 developers focused on various ideas to validate the quality of the prototype. Various testing strategies were discussed, including unit testing, integration testing, system testing and user interface testing.

**Design Implications/Decisions.** The developers devised the evaluation criteria for the system as '*new views should interact with users, present information and receive data for further processing in exactly same manner as existing views are*'. They identified the *most critical part of the system as the data collection through questionnaires* due to the negative impact of bugs on ongoing studies.

**Undertaken Design Actions.** The developers selected a pilot study that had been designed using nearly all system features and functionality. They devised a test plan to go through the study using test users on both systems in parallel. The idea behind the plan was if both systems behaved in the same manner using the same set of conditions (e.g. user, study design, data, browser etc.) then the new system was functionally reliable. The second step in the test plan was to go through all important and frequently accessed views. The existing system was equipped with a logging function. Using the log, list of URLs (possible browser requests to be mapped to controller/ actions in MVC) was generated with respect to user role and frequency. In this way the developers had a systematic test plan with a list of tasks to carry out report errors, and later verify corrections. The next section provides a more detailed account how the evaluation was performed in practice.

### 3.3    The Decision Stage

**Overview.** The evaluation of the prototype was scattered over the period of two months (see Table 1 for summary of evaluation workshops). Before each workshop bugs were fixed and code branches were merged. Team M configured a test environment that resembles the production environment to test the system. They iteratively performed testing and released alpha versions on test environment for the next round of evaluation.

**Table 1.** Prototype Evaluation during Four Workshops

| # | Tasks and Development | Evaluation Results/Feedback |
|---|---|---|
| 1 | • Installation and deployment of system on test environment | • System behaved differently in debug mode vs. release mode<br>• Bug found: error in image loading |
| 2 | • Developed comparison tool<br>• Reconfigured test environment to support comparison tool<br>• Tested critical parts of the system through questionnaires | • Testing of critical parts considered as satisfactory.<br>• Difficult to keep track of tests and verify both systems behaviours<br>• Bug found: error in JS function calls and in displaying raw HTML where it is needed |
| 3 | • Redesigned the comparison tool<br>• Implement perceptual diff. image | • Tool made the evaluation simple, easy and fast<br>• Bug found: language translation was not working on a few pages |
| 4 | • Bug fixed in both systems | • Developers agreed to release beta version |

During the workshops developers went through the list of URLs and compared the existing system with the alpha prototype. Test coverage was tracked by comparing the log table in the databases at the end of each workshop. The most critical part of the system was data collection and intervention flow. That was tested using pilot study by going through all steps of the intervention and answering questionnaires. User interfaces and stored data in the two versions of the system were analysed in three ways. *First*, the comparison of user interfaces and data was performed while logged in to each system with test users. *Second*, database records were analysed and compared. *Third*, database logs were compared. The process was repeated using different users and following different paths in the business logic. *The evaluation results of critical parts of the system were considered as satisfactory.*

Performance testing was performed indirectly by analysing and comparing average code execution times in both systems. After summative evaluation, the developer team agreed to release a version of the software to end-users for beta testing; and that beta version would go into production when the beta version showed sufficient stability. At that point, the team would switch to the Razor branch in the code repository, thus remove the need to keep two branches synchronized.

**Evaluation Implications/Decisions.** The drive for mobility adoption, if not initiated, pushed the change of the existing release process by introducing development (alpha and beta) releases on test environment before production release. This allowed for analysis and test of possible setting requirements before deploying the system on the production server. The workshops not only provided a *parallel independent testing* environment but also increased confidence level on this complex system. Developers also expressed that it was difficult to compare the existing and new system in two different browser tabs/windows.

A comparison tool was developed to simplify comparative analysis of the two code branches. An image analysis library [11] was used to visualize discrepancies between the two versions with respect to content and layout. In addition to visualizations, the tool presented the degree of discrepancy as a percentage. Images were stored in a repository to support the developers in tracking progression in the test process. The utilization of the tool supported the developers in identifying bugs caused by the conversion of a large number of views to the razor standard.

**Undertaken Design Actions.** The evaluation process led to the detection and mitigation of a number of code issues, as well a set of unanticipated refactoring measures to improve code clarity and page rendering performance. After the fourth evaluation workshop the first beta version was released for testing by end-users. A few weeks after the beta testing was finished, the system was ready for production release.

# 4    Discussion

In this paper we have investigated the impact candidate characteristics of design artefacts that are likely to impact the fitness of a design artefact to its intended application environment, how they come into play in a particular innovation process, and how they affected the evolution of the design process. We have taken our departure in the model of fitness-utility for DSR-research of Gill and Hevner [2]. As this model provides a tentative set of characteristics posing as dependent variables of DSR, we have applied these to a particular innovation process in a design project, adhering to design as artefact and design evaluation as suggested by [2, p. 24]. The artefact produced during the studied design process is viable, and its utility, quality and efficacy have been rigorously demonstrated via well-executed evaluation methods. As the model emphasizes the evolutionary fitness of a design artefact, the tentative set of design candidate characteristics was found to be useful as the point of departure of our study.

## 4.1    Fitness-Utility Characteristics

From our case, we observe that the design process evolved in a direction governed by the key ideals of the system as perceived of by the developer team. As indicated in design workshop 2, the developer team put emphasis to fitness values such as the embedding in the design system, the novelty of the mobility feature as well as the elegance of the bootstrap CSS Framework. This is also supported by the initialisation of the innovation process itself. Given the consideration that deciding to embark on any refactoring of this magnitude constitutes a risk, especially given that the system was running in production mode and that there were ongoing studies with actual participants. Any change in views without thorough testing could thus have resulted in discrepancies in research data, disruptions for users of the system, and issues for researchers to interpret the result of ongoing trials. Ultimately this could have caused undesired (negative) effects on participants' health.

However, other fitness characteristics such as the decomposability, malleability or openness of the design system were not expressed as drivers of this innovation process. Instead, the innovation diffusion rather depended on the embeddedness in the existing design system. One example of this, manifested in the degree of decomposability of the existing artefact, is that it had a layered architecture that supported the upgrade by limiting the change in one layer (i.e. presentation layer). As a result the turn towards mobility was facilitated. Likewise, we found that the alignment to technology outside of the design system itself can be seen as a key factor for driving the decisions taken. Although the artefact is not open-source but it is adopting open-source components this indirectly has an impact on the evolution of the artefact design as it has to evolve when the open design of components evolve (e.g. jQuery, jQuery plugins and planned adopting of Bootstrap CSS Framework).

Hence, the design reality tradeoffs such as resource efficiency, alignment to existing technology as well as the utility of the artefact all influenced the design process.

Following Krippendorff's [12] view of a fitness-related issue that adds a 'technological-ecological' extension to Gill and Hevner's model of fitness-utility, we argue that designers need to recognize the meaning of an *ecology* of artefacts to produce successful designs. From a technological point of view, this ecology includes the dependencies between the artefact in focus and boundary resources such as development tools, frameworks in use, et cetera. Clearly, there is a need to continually keep an artefact in sync with such boundary objects to promote artefact mutability. A trivial example from a contemporary web development setting is that a jQuery-based web application needs to be continually adapted to new versions of the jQuery framework. If not, the code will 'rot' to paraphrase Martin [13]. In order to utilize jQuery plugins, a fresh version of jQuery itself may be needed. Bad compliance with new versions of the framework will thus make it harder to utilize new plugins that support a better user experience for the users of the artefact. That is; in order to promote a software artefact's fitness to the changing design landscape, the artefact needs to continually evolve both in terms of its compliance with new requirements from its stakeholders and of its fitness to the emerging technological landscape.

## 4.2   Making Explicit Different "Usefulness" Characteristics

In addition, we found that other characteristics, both pertaining to the artefact, the design system as well as the context of the design system had a major impact on the design process. In the fitness-utility model, these characteristics are all captured as the usefulness of the design artefact (see [2, p.26:5]), as it includes "...factors of efficacy in performing the task, range of task cases performed, ease of use ease of learning, and cost-benefit in the performance of a task." In our study, we found it valuable to distinguish between the various characteristics of usefulness. The reason was that the main culprit of design choices often was to be found between different characteristics belonging to the 'usefulness' category. As an example, in workshop 3 we find decisions concerning on the one hand, the need of rigorous evaluation to guarantee the usefulness (accountability) of the system, and on the other hand the need not to delay the process too much. The motivation for the latter was two fold, a delay would result in further delays to extend the usefulness of the system by achieved mobility (ease of use) and in the same time reducing usefulness (cost-benefit in the performance of the task) due to increasing development efforts. For this reason we suggest that when designing DSR evaluation criteria for the purpose of innovation processes, it may be useful to distinguish between various characteristics of the usefulness category and acknowledge e.g. the below characteristics as a complement to the tentative characteristics of the fitness-utility model. Besides from hints found in the empirical material pertaining to making the artefact novel and elegant from a developer's perspective, other characteristics such as *robustness* and *accountability* (security and integrity) were the main foci.

The software engineering literature provides well-established practices and concepts for quality assurance. As an example, as defined by the IEEE standard [13, p.64], *robustness*, i.e. the degree to which a system or component can function correctly in the presence of invalid inputs or stressful environmental conditions, is well established as an important quality attribute [15]. Likewise, among desirable properties of design artefacts and design process, *accountability*, i.e. has attracted the attention of IS-researchers. The meaning of information accountability is that "[..] the use of information should be transparent so it is possible to determine whether a particular use is appropriate under a given set of rules and that the system enables individuals and institutions to be held accountable for misuse." [15, p.84].

As an example from our case, even though the developers devised one of the evaluation criteria for the system as '*new views should interact with users*', the openness was to cater for a type of usefulness, i.e. the accountability of the system. Furthermore, as expressed in workshop 1, enhancing user experience was a priority, rendering the software more useful by using 'technology more effectively in order to promote behaviour change' and enhance recruitment to the intervention studies e.g. via the design of the portal's layout'. However, these choices were mere means for increasing the usefulness of the artefact.

One other concrete example emanating from the one briefly discussed above is how these external ideals or requirements had major impact on the artefact quality improvement and the process of development and evaluation. From the actions taken after workshop 3, the risk of introducing changes in the production environment, with the risk of negative impact on the ongoing RCT-studies meant a focus on rigorous evaluation. Still this was no straightforward choice. To achieve a satisfactory system systematic testing was needed, however, the extra delay would require extra efforts in code synchronization (due to parallel development) and this further delaying desired step two development (i.e. *designing for mobility*). As automatic testing was ruled out, new means of comprehensive test of the new system were deemed necessary. In itself evidence of the impact of the values of the environment of the design system, rather than the design system itself, the accountability of the system could not be compromised. As a result, while analysing the source code changes during the prototype development it was found the extensive evaluation cycles paid an important role. Fig. 4 explains major events in the code change. For example sub system prototype development $(t_0-t_1)$, system prototype development $(t_2-t_6)$, prototype evaluation $(t_7-t_{20})$, and merging of branches $(t_7, t_{11}, t_{12}, t_{19})$. We can clearly see the evaluation resulted in major changes in the code, almost double than in the original development.

Summing up the empirical investigation of fitness-utility of DSR presented in this paper, we find that various ideals among developers with regards to characteristics of both fitness and usefulness impact the evolution of the design process. Given their impact, making explicit such dependent variables of DSR is imperative.

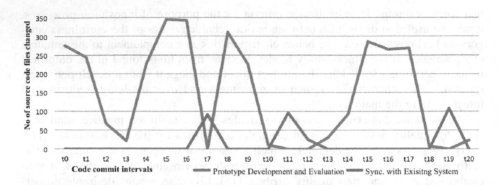

**Fig. 4.** Source Code Changes during Prototype Development and Evaluation

## 5     Conclusion

We have investigated how the DSR utility function is enacted in a development team in a process of innovation within a design system, and the characteristics, design choices and ideals that affected the emergence of the design process. We found the tentative list of Gill & Hevner [2] a useful foundation for our study. However, in light of the explicit design decisions and design activities carried out, the interaction between the characteristics, design reality tradeoffs including resource efficiency, alignment to existing technology as well as the utility of the artefact all had a continuous impacting on design choices in each of the three phases of the initial innovation process.

One the one hand, our empirical study suggests that it reasonable to propose that the fitness-utility model may benefit from a revision of its candidate characteristics to include the 'technological-ecological fit' as a new candidate. Technological-ecological fit highlights the IT artefact's relations to emerging boundary objects (e.g. plug-ins and APIs) and the way that those relations constrain and/or enable the mutability of the IT artifact. Technological-ecological fit was prevalent in the case of our inquiry, but it is not explicitly addressed in the utility-fitness model outlined by Gill & Hevner [2]. In addition, the utility of IT artefacts is highly dependent on issues related to information accountability issues and software robustness. On the other hand, given that the utility-fitness model is described at an abstract level, the proposed revisions are arguably too specific to be incorporated into the model. In either case, our empirical account of utility-fitness constitutes a contribution to the discourse on utility-fitness primarily through a rich illustration of how ideals among developers influence the emergence of a design process.

In future research, the focus of investigation is to be placed on the remaining phases of the innovation process as well as other design processes.

**Acknowledgements.** This work was conducted as part of the Uppsala University Psychosocial Care Programme (U-CARE) at Uppsala University. U-CARE is a strategic research programme funded by the Swedish Government through the Swedish Research Council. We would like to thank all anonymous reviewers for their valuable comments and suggestions.

# References

1. Hevner, A.R., March, S.T., Park, J., Ram, S.: Design science in information systems research. MIS Q. 28, 75–105 (2004)
2. Gill, T.G., Hevner, A.R.: A Fitness-Utility Model for Design Science Research. ACM Trans. Manag. Inf. Syst. 4 (2013)
3. Gregor, S., Jonas, D.: The Anatomy of a Design Theory. J. Assoc. Inf. Syst. 8, 312–335 (2007)
4. Rogers, E.M.: Diffusion of innovations. Free Press, New York (2003)
5. Baskerville, R.L., Kaul, M., Storey, V.C.: Unpacking the duality of design science. In: Thirty Second International Conference on Information Systems, Shanghai (2011)
6. Dewey, J.: Logic: The Theory of Inquiry. H. Holt and Company, New York (1938)
7. Klein, H.K., Myers, M.D.: A set of principles for conducting and evaluating interpretive field studies in information systems. MIS Q. 23, 67–94 (1999)
8. Orlikowski, W.J., Baroudi, J.J.: Studying Information Technology in Organizations: Research Approaches and Assumptions. Inf. Syst. Res. 2, 1–28 (1991)
9. Sjöström, J.: Designing Information Systems (2010)
10. Hevner, A.R.: A Three Cycle View of Design Science Research. Scand. J. Inf. Syst. 19, 87–92 (2007)
11. Cryer, J.: Resemble.js: Image analysis and comparison,
    http://huddle.github.io/Resemble.js/
12. Krippendorff, K.: The Semantic Turn: A New Foundation for Design. CRC Press, Boca Raton (2006)
13. Martin, R.C.: Design Principles and Design Patterns (2000),
    http://www.objectmentor.com
14. IEEE Standard Glossary of Software Engineering Terminology, IEEE Std. 610.12. (1990)
15. Shahrokni, A., Feldt, R.: A systematic review of software robustness. Inf. Softw. Technol. 55, 1–17 (2013)
16. Weitzner, D.J., Abelson, H., Berners-Lee, T., Feigenbaum, J., Hendler, J., Sussman, G.J.: Information accountability. Commun. ACM 51, 82–87 (2008)

# An Artifact for Improving Effective Medication Adherence

Neetu Singh and Upkar Varshney

Georgia State University, Atlanta, GA 30302-4015
{nsingh7,uvarshney}@gsu.edu

**Abstract.** In this paper, we focus on medication adherence and interventions to improve the level of medication adherence. We define Effective Medication Adherence (EMA) and study several interventions, including mobile reminders and context aware reminders, to improve the patterns of Effective Medication Adherence. The research question we address is: How context-aware reminders improve the Effective Medication Adherence? In this paper, we present a preliminary design of Health-IT artifact to implement multiple types of reminders. The performance results will be presented at the conference.

**Keywords:** Medication adherence, Interventions, Context aware reminders, Model, Health-IT artifact, Prototype Evaluation.

## 1 Introduction

Medication non-adherence is a well recognized and expensive problem in US. About 50% patients do not take their medications as prescribed and about 84% cite simple forgetfulness as the reason [1]. Medication adherence refers to the degree of conformity to the recommendations about day-to-day treatment with respect to the timing, dosage, and frequency [2]. The medication non-adherence results in $290 Billion annual cost to the US healthcare system [3]. More health benefits worldwide would result from improving adherence to existing treatments than developing any new medical treatments [4]. Although the consequences of suboptimal adherence to medications are quite variable, it clearly poses a threat to the health population [4,5,6].

In this paper, we focus on medication adherence and interventions to improve the level of medication adherence. As the average value and the pattern of medication consumption are important predictors of health outcomes, we define Effective Medication Adherence (EMA) as an attribute that can capture both of these predictors [7]. In this paper, our goal is to provide interventions, more specifically reminders and context aware-reminders, to improve the patterns of Effective Medication Adherence. The research question addressed in this study is how reminders and context aware reminders improve the patterns of Effective Medication Adherence? In this study we develop a Medication Intervention Model (MIM) as a Health-IT artifact. This intervention model will help the patients to improve the patterns of medication adherence. The novelty of MIM is that it is context sensitive and persistent. The context-aware

M.C. Tremblay et al. (Eds.): DESRIST 2014, LNCS 8463, pp. 304–311, 2014.
© Springer International Publishing Switzerland 2014

reminder will be provided to patient only if the patient had not consumed the dose at prescribed time and persistent reminder will be provided to the patient until the patient consumes the prescribed dose.

## 2    Method

Multiple IT artifacts have been defined [9]. The IT artifacts are created to enable the representation, analysis, understanding, and development of successful information systems within organizations [10]. The Design Science Research is motivated by the awareness of common problem. The effective solution of the problem is provided by developing a better interface [11]. We focus on how to incorporate interventions in the form of context-awareness in the design and evaluation of an artifact. The artifact can be implemented on wireless based smart medication management system [12] or smartphones. In this paper, artifact is developed using the guidelines [9] and plan to evaluate its effectiveness using the prototype and formal proofs [13]. The general approach followed in this paper is shown in Figure 1 and is inspired by several early approaches [8, 11, 14]. Earlier studies revealed that design science research is initiated with a significant prospect, challenging problem, or creativity/conjecture for some innovativeness in the application environment [9, 15, 16].

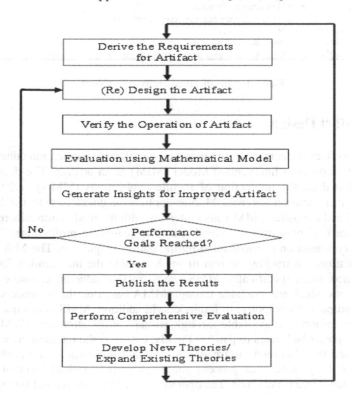

**Fig. 1.** The DSR Approach Used

**Requirements for Artifact:**
1. To support an intervention based on simple and context-aware reminders
   - Collecting real-time information from the patient and/or medication box on medication consumption
   - Deriving the context of medication consumption (the desired value and pattern of adherence, patient's needs and activities, recent consumption of doses, among others)
   - Computing the timing for reminders and context-aware reminders
   - Communicating with healthcare professionals as needed (analysis of consumption history and set of actions if not resolvable by the artifact)
2. Support for patient-mobility (preferable use of omnipresent smartphone infrastructure)
3. Assistive role to the patient (to improve the pattern of medication adherence) and healthcare professionals (not replacing the need for healthcare professionals but automating parts of the process to assist)

**Design of Artifact:**
1. Design a mobile application for medication adherence (Mobile Medication Application or MMA)
2. Utilize a smart medication dispenser that can dispense doses as necessary (Wireless Medication Box)
3. Design a server that
   - can communicate with patient and healthcare professionals (via mobile application) as needed and also with medication dispenser
   - can receive necessary dose consumption information from smart dispenser and/or the patient and can process medication consumption context of the patient
   - can generate simple and context-aware reminders as decide if and when these reminders be sent to the patient and how often
   - can analyze the consumption history and communicate with healthcare professional
4. Provide multi-network wireless access to various components (device, server) to support patient mobility

**Verification of the Artifact Operation**
1. Check if various components (application, server and medication dispenser) can interact among each other and with patient and healthcare professional
2. Check if various informational contents are received by the server
3. Check if context is generated correctly
4. Check the timing of reminders and context-aware reminders
5. Check the number of doses, reminders and consumption history for any inconsistencies

**Fig. 2.** Details of Three Steps in Our Work

# 3    Artifact Design

To study the effect of context aware reminders on effective medication adherence, we develop the Medication Intervention Model (MIM) as an artifact. The design of the artifact is based on the interaction of mobile applications (MMA) and the server (MMS) for medication adherence. Mobile application interacts with the healthcare professional and the patient. MMA also interacts with the medication adherence server to keep track of prescriptions provided by the healthcare professionals' office as well as the consumption of medication by the patient (Figure 3). The MIM supports these interactions and tracking as part of implementing the intervention for medication adherence. More specifically, MMS keeps track of adherence, side effects and dosing changes which are available through MMA based on the reminders provided to patient and patient's response to reminders. In addition, MMS keeps track of dose consumption information available through wireless medication box (WMB) which provides the prescribed doses to patient. Finally, based on the interactions with MMA and WMB and the additional information available, MMS generates a context-aware reminder for the patient. This process continues until a desired level of effective medication adherence is achieved. The operation of MIM is shown in Figure 4.

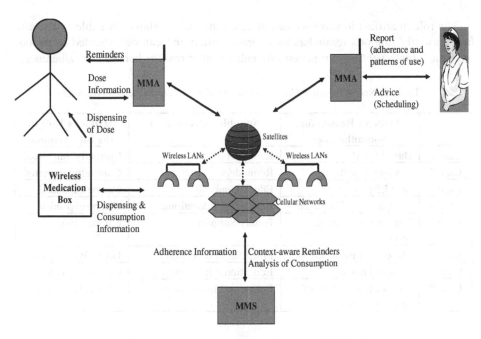

**Fig. 3.** MIM: Various Components and Information Exchange

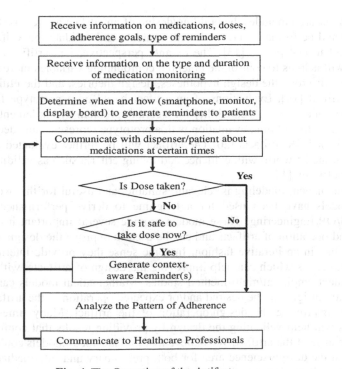

**Fig. 4.** The Operation of the Artifact

The role of artifact in various cases of non-adherence is shown in Table 1. The artifact currently supports reminders as an intervention and can be extended to include educational interventions for patients to address other reasons behind non-adherence.

**Table 1.** Non Adherence Cases and the Artifact's Role in the Intervention

|        | Primary Reason for Non-adherence | Suitable Intervention | Artifact's Role in the Intervention |
|--------|----------------------------------|-----------------------|-------------------------------------|
| Case 1 | Busy lifestyle | Reminders | Currently Supported |
| Case 2 | Cognitive Decline | Reminders | Currently Supported |
| Case 3 | Side Effects | Educational | Can be expanded |
| Case 4 | Complexity of Regimen | Reminders/Educational | Can be expanded |
| Case 5 | The length of chronic condition | Family Support | Can be expanded |
| Case 6 | The cost of medications | Financial Intervention | Difficult to expand |
| Case 7 | Lack of knowledge | Educational Intervention | Can be expanded |
| Case 8 | Lack of trust or lack of perceived need | Behavioral Interventions | Difficult to expand |

# 4    Performance Evaluation

Design research includes the building/design of an artifact as well as the evaluation of its use and performance [18]. We will evaluate and validate the artifact using prototype and formal proofs [13]. The ex-ante perspective, i.e., artificial evaluation methods will help us to control the potential confounding variables more carefully and to prove or disprove the design hypotheses, design theories, and the utility of the developed artifact [19]. Evaluations of an artifact based on a prototype facilitate the assessment of a solution's suitability for a certain problem by implementing the solution generically. In addition, evaluation with a prototype represents an adequate evaluation method for DSR artifacts [20].The artifact will be further evaluated (empirically) to demonstrate its worth with evidence addressing criteria such as validity, utility, quality, and efficacy [17].

Mathematical modeling is relevant, suitable, and useful for this work. Mathematical models have been used for a longtime to derive performance of systems in CS/DS/OR/Engineering. These models provide several important insights in the design and operation of artifacts and can be used to improve the design and operation of the artifact in an iterative fashion. In some sense they provide intermediate and immediate results which can help improving the design of artifacts, without waiting for subsequent empirical/multi-method studies. Mathematical models can provide many important insights in the desired and/or expected operation of the artifact and thus can help in improving the design/operation of the artifact. Many times, mathematical models will help validating the design by providing results that conform to expected performance of the artifact. We believe that mathematical models could be used effectively in the design science area for both preliminary and intermediate evaluation of artifacts, followed by a more empirical evaluation (Figure 5).

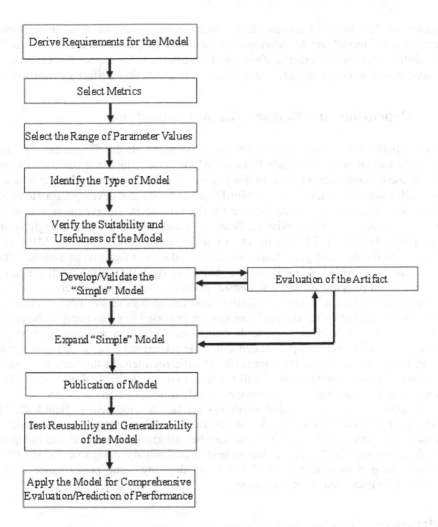

**Fig. 5.** The Use of Mathematical Model in Artifact Evaluation

We should be aware of numerous limitations and challenges in mathematical models. The development of models may take time especially when the artifact's design and operation is still evolving. Many times it is not clear what variables and metrics should be included and what parameters are utilized and where to get those values. The choice of model type is another challenge as decision on whether to use deterministic (closed-form) or stochastic (random-events) approach can affect the suitability and usefulness of model. The underlying assumptions in the model along with difficulty in validation, especially with error propagation inherent in some models, could reduce the usability of mathematical models. The complexity of models in deriving accurate results is another challenge.

The approach (Figure 5) we take in this paper is to develop simple model for quick results that can help verify the basic design and operation of the artifact and more complex models that can provide deeper understanding and more accurate results. More complex model will be developed as this work progresses and issues related to re-usability of model for other artifacts will be addressed. We expect that the comprehensive model, although complex, will be useful in predicting artifact's performance.

# 5     Conclusion and Research Recommendation

Lack of medication adherence is a serious problem. In Health-IT context, IT-based interventions can be used to study Effective Medication Adherence based on the patterns of medication consumption. In this paper, we utilize design science approach to design, develop and evaluate our Health-IT artifact. We are developing a Health-IT artifact with intelligence and persistence for the reminders. Interventions that stimulate better adherence to essential medications even slightly may meaningfully improve public health [21, 22]. The novelty of our Health-IT artifact, termed MIM, is its context-sensitiveness and persistence. The artifact does not focus on persistence alone which can be provided by many simple tools, but by utilizing the intelligence and information on patients, medication, consumption patterns, among others. It creates a sophisticated system to improve effective medication adherence. For example, the context-aware reminder to take medicine will be provided to patient only if the patient had not consumed the dose at prescribed time and persistent reminder will be provided to the patient until the patient consumes the prescribed dose. It will consider the dosing frequency and time for a particular dosing regimen. In this way the context aware reminders provided by MIM will not lead to the undesirable drug event (UDE), where more doses are taken than necessary or safe limit is crossed.

Our approach can be expanded to address artifact development in Health-IT. The designed artifact can be used to address several research problems in medication adherence and numerous interventions that can be introduced, evaluated and compared for effectiveness. In this paper, we present a preliminary design of the Health-IT artifact. Using a mathematical model, we are deriving some performance results, which will be presented at the conference.

# References

1. Sicre, A.: The Medication Non-Adherence Blog: White Coat Adherence (2007)
2. Cramer, J.A., Roy, A., Burrell, A., Fairchild, C.J., Fuldeore, M.J., Ollendorf, D.A., Wong, P.K.: Medication compliance and persistence: terminology and definitions. Value in Health 11(1), 44–47 (2008)
3. New England Healthcare Institute.: Thinking outside the pillbox: A system-wide approach to improving patient medication adherence for chronic disease. New England Health Care Institute (2009)
4. Sabatâe, E. (ed.): Adherence to long-term therapies: evidence for action. World Health Organization (2003)
5. Braithwaite, S., Shirkhorshidian, I., Jones, K., Johnsrud, M.: The Role of Medication Adherence in the US Healthcare System (2013)
6. Peterson, A.M., Takiya, L., Finley, R.: Meta-analysis of trials of interventions to improve medication adherence. American Journal of Health-System Pharmacy 60(7), 657–665 (2003)

7. Varshney, U., Singh, N.: A Framework for Studying Patterns of Effective Medication Adherence. In: Wireless Telecommunication Symposium, WTS (2013)
8. Hevner, A., Chatterjee, S.: Design science research in information systems, pp. 9–22. Springer, US (2010)
9. Hevner, A.R., March, S.T., Park, J., Ram, S.: Design science in information systems research. MIS Quarterly 28(1), 75–105 (2004)
10. March, S.T., Smith, G.F.: Design and natural science research on information technology. Decision Support Systems 15(4), 251–266 (1995)
11. Vaishnavi, V.K., Kuechler Jr., W.: Design science research methods and patterns: innovating information and communication technology. CRC Press (2007)
12. Varshney, U.: Wireless Medication Management System: Design and Performance Evaluation. In: Wireless Telecommunications Symposium (WTS), pp. 1–8 (2011)
13. Cleven, A., Gubler, P., Hüner, K.M.: Design alternatives for the evaluation of design science research artifacts. In: Proceedings of the 4th International Conference on Design Science Research in Information Systems and Technology, p. 19. ACM (2009)
14. Peffers, K., Tuunanen, T., Rothenberger, M.A., Chatterjee, S.: A design science research methodology for information systems research. Journal of Management Information Systems 24(3), 45–77 (2007)
15. Hevner, A.R.: The three cycle view of design science research. Scandinavian Journal of Information Systems 19(2), 87 (2007)
16. Iivari, J.: A paradigmatic analysis of information systems as a design science. Scandinavian Journal of Information Systems 19(2), 39 (2007)
17. Gregor, S., Hevner, A.R.: Positioning and presenting design science research for maximum impact. Management Information Systems Quarterly 37(2), 337–355 (2013)
18. Pries-Heje, J., Baskerville, R., Venable, J.: Soft design science research: Extending the boundaries of evaluation in design science research. In: Proceedings of the 2nd International Conference on Design Science Research in Information Systems and Technology, Pasadena, CA (2007)
19. Pries-Heje, J., Baskerville, R., Venable, J.: Strategies for Design Science Research Evaluation. In: Proceedingsof the 16th European Conference on Information Systems, Galway, Ireland, Paper 87 (2008)
20. March, S.T., Storey, V.C.: Design science in the information systems discipline: an introduction to the special issue on design science research. MIS Quarterly 32(4), 725–730 (2008)
21. Friedman, A., et al.: A telecommunications system for monitoring and counseling patients with hypertension. Impact on medication adherence and blood pressure control. Am. J. Hypertension 9, 285–292 (1996)
22. Haynes, R., Yao, X., Degani, A., Kripalani, S., Garg, A., McDonald, H.: Interventions to enhance medication adherence. Cochrane Database of Systematic Reviews, 1–96 (2005)

# Improving Case Management via Statistical Text Mining in a Foster Care Organization

Alfred Castillo, Arturo Castellanos, and Monica Chiarini Tremblay

Florida International University, Decision Sciences and Information Systems
{acast084,acast317,tremblay}@fiu.edu

**Abstract.** Every year more than 800,000 children in the U.S. spend time in foster care with 35% being on psychotropic medication. An increasing ratio of foster care children per case worker makes it challenging to balance their multiple roles during the lifecycle of a case. Although there are review boards for identifying cases that require special attention, scanning through all the unstructured data is time-consuming and is further complicated by poorly written, or incomplete, case note entries from the overwhelmed case workers. As part of a larger comprehensive study of a technology-centric foster care organization, we investigate a challenging nationwide problem of over-prescription of psychotropic drugs, which can lead to unnecessary deaths. We demonstrate how text mining techniques can significantly reduce the administrative requirements for auditing case notes by providing a smaller sample that is manageable yet be sensitive to exclusion of children showing evidence of psychotropic drug use. This should significantly lighten the load for case managers as they investigate possible cases.

**Keywords:** text mining, foster care, stm, design science, design artifact.

## 1 Introduction

Children in foster care are three to ten times more likely to suffer from mental health conditions (Harman, Childs et al. 2000) thus receiving behavioral health services to a greater extent compared to other children. Despite the fact that children in foster care represent less than 3% of all enrollees in the Medicaid program; they account for up to 41% of all mental health expenditures, a large part due to the use of psychotropic medication (Rubin, Matone et al. 2012). Psychotropic medication is prescribed to help them cope with behavioral problems such as attention-deficit/hyperactivity disorder (ADHD), depression, bipolar disorder, and psychotic disorders –in many cases these children are prescribed concomitant medication with dosages that are regularly used for adults. Despite their challenging lives as foster children, those with behavioral problems are frequently the ones that do not find a stable placement, limiting the possibility of reliable and consistent treatment (Zima, Bussing et al. 1999). This is dangerous especially when using: 1) antidepressants, in which adverse side effects include suicidal thoughts; 2) anti-anxiety medications, which side-effects could trigger blurred vision, drowsiness and dizziness, and nightmares; or 3) mood stabilizers,

M.C. Tremblay et al. (Eds.): DESRIST 2014, LNCS 8463, pp. 312–320, 2014.

which treat bipolar disorders but may have side effects such as hallucinations and suicidal thoughts (GAO 2011).

There are several examples of the unfortunate consequences in the news. In April of 2009, Gabriel Myers, a 7-year-old child who had been taken from his drug-abusing mother and who had been sexually abused in a previous foster home, locked himself in the bathroom and hanged from a detachable showerhead. At that time he had several psychiatric drugs prescribed –three of which were labeled as "black box" medication (the strongest advisory alert that the U.S. Food and Drug Administration issues), indicating that the drug can pose life-threatening adverse effects –including suicidal tendencies in children (Martinez 2010). Another impactful case is that of Denis Maltez, a 12-year-old autistic boy who died of "serotonin syndrome" after being prescribed several psychotropic drugs in the highest doses, dosages that are typically given to adults. In this particular case, DCF received a report from a school teacher stating that Denis was "sleeping in class, shaking, and trembling" and a second medical report from the hospital which stated that "Denis was sleepy because he was overmedicated" (Miller 4/18/2010).

To ensure safety and well being of the children, the Department of Children and Families (DCF) tracks, via the state run Safety Families Network (FSFN), all psychotropic drugs provided to children in foster care. Some of the fields include, but are not limited to, medication name, dosage prescribed, number of refills, prescribing physician, whether the drug is used as psychotropic medication, and the start and stop date. This system assumes that the information introduced by the case manager is reliable and complete, but unfortunately there are few built-in mechanisms to prevent data quality issues. For example, a generic medication to which the caseworker does not know the brand equivalent is placed as "other". Adding to data quality problems is the ability to leave blank fields (Group 2009).

The focus of this manuscript is to determine foster children that are on psychotropic medication via text mining. Because there are many interrelated behavioral indicators (e.g. child's physical, mental, or emotional well-being) of psychotropic medication use, it is important to use a combination of domain experts and literature to meaningfully evaluate the text mining outcomes. These factors are interspersed in the case notes written by the case manager when they engage with the foster children through visits or telephone calls. At a minimum there is one visit per month that is documented in a case note, but some foster children may have as many as 20+ case notes in one month. As a result, the number of case notes of all the foster children could number in the millions and makes it difficult to oversee more than a portion of records manually. This is the focus of our research question: can Statistical Text Mining (STM) help to complement current practices in classifying and prioritizing cases of psychotropic drug use in foster children? Our artifact will improve (Gregor and Hevner 2013)or complement current practices for a more efficient and effective method. In the subsequent sections we discuss our methodology, present our results and analysis, and discuss conclusions and future work.

## 2    Methodology

We follow the design science methodology proposed by (Hevner and Chatterjee 2010) to design a text-mining artifact in attempt to solve a problem that is relevant to any foster care organization. We evaluate the results of our design by benchmarking with the results given by expert case managers. Text mining is a process of knowledge discovery via a set of techniques and tools that allow for "nontrivial extraction of implicit, previously unknown, and potentially useful information from given [free-form, or textual] data" (Feldman and Dagan 1995). A conceptual framework that describes the process used in this study is that of the Cross Industry Standard Process for Data Mining (CRISP-DM) model (see Fig. 1), which has been used in a similar capacity before (Tremblay, Berndt et al. 2009). As illustrated, it is closely tied to the design science guidelines, but is specifically tailored for text mining. Although another popular model is that of Sample, Explore, Modify, Model and Assess (SEMMA), we chose CRISP-DM for the explicit emphasis on business understanding as the starting point, and its intuitive flow.

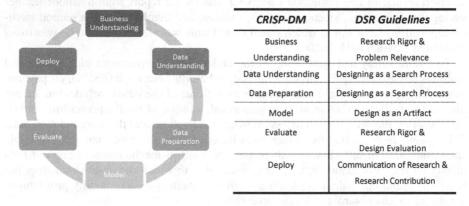

| CRISP-DM | DSR Guidelines |
|---|---|
| Business Understanding | Research Rigor & Problem Relevance |
| Data Understanding | Designing as a Search Process |
| Data Preparation | Designing as a Search Process |
| Model | Design as an Artifact |
| Evaluate | Research Rigor & Design Evaluation |
| Deploy | Communication of Research & Research Contribution |

**Fig. 1.** CRISP-DM Framework and Relation to DSR Guidelines

The steps in CRISP-DM are iterative in that results, or issues, in a current step of the framework can be improved by revisiting a previous step. In this way: not understanding the data can be mitigated by better understanding the business and how they use the data; having issues in preparing the data can be remedied by having a deeper understanding of the data's structure, distribution, and meaning; choosing between models can be limited by how the data was prepared (ex: some models do not fare well with nominal data but may be able to handle numerical, such as frequencies of occurrence); evaluation results can usually be improved by revisiting the model that generated the results and fine-tuning; the decision to deploy within an organization is based on evaluation results; and once an organization is using the deployed model it may generate new ideas, refine old ones, or change business assumptions which results in a new cycle. The underlying principle is to take due diligence at each step to prevent "garbage-in garbage-out" (GIGO) from occurring. What follows is how each step was executed for this study.

## 2.1    Business and Data Understanding

Development of a deep understanding of the foster care organization, and social work case management in general, is the result of a seven-year research relationship with a leading community based care organization. To gain a broad understanding of the organization, meetings were held with the Chief Information Officer, Chief of Clinical Services, Chief of Program Operations, Community Based Care Director, Director of Quality Assurance, senior business analyst, and several case workers. Initial meetings were face-to-face and open-ended to allow for the free-flow of ideas and the subsequent extraction of relevant issues that can be addressed by the research team as part of a comprehensive research agenda. The current issue being addressed is that of identifying children that are on psychotropic medication but are not identified in the system as such. Providing a solution to this would have a three-fold impact. First, it would save lives. Second, it would improve auditing outcomes for the organization. Finally, it would free up limited human resources for other critical tasks.

Case management is a process that involves Intake, Initial Assessment or Investigation, Family Assessment, Planning, Service Provision, Evaluation of Family Progress, and eventually Case Closure. A significant amount of time is spent on investigating, intaking, and placement tasks, but generally the case workers spend the bulk of their time performing assessments of out-of-home foster children. They must visit them monthly, take a GPS marked and time-stamped photograph of the child, and conduct an interview. Most case notes are written while off-site via a Blackberry application. Due to the tight time constraints of the case workers they generally rush to fill it out as quickly as possible in order to move on with their busy schedules. Unfortunately, the required fields of the application were designed from a minimal one-to-one cardinality perspective so that only the fields that are common to all cases are the ones with validation. Indirectly, this results in data inconsistency, as some case workers rely on filling in those more specific fields when they return to the office, but often get sidetracked and forget. Also, the rush in putting in these case notes on a mobile device lowers the data quality with the insertion of fragmented sentences and commonly misspelled words in case notes. Recent changes in state statutes now require additional information to be collected; however the process followed by case workers via system design does not ensure complete data collection.

## 2.2    Data Preparation

Among the most important data preparation activities was to solicit the help of nurse case managers to develop an accurate sample to construct a "gold standard" dataset with correctly labeled cases of our target variable, psychotropic medication use. All case notes for one particular sub-organization that manages a large portion of the foster children were manually checked and coded accurately for the month of November. This was particularly challenging because of the high reporting requirements in case management. The resulting dataset was inundated with case notes of 32 different types of varying frequency for 404 children, of which 39 were confirmed to be on psychotropic medication. After filtering out new cases, the final sample included notes on 358 children, of which 33 were confirmed to be on psychotropic medication.

Initially, it seemed promising that specific case note types (such as those for run-aways) resulted in high correlations with the target variable (taking psychotropic medications); however, the low frequency in a perfect sample population becomes almost meaningless in the imperfect larger population of interest. For this reason, the focus became on analyzing one specific type of case note: "Home Visit-Child's

Current Residence" visits had the richest contextual information about the child's case but that is the most inclusive.

All the data was retrieved from the secure front-end website via Ruby on Rails scripts using the mechanize gem. Since there is health related information contained in the various case notes we had to follow HIPAA guidelines for personal health information (PHI) identifiers. Children and case identifiers were de-identified by generating a random number and using that number for reference of the child/case.

Names are commonly de-identified by creating a lookup table of various types of nouns (first names, titles, etc.) and then parsing the text to replace any identified ones with some placeholder. Using sentence processing heuristics can help in situations where individuals' names can coincide with dictionary words by either removing them or labeling them as "ambiguous" for manual processing (Neamatullah, Douglass et al. 2008). All labels related to location, contact information, and other PHI was removed. For the free-text section, because the child and other individuals directly involved with him/her were identified in labeled sections, those names formed the lookup table for parsing the free-text. Although the dates for the case notes themselves were not particularly important, the order was, as it tells a chronologically ordered story. While processing the case notes the dates were replaced with an ordinal number (1, 2, 3...n) to represent the recency of it relative to the child's other case notes. This was all loaded into SQL server (see Figure 2).

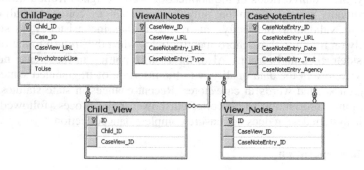

**Fig. 2.** SQL Table Structure

## 2.3     Model

Text mining can be achieved through different approaches such as keyword-based or regular expression matching, natural language processing (NLP), or machine learning algorithms. The keyword approach is typically not powerful enough for extracting information and the NLP, an ontology-based deductive approach, requires a high degree of customization (Tremblay, Berndt et al. 2009). In this paper we are going to focus on an inductive machine learning approach ideal for classification. First, an expert case manager labels a small set of case notes as "Yes" (uses psychotropic medication) and "No" (no use of psychotropic medication) –our corpus with target variable. Second, we excluded template phrases from the corpus. Once we had our gold standard, we loaded the data into WEKA–an open-source software tool that contains a collection of machine learning algorithms (Hall, Frank et al. 2009). The process followed is the one showed in Figure 3.

Modeling involves first tokenizing the text in the corpus into a large document-by-term matrix. Words can be left as is or can be reduced into stemmed words, which are not necessarily linguistically valid words (e.g. bruis: bruise, bruises, bruised). Due to every term not being equally predictive, for attribute selection we used the InfoGain evaluator, which evaluates the worth of an attribute by determining the information gain with respect to the target variable; the ranker then ranks the attributes based on the threshold value we set.

Also, we need to consider the tradeoff between sensitivity and specificity. In this study the sensitivity is the ratio of predicted children on psychotropic medication to the population of children on psychotropic medication, and specificity is the ratio of children predicted not to be on medication to all children not on medication. We included cost sensitivity to systematically force the algorithms to view the false negatives as a cost function. The cost matrix was configured with a 10 times higher cost for missing a child that is on psychotropic medication (e.g. penalizing for false negatives), than the cost for mistakenly including a child that is not on psychotropic medication. For comparison, we also omitted cost sensitivity.

The last step was to run the data into several machine-learning algorithms and evaluated the results, which we discuss in Section 3.

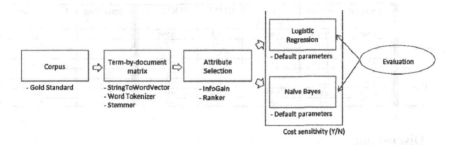

**Fig. 3.** Data mining process

# 3    Results and Evaluation

We used Logistic Regression and Naïve Bayes machine learning algorithms to develop a total of 8 models. In Table 2, we show the results for each model, and outline whether we included stemming or used whole words, and whether we applied a cost function or not. The performance of each model is compared using commonly accepted metrics: recall, precision, root mean squared error (RMSE), F-measure, and ROC curve (ratio of sensitivity to one-minus specificity). Recall (R) reflects the percentage of correct positive predictions out of all the possible positives in the training set, precision (P) reflects the percentage of correct positive predictions out of the predicted positives, while the F-measure is simply a ratio of overall goodness of fit for precision and recall. The definitions are provided in Table 1 where TP is true positives, FP is false positives, TN is true negatives, FN is false negatives, and y is the actual value that is compared to the predicted value ($\hat{y}$) for each n in the set of predictions.

Based on statistical results, the Logistic model had a better overall fit for STM than Naïve Bayes by .373 in F-measure. The best performing Logistic model resulted in 322 TN, 30 TP, 3 FN, and 3 FP. The best performing Naïve Bayes model resulted in 276 TN, 30 TP, 3 FN, and 49 FP. The discrepancies illustrates where the Logistic model outperformed Naïve Bayes. It was due to the larger number of false positives in general which significantly lowered precision. The individual stemmed terms that were found most predictive were: abilif, fight, subst, suspen, disrespect, withdraw, misus, fought, dead, dissapoint, grim, inm, dcf, diagnos. These resulted in increases to precision and a minor decrease to recall. Cost sensitivity resulted in a marginal increase in recall, for a larger decrease in precision.

**Table 1.** Formulas for Evaluation

| Precision | Recall | F-measure | RMSE |
|---|---|---|---|
| $P = \dfrac{TP}{TP + FP}$ | $R = \dfrac{TP}{TP + FN}$ | $F = \dfrac{2(P * R)}{P + R}$ | $\sqrt{\dfrac{\sum_{i=1}^{n}(y_i - \hat{y}_i)^2}{n}}$ |

**Table 2.** Evaluation results

|  | Precision | Recall | F-measure | RMSE | ROC curve | Stemming | Cost sensitivity |
|---|---|---|---|---|---|---|---|
| Logistic | **0.909** | **0.909** | **0.909** | **0.103** | **0.998** | No | No |
| | 0.717 | 1.000 | 0.835 | 0.151 | 0.998 | No | Yes |
| | 0.966 | 0.848 | 0.903 | 0.103 | 0.998 | Yes | No |
| | 0.717 | 1.000 | 0.835 | 0.151 | 0.998 | Yes | Yes |
| Naïve Bayes | 0.323 | 0.970 | 0.485 | 0.408 | 0.970 | No | No |
| | 0.267 | 0.970 | 0.418 | 0.468 | 0.970 | No | Yes |
| | **0.378** | **0.909** | **0.536** | **0.366** | **0.971** | Yes | No |
| | 0.327 | 0.970 | 0.489 | 0.409 | 0.971 | Yes | Yes |

# 4    Discussion

Which model is ultimately chosen will have different implications in practice. The 8 models illustrate this tradeoff and motivate our discussion. There are models that performed with higher precision, and others that performed with higher recall. In the former, clinical case managers have a lower load of documents to revise at the expense of missing potential positive cases. In the latter, they have a higher load of documents to review with the benefit of including more of the positive cases that are misclassified. For example, the "best" performing model (Logistic in bold) was cho-sen based on F-measure, but with a recall of 0.909 it actually misclassified 3 children that were on psychotropic medication. If this is deemed unacceptable, then the second Logistic model would be chosen, which resulted in a perfect classification of all children using psychotropic medication (recall = 1.000) at the expense of merely an additional 10 cases that were incorrectly identified as possible cases of psychotropic use (precision = 0.717). In practice these "small" additional 10 cases means the case workers would be processing 116.66% more erroneously classified records overall.

## 5    Conclusion and Future Work

This work in progress (WIP) evaluated the feasibility of using statistical text mining on case manager notes to identify foster children on psychotropic medication that have not yet been identified. The results show potential to significantly reduce the workload of clinical caseworkers by refocusing their efforts to a smaller subsample.

As in most small-scale studies, it is not without limitations. The sample was only 404 and was specifically for one organization, which may limit the generalizability. Also, the data was only for one month, which did not necessitate the creation of a corpus immune to events that occur during the lifecycle of case management.

Future work should incorporate additional datasets to further refine the model to ensure applicability to a broader audience. In addition, stemming, refining stop lists, using different algorithms that deal better with sparse matrices, and improving the gold standard by iteratively working with nurse case managers should be explored. This project focuses specifically on identifying children using psychotropic medication and preventing tragic cases like that of Gabriel Myers and Denis Maltez, but could be generalized to other contexts within the organizations, such as predicting instances of abuse and neglect.

## References

1. Feldman, R., Dagan, I.: Knowledge Discovery in Textual Databases (KDT). KDD (1995)
2. GAO, HHS Guidance Could Help States Improve Oversight of Psychotropic Prescriptions. Foster Children, U.S. Government Accountability Office (2011)
3. Gregor, S., Hevner, A.R.: Positioning And Presenting Design Science Research For Maximum Impact. MIS Quarterly 37(2) (2013)
4. Group, G.M.W.: Psychotropic Medication: For Children in Out of Home Care Business Rules with Data Entry Guidelines and Frequently Asked Questions. Special Initiatives, Florida Department of Children and Families (2009)
5. Hall, M., Frank, E., Holmes, G., Pfahringer, B., Reutemann, P., Witten, I.H.: The WEKA data mining software: an update. ACM SIGKDD Explorations Newsletter 11(1), 10–18 (2009)
6. Harman, J.S., Childs, G.E., Kelleher, K.J.: Mental health care utilization and expenditures by children in foster care. Archives of Pediatrics & Adolescent Medicine 154(11), 1114–1117 (2000)
7. Hevner, A., Chatterjee, S.: Design science research in information systems. Springer (2010)
8. Martinez, E.: After 7-Year-Old Gabriel Myers' Suicide, Fla. Bill Looks To Tighten Access To Psychiatric Drugs. CBS News (2010)
9. Miller, C.M.: Red Flags Overlooke. In: Prescription Drug Death of 12-Year-Old (April 18, 2010), http://www.psychsearch.net/red-flags-overlooked-in-prescription-drug-death-of-12-year-old/
10. Neamatullah, I., Douglass, M.M., Li-wei, H.L., Reisner, A., Villarroel, M., Long, W.J., Szolovits, P., Moody, G.B., Mark, R.G., Clifford, G.D.: Automated de-identification of free-text medical records. BMC Medical Informatics and Decision Making 8(1), 32 (2008)

11. Rubin, D., Matone, M., Huang, Y.-S., Dosreis, S., Feudtner, C., Localio, R.: Interstate variation in trends of psychotropic medication use among Medicaid-enrolled children in foster care. Children and Youth Services Review 34(8), 1492–1499 (2012)
12. Tremblay, M.C., Berndt, D.J., Luther, S.L., Foulis, P.R., French, D.D.: Identifying fall-related injuries: Text mining the electronic medical record. Information Technology and Management 10(4), 253–265 (2009)
13. Zima, B.T., Bussing, R., Crecelius, G.M., Kaufman, A., Belin, T.R.: Psychotropic medication use among children in foster care: relationship to severe psychiatric disorders. American Journal of Public Health 89(11), 1732–1735 (1999)

# Instantiation Validity in IS Design Research

Roman Lukyanenko, Joerg Evermann, and Jeffrey Parsons

Faculty of Business Administration, Memorial University of Newfoundland
St. John's, NL Canada
{roman.lukyanenko,jevermann,jeffreyp}@mun.ca

**Abstract.** Studies that involve information technology artifacts play a prominent role in Information Systems (IS) research. We argue that special attention needs to be paid to ensuring the validity of such studies. This paper makes three contributions to IS research. First, it introduces the concept of instantiation validity as broadly applicable to IS design research, and distinct from existing notions of validity. Second, the paper identifies several sources of instantiation validity threats that can arise in IS design research. Third, it points to the need for guidelines to address these threats and demonstrate validity in design research.

**Keywords:** IS research, validity, design science, instantiation validity.

## 1    Introduction

Information Systems (IS) researchers investigate the effective design and use of information technology (IT) at the individual and organizational levels. Arguably, the IT artifact lies at the core of the discipline, with central research questions addressing how information technology is designed and how the design of information technology is influenced by and impacts the environment. Given this focus, properties of IT artifacts are frequently conceptualized as intervening and dependent variables in IS theories and models. In this paper, we focus on validity issues that arise when creating or reusing IT artifacts to evaluate theories. Specifically, we focus on implemented software systems that operationalize one or more theoretical constructs. These software systems can be either created for the purpose of theory evaluation (e.g., [1]) or be existing real-world software systems identified by researchers for their special features of interest (e.g., [2]).

Typically, a construct instantiated in a software system is an independent or predictor variable in a theoretical model. The latter could be a behavioral theory that predicts and/or explains some focal phenomena [3, 4]. It can also be a theory of system design [5, 6], in which case the software instantiates some abstract design principles.

For example, Komiak and Benbasat [2] investigate the independent variables 'perceived personalization' and 'familiarity'. To establish their impact on the dependent variable of interest (adoption intentions mediated by trusting beliefs), they selected two existing software systems that were assumed to vary in the levels of perceived personalization and familiarity. In their study, the validity of a conclusion such as

M.C. Tremblay et al. (Eds.): DESRIST 2014, LNCS 8463, pp. 321–328, 2014.
© Springer International Publishing Switzerland 2014

*personalization of an IS leads to its increased adoption* depends critically on whether the chosen artifacts faithfully instantiated the underlying theoretical construct of personalization and levels thereof. This is analogous to the problem of measurement of theoretical constructs, where an inappropriately chosen measurement may fail to reveal manipulation or inadvertently measure the wrong construct. Likewise, an instantiation that is incongruent with the constructs it is intended to express fails to adequately represent its underlying construct. This may occur even when the artifact itself is a working software system and may undermine the validity of the conclusions that can be drawn from the research.

We introduce the term **instantiation validity** to specifically refer to the validity of IT artifacts as instantiations of theoretical constructs. Instantiation validity is analogous to the concepts of construct validity in survey research [7-9] and research design validity in experimental work [10]. However, executable software systems differ in important ways from "traditional" experimental stimuli, such as images or diagrams. Thus, while existing principles of validity apply to IS design research, we claim that unique challenges inherent in the design of IT artifacts warrant additional attention.

Despite the growing interest in IS design research, no established notion of the instantiation validity of artifacts exists. March and Smith [11] see the role of the artifact only as demonstrating the feasibility of a design, and are not concerned with its validity with respect to a theoretical construct. Gregg et al. [12] suggest that "researchers may elect to develop a system to demonstrate the validity of the solution" (p. 175) but do not offer criteria to establish the validity of such systems. Hevner et al. [13] state only that "rigor is derived from the effective use of the knowledge base ... Success is predicated on the researcher's skilled selection of appropriate techniques to develop or construct a theory or artifact" (p. 88). In fact, the term "validity" appears only twice in that seminal paper. A recent paper on design science research by Gregor and Hevner [6] states that artifacts are evaluated based on their "validity, utility, quality, and efficacy", where "[v]alidity means that the artifact works and does what it is meant to do" (p. 351). In their terms, a functioning artifact is necessary but not sufficient to establish instantiation validity; the artifact must also do what it is meant to do.

A notion similar to instantiation validity has been discussed in recent debates in the design science literature. Notably, Parsons and Cole [14] and Burton-Jones et al. [15] propose guidelines for evaluating scripts (artifacts) generated using theoretically-motivated variations of conceptual modeling grammars. For example, Parsons and Cole [14] encourage researchers to ensure that different scripts are informationally equivalent with respect to what is being measured, whereas Burton-Jones et al. [15] argue that informational inequivalence is sometimes inevitable. Similarly, a recent debate on "construct validity" [16, 17] focused on whether the constructed design artifact (in this case, a UML diagram) was congruent with the intended theoretical constructs. Motivating directly our notion of instantiation validity, Arazy et al. [18] claimed that the ad hoc manner in which artifacts were designed contributed to inconclusive and mediocre findings in recommender systems research, while Hovorka and Gregor [19] lament that IS design science researchers rarely explain how theoretical causality is instantiated in actual systems. These debates demonstrate awareness of the potential problem in the research community but, at the same time show the lack of concrete guidance or criteria for the establishment of instantiation validity.

This work-in-progress paper makes three main contributions. First, considering existing notions of validity, it introduces the concept of instantiation validity as an important concept in IS design research. Second, the paper explores the sources of instantiation validity threats that can arise in IS design research. Third, it points to the need for guidelines for researchers to address these threats and demonstrate the validity of a design study.

# 2     Existing Validity Research and Instantiation Validity

Validity in scientific research refers to the extent to which inferences and conclusions are warranted and justified from the empirical evidence obtained [20]. The nature and threats to validity in experiments and surveys, and ways to address or mitigate them, have been extensively discussed in the IS literature [7, 8, 21].

Survey research creates questions ("measurement items") in order for researchers to measure theoretical constructs corresponding to cognitive or emotional states of research subjects. Construct validity in survey research asks whether the measurement items are collectively a good representation of the construct and only that construct [9]. Churchill [22] and Hinkin [23] offer additional guidelines, including: employing focus groups and critical incident techniques to generate items; keeping measurement items clear, short and simple; and controlling for (or avoiding) context effects. Research on stimulus design also provides input for instantiation validity. Benbasat [10] characterizes a stimulus as faulty when it does not separate the focal theoretical construct from others. A common guideline in survey and experimental research is to use standardized measurement items (e.g., [24]) or standardized stimuli (e.g., [25]).

The norms from survey research and research design can inform guidelines for instantiation validity. For example, they suggest that a particular feature of the artifact should instantiate only one construct and that artifacts should only vary in relevant features. One could also conclude that design features should be "simple" or "atomic". It remains unclear, however, to what extent these norms can be applied to IS design studies as the nature of software presents specific threats to instantiation validity.

# 3     Threats to Instantiation Validity

Real(istic) IS artifacts are considerably more complex than the stimuli used in many experimental settings or the questionnaire items in survey research. Furthermore, rapid change in information technology introduces new ways to build IS. Moreover, whereas both theoretical constructs and measurement items are expressed using the common medium of natural language, this is not the case for software systems. We elaborate on these points by presenting threats to validity unique to IT artifacts.

## 3.1   Artifact Instantiation Space

Most IS theories are mid-range theories [4, 26, 27]; that is, they are moderately abstract (i.e., they do not purport to explain everything) but "close enough to observed data to be incorporated in propositions that permit empirical testing" [28].

This intentional generality of IS theories makes it difficult to derive specific design choices based on IS theoretical constructs (e.g., what programming language to use, how to design user interfaces, where to place navigation buttons). A typical software project may contain thousands of lines of programming code and many objects in the user-interface. Since the theoretical construct frequently lacks guidance for the exact ways to develop an IT artifact, there can be a large number of design options to choose from [27]. We call the set of possible variations in software features the *instantiation space*. As a result of a large instantiation space and limited guidance by the focal construct, there may be considerable ambiguity when instantiating a theory.

In the absence of explicit guidance, the connection from theoretical propositions to actual design is made by leveraging knowledge outside the focal theory. This may involve tacit knowledge, prior experience of developers, auxiliary theories, trial-and-error, or simply the intuition of developers [27]. Instantiations are also influenced by available technologies, developer expertise, familiarity of developers with certain development techniques, budget and time constraints.

A large instantiation space threatens instantiation validity. As there may be many ways to instantiate a theoretical construct, it is unclear how specific implementations impact evaluation results. Even small features of an artifact can produce substantial change in a dependent variable of interest. For example, Shepherd et al. [29] find "that a single horizontal line on one GSS interface led to an increase of 23 percent in ideation productivity" (p. 16). Lukyanenko and Parsons [27] argued that many implementation decisions have to be made in an ad hoc manner that may undermine theoretical predictions. Briggs et al. [30] concede that "subtle differences in interface can cause major [outcome] differences". A challenge of IS design research, therefore, is to account for the consequences of the chosen implementation and ensure that they do not interfere or interact with the variables of interest in unpredictable ways.

## 3.2    Artifact Complexity

While the threat posed by the instantiation space is due to the abstraction level and lack of theoretical guidance, the complexity of IT artifacts may exacerbate the lack of theoretical determination. In contrast to many experimental stimuli or questionnaire items, a software system is a complex entity with many interacting parts that provide the functionality to manifest one or more theoretical constructs. We identify two specific causes of threats: auxiliary features and emergent properties.

**Auxiliary Features.** The complexity of software systems allows, and often requires, the researcher to imbue the system with properties that relate to other than the focal theoretical constructs. For example, an IS designed to reflect theoretical constructs dealing with user interface design will also require realistic data for the user to interact with, a database to store data in and an operating system to execute on. Such necessary auxiliary elements, which can affect the focal properties of an IS, present threats to instantiation validity.

Returning to the example from [2], which posits that a personalized IS leads to high user acceptance, a researcher selects (or constructs) an artifact with particular features and measures user acceptance. However, the data in the system, chosen by the researcher for the study, may interact with the theoretical construct. In a simple case, users may erroneously consider the data they view in their acceptance decision. One solution is to use equivalent data. However, it may be the case that the required user interface features do not allow for equivalence of data across conditions (interaction effect), in which case this threat cannot be addressed with experimental designs.

**Emergent Properties.** The complexity of a software system may produce emergent properties and behavior, arising as a result of the components being put together. For example, presentation complexity and information overload are emergent properties of the way information is presented to a user. Unless emergent properties are part of the focal theory, they may interact with other constructs in unpredicted ways. For example, users may demonstrate low intentions to adopt a well-personalized system because of the complexity introduced to produce the effect of personalization. This would be in contrast to theoretical expectations and, more importantly, is not due to the focal construct, leading the researcher to wrongly reject her theory.

Given the nature of software artifacts in IS design research, it is unrealistic to expect any given instantiation to fully represent the underlying construct and only that construct. This is strikingly different from survey research that calls for measurement items to exhaust the content domain to be covered by the construct. The challenge becomes to ensure and demonstrate that the chosen instantiation allows the desired inferences and conclusions.

### 3.3 Artifact Cost

When IS design research uses purpose-built software artifacts to evaluate a theory, the construction of these artifacts is relatively more expensive than the development of experimental stimuli like simple pictures or diagrams. Software design, programming, and testing, even when done only for academic research, are resource-intensive. This relative cost of software artifacts can lead to validity problems that must be addressed.

Given the expense of constructing the artifact, researchers typically find themselves in the situation where only a single artifact can be constructed. In contrast to experimental research, where alternative experimental conditions can be created by the combination of different stimuli, and survey research, where multiple questions can be designed easily and cheaply, IS design research is limited to one or a very small number of artifacts. This limits the ability to use experimental designs to control for confounding effects, and the ability to demonstrate validity and reliability by comparing multiple implementations.

Artifact cost may also prevent researchers from testing multiple levels of a construct. For example, when testing the impact of personalization on adoption, a researcher may instantiate different levels of personalization. However, very high levels of personalization are likely to be costly and technologically difficult. Thus, a failure to find a significant effect may in fact be due to the researcher having instantiated in the artifact an insufficient range of levels of the focal construct.

### 3.4 Artifact Medium and Distance

In survey design, the theoretical construct and the items intended to measure it are expressed in the same medium – natural language. Thus, construction of questionnaire items can employ words already present in the definition of the construct. This process ensures a minimal "distance" and maximal congruence between the instantiated instrument and the construct (ensuring face and content validity).

As in this paper we focus on artifacts that are software systems, the instantiated artifact is expressed in different medium, executable software. Thus, there is no convenient way of judging the *distance* between the definition of the theoretical construct, and the instantiated artifact. Further, because of the complexity of the artifact, the instantiated property often cannot be trivially or directly derived from the theoretical definition, adding a "conceptual distance" between construct and instantiation. We argue that the medium shift and "distance" threatens validity. At each step of moving from construct to implementation there is a potential for confounds. Just as importantly, each of these steps requires validation which, given the instantiation space and lack of theoretical guidance, may prove difficult.

### 3.5    Technological Progress

Related to the medium shifts between construct and instantiation is the issue of technological progress. This concerns not only specific implementation technologies, such as particular programming languages and operating systems, but, more broadly, system development paradigms. For example, user interfaces are shifting from the desktop metaphor towards touch-enabled interfaces. For the design perspective, we have witnessed different paradigms, such as procedural, functional, object-oriented, and declarative. System architectures have moved from distributed, towards rich client, towards thin (or web-based) client. Additionally, and perhaps more importantly, the shift in foundational paradigms, such as system architecture, programming, and user interfaces, mean that the notion of a valid instantiation may change over time. For example, what might be regarded as a complex interaction in a mouse-based interface might become relatively simple in a touch-based interface.

These shifts in technologies imply that artifacts intended to express the same theoretical construct are designed and implemented differently over time, and will behave differently and exhibit a different user interface. This requires that validity be re-established for every instantiation.

## 4    Discussion, Future Work, and Conclusion

Establishing validity is important for developing and testing theories. The prevalence of design research in the IS discipline raises the question of validity in studies that use information technology artifacts. Considering the nature of IS design research, we raise the question of what it means for a software system to be a valid instantiation of a target theoretical construct and introduce instantiation validity as a unique concern for IS researchers and reviewers of their work.

We argue there are threats specific to instantiation validity rooted in the vast space of design choices, complexity of software systems, cost of software development, the distance between constructs and their instantiations and rapid technological change. Unless addressed, these threats may undermine inferences and conclusions drawn from the obtained empirical findings. Unless sound criteria for evaluating instantiation validity of IS design research is applied, doubts remain whether results are due to extraneous factors or attributable to idiosyncratic software development.

To begin addressing this issue, guidelines are needed for IS design research to mitigate threats to instantiation validity. Such guidelines can support researchers in constructing and using artifacts, as well as reviewers and readers in assessing the quality of IS design contributions. Our future work will focus on developing guidelines to address the threats identified in this paper. Further, we will examine the applicability and transferability of guidelines that exist for experimental and survey work, and their limitations in the design science context. We hope this paper will become a starting point for the development of guidelines for instantiation validity.

# References

1. Kamis, A., Koufaris, M., Stern, T.: Using an Attribute-Based Decision Support System for User-Customized Products Online: An Experimental Investigation. MIS Quarterly 32, 159–177 (2008)
2. Komiak, S.Y.X., Benbasat, I.: The Effects of Personalization and Familiarity on Trust and Adoption of Recommendation Agents. MIS Quarterly 30, 941–960 (2006)
3. Gregor, S.: The Nature of Theory in Information Systems. MIS Quarterly 30, 611–642 (2006)
4. Weber, R.: Evaluating and Developing Theories in the Information Systems Discipline. Journal of the Association for Information Systems 13, 1–30 (2012)
5. Gregor, S., Jones, D.: The Anatomy of Design Theory. Journal of the Association for Information Systems 8, 312–335 (2007)
6. Gregor, S., Hevner, A.R.: Positioning and Presenting Design Science Research for Maximum Impact. MIS Quarterly 37, 337–355 (2013)
7. Straub, D., Boudreau, M., Gefen, D.: Validation Guidelines for IS Positivist Research. Communications of the Association for Information Systems 13, 380–427 (2004)
8. Venkatesh, V., Brown, S.A., Bala, H.: Bridging the Qualitative-Quantitative Divide: Guidelines for Conducting Mixed Methods Research in Information Systems. MIS Quarterly 37, 21–54 (2013)
9. Cook, T.D., Campbell, D.T., Peraccio, L.: Quasi-experimentation. In: Dunnette, M., Hough, L. (eds.) Handbook of Industrial and Organizational Psychology, vol. 1, pp. 491–576. Consulting Psychologists Press, Palo Alto (1990)
10. Benbasat, I.: Laboratory experiments in information systems studies with a focus on individuals: A critical appraisal, vol. 2. Harvard Business School, Cambridge (1989)
11. March, S.T., Smith, G.F.: Design and Natural Science Research on Information Technology. Decision Support Systems 15, 251–266 (1995)
12. Gregg, D.G., Kulkarni, U.R., Vinzé, A.S.: Understanding the Philosophical Underpinnings of Software Engineering Research in Information Systems. Information Systems Frontiers 3, 169–183 (2001)
13. Hevner, A., March, S., Park, J., Ram, S.: Design Science in Information Systems Research. MIS Quarterly 28, 75–105 (2004)
14. Parsons, J., Cole, L.: What do the Pictures Mean? Guidelines for Experimental Evaluation of Representation Fidelity in Diagrammatical Conceptual Modeling Techniques. Data & Knowledge Engineering 55, 327–342 (2005)

15. Burton-Jones, A., Wand, Y., Weber, R.: Guidelines for Empirical Evaluations of Conceptual Modeling Grammars. Journal of the Association for Information Systems 10, 495–532 (2009)
16. Shanks, G., Weber, R.: A Hole in the Whole: A Response to Allen and March. MIS Quarterly 36, 965–980 (2012)
17. Allen, G.N., March, S.T.: A Research Note on Representing Part-Whole Relations in Conceptual Modeling. MIS Quarterly 36, 945–964 (2012)
18. Arazy, O., Kumar, N., Shapira, B.: A Theory-Driven Design Framework for Social Recommender Systems. Journal of the Association for Information Systems 11, 455–490 (2010)
19. Hovorka, D., Gregor, S.: Untangling Causality in Design Science Theorizing. In: 5th Biennial ANU Workshop on Information Systems Foundations (2010)
20. Brewer, M.B.: Research design and issues of validity. In: Reis, H., Judd, C. (eds.) Handbook of Research Methods in Social and Personality Psychology, pp. 3–16. Cambridge University Press, Cambridge (2000)
21. Straub, D.W.: Validating Instruments in MIS Research. MIS Quarterly 13, 147–169 (1989)
22. Churchill, G.A.: A Paradigm for Developing Better Measures of Marketing Constructs. Journal of Marketing Research, 64–73 (1979)
23. Hinkin, T.R.: A Review of Scale Development Practices in the Study of Organizations. Journal of Management 21, 967–988 (1995)
24. Moore, G.C., Benbasat, I.: Development of an Instrument to Measure the Perceptions of Adopting an Information Technology Innovation. Information Systems Research 2, 192–222 (1991)
25. Snodgrass, J.G., Vanderwart, M.: A Standardized Set of 260 Pictures: Norms for Name Agreement, Image Agreement, Familiarity, and Visual Complexity. Journal of Experimental Psychology: Human Learning and Memory 6, 174–215 (1980)
26. Kuechler, W., Vaishnavi, V.: A Framework for Theory Development in Design Science Research: Multiple Perspectives. Journal of the Association for Information Systems 13, 395–423 (2012)
27. Lukyanenko, R., Parsons, J.: Reconciling Theories with Design Choices in Design Science Research. In: vom Brocke, J., Hekkala, R., Ram, S., Rossi, M. (eds.) DESRIST 2013. LNCS, vol. 7939, pp. 165–180. Springer, Heidelberg (2013)
28. Merton, R.: On Sociological Theories of the Middle Range. In: Merton, R. (ed.) Social Theory and Social Structure, pp. 39–53. The Free Press, New York (1949)
29. Shepherd, M.M., Briggs, R.O., Reinig, B.A., Yen, J., Nunamaker, J., Jay, F.: Invoking Social Comparison to Improve Electronic Brainstorming: Beyond Anonymity. Journal of Management Information Systems 12, 155–170 (1995)
30. Briggs, R.O., Nunamaker, J., Jay, F., Sprague, J., Ralph, H.: 1001 Unanswered Research Questions in GSS. Journal of Management Information Systems 14, 3–21 (1997)

# What Kinds of Artifacts Are We Designing?
# An Analysis of Artifact Types and Artifact Relevance in IS Journal Publications

Andreas Drechsler and Philipp Dörr

Institute of Computer Science and Business Information Systems,
Universitätsstr. 2, University of Duisburg-Essen, 45141 Essen, Germany
andreas.drechsler@icb.uni-due.de

**Abstract.** In this paper, selected recent IS journal publications with an emphasis on design science are analyzed in regard to the types of artifacts which are designed (abstract designs or instantiations? / technical or social emphasis?). The findings are then connected to a recently proposed distinction of conceptual and instrumental relevance of research outcomes and discussed, whether the type of artifact matches the appropriate type of relevance. It is shown that artifacts with a technical emphasis may fall into a different relevance category than artifacts with a social emphasis. Future IS design science research projects can benefit from considering the "right" type of artifact relevance in the light of the type of artifact designed and doing so in an explicit way.

**Keywords:** artifacts, abstract artifacts, technical artifact, social artifact, socio-technical artifact, relevance, conceptual relevance, instrumental relevance.

## 1    Introduction

Around the beginning of the past decade, there was an extensive debate on how to improve the relevance of IS research [2, 6, 14]. Here, the design science paradigm is seen as a way to produce practically relevant research with an impact while still adhering to a high level of rigor [9, 10, 19]. Gregor and Hevner characterize IS design science research (DSR) as being aimed at the design of socio-technical systems, producing practically useful – and thus relevant – artifacts [7]. However, the term relevance mostly is treated as a black box in the IS literature. In contrast, Nicolai and Seidl propose a more differentiated picture on relevance in the management literature [18]. They distinguish conceptual, instrumental, and legitimative relevance of management research outcomes (see section 2.1) and are highly critical of research outcomes of instrumental relevance in the sense of "hands-on applicability". In brief, they regard it as impossible that abstract research outcomes have a direct instrumental relevance for practice.

For IS DSR, this distinction and critique warrants a closer look at the actual relevance and effective type of impact intended by DSR artifacts, since practical utility not only implies instrumental relevance, but it is also the major criterion ("dependent variable") by which DSR artifacts are to be evaluated – at least traditionally [5].

M.C. Tremblay et al. (Eds.): DESRIST 2014, LNCS 8463, pp. 329–336, 2014.

In other words, relevance is a key criterion when moving from theory to practice in DSR. Against this backdrop, the goal of this research-in-progress paper is to shed first light on this issue on a theoretical (section 2) and empirical (section 3) level. In section 2.1, the discourse in the management literature is briefly reviewed and applied to IS DSR artifacts. To prepare the subsequent empirical analysis, section 2.2 proposes a more differentiated perspective on socio-technical artifacts, distinguishing four types. The empirical analysis in section three takes four recently published MISQ DSR papers as a sample, takes a closer look whether and how they handle the issue of artifact relevance, and relates this to the types of artifacts designed. In the final section, the authors draw a conclusion and give an outlook towards further research.

## 2     Theoretical Foundations

### 2.1     Types of Artifact Relevance in IS Research

For the outcomes of management-oriented research in general, Nicolai and Seidl distinguish conceptual, instrumental, and legitimative relevance [18]. For them, research is conceptually relevant when it has the potential to guide and inspire managerial decisions and actions. A typical example they name is the identification of causal relationships through empirical research. In contrast, research is of instrumental relevance when the outcomes are intended to be immediately useful and applicable in managerial practice. They give the examples of schemes for decision support (matrixes, flow charts, etc.), forecasts, and technological rules. The latter is the link to DSR artifacts since technological rules can serve as design propositions as part of or a foundation for DSR artifacts or design theories [7, 8, 15]. The third form of research relevance – legitimative relevance – occurs when research outcomes are solely used to justify managerial action. Nicolai and Seidl characterize this form as only a latent form of research relevance. It is therefore not considered further in this paper. Due to the uniqueness of application contexts, Nicolai and Seidl are highly critical toward all forms of instrumental relevance [18]. In their view, research outcomes – such as generalized technological rules – cannot be of high utility for immediate application in specific real-world situations. In contrast, Avenier takes a constructivistic view on the bridge between academia and practice and outlines that also research outcomes with an instrumental intention first serve to "irritate" practitioners – inspire them and stimulate processes of reflection and creativity – before they take actual action [1].

Applying the distinction between conceptual and instrumental relevance to IS DSR leads to the conclusion that an abstract artifact is to be judged in terms of its conceptual relevance. Since it is not instantiated yet for a specific application context, it cannot be judged in terms of its actual utility, but only in terms of its potential utility for the class of problems it is supposed to address. Only the instantiated artifact then is to be judged by its actual utility or – in Nicolai and Seidl's terms – its instrumental relevance. This highlights the distinction between abstract artifacts and instantiations. Here, design theories contain the characteristic of "mutability" [8] which considers how well an abstract artifact can be tailored to fit to a specific application context and thus, realize its promise of potential utility through actual utility on the instance level.

One key limitation of the application of Nicolai and Seidl's distinction to IS artifacts is that they assume management-oriented research outcomes – especially since relevance is a social construct which thus differs by community. For IS research, the "MIS practitioner" is assumed as the "practitioner client" in addition to the student and scholar client [4]. As examples for MIS practitioners, Gill and Bhattacherjee explicitly name "consultants" and "industry/academic collaborators". While for the former, at least a cursory interaction with managers (when acquiring a new project and/or presenting key results) can be derived, the latter collaboration can happen on the managerial and on the technical level. Thus, it can be assumed that especially DSR publications with artifacts with a heavy emphasis on technical aspects are not aimed at a management audience, while at the same time conforming to key goals and audiences of IS research.

In addition, the validity of Nicolai and Seidl's argument against instrumental relevance – the requirement of abstraction for research outcomes – is at least questionable for IS DSR artifacts with an emphasis on technical aspects. The reason is that customizing artifacts to specific application contexts so that they can achieve their full utility is a well-covered issue in IS DSR [5, 10]. Interestingly, Avenier's counter-argument is not easily applicable either – do technical artifacts actually have an "inspirational power"? On the one hand, it can be argued "yes", since their introduction into an organization usually needs a management decision first, based on the potential utility of the abstract artifact. On the other hand, it can also be assumed that the decision is not based on inspiration, but on a structured and fact-based decision process.

As one can see already from the brief discussion above, the seemingly "simple" distinction between conceptual and instrumental relevance of socio-technical IS DSR artifacts leads to a variety of questions which require specific attention. At the same time, none of the issues raised above is entirely novel and it can be assumed that at least some of them are covered explicitly or implicitly in the existing IS DSR literature. Therefore, before the debate is pursued further on the conceptual level, it appears worthwhile to see whether and how these issues are handled in actual IS DSR publications. But before this is possible, a more differentiated perspective on socio-technical artifacts as outcome of IS DSR is needed than just distinguishing a social and a technical part of an artifact.

## 2.2    Types of Socio-technical Artifacts

To arrive at such a more differentiated perspective on socio-technical artifacts, the authors consider information systems development methodologies (ISDM) as meta-artefacts for conducting DSR [12, 20]. Since the emphases of the consideration of social and technical aspects in a designed artifact are largely dependent on the design process and the underlying paradigmatic views, it is assumed that such a paradigmatic distinction of ISDM allows a corresponding distinction of artifacts.

The first ISDM had a strong focus on the technical system. The underlying belief lied in the possibility of a "scientistic engineering theory of information systems design" [13]. Such a perspective is typically connected with the use of formal development life cycles (e.g. waterfall model) as ISDM [11]. Other ISDM focus also on the technical system, but with additional consideration of social factors, for example structured methodologies (e.g. Structured Analysis and Design Technique) which make a clear distinction between logical and physical design [11]. This happens to mitigate the negative effects of a purely technical view on information systems development such as insufficient user involvement and techno-centrism [23]. A further-reaching solution to these issues was the development of socio-technical participative ISDMs such as ETHICS [17]. They aim to achieve an optimal fit between the technical and social system and to enable users to control the developing process by giving them equal power and competence [11]. A fourth stream viewed information systems development as a largely social process [11]. Here, a well-known ISDM is the Soft System Methodology (SSM) by Checkland [3].

For the classification of IS DSR publications in this paper, these four categories (technical, technical with social consideration, integrated socio-technical, and social) are used to distinguish the type of artifacts or design theories developed in the respective articles. At the same time, the research processes employed do not necessarily have to follow the specific ISDMs mentioned above – they just served as an instrument to arrive at a more fine-grained distinction of socio-technical artifacts. It is of note that articles may eschew a clear assignment to a specific category. Thus, the two categories of "technical" and "social" are seen as forming two endpoints of a continuum. The two other categories form intermediate anchor points on this continuum around which articles can be clustered during classification.

## 3    Analysis of Artifact Types and Relevance in the IS Literature

### 3.1    Research Design

For this research-in-progress paper, four archetypical examples of articles published in MIS Quarterly are selected to provide a more in-depth analysis of the issues raised above. The articles were selected and the respective artifacts classified according to the four categories as outlined in section 2.2 as part of a larger research project, which is aimed at providing a systematic analysis of artifact types and relevance in the IS literature of the recent years. The classification was conducted and reviewed independently by at least two researchers, in order to achieve inter-coder reliability and thus, increase its validity. The intention of the in-depth analysis conducted below is to provide a foundation for discussion and feedback and also to provide insight into the classification process. A single journal – one of the two (or three) journals commonly considered as "tier 1" journals [16] – is chosen for this paper in order to account for journal-related biases. The overall goal for the overarching research project is to draw quantitative statements across all journals in the "AIS Basket of Eight" about the types of artifact and the type(s) of relevance considered. In turn, these quantitative statements are to provide a foundation to discuss implications for the IS discipline in general and DSR specifically in a larger scope.

### 3.2    Sample Analysis: Technical Artifact

The article chosen as archetypical sample of a DSR article of a technical artifact is "A Cost-Based Database Request Distribution Technique for Online E-Commerce Applications" by vanderMeer et al., published in 2012 in MIS Quarterly [25].

They develop – and explicitly state this – a theoretical model and a method for a cost-based database request distribution technique as abstract artifacts and instantiate the method for the purpose of experimental evaluation. Thus, the artifact is classified as technical. vanderMeer et al. evaluate their artifact terms of its instrumental relevance – whether its performance is superior to commercially available solutions and hence, more useful. Interestingly, they also discuss aspects of conceptual relevance: whether and when IT managers should consider changing the database request distribution technique, what implications in terms of reliability are, and how the abstract artifact should be configured for specific instances, based on database buffer sizes. This illustrates the issue of "inspirational power of (technical) artifacts" raised in the discussion on the conceptual level section 2.1 and that vanderMeer et al. recognized this – albeit implicitly – and covered the issue.

### 3.3    Sample Analysis: Technical Artifact with Social Considerations

The article chosen as archetypical sample of a DSR article of a technical artifact which additional social considerations is "Knowing What a User Likes: A Design Science Approach to Interfaces that Automatically Adapt to Culture" by Reinecke and Bernstein, published in 2013 in MIS Quarterly [21].

The artifacts they design are a method to implement cultural adaptivity of user interfaces and an instance of a culturally-adaptable system. Since the technical artifacts (two ontologies, an algorithm, user interface adaptation rules, and the instantiated system) constitute the key contribution, but are, at the same time, heavily influenced by cultural issues, the article is classified as technical with additional consideration of the social factor. The abstract artifacts (ontologies, algorithm, and adaptation rules) are distinguished from the instanced system and the article also discusses further areas for instantiation beyond the application context of task management. Hence, the authors of the article consider the abstract artifacts to be of conceptual relevance, based on the evaluation of the instanced system which was evaluated in terms of instrumental relevance (how well the system adapted to users' cultures). This highlights the interplay between the two types of relevance and abstract and instantiated artifacts. It is also of note that the article is not aimed at a managerial audience, limiting the applicability of Nicolai and Seidl's distinction.

### 3.4    Sample Analysis: Socio-technical Artifact

The article chosen as archetypical sample of a DSR article of an artifact with an integrative perspective on social and technical aspects is "Vital Signs for Virtual Teams: An Empirically Developed Trigger Model for Technology Adaptation Interventions" by Thomas and Bostrom, published in 2010 in MIS Quarterly [24] .

The designed artifact– though not explicitly called one – is a model to diagnose work in ICT-supported distributed – virtual – teams and to recognize shortcomings requiring managerial action (interventions). It is classified as socio-technical as an integrative perspective on virtual teamwork is taken, encompassing the adequacy of ICT as well as issues of trust and relationships, for example. The model is of abstract nature and explicitly characterized as being robust across application contexts. Since the authors state in the abstract that the model can be used as "diagnostic tool", they

regard it as being of instrumental relevance. At the same time, it provides five categories of overall 52 generic triggers to warrant specific interventions by a virtual team
leader. In other words, its instrumental use is intended to trigger – guide and inspire –
specific managerial action on the instance level. Hence, it eschews a clear classification as being of either conceptual or instrumental relevance. In turn, this leads to an
indication that Nicolai and Seidl's classification is not of dichotomic (or trichotomic,
if one includes legitimative relevance as well) nature. However, this issue is not reflected on explicitly in the article since application of the model to actual virtual
teams on the instance level is not elaborated on further.

### 3.5     Sample Analysis: Social Artifact

The article chosen as archetypical sample of a DSR article of a predominately social
artifact is "Control over Virtual Worlds by Game Companies: Issues and Recommendations" by Roquilly, published 2011 in MIS Quarterly [22]. This choice requires
special explanation as there were disagreements among the evaluating researchers
whether this article should indeed be classified as predominantly DSR. While the
article devotes only four out of twenty pages overall to design three recommendations
for the design of contracts – a social construct – for users of virtual worlds, it was still
the "most social" design-oriented article identified in a tier 1 journal. In additions,
these recommendations match what Nicolai and Seidl [18] call "technological rules"
(see section 2.1). They can serve as design principles for a future design theory and
are thus regarded as "precursors" of social artifacts in IS research.

The recommendations themselves are of an abstract nature, aimed at all classes of
company-run virtual worlds. The limits of applicability to specific instances are not
explicitly discussed. The first recommendation is a general one – hence, intended to
apply to all instances of virtual worlds – while the second and third take the game
company's business and gaming model, respectively, into account. All three are formulated strongly using "should". In terms of relevance, the first recommendation is
clearly seen as intended to be of instrumental relevance. The other two are of a more
conceptual relevance as they clearly distinguish specific variables (business model /
gaming model) of instances of virtual worlds, influencing the nature of the recommendation. At the same time, the "should" implies a direct – instrumental – applicability as well, without leaving room for intentional redesigns or addressing the need
for further guidance of decisions on how to design contracts on an instance level.
Thus, Nicolai and Seidl's critique (see 2.1) applies to these technological rules and
would apply likewise to abstract artifacts / design theories based upon them which do
not take into account the adjustment to specific circumstances during an instantiation.

## 4     Conclusion and Future Research

The analysis of four articles – each with a different emphasis of technical and social
elements of the socio-technical artifact – illustrated that aspects of conceptual as well
as instrumental relevance play a role for all types of artifacts. At the same time, it was
also illustrated that the two types of relevance play different roles for the different

types of artifacts and that an explicit consideration of these aspects enhances the overall contribution. While the instrumental relevance of the technical artifact was shown to be a key criterion for its utility, it was also illustrated that an explicit consideration of aspects of conceptual relevance for a managerial audience may foster its adoption in practice. For artifacts with a greater emphasis on social aspects, the sample analysis highlighted the importance of conceptual relevance for their utility for a wide range of application contexts as well the limitations of instrumental relevance without explicitly considering the difference between abstract statements and instantiations in specific contexts of application.

The expansion of the analysis to more journals and to draw quantitative statements about the types of artifacts and the type(s) of relevance that are considered or assumed is a task for future research. In parallel, it appears worthwhile to take a more systematic and in-depth look at theoretical and practical implications of the different types of relevance for different types of artifacts in IS DSR. The same applies to the development of concrete implications or guidelines for IS DSR to deal with the different types of relevance for different types of artifact – during the research process as well as for the communication of the outcomes. The same applies for relevance for different sub-groups of the target audience of "MIS practitioners" which are largely unanalyzed as well.

# References

1. Avenier, M.-J.: Shaping a Constructivist View of Organizational Design Science. Organization Studies 31(9/10), 1229–1255 (2010)
2. Benbasat, I., Zmud, R.W.: The Identity Crisis within the Is Discipline: Defining and Communicating the Discipline's Core Properties. MIS Quarterly 27(2), 183–194 (2003)
3. Checkland, P.: Soft systems methodology: a 30-year retrospective. John Wiley, Chichester (1999)
4. Gill, G., Bhattacherjee, A.: Whom Are We Informing? Issues and Recommenda-tions for MIS Research from an Informing Sciences Perspective. MIS Quarterly 33, 217–235 (2009)
5. Gill, T.G., Hevner, A.R.: A Fitness-Utility Model for Design Science Research. ACM Trans. Manage. Inf. Syst. 4(2), 5:1–5:24 (2013)
6. Gray, P.: Introduction to the Debate on the Core of the Information Systems Field. Communications of the Association for Information Systems 12(1) (2003)
7. Gregor, S., Hevner, A.R.: Positioning and Presenting Design Science Research for Maximum Impact. MIS Quarterly 37(2), 337–A6 (2013)
8. Gregor, S., Jones, D.: The Anatomy of a Design Theory. Journal of the Association for Information Systems 8(5), 312–335 (2007)
9. Hevner, A.: A Three Cycle View of Design Science Research. Scandinavian Journal of Information Systems 19(2), 87–92 (2007)
10. Hevner, A., et al.: Design Science in Information Systems Research. MIS Quarterly 28(1), 75–105 (2004)
11. Hirschheim, R., et al.: Information Systems Development and Data Modeling Conceptual and Philosophical Foundations. Cambridge Univ. Pr. (2008)
12. Iivari, J.: A Paradigmatic Analysis of Information Systems As a Design Science. Scandinavian Journal of Information Systems 19(2), 39–64 (2007)

13. Klein, H.K., Lyytinen, K.: The Poverty of Scientism in Information Systems. In: Mumford, E., et al. (eds.) Research Methods in Information Systems, pp. 131–162. Elsevier, Amsterdam (1985)
14. Kock, N., et al.: IS Research Relevance Revisited: Subtle Accomplishment, Unful-filled Promise, or Serial Hypocrisy? Communications of the Association for Information Systems 8, 1 (2002)
15. Kuechler, W., Vaishnavi, V.: A Framework for Theory Development in Design Science Research: Multiple Perspectives. Journal of the Association for Informa-tion Systems 13(6), 395–423 (2012)
16. Lowry, P., et al.: Evaluating Journal Quality and the Association for Information Systems Senior Scholars' Journal Basket Via Bibliometric Measures: Do Expert Journal Assessments Add Value? MIS Quarterly 37(4), 993–1012 (2013)
17. Mumford, E.: Designing human systems for new technology: the ETHICS method. Manchester Business School, (Manchester) (1983)
18. Nicolai, A.T., Seidl, D.: That's Relevant! Different Forms of Practical Relevance in Management Science. Organization Studies 31(9/10), 1257–1285 (2010)
19. Nunamaker Jr., J.F., Briggs, R.O.: Toward a broader vision for Information Sys-tems. ACM Trans. Manage. Inf. Syst. 2(4), 20:1–20:12 (2012)
20. Nunamaker, J. J.F., Chen, M.: Systems Development in Information Systems Research. In: Proceedings of the 23rd Hawaii International Conference on System Sciences, Kailua-Kona, pp. 631–640 (1990)
21. Reinecke, K., Bernstein, A.: Knowing What a User Likes: A Design Science Ap-proach to Interfaces that Automatically Adapt to Culture. MIS Quarterly 37(2), 427–453 (2013)
22. Roquilly, C.: Control Over Virtual Worlds by Game Companies: Issues and Rec-ommendations. MIS Quarterly 35(3), 653–671 (2011)
23. Somogyi, E.K., Galliers, R.D.: Applied Information Technology: from Data Proc-essing to Strategic Information Systems. Journal of Information Technology 2(1), 30–41 (1987)
24. Thomas, D., Bostrom, R.: Vital Signs for Virtual Teams: An Empirically Devel-oped Trigger Model for Technology Adaptation Interventions. MIS Quarterly 34(1), 115–142 (2010)
25. VanderMeer, D., et al.: A Cost-Based Database Request Distribution Technique for Online e-Commerce Applications. MIS Quarterly 36(2), 479–507 (2012)

# Extending the Fitness-Utility Model
# for Management Artifacts in IS Design Science Research

Andreas Drechsler

Institute of Computer Science and Business Information Systems,
Universitätsstr. 2, University of Duisburg-Essen, 45141 Essen, Germany
andreas.drechsler@icb.uni-due.de

**Abstract.** This paper proposes an extended fitness-utility model for management artifacts in IS DSR – such as artifacts for IT management or IT project management. It connects the elements of Gill and Hevner's fitness-utility model to different phases of an artifact lifecycle and different types of artifact relevance. It is shown that, due to the nature of management artifacts compared to IT artifacts, management artifacts are to be evaluated in terms of conceptual – and not instrumental – relevance and highlighted that different aspects of fitness are important for abstract and instantiated artifacts to sustain long-term utility. Based on these findings, a first version of an extended fitness-utility model is proposed. It is substantiated based on selected findings from empirical research about important factors for adoption of IS/IT management artifacts of practice. IS researchers who want to design IS/IT management or IT project management artifacts can use the extended fitness-utility model to explicitly consider relevant aspects of fitness already during design-time of their artifacts.

**Keywords:** fitness, utility, artifacts, relevance, management artifacts, fitness-utility model.

## 1 Introduction

Until recently, utility has been regarded as the main evaluation criterion ("dependent variable") for design science artifacts. However, Gill and Hevner propose to consider artifact fitness in addition to utility [6]. Their main arguments for considering artifact fitness are 1) to foster artifact evolution in the ongoing search for improved solutions and 2) to sustain artifact utility in changing application contexts. They develop a first version of a fitness-utility-model and illustrate its viability by drawing on a number of examples of IT artifacts (open source code, Linux versus UNIX, the SABRE airline booking system etc.). But IT artifacts are not the only research object in IS design science research (DSR). IS DSR in the domains of IS/IT management and IT project management (ITPM, in short) is mainly concerned with the development and evaluation of management artifacts, such as IT governance strategies, IT management processes, or project management methodologies [5]. Due to the different nature of management artifacts compared to IT artifacts, this research-in-progress paper argues that fitness of management artifacts is a prerequisite for adoption as well as for

M.C. Tremblay et al. (Eds.): DESRIST 2014, LNCS 8463, pp. 337–344, 2014.
© Springer International Publishing Switzerland 2014

sustained utility – and hence, relevance – of an ITPM artifact and illustrates this by means of an extension of Gill and Hevner's fitness-utility model as well as first empirical findings. In order to do so, the relevant theoretical foundations of management and IS DSR, artifact relevance, and artifact fitness are briefly reviewed in the second section. In the third section, they integrated into an extended fitness-utility model for ITPM artifacts. The fourth section covers first findings from empirical research aimed at deriving relevant factors for the usefulness and acceptance of ITPM artifacts. The paper ends with a brief discussion as well as an outlook toward future research.

## 2    Theoretical Foundations

In this section, the current state of the literature regarding management artifacts in IS DSR (section 2.1) and different types of relevance of research outcomes is briefly reviewed (section 2.2). Afterwards, Gill and Hevner's fitness-utility model [6] is described (section 2.3). The three aspects are then tied together in section 3.

### 2.1    Management Artifacts and IS DSR

In the management DSR literature, the understanding of management artifacts can be summarily characterized as any element – or combinations thereof – of a possible future organizational reality [5]. While there is no clear definition of a management artifact, Romme gives the following example: "products, services, organizational structures, organizational identities, business strategies, multiuser networks, management tools, projects, and discourses" [13]. He also highlights that management artifacts do not necessarily exist per se, but are tangible or intangible socially-constructed facts. This is unlike IT artifacts which always have a tangible component (hardware, readable or compiled program code, etc.). Particular challenges of management DSR are seen as coping with organizational phenomena such as a dynamic and complex environment leading to surprises, planned or emergent change over time, or informal or covert structures [15]. For IS DSR, management artifacts are a key research object when designing elements of IT organizations or IT project organizations [5]. To cover both domains, they are abbreviated as ITPM artifacts in the remainder of the paper.

### 2.2    Types of Relevance in Research

For the outcomes of management research in general, Nicolai and Seidl distinguish three types of relevance: conceptual, instrumental, and legitimative relevance [11]. For them, research is conceptually relevant when it has the potential to guide and inspire managerial decisions and actions. A typical example is the identification of causal relationships through empirical research. Research is of instrumental relevance when the outcomes are intended to be immediately useful in managerial practice. They give the examples of schemes for decision support (matrixes, flow charts, etc.), forecasts, and technological rules. The latter is the link to DSR artifacts since technological rules can serve as design propositions as part of or a foundation for DSR artifacts or design theories [4, 7–9]. The third form of research relevance - legitimative relevance – occurs when research outcomes are solely used to justify managerial action. Nicolai and Seidl characterize this form as only a latent form of research relevance. Consequently, legitimative relevance is not considered further in this paper. Furthermore, due to the uniqueness of every organization at any point in time, they are highly critical toward all forms of instrumental relevance. In their view, research outcomes – which are necessarily abstract – cannot be of high utility for immediate application in specific real-world situations. Here, Avenier provides a counterpoint: He takes a constructivistic view on the bridge between academia and practice and outlines that also research outcomes with an instrumental intention also first serve to "irritate" practitioners – stimulate processes of reflection and creativity – before they take actual actions and use the research outcomes in practice [3].

### 2.3    The Fitness-Utility Model for DSR

In [6], Gill and Hevner develop a fitness-utility model for DSR, in order to highlight that utility should not be the only criterion used for evaluating DSR research outcomes. They first distinguish two types of fitness: type 1 as the ability of an organism to survive over time and type 2 as the ability of an organism to reproduce and evolve over generations. Afterwards, they propose an integrated perspective on the two aspects of fitness and utility. They operationalize the fitness concept by proposing seven characteristics of fitness and one characteristic of unfitness:

- Decomposable: Artifacts which are decomposable into smaller units allow a redesign of singular units to cope with external changes, instead of having to redesign the entire artifact.
- Malleable: Artifacts which are malleable can be adapted to cope with changing environments and also be adapted to be used for unintended purposes.
- Open: Artifacts which are open for inspection and change allow their end-users a rapid adaption to changing environments. They regard the three characteristics of malleability, decomposability, and openness as complementary and enhancing each other.
- Embedded in Design Systems: When artifacts are part of systems where design and changes are common it can be expected that they evolve more rapidly than when design and change are uncommon.
- Novel: Novel artifacts – provided they are viable – can trigger and lead a wave of innovation or change for an entire landscape of artifacts.
- Interesting: Interesting artifacts may intrigue designers, researchers, or users and thus, also lead to a wave of change or innovation – especially when artifacts are novel and interesting at the same time.
- Elegant: Artifacts perceived as elegant – in addition to being functional (= useful) – may trigger positive reactions in users and therefore be adopted or used more often or be of increased longevity.
- Too useful: In contrast to the characteristics above, artifacts may also be "too useful" when they are of high utility in the present, but lack the fitness to evolve over

time to further improve their utility or to adapt to changing circumstances. In contrast, progress and improvement require the change of existing artifacts or the adoption of new, more useful ones. When artifacts are unable to respond to the former and prevent the latter (for example, due to lock-in effects), they are considered as being "too useful", eventually leading to their decline and "extinction".

Bringing these characteristics and utility / usefulness together, Gill and Hevner postulate that designs (= artifacts) need to exhibit a certain number of fitness characteristics, to be of long-term usefulness and relevance and, at the same time, need to avoid becoming "too useful".

## 3    An Extended Fitness-Utility Model for ITPM Artifacts

In order to link the three aspects of fitness, utility, and artifact relevance of ITPM artifacts, it is first important to distinguish abstract artifacts and instantiations. Abstract artifacts are designed for a class of real-world problems and are considered to be the prime outcome of DSR [7]. An abstract artifact is to be differentiated from its instantiations which constitute applications of the abstract artifacts to specific real-world situations. An instantiated artifact is considered useful in a specific application context when it helps solving the instance of the real-world problem in the context. An abstract artifact is then considered useful when several instantiations in different contexts proved to be useful. This distinction exists not only in the IS DSR literature, but also in the management DSR literature [1, 2] and therefore applies to ITPM artifacts as well [5].

Following the distinction made by Nicolai and Seidl [11] (see section 2.2), it is argued that an abstract artifact is to be judged in terms of its conceptual relevance. Since it is not instantiated yet for a specific application context, it cannot be judged in terms of its actual utility, but only in terms of its potential utility. For ITPM artifacts, this judgment is made by the IT or project executives deciding whether the abstract ITPM artifact has the potential utility to solve their particular real-world problem. Researchers may or may not be involved in this decision. Only the instantiated artifact then is to be judged by its actual utility or – in Nicolai and Seidl's terms – its instrumental relevance. And since ITPM artifacts as special instance of management artifacts are considered to be "social facts" (see section 2.1) even this instrumental relevance does not constitute a tool- or engineering-like application [12] of a management artifact, but it depends on the acceptance of the instantiated artifact by its eventual users. In the case of an IT project management methodology artifact, for example, these end-users are all members of the project team.

Adding a fitness perspective to this so far solely utility-oriented perspective, it becomes clear that both types of fitness Gill and Hevner distinguished (survival and reproduction) are relevant, but again, on different levels of artifact abstraction. The potential utility of an abstract ITPM artifact – in the perspective of an ITM or PM executive – is immediately related to their perception of its fitness to be adapted

("reproduced") to the specific situation of the organization, in order to be of actual –
and not only potential – utility. In a long-term perspective, the adapted and instantiated artifact also needs to prove its fitness – but this time in terms of survival – due
to the necessity to be adaptable to changing elements of the organization or its environment in order to sustain its utility. There is also a third fitness-related perspective,
this time during the instantiation and adaptation process of the abstract artifact itself:
the acceptance of the ITPM artifact on the end-user level depends on the extent of the
adaptability of the abstract artifact to the specific application context, so that the end-
users of the artifact can find it useful. This is not a matter of reproduction (at this
point in time the decision-maker(s) have already decided in favor of the artifact,
therefore it is going to be introduced anyway) or survival (the artifact is just being
instantiated so it is not a matter of changing an already instantiated artifact to fit to
new circumstances), but actual adaptability during the instantiation process.

For each of the three fitness-related perspectives (reproduction, survival, and adaption-during-instantiation), it is now hypothesized that different characteristics of fitness are of special importance: During the phase where ITM or project executives
decide whether an ITPM artifact is going to be instantiated ("reproduced") at all, an
artifact promising an elegant solution will probably be of high interest. Being embedded in a "design system" (for example, offered by renowned consultants or researchers) will probably also foster a positive decision. The same applies when the artifact is
open for integration with the existing management systems. In terms of novelty, it is
probably more down to the personal preference of the decision-maker: do they prefer
a well-established abstract artifact with a proven track record of utility in other contexts or are they willing to try a new and promising potential solution? However, it
can be assumed that novelty will at least help to bring an artifact to their attention.

During the instantiation process, different fitness-related qualities increase in importance. Openness for integration with the existing management systems (in an organizational perspective) and individual work routines (in an individual perspective)
is now becoming more crucial, but also effective malleability and decomposability to
adapt the abstract artifact to its application context. A similar case can made for elegance, but this time not on the solution-oriented level, but with regard to its internal
composition and internal elements. Does it, for example, prescribe cumbersome
processes or lightweight and flexible workflows? It can also be surmised that an interesting – or even exciting – artifact will hold its future end-users attention longer and
ease its acceptance [10].

In a long-term artifact survival perspective, the aspects of malleability, openness,
and easy decomposition appear of similar importance as during the initial adaptation
phase. But since it can be assumed that more incremental but regular changes are
taking place here, being embedded in a design system (for example, a continual improvement process) will foster the survival of the artifact. In this context, elegance is
a factor again, but in a third sense: that small but regular changes can be elegantly
integrated into the elements of the artifact. In addition, the issue of an artifact being
"too useful" also needs to be addressed in this phase.

Based on these considerations, an extended fitness-utility model for ITPM artifacts
is proposed as depicted in Table 1.

**Table 1.** Extended fitness-utility model for ITPM artifacts

| Phase | Decision to introduce abstract ITPM artifact | Artifact instantiation process | ITPM Artifact in use |
|---|---|---|---|
| Artifact | Abstract artifact | Abstract artifact in redesign | Artifact instance |
| Stakeholders involved | decision-makers, (consultants), (researchers) | decision-makers, change managers, end-users, (consultants), (researchers) | end-users, (change managers) |
| Utility | potential utility ⟶ actual utility | | |
| Relevance | conceptual relevance ⟶ instrumental relevance | | |
| Fitness type analogy | "reproduction" (type 2) | "adaption" | "survival" (type 1) |
| Relevant characteristics of fitness | • Novel (depending on personal preferences)<br>• Elegant (solution)<br>• Embedded in Design System<br>• Open<br>• Interesting (for decision-makers) | • Malleable<br>• Decomposable<br>• Open<br>• Elegant (composition)<br>• Interesting (for end-users) | • Malleable<br>• Decomposable<br>• Open<br>• Elegant (maintenance)<br>• Embedded in Design System<br>• Too useful? |

## 4     Fitness and ITPM Artifacts – First Empirical Findings

In this section, first evidence of the validity of the extended fitness-utility model of Table 1 is presented. The findings are taken from other research projects in the larger context of ITPM artifacts and reinterpreted in the light of the extended model. Since these research projects were not directed at an explicit validation of the model, the confirmatory power of the findings is somewhat limited. Nevertheless, in the absence of other evidence, the author regards them as sufficiently convincing to discuss them here at least briefly.

The importance of conceptual artifact relevance for the first phase – expressed in terms of perceived potential utility and perceived interest by the decision-makers – was noted in a recent study. Ten CIOs or other high-ranking IT executives of German small and medium enterprises of different sizes and industries were interviewed, in order to gain an overview about the instruments they use to direct the IT function and whether and why they used or did not use an IT balanced scorecard. The majority did not. In the light of the model, their statements are interpreted that the IT balanced scorecard (as one instance of an ITPM artifact of practice) was not interesting to them because they did not perceive it to be elegant (= lightweight) and open (= to their specific requirements for directing their IT function), even despite it was perceived as being well-embedded in a design system (= offered by consultants). Overall, it can be concluded that the instrument lacked fitness and conceptual relevance for the non-adopters and they therefore decided against adapting it.

Another research project was concerned with the introduction and application of an ITPM artifact of practice: the ITIL framework for IT service management [14]. Six cases of the introduction of the ITIL framework were analyzed by expert interviews with relevant stakeholders and document analysis. Of special note here in the interviews was the "prescribed malleability" of ITIL – that the respective organizations were required to adapt the abstract ITIL processes to their specific structures and processes. The ITIL processes were also considered to be open to incorporate existing management practices. The decomposability of ITIL was also mentioned positively, that one could concentrate on introducing one or a few processes at a time. For the long-term utility of the introduced ITIL processes, the interviewees highlighted the importance of guiding principles as well as a formalized continual service improvement process. These elements can be interpreted as elements of a "design system". To further highlight the importance of malleability and openness for long-term utility, one interviewee estimated that about four years after the initial introduction, the ITIL Change Management process they used had about only ten percent in common with the initial version of the process design.

## 5    Conclusion and Future Research

Table 1 proposes an extended fitness-utility model for IT management and IT project management (ITPM) artifacts. This extension of Gill and Hevner's model [6] is based on a separate consideration of abstract and instantiated artifacts and conceptual and instrumental relevance. It suggests considering different characteristics of fitness and different types of relevance for abstract and instantiated ITPM artifacts. It was argued that a differentiated consideration of the fitness characteristics for artifact design can foster their adoption in practice and support their sustained utility even in a long-term perspective – despite changing organizations and their environment. The arguments were also supported by initial evidence gathered in ongoing research projects, which illustrates the initial validity of the proposed extended fitness-utility model. For the design of future management artifacts the its current version suggests that one should design both for elegance and conceptual clarity so that an ITPM artefact gets adopted by management, but also for malleability, decomposability, and openness, so that the ITPM artefact can be easily instantiated and used. These characteristics furthermore allow an ex-ante evaluation of an abstract artifact before its first instantiation, providing a step toward an operationalization of the abstract requirement of "(potential) utility".

The next big step in future research is to refine the extended fitness-utility model further and to validate its elements by dedicated empirical research for each phase, in different domains, and on every stakeholder level (executives and end-users). The second big step afterwards is to transform these findings into actual design-relevant prescriptive knowledge to design abstract ITPM artifacts not only for utility, but for the relevant fitness qualities identified and validated. Furthermore, the author also considers it worthwhile to explore whether the extended fitness-utility model for ITPM artifacts applies to IT artifacts as well or which modifications are needed, based on the different characteristics of the two types of artifact.

# References

1. Van Aken, J.E.: Management Research Based on the Paradigm of the Design Sci-ences: The Quest for Field-Tested and Grounded Technological Rules. Journal of Management Studies 41(2), 219–246 (2004)
2. Van Aken, J.E., Romme, A.G.L.: A Design Science Approach to Evidence-Based Man-agement. In: Rosseau, D.M. (ed.) The Oxford Handbook of Evidence-Based Management, pp. 43–61. Oxford University Press, New York (2012)
3. Avenier, M.-J.: Shaping a Constructivist View of Organizational Design Science. Organi-zation Studies 31( 9/10), 1229–1255 (2010)
4. Bunge, M.: Scientific Research II: The Search for Truth. Springer, Berlin (1967)
5. Drechsler, A.: Design Science as Design of Social Systems - Implications for Information Systems Research. Journal of Information Technology Theory and Application 14(4) (2013) (in print)
6. Gill, T.G., Hevner, A.R.: A Fitness-Utility Model for Design Science Research. ACM Trans. Manage. Inf. Syst. 4(2), 5:1–5:24 (2013)
7. Gregor, S., Hevner, A.R.: Positioning and Presenting Design Science Research for Maxi-mum Impact. MIS Quarterly 37(2), 337–A6 (2013)
8. Gregor, S., Jones, D.: The Anatomy of a Design Theory. Journal of the Association for In-formation Systems 8(5), 312–335 (2007)
9. Kuechler, W., Vaishnavi, V.: A Framework for Theory Development in Design Science Research: Multiple Perspectives. Journal of the Association for Information Sys-tems 13(6), 395–423 (2012)
10. Mohan, K., Ahlemann, F.: Committed Use of Project Management Methodologies: Under-standing the Role of Costs, Benefits, and Psychological Needs. In: ICIS 2013 Proceedings (2013)
11. Nicolai, A.T., Seidl, D.: That's Relevant! Different Forms of Practical Relevance in Man-agement Science. Organization Studies 31(9/10), 1257–1285 (2010)
12. Pandza, K., Thorpe, R.: Management as Design, but What Kind of Design? An Appraisal of the Design Science Analogy for Management. British Journal of Management 21(1), 171–186 (2010)
13. Romme, A.G.L.: Organizational Development Interventions: An Artifaction Perspective. Journal of Applied Behavioral Science 47(1), 8–32 (2011)
14. Rudd, C.: ITIL V3 Planning to Implement Service Management. The Stationery Office, London (2010)
15. Tranfield, D., et al.: Management as a Design Science Mindful of Art and Surprise. Journal of Management Inquiry 15(4), 413–424 (2006)

# Using Coloured Cognitive Mapping (CCM) for Design Science Research

John R. Venable

Curtin University
Perth, Western Australia, Australia
j.venable@curtin.edu.au

**Abstract.** Design Science Research (DSR) is a research paradigm for research that undertakes to solve general problems through the invention and evaluation of new or improved technologies. Once DSR is completed, practitioners may make use of the new technology to solve particular instances of the generalised problem (and thereby make improvements in a problematic situation). In order to effectively solve a generalised problem, it is important (among other things) for DSR researchers to (1) understand the problem, its causes, and the conditions that allow a problem to continue or hinder its solution, (2) develop a shared problem understanding among collaborating DSR researchers, (3) creatively think of alternative potential avenues and means to solve (or reduce or alleviate) the problem, and (4) develop and convey design theories about the utility of a developed design artefact to solve a problem. This paper describes how Coloured Cognitive Mapping (CCM) can be used for these purposes in the context of DSR and provides evidence of its utility for those purposes through description of an application of CCM to DSR and more formal evaluation through teaching CCM to DSR researchers and surveying them for their opinions about its utility and features.

**Keywords:** Design Science Research (DSR), Coloured Cognitive Mapping (CCM), problem analysis, problem solving, design theory, creativity.

## 1 Introduction

Coloured Cognitive Mapping (CCM) [1, 2] is an approach for analysing problems to understand their causes and consequences and for identifying potential ways to solve the problem(s). CCM includes both a simple diagramming notation and a procedure for conducting a causal analysis of the problem and its consequences, transforming the resulting CCM into diagram concerned with solving the problem, and augmenting the diagram with potential or candidate solutions to the problem. Formalising problem understandings and potential solutions in the form of CCMs supports both clear reasoning and communication with other stakeholders and would-be problem solvers.

Design Science Research (DSR) is a research paradigm for research that undertakes to solve general problems through the invention and evaluation of new or improved technologies. Once DSR is completed, practitioners may make use of the new

M.C. Tremblay et al. (Eds.): DESRIST 2014, LNCS 8463, pp. 345–359, 2014.
© Springer International Publishing Switzerland 2014

technology to solve particular instances of the generalised problem (and thereby make improvements in a problematic situation). In order to effectively solve a generalised problem, it is important (among other things) for DSR researchers to (1) understand the problem, its causes, and the conditions that allow a problem to continue or hinder its solution, (2) develop a shared problem understanding among collaborating DSR researchers, (3) creatively think of alternative potential avenues and means to solve (or reduce or alleviate) the problem, and (4) develop and convey design theories about the utility of a developed design artefact.

This paper investigates how Coloured Cognitive Mapping (CCM) can be used for these purposes in the context of DSR and provides some initial evidence of its utility for those purposes.

The next section describes relevant literature on DSR and CCM, giving rise to a research question. Section 3 gives an overview of CCM. Section 4 describes an example of the application of CCM to an ongoing DSR project. Section 5 describes and presents the results of studies to evaluate the utility of CCM for use in DSR. Section 6 then summarises and suggests further research.

## 2     Review of Relevant Literature

This section reviews two main areas of literature: Design Science Research (DSR) and Problem Analysis. The review of DSR seeks to motivate the problem to be addressed and the significance of this research. The review of problem analysis seeks to identify existing approaches to problem analysis and the place of CCM within that context.

### 2.1     Problems in the Design Science Research Literature

As noted earlier, DSR is a research paradigm for research that undertakes to solve general problems through the invention and evaluation of new or improved technologies. There are few published definitions of DSR, but Venable and Baskerville [3, p. 142] define DSR as "Research that invents a new purposeful artefact to address a generalised type of problem and evaluates its utility for solving problems of that type".

The concept of a problem and activities to understand and define it are central to DSR. March and Smith [4, p. 251] emphasise that "Real problems must be properly conceptualized and represented, appropriate techniques for their solution must be constructed, and solutions must be implemented and evaluated using appropriate criteria." Hevner et al [5, p. 76] emphasise that design science research "is fundamentally a problem-solving paradigm." "Design science . . . creates and evaluates IT artifacts intended to solve identified organizational problems" [5, p. 77].They also state that in DSR, "Purposeful artifacts are built to address heretofore unsolved problems." [5, p. 78]. Vaishnavi and Kuechler [6] assert that the DSR process begins with the "Awareness of Problem" phase.  Peffers et al [7] state that "The development of the artefact should be a search process that  draws from existing theories and knowledge to come up with a solution to a defined problem." They further include a first step in their DSR methodology (DSRM) "Activity 1: Problem identification and motivation." In fact, in formulating DSRM, Peffers et al [7] reviewed seven articles from IS and Engineering and all seven had common design process elements similar to their Activity 1: problem identification and motivation. In this activity, the key tasks are to define the problem and show importance [7]. Sein et al [8] identify solving a class of problem as part of the essence of DSR (along with innovation). Accordingly, they include Problem Formulation as the first stage in their Action Design Research (ADR) methodology. Among other activities, Problem Formulation in ADR includes "(3) Cast the problem as an instance of a class of problems" [8, p. 5].

An important gap in the above literature is that there is little to no guidance on how to understand, represent, and define the problem to be solved. Peffers et al [7] do suggest that "it may be useful to atomize the problem conceptually so that the solution can capture its complexity". Similarly, Hevner et al [5, p. 88-89] state that "Design-science research often simplifies a problem by explicitly representing only a subset of the relevant means, ends, and laws or by decomposing a problem into simpler subproblems." Hevner et al [5] further suggest using constructs and models in the definition of the problem to be solved. "Constructs provide the language in which problems and solutions are defined and communicated [9]. Models use constructs to represent a real world situation – the design problem and its solution space [10]. Models aid problem and solution understanding and frequently represent the connection between problem and solution components enabling exploration of the effects of design decisions and changes in the real world." [5, pp. 78-79]. However, neither Peffers et al [7] nor Hevner et al [5] provide further information or guidance on how a problem may be "atomized", simplified, decomposed, or modelled.

Subsequent to DSRM's Activity 1: Problem identification and motivation, Peffers et al [7] further suggest that DSR researchers conduct Activity 2: Define the objectives for a solution. To motivate the inclusion of Activity 2 in DSRM, they state "Some of the researchers explicitly incorporate efforts to transform the problem into system objectives, also called metarequirements [11] or requirements [12], whereas for the others, these efforts are implicit as part of programming and data collection [13] or implicit in the search for a relevant and important problem. Identified problems do not necessarily translate directly into objectives for the artifact because the process of design is necessarily one of partial and incremental solutions. Consequently, after the problem is identified, there remains the step of determining the performance objectives for a solution." [7, p. 55]. Put into other words, in order to have design objectives, one needs to understand what it would mean to solve the problem. However, Peffers et al [7] do not provide suggestions for *how* a problem definition can or should be transformed into design requirements or metarequirements.

Vaishnavi and Kuechler [6], subsequent to their Awareness of Problem phase propose a second phase of "Suggestion", which is in some way similar to Activity 2 in DSRM. Like the strong connection between Activity 1 and Activity 2 in DSRM, the Suggestion phase "is intimately connected with" the Awareness of Problem phase [6, p. 7]. In the Suggestion phase, a "Tentative Design" is created. Vaishnavi and Kuechler [6, p. 7] note that "Suggestion is an essentially creative step ..." and that "if after investing considerable effort on an interesting problem a Tentative Design or at least the germ of an idea for problem solution does not present itself to the research, the idea (Proposal) will be set aside." They further note that such creative suggestions for a problem solution are identified through abductive reasoning, but then require further thinking and redesign to ensure that a tentative design is practicable for the problem for which an initial solution was abduced. Like Vaishnavi and Kuechler [6], March and Smith[4], Hevner et al [5], and Peffers et al [7] all emphasise the creative nature of DSR, which implies the need to encourage and support creativity.

A third gap in the above literature is that there is no guidance for how an initial tentative design might be creatively abduced and/or refined into a reasonable proposal to be pursued in more detail in a DSR project. How creativity can be supported and encouraged is not addressed in the above literature.

The concepts of problems, requirements, and (tentative) solution designs are addressed in the DSR literature on Design Theories [11, 14-17]. A design theory is a formal statement of the results of DSR. Once a problem definition is transformed into requirements, it can be stated as meta-requirements [11], purpose and scope using constructs [15], a problem space [14], or general requirements [16, 17]. An initial or more detailed solution design can be stated as a meta-design [11], principles of form and function, artefact mutability, and principles of implementation using constructs [15], a solution space [14], or a general design [16, 17]. A design theory includes a relationship between requirements and design that prescribes instantiating the design to achieve the requirements [11, 15, 16] or simply indicates that there is utility to be had in instantiating the design for achieving the requirements [14, 17].

A fourth gap in the literature is that there is little or no guidance for how to state requirements and designs and the relationships between them. Where do the constructs for requirements or designs come from? At what level of detail should they be presented?

Finally, none of the DSR literature reviewed above addresses issues of stakeholder involvement and obtaining agreement about the problem to be solved in a DSR project or what design features and architecture the designed solution or purposeful artefact should have. A DSR project may be done by a single person or it may involve multiple clients, funding agencies, and other people with a stake in what problem is to be solved and how a problem is solved, as well as a team of designers and technology developers. It is one thing to work alone on the above activities and another thing to develop agreement about what problem(s) a DSR project will address or what features are included in a design and how they fit together into a coherent whole (architecture). This then is a fifth gap in the DSR literature.

To summarise these research gaps, the DSR literature provides little or no guidance for how to (1) formulate and define problems, (2) transform a problem definition into solution requirements, (3) creatively reason about potential solutions, (4) formulate design theories with constructs and relationships between them at an appropriate level of detail and precision, and (5) collaborate and communicate with multiple stakeholders to reach agreement when conducting the above activities. Indeed, Hevner et al [5] themselves identify some of these gaps and their importance when they state in their Discussions and Conclusions section that "Insufficient sets of constructs, models, methods, and tools exist for accurately representing the business/technology environment." [5p. 99]. They further go on to identify the importance and impact of this problem when they state that "Orman (2002) argues that many of the equivocal results in IS behavioral-science studies can be explained by a failure to differentiate the capabilities and purposes of the studied technology." [5, p. 99-100]. Here we can interpret "capabilities" as the features of an artefact design, "purposes" as the problem to be solved and requirements, "failure to differentiate" as resulting from lack of precise representations of problems and solution designs.

## 2.2 Relevant Problem Solving Literature

There are many methods, tools, and techniques that are applied to analysing, understanding, and solving problems, including Soft Systems Methodology [18-20] and its various techniques, including Rich Pictures, CATWOE Criteria and System Definitions, and Conceptual (a.k.a. Activity) Models, Fishbone or Ishikawa Diagrams [21], Problematiques [22], Cognitive Maps and the Strategic Option Development and Analysis (SODA) and Strategy Making methods [23-27], and Coloured Cognitive Maps [1, 2]. Such methods and techniques could potentially be useful applied in DSR in order to resolve the above issues. However, by and large, they have not thus far been applied in DSR and there is no literature describing their use in DSR.

In Soft Systems Methodology (SSM) [18-20], Rich Pictures are a cartoon-like form of diagram that are used to represent the problem and its context, including stakeholders, organisations, resources, physical and abstract phenomena, processes, barriers (to solution), agreements, and the concerns of stakeholders. They are good tools for understanding a problematic situation. The CATWOE Criteria (a pneumonic for Customer, Actor, Transformation, Weltanschaung (or World-view), Owner, and Environment) are used as criteria to form or evaluate the completeness of a System Definition, which is a plain-language statement describing a system (in the general systems sense) that would solve a problem. Conceptual Models (a.k.a. Activity Models) are simple process model diagrams that identify the different activities (and the precedence linkages between them) that are necessary and sufficient to achieve the Transformation within a stated CATWOE/System Definition, within the constraints contained in the CATWOE/System Definition. SSM provides much guidance on how to use these tools/techniques to analyse problems and especially provides advice on sharing understandings and obtaining agreement on what problem to solve and defining what solution to seek. However, SSM does not provide much advice about or tools that direct support modelling and analysis of the causes of a problem or how to match solutions to a problem beyond obtaining agreement.

All of the other tools/techniques above, including Fishbone Diagrams [21], Cognitive Maps, SODA, and Strategy Making [23-27], Problematiques [22], and Coloured Cognitive Mapping [1, 2] are forms of causal analysis. Fishbone Diagrams and Problematiques focus on understanding the causes of problems. Cognitive Maps can be used to model either problems and their causes and consequences or to model goals and potential actions and strategies for achieving those goals, although SODA and Making Strategy focus largely on the latter. Coloured Cognitive Mapping (CCM) [1, 2] specifically addresses both causal analysis of problems as well as determining strategies for solving a problem. In particular, it includes a process for taking a CCM of a problem and its causes and transforming it into a CCM of potential solutions to a problem. This is similar (if not identical) to transforming a problem definition into a requirements specification for a solution. CCM can be used to model both specific (situated) problems and the generalised problems that are addressed in DSR. Therefore CCM is a good candidate for use in early stages in DSR. This conclusion from the literature gives rise to the following research questions:

1. How can Coloured Cognitive Mapping be used to support problem analysis, definition, creative suggestion, and solution requirements specification in DSR?

2. Does Coloured Cognitive Mapping provide utility to Design Science Researchers for problem analysis, definition, creative suggestion, and solution requirements specification in Design Science Research?

Having identified some problems with DSR, a potential solution approach in CCM, and our research questions, we now turn to a description of CCM.

# 3    Overview of Coloured Cognitive Mapping (CCM)

Coloured Cognitive Mapping [1, 2] was developed to facilitate understanding the causes and consequences of problems and then to transition to reasoning about potential means to solve a problem. He proposed that CCM could be used to analyse problematic contexts for reasoning systems [2] as well as for requirements analysis for information systems development [1]. Either way the approach is the same.

The CCM approach includes both a diagramming notation and a three step process for using the notation to analyse a problem and come up with candidate solutions. It also includes a conceptualisation of two forms of CCMs: (1) a CCM of "the problem as difficulties", which focuses on the problem, what is undesirable about it, and what causes the problem and allows it to persist, and (2) a CCM of "the problem as solutions", which focuses on the solution of the problem, what benefits would accrue from solving the problem, what causes of the problem might be reduced or eliminated to solve the problem, and how such problem causes might be reduced or eliminated. Figure 1 gives a typical pattern for each form of CCM and shows the CCM notation. The wording of each node in figure 1 suggests the kinds of concepts and words that might be included in a CCM.

CCMs extend the Cognitive Map diagram notation of Eden and Ackerman [23, 24, 26] by colouring nodes (see figure 1). Nodes that are coloured red (or otherwise annotated, e.g. by node shape or bolding of text) indicate that the node is undesirable, while nodes that are coloured green (or otherwise annotated, e.g. by shape or non-bold text) indicate that the node is desirable. Shape and bold/non-bold text are used as a redundant cue for desirability because some people are colour blind. Like ordinary cognitive maps, the text within a node has two poles: a primary pole, the text in which indicates the central meaning of the node, and a secondary pole, the text of which provides a contrast to the primary pole. These are separated by an ellipsis symbol ("…"). The text in a node is read as "[primary pole text] as opposed to [secondary pole text]". For example, the text in the upper left node in figure 1 is read as "Problem consequence as opposed to absent or reduced". The secondary pole in a node is important. For example, the node "boring lectures … interesting lectures" is quite different from "boring lectures … no lectures".

Like ordinary cognitive maps, in addition to nodes, CCMs include arrows to indicate causality (see figure 1). The node at the tail of the arrow causes the node at the head of the arrow. Causality can mean full or partial causality; the arrow doesn't indicate the degree or strength of the causality. Synonyms for such causality of arrows in CCMs include causes, facilitates, increases, contributes to, permits, enables, leads to, and more. For example, the upper left arrow in figure 1 indicates that "problem causes problem consequence". Arrows may optionally be annotated with a minus sign. If there is a minus sign on an arrow, it means that the node at the tail of the arrow causes the secondary pole of the node at the head of the arrow. Alternatively, a node at the

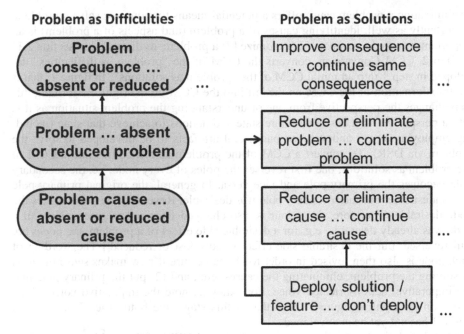

**Fig. 1.** Notation and patterns for two forms of Coloured Cognitive Maps [2]

tail of an arrow with a minus sign can be said to detract from, reduce, prevent, disable, or hinder the primary pole of the node at the head of the arrow.

The three step process proposed by Venable [2] includes (1) Problem Diagnosis, (2) CCM Conversion, and (3) Solution Derivation.

Step 1, Problem Diagnosis, focusses on developing a CCM of the problem as difficulties, i.e. it develops a CCM along the lines of the pattern on the left side of figure 1. The focus here is on understanding the problem (and developing a *shared* understanding), how it operates and why it is undesirable. Problem Diagnosis begins with one or more statement(s) of the problem (or problems if there are several) itself, as in the middle of the left side of figure 1. It then adds nodes that explore the consequences of the problem, i.e. they are caused by the problem. The consequences of the problem explain why the problem is undesirable and give an idea of the significance of the problem and why one would want to solve it. Problem consequences are usually placed above the problem and must be connected by an arrow from the problem to the consequence. While problem consequences are usually undesirable, there may be desirable side-effects (which are then coloured green instead of red). There can be *many* consequence nodes on a CCM and there may also be consequences of consequences, consequences of consequences of consequences, and so on. Problem diagnosis next adds nodes for causes of problems, which are generally placed below the problem and must be connected by an arrow from the cause to the problem. Like consequences, there may be many causes for a problem as well as causes of causes, causes of causes of causes, and so on. Understanding the causes and enablers of problems is important in order to identify potential ways to solve the problem. Reducing or eliminating a problem cause offers a potential means to reduce or solve a problem. Importantly as well, identifying causes of a problem (and aspects of a problem) is an important way to decompose [5] or atomize [7] a problem, as discussed in section 2.1.

Step 2, CCM Conversion, converts the CCM of the "problem as difficulties" developed in step 1 into an initial CCM of the "problem as solutions". In figure 1, that is the transformation of the CCM on the left into the CCM on the right. Performing this step changes the perspective from one of understanding the problem situation as it is into a perspective of a desirable future state and actions to achieve that state (including employing as yet undeveloped purposeful artefacts to be developed to solve the problem via DSR). To convert a CCM of the problem as difficulties into a CCM of the problem as solutions, one first reverses the poles of every node, i.e. the secondary pole becomes the primary pole and vice versa. In general, the original primary pole was undesirable, but the secondary pole was desirable. Reversing the poles makes the node desirable. Therefore, the colour is also changed from red to green. [Note, if a node was already desirable, e.g. for a desirable side effect of a problem, the nodes are still reversed, but the desirable side effect is now lost or reduced.] The wording of each node is also then revised in order to (1) make sure it now makes sense in terms of solving the problem, eliminating the causes, etc., and (2) put the primary pole into the imperative, action-oriented voice. For example, note the imperative voice of the nodes on the right in figure 1. Note that at this stage, the bottom level of nodes in figure 1 has not yet been developed.

Step 3, Solution Derivation, augments the initial CCM of the problem as solutions developed in step 2 with further nodes that suggest *how* the problem and/or its causes can be reduced or eliminated. The purpose here is to come up with an adequate set of options for solving the problem, understand how they fit into the causal model of solving the problem (the problem as difficulties), and ultimately to make decisions about what actions to take (including, e.g. what new purposeful artefact features do design and evalaute in a DSR project). Coming up with candidate solutions, particularly envisioning new purposeful artefacts, requires some creative thought, but having a detailed understanding of a problem and its causes opens up many potential avenues for reducing or eliminating causes and achieving the goal of solving the problem as a whole. Solving a problem requires taking action, so nodes added need to be action-oriented and in the imperative voice, like the nodes derived in step 2. At this stage, one can brainstorm potential ways to address each of the causes, then consider which action node or what set of action nodes is [most] likely to sufficiently solve the problem and is feasible within existing resources. Where purposeful technology artefacts to solve a problem already exist, their application can be the topic of a node and connected to reducing one or more causes or the problem itself. Where purposeful technology artefacts are envisioned, but do not yet exist, taking action in the form of DSR may then be considered. In the context of DSR, one or more envisioned purposeful technology artefact node may be selected for one or more DSR projects.

Carefully employing the above process should pay dividends for DSR projects by (1) ensuring a thorough problem understanding so that its significance is clear and it is less likely to solve the wrong problem or work on developing a new purposeful artefact that is unlikely to solve the problem, (2) encouraging consideration of how to solve the problem from many angles, which encourages creativity, (3) developing a shared understanding and agreement about what DSR is to be done and why it is being done (the purpose and anticipated utility of the purposeful artefact), and (4) supporting design theory formation. Concerning support for design theory formation: (1)  CCM nodes concerning solving the problem and making an improvement form the meta-requirements [11] or general requirements [14, 16] in a design theory, (2) CCM nodes concerning artefact employment and features (together with their later more detailed design components and connections) form the meta-design [11]or general design [14, 16] in a design theory, and (3) the arrows between these nodes form the connection (utility relationship) between the meta-design and the meta-requirements [11].

# 4    An Example Application of CCM to DSR

The author has used the CCM approach together with colleagues at the start of a number of DSR projects. One example involved a group interested in conducting DSR to develop tools and systems to provide technology-assisted assessment of student assignment work. The author facilitated (and contributed to) an informal workshop to explore the problem. As the researchers were also all teachers, they could envisage themselves as future users of whatever technology-supported assessment systems or tools were developed. Thus all participants had more than one stakeholder role. The workshop was held in a colleagues (large) office with a large whiteboard. Figure 2 shows the whiteboard at the end of the session.

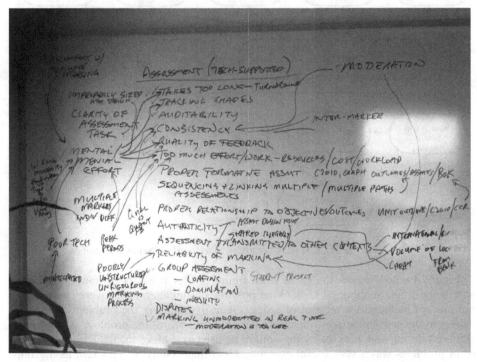

**Fig. 2.** Whiteboard after initial session analysing assessment marking problem

During the session, colleagues were invited to brainstorm to identify problems around the topic of assessment of student work. Problems were listed in random order as they were suggested. Each of the different items/nodes raised was discussed and clarified to the satisfaction of the participants. Next, the list was reviewed and the problems upon which the group wanted to work were identified. Next, causes were identified and connected to the problem "nodes" (text strings) with causal arrows. Other nodes continued to be added, sometimes with causes simply noted as bullet points underneath. The problems identified at the start are all listed at the centre of figure 2. Problems ticked in red, particularly those with two ticks, were the problems the group decided they would like to work on. Note that the group chose not to explore the consequences of the problem(s) at that time. Note as well that the group did not take time to dress up and improve the CCM into a properly formatted one. Many of the problem nodes were not initially stated clearly as problems and none of the nodes had secondary poles. Having computer-based support for projecting and editing the CCM might have improved the elegance of the resulting diagram. Nonetheless the exercise was considered by all to be useful and it provided a basis for drawing a more formalised CCM. Figure 3 below provides an extract of portions of the resulting CCM of the problem as difficulties.

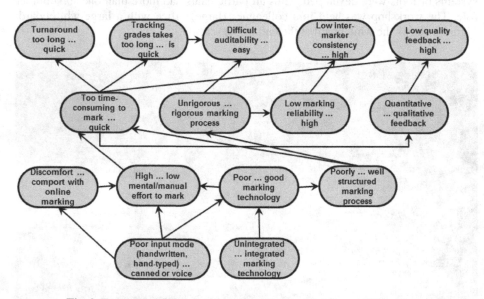

**Fig. 3.** Example of CCM of Assessment Marking Problem as Difficulties

Figure 4 below shows the CCM from figure 3 after it has been transformed and with some solution options added. Other possible design alternatives were considered, but are not included for reasons of space. Overall, exploring the problems and their causes in the problem space, converting the map into one of the problem as solutions, and considering how new technology might be used to achieve the reduction in causes or in problems was a very useful exercise. Most importantly, using CCM as a group greatly facilitated developing a shared understanding of the problem space and the areas on which the group could agree to work.

Within figure 4, the node(s) at the bottom of the figure that are chosen by the DSR researcher for their purposeful DSR artefact(s) correspond to the meta-design (or generalised design) in a subsequent design theory while the nodes that represent solving the problem and/or its implications represent the meta-requirements (or generalised requirements) in a design theory that formalises the knowledge resulting from the research.

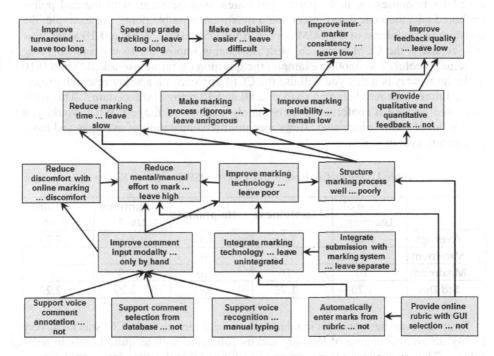

**Fig. 4.** Example of CCM of Assessment Marking Problem as Solutions

## 5    An Evaluation of CCM for DSR

To more rigorously evaluate CCM for DSR in practical use, the author conducted a number of workshops in which he has taught the framework. During the workshops, attendees applied CCM to their own research (if possible) or to a fictional piece of design science research. Workshop attendees were a mix of experienced researchers, early career researchers, and PhD students. Three workshops were conducted at three different locations. In all there were 22 attendees. During the workshops, nineteen attendees applied CCM to their own research and three applied it to a fictional DSR example.

At the conclusion of the workshop, attendees were asked to complete a short questionnaire evaluating the use of CCM for DSR. The questionnaire included quantitative questions concerning the CCM approach's ease of learning, usefulness, and helpfulness for their research (only for those who applied it to their own research), as well as ratings of the likelihood that the respondent would continue to use CCM for their research (again only for those who applied it to their own research) and that they would use CCM on future DSR projects (all participants). The questionnaire also invited open comments to identify problematic areas, good and useful areas, perceived benefits, and suggestions for improving the CCM approach for DSR. All attendees completed the questionnaires.

Table 1 presents the results of the quantitative questions. Quantitative questions asked for responses on an 11 point, zero-to-ten numeric scale, with the end points anchored on a theoretical zero point and a maximum possible point. For example, the question on usefulness of the CCM approach for DSR asked "2. On a 0-10 scale, how easy to use is the CCM approach, with zero being impossible to use and 10 being extremely useful?" As another example, the question on future use asked "On a 0-10 scale, how likely is it that you will use the CCM approach on another research project in the future, with zero being no chance at all and 10 being 100% certain?" This scale was used because it conforms to a commonly understood usage ("What would you give it out of 10?"), which also allows meaningful computation of averages and has a convenient midpoint of 5.

**Table 1.** Quantitative Results of CCM for DSR Evaluation Survey

|         | Ease of Learning | Usefulness | Helpfulness | Continue Use? | Future Use? |
|---------|------------------|------------|-------------|---------------|-------------|
| Average | 8.05             | 7.95       | 7.47        | 7.16          | 7.53        |
| Minimum | 3                | 3          | 4           | 3             | 2           |
| Maximum | 10               | 10         | 10          | 10            | 10          |
| Std Dev | 1.70             | 1.76       | 1.81        | 2.27          | 2.20        |

From the quantitative results in table 1, the reader can see that CCM was rated very highly on average in ease of learning and usefulness as well as quite highly in helpfulness. The answers concerning rating of likelihood that the attendees would continue to use the CCM approach and/or would use it on future DSR projects further indicate the utility of the CCM approach to participants. While average ratings were generally high, not all individual ratings were high, indicating that the CCM approach was not universally considered to have high utility for every researcher. Generally lower ratings were given by highly experienced researchers, for whom presumably their experience makes problem analysis a more intuitive and familiar practice.

The post-workshop questionnaire also contained a number of questions asking for open comments on strengths and benefits, weaknesses and problematic areas, and suggestions for improvement (e.g. 10. "What three suggestions would you make for improving the CCM approach?").

Benefits and strengths of the CCM approach cited included the following:

- Problem formulation seems much easier.
- Simple, logical, and incremental.
- It can be a good conceptual tool to explore, discover and examine the problem space and to make a connection to the solution space.
- Transition from description of problem to identification of (potential) solutions

- Stage 2 gave me a good tool to clarify what I need to do.
- Encourages rational thinking.
- Provide an extremely logical way of thinking about my research questions.
- The visualisation of a problem is good and effective.
- Force me to think outside the box.

Weaknesses/problematic areas of the CCM approach cited included the following:

- Identifying relevant nodes.
- Initial problem map.
- Formulating causal relationship was hard.
- Making sure the (causal) links are valid - easiness of relating things to each other.
- I need more time to think what is cause and what is effect in some cases.
- Polarity is an issue - not a straightforward exercise. Not being clear on what is desirable.
- Scoping - where do the problems and consequences end? When do we stop analysing?
- Some concepts can't be reversed easily.
- CCM conversion.

The respondents made a number of useful suggestions for improving the CCM approach, including the following:

- Perhaps could benefit from identification of the perspective from which consequences are framed, i.e. whose problem is this? Are problems different for different actors?
- Maybe call "problems as solutions" "problems as opportunities" instead.
- Trade off analysis when not all alternative solutions can be implemented.
- How to evaluate solutions.
- Provide some heuristics for scoping.

The first suggestion is important where different stakeholder have different interests and perspectives. Of course one could annotate nodes according to the stakeholders for whom the node is relevant or appropriate.

As yet, the above suggestions have not yet been incorporated into the CCM approach or evaluated. However, it is likely that the CCM approach will continue to evolve over time as we gain more experience with it and make various small (or possibly large) improvements to adapt it for use in DSR.

The evaluation through teaching in workshops and with limited application to participants' research has some significant limitations. First, the author was available to answer questions and provide suggestions. Second, the approach was not used in a group, so its utility for working in a group was not evaluated. Third, the CCM approach was not used to explicitly draft or construct a design theory, so its utility for that purpose was also not evaluated.

## 6     Conclusion

This paper has proposed the adaptation and use of Coloured Cognitive Mapping as a technique to support the early stages of Design Science Research and address the gaps in the DSR literature concerning how to analyse a problem in the context of DSR as well as how to identify and suggest potential or candidate design artefact alternatives. The paper has identified five main benefits of employing CCM to analyse problems in DSR: (1) improving understanding of a problem to be solved in DSR, its causes, and the conditions that allow a problem to continue or hinder its solution, (2) ability to transform a problem into solution requirements during step 2 of the CCM process, (3) improved ability to develop a shared problem understanding among collaborating DSR researchers, (4) improved ability to creatively think of alternative potential avenues and means to solve (or reduce or alleviate) the problem, i.e. possible artefacts to develop and evaluate, and (5) improved ability to develop and convey design theories about the utility of a developed design artefact to solve a problem, address all five of the research gaps identified toward the end of section 2.1.

The CCM approach has been evaluated in two ways. The author and colleagues have applied the CCM approach at early stages of DSR projects, illustrating its potential to support groups to reach a shared understanding and suggest design alternatives. The author has further evaluated the CCM approach by teaching it in workshops and surveying workshop participants for their opinions about the approach, from which feedback is largely quite positive.

Limitations of the evaluations conducted suggest that further research is needed to apply the approach throughout live projects not conducted by the author and to more rigorously evaluate the approach against the hypothesised benefits identified above.

## References

1. Venable, J.R.: Supporting Problem Formulation in IS Development with Coloured Cognitive Maps. In: Conference Supporting Problem Formulation in IS Development with Coloured Cognitive Maps. National University of Ireland, Galway (Year)
2. Venable, J.R.: Coloured Cognitive Maps for Modelling Decision Contexts. In: Conference Coloured Cognitive Maps for Modelling Decision Contexts. CEUR Workshop Proceedings (Year)
3. Venable, J.R., Baskerville, R.: Eating Our Own Cooking: Toward a More Rigorous Design Science of Research Methods. Electronic Journal of Business Research Methods 10, 141–153 (2012)
4. March, S.T., Smith, G.F.: Design and natural science research on information technology. Decision Support Systems 15, 251–266 (1995)
5. Hevner, A.R., March, S.T., Park, J., Ram, S.: Design Science in Information Systems Research. MIS Quarterly 28, 75–105 (2004)
6. Association for Information Systems, http://desrist.org/design-research-in-information-systems/
7. Peffers, K., Tuunanen, T., Rothenberger, M.A., Chatterjee, S.: A Design Science Research Methodology for Information Systems Research. Journal of Management Information Systems 24, 45–77 (2008)

8. Sein, M.K., Henfridsson, O., Purao, S., Rossi, M., Lindgren, R.: Action Design Research. MIS Quarterly 35, 37–56 (2011)
9. Schön, D.A.: The Reflective Practitioner: How Professionals Think in Action. Basic Books, New York (1983)
10. Simon, H.A.: The Sciences of the Artificial. MIT Press, Cambridge (1996)
11. Walls, J.G., Widmeyer, G.R., El Sawy, O.A.: Building an information system design theory for vigilant EIS. Information Systems Research 3, 36–59 (1992)
12. Eekels, J., Roozenburg, N.F.M.: A methodological comparison of the structures of scientific research and engineering design: Their similarities and differences. Design Studies 12, 197–203 (1991)
13. Archer, L.B.: Systematic method for designers. In: Cross, N. (ed.) Developments in Design Methodology, pp, pp. 57–82. Wiley, London (1984)
14. Venable, J.R.: The Role of Theory and Theorising in Design Science Research. In: Conference The Role of Theory and Theorising in Design Science Research (Year)
15. Gregor, S., Jones, D.: The Anatomy of a Design Theory. Journal of the Association for Information Systems 8, 312–335 (2007)
16. Baskerville, R., Pries-Heje, J.: Explanatory Design Theory. In: Business & Information Systems Engineering 2010, pp. 271–282 (2010)
17. Venable, J.R.: Rethinking Design Theory in Information Systems. In: vom Brocke, J., Hekkala, R., Ram, S., Rossi, M. (eds.) DESRIST 2013. LNCS, vol. 7939, pp. 136–149. Springer, Heidelberg (2013)
18. Checkland, P., Holwell, S.: Information, Systems, and Information Systems. Wiley, Chichester (1999)
19. Checkland, P.: Systems Thinking, Systems Practice. Wiley, Chichester (1981)
20. Checkland, P., Scholes, J.: Soft Systems Methodology in Action. J. Wiley, Chichester (1990)
21. Ishikawa, K.: Guide to Quality Control. Union of Japanese Scientists and Engineers (JUSE), Tokyo, Japan (1956)
22. Roberts, P.: Systems and the Problematique. Futures 27, 730–740 (1994)
23. Ackermann, F., Eden, C.: SODA – Journey Making and Mapping in Practice. In: Rosenhead, J., Mingers, J. (eds.) Rational Analysis for a Problematic World Revisited. Wiley, Chichester (2001)
24. Eden, C.: Cognitive Mapping: a review. European Journal of Operational Research 36, 1–13 (1988)
25. Eden, C., Ackermann, F.: Making Strategy: The Journey of Strategic Management. Sage, London (1998)
26. Eden, C., Ackermann, F.: SODA - The Principles. In: Rosenhead, J., Mingers, J. (eds.) Rational Analysis for a Problematic World Revisited. Wiley, Chichester (2001)
27. Bryson, J.M., Ackermann, F., Eden, C., Finn, C.B.: Visible Thinking: Unlocking causal mapping for practical business results. Wiley, Chichester (2004)

# Towards a More Cognitively Effective Business Process Notation for Requirements Engineering

Carel Miske, Marcus A. Rothenberger, and Ken Peffers

Department of MET, University of Nevada, Las Vegas, NV
miskec@unlv.nevada.edu,
{marcus.rothenberger,ken.peffers}@unlv.edu

**Abstract.** We are developing a semi-formal business process modeling notation based on the modification of theatrical blocking notation that is more cognitively effective for application in requirements engineering communication than extant notations. The Socio-Technical System Notation (STSN) incorporates ontological, semantic, and visual design improvements over extant languages that were pinpointed by prior research as areas for improvement to existing notations, such as the UML and BPMN, for the purpose of reducing the likelihood of errors and misinterpretation during the encoding and decoding processes. The research-in-progress paper follows a design science research approach to motivate the development of the STSN, to present a prototype of the notation, and to set the stage for the empirical evaluation of the language based on its design objectives. The research presents a process notation that enables the encoding of more detailed requirements information into a visual representation than extant notations.

**Keywords:** conceptual modeling, requirements engineering, cognitive effectiveness, business process modeling, notation design.

## 1 Introduction

The standard rationale for conceptual modeling during the requirements engineering (RE) process is that visual representations of the system and processes mitigate risks associated with incorrect and incomplete requirements specifications by acting as a means for eliciting, analyzing, agreeing, and communicating domain knowledge [1, 2]. Further, these models assist with framing the problem scope, establishing system boundaries, and overcoming the perception gaps between the goal and process oriented problem domain and the machine oriented solution domain [1, 3]. Ideally, conceptual models help to establish a common-ground understanding and shared mental model of the system among project stakeholders, and thereby increase the efficiency and effectiveness of problem solving and developing an apposite solution during the RE process [4]. However, the persistently significant level of requirements-related IT project failures [5, 6] indicates that there remains room for improvement in the RE communication process despite the advances in available modeling notations.

M.C. Tremblay et al. (Eds.): DESRIST 2014, LNCS 8463, pp. 360–367, 2014.
© Springer International Publishing Switzerland 2014

A potential source for the disparity between the intention and realization of the goals for RE conceptual modeling is that the development of the de facto standard languages used, the Unified Modeling Language (UML) and Business Process Model and Notation (BPMN), has not been focused on expressly facilitating the cognitive effectiveness and ease of use of these languages as communication tools [7-9]. Further, analyses of these languages indicate inherent ontological, semantic, and visual design factors that may limit their utility in RE communications because of the potential for ambiguity, cognitive overload, and practitioner error during encoding and decoding [10-12]. This suggests that attention to the standards applied to the analyses of these notational languages may potentially improve RE communications and reduce the incidence of requirements-related project failures. However, a comprehensive revision of these languages would be exceedingly broad in scope and fundamentally incompatible with their purposes.

We propose the Socio-Technical System Notation (STSN) as a prototype language designed as a comprehensive solution to this problem and initially apply its scope to business process diagramming. The informal iconical form of theatrical blocking notation (TBN) serves as the basis for STSN. We chose it because of its utility in cross-functional communication in the theatrical industry. We intendedly designed the notation for ontological and semantic clarity and completeness, based upon the ontological work of Bunge [13, 14] and Wand, and Weber (BWW) [15, 16] and Moody's Semantic Clarity Model (MSCM) [11]. The visual design was informed by Moody's Physics of Notations Theory (PoNT) [11]. The comparative empirical evaluation of the STSN will require test subjects to encode and de-code business processes in STSN and UML Activity Diagrams (AD). In addition, the decoding process evaluation includes recognition, recall, and transfer tests to measure user retention and understanding as indicators of the cognitive effectiveness of the languages [17].

This research contributes to information systems (IS) with a theoretical solution for mitigating risks associated with communication problems in RE in the form of a visual notation artifact. The artifact is designed as an efficient means for creating cognitively effective visualizations of business processes. The resulting artifact may also have utility for business process management and (re)engineering, supply chain management, and other disciplines where activities and data flow inform decisions.

## 2    Identification of the Problem

The need to bridge the socio-cognitive differences that shape the way business stakeholders and developers frame problems and engage in sense making is an intrinsic challenge for information systems RE [3]. Recent research supports the importance of overcoming this perception gap to mitigate project performance risks [18]. Failure to bridge this gap may reduce innovation, value creation, and efficiency during the software development process [19-21].

RE is an inherently complex and human-centered discipline. The success of the RE process is challenged by many factors, including the heterogeneous needs of the business stakeholders [22, 23] and the complexity and dynamism of contemporary business and IS [24]. Because of the many risk factors associated with ambiguous and uncertain requirements and change management, the degree of success in executing the RE process has a critical influence on project outcome [25-28].

To overcome these obstacles, RE practitioners strive to communicate the complexity and interconnectivity of IS requirements in a way that is mutually understandable to business stakeholders and developers [24]. Natural languages alone do not provide an unambiguous communication tool for conveying the complexity of business processes and IS [29]. The cognitive theory of multimedia learning (CTML) [17], based upon dual coding theory [30], supports the potential for enhanced cognitive effectiveness, and thereby communication efficacy, through supplementing textual or verbal information with diagrams during RE communication. Consequently, supplementing natural language communication with visual notation languages during RE should facilitate improved domain understanding, system and process analysis, decision making, cognition, and communication between the business stakeholders and developers [1, 4]. However, RE practitioners must be proficient in selecting and using the modeling language(s) that enable accurate and complete visual representation of the problem domain with the desired perspective(s) for analysis [23]. Otherwise, RE practitioners risk diminishing the efficacy of the communication and design process by providing inaccurate, incomplete, unnecessary, redundant, or ambiguous information in diagrammatic form.

The de facto standard notations used for RE system and process diagrams, BPMN, for business process modeling, and UML, for systems modeling, are not explicitly designed to facilitate the intuitive creation and interpretation of diagrams by novice language users or to bridge the perception gaps among stakeholders by managing complexity at higher levels of detail, agility, and diagramming [7-9]. As these notations evolved from the tradition of workflow diagrams, they relied primarily on abstract geometric shapes rather than "semantically immediate" icons [11, p. 765] and placed little emphasis on visual designs to improve usability and cognition through the application of relevant theories such as Bertin's eight visual variables [31] or Mayer's CTML [17]. They also do not provided visual constructs for mapping goals to actions [7, 9] that give purpose to the activity [23] and are required by the definition of an activity in a social system [14]. Further, the results of analyses of the ontological and semantic mapping of these notations indicate that there are extant concerns with the clarity and completeness of these languages and the impact of these restrictions on the cognitive effectiveness and expressiveness of diagrams created in these languages [12, 32-35]. The complexity and interconnectivity of problem domains that fall outside of the intentions and philosophy of these notations may exacerbate these limitations. The implication of these analyses is that a language specifically designed to adhere to the principles of these recommended notational design theories would serve as an instrument to facilitate improved RE communications.

# 3     Objectives of the Solution

For the STSN to provide a design research contribution by improving RE communications, the notation system should satisfy the following objectives: it must (1) be ontologically and semantically clear and complete as defined by the BWW ontology and MSCM; (2) be easy to learn and to use; and (3) facilitate greater recognition, recall, and transfer, when compared with the UML AD. We compare STSN's performance to that of the

UML AD because of high adoption rates and long implementation history. The overall set of objectives was derived from analyses of the factors that limit the utility, expressiveness, and cognitive effectiveness of the UML AD as a communication tool.

## 4    Design and Development

The language constructs necessary for the satisfaction of the objectives of the solution were designed into the STSN notation during the conversion process of TBN into a socio-technical system business process notation. Objective (1) required the creation of language constructs in full support of (a) the BWW ontology, the de facto standard for evaluating ontological completeness and clarity as a measure of the semantic construction of software engineering conceptual modeling notations, and (b) the MSCM. Objectives (2) and (3) required the practical application of the design principles from the PoNT and the evaluation of the utility of the notation through empirical testing.

The TBN language was selected because it serves as a common-ground tool for decision-making, training, analysis, and design and as a means to create an historical record of the production within the domain of theatre [36]. By tradition, this relatively intuitive, actor-oriented language enables the rapid, live recording and easy modification of the detailed complexity of actors interacting with other actors and objects within their environment and being acted upon by external factors. It therefore serves within the theatrical domain similar purposes as required of diagramming within the RE domain. In its iconical forms, TBN inherently facilitates semantic immediacy and provides the combination of text and graphics recommended by the CTML. These attributes combined with over a century of successful use in theatre recommended the adaptation of the TBN to achieve the goals of this research.

The primary weakness of the TBN is a lack of standardization. Although common sets of notational symbols are included in theatrical curricula and reference books, stage managers primarily develop their modeling style through apprenticeship and experience [36]. Beyond a few basic symbols and common variants, TBN is primarily an ad hoc notation, similar to the Rich Pictures used in Soft Systems Methodology [37]. Therefore, although TBN could theoretically mitigate many of the aforementioned RE communication challenges, the informal nature of TBN prevents a standardized application of the notation directly to the more formal and complex RE problem space. Fig. 1 is a simple example of a business process recorded directly in TBN.

TBN is concerned with physical movement and the relative and absolute positioning of things within the environment and is temporally linked to the script. In contrast, business processes are concerned with workflows and must have internal methods of depicting temporal changes. Therefore, the STSN required the addition of both the semantic constructs and syntax for depicting these concerns. For this initial phase of the design, we selected Hofstede et al.'s workflow patterns [38] because of their level of completeness and standardization. As these models have been applied to analyses of the UML AD and BPMN their use also enables a comparative evaluation of the relative completeness of the STSN. An example of the STSN is depicted in Fig. 2.

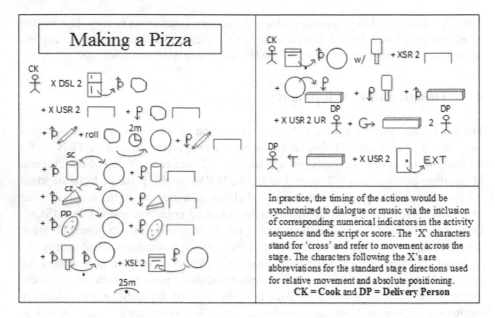

**Fig. 1.** An example of a heavily iconical form of TBN

The STSN is intended to supplement existing diagrams in the UML by providing the means for encoding more detailed requirements information into a more cognitively effective representation of business processes. The socio-technical viewpoint of the notation enables an enhanced depiction of the interaction of humans and technology from the standpoint of the actors (both human and artificial) within the system. The reliance upon icons enhanced with text is recommended by the CTML for communication efficacy and cognitive effectiveness. The summary goal of the STSN is to assist with overcoming the perception gap during the RE process by providing a comparatively humanistic and intuitive method for decoding information and to enable the effective encoding of complex system information.

## 5     Evaluation

The artifact will be evaluated in an experimental setting with the treatment group interacting with the STSN and the control group interacting with the UML AD, both, for the purpose of interpreting the notation and for encoding requirements. The evaluation will follow guidelines for the empirical evaluation of conceptual models from Burton-Jones et al. [39] and Gemino and Wand [4]. Diagram interpretation will include tests for recognition, recall, and transfer. Encoding will require the creation of a simple business process diagram. Perceived ease of use will be assessed based upon the guidelines provided by Moore and Benbasat [40].

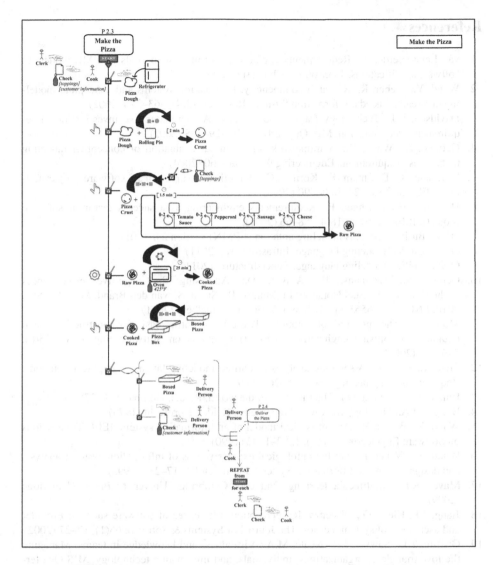

**Fig. 2.** STSN diagram demonstrating the use of custom and generic objects

# 6    Conclusion

This research contributes to the IS body of knowledge by proposing a theoretical solution for mitigating risks associated with communication problems in RE. The solution takes the form of a visual notation artifact designed as an efficient means for creating cognitively effective visualizations of complex business processes. It also contributes to the study of notational design through a demonstration and evaluation of the application of relevant theories intended to enhance the communications efficacy of notations.

# References

1. van Lamsweerde, A.: Requirements engineering: From system goals to UML models to software specifications. John Wiley, Chichester (2009)
2. Wand, Y., Weber, R.: Research commentary: Information systems and conceptual modeling–a research agenda. Information Systems Research 13(4), 363–376 (2002)
3. Davidson, E.J.: Technology frames and framing: A socio-cognitive investigation of requirements determination. MIS Quarterly 26(4), 329–358 (2002)
4. Gemino, A., Wand, Y.: A framework for empirical evaluation of conceptual modeling techniques. Requirements Engineering 9(4), 248–260 (2004)
5. El Emam, K., El Emam, K., Koru, A.G.: A replicated survey of IT software project failures. IEEE Software 25(5), 84–90 (2008)
6. Hofmann, H.F., Lehner, F.: Requirements engineering as a success factor in software projects. IEEE Software 18(4), 58–66 (2001)
7. OMG: Business process modeling notation (BPMN) version 2.0. (2011)
8. OMG: Unified modeling language: Infrastructure. (2011)
9. OMG: Unified modeling language: Superstructure. (2011)
10. Genon, N., Heymans, P., Amyot, D.: Analysing the cognitive effectiveness of the BPMN 2.0 Visual Notation. In: Malloy, B., Staab, S., van den Brand, M. (eds.) SLE 2010. LNCS, vol. 6563, pp. 377–396. Springer, Heidelberg (2011)
11. Moody, D.: The "physics" of notations: Toward a scientific basis for constructing visual notations in software engineering. IEEE Transactions on Software Engineering 35(6), 756–779 (2009)
12. Siau, K., Tian, Y.: A semiotic analysis of unified modeling language graphical notations. Requirements Engineering 14(1), 15–26 (2009)
13. Bunge, M.A.: Ontology I: The furniture of the world. Reidel, Dordrecht (1977)
14. Bunge, M.A.: Ontology II: A world of systems. Reidel, Dordrecht (1979)
15. Wand, Y., Weber, R.: An ontological model of an information system. IEEE Transactions on Software Engineering 16(11), 1282–1292 (1990)
16. Wand, Y., Weber, R.: On the ontological expressiveness of information systems analysis and design grammars. Information Systems Journal 3(4), 217–237 (1993)
17. Mayer, R.E.: Multimedia learning, 2nd edn. Cambridge University Press, Cambridge (2009)
18. Jiang, J.J., Klein, G., Discenza, R.: Perception differences of software success: Provider and user views of system metrics. The Journal of Systems & Software 63(1), 17–27 (2002)
19. Griffith, T.L., Sawyer, J.E., Neale, M.A.: Virtualness and knowledge in teams: Managing the love triangle of organizations, individuals, and information technology. MIS Quarterly 27(2), 265–287 (2003)
20. Mohtashami, M., Marlowe, T., Kirova, V., et al.: Risk management for collaborative software development. Inf. Syst. Manage. 23(4), 20 (2006)
21. Vlaar, P.W.L., van Fenema, P.C., Tiwari, V.: Cocreating understanding and value in distributed work: How members of onsite and offshore vendor teams give, make, demand, and break sense. MIS Quarterly 32(2), 227–255 (2008)
22. Holmström, J., Sawyer, S.: Requirements engineering blinders: Exploring information systems developers' black-boxing of the emergent character of requirements. European Journal of Information Systems 20(1), 34–47 (2011)
23. Nuseibeh, B., Easterbrook, S.: Requirements engineering: A roadmap. In: Proceedings of the Conference on the Future of Software Engineering, Limerick, Ireland. ACM, New York (2000)

24. Jarke, M., Loucopoulos, P., Lyytinen, K., et al.: The brave new world of design requirements. Inf. Syst. 36(7), 992–1008 (2011)
25. Chen, Y., Bharadwaj, A.: An empirical analysis of contract structures in IT outsourcing. Information Systems Research 20(4), 484,506,604 (2009)
26. Jiang, J.J., Klein, G., Wu, S.P.J., et al.: The relation of requirements uncertainty and stakeholder perception gaps to project management performance. The Journal of Systems & Software 82(5), 801–808 (2009)
27. Keil, M., Cule, P.E., Lyytinen, K., et al.: A framework for identifying software project risks. Association for Computing Machinery. Communications of the ACM 41(11), 76 (1998)
28. Wallace, L., Keil, M.: Software project risks and their effect on outcomes. Commun. ACM 47(4), 68 (2004)
29. Yang, H., de Roeck, A., Gervasi, V., et al.: Analysing anaphoric ambiguity in natural language requirements. Requirements Engineering 16(3), 163–189 (2011)
30. Paivio, A.: Mental representations: A dual coding approach. Oxford University Press, New York (1986)
31. Bertin, J.: Semiology of graphics: Diagrams, networks, maps, 1st edn. ESRI Press (2010)
32. Recker, J., Rosemann, M., Krogstie, J.: Ontology- versus pattern-based evaluation of process modeling languages: A comparison. Communications of AIS 2007(20), 774–799 (2007)
33. Recker, J., Rosemann, M.: The measurement of perceived ontological deficiencies of conceptual modeling grammars. Data Knowl. Eng. 69(5), 516–532 (2010)
34. Weber, R.: Conceptual modelling and ontology: Possibilities and pitfalls. J. Database Manage. 14(3), 1 (2003)
35. Moody, D., van Hillegersberg, J.: Evaluating the visual syntax of UML: An analysis of the cognitive effectiveness of the UML family of diagrams. In: Gašević, D., Lämmel, R., Van Wyk, E. (eds.) SLE 2008. LNCS, vol. 5452, pp. 16–34. Springer, Heidelberg (2009)
36. Fazio, L.: Stage manager: The professional experience. Focal Press, Boston (2000)
37. Checkland, P., Scholes, J.: Soft systems methodology in action. Wiley (1990)
38. ter Hofstede, A.H.M., Kiepuszewski, B., Barros, A., et al.: Workflow patterns. Distributed and Parallel Databases 14(1), 5–51 (2003)
39. Burton-Jones, A., Wand, Y., Weber, R.: Guidelines for empirical evaluations of conceptual modeling grammars*. Journal of the Association for Information Systems 10(6), 495–532 (2009)
40. Moore, G.C., Benbasat, I.: Development of an instrument to measure the perceptions of adopting an information technology innovation. Information Systems Research 2(3), 192–222 (1991)

# Social Data Analytics Tool (SODATO)

Abid Hussain[1] and Ravi Vatrapu[1,2]

[1] CSSL, Department of IT Management, Copenhagen Business School, Denmark
[2] MOTEL, Norwegian School of Information Technology (NITH), Norway
{ah.itm,vatrapu}@cbs.dk

**Abstract.** This paper presents the Social Data Analytics Tool (SODATO) that is designed, developed and evaluated to collect, store, analyze, and report big social data emanating from the social media engagement of and social media conversations about organizations.

**Keywords:** social media, data science, computational social science, big data analytics.

## 1 Introduction

Big social data that is generated by the social media engagement and social software utilization of a company results in both operational issues and managerial challenges [5, 8]. With the wide spread adoption of social media for organizational purposes, there is a clear need for developing concepts, methods, and tools that systematically analyze big social data. In recent years, researchers have emphasized that technical advancements are required to deal with the situation [10]. Such requirements include the modeling of social data on individual and collective levels as well as identification of unified methods to process social data [1, 4, 9]. In this paper, we report on the design, development and features provided by a theoretically informed and methodologically grounded IT artefact (SODATO) that addresses the diverse but interrelated issues associated with social data.

The remainder of the paper is organized as follows. *Section 2* describes the design of the IT artefact in terms of the problem statement, use cases, intended user groups, and technical architecture. *Section 3* presents the *Action Design Research* (ADR) method [7] and describes how ADR informed the design, development and evaluation of SODATO. *Sections 4* and *5* report on the significance of the IT artefact to researchers and practitioners respectively. *Section 6* summarizes the ADR evaluation of SODATO.

## 2 Design of the IT Artefact

### 2.1 Problem Statement

From an academic standpoint, Zeng [10] identified the unique technical challenges in social media analytics due to unstructured data across networks and observed that

M.C. Tremblay et al. (Eds.): DESRIST 2014, LNCS 8463, pp. 368–372, 2014.

data has not been treated systematically in data and text mining literature. Wang [9] argued that social computing is changing the way we interact, identified a need for modeling of social data on both individual and collective level, and called for new analytical techniques and IT artefacts for social data analytics. Quite a few organizations have been falling behind in adopting the social media due to lack of understanding of its diverse scope [3]. Kietzmann et al. [4] urged organizations to take social media engagement seriously. They argued that since social media sites are diverse in functionality and scope, there is a need of identifying uniformed and generic methods to analyze social data from different sites. Finally, Chen et al. [1] describe the state of data analytics and state that social media analytics is essentially different from traditional Business Intelligence and more research is needed in order to design methods and techniques for drawing insights from social data. From an industry standpoint, many commercial software vendors (such as Radian6[1], IBM Cognos Customer Insight[2], SAS[3], Social Bakers[4]) are providing software applications to monitor, measure, and manage social data. However, an important problem with existing commercial applications is that there is little-to-no empirical research on the data provenance, efficacy, effectiveness, and impact of the different social media metrics and key performance indicators employed. Further, there is no provision of "raw data" as such or transparency about the algorithms, formulas, and metrics from a data science technical perspective as well as an organizational perspective of business analytics. We term this lacuna in the current theoretical knowledge, empirical findings, and industry practice as the **Gulf of Social Media Analytics**. The primary objective of this paper to briefly present the design, development and evaluation of an IT artefact (Social Data Analytics Tool, SODATO) to bridge the Gulf of Social Media Analytics. To achieve this, we have developed a unified framework [6] consisting of a theory of social data, a conceptual model, a formal model, technological architecture and finally, the software tool itself which is the focus of this paper.

## 2.2 Use Cases

One use case is for the campaign strategist of a political party can utilize SODATO in order to fetch Facebook walls. A second use case is that the social media manager at an organization can use SODATO to fetch their social data and extract meaningful and actionable insights on content performance (such as which post types are most popular amongst the users and explore correlations to sales and other in-house data from ERP and CRM systems).

## 2.3 Intended User Groups

Analyzing the use cases mentioned, the target end users of SODATO can be listed as researchers, analysts, social media managers, chief listening officers, and trainee analysts (for example, students in social media management and social data analytics courses).

---

[1] www.radian6.com

[2] http://www-01.ibm.com/software/analytics/cognos/

[3] http://www.sas.com/software/customer-intelligence/
social-media-analytics/

[4] www.socialbakers.com

## 2.4    Technical Architecture

Please refer to [6] for the unified framework of theory, conceptual model, and formal model of social data together with an illustrative example and a demonstrative case study. Figure 1 presents schematic of SODATO. SODATO can be accessed from http://cssl.cbs.dk/sodato

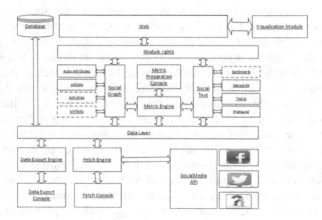

**Fig. 1.** Schematic of the Social Data Analytics Tool (SODATO)

Technically, SODATO utilizes the APIs provided by the social network vendors for example Facebook open source API named as Graph API. SODATO is a combination of web as well as windows based console applications that run in batches to fetch data and prepare data for analysis. The Web part of the tool is developed using HTML, JavaScript, Microsoft ASP.NET and C#. Console applications are developed using C#. Microsoft SQL Server is used for data storage and data pre-processing. SODATO provides a generic method for retrieving, storing and analyzing social data. SODATO can be utilized by practitioners as well as researchers in order to obtain a detailed understanding of trends, dynamics, and mechanisms in the domain of Facebook currently (and scalable to different online social media platforms). Specifically, SODATO supports descriptive, prescriptive and/or predictive analytics in terms of *the social graph* (actors involved, artefacts created, actions taken, activities engaged) and *social text* (sentiments expressed, topics discussed, pronouns addressed, and keywords mentioned) [8].

## 3    Design Science Methodology

SODATO has been developed based on the design principles defined by Action design Research methodology [7]. The development process started in 2011 when the alpha version of SODATO was released with the name SOGATO [2]. The development process started with the basic problem formulation jointly informed by the literature in the domain of social media analytics. Developers, researchers, trainee social media analysts and organizations constituted the ADR team of SODATO. There have been multiple iterations informed by the second phase of ADR, *Building intervention and evaluation* (BIE). Each iteration contributed towards the IT artefact as well as the knowledge body within the domain of social media analytics. Finally, reflections and learnings from the ADR process are currently being actively reported through both academic publications and workshops. . Table 1 presents the First BIE cycle of ADR [7] for SODATO.

**Table 1.** First BIE Cycle for SODATO

| SODATO: RELEASE ONE | | | | |
|---|---|---|---|---|
| Actor: Type | Evaluation: Examples | Feedback: Examples | Contribution: Ensemble Artefact | Contribution: Science |
| Researchers | Danish election 2011 Social media analysis | Large walls cannot be fetched using web version<br><br>Statistics are performing slow | Batch processing introduced<br><br>Pre- Processing of fetched data built | Empirically informed modifications to the descriptive model of social data |
| Trainee Analysts | Social media projects with real-world case companies | Multiple requests for walls for multiple users<br><br>User interface issues | Authorization system developed<br><br>User interface improved | |
| Practitioners | Interaction with trainee analysts | Statistics needed to be developed that suited the case company's industry sector and social media use | Custom metric module was developed | |

# 4    Significance to Research

SODATO incorporates innovative features that provide value to the researchers. The development of the tool in theoretically grounded [6] and follows industry standards in software engineering. SODATO addresses the commercial tools' lack of attention to data fetch procedures by implementing systematic data collection procedures, logging, and error recovery options. Due to the complex data structure of Facebook when compared to Twitter, there has been far less research using Facebook data comparatively and SODATO enables researchers to fill this knowledge gap by provisioning facebook social data. As far as we know, there does not exist a social media analytics tool in the literature that is designed and developed using design science principles. Neither could we find any generic method that could uniformly be applied for building other application in the same domain of knowledge. Hence we believe that this artefact is a contribution for information systems in general and design science research in particular. At the operational level, SODATO provides unique (as of yet) features to researchers as stated below:

• SODATO can fetch and store historic data right from start of Facebook time (we are yet to find this in a commercial tool)
• SODATO provides very high level of transparency in data fetching and calculates data provenance

• Researchers are able to fetch the data using the tool and can export large sets of data and do analysis using modelling, statistical and/or coding tools of their choice such as Microsoft Excel, IBM SPSS, R, MatLab etc.
• Domain specific features for projects in fields such as Political Science, Marketing, Finance, and Sustainability.

## 5  Significance to Practice

SODATO provides state-of-the-art functionality for descriptive, predictive, and prescriptive analytics of big social data for organizations. It differs from existing commercial tools in the sense that it can be used as a strategic tool for fetching the complete online social data record of an organization on the platform of Facebook. Different insights can be generated from different analysis methods provided by the tool such as sentiments analysis, keyword analysis, actor attribute analysis, content performance analysis, social influencer analysis and integrative analytics with in-house data from web analytics, ERP and CRM systems.

## 6  Evaluation

As mentioned earlier, we adopted the ADR model [7] for design and development and the current state of the tool is informed by iterations over three years where trainee analysts, researchers and practitioners have been evaluating the tool (see Table 1 for the first BIE cycle).

## References

1. Chen, H., Chiang, R.H., Storey, V.C.: Business intelligence and analytics: from big data to big impact. MIS Quarterly 36, 1165–1188 (2012)
2. Hussain, A., Vatrapu, R.: SOGATO: A Social Graph Analytics Tool. In: The 12th European Conference on Computer Supported Cooperative Work 2011 (2011)
3. Kaplan, A.M., Haenlein, M.: Users of the world, unite! The challenges and opportunities of Social Media. Business Horizons 53, 59–68 (2010)
4. Kietzmann, J.H., Hermkens, K., Mccarthy, I.P., Silvestre, B.S.: Social media? Get serious! Understanding the functional building blocks of social media. Business Horizons 54, 241–251 (2011)
5. Lovett, J.: Social Media Metrics Secrets. Wiley (2011)
6. Mukkamala, R., Hussain, A., Vatrapu, R.: Towards a Formal Model of Social Data. IT University Technical Report Series TR-2013-169 (2013), https://pure.itu.dk/ws/files/54477234/ITU_TR_54472013_54477169.pdf
7. Sein, M., Henfridsson, O., Purao, S., Rossi, M., Lindgren, R.: Action design research. MIS Quarterly 35, 37–56 (2011)
8. Vatrapu, R.: Understanding Social Business. In: Akhilesh, K.B. (ed.) Emerging Dimensions of Technology Management, pp. 147–158. Springer, Heidelberg (2013)
9. Wang, F.-Y., Carley, K.M., Zeng, D., Mao, W.: Social computing: From social informatics to social intelligence. IEEE Intelligent Systems 22, 79–83 (2007)
10. Zeng, D., Chen, H., Lusch, R., Li, S.-H.: Social media analytics and intelligence. IEEE Intelligent Systems 25, 13–16 (2010)

# Travel Safety: A Social Media Enabled Mobile Travel Risk Application

Kay Noyen[1] and Felix Wortmann[2]

[1] ETH Zurich, Information Management, Zurich, Switzerland
knoyen@ethz.ch
[2] University of St. Gallen, Technology Management, St. Gallen, Switzerland
felix.wortmann@unisg.ch

**Abstract.** We present the design artifact Travel Safety, a mobile travel risk information system (IS). Besides offering general travel risk information, the iPhone application leverages social media, in particular Twitter, to source travel risk information from multiple foreign offices. This provides a comprehensive real-time information base for the application and enables dispatch of automatic travel warnings. On the basis of Travel Safety we want to explore if content from social media can be leveraged to increase the attractiveness and usage of applications. Furthermore, we want to understand critical success factors in the context of using social media content. Travel Safety was evaluated in a large field study with 422 participants. The study reveals that applications can indeed successfully be enriched by social media content. However, our results also reveal that a fully automated sourcing of social media content without human content management bears significant challenges.

**Keywords:** Social Media, Mobile Applications, Travel Risk.

## 1    Introduction

Travel risk applications are becoming more and more established in the corporate landscape. Many global corporations equip their employees with IS like [1] and [2]. The promise of these pervasive systems is to manage potential risks before and actively safeguard employees during their travels. However, the high cost of travel risk data feeds has so far prevented broad adoption of travel risk IS. In this paper, we propose a design artifact that, besides offering well-known basic travel risk related features, particularly general travel risk information per country and an integrated emergency call, sources travel risk information from Twitter. Our experience has shown that only the basic features do not drive high usage of the application. Therefore, we investigate the potential of integrating real-time travel risk information sourced from Twitter into the application. By following this research avenue we address two fundamental research questions, i.e. "Can content from social media be leveraged to increase the attractiveness and usage of applications?" and "What are critical success factors in the context of using social media content in applications?"

M.C. Tremblay et al. (Eds.): DESRIST 2014, LNCS 8463, pp. 373–377, 2014.

## 2    Design of the Artifact

The core requirement of travel risk applications is to provide current, reliable and relevant travel risk information [3]. Travel Safety is designed to source this information from Twitter, instead of obtaining it from expensive commercial providers. In doing so, we followed the design science research paradigm [4,5,6]. Fig. 1 shows the data integration process. The process is fully automated and does not require active human content management. Tweets are aggregated from foreign offices (e.g. the German Federal Foreign Office Twitter account). After detecting the language of each tweet, countries are identified by matching potential country names. Irrelevant content is filter by excluding key words. Finally, a risk indicator graph is generated per country by counting the tweets mentioning the respective country in the aggregated tweets.

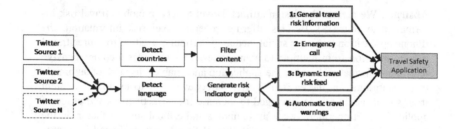

**Fig. 1.** Data integration process and Travel Safety features

### 2.1    Features

Travel Safety comprises two basic and two Twitter-based features:

1. **General Travel Risk Information:** Travel Safety includes a collection of travel facts listed by country. These facts range from local emergency numbers to vaccination recommendations, drunk driving laws, addresses of embassies and visa requirements. An example is shown in fig. 2b.

2. **Emergency Call:** Travel Safety displays local emergency numbers for registered travel destinations. Users can initiate calls to local police, fire stations, and hospitals. Additionally, users can directly call the assistance number of the provider of the application (automobile club). This is shown in fig. 2c.

3. **Dynamic Travel Risk Feed:** By selecting a country on the real-time risk map in fig. 2a, users can view the country's risk indicator graph and the corresponding tweets. This provides detailed information about the current situation in all countries in the world. Fig. 2d shows an example.

4. **Automatic Travel Warnings:** Travel Safety allows its users to register their travels and receive automatic travel warnings per SMS and/or push-notification by country. An example is shown in fig. 2e.

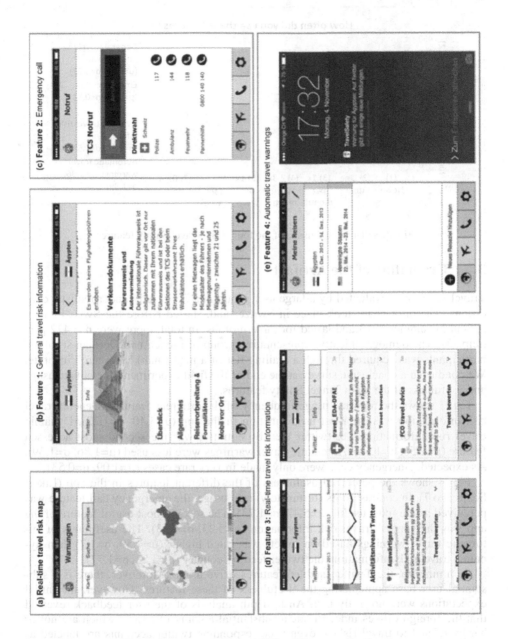

**Fig. 2.** Screencast of Travel Safety iPhone application

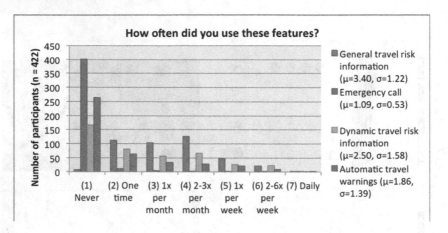

**Fig. 3.** Self-reported usage of the four main Travel Safety features

# 3    Evaluation of the Artifact

Travel safety was evaluated by a large user group in a field study under realistic conditions. The pilot phase took place in Switzerland, started before the Swiss holiday season in summer 2013 and lasted for three months. In total, there were n = 422 participants. The demographically representative group of French and German speaking participants was acquired through a mailing list of a major market research institute. We conducted a conclusive survey at the end of the field experiment to evaluate usage and usefulness of the main Travel Safety features.

Fig. 3 shows the reported usage frequency of the different features. General travel risk information was the most used function in the app (μ=3.40, σ=1.22). Dynamic travel risk information, i.e. twitter feed by country, was the second most accessed feature (μ=2.50, σ=1.58). Automatic travel warnings were less used (μ=1.86, σ=1.39). As expected, emergency calls were only made in very rare cases (μ=1.09, σ=0.53).

Fig. 4 shows the perceived usefulness of the different features in the app (Likert Scale 1 to 7). In contrast to its (fortunately) rare usage, the emergency call feature was perceived as the most useful (μ=5.47, σ=1.73). The second most useful feature of the app was the general travel risk information (μ=5.35, σ=1.53). The usefulness of automatic travel warnings based on tweets was rated higher (μ=4.59, σ=1.7) than dynamic travel risk information, the twitter feed by country (μ=3.58, σ=1.77).

Summing up, the Twitter-enabled features drive usage. Moreover, there is a substantial user base appreciating the usefulness of these features. However, the initial expectations were not fully met. An in depth analysis of the user feedback revealed that the foreign offices indeed issue a substantial amount of tweets which are not or hardly related to travel risks – even if corresponding twitter accounts are labeled as "dedicated to travel risks". After investigating the potential of more sophisticated filtering approaches, we have to conclude that fully automated sourcing of social media content without any human involvement has strong limitations. While we will certainly improve automatic filtering in our next design iteration, we strongly believe that we also have to build upon human computation [7], i.e. encourage users to get involved into content management e.g. by classifying risk-tweets as irrelevant.

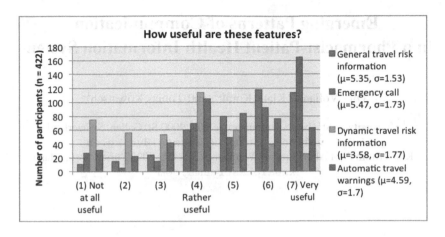

**Fig. 4.** Perceived usefulness of the four main Travel Safety features

# References

1. Aon WorldAware Solutions, http://www.aon.com
2. Drum Cussac Risk Management Platform, http://www.drum-cussac.com
3. Löwenheim, O.: The responsibility to responsibilize: foreign offices and the issuing of travel warnings. International Political Sociology 1(3), 203–221 (2007)
4. Hevner, A.R., March, S.T., Park, J., Ram, S.: Design science in information systems research. MIS Quarterly 28(1), 75–105 (2004)
5. Peffers, K., Tuunanen, T., Rothenberger, M.A., Chatterjee, S.: A design science research methodology for information systems research. Journal of Management of Information Systems 24(3), 45–77 (2007)
6. Gregor, S., Hevner, A.R.: Positioning and presenting design science research for maximum impact. MIS Quarterly 37(2), 337–355 (2013)
7. Von Ahn, L.: Human computation. In: 46th ACM/IEEE Design Automation Conference. IEEE (2009)

# Emerging Patterns of Communication
# in a Pharmacist-Patient Health Information System

Dirk Volland[1], Klaus Korak[2], and Tobias Kowatsch[1]

[1] University of St. Gallen, Dufourstrasse 40a, 9000 St. Gallen, Switzerland
{dirk.volland,tobias.kowatsch}@unisg.ch
[2] Konsortium Pilot AlphaStreams, Weinbergstr. 56/58, 8092 Zürich, Switzerland
kk@alphastreams.com

## 1    Introduction

Communication between healthcare professionals and patients is a major determinant of patients' satisfaction, patients' adherence, health outcomes, and ultimately of healthcare costs [1]. In most cases, however, personal communication between a healthcare professional and a patient is restricted to episodic face-to-face encounters. Once the face-to-face encounter comes to an end, structured communication ends. The absence of structured communication in time intervals between face-to-face encounters is a defining characteristic of current healthcare professional-patient interaction [2,3]. As a consequence, healthcare professionals lack the ability to guide patients outside the institutional space and to adjust supportive measures depending on particular situations and needs that arise during the therapeutic process.

Pharmacist-Patient Health Information Systems (PPHIS) aim to address this limitation by enabling structured communication between a pharmacist and a patient subsequent to their episodic face-to-face encounter [2,3]. In multiple build and evaluation cycles and in close collaboration with 21 Swiss pharmacies over the duration of three years, a PPHIS prototype has been developed and continuously improved, following the design science research paradigm [4,5]. Research in this field has resulted in design principles for PPHIS [2], in the development of several PPHIS prototypes, and suggested a methodology for evaluating emerging patterns of communication between pharmacists and patients [3].

The current work builds upon this research and asks the following research question: What patterns of communication emerge in a PPHIS? This work specifically focuses on nutrition counseling in the context of diabetes mellitus and obesity. Nutrition counseling was so far limited to the face-to-face encounter in the pharmacy. Guidance of the patient and support of behavioral changes outside the pharmacy was not available in traditional counseling regimens although its effectiveness has been shown [6]. Nutritional counseling employing the PPHIS allows for structured communication subsequently to the face-to-face encounter, thus fundamentally expanding and augmenting healthcare professional-patient communication. In the following, the PPHIS and first results are described.

M.C. Tremblay et al. (Eds.): DESRIST 2014, LNCS 8463, pp. 378–382, 2014.

## 2    Design of the Artifact

The design of the artifact is based on the design principles and instantiation of genres for PPHIS as described in [2,3]. The developed PPHIS prototype consists of (1) a tablet-PC application that enables communication and monitoring of patients by pharmacists, (2) a smartphone application[1] used by patients that guides them along the defined interaction-template as configured by the pharmacist and allows for communication with the guiding pharmacists[2], and (3) a mobile backend service to synchronize the usage data of the different clients.

During the face-to-face encounter with the patient, the pharmacist uses the tablet-PC to choose among a variety of interaction-templates based on indication or drug. These templates define at which time-points specific forms of communication become available for the patient and therefore enable pre-defined and structured communication after the patient's pharmacy-visit. As an example, a template may be configured so that the patient receives a defined information element on the second day following a pharmacy visit or is asked for a photo documenting therapeutic progress on day four. Currently templates for antimicrobial therapy, skin diseases, pain management, and nutrition counseling for obesity and type 2 diabetes are implemented.

Fig. 2 shows an annotated screenshot of the tablet-PC application. After adding a patient to the system, a personal code is generated that is sent to the patient via SMS including a link to the app. The patient is then asked for this code as shown in Fig. 1 (Screen 1). Screen 2 shows the main screen visualizing the interaction-template over the specified duration. Screen 3 is specific to the type of communication item and may include e.g. a photo function or a status update. Screen 4 shows the dialog function with the possibility for spontaneous communication. This dialog is also available to the pharmacist on the tablet-PC whenever situation-dependent communication or feedback is needed, complementing the pre-defined communication process.

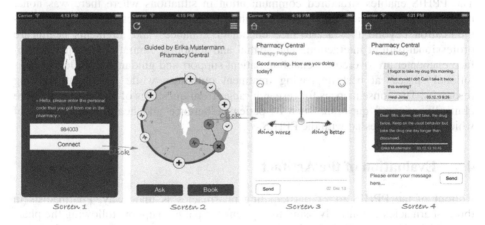

**Fig. 1.** Patient's user interface screens on a smartphone

---

[1] https://itunes.apple.com/ch/app/alphastreams/id579920749?mt=8
[2] https://itunes.apple.com/ch/app/as-cockpit/id687267702?mt=8

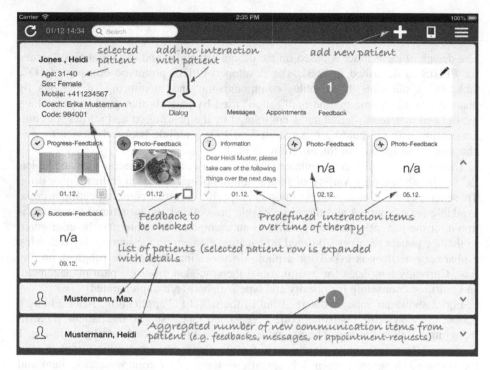

**Fig. 2.** Pharmacist's user interface main screen on a tablet-PC

## 3    Significance to Research and Practice

The PPHIS enables structured communication in situations where there was none, impacting both practice and research. From a practical perspective, structured communication beyond the face-to-face encounter enhances and augments healthcare professional-patient interaction. The spatial and temporal limitations of the face-to-face encounter are overcome, enabling patient support and guidance outside the institutional spaces, at best improving treatment outcomes while leveraging existing resources. The consequences for research range from questions of HIS design to more clinically oriented questions such as patient adherence and health outcome, all of which can be addressed with the PPHIS.

## 4    Evaluation of the Artifact

Rollout of the PPHIS to 21 participating pharmacies is underway. Pharmacists in three pharmacies are already using the system for patient support following the pharmacy visit. The current evaluation focuses on three customers in a Swiss pharmacy that have participated in the nutrition counseling. Patients were guided by a pharmacist with an educational background in nutrition counseling for one week subsequent to the pharmacy visit. Previously, nutrition counseling consisted of an initial 45-minute session in the pharmacy where the specific situation was discussed and several recommendations for nutrition intake were derived that the patient should follow. In a subsequent second meeting, after one or two weeks, it was discussed how the patient was able to follow the recommendations.

With the introduction of the PPHIS, the pharmacist also provided guidance and support once the patient had left the pharmacy. The nutrition-counseling interaction-template is specified for seven days and includes four information-elements that are generated by the system and customized by the pharmacists (e.g. the recommendations agreed upon). In addition, patients are reminded every morning to document food intake throughout the day. Patients were also able to ask questions and to make additional comments with regard to their food intake. The pharmacist was informed when a new photo of a meal or message was available and could advice accordingly.

On the last day of the follow-up, the patients received a survey within the app. Table 1 shows the items of the survey that are based on "relative advantage" [7], the "information-, motivation-, and strategy model" [1], and the net promoter score (NPS) [8].[3] All items except the NPS were rated on a 7-item Likert scale from "strongly disagree" to "strongly agree". Results demonstrate that patients perceived the PPHIS as very useful, felt better supported, and would recommend it to their friends (NPS). Table 1 also shows the communication frequency between pharmacist and patient. Patients documented between 7 and 33 photos of food intake and wrote between 10 and 44 messages to the pharmacist. The pharmacist communicated between 9 and 29 times to the patient and checked all the photos.

**Table 1.** Frequencies & Survey Results

| Patient | Sex | Age | # Photos | # Messages from Patient | # Messages from Pharmacist | Follow-up useful | Information helpful | More motivated | Better supported | Net Promoter Score | Why would you recommend or not recommend it? |
|---|---|---|---|---|---|---|---|---|---|---|---|
| 1 | F | 41-50 | 7 | 10 | 9 | 6 | 3 | 6 | 6 | 6 | Easy to use. Don't like taking photos, but the tips from the pharmacist are really helpful. |
| 2 | M | 19-30 | 32 | 23 | 29 | 7 | 6 | 7 | 7 | 9 | It is very personal and innovative. |
| 3 | F | 19-30 | 33 | 44 | 27 | 7 | 7 | 7 | 7 | 10 | I would recommend it, because it is fun and the tips can be directly applied. I was much more aware of food selection. |

Analyzing communication, the patterns described in Table 2 emerged between pharmacist and patient. Table 3 shows the emerging communication patterns from patient to pharmacist (single messages may relate to multiple patterns, but also to no pattern).

---

[3] The complete survey with full-length questions can be requested from the first author.

**Table 2.** Communication patterns of pharmacist

| Pattern | Examples | # |
|---|---|---|
| Informational messages | "This meal has too much fat in it. Try to avoid the sauce." | 18 |
| Strategic messages | "Vegetables or fruit should be eaten 5 times a day." "Use the sauce only for the meat not the vegetables." | 12 |
| Motivational messages | "Very good meal." "You are getting much better." | 11 |
| Requesting information | "Send me a photo of the ingredients label" | 10 |
| Providing tips/alternatives | "The pasta sauce should include more tomatoes." "Eat more of the bread that helps against the hunger." | 9 |
| Answering questions | "Dark bread is usually better than French bread, because it has less sugar." | 6 |

**Table 3.** Communication patterns of patients

| Pattern | Examples | # |
|---|---|---|
| Commenting on photos/meals | "I ate only half of the meal ;-)" "I drank two liters today." | 45 |
| Commenting on behavior or progress | "Could not eat something else because I was in meeting all day." "Headache is getting better". | 25 |
| Asking for information or advice | "Which cereal is better: With chocolate or honey?" "What are the properties of pumpkin oil?" | 7 |

# References

1. DiMatteo, M.R., Haskard-Zolnierek, K.B., Martin, L.R.: Improving patient adherence: a three-factor model to guide practice. Health Psychology Review 6(1), 74–91 (2012)
2. Volland, D., Korak, K., Brückner, D., Kowatsch, T.: Towards Design Principles for Pharmacist-Patient Health Information Systems. In: vom Brocke, J., Hekkala, R., Ram, S., Rossi, M. (eds.) DESRIST 2013. LNCS, vol. 7939, pp. 519–526. Springer, Heidelberg (2013)
3. Volland, D., Korak, K., Kowatsch, T.: Improving Patient's Adherence by Enabling Pharmacist-Patient Communication Beyond Face-to-face Encounters: An Analysis of Genres of Pharmacist-Patient Health Information Systems, Multikonferenz Wirtschaftsinformatik (MKWI) 2014, Paderborn, Germany (2014)
4. Gregor, S., Hevner, A.: Positioning and presenting design science research for maximum impact. MIS Quarterly 37(2), 337–355 (2013)
5. Hevner, A., March, S., Park, J., Ram, S.: Design science in information systems research. MIS Quarterly 28(1), 75–105 (2004)
6. Bradley, D.W., Murphy, G., Snetselaar, L.G., Myers, E.F., Quails, L.G.: The incremental value of medical nutrition therapy in weight management. Managed Care 22(1), 40–45 (2013)
7. Moore, G.C., Benbasat, I.: Development of an instrument to measure the perceptions of adopting an information technology innovation. Information Systems Research 2(3), 192–222 (1991)
8. Reichheld, F.F.: The one number you need to grow. Harvard Business Review 81(12), 46–55 (2003)

# Impacts of In-memory Technology on Data Warehouse Architectures – A Prototype Implementation in the Field of Aircraft Maintenance and Service

Tobias Knabke[1], Sebastian Olbrich[1], and Sarah Fahim[2]

[1] Mercator School of Management, University of Duisburg-Essen, Duisburg, Germany
tobias.knabke@stud.uni-due.de,
sebastian.olbrich@uni-due.de
[2] Ruhr-Universität Bochum, Bochum, Germany
sarah.fahim@rub.de

**Abstract.** Given today's dynamic market situations, organizations need to internalize the capability to react flexibly on external and internal driven changes. Of course this capability must be supported by the IS landscape. This holds particularly true in the field of aircraft maintenance. For a service provider it is critical to know the age and structure of its equipment pool. This information is vital in offering processes to attract potential customers and to meet service level agreements of existing clients. As current Business Intelligence (BI) architectures fall short in supporting these processes in adequate time and flexibility, we introduce a prototype using an in-memory based BI architecture. The presented artifact proves to have the capability to support business critical processes in a new way. This leads to faster analyses supported by the BI system and also indicates enhanced agility for BI in terms of flexibility and adaptation.

**Keywords:** In-Memory Databases, Business Intelligence, Data Warehouse Architecture, Prototype.

## 1 Motivation and Use Case

Today Information Systems (IS) support almost all business operations and are often closely connected to a company's strategy. In increasingly dynamic and globalized market situations institutions need to adjust their strategies and enable their IS to respond quickly to changing customer preferences in order to stay competitive [1]. Yet, achieving agility in Business Intelligence (BI) as a distinct class of dispositive IS is not trivial but an ongoing challenge in multiple industries [2, 3]. Flexibility and quick adaptions according to customer requirements are also a major challenge in the presented use case from the aircraft maintenance, repair and overhaul (MRO) industry. One critical requirement is to simulate and calculate prices for individual service and maintenance contract offers. This is a rather challenging task as the necessary components (materials or parts) are distributed in stocks all over the world and several regulations on the use apply, e.g. legal or individual customer agreements. Thus, the service provider needs to keep track of which parts for repair and maintenance are

M.C. Tremblay et al. (Eds.): DESRIST 2014, LNCS 8463, pp. 383–387, 2014.

kept at what location. In addition, diverse master data information like age, compatible aircraft types or financial value of the component is necessary – both with current and historical information. For instance, it is allowed to install pre-used parts on a plane. Hence, it is quite a profitable business to look for such parts in stocks and provide them as cheaper replacement after maintenance or repair. Yet, some service contracts forbid the usage of parts older than the plane itself.

These and similar requirements can hardly be met with acceptable response times or without re-loading the complete data set. This is especially true if today's enterprise data warehouses (DWH) with its layered scalable architectures (LSA) are used in combination with disk-based databases (DBDB). Some evidence suggests that technologies like in-memory (IM) may positively affect the agility of BI and can act as technology enablers for new business scenarios [4]. This leads us to the following design questions:

- How can new technologies like IM support business processes as the one above?
- What are the impacts on current (Enterprise) DWH architectures?

Details of the use case challenges within a DBDB based DWH environment with LSAs are explained next. Afterwards, the design and the implementation of the artifact are introduced. We close this paper with our intended contribution, limitations as well as an outlook to future research activities.

## 2      Problem Statement and Background

Since the use case combines high data volumes and different source systems as well as analytical applications, it is located in the field of BI and Business Analytics in particular. As IS support, the field of BI can be summarized as a set of technologies, applications, and processes for gathering, storing, accessing, and analyzing data that helps users to make better decisions [5]. It supports decision makers through business analyses on the basis of internal and external data [6–8] and thus contributes to the organization's competitiveness and sustainable development. In the presented scenario of an aircraft MRO service provider the analyst is interested in the current and historical inventory development of components used for aircraft MRO services, in particular:

- Inventory monitoring on unique material basis over time, e.g. value and age
- Distribution of assets grouped by age with reference to compatible aircraft types
- Simulation and calculation of financial impacts on service contracts

The real world example consists of several hundred million records. Material movements, availability per (distributed) stock and value of the components are only a few characteristics that need tracking. The underlying data is used for several other analytic applications. It is extracted from the source systems into a DWH using a traditional BI approach. This general understanding of BI is based on two central underlying design assumptions:

1. Layered scalable architecture also known as (Enterprise) DWH [9, 10]
2. Persistent data storage based on DBDB

Traditional BI architectures store data physically in each of the several layers in the DWH/LSA structure. Data organization is usually de-normalized, using multi-dimensional data storage concepts like star schema [9], extended/enhanced star schemes that apply vendor specific features (e.g. as for SAP BW) or snowflake schema [9]. The multi-layered LSA combined with multi-dimensional models are required to achieve acceptable response times with DBDBs, but result in multiplication of data and inflexible data modeling.

Different from other existing applications the data for the presented scenario is required on a very granular basis - even for analysis. Starting from material movements it needs to be analyzed what components are currently and have been in stocks over time. Another challenge is the many-to-many relationship (n:m) of component and aircraft type. One component may fit to several aircraft types. In return, one aircraft consists of several components. This is maintained in "aircraft part lists" (APL) that map these relationships. These maintenance lists are then used to calculate service contract rates as they can also represent the scope of a service offering. Hence, the transactional data (material movements) needs to be connected to aircraft types via APLs. However, this would boost the data volume in a de-normalized DWH approach with only physical layers - for each material and aircraft type combination one physical record is be needed to meet performance requirements. With this procedure 100 million records could easily turn into several billion records. Especially if adding or deleting a mapping in the APL requires a data reload. Traditional BI architectures with physical DWH layers [10] or common modeling techniques like slowly changing dimensions are not able to solve this issue - a conflict regarding the goals of efficiency and agility.

## 3    Design of the Artifact

The running prototype[1] is implemented based on the semi-virtual DWH architecture depicted in Fig. 1 using IM databases as suggested in [11]. The IM based prototype utilizes column-oriented data storage on a relational database model. Thus, a multiplication

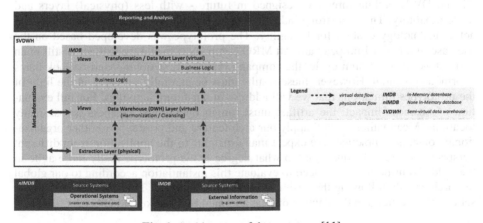

**Fig. 1.** Architecture of the prototype [11]

---

[1] For a screencast demo of the running prototype please contact the authors.

of records as described in section 2 with the multi-dimensional, cube based approach is no longer necessary. Instead, physical layers only required for performance reasons are omitted. Logical views/joins are used and calculations are performed by the database in-memory.

Fig. 2 gives a first impression of the provided analysis functions of the prototype. The implementation is based on commercial, out-of-the-box software using only default functionalities without custom development or programming.[2]

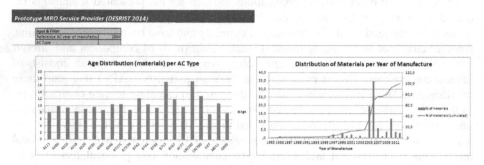

**Fig. 2.** Screenshot of the prototype

# 4     Contribution and Outlook

Our goal is to contribute to agility in the field of IS and BI in particular. Therefore, we implemented an artifact of the semi virtual DWH concept for more agile BI intro-duced in [11]. By instantiating this IM based approach we could overcome the architectural and performance critical issues related to the presented use case within traditional BI environments. The presented business process from the MRO service in the aircraft industry is just now enabled adequately with our enhanced BI/DWH archi-tecture. Furthermore, these first results show that IM technology may change the way BI and DWH architectures are designed in future - with less (physical) layers and more flexibility. This is a strong indication for our hypothesis that IM technology can act as technology enabler for BI agility. The prototype was developed based on the use case of a major European aircraft MRO company. Despite the artifact is still in an early stage of the design cycle, the company realized first savings and outlook bares enormous potential. However, these results must be carefully reflected in the light of the prototypes limitations that we will address in our future activities. For full evalua-tion of business impact, the artifact must run in operational business across many locations. Meanwhile, we will apply our architecture and prototype to other organiza-tional contexts in practice. We expect many insights to the application from different perspectives – e.g. the question "to what degree is the prototype really more agile in the field?". Furthermore, we need to evaluate this instantiation according to our global research agenda following the design science approach [12]. This can be based on the set of agility criteria in the context of BI elaborated by Knabke and Olbrich [13].

---

[2] The artifact was implemented with SAP BW (Version 7.31) on HANA (Version 1.00.70) using SAP BO Analysis (Edition for MS Office) (Version 1.4.1.2585) as frontend tool.

# References

1. Gandossy, R.: The Need for Speed. Journal of Business Strategy 24, 29–33 (2003)
2. Cockburn, A.: Agile software development Addison-Wesley. Addison-Wesley, Boston (2002)
3. Moss, L.: Beware of Scrum Fanatics On DW/BI Projects. EIMInsight Magazine 3 (2009)
4. Plattner, H., Zeier, A.: In-Memory Data Management. An Inflection Point for Enterprise Application. Springer, Heidelberg (2011)
5. Chamoni, P., Gluchowski, P.: Integrationstrends bei Business-Intelligence-Systemen. CG 04 46, 119–128 (2004)
6. Chung, W., Chen, H., Nunamaker, J.F.: A Visual Knowledge Map Framework for the Discovery of Business Intelligence on the Web. CCN 2005 21, 57–84 (2005)
7. Watson, H.J., Wixom, B.H.: The Current State of Business Intelligence. WW 2007 40, 96–99 (2007)
8. Abbasi, A., Chen, H.: CyberGate: A System and Design Framework for Text Analysis of Computer-Mediated Communication. WW 2001 32, 811–837 (2008)
9. Kemper, H.-G., Mehanna, W., Unger, C.: Business Intelligence - Grundlagen und praktische Anwendungen. Eine Einführung in die IT-basierte Managementunter-stützung Vieweg, Wiesbaden (2006)
10. Hahne, M.: Design des Enterprise Data Warehouse. Modellieren mehrschichtiger Architekturen. BI-Spektrum 5, 8–12 (2010)
11. Knabke, T., Olbrich, S.: Towards agile BI: applying in-memory technology to data warehouse architectures. In: Lehner, W., Piller, G. (eds.) Innovative Unternehmensanwendungen mit In-Memory-Data-Management. Beiträge der Ta-gung IMDM 2011, Mainz, December 2, pp. 101–114. Köllen Druck+Verlag GmbH, Bonn (2011)
12. Hevner, A., March, S.T., Park, J., Ram, S.: Design Science Research in Information Systems. WW 2001 28, 75–105 (2004)
13. Knabke, T., Olbrich, S.: Understanding Information System Agility – The Example of Business Intelligence. In: Proceedings of the 46th Annual Hawaii International Conference on System Sciences, pp. 3817–3826 (2013)

# Integration of Information Retrieval in Creativity Support: A Prototype to Support Divergent Thinking

Dominik Siemon and Susanne Robra-Bissantz

Chair Information Management, University of Braunschweig, Germany
{d.siemon,s.robra-bissantz}@tu-bs.de

**Abstract.** Creativity support has been adressed in various fields of studies and already entered information technology with the development of different tools in order to enable, foster and improve the creative stage. In this paper we outline our approach of supporting the divergent thinking process during the generative stage by using information extraction and information retrieval methods as well as social media for the actual supporting content. A prototype that offers an automated support and that tries to produce a broad benefit for the idea generator was developed and will further be evaluated according to current design science guidelines.

**Keywords:** Creativity support system, divergent thinking, information retrieval.

## 1    Introduction and Design Theory

Both, creativity and the generation of ideas are processes, which can arise autonomous and independent from the environment. However supporting this processes can enhance the idea itself. This creativity support can be done in traditional ways or with the help of information technology by specific software tools, interactive interfaces or rich visualization- and searching tools [1]. Usually these tools support the recording and management of ideas, rather than supporting the actual generative creativity process [1]. This generative process describes the production of ideas during the stage of creative thinking [2,3]. Creative thinking is defined as the capability of an individual to form associations, develop patterns and possess a certain degree of abstraction, which is essentially based on a divergent reasoning process as developed by the psychologist J.P. Guilford [4]. This divergent thinking offers a subjective consideration, enabling mental leaps [5] and breaking away from familiar structures, in order to generate new patterns and solutions [4]. In our research we concentrate on the support of the generative process by the aid of our prototype, which facilitates divergent thinking. The prototype is designed to support engineers, scientists, product managers or artists to make new discoveries and evaluate ideas or to support problem-solving processes. A common method for supporting the creative thinking process is to explore and search for inspiration, which has already been integrated into different IS, such as search engines [1]. The underlying principle of these techniques is, that the individual generating the idea is aware of the actual support he is seeking [6]. An individual seeking for inspiration with the help of a search engines is aware of the

M.C. Tremblay et al. (Eds.): DESRIST 2014, LNCS 8463, pp. 388–392, 2014.
© Springer International Publishing Switzerland 2014

terms he is using for his search. Therefore an additional benefit, which generates new patterns and finds unknown issues, is not necessarily provided [6, 7]. Possible reliefs for this problem might be specific search engines, especially made for the generation of associations and patterns [6]. Nevertheless, the individual is always aware of the initial query (terms) he is using for seeking support [6, 7]. In our approach we attempt to avoid this awareness by using information extraction (IE) to analyze written ideas and information retrieval (IR) methods to query data sources to support the creative process of the idea generator.

## 2    Design of the Artifact

### 2.1    Information Retrieval for Creativity Support

IE is the process of extracting and obtaining data from given resources i.e. from a document, which contains full-text or other data. IE algorithms try to reduce documents to a more dense and short representation. Furthermore IR selects a set of documents based upon a given query [8]. This is why IE systems work essentially by means of convergent information processing [9]. Analyzing the given idea will thus not support the divergent thinking process, because it simply extracts the basic information from the idea. No new patterns or solutions can be found upon these analyses [9]. Therefore new issues must be evaluated rest upon the results of the analyses to support the actual divergent thinking process. This process takes part in the next step, where specific data sources will be queried for potential supportive information. This information can therefore stimulate inspiration, emerge new association or empower users to be more creative [7], [9].

The main difference is thus not the active search for creativity support by the idea generator but the automated process by the system, which can expand the information horizon of the idea generator and support the actual creativity process [6]. For this to work effectively the IR must operate precisely and a data source must be selected that provides potential associations and inspiration. The following chapter explains this approach and the developed prototype in more detail and shows the technical capabilities of the artifact [10]. A reasonable data source is difficult to determine, as it depends on the manner of ideas being generated. An idea generation process has usually a specific topic and a goal to solve certain problems or to achieve specific tasks. Thus all ideas can be categorized before the support can take affect and specific data sources can be determined. However data sources shouldn't rely on topic restrictions, because supporting content can also be found in unrelated data sources [6], [9].

### 2.2    Implementation

In the course of this research, a web-based prototype for supporting the generation of ideas was developed. The prototype captures written ideas (see Fig. 1, S1) and analyses them with a designed IE algorithm (see Fig. 1, S2). This IE algorithm is based upon the bag-of-words model[1], representing the idea in a predefined amount of valued words (list), which will be used to query designated data sources.

---

[1] The bag-of-words model is a document representation, where a text (document) is represented by an ordered set (bag) of words by their frequency of occurrence in the text.

This list is ordered by the appearance of a word with a weightage relative to the number of all valued words (words without stop words). The outcome of this algorithm is a ranked list of valued terms, which represents the written idea (see Fig. 1, S2). In a set of combinations, these valued terms will then be used to query several data sources (see Fig. 1, S3).

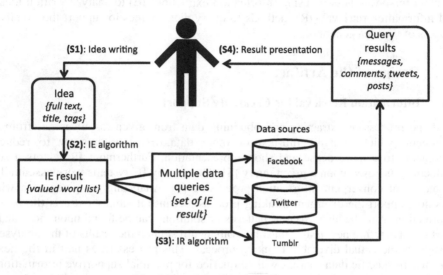

**Fig. 1.** Functionality of the prototype

Different data sources can obtain variable types of information and can thus support the creativity process in diverse ways. Special databases applied for different fields of problems and information can be used to find creativity supporting content. In our approach we defined social media applications as data sources.

Social media refers to applications, where users interact in social networks and create and share content. The popularity of social media applications is immense, which results in a big amount of data created by users all over the globe. The democratization of knowledge and information supports the transformation of the user from a mere (information) consumer to a producer. The widespread access and the high usage of social media turns it into a data source with a wide range of topics, that is not restricted to specific users [11]. Our approach queries the services Facebook, Twitter and Tumblr via the API's and their REST[2] architectural hypermedia data system. All queries aim for the main text or message written by the users, e.g. the tweets, messages and posts. The results are saved into a valued list and are presented to the idea generator inside the web application, offering to read the messages, delete unrelated results or mark them as important (see Fig. 1, S4). The following screenshot (Fig. 2) shows the presentation view with the IR results, arranged by their relevance towards the idea.

---

[2] REST stands for Representational State Transfer and describes a concept of resource access for Web applications.

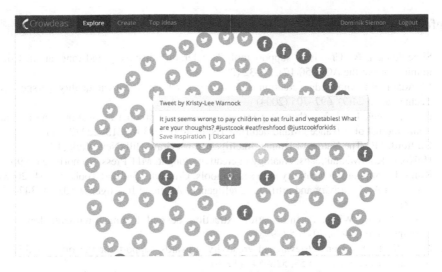

**Fig. 2.** Presentation view with the IR results

General IR algorithms underlie a strict effectiveness on how the results obtain a certain quality towards the query. This quality can be defined by the relevance theory, identified by Saracevic, which explains how well a retrieved document meets the query [12]. According to the nature of creativity supporting content, these general relevance restrictions can be neglected [6], [9].

## 3    Evaluation of the Artifact and Future Research

We aim to evaluate the utility, quality and efficacy of the artifact [10] by defining a prior aspect in this research. This aspect is the theory in what way the IE algorithm can represent the idea in a respectful way. To evaluate this, subjects will be asked to write down ideas, which will be analyzed by the IE algorithm. The extracted results will be presented to the idea generators and feedback on how well the IE worked will be collected. After that, the main hypothesis will be evaluated with two focal groups. One group will be assisted by the prototype whereas the other group will receive no assistance. Experts will give the two groups the same tasks or problems to solve over a specific time period.

The experts will then evaluate the ideas according to their quality [13]. Assessing and evaluating the quality of ideas, especially by influencing and supporting the creative stage, is difficult and complex. Terasa M. Amabile defined an approach on how to measure creativity by setting special dimensions [14]. The experts, who issued the tasks and problems to the subjects, will use this approach to assess the ideas. In addition to that, the subjects will be asked if the information found by the algorithm was able to support the idea generation stage.

# References

1. Shneiderman, B.: Creativity support tools: accelerating discovery and innovation. Communications of the ACM 50(12), 20–32 (2007)
2. McAdam, R.: Knowledge creation and idea generation: a critical quality perspective. Technovation 24(9), 697–705 (2004)
3. Li, Y., Wang, J., Li, X., Zhao, W.: Design creativity in product innovation. The International Journal of Advanced Manufacturing Technology 33(3-4), 213–222 (2007)
4. Guilford, J.P.: The Nature of Human Intelligence. McGraw-Hill, New York (1967)
5. Holyoak, K.J.: Mental leaps: Analogy in creative thought. MIT Press, Cambridge (1996)
6. Kules, B.: Supporting creativity with search tools. Creativity Support Tools, 53–64 (2005)
7. Boden, M.A.: Creativity and artificial intelligence. Artificial Intelligence 103(1), 347–356 (1998)
8. Gaizauskas, R., Wilks, Y.: Information extraction: beyond document retrieval. Journal of Documentation 54(1), 70–105 (1998)
9. Ford, N.: Information retrieval and creativity: towards support for the original thinker. Journal of Documentation 55, 528–542 (1999)
10. Hevner, A.R., March, S.T., Park, J., Ram, S.: Design science in information systems research. MIS Quarterly 28(1), 75–105 (2004)
11. Asur, S., Huberman, B.A.: Predicting the Future with Social Media. In: 2010 IEEE/WIC/ACM International Conference on Web Intelligence and Intelligent Agent Technology (WI-IAT), pp. 492–499 (2010)
12. Saracevic, T.: RELEVANCE: A review of and a framework for the thinking on the notion in information science. Journal of the American Society for Information Science 26, 321–343 (1975)
13. Voigt, M., Bergener, K., Becker, J.: Comprehensive Support for Creativity-Intensive Processes. Business & Information Systems Engineering 5(4), 227–242 (2013)
14. Amabile, T.M.: Creativity in context: Update to "The Social Psychology of Creativity". Westview Press, Boulder (1996)

# AmbiTune: Bringing Context-Awareness to Music Playlists while Driving

Patrick Helmholz, Sebastian Vetter, and Susanne Robra-Bissantz

Chair Information Management, University of Braunschweig, Germany
{p.helmholz,s.vetter,s.robra-bissantz}@tu-bs.de

**Abstract.** The usage of online music content and mobile devices is becoming more and more a part of our daily lives. In recent years, research on contextual music recommendation has emerged and new services have been introduced. Driving is one of the most common listening situations. It differs from other listening situations in that the main focus is on driving, which means the mental load is higher. The scenario of listening to music while driving has been neglected in past research and is therefore reflected by the limited integration of textual music adaptation in car radios or infotainment systems. This paper presents the results of a preliminary study involving a driving simulator created to analyze the effects of various types of music on subjects while driving. As the results of the subjective measure show, there is a strong influence on the mental load of participants listening to fast-paced music while driving. According to these findings, a first prototype of an application was implemented allowing the driver to adjust the music selection with respect to the mental load as well as personal preference. This application uses contextual parameters and performs as a research prototype for future real-driving studies.

**Keywords:** Music recommendation, driving context, context-awareness, mental load.

## 1 Introduction

Context-awareness forms a core concern in ubiquitous computing and goes hand in hand with today's extensive use of sensor technology [1]. The importance of context is even greater when users move away from traditional desktop computing environments. Thanks to mobile computing devices, users can access information and services in different surroundings and situations. The needs of users may vary depending on the context, and context-aware systems can adapt to provide the relevant services or infotainment [2]. In the field of music services, the use of context-aware systems is relatively new. However, as context-aware systems become increasingly popular through mobile devices and online streaming services, it is arguable that people now actively use them in everyday listening contexts to a much greater extent [3]. Here mobile music recommender services can benefit by taking the user's context (e.g. location, emotion or speed) into consideration [4]. Research has shown that a positive relation exists between the affective qualities of the listening situation and the preference for music that augments these qualities [5].

M.C. Tremblay et al. (Eds.): DESRIST 2014, LNCS 8463, pp. 393–397, 2014.
© Springer International Publishing Switzerland 2014

While driving a car, many people turn down the volume or change the music if they are in a complex driving situation [6]. Stutts et al. (2003) study pointed out that 91% of drivers constantly manipulate audio-controls while driving [7]. This behavior shows that driving is a unique listening situation, because the context changes very quickly influencing the mental load of the driver [6] and his music preference [4]. Therefore it is necessary to have a dynamic and context-aware music recommender system that adapts to the driving situation. As this research follows the iterative design science methodology [8], including a preliminary study to analyze the effect of music while driving, a study-related prototype of an application to adjust the music selection based on contextual parameters is presented. This application performs as a research prototype for further real-driving studies to situation-oriented music recommendation while driving.

## 2        Preliminary Study

A driving simulator study was designed to analyze the effect of music with different tempos, arousal and valence on the mental load and performance of drivers. This ex ante evaluation is used for the purpose of deciding which factors of music are relevant for a first prototype [9].

In the driving experiment, the participants had to frequently name their subjective mental load while ten short music samples from well-known artists were played. The ten samples were selected and evaluated in a short preceding online survey. Besides the subjective measure, driving performance data, like velocity and distance to a lead car were recorded in a logfile. In addition, biofeedback of the participants was recorded using skin conductance and temperature sensors. Twelve females and 28 males with an average age of 22.78 (SD = 2.675) and at least two years of driving experience (Mean = 5.05, SD = 2.375) participated in the experiment. They were separated into three groups, two with differing playlists and one without music.

The experiment was separated into two main driving tasks. In the first ten minutes, the participants were instructed to follow a lead car with a realistic, self-chosen distance. In the second portion of the experiment, the participants were allowed to drive with a realistic, self-chosen speed less than 110 km/h without a lead car. The subjective measure showed that the fast-paced and high-arousal music had a strong influence on the mental load of the participants. This increased mental load can affect the driver in complex driving situations and cause critical situations.

## 3        Design of the Artifact

AmbiTune, an application for Android smartphones, was implemented as a first prototype to consider the context for music playlists while driving. The application operation process for an exemplary drive is presented in Figure 1. The figure shows the context data processing with the single songs in the sub-playlists as final output.

AmbiTune uses the GPS sensor of the smartphone and the prediction engine of a former prototype of the research group to perform the prediction of the route trajectory, which is described as the upcoming course of the road in geographical terms as well as in terms of time (see [10]). This route trajectory is used as a first data input for the application to determine the playlist length for the current trip (see Fig. 1, steps 1 and 2).

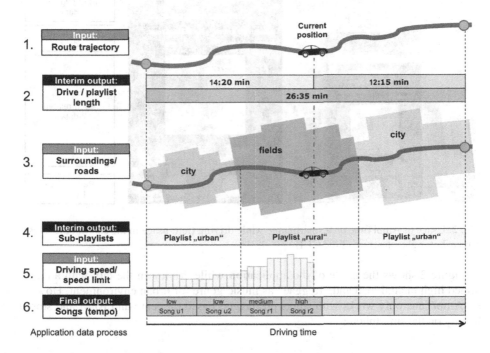

**Fig. 1.** Concept of AmbiTune: Adapting the music to the surroundings and driving speed

Based on the position data of the route trajectory, it is possible to perform a query to the OpenStreetMap (OSM)[1] database consecutively. This query returns XML-Code with the whole map data according this position. Due to this code, it is possible to filter and generate aggregated surroundings (e.g. urban or rural) for the current trip. The interim output separates the whole playlist (length) into different sub-playlists according to the varying surroundings of the road (see Fig. 1, steps 3 and 4). The user can use the personal profile to associate different music genres to the sub-playlists (e.g. country for rural, reggae for urban). On the basis of the consecutively recorded GPS position data, it is possible to interpolate the actual driving speed. Using the driving speed regarding the surroundings and the actual speed limit (also from the OSM database), driving phases with a high mental load can be identified and the music adjusted accordingly (see Fig. 1, steps 5 and 6). According to the preliminary study, slower songs with low Beats Per Minute (BPM) rates are selected for driving phases with a high mental load. The final output of the application is a context-aware music playlist for the current trip in which the music is selected according to the surroundings of the street as well as the mental load of the driver (see Fig. 1, step 6).

---

[1] OSM is an open source collaborative project to create a free editable map of the world.

**Fig. 2.** Usage of AmbiTune on a smartphone while driving (left: usage in the car, middle: closer screenshot, right: structure of the GUI)

Figure 2 shows the usage of the application while driving in the city with a determined high mental load and "Reggae" as music genre for urban environment. However, AmbiTune only works with songs pre-tagged based on genre and BPM and stored locally on the smartphone.

## 4    Significance of the Artifact

*Significance for Research:* Reviewing other papers in this field of research, we identified a lack between theoretical basic research and prototyping. Our prototype shows in which way user profiled music preferences could be combined with the automatic adaption of the music to the actual context while driving. Our approach also combines sensory data from the smartphone with filtered data from the Internet to adapt the music. In addition, the prototype itself is designed for further research, as the anonymized data can be analyzed subsequently.

*Significance for Practice:* In consideration of increased interest and standardization[2] of data exchange between applications and car, the integration of this prototype directly into the car system is imminent. For this reason, we are currently working with a large automobile manufacturer to implement this prototype into the car for real-driving studies.

## 5    Conclusion and Future Work

The findings of the driving simulator study demonstrate that music has a direct influence on driving performance. In addition, it was shown by a prototype that it is

---

[2] See www.openautoalliance.net

possible to adapt the music to the driving route by using different context parameters. Since this presents an early prototype, not all research has been conducted. In the next step, the prototype will be evaluated in a real-driving study in cooperation with the automotive industry. In order to offer a wider selection of music for the study, a connection to the music streaming service Spotify will be tested. As we are unaware of the users' situations, it is unclear if every driver has to be treated the same way and which parameters are needed to create a good service for a specific user. Therefore it is necessary to integrate the user early in the innovation process of the application. A not yet implemented situation-oriented feedback channel could be used to receive the user's ideas and needs for further research and adaption of the prototype.

# References

1. Jonsson, K., Holmström, J., Lyytinen, K., Nilsson, A.: Desituating context in ubiquitous computing: Exploring strategies for the use of remote diagnostic systems for maintenance work. International Journal of Actor-Network Theory and Technological Innovation 2, 40–55 (2010)
2. Kaminskas, M., Ricci, F.: Contextual music information retrieval and recommendation: State of the art and challenges. Computer Science Review 6, 89–119 (2012)
3. North, A., Hargreaves, D., Hargreaves, J.: Uses of Music in Everyday Life. Music Perception: An Interdisciplinary Journal 22 (2004)
4. Wang, X., Wang, Y., Rosenblum, D.: A daily, activity-aware, mobile music recommender system. In: Proceedings of the 20th ACM International Conference on Multimedia, pp. 1313–1314. ACM, New York (2012)
5. North, A.C., Hargreaves, D.J.: Situational influences on reported musical preference. Psychomusicology: A Journal of Research in Music Cognition 15, 30–45 (1996)
6. Dibben, N., Williamson, V.J.: An exploratory survey of in-vehicle music listening. Psychology of Music 571–589 (2007)
7. Stutts, J., Feaganes, J., Reinfurt, D., Rodgman, E., Hamlett, C., Gish, K., Staplin, L.: Driver's exposure to distractions in their natural driving environment. Accid. Anal. Prev. 37, 1093–1101 (2005)
8. Peffers, K., Tuunanen, T., Rothenberger, M.A., Chatterjee, S.: A Design Science Research Methodology for Information Systems Research. Journal of Management Information Systems 24, 45–77 (2007)
9. Pries-Heje, J., Baskerville, R., Venable, J.R.: Strategies for Design Science Research Evaluation. In: Golden, W., Acton, T., Conboy, K., van der Heijden, H., Tuunainen, V.K. (eds.) 16th European Conference on Information Systems, ECIS 2008, Galway, Ireland, pp. 255–266 (2008)
10. Helmholz, P., Ziesmann, E., Robra-Bissantz, S.: Context-Awareness in the Car: Prediction, Evaluation and Usage of Route Trajectories. In: vom Brocke, J., Hekkala, R., Ram, S., Rossi, M. (eds.) DESRIST 2013. LNCS, vol. 7939, pp. 412–419. Springer, Heidelberg (2013)

# Designing an Information System
# for Residential Heating and Ventilation
# to Improve Comfort and Save Energy

Thomas von Bomhard[1], Dominic Wörner[2], and Felix Wortmann[1]

[1] Institute of Technology Management, University of St. Gallen
{thomas.vonbomhard,felix.wortmann}@unisg.ch
[2] Department of Management, Technology and Economics, ETH Zurich
dwoerner@ethz.ch

**Abstract.** Large amounts of energy are wasted because heating systems run round-the-clock even though residents are out or occupy only a small part of their home. Major reasons for this behaviour are the non-intuitive heating controls and missing direct feedback about the heating activity or even energy consumption. In addition, bad ventilation behaviour, e.g. tilted windows, may lead to unhealthy room climate as well as significant heat losses. To address these problems, we analysed the requirements for a supporting information system. We present a first prototypical implementation of an individual-room heating and ventilation system which combines automation, an intuitive user interface and supporting feedback. This should empower residents to achieve energy-efficient heating and improved comfort.

## 1 Introduction

In Germany, 71% of energy consumed by residential buildings is due to space heating [1] distinguishing it as a powerful lever for energy-efficiency measures. Besides weather, thermal properties of the building, and the heating system, user behaviour determines the energy consumption for residential space heating. Concerning the latter point, there are three simple options for saving energy: (1) decreasing setpoint temperatures permanently, (2) turning down the heating when a room/home is not occupied, and (3) correct ventilation behaviour. However, executing on these options might challenge users' comfort and ultimately motivation to preserve energy. More specifically, users have to remember lowering setpoints when leaving, they might have to tolerate unpleasant temperatures and they don't get any direct feedback about the effect of their effort.

In the 70s and 80s, programmable thermostats were developed to overcome some of the aforementioned issues. But most users struggle to program their heating schedule due to the bad usability of such devices [2]. Moreover, it can be quite challenging to define a suitable schedule if residents' daily routines change. These challenges are addressed by a new generation of *connected thermostats* enabling intuitive user interaction via smartphone interfaces and in some cases

M.C. Tremblay et al. (Eds.): DESRIST 2014, LNCS 8463, pp. 398–402, 2014.
© Springer International Publishing Switzerland 2014

even providing presence-based heating capabilities. The most known product in this category is the learning thermostat by NEST Labs[1] in the US. Another similar solution for European heating systems was developed by the startup tado[2] in Germany. Both solutions replace the central thermostat, which controls the heating according to the temperature of a single zone in the building. While this approach is cost-efficient it often leads to under- or oversupply of particular rooms and setback strategies can only be applied on the whole dwelling.

Contributing to the recent IS stream of *Energy Informatics* [3], we applied information systems thinking and skills to design a prototype IS helping residents to achieve energy-efficient heating and improved comfort.

## 2  Requirements Analysis

### 2.1  Conceptual Approach

In contrast to NEST, tado and several academic implementations [4, e.g.], which are *smart* or *intelligent* central thermostats, we pursue a decentralised, individual-room approach by controlling the hot water flow at each individual radiator. Therefore our system can, in contrast to the former, also be used in multi-family homes with central heating. There are already solutions of controllable radiator valves (CRVs) with additional smartphone- and web-based interfaces. They ease the process of creating a schedule as well as adding the convenience of remote control. However, we wouldn't call them *smart*, since they lack the ability to automatically adapt the schedule to changing user behaviour. For example, NEST tries to learn a schedule and temperature preferences by analysing user interactions with the system and by leveraging a PIR presence detector. Tado utilises the geolocation capabilities of smartphones to infer the distance of residents to their homes and to adjust the setpoints accordingly. To our knowledge, decentralised control approaches with such capabilities do not exist so far.

Moreover, as shown by Frontczak et al. [5], humidity and air quality are important factors influencing residents' comfort. Therefore it is necessary to make people aware of poor room climate and to foster optimal ventilation. Of course, most people have their own ventilation habits to overcome bad climate conditions, but due to feedback information, ventilation is often suboptimal in terms of energy efficiency and even comfort gains. For example, many people keep their windows tilted in winter, which leads to minor air exchange but tremendous heat loss. Similarly, people try to overcome dry air in winter by opening a window which often leads to the opposite effect since the outside air may contain even less humidity.

### 2.2  Fundamental Requirements

On the basis of our conceptual approach we can formulate key requirements for a heating and ventilation information system:

---

[1] https://nest.com/thermostat/
[2] https://tado.com

- **Comprehensible Individual-Room Heating Control:** The heating system is generally slow in response to user interaction. As a result, residents tend to set the heating to maximum when they feel cold, thereby often wasting energy. Thus, we require the IS to give immediate feedback in form of an estimated heat-up time to the desired temperature. Furthermore, it should be visible when the system is active, i.e. heating up. CRVs often have built-in room temperature sensors. However, due to the proximity of the CRVs to the radiator this can lead to deviations of several degrees to the actual room temperature. Therefore, we require an independent temperature sensor per room.
- **Presence-Based Automatic Scheduling:** Similar to NEST's and tado's approach, the system should be capable of scheduling the room temperature automatically such that on the one hand the user's comfort temperature should always be reached when a room is occupied, and on the other hand the temperature should be maximally decreased when a room is empty. This *smart* feature is not trivial to implement, because it has to strike balance between energy savings and comfort. Furthermore, privacy and automation complexity have to be considered from a user perspective. (cf.[6])
- **Easy-to-Use Manual Scheduling:** Since automatic scheduling may not be the optimal solution in every case, we require an easy-to-use manual schedule which can be edited remotely. Thus, the user should be able to adjust the schedule as soon as unexpected changes in his daily routine occur.
- **Room Climate Assistant:** The system should analyse temperature, humidity and air quality of a room to provide actionable information for optimising the room climate.

## 3  Design of the Artifact

In the following, we give a brief technical overview of our system. Afterwards, we show how the requirements have been implemented.

### 3.1  System Implementation

- **Connected Room Climate Sensors:** Off-the-shelf wireless sensors (Netatmo[3] weather station) provide temperature, humidity and air quality ($CO_2$ concentration) measurement data in 5min resolution which is accessible through a cloud-based API.
- **Controllable Radiator Valves (CRV):** Commercial motorised valves (eQ-3 Homematic[4] ) allow to control setpoints remotely and can be installed by residents in minutes.
- **Home Controller:** A low-cost, embedded computer (BeagleBone Black) relays data and control signals between the local CRVs and our backend server.

---

[3] http://www.netatmo.com
[4] http://www.eq-3.de/homematic-197.html

- **Backend:** Besides the storage of measurement and user interaction data, it provides the platform to implement *intelligent* features.
- **Smartphone app:** The main user interface is an iOS smartphone app that gives users control of their heating and feedback about their room climate.

## 3.2 Feature Implementation

In the following, we present how we have implemented the requirements and how an user can interact with our system.

After choosing a room via a list menu in the app a temperature view will be displayed (see Fig. 1a). In the centre of the screen, the current room temperature is shown. The up/down arrows illustrate if the room is currently heating up or cooling down. On the right, the CRVs temperature measurement and valve opening are shown. The status message on the top explains what the systems is doing. During heating it entails an estimated heat-up time to the desired temperature which is calculated by taking previous heat-up procedures into account. Furthermore, the room temperatures and setpoints for the day can be visualised by turning the app to landscape view (see Fig.1d).

In Fig. 1c, a heating schedule for a week, divided in two schedules, one for workdays and one for the weekend can be seen. The schedule allows to set time intervals for typical heating modes: comfort-mode (indicated by a "couch" icon), sleep-mode (indicated by a "Zzz"-icon) and away-mode (indicated by a "walking man" icon). Each heating mode has a selectable temperature setpoint associated with it. The user can simply change the schedule by moving one of the knobs to the left or right. Compared to any user interface of a radiator thermostat, we claim that this is a strong usability improvement.

Presence-based automatic scheduling is implemented similarly to tado's approach by leveraging the smartphone location services. Temperature setpoints are lowered depending on the distance of the resident to his home. But, in contrast to tado, the user can choose which room (instead of the whole dwelling) should be controlled by this feature. Hence, our approach offers more flexibility and convenience, especially if some residents are not smartphone users or do not want to share their location for privacy reasons.

The air quality screen (see Fig.1b) shows the current $CO_2$-Level in ppm (parts per million), an informative feedback text and a smiley icon which empowers the user to judge the air quality at a quick glance. If ventilation is appropriate, the feedback text entails a reasonable ventilation time, which is estimated based on the current $CO_2$-Level and previous ventilation procedures.

Similarly to the air quality screen, a humidity screen is available. There, the user is warned about moldiness risk if the humidity is higher than 70%. If the indoor humidity is too low ($<30\%$), the system recommends opening a window only if the humidity levels outside are high enough.

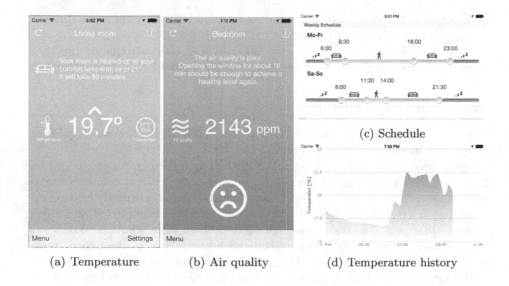

(a) Temperature          (b) Air quality          (d) Temperature history

## 4    Forthcoming Evaluation of the Artifact

Currently our system is running in five dwellings with friendly users in order to achieve a stable system from a technological point of view. For the next heating season, we plan to equip additional 10-20 comparable dwellings in multi-family homes in order to evaluate energy savings, influence on ventilation behaviour, user satisfaction, and the general usability of the system. Energy savings and influence on ventilation behaviour can be measured (approximately) using the room climate sensor measurements. User satisfaction and usability will be evaluated by interviews.

## References

1. BMWi: Bundesministerium für Wirtschaft und Technologie: Energiedaten nationale und internationale Entwicklung (Gesamtausgabe), BMWi Referat III C 3 (2012)
2. Peffer, T., Pritoni, M., Meier, A., Aragon, C., Perry, D.: How people use thermostats in homes: A review. Building and Environment 46(12), 2529–2541 (2011)
3. Watson, R.T., Boudreau, M.C., Chen, A.J.: Information Systems and Environmentally Sustainable Development: Energy Informatics and New Directions for the IS Community. MIS Quarterly (1), 23–38 (2010)
4. Gupta, M., Intille, S.S., Larson, K.: Adding GPS-control to traditional thermostats: An exploration of potential energy savings and design challenges. In: Tokuda, H., Beigl, M., Friday, A., Brush, A.J.B., Tobe, Y. (eds.) Pervasive 2009. LNCS, vol. 5538, pp. 95–114. Springer, Heidelberg (2009)
5. Frontczak, M., Andersen, R.V., Wargocki, P.: Questionnaire survey on factors influencing comfort with indoor environmental quality in Danish housing. Building and Environment 50, 56–64 (2012)
6. Yang, R., Newman, M.W., Forlizzi, J.: Making sustainability sustainable: Challenges in the design of eco-interaction technologies. In: Proc. of the SIGCHI Conference on Human Factors in Computing Systems. ACM (2014)

# A Visualization Approach for Reducing the Perceived Complexity of COBIT 5

Yannick Bartens[1], Steven de Haes[2], Linda Eggert[3], Leonard Heilig[1], Kim Maes[2], Frederik Schulte[1], and Stefan Voß[1]

[1] Institute of Information Systems, University of Hamburg, Hamburg, Germany
{yannick.bartens,leonard.heilig,
frederik.schulte,stefan.voss}@uni-hamburg.de
[2] Information Technology Alignment and Governance Research Institute,
University of Antwerp – Antwerp Management School, Antwerp, Belgium
{steven.dehaes,kim.maes}@uantwerpen.be
[3] Institute for Risk and Insurance, University of Hamburg, Hamburg, Germany
eggert@hzv-uhh.de

**Abstract.** COBIT 5 is positioned in the market as a de-facto standard for enterprise governance of IT. Relevant literature and management experience, however, indicate that the adoption of the framework is challenging due to its perceived complexity. In this paper we present a software prototype aiming to promote the understanding of COBIT 5, its components and their relationships by means of information visualization, thus facilitating its usage and adoption in scientific and practical context. The current state of evaluating the prototype is outlined.

**Keywords:** COBIT 5, IT governance, information visualization, prototype.

## 1 Introduction

IT governance, recently rebranded as "enterprise governance of information technology" (EGIT), can be considered as a key concept in pursuing the creation of business value through suitable application of information technology (IT) [1]. The adoption of COBIT 5 has been ascertained as a measure for the application of EGIT in practical environments [2]. However, this adoption in organizations is widely described as challenging due to the high perceived complexity of COBIT 5 [2, 3]. In contrast to objectively measureable complexity, perceived complexity results from the distinctions made by a subjective observer [4]. Moreover, the academic knowledge base to analyze and leverage COBIT 5 from a research perspective is limited and needs to be extended to facilitate adoption in academia [2]. In this paper we present a prototype leveraging the utilization of COBIT 5 by means of information visualization.

To address these problem statements, and building on the work of Ware [5] and Keller & Tergan [6], we present a software prototype as an information visualization tool. Different from the current textual representation of COBIT 5, visual information depicts a more comprehensible way of representation, assisting in "coping

M.C. Tremblay et al. (Eds.): DESRIST 2014, LNCS 8463, pp. 403–407, 2014.
© Springer International Publishing Switzerland 2014

with subject-matter complexity and ill-structuredness" [6], making knowledge and information explicit and allowing to generate, retrieve, elicit, (re-)structure, evaluate, locate and access information. Hence, our goal is to derive design requirements on information visualization [6] in order to develop an artifact addressing the above mentioned problems.

The software prototype represents an artifact in the sense of design science research [7] aiming to be valuable for application in practice and science, especially in supporting the understanding of the components of COBIT 5 and their relationships and in building an instrument usable for research. Our research applies the methodology outlined by Gregor and Hevner [8], albeit due to space limitations only an abbreviated synopsis of the conducted literature review can be provided.

## 2    Design of the Artifact

We address insight generation through the adaption of certain design principles [9], which are outlined in Table 1. They are to be implemented by the prototype together with other more generic requirements for information visualization.

**Table 1.** Aggregated design requirements as derived from literature

| Design Requirements | Sources |
|---|---|
| **D.1: Provide Overview** | [9–12] |
| The provision of an abstracted overview helps understanding the overall picture of a dataset and promotes further exploration. In addition, it allows the differentiation of known and unknown information, therefore enabling the exploration and generation of new knowledge. | |
| **D.2: Adjust** | [9, 11, 12] |
| Adjustment of the level of abstraction and/or range of selection serves the purpose of sense-making and test of hypothesis. This way of filtering helps to explore a large amount of data and enables the selection of demand-specific information. Reducing the amount of the search and working memory load needing more detailed facts can be extracted. | |
| **D.3: Detect Pattern** | [9, 10] |
| Pattern detection refers to accessing specific distributions, trends, frequencies or structures within a dataset. This also enables both finding demand-specific information and the discovery of new knowledge as well as the test of hypothesis and development of new questions. | |
| **D.4: Match Mental Model** | [9, 11] |
| Through visualization the gap between data and a user's mental model of it can be decreased, thus reducing the cognitive load in understanding, increasing perceived familiarity and linkage of information to real-world knowledge. A visual representation transforms information into a physical space for effective exploration. | |

Resembling a specific instantiation of our artifact, the COBIT 5 Visualization Prototype is developed on a strict transformation of the COBIT 5 enabling processes publication [13], specifically designed to address the elicited requirements. The used technologies include HTML5, a tailored JavaScript (GoJS) library, and PHP5/MySQL for the dynamic components. The visualization is generated via GoJS with the assistance of an HTML5 canvas [14]. By this, we reduce barriers such as location dependencies for accessibility, plugin usage, and high resource requirements. Thus, the platform independent usage on mobile devices like smartphones and tablets is possible.

Fig. 1 illustrates the graphical user interface (D.1, D.3, D.4) with an already applied filter for demand-specific display (D.2, D.3). Our prototype visualizes the practices of the COBIT 5 process reference model in a graph-like structure, projecting practices as vertices and their interfaces as edges. The in- and outputs between those interfaces are presented as textual descriptions, similar to edge weights in graph theory. Functionalities of our instantiation include a recurring layout of the visualization (D.1, D.3, D.4) as well as navigation functions like zoom, pan and move (D.1, D.2, D.3). The practices are clustered in their respective domains and color-coded accordingly (D.1, D.3, D.4). When selecting one or more practices their in- and outputs as well as the connected first-degree vertices will be highlighted (D.2, D.3, D.4). The data of the selected elements will be given to the user in a table to the right hand side (D.3, D.4) in order to ensure the provision of the completeness of data (D.2 and D.3). In addition filters for selection and display limitation on processes, domains and superior goals levels are available, in future versions complemented by a search function for the aforementioned options plus the in- and outputs (D.1, D.2, D.3).

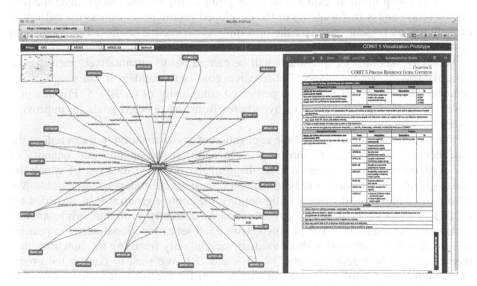

**Fig. 1.** Graphical representation of the prototype

# 3    Significance to Research and Practice

COBIT 5 and its associated suite of products is a large, multifaceted and complex set of guidance. The framework is systematically designed to encompass the complete investment life-cycle, with both governance and management aspects. The perceived complexity gives rise to the need for research on COBIT 5 as an artifact. As indicated by De Haes et al. [2], there is a need to investigate the design and internal consistency of COBIT 5, or lack thereof. The COBIT 5 Visualization Prototype developed in the context of this paper can be leveraged in more analytical research programs to check for internal consistency and embedded design patterns in COBIT 5. Furthermore, the prototype is estimated to leverage the adoption of COBIT 5 in practice.

Specifically, we seek to address the difficulty of the implementation and transformation of existing environments, which already have implemented COBIT 5. The potential of our idea and its implementation was approved by experienced network members, from academia and practice, of the institutions involved in this paper.

It has to be noted that comparable approaches on visualization of the COBIT 5 knowledge base have not been made yet. A reconfirmation was obtained by direct correspondence with ISACA. In conclusion, our artifact and its instantiation can be truly considered a novelty and highly innovative from a practical point of view.

## 4     Evaluation of the Artifact

As envisaged in the design science research paradigm, the evaluation of an artifact is divided into qualitative and quantitative phases. To align with this approach our artifact will undergo two separate but consecutive evaluation rounds (e.g., as in [15]):

In a first step multiple explorative focus groups [16] are used to evaluate the perceived utility and actual usability of the developed prototype as well as the collection of feedback on possible tasks for the upcoming experimental studies. The conduction of the explorative focus groups is currently in progress.

Secondly, laboratory experiments will be carried out to quantitatively measure the effectiveness of our prototype. The research goal is to validate if the usage of the proposed prototype will reduce the perceived complexity of COBIT 5. For this purpose, we derived a testable set of hypotheses from the pursued goals on improving COBIT 5 with our prototype.

The experiment investigates if the application of a visualization tool can reduce the time needed for retrieval of information. In addition, the quality and quantity of retrieved information is assessed. The shape of the provided data out of which demand-specific information is to be generated represents the independent variable. We differentiate into three different configurations; the control group will be provided the COBIT 5 framework in an unaltered version as currently available, while another group will use a version of our prototype with a full set of functionalities. The remaining group will be provided with a modified version, only featuring the functionalities based on the design requirements D.1, D.3 and D.4. We seek to consult the procedures outlined by North [17] and Carpendale [18] for the advanced measurement of the dependent variables.

**Acknowledgments.** The presented prototype is not yet available for distribution as the content of the referenced COBIT 5 knowledge base is copyrighted material of ISACA and was used for demonstration and proof of concept purposes only.

# References

1. De Haes, S., Van Grembergen, W.: Moving From IT Governance to Enterprise Governance of IT. ISACA Journal 3, 21 (2009)
2. De Haes, S., Van Grembergen, W., Debreceny, R.S.: COBIT 5 and Enterprise Governance of Information Technology: Building Blocks and Research Opportunities. Journal of Information Systems 27, 307–324 (2013)
3. Williams, P.: A Helping Hand with IT Governance,
   http://www.computerweekly.com/opinion/
   A-helping-hand-with-IT-governance (2006) (last access February 27, 2014)
4. Schlindwein, S.L., Ison, R.: Human Knowing and Perceived Complexity: Implications for Systems Practice. Emergence: Complexity & Organization 6(3), 27–32 (2004)
5. Ware, C.: Information Visualization: Perception for Design. Elsevier, Amsterdam (2012)
6. Keller, T., Tergan, S.-O.: Visualizing Knowledge and Information: An Introduction. In: Tergan, S.-O., Keller, T. (eds.) Knowledge and Information Visualization. LNCS, vol. 3426, pp. 1–23. Springer, Heidelberg (2005)
7. Hevner, A.R., March, S.T., Park, J., Ram, S.: Design Science in Information Systems Research. MIS Quarterly 28(1), 75–105 (2004)
8. Gregor, S., Hevner, A.R.: Positioning and Presenting Design Science Research for Maximum Impact. MIS Quarterly 37(2), 337–355 (2013)
9. Yi, J.S., Kang, Y., Stasko, J.T., Jacko, J.A.: Understanding and Characterizing Insights: How Do People Gain Insights Using Information Visualization? In: Proceedings of the BELIV 2008, pp. 4:1–4:6. ACM, New York (2008)
10. Dang, Y., Zhang, Y., Hu, P.J.-H., Brown, S.A., Chen, H.: Knowledge Mapping for Rapidly Evolving Domains: A Design Science Approach. Decision Support Systems 50, 415–427 (2011)
11. Börner, K., Chen, C., Boyack, K.W.: Visualizing knowledge domains. Annual Review of Information Science and Technology 37(1), 179–255 (2003)
12. Shneiderman, B.: The Eyes Have It: A Task by Data Type Taxonomy for Information Visualizations. In: Proceedings of the 1996 IEEE Symposium on Visual Languages, pp. 336–343 (1996)
13. ISACA (ed.): COBIT 5: Enabling processes. ISACA, Rolling Meadows (2012)
14. Grady, M.: Functional Programming Using JavaScript and the HTML5 Canvas Element. Journal of Computing Sciences in Colleges 26(2), 97–105 (2010)
15. Müller, O., Debortoli, S., Seidel, S.: MUSE: Implementation of a Design Theory for Systems that Support Convergent and Divergent Thinking. In: vom Brocke, J., Hekkala, R., Ram, S., Rossi, M. (eds.) Design Science at the Intersection of Physical and Virtual Design, pp. 438–445. Springer, Heidelberg (2013)
16. Tremblay, M.C., Hevner, A.R., Berndt, D.J.: Focus Groups for Artifact Refinement and Evaluation in Design Research. Communications of the Association for Information Systems 26, 599–618 (2010)
17. North, C.: Toward measuring Visualization Insight. IEEE Computer Graphics and Applications 26(3), 6–9 (2006)
18. Carpendale, S.: Evaluating Information Visualizations. In: Kerren, A., Stasko, J.T., Fekete, J.-D., North, C. (eds.) Information Visualization. LNCS, vol. 4950, pp. 19–45. Springer, Heidelberg (2008)

# Supporting Technical Customer Service Processes: A Design-Centered Approach

Gerald Däuble, Inga Schlömer, Boris Böttcher, and Markus Nüttgens

University of Hamburg, Department of Business Administration, Hamburg, Germany
{gerald.daeuble,inga.schloemer,boris.boettcher,
markus.nuettgens}@uni-hamburg.de

**Abstract.** Services gain importance when it comes to overall revenue structures of industrial companies. Product-Service Systems (PSS) are seen as a way to diversify from competition and establish a unique selling proposition. Services being on the rise - service productivity becomes vital. With a design-centered approach requirements such as information needs of technical customer service are iteratively transferred into a prototype of a mobile support system for technical service staff. In order to ensure efficiency, effectiveness, usefulness and utility of the artefact several evaluation methods are applied within iterative design cycles.

**Keywords:** Technical Customer Service, Service Technician, Mobile Assistance System, Mobile Support System, Prototype, Design Science.

## 1 Introduction

Services gain importance when it comes to overall revenue structures of industrial companies [1]. One reason is global competition and increased market transparency making (product) prices more comparable [2]. Product-Service systems (PSS) are seen as a way to diversify from competition and establish a unique selling proposition [2,3]. By addressing after-sales markets the traditional product life cycle is extended. Besides an efficient production of products, efficient (after-sales) services are emphasized. While productivity of industrial production has been the subject of investigation for decades [4,5], service productivity is a comparably new field of research. This applies to methods of planning services as well as establishing measures for monitoring, decision support and continuous improvement. Within our cooperation with several companies providing technical customer service it became obvious that different obstacles have to be faced in order to increase service productivity[1]. Besides matters of operational and organizational structure information can be seen as a critical success factor. Companies in the area of technical customer service dispatch technicians

---

[1] The underlying projects for this paper ("EMOTEC" and "HALLO SME") are funded by BMBF (German Federal Ministry of Education and Research), BMWi (Federal Ministry for Economic Affairs and Energy) and supervised by PT-DLR (project references: BMBF 01FL10023, BMWi 01MU12029A).

M.C. Tremblay et al. (Eds.): DESRIST 2014, LNCS 8463, pp. 408–412, 2014.

to customer's sites for repair and maintenance tasks. As well as efficient dispatching and logistics this requires extensive planning when it comes to necessary tools, spare parts and documentation. Hence interaction between technicians and the back office is vital. As an example: after completion of a service task a - often paper based - work order document is filed and transferred to the back office. This often occurs on a daily basis. As a result interaction and reaction to internally or externally triggered changes is obviously limited (e.g. incoming high priority request, exceeding of planned time, etc.). From a back office's perspective executing service tasks at a customer's site often can be seen as a „black box".

The goal of this project is to uncover and understand information needs in the area of technical customer service and to provide technicians with the right information at the right time using an innovative IT artefact. Furthermore efficient interaction between service technician and back office is the aim of this project.

## 2    Design of the Artifact

Improving technical customer services can be separated in two areas: First - providing technicians adequately with required information in order to ensure efficient maintenance while assuring service quality at complex tasks. Second - improving administrative processes by automated integration of information from different sources. This reduces manual administrative efforts from a technician's perspective and enables transparency from the back office's point of view. Both areas are addressed through the design of a tablet based mobile assistance system for service technicians, which provides adequate information from a variety of sources context-sensitive at any time throughout a service task. Furthermore it is aimed at supporting interaction between back office and service technician. Besides the aforementioned complexity and the broad variety of tasks carried out by technical service staff, the strategic position of technicians is noteworthy. The technician's role as the point of service is being refined to a point of sale due to the potential of having a technical sales person right at the customer's site with deep knowledge of the customer's organization. This approach consequently adds information requirements to the range of tasks and responsibilities. Current requirements concerning technical and planning information are amended by financial and customer relationship information. Against this background, the technician and his requirements are the main focus of the presented design process of the IT artefact. The Design-Science Research Guidelines by Hevner et. al underlie this research process [6]. To gain relevance in an iterative research process the project is performed in a user-centered design (UCD) approach. A user-centered life cycle for product development describing a process of four iterative steps is used as follows: 1. Specify context of use, 2. Specify requirements, 3. Produce design solutions and 4. Evaluate designs [8]. Specific use cases in the field of repair and maintenance were defined and empirical data was collected in cooperation with a leading international company providing complex technical products in the area of intralogistic. In an iterative approach, starting from compiled process models (event-driven process chains) first scribbles and functional descriptions, mock-ups, design studies and a prototype were developed. The prototype is set up on a ruggedized iPad for field and laboratory testing. The following link leads to a screencast video presenting the prototype in its current state: http://youtu.be/8plInkVAebk

# 3    Significance to Research

An extensive literature review on requirements of technical customer service has been conducted and published [19]. Those requirements were triangulated [9,10] with results from shadowing service technicians in real world scenarios and results from expert interviews [19]. In the first step, the context (service technicians using a mobile assistance system supporting technical and administrative tasks) was specified. The context consists of user, work task, motives for use, work equipment, physical and social environment [7]. Five researchers were shadowing ("participant observation" [9]) service technicians in two countries for over 200 hours. The method of shadowing allowed insights into the work flow, the frequency of activities, sub-steps, terminology, errors and possible interference potential. The resulting use cases cover the whole process from leaving their homes in the morning, approaching the customer's site, identifying service object(s), conducting repair or maintenance, completing administrative tasks and leaving the customer's site. Overall 77 service processes have been documented as event-driven process chains and analyzed in detail. To bridge the gap between self-perception and experience of the technical service, interviews were conducted in addition [11,12]. Hence information was identified to be a crucial success factor in the area of technical customer service, the design of an artefact closing - or narrowing - this gap is aspired. In order to support service technicians by improving the mobile provision of information a Design-Science approach was applied. Results (instantiations) of the design cycles can be analyzed and evaluated against academia and practice [13]. The presented artifact contributes new knowledge to the prescriptive knowledge base. The contribution contains a current state of the art concerning requirements in the domain of the technical customer service [19], information needs of service technicians [19], investigation and documentation of real world service processes, design approaches and results from the outstanding deployment of the final artefact in real world scenarios including evaluation. In terms of generalizability in a further step it will be verified if and how the artefact can be applied to other domains and cases.

# 4    Significance to Practice

Adequately providing information to mobile service technicians in order to improve efficiency and maintain the level of pursued quality is the aim of the industry. Closely related to chapter 3 significance to practice is ensured by involving service technicians into the design cycles. By the aforementioned approach of triangulation the practical perspective is embedded in our approach. Besides iteratively refining the artefact, diffusion of this research's results already is initiated. To ensure contribution to the practical audience a close cooperation with the German Institute for Standardization (DIN) exists. It is aimed at compiling a specification providing a guideline for designing mobile information systems in the area of technical customer service. In order to involve a broader audience several practitioners' conferences and trade shows were attended critically discussing strengths and weaknesses of the prototype.

# 5     Evaluation of the Artifact

Evaluation allows making a statement to what extent an artifact is closing or narrowing the underlying research gap and shows the extent to which objectives have been attained [14,15]. The utility of the artefact is opposed with the initial goal in order to state if and how objectives are achieved. According to the project's goals of improving productivity and empowering service technicians, usability, efficiency and effectiveness are being evaluated. The following table describes different evaluation approaches.

**Table 1.** Evaluation of the artefact (instantiation)

| *Goal/Question* | *Approach* |
| --- | --- |
| **Effectiveness:** Does the prototype provide all required information in order to complete defined service processes (use cases)? | Ex-post analysis based on documented use cases |
| **Efficiency:** Does the improved user interface promote time savings? Which improvements can be achieved applying usability methods? | Laboratory experiment: eye tracking to analyze the design of the user interface in detail |
| **Effectiveness, Efficiency:** Which details can be improved within the next iteration of the prototype? | Expert interviews with different stakeholders (technicians, management), eye tracking to analyze plausibility and obstacles |
| **Effectiveness:** Does the prototype affect the error ratio? | Field study/observation of initially defined use cases and comparison with documented use cases |
| **Efficiency:** At which points of the service process using the prototype is more efficient than the status quo? Can aspired time savings be achieved? | Field study/observation of initially defined use cases and comparison with documented use cases |
| **Efficiency:** Does the real time functionality improve interaction between service technician and back office? | Field study/observation of initially defined use cases and comparison with documented use cases |

Eye tracking experiments provide valuable insights from a service technician's perspective and allow - compared to just measuring time - to analyze for example how measured times are composed and how to continuously improve interaction between technician and IT system [16,17,18].

# References

1. Federal Statistical Office Germany: Pressekonferenz 'Bruttoinlandsprodukt 2012 für Deutschland', Statement von Präsident Roderich Egeler (2013)
2. Baines, T.S., Lightfoot, H.W., Evans, S., Neely, A., Greenough, R., Peppard, J., Roy, R., Shehab, E., Braganza, A., Tiwari, A., Alcock, J.R., Angus, J.P., Bastl, M., Cousens, A., Irving, P., Johnson, M., Kingston, J., Lockett, H., Martinez, V., Michele, P., Tranfield, D., Walton, I.M., Wilson, H.: State-of-the-art in product-service systems. Proceedings of the Institution of Mechanical Engineers, Part B: Journal of Engineering Manufacture 221(10), 1543–1552 (2007)
3. Tukker, A.: Eight types of product–service system: eight ways to sustainability? Experiences from SusProNet, Bus. Business Strategy and the Environment 13(4), 246–260 (2004)
4. Lehmann, C., Koelling, M.: The Productivity of Services: A systematic literature review. In: RESER, 20th Anniversary Conference, Gothenburg, Sweden (2010)
5. Lasshof, B.: Produktivitätvon Dienstleistungen: Mitwirkung und Einfluss des Kunden. Dt. Univ.-Verlag, Wiesbaden (2006)
6. Hevner, A.R., Ram, S., March, S.T., Park, J.: Design Science in Information Systems Research. MIS Quarterly 28(1), 75–105 (2004)
7. DIN EN ISO 9241-11:1999-01: Ergonomic requirements for office work with visual display terminals (VDTs) - Part 11: Guidance on usability (ISO 9241-11:1998); German version EN ISO 9241-11:1998. Beuth, Berlin (1999)
8. ISO/TR 18529:2000 Ergonomics – Ergonomics of human-system interaction – Human-centred lifecycle process descriptions. Beuth, Berlin (2000)
9. Myers, M.D.: Qualitative research in business and management. Sage, Thousand Oaks (2013)
10. Mingers, J.: Combining IS research methods: towards a pluralist methodology. Information Systems Research 12(3), 240–259 (2001)
11. Kuniavsky, M.: Observing the user experience a practitioner's guide to user research. Morgan Kaufmann Publishers, San Francisco (2003)
12. Holtzblatt, K.: Rapid contextual design: a how-to guide to key techniques for user-centered design. Elsevier/Morgan Kaufmann, San Francisco (2005)
13. Gregor, S., Hevner, A.R.: Positioning and Presenting Design Science Research for Maximum Impact. MIS Q. 37(2), 337–355 (2013)
14. Becker, J.: Wissenschaftstheorie und gestaltungsorientierte Wirtschaftsinformatik. Physica-Verlag, Heidelberg (2009)
15. Österle, H., Becker, J., Frank, U., Hess, T., Karagiannis, D., Krcmar, H., Loos, P., Mertens, P., Oberweis, A., Sinz, E.J.: Memorandum zur gestaltungsorientierten Wirtschaftsinformatik, Schmalenb. Zeitschriftf. betriebsw. Forsch. 62, 664–672 (2010)
16. Pernice, K., Nielsen, J.: How to Conduct Eyetracking Studies. Fremont (2009)
17. Wallach, D., Scholz, S.C.: User-Centered Design: Why and How to Put Users First in Software Development. In: Maedche, A., Botzenhardt, A., Neer, L. (eds.) Software for People, pp. 11–38. Springer, Heidelberg (2012)
18. Ericsson, K.A., Simon, H.A.: Verbal reports as data. Psychological Review 87(3), 215–251 (1980)
19. Matijacic, M., Fellmann, M., Özcan, D., Kammler, F., Nüttgens, M., Thomas, O.: Elicitation and Consolidation of Requirements for Mobile Technical Customer Services Support Systems – A Multi-Method Approach. In: Proceedings of the 34. ICIS, Milan, Italy (2013)

# An Art-Based IS for Improving Room-Climate

Paul Rigger and Felix Wortmann

University of St. Gallen, Dufourstrasse 40a, 9000 St. Gallen, Switzerland
{paul.rigger,felix.wortmann}@unisg.ch

**Abstract.** Indoor room-climate influences our everyday life on many levels. High room temperature decreases our productivity and our ability to concentrate. Moreover, many medical conditions can be traced back to bad indoor room-climate. In this paper we present an information system (IS) for room-climate monitoring. Our system is an informative art system being equipped with standard room climate sensors for temperature, humidity and carbon dioxide. In contrast to conventional monitoring systems a display embedded in a standard art frame presents the current room climate on the basis of classical art. Changing room conditions are reflected in the painting in real-time. By implementing the presented IS we pursue a research avenue which is dedicated to a more fundamental research questions: "Are hedonic, art-based IS superior to utilitarian, non-art-based IS in respect to usage and impact?

**Keywords:** Human-computer interaction, ambient displays, art information systems, pervasive computing.

## 1 Introduction

In 1983 the World Health Organization defined the sick building syndrome, describing the influence of poor indoor climate on human beings, causing discomforts and health risks. Symptoms include negative effects on eyes, nose, throat and lower airways, skin reactions, non specific hypersensitivity, mental fatigue, headache, nausea, and dizziness among people staying in respective buildings [1].

In contrast to the latest generation of professional buildings, older professional buildings and residential homes are rarely equipped with an automatic ventilation system and fresh air is usually provided through opened windows. However, sensing room climate can be very hard for humans. While we have a good sense for temperature, humidity levels are only recognized with a delay of hours, e.g. on the basis of a dry throat. Even worse, carbon dioxide levels cannot be sensed directly at all. Information technology can be a remedy to these challenges. Though, engaging people tracking their room climate on the basis of sensor systems is far from being easy. While reading the values on a standard gauge is not very appealing, starting up one of the latest room climate smartphone apps on a regular basis is cumbersome. Furthermore, providing enough help to interpret room climate data is challenging.

To address the depicted challenges we propose an art-based IS. Thereby, we pursue a broader research avenue which is dedicated to a fundamental research questions:

M.C. Tremblay et al. (Eds.): DESRIST 2014, LNCS 8463, pp. 413–417, 2014.
© Springer International Publishing Switzerland 2014

"Are hedonic, art-based IS superior to utilitarian, non-art-based IS in respect to usage and impact?

## 2    Design of the Artifact

### 2.1    Problem Statement

Having analyzed and tested multiple of the currently available solutions in real life, from standard gauges[2] to more sophisticated internet-enabled sensors [3], the following key problems can be identified [4]:

- **Complex User Interfaces and Non-self-explanatory Presentation of Data:** Displaying blunt data on a gauge or a digital display requires a lot of prior user knowledge to be effective. Data has to be interpreted and compared against known target values. While interpretation of temperature can be performed by an average user, e.g. interpreting $CO_2$ values in parts per million (ppm) can indeed be very challenging.
- **Lack of Systematic Engagement:** Room climate is specific for each individual room and has to be measured continuously when the user is present. Furthermore, the room climate IS should specifically engage the user in case of poor room climate conditions. Standard room climate systems tend to keep the level of engagement constant, thereby losing the users intention already during periods of good room climate.
- **Long-Term Usage Challenges:** As discussed, current systems lack self-explanatory user interfaces and do not engage the user when the room climate conditions worsen. This ultimately challenges their long-term usage and impact. However, there is a new generation of internet-enabled system using smart phone apps or other mobile front-end devices to display information. While these systems overcome some of the discussed challenges they bring their own set of issues. Starting up an app is cumbersome compared to an always visible measurement device. Push notifications can be used as a remedy to inform the user even if she does not start the app. However, these notifications are often perceived as intrusive and disturbing, especially when not being in the corresponding room currently having bad conditions.

### 2.2    Requirement Analysis

Preliminary research in the context of our work can be found under terms such as "ambient information systems" [5],"informative art systems" [6], or "peripheral displays". Various articles derive design principles for successful ambient information systems [6–10]. Building upon this body of knowledge we derive four key design requirements to develop our prototype:

- **Connect to People Emotionally:** We want to go beyond designing a system that builds upon rationality and cognitive thinking, i.e. leverage emotions and psychological incentives [9].

- **Draw Attention Only When Necessary:** We want to build a monitoring device that is unobtrusive and remain so unless attention is really necessary. The device should integrate seamlessly into the surroundings [11].
- **Provide Choice:** The design of the artifact is supposed to foster usage and post acceptance. Therefore, we want to leverage the advantages of personalization [12] and allow the user to customize the solution to a specific taste [8].
- **Learn from the Past:** Apart from having the current room climate displayed on spot with the display, a smartphone application allows to analyze the data in more depth whenever a user wants. To enable rich feedback of the room climate this application also allows a review of historical data.

### 2.3    Design and Features of the Artifact

The goal of this research is to build a room-climate monitoring system that fosters usage and post acceptance by integrating an innovative user interface, descriptive and injunctive feedback [13] and recommendations for improvements. We do so by implementing a hedonic user-interface by incorporating art.

Therefore we build a standard wooden art frame that is equipped with standard room climate sensors, and internet-capable minicomputer and a LCD display to illustrate art. In contrary to a standard framed picture, the displayed art gets modified in real time according to the continuously measured room climate.

Our first prototype "Quantified-Art" shows Marilyn Monroe and manipulates her face in case of room climate changes. As pointed out by [8] the idea behind using a face is that it is easily recognized including changes in the appearance. More specifically, low temperature is presented by coloring the lips of Marilyn Monroe blue. Likewise high temperatures, exceeding a predefined threshold, transform the lips neon yellow for Marilyn Monroe. The intensity of the lips color reflects the extent that the threshold is being exceed/fallen below. The room's humidity level is presented by modification of the skin. Values below a threshold are depicted as a dry skin with cracks. Exceeding the optimal humidity value forms droplets on the skin. Likewise, the indoor carbon dioxide level is presented by a modification of the skin. The level of exceedance of each measurement is presented by the intensity of the modification. The modification is done in real-time by software deployed on the minicomputer.

**Fig. 1.** Modifications according to room-climate conditions (from left: 1. Low temperature, high temperature, low humidity, high humidity, high carbon dioxide level)

The Quantified-Art display was developed using a 23-inch TFT-LCD panel. Having a brightness of $250cd/m^2$ and viewing angles of $89°$ in each direction the displays are not recognized as displays but as a normal print of art. A wooden frame hides the metallic edges of the panel and provides enough space in the back of the display to house the sensors, the computer and electrical power supply. The Raspberry Pi [14], a Linux based small computer, in the back of the display was used to interact with the sensor and display the art using the built in graphic chip. The Raspberry Pi provides 16 GPIO (general purpose input output) and SPI, I2C as well as an AURT interface to connect sensors. Sensing room climate levels we used the K33 OEM [15] module from Sense Air measuring carbon dioxide concentration with a no dispersive infrared sensor. Communicating with the Raspberry Pi the sensor provides a UART interface.

Beside the Quantified-Art display we provide the user with a web portal to change settings. This way the display itself stays a true plug and play product without a complicated user interface. After login with the corresponding Quantified-Art identification the user can change the displayed art as well as adapt the behavior of the art corresponding to the measured room climate. Apart from having the current room climate displayed on spot with the quantified-art display, a smartphone application allows the user to check the room climate on the go

In order to provide the described functionalities, we need a comprehensive architecture. We use a standard SQL database (PostgreSQL) [16] to store historical data, handle user administration and provide threshold data. In addition, the database is linked to a second database where all the art content is available for download. All front-end devices communicate with the backend over a middleware written in NodeJS [17] and deployed on the server. The middleware allows posting new values or users on the backend without accessing the database itself. The same applies to getting data from the server. The devices request specific data (e.g. temperature over the last 24 hours) and the middleware provides it from the backend.

## 3    Evaluation of the Artifact and Further Research

During a pre-evaluation phase the prototype is currently demonstrated in a real world setup and potential users evaluate the artifact via an item-based questionnaire. In a first step, we try to understand the influence of our artifact on motivation as a driver for usage. Based on [18, 19] there are different motivations driving human action. Fun and enjoyment are a fundamental source of intrinsic motivation. Furthermore, usefulness and willingness to learn are a second source of so-called internalized extrinsic motivation. This first stage of testing allows the evaluation of the effectiveness of the prototype building upon the work of [20].

In a longitudinal field study the prototypes will be tested in 50 classrooms of a secondary school. The logging of the actual room climate allows A/B testing for the long-term impact of the proposed system compared to classrooms with standard or without any room-climate monitoring system. In addition to quantitative log data, the qualitative feedback of 800 students and teaching stuff will be collected.

By evaluation and redesigning the proposed prototype we intend to derive a design theory for art-based IS. Besides room climate data further research could expand the focus to other domains. Indeed, we are currently discussing with leading diabetic health care researches to use an art-based IS to monitor and improve blood sugar levels of diabetic patients.

# References

1. Skov, P., Valbjørn, O., Pedersen, B.V.: Influence of Indoor Climate on the Sick Building Syndrome in an Office Environment. The Danish Indoor Climate Study Group. Scandinavian Journal of Work, Environment & Health 16, 363–371 (1990)
2. Climatemeter Temperature/Humidity - Lufft, http://www.lufft.com/en/products/temperaturehumidity/climatemeter-511099 (accessed February 28, 2014)
3. The Netatmo Weather Station, http://www.netatmo.com/en-US/product (accessed February 28, 2014)
4. blinded for review
5. Pousman, Z., Stasko, J.: A Taxonomy of Ambient Information Systems. In: Proceedings of the Working Conference on Advanced Visual Interfaces - AVI 2006, p. 67. ACM Press, New York (2006)
6. Redström, J., Skog, T., Hallnäs, L.: Informative Art. In: Proceedings of DARE 2000 on Designing Augmented Reality Environments - DARE 2000, pp. 103–114. ACM Press, New York (2000)
7. Streitz, N.N.A., Rocker, C., Prante, T., van Alphen, D., Stenzel, R., Magerkurth, C.: Designing Smart Artifacts for Smart Environments. Computer 38, 41–49 (2005)
8. Ferscha, A.: A matter of taste. In: Schiele, B., Dey, A.K., Gellersen, H., de Ruyter, B., Tscheligi, M., Wichert, R., Aarts, E., Buchmann, A.P. (eds.) AmI 2007. LNCS, vol. 4794, pp. 287–304. Springer, Heidelberg (2007)
9. Nakajima, T., Lehdonvirta, V.: Designing Motivation Using Persuasive Ambient Mirrors. Personal and Ubiquitous Computing 17, 107–126 (2011)
10. Matthews, T., Forlizzi, J., Rohrbach, S.: Designing Glanceable Peripheral Displays. UC Berkeley (2005)
11. Hallnäs, L., Redström, J.: Slow Technology – Designing for Reflection. Personal and Ubiquitous Computing 5, 201–212 (2001)
12. Kulkarni, A.: Design Principles of a Reactive Behavioral System for the Intelligent Room. Bitstream: The MIT Journal of EECS Student Research, 1–6 (2002)
13. Loock, C., Staake, T., Thiesse, F.: Motivating Energy-Efficient Behavior with Grenn IS: An Investigation of Goal Setting and the Role of Defaults. MIS Quaterly 37, 1313–1332 (2013)
14. Raspberry Pi | An ARM GNU/Linux box, http://www.raspberrypi.org (accessed February 28, 2014)
15. CO2Meter.com CO2, Temperature, Humidty, Environmental Data Logger, http://www.co2meter.com/collections/co2-sensors/products/k33-environmental-logger-co2-sensor (accessed February 28, 2014)
16. PostgresSQL, http://www.postgresql.org (accessed February 28, 2014)
17. node.js, http://nodejs.org (accessed February 28, 2014)
18. Deci, E., Ryan, R.: The "What" and "Why" of Goal Pursuits: Human Needs and the Self-Determination of Behavior. Psychological Inquiry 11, 227–268 (2000)
19. Ryan, R.M., Deci, E.L.: Self-determination theory and the facilitation of intrinsic motivation, social development, and well-being. The American Psychologist 55, 68–78 (2000)
20. Van der Heijden, H.: User Acceptance of Hedonic Information Systems. MIS Quarterly 28, 695–704 (2004)

# RUPERT: A Modelling Tool for Supporting Business Process Improvement Initiatives

Florian Johannsen[1] and Hans-Georg Fill[2]

[1] Chair of Business Engineering, University of Regensburg, Germany
florian.johannsen@wiwi.uni-regensburg.de
[2] Research Group Knowledge Engineering, University of Vienna, Austria
hans-georg.fill@univie.ac.at

**Abstract.** Business process improvement (BPI) will be a high priority topic for CEOs in the near future. Currently available BPI approaches, however, lack means for adequately codifying, documenting and processing knowledge created in a BPI project. Therefore we developed RUPERT (**R**egensburg **U**niversity **P**rocess **E**xcellence and **R**eengineering **T**oolkit), which is a tool for managing knowledge in a BPI project, covering all stages of the knowledge lifecycle. In this paper, we describe the design and implementation of RUPERT.

## 1 Introduction

Developments in information technology (e.g. Web 2.0) have brought about high market transparency leading to rapidly changing consumer requirements in recent years [1, 2]. At the same time, increasing market pressure forces companies to reduce costs and to reengineer resp. optimize business processes to be more efficient [3, 4]. To face these challenges, business process improvement (BPI) has been a key subject for CEOs in the recent past and will remain a high priority area to achieve process excellence [4, 5]. A major success factor for BPI projects is the participation of employees engaged in a business process under consideration (see [6]). In a BPI project, the project participants' tacit process knowledge (e.g. of process weaknesses, etc.) is transformed into explicit knowledge which needs to be codified, communicated and processed adequately. However, the management of process knowledge is a topic so far strongly neglected in current BPI approaches (e.g. [2, 7, 8]). Knowledge management tools (KM tools) provide a solution for this shortcoming since they do not only enable to store knowledge suitably but also facilitate the knowledge transfer within a company or across enterprise boundaries [9, 10].

In practice, KM tools are used for supporting all stages of the knowledge lifecycle [10]. Whereas the benefits of KM tools are commonly known (e.g. for innovative product development [9]), their potential for supporting BPI projects has not been investigated in detail yet. A possible explanation might be the lack of KM tools adapted to the specific needs of BPI practitioners. We thus contribute to the effective management of knowledge created in a BPI project, by the prototypical development of the tool "RUPERT" (**R**egensburg **U**niversity **P**rocess **E**xcellence and **R**eengineering **T**oolkit). RUPERT builds on the so-called "BPI roadmap" which we developed

M.C. Tremblay et al. (Eds.): DESRIST 2014, LNCS 8463, pp. 418–422, 2014.
© Springer International Publishing Switzerland 2014

during an earlier stage of our research (see [20]). The BPI roadmap is a manageable set of well-established BPI techniques covering all mandatory stages of a BPI project (see e.g. [11]) and has been evaluated in different BPI project settings. Several challenges were associated with the implementation of RUPERT. First, all techniques of the BPI roadmap were supposed to be considered by the tool. Second, the tool needed to be intuitively operable in terms of the handling of the tool and the application of the techniques. The realization of the techniques in the form of an IT-based modelling tool was thus promising for effectively codifying, communicating as well as processing knowledge in practice (see [12]). Third, the tool was meant to support all phases of the knowledge lifecycle [10] in the context of a BPI project. Besides knowledge generation and sharing this also included the automatic creation of reports enabling the analysis of knowledge captured. In the following, we introduce the tool "RUPERT" and emphasize key aspects of its implementation. The remainder of the paper is structured as follows: In section 2, we provide information on the design of the prototype and justify its implementation using a metamodelling platform. Afterwards, we highlight the contribution of the prototype. Section 4 describes the evaluation results gained in a pre-test. The paper concludes with a summary and an outlook.

## 2    Design of the Artifact

Recent studies (see [4]) have shown that process improvement initiatives increasingly abandon holistic BPI approaches, which are often perceived as over dimensioned or inefficient. Instead a manageable set of BPI techniques is preferred (see [4]). Therefore, we have developed a BPI roadmap in a long-term cooperation with an automotive bank, which builds on eleven well-established BPI techniques (see [20]).

The BPI roadmap starts with the *SIPOC Diagram*, visualizing the business process. Afterwards, the *CTQ-/CTB-Matrix* is used to identify customer requirements and *Performance Indicators* are defined for measuring the process performance. By means of the *Measurement Matrix* and the *Data Collection Plan*, the Performance Indicators are prioritized and operationalized. As soon as the process data has been collected, the current process performance is analyzed via *Histograms* resp. *Scatterplots*. Then, problem causes are identified via *Ishikawa Diagrams* and corresponding solutions are developed with *Affinity Diagrams*. After implementing these, means for mitigating unexpected process variances are formulated (*Reaction Plan*) and the process performance is continuously controlled (*Control Charts*). These BPI techniques were transformed into conceptual model types. The *conceptualization* as model types and metamodels is described in an earlier work [20]. We chose this approach because conceptual models have proven as a very effective means for organizing, creating, distributing and preserving knowledge in practice [12]. The model types of the BPI roadmap are interrelated with one another. Results that are produced once can be referenced by other model types. The integrated metamodel of the BPI roadmap linking the technique-specific metamodels by common key concepts (e.g. "critical-to-quality-factors") was the main result of the **design phase**. Each metamodel was formalized (**formalization phase**) using the FDMM formalism, which enabled their mathematical description [13]. This is an important step, since it allows the user to formally define, analyze and evaluate the syntax of the modelling language to be implemented [14]. The formal specification served as input for the implementation of the metamodels via the ADOxx metamodelling platform [13, 15] (**development phase**). An example for the formalization of the metamodel for the *Measurement Matrix Model* as FDMM code is given in Fig. 1. This figure also shows screenshots of the *CTQ-/CTB-Model* and the *Performance Indicator Model*. Further, an excerpt of the ADOxx Library Language (ALL) is shown, which is used for describing user-defined metamodels that are derived from the ADOxx meta²model [15].

In general, metamodelling platforms provide great benefits when implementing metamodels, since classes and their relations can be implemented without programming effort (see [15]). Further, an environment for the storage, user interaction and the creation of models, as well as the creation of an installation package for the resulting modelling tool is provided automatically [16]. The ADOxx metamodelling platform (www.adoxx.org) has been successfully applied in various research and industrial projects for more than 15 years and has constantly been developed further [15].

The architecture of ADOxx builds on a database-driven client-server repository providing a multi-user environment with several components to realize modelling methods [15]. The platform proved well-suited for implementing "RUPERT" considering the challenges as stated in section 1. In particular, the querying functionality of ADOxx [15], in the form of the ADOxx query language (AQL), allows to automatically generate user-defined reports and to analyze the knowledge captured.

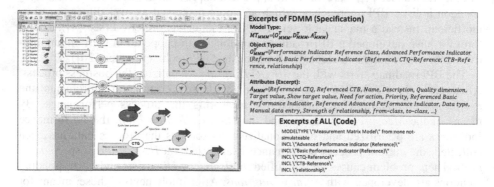

**Fig. 1.** Examples for model types, FDMM and ALL code

## 3    Significance of the Research

RUPERT contributes to the appropriate documentation, communication and processing of knowledge in BPI projects, supporting all stages of the knowledge lifecycle from capitalizing, sharing, retrieving, to the creation of knowledge concerning the business process to be improved (see [10, 21]). In doing so, a solution for the goal-oriented management of knowledge in BPI projects is proposed. Potential users of the tool are all members of a project team involved in a BPI project. Since the models are stored in a repository and the BPI roadmap covers all stages of a BPI project, process knowledge once captured can be retrieved and reused at any time. Therefore the *capitalization of knowledge* (see [10]) is supported. The tool enables to share process knowledge (*knowledge sharing*) (see [10]), since ADOxx builds on a client-server approach, allowing all project members to access the models and results. By the querying functionality of ADOxx, process knowledge can be systematically retrieved from the models e.g. in the form of user-adapted reports (*knowledge retrieval and querying*) (see [10]). These reports support decision making, since the insights gained can be used for deriving problem-specific solutions. Finally, *knowledge creation* (see [10]) is supported, as the model types of the BPI roadmap guide the systematic transformation of employees' implicit knowledge to explicit process knowledge.

## 4    Pre-test for a Usability Study

RUPERT represents a proof-of-concept (see [17]) for the previously developed BPI roadmap. The FDMM formalism was used to analyze the soundness and correctness of the created metamodels. In a next step, the usability of RUPERT is to be evaluated in an extensive laboratory experiment with a target sample size between 60 to 100 participants. For that purpose, a pre-test with seven master students (business informatics) of a German university was conducted to evaluate the material developed for the usability study of RUPERT. The material was based on a case study from a real life BPI project at an automotive bank. Based on a given problem statement, the participants were asked to systematically derive solutions for process improvement using the tool "RUPERT". To assess usability, the dimensions efficiency, effectiveness and subjective usability (SUMI) were referred to (see [18]). Effectiveness was judged by the quantity and quality of solutions developed, whereas the "temporal efficiency" was measured by the relation of effectiveness and task time (see [18]). The subjective usability was determined based on the SUMI questionnaire [19]. The results received from the pre-test confirmed the suitability of the material for a larger usability study. The students did well in developing solutions using RUPERT, even though they did not have domain specific knowledge on automotive banks. It took the participants between 58 and 62.5 minutes to complete the case study. The review of participants' solutions (to assess effectiveness) was done by two researchers to reduce subjectivity. Participants perceived the SUMI questions as well-formulated and unambiguous. The download and installation of RUPERT in a computer lab took about 20 minutes. In addition to master degree students, we plan to evaluate RUPERT with practitioners.

## 5    Conclusion

In this paper, we describe the prototypical implementation of RUPERT. The tool supports the management of emerging knowledge in BPI projects and thus contributes to current BPI research. RUPERT serves as a proof-of-concept for the so-called "BPI roadmap" that was developed and evaluated at a prior stage of this research. In that context, the formalization of the metamodels of the BPI roadmap (via FDMM) proved to be a mandatory step for assessing their correctness prior to implementation. Whereas the BPI roadmap was already evaluated in practice, an extensive evaluation of RUPERT has not been done yet. In future work, RUPERT will thus be evaluated in larger settings in both academia and practice. Further information on RUPERT (screenshots, use case, etc.) as well as the prototype (as an MS Windows installation package) is available at: http://www.omilab.org/web/rupert/home

# References

1. Sharma, G., Baoku, L.: Customer satisfaction in Web 2.0 and information technology development. Information Technology & People 26, 347–367 (2013)
2. Seethamraju, R., Marjanovic, O.: Role of process knowledge in business process improvement methodology: A case study. BPMJ 15, 920–936 (2009)
3. Heckl, D., Moormann, J., Rosemann, M.: Uptake and success factors of Six Sigma in the financial services industry. Business Process Management Journal 16, 436–472 (2010)
4. Davis, D.: 3rd Biennial PEX Network Report: State of the Industry - Trends and Success Factors in Business Process Excellence (2013)
5. McDonald, M.P., Aron, D.: Reimagining IT: The 2011 CIO Agenda. Gartner (2011)
6. Siha, S.M., Saad, G.H.: Business process improvement: empirical assessment and extensions. Business Process Management Journal 14, 778–802 (2008)
7. Zellner, G.: A Structured Evaluation of Business Process Improvement Approaches. Business Process Management Journal 17, 203–237 (2011)
8. Adesola, S., Baines, T.: Developing and evaluating a methodology for business process improvement. Business Process Management Journal 11, 37–46 (2005)
9. Vaccaro, A., Parente, R., Veloso, F.M.: Knowledge management tools, interorganizational relationships, innovation and firm performance. Technological Forecasting and Social Change 77, 1076–1089 (2010)
10. Xu, Y., Bernard, A., Perry, N., Lian, L.: Managing knowledge management tools: a systematic classification and comparison. Management and Service Science (2011)
11. Pande, P., Neuman, R., Cavanagh, R.: The Six Sigma Way: How GE, Motorola, and other top companies are honing their performance. McGraw-Hill, New York (2000)
12. Anaby-Tavor, et al.: Insights into enterprise conceptual modeling. Data & Knowledge Engineering 69, 1302–1318 (2010)
13. Fill, H.-G., Hickl, S., Karagiannis, D., Oberweis, A., Schoknecht, A.: A Formal Specification of the Horus Modeling Language Using FDMM. In: Proceedings Wirtschaftsinformatik, Paper 73, Leipzig (2013)
14. Fill, H.-G., Redmond, T., Karagiannis, D.: FDMM: A Formalism for Describing ADOxx Meta Models and Models. In: Proceedings 14th ICEIS, pp. 133–144 (2012)
15. Fill, H.-G., Karagiannis, D.: On the Conceptualisation of Modelling Methods Using the ADOxx Meta Modelling Platform. EMISA - An International Journal 8 (2013)
16. Clark, T., Sammut, P., Willans, J.: Applied metamodelling (2008)
17. Hevner, A.R., March, S.T., Park, J., Ram, S.: Design Science in Information Systems Research. MIS Quarterly 28, 75–105 (2004)
18. Bevan, N.: Measuring usability as quality of use. Software Quality Journal 4 (1995)
19. Kirakowski, J., Corbett, M.: SUMI: The software usability measurement inventory. British Journal of Educational Technology 24, 210–212 (1993)
20. Johannsen, F., Fill, H.-G.: Codification of knowledge in business process improvement projects. Paper Conditionally Accepted for ECIS 2014, Tel Aviv (2014)
21. Alavi, M., Leidner, D.E.: Review: Knowledge management and knowledge management systems: Conceptual foundations and research issues. MIS Quarterly 25, 107–136 (2001)

# Corporate Navigator App –
# A New-Generation Management Support System

Jörg H. Mayer[1], Claudia Koschtial[2], Jens Hartwig[3], and André Röder[3]

[1] University of St. Gallen, Institute of Information Management,
Müller-Friedberg-Strasse 8, 9000 St.Gallen, Switzerland
joerg.mayer@unisg.ch
[2] Freiberg University of Technology, Institute of Information Management,
Silbermannstr. 2, 09599 Freiberg, Germany
claudia.koschtial@bwl.tu-freiberg.de
[3] Darmstadt University of Technology, Chair of Accounting and Auditing,
Hochschulstrasse 1, 64289 Darmstadt, Germany
{jens.hartwig,a.roeder}@stud.tu-darmstadt.de

## 1  Design Problem

As an umbrella term, *management support systems* (MSS) cover management information systems, decision support systems, executive information systems, and – more recently – knowledge management, and business intelligence (BI) systems for managers [1]. By serving as their central, hands-on, day-to-day source of information, MSS help managers to perform their jobs more productively and efficiently [2].

Their redesign is currently an interesting and relevant subject for two reasons. Firstly, managers have to make decisions faster than they have in the past and want *self-service MSS* to support them in doing so [3, 4]. Secondly, *mobility* is one of the most visible trends in information systems (IS) and companies expect mobile IS to make their workforce – including their managers – more efficient [5]. In parallel, multi-touch, direct-manipulation user interfaces have raised managers' expectations of easy-to-use *smart devices* (hardware perspective) [6] and, thanks to Apple's million-dollar slogan "There's an app for that," manager awareness of *apps* (small capsulated software programs) is constantly growing (software perspective) [7].

The objective of this article is to lay out a self-service app for investigating the boundaries of mobile MSS. Taking the Corporate Navigator as an example, a joint MSS developed by a manager focus group from large international companies [8], the prototype on hand complements managers' stationary reporting working routines when they are mobile.

## 2  Requirements Analysis and Conceptual Design

**Corporate Navigator Prototype:** Applying a business-to-IT architecture and based on our prior work [9], two characteristics distinguish the Corporate Navigator as a new-generation MSS prototype from its predecessors: It consistently integrates *four*

M.C. Tremblay et al. (Eds.): DESRIST 2014, LNCS 8463, pp. 423–427, 2014.
© Springer International Publishing Switzerland 2014

*IS design layers* (strategic positioning, conceptual design, business/IT alignment, and IT components) so that it can react flexibly to changing business requirements. In doing so, a *three-step standard reporting* ensures that information is synthesized hierarchically and presented in a condensed format for manager self-service [10]. The *Corporate Portfolio* (A) provides a graphical overview of a company's financial performance with just three KPIs: reward, risk, and relevance. The *Corporate Dashboard* (B) is a one-page report with detailed KPIs structured into five information clusters: financial accounting, management accounting, cash flow and liquidity management, compliance management, and program management. Finally, *Corporate Analyses* (C) cover about ten standard analyses and a flexible periphery for ad-hoc reporting, non-routine information, and links to the transaction systems.

The Corporate Navigator prototype is based on an SAP platform including SAP ERP 6.0 as the enterprise resource planning system, BW 7.3 as the data warehouse, and SEM-BCS 6.34 as the business application.

**Objective:** The current research project "self-service MSS app" is aimed at aligning the upcoming requirements of managers with "modern" IS capabilities in two respects. The intention is to deliver a *mobile version* of a stationary Corporate Navigator reporting [9] which can be navigated by managers themselves and to complement the MSS content *"beyond the financials"* [11].

Thus, the app design followed the *"mobile first"* paradigm [12] anticipating smaller design elements (most often less than 10") and alternative input methods such as touch, by introducing new navigation concepts [2]. One example of such a new "mobile first" design is Microsoft's tile design which naturally embraces touch gestures by offering wide-spaced interactive buttons [13].

**Project:** A two-person BI team and four IS researchers started a five month project in October 2013 with the manager focus group named in Sect. 1. Firstly, they evaluated different *frontend applications* focusing on easy-to-use IS handling, compatibility with the SAP Business Warehouse, and state of the art mobile capabilities [14]. The Corporate Navigator app (see the prototype on hand) is based on the winner of this software evaluation MicroStrategy 9.3.1 [15].

Secondly, regarding the end-user device, the manager focus group voted for *tablets* as its new MSS smart devices. One reason in that discussion was that tablets are expected to exceed portable PCs (notebooks and hybrids) in units shipped in 2013 [16] and, as Apple still dominates the tablet market in terms of hardware sold [17] we set up the Corporate Navigator app as a mobile first MSS design on an iPad.

## 3    Implementation and Demonstration

Based on the findings of prior research on mobile MSS [18] and complementing feedback during the MSS design from the manager expert focus group in another workshop during the design, a final workshop presenting the results the manager focus group and a first implementation at one of the large international companies [8], implementing the Corporate Navigator app taught us four lessons learned.

Firstly, *microcharts* – a new type of graphics [19] – help to expose important KPIs in a condensed manner (especially when using dashboards). Bullet graphs are an example within the new types of graphics which show a KPI's actual value in the context of its budget or forecast value. More important, *sparklines* which present time series of important KPIs rather than showing just a single value were well received. In doing so, detailed information on demand should be available as well. A *mouse-over feature* or similar input gestures like tap on a touch-sensitive user interface should be an intuitive way to navigate to these details. This feature enables managers to be aware of the relevant information while being able to obtain further knowledge.

Secondly, *value-driver trees* enable managers to better understand their business by a KPI's decomposition of relevant figures such as EVA (economic value added). Each value driver's (mathematical) inner structure has to be visible and accessible on the app. Combined with *sliders* to vary the most important levers, value-driver trees offer a rich, but easy-to-use way of performing what-if analyses. The results of manipulations are calculated "on the fly" when changing the value drivers and expose information for scenarios such a most probable, best case or even worst case.

Thirdly, since collaboration is gaining importance in managerial decision-making, our new MSS app supports several forms focusing on commenting [20]. Besides comments within the report or at important KPIs, a *collaboration bar* is a new Corporate Navigator feature. This bar is designed to follow the concept of "show more" and thus is only visible on demand, by sliding it in from the screen side, for example. The bar itself covers comments by managers and their supporting staff in chronological or other orders (time, sender, importance, etc.).

Fourthly, a predefined *exception reporting* process was implemented within the app. Exception reports are being pushed to managers' devices as notification. In a notification, a description is given to choose whether or not to follow the lead by switching to the app. In the app, managers are then able to do instant analyses and reply with edits or comments without leaving the app. Copying and pasting screenshots into an email program becomes superfluous as a result. The "push"-function can be triggered manually by supporting staff, as well as by automatic thresholds. Furthermore, as one of our final lessons learned, an MSS exception reporting should enable managers to subscribe to individual reports or KPIs to receive incremental updates or the reports they subscribed to per se.

## 4    Evaluate

For *research purposes*, the Corporate Navigator enables researchers to better understand new MSS app design and manager self-service. Thus, it should be a rigorous starting point for future research. The MSS app exposes essential management reporting artifacts such as Corporate Portfolio, Corporate Dashboard, and Corporate Analysis. With its modular design, it integrates not just further reporting elements such as an environmental scanning system, but even improves the non-functional perspective of a "modern" management report design.

For *practice purposes*, the Corporate Navigator app accommodates the changing MSS requirements of new-generation managers, especially when they are mobile. Thus, the Corporate Navigator app should increase the business value of IS by presenting the most relevant KPIs in a manner that is comprehensive in terms of content, but nonetheless brief and intuitive. Using the new MicroStrategy frontend gives the user interface a "look & feel" which covers managers' requirements.

Furthermore, *tablets* accessing MSS can create their own use case in three ways [6]: They can serve as (a) an advanced PDF reader more efficiently than smartphones, (b) they are handier to serve as an electronic typewriter for complex emailing, especially when office documents are attached, and (c) tablets are starting to become managers' preferred device for simple ad-hoc analysis "on the fly."

# 5     Avenues for Future Research

Since descriptive analytics is often integrated into today's MSS and even models, which predict the future under incorporation of historic data (predictive analytics) become more and more common in BI solutions [21]. We propose *prescriptive analytics* as a next step in MSS design. It origins from operations research and uses mathematical optimization and simulation to suggest optimal behavior [22] or decisions [23]. Thus, a first avenue for future research is to evaluate the benefits of prescriptive analytics incorporated in MSS and its acceptance by managers.

The relevance of *self-service MSS* for managers should be examined as well. Adequate forms of visualizations, tailored to the management's needs, could yield more insights and therefore improve decision-making. Especially reoccurring analyses, e.g. the effects of currency or material price changes, could be done by the managers themselves and pre-calculated by the MSS to keep IS response times short and proactive.

Future research should also examine the benefit of *real-time management* based on new in-memory technology for MSS. Furthermore, a prioritization of managers' most important *MSS use situations* should be interesting for future research and, in doing so, managers exposed their mobile offline situations [6, 14].

Finally mobile MSS should also support "fun and enjoyment." This should be examined more in detail from a manager's perspective.

# References

1. Carlsson, S.A., Henningsson, S., Hrastinski, S., Keller, C.: An Approach for Designing Management Support Systems: The Design Science Research Process and Its Outcomes. In: Proceedings of the Fourth International Conference on Design Science Research in Information Systems and Technology (DESRIST), pp. 1–10. ACM, New York (2009)
2. Clark Jr., T.D., Jones, M.C., Armstrong Curtis, P.: The Dynamic Structure of Management Support Systems: Theory Development, Research Focus, and Direction. MIS Quarterly 31(3), 579–615 (2007)
3. Stodder, D.: Achieving Greater Agility with Business Intelligence: Improving Speed and Flexibility for BI, Analytics, and Data Warehousing. TDWI Research, Renton, USA (2013)
4. Mayer, J.H.: Current Changes in Executive Work and How to Handle Them by Redesigning Executive Information Systems. In: Mancini, D., Vaassen, E., Dameri, R.P. (eds.) Accounting Information Systems for Decision Making, vol. 3, pp. 134–155. Springer, Heidelberg (2013)
5. Ladd, D.A., Datta, A., Sarker, S., Yanjun, Y.: Trends in Mobile Computing within the IS Discipline: A Ten-Year Retrospective. Communications of AIS (CAIS) 27(17), 285–306 (2010)
6. Mayer, J.H., Stock, D., Winter, R., Scholl, N.: Management Support Systems on Different Devices—A Business Perspective Accommodating Managers' Growing Range of Use Situations. In: Proceedings of the Fourty Seventh Annual Hawaii International Conference on System Sciences (HICSS), pp. 285–306. IEEE, Waikoloa (2014)

7. Apple Inc., `http://www.youtube.com/watch?v=szrsfeyLzyg` (accessed January 15, 2014)
8. Competence Center "Management Support Systems", `http://uss.iwi.unisg.ch` (accessed January 15, 2014)
9. Mayer, J.H., Winter, R.: New-Generation Managers and Their IS Support—Getting It Right with the Corporate Navigator. In: vom Brocke, J., Hekkala, R., Ram, S., Rossi, M. (eds.) DESRIST 2013. LNCS, vol. 7939, pp. 432–437. Springer, Heidelberg (2013)
10. McKinsey & Company, `http://www.mckglobal.com/Connect/BTO/ SAP_Corporate_Navigator/SAP_CN_03_online_en/index.html`(accessed January 15, 2014)
11. Mayer, J.H.: Using The Kano Model To Identify Attractive User-Interface Software Components. In: George, J.F. (ed.) Proceedings of the 20th International Conference on Information Systems (ICIS), Orlando, USA. HCI, vol. 314, pp. 1–17 (2012)
12. Voas, J., Michael, J.B., van Genuchten, M.: The Mobile Software App Takeover. IEEE Software 29(4), 25–27 (2012)
13. Microsoft, `http://msdn.microsoft.com/en-us/library/windowsphone/ design/jj662929(v= vs.105).aspx` (accessed January 15, 2014)
14. Mayer, J.H., Quick, R., Hauke, J.: Taking a New-Generation Manager Perspective to Develop Interface Designs. In: Pennarola, F., Becker, J. (eds.) Reshaping Society Through Information Systems Design. Proceedings of the Thirty Fourth International Conference on Information Systems (ICIS), pp. 1–16. AIS, Italy (2013)
15. MicroStrategy, `http://www.microstrategy.com/platforms/ analytics/business-intelligence` (accessed December 10, 2013)
16. International Data Corporation (IDC), `http://www.idc.com/ getdoc.jsp?containerId=prUS24314413` (accessed October 30, 2013)
17. The NPD Group, Inc., `https://www.npd.com/wps/portal/npd/us/news/ press-releases/u-s-commercial-channel-computing-device-sales- set-to-end-2013-with-double-digit-growth-according-to-npd` (accessed October 15, 2013)
18. Mayer, J.H., Röder, A., Hartwig, J., Quick, R.: A Self-Service MSS Design from a New-Generation Manager Perspective, research paper. University of St.Gallen and Darmstadt University of Technology. St.Gallen and Darmstadt (2014)
19. Frishberg, L.D.: Interactive sparklines: A dynamic display of quantitative information. In: CHI 2011 Extended Abstracts on Human Factors in Computing Systems (CHI EA 2011), pp. 589–604. ACM, Vancouver (2011)
20. Feistenauer, H., Mayer, J.H., Quick, R.: A First Perspective on Requirements of New-Generation Managers for Collaboration Technology to be Integrated into Management Support Systems. In: Johnson, R., Djamasbi, S. (eds.) The Twelfth Annual Pre-ICIS Workshop on HCI Research in MIS, Mailand, Italy (poster presentation) (2013), `http://sighci.org/index.php?page=pre-icis2013` (accessed January 02, 2014)
21. Chen, H., Chiang, R.H., Storey, V.C.: Business Intelligence and Analytics: From Big Data to Big Impact. MIS Quarterly 36(4), 1165–1188 (2012)
22. Ghasemi, S., Ghasemi, M., Ghasemi, M.: Knowledge Discovery in Discrete Event Simulation Output Analysis. In: Pichappan, P., Ahmadi, H., Ariwa, E. (eds.) INCT 2011. CCIS, vol. 241, pp. 108–120. Springer, Heidelberg (2011)
23. Sharda, R., Asamoah, D.A., Ponna, N.: Business analytics: Research and teaching perspectives. In: Proceedings of the ITI 2013 35th International Conference on Information Technology Interfaces, pp. 19–27. IEEE, Cavtat (2013)

# Mass Shooting Incident Response Optimization System:
## Development of Situational Aware Incident Response System

Joana Monteiro, Shuai Yuan, Abhiram Upadhya, Pavankumar Mulgund, Megha Malaviya, and Raj Sharman

State University of New York at Buffalo, NY
{joanaalu,shuaiyua,abhiramk,pmulgund,meghamal, rsharman}@buffalo.edu

**Abstract.** The number of mass shooting incidents have shown an increase from 2000 to now. With the increased number in this type of incident the number of victims has also increased. Post incident analysis reports suggest improvements in situational awareness could have reduced the number of deaths during the incidents. The application extends primary triage as an input to situational awareness, use of heuristic methods for efficient search for victims and optimized route for reaching victims and extraction. This research also proposes an inclusive process of dealing with the incident starting from when active shooter is neutralized to the point when victims are extracted from the scene, from the viewpoint of Emergency Medical Services (EMS).

**Keywords:** Situational awareness, computer aided triage, active shooting, incident response, Design Science.

## 1 Introduction

On July 20th 2012 during the midnight premiere of the Batman movie a lone gunman entered theatre #9 at the Century Aurora 16 Multiplex, in Colorado. He killed 12 and wounded 58 people. Most of the victims were admitted with gunshot wounds, while others were treated for injuries sustained during the ensuing chaos (Aurora FD, 2012).

Victims at the back of the theater, some who were among the more severely wounded, did not receive attention immediately. The victims at the front of the screening room (some who had less severe injuries), received response attention first. Some of the victims in the back of the room died as a consequence of not receiving attention on priority.

The design of our solution addresses some of the gaps in the response efforts to a mass shooting incident, by contributing to the increase of situational awareness and efficiency in the victim triage and extraction process.

Situation awareness is the perception of environmental elements with respect to time and/or space, the comprehension of their meaning, and the projection of their status after some variable has changed, such as time, or some other variable. In many dynamic work situations, no single individual can acquire the varied and often rapidly expanding information needed for success. Individuals must work together to collect,

M.C. Tremblay et al. (Eds.): DESRIST 2014, LNCS 8463, pp. 428–432, 2014.

analyze, synthesize and disseminate information throughout the work process (Sonnenwalda & Pierceb, 2000).

This application provides mechanisms for the input of relevant information by EMS though the use of mobile apps, facilitating situational awareness during shooting incidents. The central feature of this artifact is that it leverages theory to develop a shortest path discovery algorithm which uses weights provided by the first wave of responders regarding difficulty in navigating obstacles; and allows second and third wave responders to easily make their way to victims and ambulances.

## 2    Design of the Artifact

This paper proposes an artifact structure follows the ICS (Incident Command System) 100 framework.

### 2.1    Process Flow

The first wave of responders equipped for primary triage reach the site of the incident. They perform what is called a hasty/heuristic search to reach the site of the shooting as close as possible. En route to the site the responders update the command center and subsequent teams regarding the obstacles they encounter when trying to reach the victims. As and when the triage specialists find injured victims they perform STARTTriage and using the MSIROS system capture the following details a) Triage status; b) Scan the RF tag of triage tag; c) Take the picture of the victim and then move on to next victim. The information entered by them is sent directly to the command center and is available for all field personnel through mobile devices. This information increases the situational awareness of all the participants of the response. The $2^{nd}$ wave of responders enters the incident location equipped with the information provided by wave 1 responders and will respond to the identified choke points. They will reach the victims using the short path algorithm. As and when they find victims they perform STARTTriage and update the database. The information flow from these waves refines the situational awareness data, allowing the $3^{rd}$ wave of responders to perform a grid search of the entire incident perimeter with increased situational awareness. The evacuation also is performed based on shortest path using optimal evacuation route. The algorithm can be refined as and when more information becomes available.

### 2.2    System Architecture

Our system will have two interfaces, one mobile app for the first responders and a web app that allows the command center to visualize updates in real time. The back end of this system is a central database which will get real time updates from the mobile app as well as the command center web app.

The mobile app will allow for: victim status and images to be captured at triage; shortest path to be visualized and modified; input to be provided on situational awareness factors.

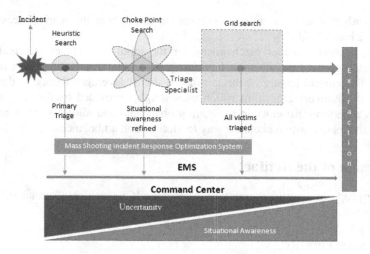

**Fig. 1.** MSIROS Process Flow

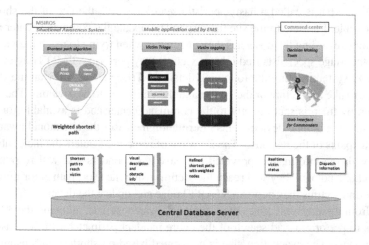

**Fig. 2.** MSIROS System Architecture

# 3    Significance to Research

## 3.1    Design Science Methodology

Using Hevner et al (2004) guidelines for Design Science Research we identify the following aspects that break the main paradigms identified by this body of literature:

- Research Rigor (G5): The construction of this artifact relies not only on the implementation of existing triaging protocols, and emergency response effort frameworks, but also on the adaptation of existing short path algorithms. The evaluation of the model proposed will rely on existing methods. (See section 5 below)

- Research Contributions (G4): The proposed artifact provides a deeper under-standing and a positive effect of the impact of response times on shooting incident outcomes. It also provides a more efficient triage mechanism that will ultimately lead to less loss of life. This artifact follows the suggested guidelines for Design Science Research (Hevner et al, 2004)

- Design as an Artifact (G1): The artifact proposed creates an instantiation that provides a model for emergency response efforts, through the use of both the front end apps and the algorithm for the creation of response focus nodes. A back end data-base will be updated in real time.

Other guidelines included in Hevner et al.'s (2004) body of work, like Problem Relevance (G2), Design As A Search Process (G6), Design Evaluation (G3), and Communication (G7) have also been taken into consideration during this process.

### 3.2  Shortest Path Algorithm

Finding the shortest path based on assigned weights to reach the victims when the EMS teams move into the building and to evacuate through an optimal route presents an interesting challenge in case of disaster situation. Dijkstra's and Bellman–Ford's algorithms both solve single-source shortest path problems, computing paths from a single source vertex to all of the other vertices in a weighted digraph. The Bellman–Ford algorithm is more flexible since it allows negative arc weights. For the purpose of eliminating the looping behavior, adaptive distributed shortest path algorithms like Humblet. (1991) have been suggested.

Specifically for evacuation problem, Pu, S., & Zlatanova, S. (2005) suggest an evacuation route calculation method taking dynamic environment and human factors into consideration. An integrated real-time evacuation route planning method including real-time data acquisition, risk distribution calculation, and evacuation route formula-tion for high-rise building fires is proposed in Han, Z., etc. (2013). The situational awareness factors are combined in the concept of "total risk", which is calculated by the fast marching level set method.  Filippoupolitis, A., & Gelenbe, E. (2009) propose a distributed decision support system that computes the best evacuation routes in real-time during an emergency situation inside a building. This system is composed of decision nodes inside building and sensor nodes that provide information about the intensity of hazard. Each decision node computes the best evacuation direction using only local information.

## 4    Significance to Practice

Our system is dedicated to assist the first responders in primary triage and tagging of victims with real time updates for increased situational awareness. The system assists first responders in finding shortest paths to particular areas in the incident site by providing weighted obstacle information and using it in the algorithm. The use of this system reduces the response time in a disaster and increases the accuracy of resource allocation and situation assessment. We believe that this artifact is not only imple-mentable but also provides relevance to the DS research just like Benbasat & Zmud (1999) propose.

# 5    Evaluation of the Artifact

The artifact has been validated during its creation through literature referencing as well as interviews with emergency response professionals. The future evaluation of the completed artifact prototype includes further technical experiments and illustrative scenarios which are the most appropriate for instantiations and algorithms (Peffers et al. 2012). Due to the nature of the shootings scenarios subject based experiments and action research are not appropriate (Venable et al. 2012).

# References

1. Aurora FD, Century Theater Shooting. Aurora Fire department preliminary incident analysis (2012)
2. ESRI, Public Safety and Homeland Security Situational Awareness, ESRI (2012)
3. Benbasat, I., Zmud, R.W.: Empirical Research in Information Systems: The Practice of Relevance. MISQ 23(1), 3–16 (1999)
4. Benson, M., Koenig, K.L., Schultz, C.H.: Disaster triage: START, then SAVE—a new method of dynamic triage for victims of a catastrophic earthquake. Prehospital and Disaster Medicine 11(02), 117–124 (1996)
5. Hevner, A., March, S., Park, J., Ram, S.: Design Science in Information Systems Research. MISQ 28(1), 75–105 (2004)
6. Peffers, K., Rothenberger, M., Tuunanen, T., Vaezi, R.: Design Science Research Evaluation. In: Peffers, K., Rothenberger, M., Kuechler, B. (eds.) DESRIST 2012. LNCS, vol. 7286, pp. 398–410. Springer, Heidelberg (2012)
7. Pu, S., Zlatanova, S.: Evacuation route calculation of inner buildings. In: Geo-information for Disaster Management, pp. 1143–1161. Springer, Heidelberg (2005)
8. Sonnenwald, D., Pierce, L.: Information behavior in dynamic group work contexts: interwoven situational awareness, dense social networks and contested collaboration in command and control. Information Processing and Management 36, 461–479 (2000)
9. Venable, J., Pries-Heje, J., Baskerville, R.: A Comprehensive Framework for Evaluation in Design Science Research. In: Peffers, K., Rothenberger, M., Kuechler, B. (eds.) DESRIST 2012. LNCS, vol. 7286, pp. 423–438. Springer, Heidelberg (2012)

# Emotionally Responsive Virtual Counselor
# for Behavior-Change Health Interventions

Reza Amini, Christine Lisetti, and Ugan Yasavur

School of Computing and Information Sciences,
Florida International University,
Miami, Florida 33199
{ramin001,ugan.yasavur}@fiu.edu,
lisetti@cis.fiu.edu

**Abstract.** In this paper, we discuss a novel approach to design an emotionally responsive system in the context of virtual health interventions for behavior change. We describe the system's design with a focus on enabling a multimodal Embodied Conversational Agent (ECA) to deliver the interventions **empathetically**. This is done by adapting its verbal and non-verbal behavior, in real-time, to those of the clients. Our current approach is based on a successful existing patient-centered intervention for behavior change - the Drinker's Check-Up (DCU). Although, the DCU uses a text-only web interface, it has been reported to reduce alcohol consumption in problem drinkers. We discuss the results of users' evaluation of the DCU intervention compared to the same intervention delivered with empathic and non-empathic ECAs. Results show that, the empathic virtual counselor has better acceptance than the other two systems.

## 1    Introduction

A substantial amount work is done in developing natural user interfaces using different input modalities such as text, mouse click, touch screen gesture, and speech. However, in the application domains that involve emotionally sensitive contents, discarding affective signals and not adapting the system's behavior to user's affective states is an obvious shortcoming. Specially, health behavior change is a highly sensitive domain. In this paper, we discuss our emotionally responsive system design in health behavior change.

Computer-based approaches are being used in delivering health interventions. They were reported as effective ways of making people aware of their unhealthy life styles and motivating them to change these behaviors [1], [2]. Even though, the effectiveness of the computer based applications are supported by many studies, the attrition rates are still very high [3]. We believe that our emotionally responsive design approach has the potential to better engage the users by providing additional channels of emotional interaction. Better engagement in the computer health interventions can increase the strength of the user-system connection which itself leads to lower dropout rates and better outcomes consequently.

Embodied Conversational Agents (ECAs) are being used for delivering health material and envisioned to be helpful in computer-based therapy [4]. In a recent comprehensive

M.C. Tremblay et al. (Eds.): DESRIST 2014, LNCS 8463, pp. 433–437, 2014.
© Springer International Publishing Switzerland 2014

literature review of active assistance technologies in health-related behavior change systems [5], dialogue systems and ECAs are identified as emerging technology themes in the behavior change systems field.

For example, the MIT FitTrack [6] uses an ECA to investigate the ability to establish and maintain a long-term working alliance with users in a behavior-change context. It creates rapport using social and empathic dialogs, politeness, and nonverbal behaviors (e.g., smile). Comparing to an equivalent agent without any social-emotional, this agent was reported as more respected, liked, and trusted. Also, Schulman et al. [7] designed a conversational agent as a virtual counselor for health behavior change. They use techniques drawn from MI to enhance client motivation and confidence to change. Users reported satisfaction from using this system.

Although these health systems have shown some promising results, they miss the empathizing ability which supports the clients emotionally and helps them overcome their negative affects [8]. Empathizing helps the counselor to adapt his/her behavior to the clients' affective states, which itself engages the clients, motivates them to use the system in long-term, and motivates them to change their unhealthy behaviors.

However, the systems mentioned above are not emotionally responsive, they operate using only a single input channel, which consists of button clicks, and discard the experienced emotions. Therefore, they cannot engage the clients enough to the interaction and motivate them to continue the interaction and attend the follow-up sessions [1], [2], instead of dropping out which is a significant intervention problem [3].

Among different unhealthy behaviors, we selected excessive drinking as our target behavior. and based our work on a computer-based intervention called the Drinker's Check Up (DCU) [9]. It uses a patient-centered counseling technique called Motivational Interviewing (MI) to motivate people to change their unhealthy alcohol consumption behaviors. The DCU is reported to be able to decrease alcohol consumption by an average of 50% in a 12 month follow-up.

In this research, we have developed an Empathic On-Demand Virtual Health Counselor (Emp-ODVIHC) which delivers the computer-based Brief Motivational Interventions (BMIs) through an ECA (shown in Fig. 1).

**Fig. 1.** Emo-ODVIHC Amy in her office

## 2    Health Counselor System Architecture

We have developed an emotionally responsive animated character. It perceives the client's facial expressions and utterances during the health interaction and provides both empathic **non-verbal** expressions (emotional facial expressions, head nods, eyebrow movements), and **verbal** reflections.

Our system architecture is composed of 3D animated character, dialogue manager, and empathy model. The system architecture is described in detail in [10], [11]. In this article, our focus is on the **Empathy Model,** which consists of an **Affective Module** and a **Cognitive Module.** The **Empathy model** is the main component which enables the user-system emotionally responsive communication.

The Empathy Model captures user's facial expressions and head movements in real-time to assess the user's most probable affective states, then combines it with affect related information elicited from utterances to decide about the counselor's empathic responses. The Affective Module is responsible for fast and reactive responses such as simple verbal reflection of user's answers and head posture mimicry (to create closeness and mutual gaze with the client). The Cognitive Module on the other hand, is responsible for feedbacks that need more thinking and decision making before expression, such as facial expressions, and head nods.

## 3    Experiment and Evaluation

Clients attended the first session of an interview with our virtual counselor, which includes the AUDIT [12] psychometric instrument to assess their alcohol dependence. The default counselor was a Caucasian female (AMY). We have implemented three conditions for the experiment:

1. **Text-only** Drinker's Check-Up (DCU): during the session, the exact same content of the DCU [9] is delivered to the user using text-only web page frames.
2. **Non-empathic** counselor: during the interview, Amy shows a neutral facial expression, and does not empathize with the user at all.
3. **Empathic** counselor: during the counseling session, Amy expresses different emotional facial expressions (happy, sad, concerned, surprised, and neutral); head gesture (nod); big/subtle smile; head posture mimicry (pitch, yaw, roll); eyebrow movement; mutual gaze; and lip synchronized verbal reflections.

We hypothesize that counselors with different delivery modalities (i.e., virtual character vs. text) and different levels of empathizing abilities have different effects on the quality of the interaction with users.

Participants were recruited from volunteer university students through fliers and emails. They were randomly assigned to one of the three conditions. From the total number of 81 subjects, 26 were assigned to the empathic counselor, 25 to the non-empathic counselor, and 30 to the text-only version.

Based on the Heerink's model [13], we designed an online after-experiment questionnaire to evaluate the character's user's acceptance (including Attitude (ATT), Intention to Use (ITU), Perceived Enjoyment (PENJ), Perceived Ease of Use (PEOU), Perceived Sociability (PS), Perceived Usefulness (PU), Social Presence (SP), Trust (TRUST), Anxiety (ANX), and Social Influence (SI)).

### 3.1    Results and Discussion

The clients' answers are analyzed using the Mantel-Haenszel-Chi-Square statistical method (df = 1, and Bonferroni corrected alpha = 1.7%) with two null hypotheses: (1) text-only and non-empathic counselor have the same effects on the users; and (2) empathic and non-empathic counselors have the same effects on the users.

Also, we compared the mean values of subjects' responses in each category to show the possible system improvements/deteriorations. Results show that:

1. In all the categories except PEOU, ANX, and SI, when comparing the empathic condition with the other two conditions using Chi-Square, $p < 0.017$, which rejects the second null hypothesis. Therefore, adding the **empathizing ability** significantly affects the user acceptance and perceived character features.
2. In all categories except PS, when comparing the textual system and the non-empathic counselor, $p > 0.017$, which approves the first null hypothesis. So, adding a **non-empathic character** does not affect significantly the users perceptions.
3. As shown in Fig. 2, except in ANX and PEOU, in all the categories, **empathic** counselor outperformed both textual system and the non-empathic counselor. Positive anxiety mean values show that subjects did not feel anxious when using these systems. Positive PEOU values indicate that the clients perceived all conditions easy to use. However, the clients prefer a character interface rather than a pure textual intervention.
4. As shown in Fig. 2, mean values show that, in ATT, ITU, PEOU, SP, and LIKE, non-empathic counselor outperforms that textual system. Whereas, in PENJ, PS, PU, TRUST, SI, PI, and PS the textual system outperforms the non-empathic counselor.

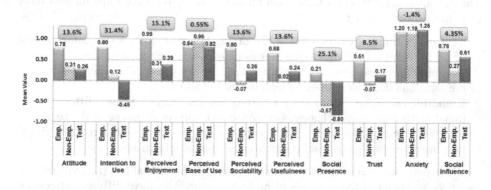

**Fig. 2.** User acceptance mean values. Percentages show improvement of empathic over textual.

## References

[1] Vernon, M.: A review of computer-based alcohol problem services designed for the general public. J. Subst. Abuse Treat. 38(3), 203–211 (2010)
[2] Portnoy, D.B., Scott-Sheldon, L.A.J., Johnson, B.T., Carey, M.P.: Computer-delivered interventions for health promotion and behavioral risk reduction: A meta-analysis of 75 randomized controlled trials, 1988-2007. Prev. Med. (Baltim) 47(1), 3–16 (2008)

[3] Dunn, T.L., Casey, L.M., Sheffield, J., Newcombe, P., Chang, A.B.: Dropout from computer-based interventions for children and adolescents with chronic health conditions. J. Health Psychol. 17(3), 429–442 (2012)

[4] Lisetti, C.L.: Embodied Conversational Agents for Psychotherapy. In: Proc. of the CHI 2008 Conf. Workshop on Technology in Mental Health, pp. 1–12 (2008)

[5] Kennedy, C.M., Powell, J., Payne, T.H., Ainsworth, J., Boyd, A., Buchan, I.: Active Assistance Technology for Health-Related Behavior Change: An Interdisciplinary Review. J. Med. Internet Resour. 14(3) (2012)

[6] Bickmore, T.W., Picard, R.W.: Establishing and maintaining long-term human-computer relationships. ACM Trans. Comput. Interact. 12(2), 617–638 (2005)

[7] Schulman, D., Bickmore, T.W., Sidner, C.L.: An Intelligent Conversational Agent for Promoting Long-Term Health Behavior Change using Motivational Interviewing. In: AAAI Spring Symposium Series, pp. 61–64 (2011)

[8] Greene, J.O., Burleson, B.R.: Handbook of Communication and Social Interaction Skills. Lawrence Erlbaum Associates, Inc., Publishers (2003)

[9] Hester, R.K., Squires, D.D., Delaney, H.D.: The Drinker's Check-up: 12-month outcomes of a controlled clinical trial of a stand-alone software program for problem drinkers. J. Subst. Abuse Treat. 28(2), 159–169 (2005)

[10] Lisetti, C., Amini, R., Yasavur, U., Rishe, N.: I Can Help You Change! An Empathic Virtual Agent Delivers Behavior. ACM Trans. Manag. Inf. Syst. 4(4), 1–28 (2013)

[11] Amini, R., Lisetti, C., Yasavur, U., Rishe, N.: On-Demand Virtual Health Counselor for Delivering Behavior-Change Health Interventions. In: IEEE International Conf. on Healthcare Informatics 2013 (ICHI 2013), vol. 1 (2013)

[12] Babor, T.F., Higgins-Biddle, J.C., Saunders, J.B., Monteiro, M.G.: AUDIT: The Alcohol Use Disorders Identification Test. Guidelines for use in primary health care, 2nd edn. World Health Organization, Department of Mental Health and Substance Dependence, p. 39 (2001)

[13] Heerink, M., Krose, B., Evers, V., Wielinga, B.: Measuring acceptance of an assistive social robot: A suggested toolkit. In: The 18th IEEE Int'l Symp. on Robot and Human Interactive Commun., RO-MAN 2009, pp. 528–533 (2009)

# Green e-community: Sensemaking in Environmental Sustainability Transformations

Stefan Seidel[1], Leona Chandra[1], Nadine Reuter[1], Daniel Stieger[2], and Michael Gau[1]

[1] Institute of Information Systems, University of Liechtenstein, Vaduz, Liechtenstein
[2] Strategic Management and Leadership, University of Innsbruck, Innsbruck, Austria
{stefan.seidel,leona.chandra,nadine.reuter,michael.gau}@uni.li,
daniel.stieger@uibk.ac.at

**Abstract.** This paper reports on an action design research study that aims to identify design principles for information systems (IS) that allow for sensemaking in the context of environmental sustainability transformations. Green e-community is presented as a prototype that instantiates a set of initial design principles and provides the foundation for subsequent rounds of building and evaluation to further develop the design principles.

**Keywords:** green IS, sensemaking, affordance, sustainability transformation.

## 1 Introduction

Information Systems (IS) play a key role in assisting organizations to become more environmentally sustainable [1]. It has been suggested that IS play an important role in transforming business processes to be less hazardous to the environment, for instance, through monitoring, work virtualization, and sensemaking [2, 3]. In this paper, we report on an action design research study that aims to identify design principles for IS that allow for sensemaking in organizational sustainability transformations. Specifically, we describe a prototype, "Green e-community," that was developed within the project in order to implement and evaluate an initial set of design principles.

Sensemaking occurs when individuals in organizations "frame, interpret, and understand the multilayered and complex issues related to the environmental sustainability transformation" [2]. It begins when individuals recognize an inadequacy of their current understanding of situations and events [4], for instance, in responding to changes in regulatory requirements [3] or to new, emergent goals related to environmental sustainability [2]. This comprehension allows individuals in organizations to explicitly understand the situation and enables the enactment of new interpretations into organizational actions [4, 5]. Consequently, sensemaking serves as a launch pad for action [4] and thus provides an important basis for organizational change.

In formulating design principles, we draw on the concept of affordance, which describes the potential uses one can make from technology [6, 7] and which is consistent with the socio-technical approach in information systems [6, 8]. The theoretical lens of affordance acknowledges that information systems do not deterministically lead to a certain effect but, instead, provide actionable spaces that actors may enact in

M.C. Tremblay et al. (Eds.): DESRIST 2014, LNCS 8463, pp. 438–442, 2014.

light of specific action goals—in this case related to environmental sustainability. It further allows us to explain which features of information systems afford which user behaviors, in order for sensemaking to occur.

## 2    Design of the Artifact

### 2.1    Affordances and Design Principles

Based upon prior theory, we identified affordances that are required for sensemaking to occur in environmental sustainability transformations [4, 5]. IS for sensemaking in sustainability transformations should afford (a) disruptive ambiguity and surprise, (b) noticing and bracketing, (c) engagement in an open and inclusive dialog, as well as (d) presumptive disclosure and action planning. From these affordances, design principles and their prototypical implementation were derived. Table 1 provides an overview of one exemplary design principle, including a prototypical implementation.

Table 1. Example of affordance, design principle, and prototypical implementation

| Affordance | Design principles | Prototypical implementation |
|---|---|---|
| Disruptive ambiguity and surprise | In order to afford disruptive ambiguity and surprise, the IS artifact should provide novel information in the form of environmental facts, observations or general behavior | Presentation of indicators through read-only web-platform: paper, plastic cup, paper towel, and waste production. |

### 2.2    Green e-community Prototype

Green e-community is a web-based prototype, where multiple users can engage in a sensemaking process. It provides facts about the current situation at the case organization and the environmental sustainability initiative, thereby triggering disruptive ambiguity and surprise. It allows individuals to store and label ideas (noticing and bracketing), and to engage in an open and inclusive dialog. Finally, it allows users to highlight potential action, thereby affording presumptive thinking and action planning. This prototype consists of a number of main views.

The **"Create a topic"** view allows users to start new discussions (topics). Users can provide a title and short description. Both verbal and visual contents can be recorded. This view is thus intended to afford noticing and bracketing.

The **"Explore topics"** view allows users to access all topics available. Topics can be ordered based on either chronology or the number of comments and ratings. For each topic, relevant data and information can be provided in order to trigger disruptive ambiguity and surprise. Figure 1, for instance, shows some information with regards to the number of plastic cups used at the case organization.

Users can select topics and engage in a discussion (i.e., post comments). Each comment can be rated on three criteria, namely whether the comment is important and whether it is problem-centric or solution-centric. While an author may view a comment as a solution, others may rate it rather as a problem. Therefore, the rating result

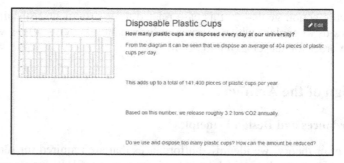

**Fig. 1.** The topic view: triggering disruptive ambiguity and surprise

reflects the opinion of the majority of users. All topics and comments are stored and labeled in the form of an ongoing web-based discussion, where direct reply to specific topics is enabled. Figure 2 shows a comment that was made in the topic "Disposable Plastic Cups" and that has been rated as solution-centric by a majority of raters.

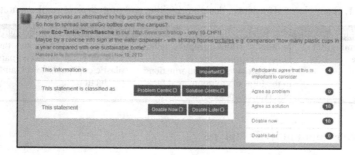

**Fig. 2.** Adding and rating comments

The **"Community"** view allows users to engage in an open and inclusive dialog with other users, they can see who else has joined the platform. The aim is to create a sense of community. Users can also send messages directly to other members. Open access to all users without any exception or any hidden filter is thus provided. Inclusion and democratization of information are further facilitated by the rating functionality that implies that users can express their own opinions which in turn influence the action plan or perhaps even the outcome itself.

The **"Action Plan"** view summarizes those comments, where users have voted that they are a solution. A list of proposed solutions is displayed separately, in order to draw attention to them and to create awareness that they can actually be implemented in the near future, hence a launching pad for actions.

## 3    Significance to Research

The development and evaluation of Green e-community is an integral part of an action design research project [9]. Through this research, we aim to design a purposeful information systems artifact that contributes to the creation of affordances for sensemaking in environmental sustainability transformations. At the same time we learn from this process and propose design principles for a class of information systems that allow for sensemaking in environmental sustainability transformation. These in turn lead to an enhancement of our understanding in using the concept of affordance as an appropriate theoretical lens to study the design of information systems.

Furthermore, this prototype provides an instantiation that can be used to explore which features of information systems afford which user behaviors, in order for sensemaking to occur. As the result, the causes of the impacts that information technology bears in this specific transformational context [7] become noticeable. Consequently, the result of this study can be expected to make a contribution to the emergent body of literature on green information systems [10-12].

## 4     Significance to Practice

Designers and practitioners will benefit from the guidelines that are developed through the implementation and evaluation of Green e-community. Resulting from the action design research process, a set of theoretically grounded, and empirically eva-luated, design principles is at our disposal. While Green e-community is one possible implementation of IS artifact that affords sensemaking in a sustainability transforma-tion, the design principles are aimed to provide a sufficient level of abstraction to be generalized beyond the specific context that was studied.

## 5     Evaluation of the Artifact

Green e-community is evaluated by employing mixed methods. First, quantitative and qualitative data is gathered through users' behavioral record while working with the prototype. Second, qualitative data is collected by conducting focus group discussion that are intended to gain a deeper insight about users' experience with the artifact as well as acquire valuable feedback for its further improvement. Despite the behavioral record in hand, it lacks the depth and data concerning users' perception and the motives behind their behaviors. This combination ensures the completeness and comprehensiveness in our data.

There are three main variables to be evaluated through these methods. The first one is whether the affordances we intended are actually perceived by users. The second one is how many topics, comments, and action plan items are generated during the phase of intensive use. They reflect the process and outcome of sensemaking in sustainability transformation. Finally, users' self-report on how Green e-community support them in their attempts to become more sustainable is the third variable.

**Acknowledgements.** This research is funded by the Research Fund of the University of Liechtenstein (Forschungsförderungsfonds der Universität Liechtenstein).

# References

1. Thibodeau, P.: Gartner's Top 10 Strategic Technologies for 2008. Computerworld (2007)
2. Seidel, S., Recker, J., vom Brocke, J.: Sensemaking and Sustainable Practicing: Functional Affordances of Information Systems in Green Transformations. MIS Quarterly 37, 1275–1299 (2013)
3. Butler, T.: Compliance with institutional imperatives on environmental sustainability: Building theory on the role of Green IS. The Journal of Strategic Information Systems 20, 6–26 (2011)
4. Weick, K.E., Sutcliffe, K.M., Obstfeld, D.: Organizing and the Process of Sensemaking. Organization Science 16, 409–421 (2005)
5. Weick, K.E.: Sensemaking in Organizations. SAGE Publications, Inc., Thousand Oaks (1995)
6. Leonardi, P.M.: Materiality, sociomateriality, and socio-technical systems: What do these terms mean? How are they different? Do we need them? In: Leonardi, P.M., Nardi, B.A., Kallinikos, J. (eds.) Materiality and Organizing: Social Interaction in a Technological World, pp. 25–48. Oyford University Press, Oxford (2012)
7. Markus, M., Silver, M.: A foundation for the study of IT effects: A new look at DeSanctis and Poole's concepts of structural features and spirit. Journal of the Association for Information Systems 9, 609–632 (2008)
8. Robey, D., Anderson, C., Raymond, B.: Information Technology, Materiality, and Organizational Change: A Professional Odyssey. Journal of the Association for Information Systems 14, 379–398 (2013)
9. Sein, M.K., Henfridsson, O., Purao, S., Rossi, M., Lindgren, R.: Action design research. MIS Quarterly 35, 37–56 (2011)
10. Elliot, S.: Transdisciplinary Perspectives on Environmental Sustainability: A Resource Base and Framework for ITEnabled Business Transformation. MIS Quarterly 35, 197–236 (2011)
11. Watson, R.T., Boudreau, M.-C., Chen, A.J.: Information systems and environmentally sustainable development: energy informatics and new directions for the IS community. MIS Quarterly 34, 23–38 (2010)
12. Melville, N.: Information systems innovation for environmental sustainability. MIS Quarterly 34, 1–21 (2010)

# Task and Process Support in ERP Systems

Tamara Babaian, Wendy Lucas, and Jennifer Xu

Computer Information Systems Department,
Bentley University,
Waltham, MA 02452
{tbabaian,wlucas,jxu}@bentley.edu

**Abstract.** We present a proof-of-concept prototype that demonstrates novel collaborative features for supporting enterprise system users. The purpose of the prototype is to illustrate the implementation of design principles derived from field studies of Enterprise Resource Planning system (ERP) users. Its novel features are designed to improve the users' understanding of the business context of their interactions with the system and help them learn to operate it by viewing how tasks have been performed in the past.

## 1 Introduction and Motivation

Enterprise Resource Planning systems (ERPs) are widely used for automating business processes, yet they are notorious for their complex and unintuitive user interfaces. The generic design of those interfaces, which support a broad variety of business practices, makes them inordinately complex for users to master on their own. We have developed a set of design principles [3], models, and algorithms [1,2,4,5] for building enterprise systems using the human-computer collaboration paradigm [3]. These principles grew out of field research investigating and documenting the usability issues experienced by ERP system users [3]. The development of these design principles was guided by collaboration theory.

In this paper, we present an integrated proof-of-concept prototype that implements some of these design principles. A relatively small number of tasks have been implemented when compared to a real ERP system. Our goal, however, is to demonstrate a novel design approach and illustrate the principles from [3] with concrete implementations. Since the design features require real-time logging of interactions and access to the Task-Interface-Logging (TIL) framework [1,4] underlying our implementation, it is not currently possible to integrate these features into an existing ERP system.

The functionality of an enterprise system traditionally lies within the set of business tasks and processes that it implements. Although individual users are typically exposed to a small subset of tasks, successful operation of the system requires a broader understanding of how individual tasks are related. The relationships between tasks and processes, their associated business contexts, and the flow of business data through them are largely hidden behind opaque interfaces. This creates huge obstacles to the users' understanding of where their responsibilities fit in, how to identify and complete related tasks, and where to look for data that is pertinent to their tasks. Users are also intimidated by the enormity of organizational data that is often presented to

M.C. Tremblay et al. (Eds.): DESRIST 2014, LNCS 8463, pp. 443–447, 2014.

them in an unfiltered, un-optimized manner, thereby discouraging independent exploration of the rich informational and operational resources offered by the system.

In adopting the human-computer collaboration paradigm, we recognize that the user alone cannot handle the cognitive load associated with learning and utilizing such a complex system. The system must include features that will educate and guide users so that they can achieve greater effectiveness in performing their tasks. To that extent, we have designed and implemented the TIL [1,4] framework in which an ERP system's tasks, task interfaces, task composition into processes, and the history of all system-user interactions, are embedded in the system's data model. Using the information in TIL, our prototype implements the following features:

- Interactive visualizations of the process currently being performed, and
- On-demand, automated demonstrations of how to execute a task.

We describe these features in the next section.

## 2     Task and Process Support in ERP Prototype

The overarching design goal of this project is to provide a mechanism by which the system can provide the user with useful guidance and assistance in:

- learning or recalling how to perform a specific task or process,
- understanding the task context and the flow of business data through tasks and processes, and
- reviewing the detailed history of tasks and documents related to the task that is currently being performed by the user.

These goals are supported by two features, an Interactive Process and Process Instance Visualization and an Automated Task Playback. Before presenting them, we provide some definitions regarding the TIL model (see [1,4] for a full description), which serves as a supporting infrastructure to our implementation. In the TIL framework, a process is a predefined set of tasks. Two tasks are connected when an output of one is used as an input to another; thus, the flow of data objects links the tasks within a process. A process instance is defined as a set of concrete instances of the tasks comprising a process that are executed by a user. Task and process descriptions are a part of the TIL model. Process instances are automatically reconstructed from the Log portion of the model in real time, using algorithms presented in [4].

### 2.1     Interactive Process and Process Instance Visualization

Figures 1 and 2 show our Prototype ERP window as it appears when a user is working on *Add Goods Receipt* task. The left pane of the window presents a traditional form-based page for entering data. The right pane contains the tabs that display information about the business process (*Purchasing*) encompassing the *Add Goods Receipt* task currently being performed by the user. The top white rectangle presents a choice of two tabs: Process Graph and Process Instance Graph.   The **Process Graph** view (Fig. 1) displays information about the Purchasing process in general, including individual tasks and data flow between them.   The **Process Instance Graph** view (Fig 2.)

presents information about the current task instance being worked on as well as the other related task instances within the same process. The rectangular pane on the bottom of the right side shows process details that are displayed when a user clicks on the components of a graph. Below we discuss the details of each view.

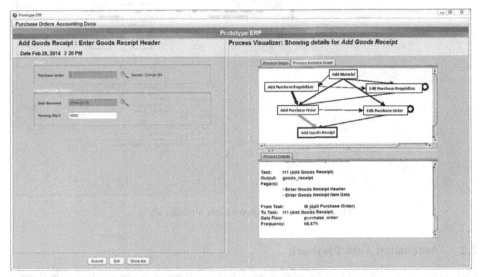

**Fig. 1.** Process Graph Visualization

Figure 1 shows the Process Graph and the Process Detail panes on the right side of the window. The user can interact with the Process Graph by clicking on tasks and arrows, with the latter representing the flow of a data object between tasks. Clicking on a task causes the Process Detail window to display detailed information on the task, including its name, id, and the number and names of the interface pages associated with it. Clicking on an arrow displays information on the data object that is passed between the two tasks and the frequency of this transition. For example, the highlighted link from *Add Purchase Order* to *Add Goods Receipt* represents a *purchase_order* object that is created by the former task and used by the latter. This information and statistics on how frequently a completed *purchase_order* object is passed by an *Add Purchase Order* task to an *Add Goods Receipt* task is displayed in the Process Detail pane. The thickness of the arrow is proportional to that frequency.

The Interactive Process Instance Visualization shown in the right pane in Figure 2 provides information on the concrete task instance of the Purchasing process that the user is working on in the left pane. Note that the Process Instance Graph shows a subset of tasks from the Purchasing process displayed in Figure 1, including only tasks that have already been completed or are in progress. Clicking on a box representing a task instance causes the window to display information on the users who executed the task, task time stamps, completion status, and the output data object produced by the task. The Interactive Process Instance Visualization allows a user to trace back through the entire process chain from the document that is currently being worked on to all other related data objects, find the task instances that were enacted to produce those related objects, and identify the users who performed those tasks.

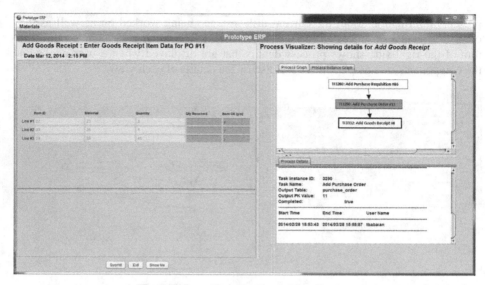

**Fig. 2.** Process Instance Graph Visualization

## 2.2 Automated Task Playback

ERP users often consult a colleague, a help desk, or their own notes when experiencing difficulty with some part of a task or learning how to do it for the first time. User difficulties stem from not knowing which fields to fill in, what data to enter and in what order or format, and how to access a related task [3]. We have implemented the system capability of replaying a prior system-user interaction, which serves as a tutorial demonstration of a task interface. These demonstrations are generated in real time based on the usage Log data collected and stored within the TIL data model [2].

To enact the Playback feature, a *ShowMe* button is included in each task interface. Upon clicking it, the system displays a page that asks the user to provide optional parameters for selecting a past execution of the task for playback. The parameters include the user whose interaction will be visualized, the beginning and end dates defining the interval in which the task instance occurred, the type of document produced by the task, a specific document number, and the process within which the task occurred. These parameters are used by the system to identify the corresponding task instances, which are then presented in a list to the user. If no parameters are entered by the user, the system presents only the task instances corresponding to the user's current task. The user picks a particular task instance and the system dynamically creates a script, based on the interaction data in the Log, and plays it as an animation in a separate Playback window.

## 3     Discussion

**Significance to Research.** Due to space limitations, we refer the reader to [2,3,5] for a review of the related literature and a discussion of how the presented features differ from the existing approaches reported in research and implemented commercially. The presented prototype makes the following research contributions:

- it illustrates the use of collaboration theory in guiding the design and implementation of large organizational systems,
- it validates the suitability of the TIL framework as a supporting infrastructure to the system-partner approach to interface design, and
- it presents novel types of user support, namely interactive process and task visualizations and on-demand task tutorials that are dynamically generated based on the automatic logging of user interaction data within the TIL framework.

**Significance to Practice.** This approach addresses common concerns of ERP users regarding the opacity of the business processes, which significantly impairs the users' ability to operate the system. The presented prototype demonstrates low-cost alternatives to time- and labor-intensive approaches to educating and supporting users via training seminars, help desks, and peer-to-peer communication.

**Evaluation of the Artifact.** We are planning a laboratory study for evaluating the usefulness of the Process Visualizations. An empirical evaluation of the asymptotic time complexity of the algorithms is also underway. Finally, we are planning on discussing the features presented here with field users in order to assess their usefulness.

**Acknowledgement.** We are grateful to Taylor Gordon, an undergraduate student who contributed to the development of the prototype.

# References

1. Babaian, T., Lucas, W.: Modeling Data for Enterprise Systems with Memories. Journal of Database Management 24(2), 1–12 (2013)
2. Babaian, T., Lucas, W.: Composing Interface Demonstrations Automatically from Usage Logs. In: Cordeiro, J., Maciaszek, L.A., Filipe, J. (eds.) ICEIS 2012. LNBIP, vol. 141, pp. 376–392. Springer, Heidelberg (2013)
3. Babaian, T., Lucas, W., Xu, J., Topi, H.: Usability through System-User Collaboration: Deriving Design Principles for Greater ERP Usability. In: Winter, R., Zhao, J.L., Aier, S. (eds.) DESRIST 2010. LNCS, vol. 6105, pp. 394–409. Springer, Heidelberg (2010)
4. Lucas, W., Babaian, T.: Implementing Design Principles for Collaborative ERP Systems. In: Peffers, K., Rothenberger, M., Kuechler, B. (eds.) DESRIST 2012. LNCS, vol. 7286, pp. 88–107. Springer, Heidelberg (2012)
5. Lucas, W., Xu, J., Babaian, T.: Visualizing ERP Usage Logs in Real Time. In: Proceedings of the 14th International Conference on Enterprise Information Systems (ICEIS 2013), pp. 83–90 (July 2013)

# Personalized Medication Adherence Motivating and Reminding System (PMAMRS)

Pavankumar Mulgund, Wencui Han, Raj Sharman, Abhiram Upadhya,
Srikanth Reddy Bandi, Vishwanath Miriyapalli, Kunal Jiwane,
Ranjit Singh, and Gurdev Singh

State University of New York at Buffalo, NY
{pmulgund,wencuiha,rsharman,abhiramk,sbandi2,vmiriyap,
kunaljiw,rs10,gsingh4}@buffalo.edu

**Abstract.** Medication non adherence reduces quality of care, causes unnecessary cost and negatively affects the quality of life of the patients. Using community engagement approach and adopting design science research guidelines, this research develops a prototype to motivate and improve patient prescription adherence.

**Keywords:** prescription adherence, compliance, IT intervention, risk propensity, Myers Briggs Type Indicator (MBTI), patient centered care.

## 1 Introduction

The problem of medication non adherence has grown manifolds in gravity. It has led to an increase in avoidable morbidity in chronic patients, reduced quality of care and has burdened the economy with unnecessary costs in the form excess hospitalizations, different or higher medication etc. In fact, United States loses about to 300 billion USD every year. With aging population and increased cost of health care services, the need for interventions that can increase and encourage medication adherence have become an absolute necessity. The information technology also has a great potential to help enhance the cause of adherence. The technology can be used to build systems that remind, motivate and monitor the patient's adherence to medications.

We have developed a reconfigurable IT system that assesses the personality and risk propensity of the patient by the responses made to a survey included in the user profile and subsequently tailors the messages by adapting language, tone, type (text, video and audio etc.) and frequency of the communication We have also developed features based on accessibility principles to help the elderly and people with disabilities to use the system.

## 2 Background and Motivation

Literature suggests that factors related to non-adherence include regimen complexity (Claxton et al., 2000; Fish and Lung, 2001), memory and recall (Kessels, 2003; Piette et al., 2000), depression (DiMatteo et al., 2000), social support (DiMatteo, 2004) and

M.C. Tremblay et al. (Eds.): DESRIST 2014, LNCS 8463, pp. 448–452, 2014.

patient belief (Horne et al., 2005). We studied the existing mobile medication reminder applications in market and found that most of these factors were not considered in the design of these applications and adherence motivation applications were nonexistent. The literature and product surveys bought out some significant short comings of the current applications and tools used for enhancing medication adherence. First, the kind of intervention required to make patients adhere to the medication regimen varies for different patients. Second, the systems so far have only 'reminded' patients about medications and not motivated them to adhere to the regime. This kind of systems are highly inadequate when we know 70% non-adherence is intentional. The current systems have also not leveraged the proven theories such as MBTI and theory of rational choice to classify the personality types and risk propensity of the individual. This information can be vital and can be used to design high impact reminders or motivational messages. Third, the systems today do not provide any kind of reporting capabilities which can be used to study the long term adherence of the patients in case of chronic conditions such as diabetes or hypertension.. Fourth, the reminder systems have largely ignored the role of the family members in helping patient adhere to the medication regime. Patient with strong family ties tend to adhere to medication 13% more than others. Finally perhaps the most important of all, the systems today are built by software engineers or IT folks who think they know how medical professionals work and what the patient needs or wants. There have hardly been any community engagements to interact, elicit and understand what kind of a reminders or motivational messages the patients, family members and other stakeholders need based on factors such as patient condition, patient's knowledge and competence, age, religious beliefs and value systems.

## 3     Process Flow

The patient answers a few questions designed based on the Myers Briggs Type Indicator (MBTI) and rational behavioral theory. The system also records Age, personal profile, Educational profile, Relatives/Guardians information, Medical History, Allergies and existing conditions. The system subsequently classifies the patient as either the thinking type or feeling type personality. It will also rate the patient as risk seeking or risk averse. Based on the personality type and risk rating, the motivational messages will be sent to patient on mobile. The system will remind the patient as the predefined time. With each reminders personalized motivational content either as message or audio will be delivered to the patient. The system will also remind the patient as the predefined time. With each reminders some motivational content wither as message

**Fig. 1.** Functionalities

or audio will be delivered to the patient. The system will also keep record of the medication adherence of the patient. This information will be used further for various analysis and decision making processes. The system will also keep record of the medication adherence of the patient. This information will be used further for various analysis and decision making processes. The system will also keep record of the medication adherence of the patient. This information will be used further for various analysis and decision making processes. The hospital, physician or family members can send out videos, messages, voice messages and appreciations to motivate adherence. A non-compliance alert should also be generated when a patient compliance falls bellows a threshold set for each of the risk levels. Pharmacist also gets notifications every month 5 to 7 days before the patient inventory of medication is completely emptied.

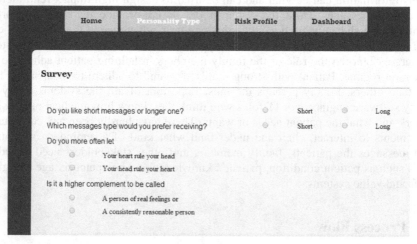

**Fig. 2.** Partial Screen

The patient information and questionnaire screen is displayed above in Figure 2. Figure 3 shows how the system is set is and the subsequent message received.

**Fig. 3.** Reminder message and compliance report

## 3.1     Design Science Considerations

| Guideline | Description |
|---|---|
| Design as an Artifact | The PMAMRS is a viable prototype. It is model demonstrates how successful interventions developed and used for the benefit of the patients |
| Problem Relevance | To develop technology solutions to the burning issue of Medication Non Adherence |
| Design Evaluation | The prototype is built on the strong foundations of Object Oriented Design methods leading to a highly modular design. The User Interface is developed by inputs from the actual users and their subsequent validation of the interfaces.<br>The experts in the field have validated the design of messages.<br>The messages were surveyed on number of people and the messages were statistically validated. |
| Research Contributions | The need of user inputs, feedbacks and statistical analysis and their subsequent application in coming up with reconfigurable user interface which is accessible and highly usable |
| Research Rigor | The prototype is developed based on a substantial research on compliance models and theories, theories of patient behaviors, personality type indicator, theory of rational choice and surveys inputs of various stakeholders in community and their statistical analysis |
| Design as a search process | The prototype designed uses some technological means to a social cause that has great societal ramifications. |
| Communication of research | The intention is to communicate about the motivation and need for the product and demonstrate the impact of this technological intervention on medication adherence |

## 3.2     Accessibility Considerations

We have followed the accessibility considerations from W3C's Web Content Accessibility Guidelines (WCAG) to develop the prototype which can be used for people with disabilities. The screen designs, color choice, notification/Alert contents,  key board support, voice based notification features are all put in place to ensure that people with disabilities such as color blindness, low/partial vision etc. can use the product with ease.

# 4    Conclusion

We intend to make a meaningful contribution to the areas of medication non adherence by developing impact interventions using information technology as a catalyst. The foundation of the prototype is the culmination of research in compliance behavioral theories, personality types, theory of rational choice, community engagement and involvement and primary analysis of surveys of various stakeholders. Finally, we hope that our efforts will help a make a difference in the lives of the patients.

# References

1. Concordance, adherence and compliance in medicine taking
2. Claxton, A.J., Cramer, J., Pierce, C.: A systematic review of the associations between dose regimens and medication compliance. Clinical Therapeutics 23(8), 1296–1310 (2001)
3. DiMatteo, M.R.: Social support and patient adherence to medical treatment: A meta-analysis. Health Psychology 23(2), 207–218 (2004)
4. DiMatteo, M.R., Lepper, H.S., Croghan, T.W.: Depression Is a risk factor for noncompliance with medical treatment: Meta-analysis of the effects of anxiety and depression on patient adherence. Archives of Internal Medicine 160(14), 2101–2107 (2000)
5. Fish, L., Lung, C.L.: Adherence to asthma therapy. Annals of Allergy, Asthma and Immunology 86(6), 24–30 (2001)
6. Horne, R., Weinman, J., Barber, N., Elliott, R., Morgan, M., Cribb, A.: Concordance, adherence and compliance in medicine taking, pp. 40–46. NCCSDO, London (2005)
7. Kessels, R.P.: 'Patients' memory for medical information. Journal of the Royal Society of Medicine 96(5), 219–222 (2003); Piette, J., Weinberger, M., and McPhee, S.J.: The effect of automated calls with telephone nurse follow-up on patient-centered outcomes of diabetes care. Medical Care 38(2), 218–30

# A Language-Independent Model Query Tool

Patrick Delfmann, Hanns-Alexander Dietrich, Jean-Marie Havel,
and Matthias Steinhorst

European Research Center for Information Systems (ERCIS),
University of Münster, Leonardo-Campus 3, 48149 Münster, Germany
{delfmann,dietrich,steinhorst}@ercis.de,
j_have07@uni-muenster.de

**Abstract.** This paper introduces a prototype implementing a visual graph-based model query language. Querying models refers to identifying particular fragments in the model that comply with a predefined pattern query. The language takes advantage of the fact that models of any type and modelling language can conceptually be represented as a labeled graph. As a consequence the query language remains flexible and is not restricted to specific model types or languages. The language supports topologically exact as well as similar pattern matching and includes additional constraints and attributes in the matching process. In doing so, the language is applicable to many different analysis tasks. Following the design science approach we develop and demonstrate a prototype of such a language which allows for visually defining a pattern query and visually representing the results of the pattern matching process.

**Keywords:** Conceptual model analysis, model querying, pattern matching.

## 1    Introduction and Problem Statement

Querying conceptual models to detect patterns in them (i.e., model fragments complying with predefined structural and semantic properties) is the basis for many analysis tasks, such as business process weakness detection or business process compliance checking. For instance, a business rule prescribing that a credit application has to be checked twice by two different persons in a business process before the credit can be granted relates to a specific process model pattern as follows: a process model check activity has to be followed by another process model check activity over a control flow path. Both have to be related to the same document, and the activities have to be performed by different persons. By matching such a pattern against a business process model, we can determine whether or not the process is compliant. Corresponding examples can be found for several further application scenarios.

Many companies are nowadays maintaining large model collections containing models of different types and languages [1]. These model collections are used as a means of analyzing particular aspects of corporate reality [2]. Due to the variety of different analysis tasks and the complexity of these collections [3], such an analysis is becoming increasingly difficult. The research community has proposed many analysis approaches to that end. However, they are mostly restricted to a certain modelling

M.C. Tremblay et al. (Eds.): DESRIST 2014, LNCS 8463, pp. 453–457, 2014.
© Springer International Publishing Switzerland 2014

language or to a specific analysis scenario, even though any model can be conceptually represented as a labeled graph which could then be queried. Further, they often only provide rather basic means for querying. In particular, only very few approaches implement functionalities such as querying attributes other than the type or the label or further constraints on model paths and loops (cf. Section 2.4). Furthermore, it is mostly not possible to visualize the querying results within the model collection, which is essential for further use of the results. Instead, many query approaches only return the model containing a particular pattern occurrence. Therefore, the paper introduces a tool prototype including a novel query language supporting the described functionalities (cf. Section 2.4). It was developed following the design science paradigm [4].

## 2    Design of the Artifact

**Scenarios.** The range of analysis tasks the query language supports is manifold. Querying models is concerned with identifying predefined model fragments (the patterns) with (partly) given structural characteristics and (partly) given contents. Querying models serves different business purposes including compliance checking [5], weakness detection [6], model translation [7], detecting structural or behavioral conflicts [8], and model abstraction [9].

**Features.** The features the query language provides include pattern identification techniques as well as means to visually draw a pattern query and to display the results. As our querying language is implemented as a plugin for a meta-modelling tool operating on models represented as labeled graphs, it is able to support arbitrary conceptual model types and languages (F1). Further, it is able to include arbitrary attributes of nodes and edges in the matching process (F2). To identify exact matches it provides means to query isomorphic fragments consisting of elements having relations and elements having in- /output relations (F3). To be able to detect similar topological structures, it is able to search for paths and loops (F4). Moreover, these paths and loops may contain a variety of constraints such as the containment or exclusion of defined elements or sub-patterns (F5). Patterns can be combined and can contain sub-patterns (F6). Attributes of nodes and edges of the pattern can be expressed as variables and put into relation in form of logic expressions (F7). Patterns can be visually drawn (F8). Finally, the result of the query can be visually displayed within the searched models (F9).

## 3    Significance to Research and Practice

**Significance to Research.** In graph theory, finding exact matches is known as the problem of subgraph isomorphism for which several algorithms have been proposed [10]. Subgraph isomorphism algorithms create a mapping in which nodes of the pattern are mapped to counterparts of the model. Isomorphic matching does not allow mapping edges to paths of arbitrary length. However, in the context of conceptual model analysis it is necessary to also identify paths or previously unknown length (cf. F4). This problem is known as subgraph homeomorphism which is computationally very complex. Therefore, we introduce a novel problem called relaxed subgraph isomorphism. Hereby, nodes of the pattern graph are matched to exactly one equivalent node of the model. However, an edge may also be mapped to a path (cf. F4 and F5). Further, the nodes and edges of a pattern can be annotated with attributes, which are included in the checking process. An edge can be either directed, undirected or of any direction. Thus a model is represented as a labelled mixed multi-graph. Our algorithm is able to solve a pattern matching problem as described above (cf. F3 and F4).

**Significance to Practice.** Our approach's sophisticated functionalities, its language independency, and its applicability to a variety of analysis scenarios make it interesting for practitioners. Most importantly, it provides a convenient means of drawing a pattern query instead of writing formal expressions which is error prone [11] or unfeasible for non-experts. Finally, the result of the analysis can be visually displayed and browsed.

## 4    Demonstration

The pattern matching process starts with defining a query (cf. Figure 1). The query is drawn visually (cf. F8). A pattern query consists of nodes and edges, which can be further specified. An element's type can be specified according to the used modelling language (cf. icon at the bottom-right corner of a node). Further, a caption match expression for the label can be specified which is set to a wildcard by default.

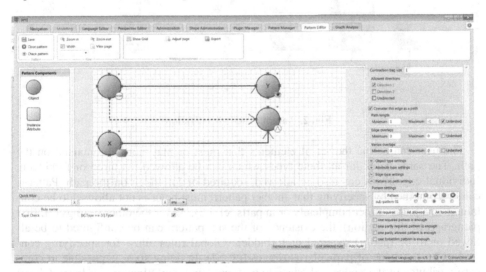

**Fig. 1.** Pattern editor

The allowed directions of an edge can be set to either be undirected, directed or of any direction. It is also possible to provide a caption match expression as well as to define the type of the edge. Further attributes can be attached to nodes and edges. Such a pattern query consisting of nodes, plain edges, and attributes thus allows for searching for exact pattern matches.

In order to define topologically similar structures, an edge can be specified to be considered as a path (edge-path mapping). The available edge settings then allow defining a min/max path length, edge overlaps and vertex overlaps. A vertex overlap could, for example, represent a loop starting and ending in an XOR-split which may thus be visited multiple times. An edge overlap can represent a loop in which a certain path is possibly passed multiple times. It is important to notice that both notions of overlaps are different. Further, it is possible to define edge and vertex overlaps globally which allows to define whether two different paths are allowed to cross each other at a certain node (global vertex overlap) or within a certain path (global edge overlap).

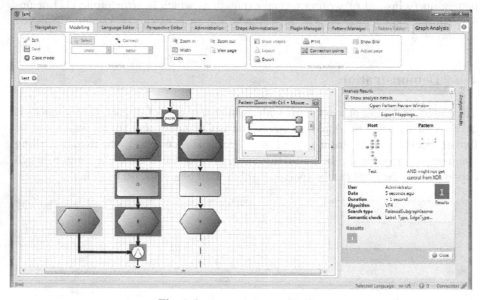

**Fig. 2.** Pattern match visualization

The user can define the set of elements that must or may not be contained on the path. The same holds for attribute types which can be allowed, required or forbidden. Individual edge types can also be allowed, required or forbidden on the path. Patterns can be combined by specifying that another pattern must be or is not allowed to be contained on a path – either completely or in parts (cf. F6). As for the other settings (cf. first paragraph of this section), the existence of the sub-pattern can be configured to be allowed or to be (partly) required or forbidden. Global rules allow for specifying constraints on the value of particular attributes (cf. F7). In doing so, it is possible to compare attributes of the nodes and edges (e.g., type, label, NoOfIncomingEdges). Global rules can be defined using logic expressions (e.g., "[X].Caption == [Y].Caption").

Once the pattern query is visually defined, the analysis can be performed. The user is prompted to select the models which are to be queried. The results are displayed together with analysis statistics. The results are highlighted in the models and can be browsed (cf. F9, Figure 2).

## 5    Contributions, Limitations, and Outlook

In this paper, we developed a modelling language independent model query tool which is able to support multiple analysis scenarios by providing sophisticated means of defining pattern queries visually. We hence contribute to the range of existing approaches, because the functionalities provided by our prototype are only partly given in research by now. A limitation of our approach is that it only supports querying structural properties and does not allow for identifying conflicts within the execution semantics of a model. Future work will evaluate the application potential of the query language in real world model analysis scenarios.

## References

1. Davies, I., Green, P., Rosemann, M., Indulska, M., Gallo, S.: How do practitioners use conceptual modeling in practice? Data & Knowledge Engineering 58, 358–380 (2006)
2. Dijkman, R.M., La Rosa, M., Reijers, H.A.: Managing Large Collections of Business Process Models - Current Techniques and Challenges. Computers in Industry 63, 91–97 (2012)
3. Dijkman, R.M., Dumas, M., van Dongen, B., Käärik, R., Mendling, J.: Similarity of business process models: Metrics and evaluation. Information Systems 36, 498–516 (2011)
4. Peffers, K., Tuunanen, T., Rothenberger, M.A., Chatterjee, S.: A design science research methodology for information systems research. Journal of Management Information Systems 24, 45–77 (2007)
5. Knuplesch, D., Ly, L.T., Rinderle-Ma, S., Pfeifer, H., Dadam, P.: On Enabling Data-Aware Compliance Checking of Business Process Models. In: Parsons, J., Saeki, M., Shoval, P., Woo, C., Wand, Y. (eds.) ER 2010. LNCS, vol. 6412, pp. 332–346. Springer, Heidelberg (2010)
6. Becker, J., Bergener, P., Räckers, M., Weiß, B., Winkelmann, A.: Pattern-Based Semi-Automatic Analysis of Weaknesses in Semantic Business Process Models in the Banking Sector. In: Proc. of the European Conference on Information Systems (ECIS 2010), Pretoria, South Africa (2010)
7. Ouyang, C., Dumas, M., ter Hofstede, A.H.M., van der Aalst, W.M.P.: Pattern-Based Translation of BPMN Process Models to BPEL Web Services. International Journal of Web Services Research 5, 42–62 (2008)
8. Mendling, J., Verbeek, H.M.W., van Dongen, B.F., van der Aalst, W.M.P., Neumann, G.: Detection and prediction of errors in EPCs of the SAP reference model. Data & Knowledge Engineering 64, 312–329 (2008)
9. Polyvyanyy, A., Smirnov, S., Weske, M.: Business Process Model Abstraction. In: Brocke, J., Rosemann, M. (eds.) Handbook on Business Process Management 1, pp. 149–166. Springer, Heidelberg (2010)
10. Foggia, P., Sansone, C., Vento, M.: A Performance Comparison of Five Algorithms for Graph Isomorphism. In: Proceedings of the 3rd IAPR TC-15 Workshop on Graph-based Representations in Pattern Recognition, pp. 188–199 (2001)
11. Becker, J., Bergener, P., Delfmann, P., Weiß, B.: Modeling and Checking Business Process Compliance Rules in the Financial Sector. In: Galletta, D.F., Liang, T.-P. (eds.) Proc. of the International Conference on Information Systems (ICIS 2011). Association for Information Systems (2011)

# Author Index